Hidden Florida

The Adventurer's Guide

Third Edition

"It's a guide to the Florida beyond the billboards, mega-attractions and traffic-snarled cities."
—*Atlanta Journal and Constitution*

"This book goes into considerable detail on the state's history and geology and details sights, accommodations, dining spots, nightlife, trails, camping and motoring."
—*Toronto Star*

"The authors have unearthed some truly hidden treasures."
—*Miami Herald*

"Where else could you find out about Grandma Newton's Bed and Breakfast in the Everglades or Lone Cabbage Fish Camp near Cocoa?"
—*New Orleans Times-Picayune*

"In addition to major attractions, it leads readers to little-known towns, secluded beaches and remote wilderness areas."
—*Washington Times*

"There are numerous consumer travel guides to Florida, *Hidden Florida* is one of the best."
—*Jewish Weekly News*

"Captures the flash and soul of Florida, from Daytona to the Everglades. This guidebook is thorough!"
—*National Motorist*

Executive Editor Ray Riegert

Hidden Florida

The Adventurer's Guide

Third Edition

Stacy Ritz, Candace Leslie

Marty Olmstead and Chelle Koster Walton

Ulysses Press

Published by: Ulysses Press
P.O. Box 3440
Berkeley, CA 94703-3440

Library of Congress Catalog Card Number 92-81059
ISBN 0-915233-66-5

Printed in the U.S.A. by the George Banta Company

10 9 8 7 6 5 4

Production Director: Leslie Henriques
Managing Editor: Claire Chun
Research Associate: Roger Rapoport
Editors: Joanna Pearlman, Judith Kahn

Editorial Associates: Wendy Ann Logsdon, Laurie Greenleaf, Cynthia Price
Illustrator: Timothy Carroll
Cartographer: Robert Lettieri
Cover Designers: Bonnie Smetts, Leslie Henriques
Indexer: Sayre Van Young

Cover Photography: Front cover photo by Unlimited Collection/Superstock; back cover photos by Steve Starr

Distributed in the United States by Publishers Group West, in Canada by Raincoast Books, and in Great Britain and Europe by World Leisure Marketing

Printed on Recycled Paper 

Notes from the Publisher

Throughout the text, hidden locales, special features, remote regions, and little-known spots are marked with a star (★).

* * *

An alert, adventurous reader is as important as a travel writer in keeping a guidebook up-to-date and accurate. So if you happen upon a great restaurant, discover a hidden locale, or (heaven forbid) find an error in the text, we'd appreciate hearing from you. Just write to:

Ulysses Press
P.O. Box 3440
Berkeley, CA 94703

* * *

It is our desire as publishers to create guidebooks that are responsible as well as informative. The danger of exploring hidden locales is that they will no longer be secluded.

We hope that our guidebooks treat the people, country and land we visit with respect. We ask that our readers do the same. The hiker's motto, "Walk softly on the Earth," applies to travelers everywhere . . . in the desert, on the beach and in town.

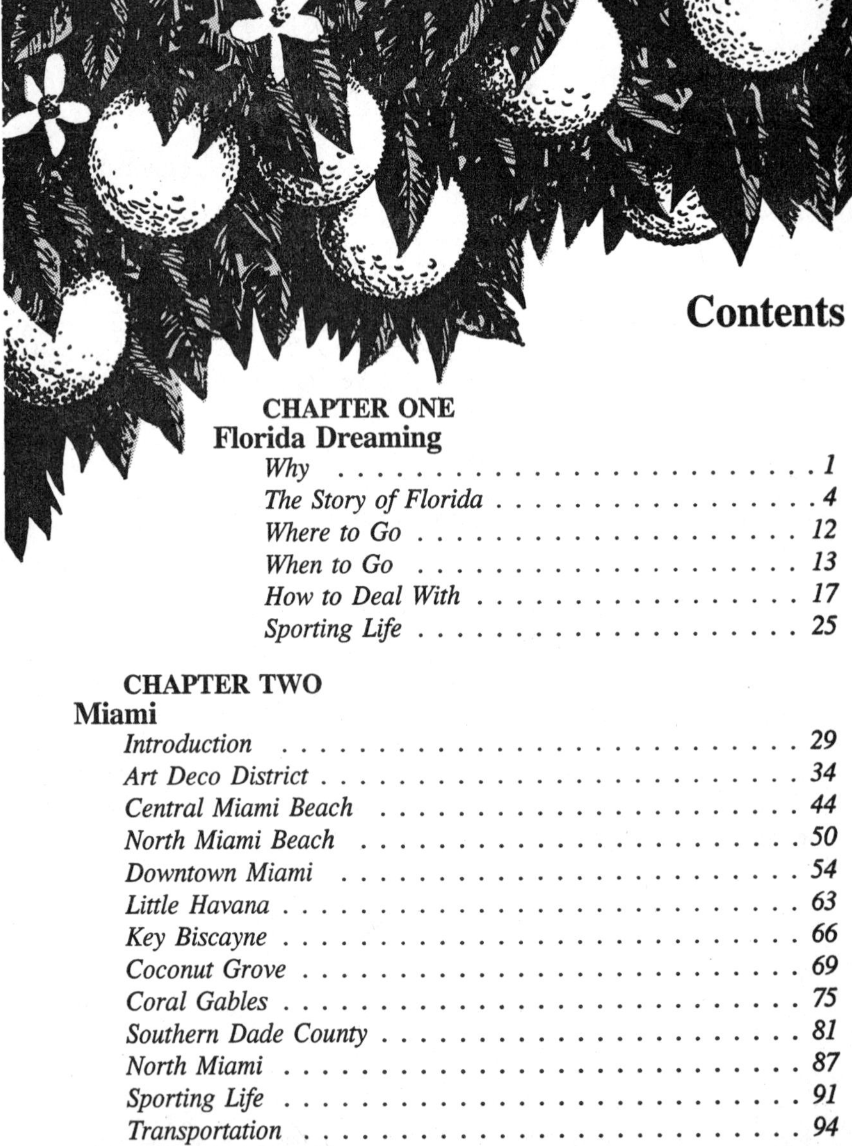

Contents

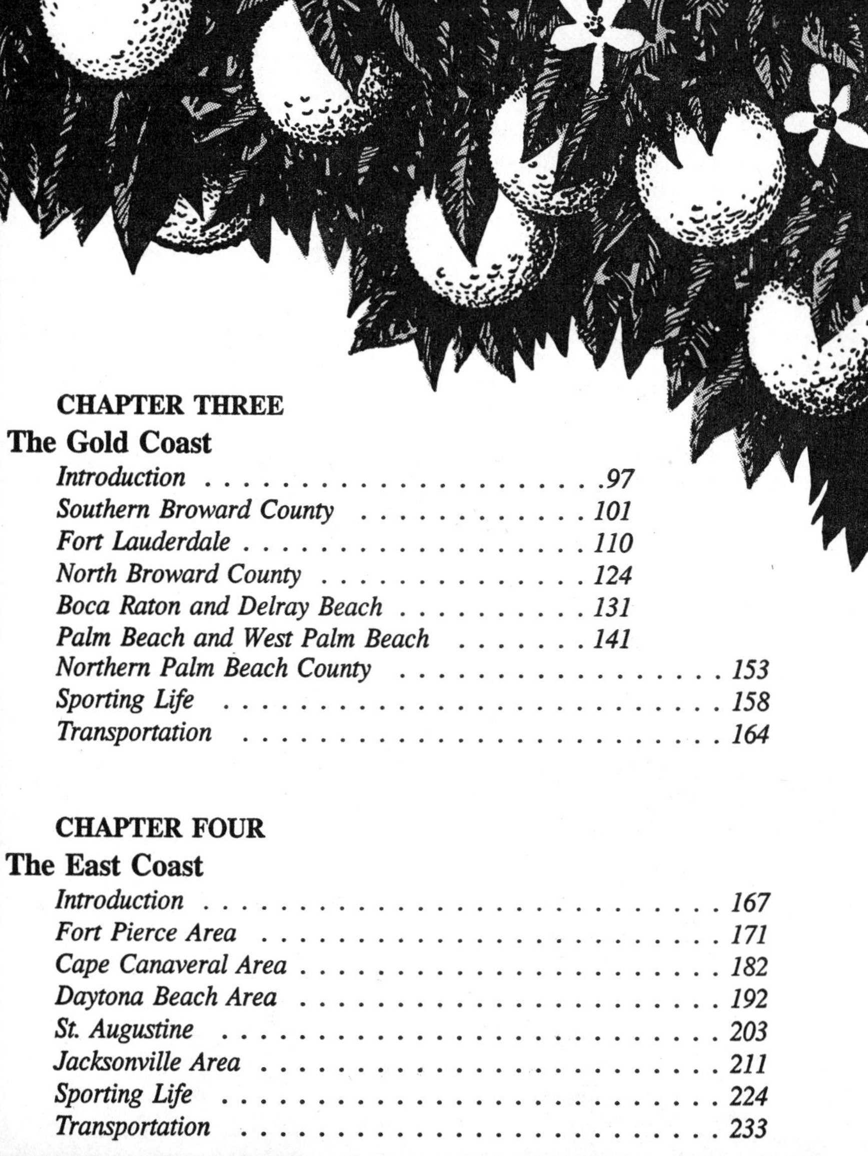

CHAPTER THREE

The Gold Coast

CHAPTER FOUR

The East Coast

CHAPTER FIVE
Central Florida

CHAPTER SIX
The Everglades and Keys

CHAPTER SEVEN
The West Coast

CHAPTER EIGHT
The Panhandle

SPECIAL FEATURES

MAPS

FLORIDA

DREAMING

CHAPTER ONE

Florida Dreaming

The Why, Where, When and How of Traveling in the Sunshine State

---

Why

Florida. Even its colorful name conjures up a variety of visions—delicate orchids, waving palms, tropical waters, white sands, fresh orange juice and, especially for winter-dodgers, welcome and dependable warmth. Shaped like a green thumb pointing into the sea, Florida is probably the United States' most recognizable piece of land. A century of dynamic public relations has also kept Florida in the public eye, from the heralding of the first railroads that carried vacationers deep into tropical paradises to the newest Disney ventures that now reportedly attract more visitors than any other spot in the world.

To squeeze a place like Florida into one book is like trying to compress a bushel of oranges into a can of concentrate. From the Georgia line to the outermost of the Dry Tortugas, from historic Pensacola to bustling, rhythmic Miami, Florida has so many dimensions that to discover them all would require return visits, many, many of them. Though no spot in the state is more than 60 miles from salt water, the beaches differ greatly from coast to coast. Of the many freshwater lakes, springs, streams and rivers, each has its own unique character, inhabitants and delights. Even the cities are all different, from gracious Old South Tallahassee to booming Ft. Lauderdale to historic Key West.

Old and new are celebrated fervently in Florida. Exhibits of Spanish treasures, re-enactments of pirate invasions, and hikes along trails once trekked by early explorers carry you back into the state's colorful and fascinating past, while cutting-edge tours of the Kennedy Space Center and mind-boggling EPCOT experiences thrust you into the anything-is-possible future. Getting in and out and around Florida is easy, too. Modern highways zip up and down and across the entire state; major airlines and trains keep the runways and tracks humming.

Yet, despite its rapid development, its remarkable tourism and its "upfrontness," Florida still possesses many hidden treasures. If you leave the massive freeways and look beyond the billboards, meander down the city side streets, walk the wilderness trails, visit the small towns, you will find them.

This book is designed to help you explore this great state. It will take you to countless popular spots and offer advice on how best to enjoy them. It will also lead you into many off-the-beaten-path locales, the places one learns about by talking with folks at the local café or with someone who has lived in the area all his life. It will acquaint you with the state's history, its natural habitats and its residents, both human and animal. It will recommend sights that should not be missed. It will suggest places to eat, to lodge, to play, to camp, with consideration for varying interests, budgets and tastes.

The traveling part of the book begins in Miami, presenting in Chapter Two the delights of this ever-popular, multifaceted city with its glittering beaches and Latin beat. Chapter Three heads up the Atlantic Gold Coast, through Palm Beach and Fort Lauderdale, along the pièce de résistance beaches that have attracted some of Florida's wealthiest visitors and residents. The future and the past are presented in Chapter Four, which explores space technology and fishing villages as it travels the East Coast for 300 miles through Daytona, Jacksonville and historic St. Augustine. Central Florida's horse farms and cattle ranches, Lake Okeechobee, the beautiful Ocala National Forest and, of course, Walt Disney World are only a sampling of the startling contrasts you will discover in Chapter Five.

Chapter Six heads south into the Everglades region and then down through the jewel-like Florida Keys. Artful Sarasota, urban St. Petersburg and Tampa, and isolated Cedar Key are some of the places Chapter Seven explores as it travels along the popular gulf beaches and into the rural inland areas of the West Coast. Chapter Eight traverses the Panhandle from the Suwannee River to the Alabama line, visiting Tallahassee and Pensacola, white quartz-sand beaches and inland parks, forests, springs and rivers.

What you choose to see and do is up to you. The old cliché that "there is something for everyone" pretty well rings true in Florida. It is proven by the numbers of retired people who return annually or settle down here, by the families who pour in each summer as soon as school is out, by the sportsfolk and sports fans, by the lovers of the out-of-doors as well as the

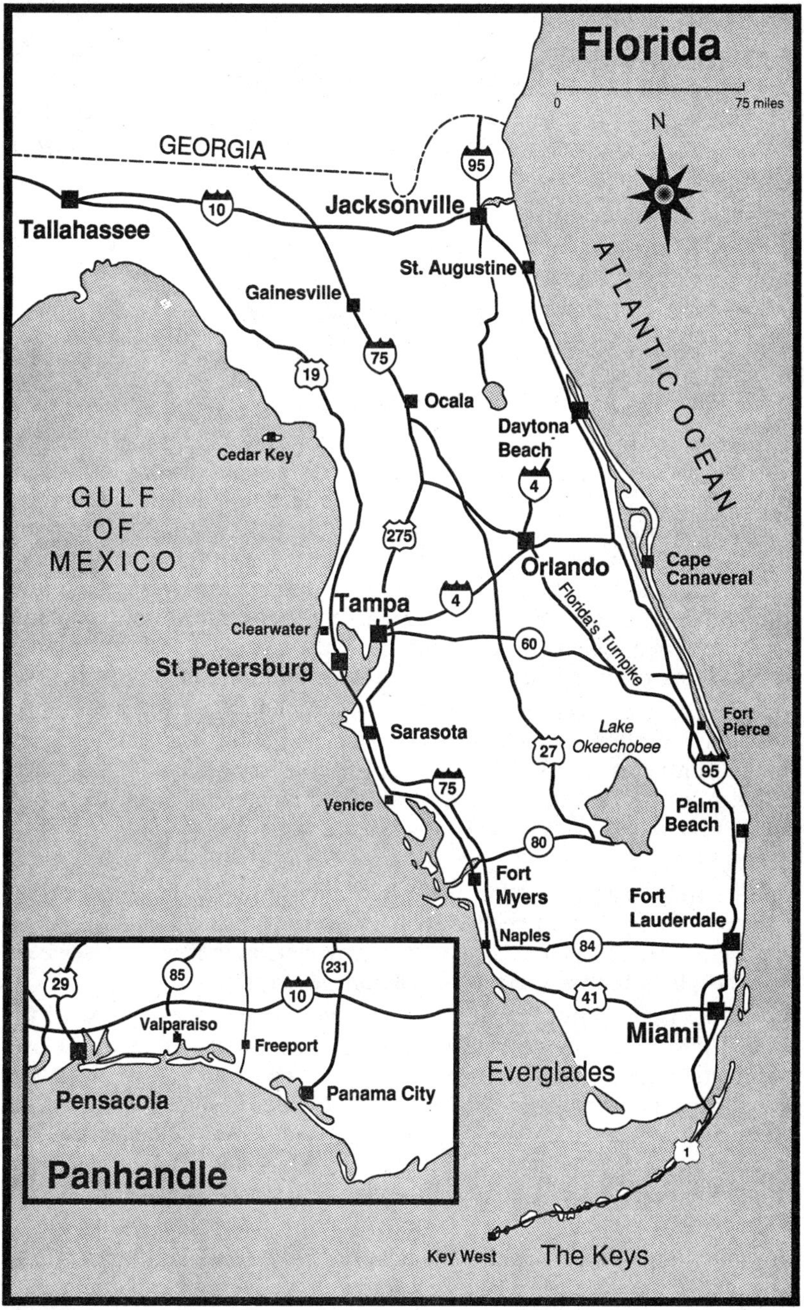

Florida
0
75 miles
N
GEORGIA
95
10
Jacksonville
Tallahassee
St. Augustine
ATLANTIC OCEAN
Gainesville
75
19
Ocala
Daytona Beach
Cedar Key
4
GULF OF MEXICO
275
Orlando
Cape Canaveral
Florida's Turnpike
Tampa
4
Clearwater
60
St. Petersburg
Fort Pierce
Sarasota
Lake Okeechobee
27
95
75
Venice
Palm Beach
80
Fort Myers
Fort Lauderdale
Naples
84
41
Miami
Everglades
1
Key West
The Keys
29
85
231
10
Valparaiso
Freeport
Pensacola
Panama City
Panhandle

fanciers of the fast lane. For sun-worshippers, there are few places more satisfying than the Sunshine State.

There is a saying that promises, "Once you get Florida sand in your shoes, you will always return." Many visitors will swear it's true, and so will thousands of permanent residents who have wended their ways here from all over the country and the world and hope to stay forever. May it prove true for you, too.

The Story of Florida

GEOLOGY

Compared to most land masses, Florida is a mere child, having emerged from the sea as recently as 20 to 30 million years ago. For eons its bedrock lay beneath the warm ocean waters, slowly collecting sediment and forming limestone deposits that would one day break the surface and become a new land. Washed by waves, worn by wind and rain, the mass enlarged and shrank as Ice Age glaciers formed and reformed, intermittently raising and lowering the level of the sea. Following the Ice Age, centuries of heavy rain filled limestone scars and caves created by the changing seas. Springs appeared, hints of the giant aquifers that were aborning underground.

The constant wearing by warm sea waves, wind and rain has resulted in a land that often seems as level as a banquet table. The state's highest point, an unspectacular 345 feet, is found near its far northern border, where rolling hills are heralded as relief from the monotonous flatness.

But the limestone that serves as anchor—much of it covered with sand, some with red clay or soils rich enough to nourish superb vegetables and fruits—offers up a variety of treasures beneath its ever-eroding, brittle crust. In some places fresh water bubbles up in tiny sinkholes and sensational springs; in others, bones of mammoths attest to a busy Pleistocene period; elsewhere, rich phosphate rock summons new mining enterprises.

While not readily apparent to the casual traveler, the state is usually divided into several basic land regions that can be identified with closer examination. Like a watery fringe, the Atlantic and Gulf coastal plains surround the state, extending inland as far as 60 miles in some places. Mostly quite level and low, they are often wooded and dense; offshore they take the form of sand bars, coral reefs, lagoons and islands. The farthest bit of fringe, the Florida Keys, consist of oolitic limestone and coral rock. East of the Keys lies the only living coral reef in the continental United States.

The southernmost mainland region, the Lake Okeechobee-Everglades Basin, contains the state's major swamp area, though great portions have been drained and converted to agricultural land. This area is dominated by the Everglades, a giant "river of grass" flowing from Lake Okeechobee, and its neighboring Big Cypress Swamp.

The central ridge and lakes region extends through the middle of the state from the Okefenokee Swamp southward to Lake Okeechobee. Dotted with numerous lakes, this gently rolling area also offers up clear, cold springs.

In the north, the Tallahassee Hills region is a narrow, eroded plateau running about 100 miles from east to west. Next to it lie the Marianna lowlands, filled with sinkholes caused by the dissolution of the limestone strata. Between the Perdido and Apalachicola rivers in the Panhandle, the western highlands rise to the state's highest elevations. Streams and clear rivers meander here between broadly rolling hills and empty into the ever-present sea.

HISTORY

EARLY EXPLORATION Modern archaeologists tell us that human beings have been harvesting the waters, roaming the hills and wading the swamps of Florida for at least 12 centuries. Little remains of the early wanderers but bits and pieces of tools and artifacts, mystifying mounds and occasional piles of refuse deposited by generations of these early partakers of oyster-on-the-half-shell. When Europeans arrived in Florida, they encountered a number of resident Indian tribes. Apalachees roamed western regions; Timucuans spread from east of the Aucilla River down to Tampa Bay; warlike Calusas resided in the Everglades. Smaller tribes such as the Tequestas and Ais struggled among the larger groups.

Written Florida history begins in 1513 when Juan Ponce de León arrived on the northeastern coast, probably near present-day St. Augustine, and claimed the land for Spain. Lovely legend tells us he was searching for a bubbling magical "fountain of youth," although one suspects he might have been equally contented with a great cache of gold, also purported to be lying in wait for ambitious treasure-seekers. Though Ponce de León was to fulfill none of his dreams, he did grace the territory with its romantic name, "Florida," in honor of Spain's Easter holiday, *Pascua Florida* or "feast of flowers."

Ponce de León left, after exploring the eastern coast, to return again in 1521, this time with the hopes of setting up a little colony on the southwestern side of the peninsula. Unfriendly Indians soon squelched this plan, but by then Florida's reputation as a place worth struggling to gain had begun to take hold. Cabeza de Vaca came and took back tales of his wanderings among the Indians; Hernando de Soto explored from present day Tampa Bay to Tallahassee before dying of fever. In 1559, Tristan de Luna tried to set up a colony on Pensacola Bay, but hardships and hurricanes put an end to the struggles after only two years.

Within a few years of de Luna's efforts, the French began exploring Florida. René Goulaine de Laudonnière established a little bastion, Fort Caroline, at the mouth of the great northward-flowing St. Johns River. These French inroads challenged the Spanish to work even faster and harder. In 1565, Pedro Menéndez de Aviles arrived on the northeast coast and established what would become the first permanent settlement in the present-day United States—St. Augustine.

Menéndez promptly set about removing the French, converting Fort Caroline into San Mateo, only to see it recaptured with much loss of life two years later. But Spanish progress continued across northern Florida in the form of a chain of forts and missions established to convert the Indians to Christianity. With the Spanish grip seemingly secure, the English steered clear of Florida. They established their first colonies far to the north, away from the threat of Spanish power, although Sir Francis Drake did manage to raid struggling St. Augustine in 1586.

By the early 1700s, English colonists began causing trouble for the Spanish, particularly in present-day South Carolina and Georgia. Little by little, they trickled south, laid waste the missions between St. Augustine and Pensacola, destroyed the little "first colony" and killed many of the Indians. Meanwhile, the French had their eyes on Florida's far western coast; they captured Pensacola in 1719. As Spain's hold grew weaker, England's desire for the territory strengthened. Finally, in 1763, following the devastating Seven Years' War, Spain traded Florida for Cuba, abandoning the glorious dreams of eternal youth, gleaming treasure and religious conversion for which her explorers, settlers and missionaries had struggled.

WAR AND INDIAN CONFLICTS England had great plans for Florida. The territory was divided into two sections—East and West Florida—with capitals at St. Augustine and Pensacola. Settlers were promised land grants and other benefits; areas were mapped in detail; tentative peace was made with some of the Creek Indians, who had been gradually moving into the territory and down the peninsula. But the English were able to fulfill few of their hopes in Florida, since they had to turn their attention to the American Revolutionary War.

Though both East and West Florida remained loyal to the British, when the dust had cleared following the American Revolution, Spain had regained the two territories and their capitals. Colonizing began in earnest. Spain offered generous land grants both to its own people and to the new Americans. Florida also became an accessible and safe haven for escaping slaves from the new states.

Conflict between Indians and settlers, which had raged through much of Florida's brief history, became more and more serious. By this time, most of the original tribes had been killed or scattered, victims of European exploration, raids and wars, but as the 18th century progressed, more Creek and other southeastern Indians had been filling the void. They became known as "Seminoles," a name derived, most likely, from "siminoli," meaning exiles or wanderers. On a pretext of hunting down runaway slaves, Andrew Jackson led troops into northern Florida in 1817 and attacked Indian settlements, precipitating the First Seminole War.

Indian wars and other assorted skirmishes and problems finally encouraged Spain to sell the territory to the United States in 1821. Andrew Jackson became the first territorial governor. The two "Floridas" were united for good. Two men were assigned the task of locating a new capital. Setting out in opposite directions, one from St. Augustine and one from Pensacola, they rendezvoused among the rolling hills of the central Panhandle, where Tallahassee became the seat of government.

As in many other parts of the country, the Indians struggled to hold onto their homeland. But the settlers found them an "annoyance," and the government decided to have them removed to Indian Territory west of the Mississippi. As president in 1835, Andrew Jackson declared the Second Seminole War, hoping to get rid of the Indians in short order. But he had not reckoned with the Seminoles' commitment to fight for what was theirs. From their midst rose a powerful leader, Osceola, whose skill and dedication gained respect even from those who fought against him. Only after investing seven years, 1500 lives and $20 million was the government able to declare a victory. At last, under dreadful conditions, most of the surviving Seminoles were removed to Indian Territory.

Several hundred Indians, however, escaped into the Everglades to spend the rest of the century living a nomadic life in the swamp. Today their descendants number about 2000 living in two separate groups—1500 Seminoles and 500 Miccosukees, many still following the traditional Everglades lifestyle. They finally resumed official relations with the United States in 1962, 125 years after their self-imposed independence.

In 1845, Florida became a state with a plantation-type economy and a population centered mostly in its northern regions. Though it seceded from the Union during the Civil War, no major battles were fought within its borders and Reconstruction was somewhat less painful than in many other southern states. Even after the war, northern Florida remained an agricultural belt. Its hard-working farmers and later rural settlers became known as "crackers," a nickname of debated origin but one that has come to be associated with folks whose roots lie deep in Florida soil.

TREASURE ALONG THE COASTS Not until the 1880s would the peninsula to the south begin to reveal its tremendous treasures. At this time, two millionaires with dreams as grand as Ponce de León's made accessible the sea-surrounded paradise and set in motion a land development that, though it has had some tough moments of hesitation, has steamrolled through the 20th century.

It all began when Henry B. Plant and Henry Flagler built railroads down each coast, establishing lavish resorts in tropical settings that attracted visitors, speculators and the thousands of workers that such projects require. This increasing accessibility also opened up new industries such as phosphate mining, sponge fishing, cigar making and citrus growing. Immigrants, attracted by the new industries, settled in various regions where some of their descendants still reside today. Greek sponge fishers established a major industry at Tarpon Springs. Cubans and Spaniards came to work at the cigar factories at Ybor City in Tampa. Other communities were established by Scots, Jews and Slovaks.

Swamps were drained, and more rich farmland became accessible. Real estate boomed until 1926, when, with the rest of the country, it busted. Depression, hurricanes and the Mediterranean fruit fly all took their toll until World War II. Then the all-weather state became a major military training ground and the economy began climbing once again.

MODERN TIMES The years since the war have been one continuous boom, filled with promise and prosperity. As some of the old industries continue to thrive, new ones, from international banking to electronics and plastics, move in with a steady flow. Most spectacular of these is space exploration, headquartered at Cape Canaveral.

Over 40 million tourists come to Florida each year, attracted as always by the warm winter climate and the beaches. But new dimensions have been added even to tourism with the coming of professional sports, renewed emphasis on the state's colorful history and, above all, sophisticated theme parks such as Walt Disney World and EPCOT Center.

The permanent population is also swelling as dramatically as waves in a hurricane. Large influxes of Cuban refugees in the early 1960s and in 1980 have changed the face of Miami. Central Americans are also arriving in search of new lives. Retirees contribute to Florida's senior population—larger than that of any other state—which brings with it increased leisure time, volunteer manpower and a growing need for health care. By the year 2000, it is expected that more new people will be moving into Florida than to any other state in the nation, making it not only one of the most populous states, but also one of the most diverse.

Dreams of gold and eternal youth have been replaced by promises of dollars, pleasant retirements and the good life in a land where the sun almost always shines and snow almost never falls. But there is a nagging cloud on the horizon that may affect Florida's future as forcefully as the explorers and the railroads impacted her past. It is a cloud observed by many who feel Florida has grown much too fast, that care and caution have been thrown to the winds of profit and growth. In its shadow are predictions of what could happen one day to a land that has developed too quickly, whose supply of crystal water has gone unchecked, whose pollution may kill the hand that feeds.

But there are encouraging signs. In 1968, Florida wrote a new constitution with the coming century in mind. Recent actions at the capital have resulted in the state's acquiring more wild areas and preserves. Archaeological exploration of Spanish missions, Indian sites and shipwrecks has kindled interest in forgotten history. Florida heritage is rich. It may well have much to teach about where the real treasures lie.

FLORA

Lying on the edge of the tropic latitudes, Florida boasts a "best of both worlds" plant life. At least 344 species of trees, about 80 percent of those native to the United States, grow here. Pines are the most prolific; pine forests cover most of north and northwest Florida, where sweet gum, red maple and tulip trees also abound. The majestic sabal palm, Florida's state tree, is the most widely distributed in the state, flourishing in most any type of soil.

Other dominant trees include magnolia and cypress, Florida hickory and numerous varieties of oak. Caribbean representatives, abundant in the subtropical regions to the south, include mahogany, gumbo-limbo and many other species of palm, including the handsome royal and coconut palms. Cabbage palmetto can be found in coastal regions throughout the state. Because lumbering was one of the state's earliest industries, few virgin stands remain.

Many Florida plants are sensitive to subtle changes in moisture, resulting in river bottoms and low hammocks full of water oaks and varieties of gum, river banks and lake shores abundant in cypress, and high, dry regions supporting pines, post oak and turkey oak. Wildflowers, many of them natives, may be found in any season. Bladderwort, duckweed and wild iris thrive in marshes and shallow water. Beautiful but not beloved, the fast-growing flowering water hyacinth can choke whole rivers and streams in a short time.

To the south, especially in the Everglades, native orchids and air plants provide an exotic beauty. The rolling northern regions are noted for abundant displays of azaleas and camellias. Oleanders, hibiscus, poinsettias, gardenias, jasmine, trumpet vine and morning-glory thrive almost everywhere. For brilliant floral displays, nothing can match a blooming royal poinciana or a colorful shower of bougainvillea, common where temperatures do not dip too low.

FAUNA

Early Florida explorers reported amazing numbers of animals everywhere they went. Even veteran travelers living today can recall the abundance of birds soaring above the Tamiami Trail when it was still a new roadway. Today, 90 percent of Everglades birds are gone, and ever-increasing civilization has reduced the mammal and reptile population considerably. However, in the protected areas where natural habitats remain, native wildlife still thrives and Florida remains a zoological wonderland.

Of the 84 land mammals still found in the state, the black bear, gray fox, puma and wild cat are the rarest. Deer are common in many regions, except for the tiny Key deer, whose dwindling population is now limited to one spot in the Florida Keys. Abundant are squirrels, rabbits, raccoons and opossums; less prolific are otters and minks, long trapped for their pelts. Armadillos poke around noisily for insects; wild boar and feral hogs can be encountered in many wooded areas.

Once common in Florida but long a victim of civilization, the gentle manatee, or sea cow, is dwindling in numbers despite efforts to save it. These bulky, homely animals may be observed in several protected areas. They often feed trustingly at the water's surface close to boaters and fishermen, where they can become victims of motor blades and abandoned tackle.

Alligators live in lakes, rivers and marshy areas throughout the state. Long protected by law, they can be seen in various parks as well as in the wild and, for safety, should be respected. Their cousin, the American crocodile, is endangered and rare.

A variety of snakes thrive in Florida; the poisonous ones include rattlesnake, coral snake, cottonmouth moccasin and copperhead. Frogs, lizards and turtles, including loggerhead sea turtles, can often be seen.

Birdwatchers have listed over 400 species and subspecies of birds throughout the state. In marshes and swamps one can often spot ibis, herons and egrets. Ospreys nest on telephone poles in the Keys. Endangered species such as roseate spoonbills and woodstorks are drastically reduced in number, but are still present in the Everglades.

Coastal regions abound in shore birds such as the brown pelican, varieties of gull, sandpipers and terns. Ducks, geese and many other migratory birds make their winter homes in Florida. Natural rookeries, protected sanctuaries and a thriving Audubon Society contribute to the maintenance of the rich bird life in the state.

One of Florida's most popular mammals resides in the sea. The sleek dolphin, popular with humans because of its high intelligence and friendliness displayed in captivity, can also present an enchanting spectacle as it sports alongside a beach or among boaters in a bay.

NATURAL HABITATS

Human beings have altered so much of Florida that it's almost possible to believe condominiums and sprawling resort complexes have replaced whatever natural environs once existed. Fortunately, this is not entirely so. A broad variety of habitats still exists, many of them protected in the state's numerous parks and preserves.

With more than 8000 miles of tidal coastline and hundreds of freshwater lakes, ponds and springs, many Florida habitats are watery affairs. The coastal zones along the Gulf of Mexico and the Atlantic Ocean include mangrove swamps, salt marshes and the barrier islands. Here estuaries, complex and delicately balanced ecosystems formed where fresh and salt water mix, are born. They are crucial and fragile nurseries for many important species.

Throughout the state lie swamps of many varieties, each distinctive and curiously mysterious. For example, on the Georgia line lies the Okefenokee Swamp, a cypress bog with towering trees. Dwarf cypress, on the other hand, distinguishes swamps of the Everglades. Flood plain swamps along river banks often lie underwater for several months. Shrub bogs are often found in pine forests.

Pinelands make up Florida's most extensive habitats. Slash pine flatwoods abound in the state's national forests, where trees are tall and close above low, dry ground or dense, swampy areas. Longleaf pines dominate sandhill communities, creating parklike forests on rolling sandy hills. Sand pine scrub, unique to Florida, is probably a remnant of an ancient desert scrub that once covered portions of California, Mexico and dry areas of the Gulf. Today it can be found along the coast and on ancient central Florida dunes.

Hardwood hammocks, or forests, are where the big trees reside. They are quite varied and may be found in many differing forms throughout the state. The hammocks are home to much of Florida's great array of wildlife. Near the shore lie coastal and lowland hammocks, abundant in cabbage palms, oaks and red cedars. From the red clay soil in the central Panhandle grow the southern mixed hardwoods, the tag-end of the forests of the Appalachian range. Massive spreading live oaks, draped with hoary Spanish moss, are found in live oak hammocks throughout the state. Tropical hammocks of southern Florida are perhaps the most intriguing, for here northern and Caribbean trees grow together—live oaks side-by-side with gumbo-limbo, mahogany and poisonwood.

Other habitats, each with their own character, include savannahs, coral reefs beneath the surface of the Atlantic Ocean, native prairies, freshwater marshes and the unique Everglades.

For a delightful and detailed guide to the diversity of Florida's natural world, from undersea regions to tidal creeks, consult *Florida, Images of the Landscape*, by James Valentine (Westcliffe Publishers).

Where to Go

Selecting Florida as a vacation destination is easy; deciding where to go is another matter. The state is so vast and varied that it would take many visits to experience all it has to offer. To help you decide, here are brief descriptions of the regions presented in this book, but they are only teasers. To get the whole scoop, read the more detailed introductions to each chapter, then delve into the material on the regions that appeal to you most.

This book begins in Miami, heads northward up the East Coast, then explores Central Florida. Next it heads south and west to the Everglades and Keys, then travels up the West Coast and finally makes a zigzag journey across the Panhandle. Each area is distinctive; put together they create a rich tapestry of the urban, the wild and the historical.

Miami is the stuff that brochures and television shows are made of. If you fly in, you will likely get a good view of glittering Miami Beach and the glorious Atlantic that attracts millions of visitors each year. You will also see the massive hotels and condominiums that hide the coastal expanse from all but the guests. The area is most definitely urban. Spanish is spoken as freely as English, a sign of the growing Latin American population. Hispanic entertainment and businesses, Cuban-style food, and ethnic music and language give sections of Miami the feel of a cosmopolitan Latin city.

Along the Atlantic, the **Gold Coast** stretches northward from the outskirts of Miami to Jupiter Inlet. Beautiful beaches and constant development mark much of this region, whose two major cities are booming Fort Lauderdale, with its miles of navigable canals, and wealthy, exclusive Palm Beach. Communities surrounding these two anchors reflect varying personalities, but just about everywhere tourists descend in winter to bask on the beaches.

The **East Coast**, stretching about 300 miles, has areas that are developing with a vengeance. But it also includes regions of near repose, especially in the area up toward the Georgia line. Ocean beaches are accessible along nearly the entire route, from auto-crazy Daytona Beach through old-fashioned fishing villages to almost-hidden Amelia Island. History is celebrated in St. Augustine and is being made at the Kennedy Space Center at Cape Canaveral. The busy seaport of Jacksonville is the major city along this coast.

Even though it boasts no beaches, perhaps the greatest variety of all can be found in **Central Florida**. Here cattle and horses graze on rolling hills, and the beautiful St. Johns River winds northward through the Ocala National Forest, where springs bubble like crystal. Citrus reigns in many areas. Lake Okeechobee struggles for survival as it nourishes fabulous farms. But the single resident of Central Florida that put the place securely on the globe's tourist map is Walt Disney World, near Orlando and Kissimmee. Sleepy towns have become cosmopolitan centers as visitors flock from across the world to this irresistible attraction.

Just beyond Miami's city lights, to the west and south lie the **Everglades and Keys,** two distinctive gifts of nature. Despite its swampy environment, the Everglades is a paradise for nature lovers and birdwatchers, offering up secrets found nowhere else on earth. To the south, the Florida Keys lie like a chain of island beads dividing the Gulf of Mexico from the Atlantic Ocean. Paralleling their eastern shoreline, the only living coral reef off the mainland United States attracts divers and explorers of every level of expertise.

The **West Coast,** from Marco Island to Cedar Key, varies greatly in pace and environment. From Fort Myers up through the Tampa/St. Petersburg area, growth abounds and travelers flood the region in the high season. But many of the communities, such as Sarasota, Tarpon Springs and isolated Cedar Key, have managed to keep their charm. Gulf beaches are fine along most of this coastline, until you reach the marshy spot where the highway veers inland. Here the pace slows down a bit, and wilderness areas offer experiences with an earlier, more natural Florida.

The **Panhandle** area includes everything north and west of the Suwannee River all the way to the Perdido River near historic Pensacola. Except for a few glitzy stretches of developed Gulf shore west of Panama City, the Panhandle reflects much of Old Florida. There are deep forests, clear springs, incredibly beautiful white sand beaches, freshwater lakes and rivers and historic sites. Tallahassee, the state capital, is a mixture of new cosmopolitan and Old South. An author once dubbed this region "the other Florida," and so it remains today.

When to Go

SEASONS

It's said that the *St. Petersburg Evening Independent* newspaper, vowing to give away free editions on days when the sun refuses to shine, has had to keep its promise no more than four times in any one year. No wonder Florida is called the Sunshine State. The weather stays balmy nearly all year in most regions, boasting a pleasant semitropical atmosphere. While Florida can also get both colder and hotter from time to time than one might expect, the state justifiably claims year-round weather nearly as perfect as can be found in the continental United States, especially for lovers of warmth and sun.

Generally the "shoulder seasons," spring and fall, bring the most pleasant days and nights in all but the southernmost regions of Florida, where winter is the favored time. Throughout the state, summers tend to be wet, hot and humid. Winters are drier, mild and sunny with moderate readings, though in the northern regions there can be periods when temperatures drop into the 20s and even occasional snow. From Central Florida southward, freezing can occur occasionally in all but the most southerly regions.

Curiously, with an average rainfall of 53 inches, the "Sunshine State" is also one of the nation's wettest. But rainfall is uneven: an area may be suffering drought conditions, only to have many inches of precipitation dumped on it from an offshore hurricane.

In general, southern Florida's winter high temperatures average in the upper 70s, with lows dropping only into the 50s. Northwest Florida has winter highs averaging around 67° and lows averaging 44°. Central Florida's temperatures range appropriately between those of its northern and southern neighbors. Summer temperatures are far more uniform throughout the state; average highs hover around 90° with lows seldom falling below 70°. While summer can bring hot afternoons, offshore breezes keep life comfortable in most regions near the coast.

Hurricanes, though they can be devastating, need not keep one away during the fall. Usually developing in September, hurricanes have also been known to occur much later. (Ironically, the worst storm in decades, Hurricane Andrew, which struck in 1992, occurred in August.) Unlike many other weather phenomena, they come with plenty of warning, allowing visitors either to batten down or depart for inland locations.

Generally temperate seasons, refreshing cold springs, breezy beaches and an abundance of air conditioning all contribute to making Florida a good year-round destination.

CALENDAR OF EVENTS

If life is a cabaret, then Florida is a fiesta. There are annual celebrations of just about everything from pirates to possum. Check with local chambers of commerce (listed in regional chapters of this book) to see what will be going on when you are in the area. Below is a sampling of some of the biggest events.

JANUARY

Miami: One of the largest post-season football games, the **Orange Bowl Classic**, kicks off the New Year. The **Art Deco Weekend Festival,** with the "Moon Over Miami Ball," takes place in South Miami Beach.

East Coast: In Daytona Beach, there is a week-long showcase of the **Ringling Brothers and Barnum & Bailey Circus.**

West Coast: The blessing of the sponge fleet, diving for the cross, Greek foods and festivities mark **Epiphany Day** in Tarpon Springs.

FEBRUARY

Miami: Over 300 artists and more than a million visitors celebrate the annual **Coconut Grove Arts Festival.** The **Miami International Boat Show** at

Miami Beach displays craft from just about every major manufacturer and offers free sailing clinics.

East Coast: The **Daytona 500** marks the culmination of **Speed Weeks** with a 200-lap stock car race at the Daytona International Speedway.

Central Florida: For ropin', ridin' and square dancin' on horseback, head over to Kissimmee's **Silver Spurs Rodeo,** the oldest rodeo in the state.

West Coast: The **Edison Pageant of Lights** commemorates Fort Myers' most famous resident. A pirate ship and accompanying flotilla invade Tampa to kick off the **Gasparilla Invasion and Parade,** as business folk turn pirate-for-a-day.

MARCH

Miami: A nine-day Hispanic celebration, **Carnival Miami,** culminates with a dynamic block party known as **Calle Ocho**. The two-week **Lipton International Players Championship** on Key Biscayne features top tennis players from around the world.

Central Florida: Top name performers appear at the **Kissimmee Bluegrass Festival.**

West Coast: A **Medieval Fair** brings jousters, minstrels and fair damsels to the grounds of the Ringling Museum in Sarasota. Tampa's **American Grand Prix Championship** is one of the country's premier horse jumping events.

Panhandle: You can see daring feats at the "greatest collegiate show on earth," **Florida State University's "Flying High" Circus Homeshow** in Tallahassee.

APRIL

Miami: Race cars whiz through downtown streets during the **Miami Grand Prix.**

Gold Coast: The **United States/International Challenge Cup** is a world-class croquet event held at Palm Beach Gardens.

East Coast: The **Bausch & Lomb WITA Tennis Championship** on Amelia Island draws top national and international talent.

Central Florida: At Lake Wales, the **Bok Tower Easter Sunrise Service** followed by carillon music has been celebrated since the 1940s.

Everglades and Keys: Runners set out from Marathon for a dash over the sea in the annual **Seven Mile Bridge Run**. Shell blowers participate in Key West's **Conch Shell Blowing Contest.**

MAY

Gold Coast: Florida's largest outdoor jazz festival, **Sunfest** at West Palm Beach, features top names and offers plenty of side events.

Everglades and Keys: The annual **Key West Fishing Tournament** has nine divisions and is held throughout the Lower Keys.

Panhandle: **Chautauqua** lives again at DeFuniak Springs, once winter home of the great American cultural movement.

JUNE

Panhandle: Pensacola's **International Billfish Tournament** is one of the largest on the Gulf, with awards exceeding $150,000. The **Fiesta of Five Flags**, also in Pensacola, is a week-long celebration with historic re-enactments, sporting events, art shows and more.

JULY

Many communities celebrate the **Fourth of July** with parades, fireworks and other festivities.

Everglades and Keys: South Florida ethnic groups join together at the Miccosukee Indian Village for the **Miccosukee Annual International Crafts and Music Festival**. Storytelling, arm-wrestling, fishing tournaments and look-alike contests highlight Key West's week-long **Hemingway Days**, honoring the man and his works.

AUGUST

Gold Coast: A sand castle contest, winetasting and an arts and crafts fair are just a few of the festivities during the month-long **Boca Festival Days** in Boca Raton.

SEPTEMBER

Gold Coast: Homemade rafts race through downtown Fort Lauderdale in the **New River Raft Race**.

East Coast: In St. Augustine, the **Annual Maritime Festival** features seafood, sailboat races and a costume ball.

Central Florida: For fast cars and lots of action, be at the **Pepsi 400 Nascar Winston Cup Series** in Daytona Beach. The **Annual Bartow Youth Villa Classic** benefits youth projects with an open golf tournament, dance, fashion show and more.

Panhandle: For two weekends the **Pensacola Seafood Festival** celebrates one of the state's oldest industries.

OCTOBER

Miami: Latin residents celebrate during Miami's **Hispanic Heritage Festival.**

East Coast: Jacksonville's **Florida National Jazz Festival** is a free outdoor event in Metropolitan Park with top-name performers.

Panhandle: The banks of the Suwannee River are a perfect setting for the **Bluegrass Camp-o-ree** at Live Oak.

NOVEMBER

Miami: Liberty City's **Sunstreet Festival** showcases Afro-American music, arts and sports.

Central Florida: Turn your gaze upward for exciting performances at the **Annual Florida State Air Fair** at the Kissimmee Municipal Airport.

Panhandle: The **Annual Florida Seafood Festival** at Apalachicola honors one of the area's most thriving industries. Artists from across the country gather in Pensacola's Seville Square for the **Great Gulf Coast Arts Festival.**

DECEMBER

Candlelight tours, parades and Santa festivals highlight many communities throughout December.

Miami: **Art in the Heart of Miami Beach** has an art and entertainment lineup. In Coral Gables, the **Junior Orange Bowl International Championships** draws hundreds of under-18 players from around the world including the United Kingdom, Taiwan, Sweden and Africa.

East Coast: Jacksonville's **Gator Bowl Classic** matches two of the country's top football teams.

Panhandle: Sparkling sea craft parade on the Intracoastal Waterway for the **Pensacola Beach Christmas Parade and Decorated Boat Procession.**

How to Deal With . . .

VISITOR INFORMATION

For a free copy of the *Florida Vacation Guide*, contact the **Florida Department of Commerce** (Division of Tourism, Direct Mail Warehouse, 126 West Van Buren Street, Tallahassee FL 32399; 904-488-3104). Most small towns have chambers of commerce or visitor information centers; many of them are listed in *Hidden Florida* under the appropriate regions.

For visitors arriving by automobile, Florida hosts five **Welcome Centers** that provide fresh orange juice, maps and lots of guidance from 8 a.m. to 5 p.m. daily. These are located near the border on Route 10, west of Pensacola; in the new Capitol Building, Tallahassee; on Route 75, north of Jennings; on Route 95, near Yulee; and three miles north of Campbellton on Route 231.

PACKING

Unless you plan to spend your Florida trip dining in ultra-deluxe restaurants, you'll need much less in your suitcase than you might think. For most trips, all you'll have to pack are some shorts, lightweight shirts or tops, cool slacks, a couple of bathing suits and cover-ups, and something *very casual* for any special event that might call for dressing up.

The rest of your luggage space can be devoted to light "beach reading" and a few essentials that should not be forgotten (unless you prefer to shop on arrival). These include good sunscreens (preferably not oils), high-quality sunglasses and some insect repellant, especially if you are traveling in the summer or heading to the far south even in winter. If you're planning to spend a lot of time outdoors—where fire ants or stinging jellyfish might be a concern—take along a small container of a papain-type meat tenderizer. It won't keep the varmints away, but it will ease the pain should you fall victim.

Take along an umbrella or light raincoat for the sudden showers that can pop out of nowhere. If you visit North or Central Florida in the winter, you would be wise to take a warm jacket or coat. Even in the far south, a sweater can be welcome on occasional winter days.

Good soft, comfortable, lightweight shoes for sightseeing are a must. Despite its tropical gentleness, Florida terrain doesn't treat bare feet well except along the shore or beside a pool. Sturdy sandals will do well. If you plan to do any hiking in the wetlands (and wetlands can show up where you might not expect them), wear canvas shoes that you don't mind wading in.

Serious scuba divers will probably want to bring their own gear, but it's certainly not essential. Underwater equipment of all sorts is available for rent wherever diving is popular. Many places also rent beach toys and tubes for floating down rivers. Fishing gear is also often available for rent.

Campers will need basic cooking equipment and, except in winter, can make out fine with only a lightweight sleeping bag or cot and a tent with good screens and a ground cloth. A canteen, first aid kit, flashlight and other routine camping gear should be brought along.

If you find you can't seem to walk a beach without picking up shells, take a plastic bag for hauling treasures. A camera is good, too; Florida sunsets are sensational. Binoculars enhance both birdwatching and beachwatching. And don't, for heaven's sake, forget your copy of *Hidden Florida.*

HOTELS

Lodgings in Florida run the gamut from tiny one-room cabins in the woods to glistening highrise condominiums in which every room faces the sea. Bed and breakfasts are relative newcomers to much of Florida, but they are there for the finding. Chain motels line most main thoroughfares and mom-and-pop enterprises still successfully vie for lodgers in every region.

Large hotels with names you'd know anywhere appear in most centers of any size. Poshest of all are the upscale resorts. Here one can drop in almost from the sky and never have to leave the grounds. In fact, you can take in all the sports, dining, nightlife, shopping and entertainment needed to make a vacation complete, although you may miss the authentic Florida.

Other Florida lodgings offer more personality, such as historic inns or little hotels where you can eat breakfast with the handful of other guests. And when spending a week at the beach, there's nothing like an old-fashioned beach house, preferably on stilts, where the salt-laden wind blows in off the water and the mockingbirds sing outside in the trees.

Whatever your preference and budget, you can probably find something to suit your taste with the help of the regional chapters in this book. Remember, rooms are scarce and prices rise in the high season, which is generally summer in the Panhandle and winter to the south. Off-season rates are often drastically reduced in many places, allowing for a week's, or even a month's stay to be a real bargain. Whatever you do, plan ahead and make reservations, especially in the prime tourist seasons.

Accommodations in this book are organized by region and classified according to price. Rates referred to are high-season rates, so if you are looking for low-season bargains, it's good to inquire. *Budget* lodgings generally are less than $50 per night for two people and are satisfactory and clean but modest. *Moderate*-priced lodgings run from $50 to $90; what they have to offer in the way of luxury will depend on where they are located, but they generally offer larger rooms and more attractive surroundings. At a *deluxe* hotel or resort you can expect to spend between $90 and $130 for a double; you'll generally find spacious rooms, a fashionable lobby, a restaurant and often a group of shops. *Ultra-deluxe* facilities, priced above $130, are a region's finest, offering all the amenities of a deluxe hotel plus plenty of extras.

If you crave a room facing the surf, be sure to ask specifically. Be warned that "waterfront" can mean bay, lake, inlet or even a slough in some cases. If you are trying to save money, lodgings a block or so from the beach often offer lower rates than those within sight of the waves and, because Florida beaches are open to the public, are often worth the short stroll.

RESTAURANTS

Eating places in Florida seem to be as numerous as the fish in the sea, and fish is what you will find everywhere. Whether catfish from a river or pompano from the surf, you can almost always count on its being fresh and prepared well. Each region has its specialties, its ethnic influences and its gourmet spots.

Within a particular chapter, restaurants are categorized geographically, with each restaurant entry describing the establishment according to price.

(Text continued on page 22.)

Florida Cuisine

With salt water on three sides and rivers, lakes and streams abounding in its interior, seafood and freshwater fish top the list of Florida foods. From the ocean and Gulf come fresh pompano, scamp, grouper, shrimp, yellowfin tuna and mullet, and the list goes on and on. Each region serves up its own special dishes from its particular waters—oysters-on-the-half-shell from Apalachicola Bay in the Panhandle, smoked mullet from the Gulf, conch chowder and fritters in the Keys. Inland there's nothing tastier than well-fried catfish. Florida lobster, a giant crawfish, gives Maine a run for its money. Alligator tail shows up on Everglades-area menus. Stone crab, available from October to May, is even a humane dish—while you are dining on the claw meat of this accommodating creature, he is busy growing a new claw for the next year.

No matter where you live, you have undoubtedly partaken of Florida citrus fruits and mixed water into a can of Florida concentrated juice. In many areas, in the winter months, you can see oranges, grapefruit, limes and tangelos right alongside the road, both on trees and for sale at inviting roadside stands. Varieties seem endless, with some fruit offering special qualities such as remarkable sweetness or no seeds. A freshly picked, easily peeled tangerine is an entirely different item from its stored-and-transported grocery-store cousin. Late fruits, such as valencia oranges and seedless grapefruit, are available into June and July. Even out of season, you'll find citrus products—marmalades, novelty wines, calamondin and kumquat jellies and lemon candies. Key lime pie is a traditional dessert from the Keys, made originally from the tiny yellow limes that grow there.

Exotic fruits have joined the list of Florida produce, familiar ones such as mangos, avocados and papayas and lesser-known zapotes, lychees and guavas. Coconuts grow in backyards in southern Florida. Swamp cabbage yields up its heart as the chief delicacy in "hearts of palm" salad. Winter vegetables and fruits thrive in the drained Everglades regions, where you can stop and pick strawberries, peppers, tomatoes or whatever else is left over from the great quantities shipped across the United States. In the northern and central regions of the state, pecans and peanuts are popular Florida treats; southern pecan pie is a rich, calorie-laden delicacy. Sugar cane and sorghum are still turned into syrup and molasses in some areas.

Ethnic foods have long influenced Florida cuisine. Throughout the state you will discover Greek dishes and salads originally introduced by the sponge fishers of Tarpon Springs. Cuban fare such as picadillo, black beans and yellow rice and fried plantains entered southern Florida when travel from the island neighbor was unrestricted. The Minorcan influence around the St. Augustine area reveals itself in pilau, a spicy stew of rice, vegetables, seafood and chicken. Creole cooking is enjoyed in the Panhandle in rich seafood gumbos and jambalayas. In the Everglades area you can try Indian fry breads and mashed cassava roots.

Lately, inventive young chefs are using local fruits and other tropical ingredients to create a new style of cooking. Seafood, chicken, lamb and beef get tropical treatments, and are often grilled, smoked or blackened. Some call it "tropical fusion" or "nuevo Cubano," while others deem it "new Florida cuisine." Whatever the name, one thing is certain: This brand of cooking is marvelously adventurous. After all, where else can you find Key lime pasta or grilled grouper with mango salsa, plantains and purple potatoes?

Of course, Floridians still relish these down-to-earth comfort foods. Diners and counter-service cafés, which serve mounds of food for a few dollars, are there to be found. And, with over 20,000 ranches statewide, a good barbecued steak is held sacred by many Floridians.

Good old-fashioned southern cooking and soul food are also an integral part of Florida cuisine, especially in northern and central Florida. Southern fried chicken, though not popular with the cholesterol-conscious, is a beloved delicacy, and fried fish is usually served with a choice of grits or hushpuppies. (The latter are fried balls of cornbread that hunters and fishermen were said to have tossed to their dogs to keep them quiet while supper was being prepared following a successful foray.) In most places, you'll be served breakfast with grits, a true southern dish and a tasty one when eaten with butter.

Winemaking is relatively new to Florida but is becoming serious business. Wild grapes are native to many regions of the state, a good predictor of possible future success. There are wineries in the Panhandle, near Jacksonville and in Tampa. These fledgling operations are gaining a reputation for Florida; keep your eye on them.

Dinner entrées at *budget* restaurants usually cost $8 or less. The ambience is informal, service usually speedy and the crowd often a local one. *Moderately* priced restaurants range between $8 and $16 at dinner; surroundings are casual but pleasant, the menu offers more variety and the pace is usually slower. *Deluxe* establishments tab their entrées from $16 to $24; cuisines may be simple or sophisticated, depending on the location, but the decor is plusher and the service more personalized. *Ultra-deluxe* dining rooms, where entrées begin at $24, are often the gourmet places; here cooking has become a fine art and the service should be impeccable.

Some restaurants change hands often and are occasionally closed in low seasons. Efforts have been made in this book to include places with established reputations for good eating. Breakfast and lunch menus vary less in price from restaurant to restaurant than evening dinners.

TRAVELING WITH CHILDREN

Any state that boasts gentle beaches, developed campgrounds and Mickey Mouse is bound to be a good place to take children. Plenty of family adventures are available in Florida, from manmade attractions to experiences in the wild. A few guidelines will help make travel with children a pleasure.

Book reservations in advance, making sure that the places you stay accept children. If you need a crib or extra cot, arrange for it ahead of time. A travel agent can be of help here, as well as with most other travel plans.

If you are traveling by air, try to reserve bulkhead seats where there is plenty of room. Take along extras you may need, such as diapers, changes of clothing, snacks and toys or small games. When traveling by car, be sure to take along the extras, too. Make sure you have plenty of water and juices to drink; dehydration can be a subtle problem.

A first-aid kit is a must for any trip. Along with adhesive bandages, antiseptic cream and something to stop itching, include any medicines your pediatrician might recommend to treat allergies, colds, diarrhea or any chronic problems your child may have.

If you plan to spend much time at the beach, take extra care the first few days. Children's skin is usually more tender than adult skin, and severe sunburn can happen before you realize it. A hat is a good idea, along with a reliable sunblock. And be sure to keep a constant eye on children who are near the water.

For parents' night out, many hotels provide a dependable list of baby sitters. In some areas you may find drop-in child care centers; look in the yellow pages for these, and make sure you choose ones that are licensed.

Many towns, parks and attractions offer special activities designed just for children. Consult local newspapers and/or phone the numbers in this guide to see what's happening where you're going.

BEING AN OLDER TRAVELER

As millions have discovered, Florida is an ideal place for older vacationers, many of whom turn into part-time or full-time residents. The climate is mild, the terrain level, and many destinations offer significant discounts for seniors. Off-season rates make most areas exceedingly attractive for travelers on limited incomes. Florida residents over 65 can benefit from reduced rates at most state parks, and the Golden Age Passport, which must be applied for in person, allows free admission to national parks and monuments for anyone 62 or older.

The **American Association of Retired Persons (AARP)** (3200 East Carson Street, Lakewood, CA 90712; 310-496-2277) offers membership to anyone over 50. AARP's benefits include travel discounts with a number of firms; escorted tours and cruises are available through **AARP Travel Service** (400 Pinnacle Way, Suite 450, Norcross, GA 30071; 800-927-0111).

Elderhostel (75 Federal Street, Boston, MA 02110; 617-426-7788) offers reasonably priced, all-inclusive educational programs in a variety of Florida locations throughout the year.

Be extra careful about health matters. In addition to the medications you ordinarily use, it's a good idea to bring along the prescriptions for obtaining more. Consider carrying a medical record with you—including your medical history and current medical status as well as your doctor's name, phone number and address. Make sure that your insurance covers you while away from home.

BEING DISABLED

Florida is striving to make more and more destinations fully accessible to the disabled. For information on the regions you will be visiting, contact the **Center for Independent Living,** which has branches in Miami (1335 Northwest 14th Street, Miami, FL 33125; 305-547-5444); Winter Park (700 North Denning Drive, Winter Park, FL 32789; 407-623-1070); Rockledge (1825-A Cogswell Street, Rockledge, FL 32955; 407-633-6182); Gainesville (1023 Southeast 4th Avenue, Gainesville, FL 32601; 904-378-7474); Tampa (12310 North Nebraska Avenue, Suite F, Tampa, FL 33612; 813-975-6560); Tallahassee (1380 Ocala Road, Apt. H-4, Tallahassee, FL 32304; 904-575-9621); and Pensacola (513 East Fairfield Drive, Pensacola, FL 32503; 904-435-9343).

Providing helpful information for disabled travelers are the **Society for the Advancement of Travel for the Handicapped** (347 5th Avenue, Suite 610, New York, NY 10016; 212-447-7284), **Travel Information Center** (Moss Rehabilitation Hospital, 1200 Tabor Road, Philadelphia, PA 19141; 215-329-5715), **Mobility International USA** (P.O. Box 3551, Eugene, OR 97403; 503-343-1284), **Flying Wheels Travel** (P.O. Box 382, Owatonna,

MN 55060; 800-535-6790). **Travelin' Talk** (P.O. Box 3534, Clarksville, TN 37043; 615-552-6670), a networking organization, also provides information for disabled travelers.

Reserve ahead to experience **Trout Pond**, a special recreation area for the handicapped, located near Tallahassee in the Apalachicola National Forest (Watully Ranger District, Route 6, Box 7860, Crawfordville, FL 32327).

BEING A FOREIGN TRAVELER

PASSPORTS AND VISAS Most foreign visitors need a passport and tourist visa to enter the United States. Contact your nearest United States Embassy or Consulate well in advance to obtain a visa and to check on any other entry requirements.

CUSTOMS REQUIREMENTS Foreign travelers are allowed to carry in the following: 200 cigarettes (or 100 cigars), $400 worth of duty-free gifts, including one liter of alcohol (you must be 21 years of age). You may bring in any amount of currency but must fill out a form if you bring in over $10,000 (U.S.). Carry any prescription drugs in clearly marked containers. You may have to produce a written prescription or doctor's statement for the customs officer. Meat or meat products, seeds, plants, fruits and narcotics are not allowed to be brought into the United States. Contact the United States Custom Service (1301 Constitution Avenue Northwest, Washington, DC 20229; 202-566-8195) for further information.

DRIVING If you plan to rent a car, an international driver's license should be obtained before arriving in the United States. Some car rental agencies require both a foreign license and an international driver's license. Many also require a lessee to be at least 25 years of age; all require a major credit card.

CURRENCY United States money is based on the dollar. Bills generally come in denominations of $1, $5, $10, $20, $50 and $100. Every dollar is divided into 100 cents. Coins are the penny (1 cent), nickel (5 cents), dime (10 cents) and quarter (25 cents). Half-dollar and dollar coins are rarely used. You may not use foreign currency to purchase goods and services in the United States. Consider buying traveler's checks in dollar amounts. You may also use credit cards affiliated with an American company such as Interbank, Barclay Card and American Express.

ELECTRICITY Electric outlets use currents of 110 volts, 60 cycles. For appliances made for other electrical systems, you need a transformer or other adapter.

WEIGHTS AND MEASURES The United States uses the English system of weights and measures. American units and their metric equivalents are: 1 inch = 2.5 centimeters; 1 foot (12 inches) = 0.3 meter; 1 yard (3 feet) = 0.9 meter; 1 mile (5280 feet) = 1.6 kilometers; 1 ounce = 28 grams; 1 pound (16 ounces) = 0.45 kilogram; 1 quart (liquid) = 0.9 liter.

The Sporting Life

CAMPING

Florida offers a variety of camping opportunities from primitive camping in wilderness areas to recreational vehicle parks that resemble fashionable resorts. For a listing of state parks and recreation areas, send for the *Florida State Parks Guide* (Department of Natural Resources, Florida Park Service, 3900 Commonwealth Boulevard, Tallahassee, FL 32399; 904-488-9872).

For information on camping in state forests, contact the **Department of Agriculture and Consumer Services** (Division of Forestry, 3125 Conner Boulevard, Tallahassee, FL 32399; 904-488-6727). Information on camping in national forests may be obtained from the **U.S. Forest Service** (Suite 4061, 227 North Bronough Street, Tallahassee, FL 32301; 904-681-7265). For information on national parks and seashores, contact the **National Park Service** (P.O. Box 2416, Tallahassee, FL 32316; 904-561-9106).

The **Florida Campground Association** (1638 North Plaza Drive, Tallahassee, FL 32308; 904-656-8878) puts out an annual *Florida Camping Directory* of over 200 private campgrounds and RV parks. Also, see the "Beaches and Parks" section in each chapter of this book to discover where camping is available in various areas of the state. An excellent book for visitors planning to camp in the state is *Florida Parks*, by Gerald Grow.

WILDERNESS PERMITS

Primitive campsites are provided in certain state parks and recreation areas. You need a permit for wilderness camping away from designated sites in national forests and in certain wilderness areas of national parks and seashores. To obtain permits and information contact individual sites, as found in the "Beaches and Parks" sections of the regional chapters of this book.

The **Florida Trail Association** (P.O. Box 13708, Gainesville, FL 32604; 904-378-8823) is creating a hiking trail from Big Cypress Preserve to the Panhandle. Much of it has been completed. By joining the association, you can hike private lands crossed by the trail and obtain maps.

BOATING

From paddle boat to cruise ship, just about every imaginable method of ploughing the waters is available in Florida. You can bring your own boat and travel the Intracoastal Waterway or laze away the day on a quiet lake with a fishing pole. And if you have no boat, you can rent or charter a craft of just about any size or speed. Each chapter in this book offers suggestions on how to go about finding the vessel of your choice. Most marinas and other rental agencies will arm you with maps and advice.

Regional chart packets for boaters and divers may be obtained by contacting the **Department of Commerce** (Office of Sports Promotion, 107 West Gaines Street, Tallahassee, FL 32399; 904-488-8347). Boating regulations and safety information may be obtained from the **Department of Natural Resources** (Florida Marine Patrol, Boating Safety Section, 3900 Commonwealth Boulevard, Mail Station 630, Tallahassee, FL 32399; 904-488-5757).

Canoeing is popular throughout Florida. To obtain the *Florida Recreational Trails System—Canoe Trails* brochure contact the **Florida Department of Natural Resources** (Florida Park Service, 3900 Commonwealth Boulevard, Mail Station 585, Tallahassee, FL 32399; 904-487-4784). *Canoeing the National Forests in Florida* is available from the **U.S. Forest Service** (227 North Bronough Street, Suite 4061, Tallahassee, FL 32301; 904-681-7265).

WATER SAFETY

Few places match Florida for the variety of water sports available. Swimming, scuba diving, snorkeling or just basking on a float are options wherever you can get to the shore, spring, lake or river. Surfing is popular on certain ocean and Gulf beaches when the wind is up. Drownings do occur now and then in all these places, but they can be avoided as long as you respect the power of the water, heed appropriate warnings and use good sense.

Wherever you swim, never do it alone. In the ocean or Gulf, if the surf is high, keep your face toward the incoming waves. They can bring unpleasant surprises even to the initiated. If you go surfing, learn the proper techniques and dangers from an expert before you start out. Respect signs warning of dangerous currents and undertows. If you get caught in a rip current or any tow that makes you feel out of control, don't try to swim against it. Head across it, paralleling the shore. Exercise caution in the use of floats, inner tubes or rafts: unexpected currents can quickly carry you out to sea.

Jellyfish stings are commonly treated with papain-type meat tenderizers. If you go scalloping, swim in or wade around in murky waters where shellfish dwell, wear canvas shoes to protect your feet.

Remember, you are a guest in the sea. All rights belong to the creatures who dwell there, including sharks. Though they are rarely seen and seldom attack, they should be respected. A wise swimmer who spots a fin simply heads unobtrusively for shore. On the other hand, if dolphins are cavorting in your area, don't worry they may put on quite a show.

Tragedies occur annually in springs, often to scuba divers who venture into deep caves and become disoriented or swim in off-limits areas. Spring diving is not for novices; accomplished divers should accompany every outing. Alligators have been known to drown swimmers or divers who venture into off-limits areas. Pay attention to warning signs; they mean what they say.

Life jackets are a must if you want your boating trip to end happily. This goes for canoes as well as larger and faster craft. And never, never take your eyes off a child who is near the water, no matter how calm conditions may appear. With so much wonderful water available in Florida, the best protection is to know how to swim, and to use your good sense.

FISH AND FISHING

Over 60 varieties of commercial fish are gathered from Florida waters; shellfish are harvested along all the coasts; and bass and bream almost jump from hook to frying pan beside freshwater streams. Florida is an angler's paradise. How you approach the sport is up to you. You can dangle a hook from a cane pole into a sluggish slough or chase bonefish in the Keys. You can spend the day casting off an abandoned bridge or haul in tarpon from a rollicking charter boat. You can gather scallops with your hands and a bucket in the shallows or catch blue crabs in a net. You may even find yourself casting a seine for mullet along the beach on an autumn morning.

Freshwater fishing is prime in many Florida waters. The state calls itself the "Largemouth Bass Capital of the World" because of the abundance of this freshwater fish, especially in the northwest. Several species of catfish and members of the sunfish family, such as bluegills, shellcrackers and crappie, abound in large lakes and backroad ponds and canals. Speckled perch are sought out during their spring spawning period, especially in the Lake Okeechobee area. Panfishing season begins with the coming of spring throughout the state and continues through the winter in the far south.

Saltwater fish are varied and abundant in the Gulf and ocean off the shores of the entire state. Common varieties include pompano, mackerel, bluefish, redfish, snapper, snook, grouper and trout. Tarpon, sailfish, marlin and shark challenge sportsfishers eager for a tussle. Crawfish, oysters, stone crabs, clams and scallops may also be harvested in season from the sea.

Salt and freshwater fishing requires a license unless you are fishing from a boat or pier that has its own license. Many bait and tackle shops and sporting goods stores around the state can provide you with the proper documentation. For further information contact the **Department of Natural Resources** (Florida Marine Patrol, Support Services, 3900 Commonwealth Boulevard, Tallahassee, FL 32303; 904-487-3122) or a local marina.

If you'd like to try a kind of fishing that's new to you, you will find guide services available just about everywhere boats are rented and bait sold. Charter fishing is the costliest way to go out to sea; party boats take a crowd but are less expensive and usually great fun. On rivers, lakes and tiny hidden streams, guides can show you the best place to throw a hook or skim a fly.

There are also fish to be viewed in Florida. A face mask, with or without a snorkel, will open up an undersea world of incredible beauty, whether it be in a crystal spring, along the shore or out among the reefs. In fact, colorful tropical fish may well be some of Florida's loveliest hidden treasures.

MIAMI

CHAPTER TWO

Miami

A throbbing pulse on Florida's southeastern tip, Miami has been viewed for much of this century as America's tropical dream destination. Longing for escape and a large dose of sunshine, visitors have continually sought out the palm-fringed beaches and sapphire waters of this carefree realm.

But like most idyllic locales, Miami and its environs embody far more than postcard-perfect beaches. Intertwined in this 2000-square-mile megalopolis are chic bayside villages, exclusive islands, grand Mediterranean areas and an array of skyscrapers. Across the pancake-flat terrain also lies a maze of bewitching waterways, traffic-choked highways and sprawling residential regions. A close inspection will even reveal a bit of the mangrove wilderness that served as the birthing place of this great resort center.

Miami's story is one of overnight success, a place built so fast and loved so soon that it's easy to forget how young it really is. Little more than a fishing village when it was incorporated in 1896, Miami didn't really evolve as a city until its frenetic 1920s land boom.

Likewise, as late as 1910, that silvery thread of barrier islands called Miami Beach was still awash with avocado and mango plantations. Not until the following decade did the ten miles of coastline finally burst with plush hotels and communities that were immediately frequented by celebrities.

The tale's prologue, however, trickles back to 1513 when Spaniard Ponce de León first set foot on this island strand. He encountered perilous coral reefs and mosquito-infested scrublands that made navigation difficult, even for the Calusa and Tequesta Indians who inhabited the shores. Back then, the Tequestas called the swamplands Lake of Mayaime, or "very large" lake, referring to northwestern Lake Okeechobee. The passage of time transformed the words into Miami.

It wasn't a grand lake, however, that drew railroad magnate Henry Flagler to the state's southern reaches in 1896. Rather, it was a fragrant bouquet of orange blossoms, sent by an astute pioneer named Julia Tuttle. When an unusually harsh freeze killed citrus groves as far south as West Palm Beach, where Flagler had created an elite vacation community, Tuttle dispatched the blooms as proof of warmer climes to the south. Previously skeptical of Miami's treasures, Flagler was at last convinced.

Flagler's railroad fueled progress in the area, bringing curious northern settlers to a land of warm ocean breezes and sunshine. New Jersey businessman John Collins was one of the first to catch a train southward to inspect a yet unseen coconut plantation he had purchased on Miami's barrier islands. Enchanted by the scene, he planted more fruit trees and began constructing a wooden bridge that would link these windswept isles to the mainland.

By 1913, Collins went broke with only half the bridge built and turned for help to Carl Fisher, inventor of the auto headlight and owner of the Indianapolis Speedway. A shrewd businessman, Fisher finished the bridge in exchange for a swath of island property, then set about molding his new sandspur into beach-rimmed isles with pretty shopping plazas, golf courses, hotels and waterfront homes.

When the 1920s land boom struck, Miami was primed. "Binder boys" stood on street corners hawking real estate for mere pennies, land that turned thousands of investors into overnight millionaires. Dazzled by this newfound investment, wealthy industrialists built fancy oceanfront estates and began shaping the downtown area. To the south, Staten Islander Ralph Munroe formed a quaint bayside village while pioneer George Merrick carved a Mediterranean-style community out of palmetto fronds.

Waves of "tin can tourists" arrived from the frigid north, setting up tents and other makeshift homes along Miami's shores. "Miami or Bust" read the signs that sprinkled highways across the country. Suddenly, Miami Beach was the dream vacation of every red-blooded American.

But the dream was temporarily dashed in 1926 when a perilous hurricane proved that even paradise can go awry. Nearly 400 people were killed and thousands of buildings destroyed or damaged. Then the Depression hit. The area fell into a lull until the mid-1930s, when a new building boom changed the look of southern Miami Beach: art deco architecture began sprouting everywhere. Radiant pastel buildings sporting geometric and streamlined moderne designs—deemed visual metaphors of progress—breathed new life into the area.

During the next two decades, central Miami Beach was a flurry of activity as more glitzy hotels took their places on the sand and posh neighborhoods sprouted along the waterways. At the same time, cultural change was

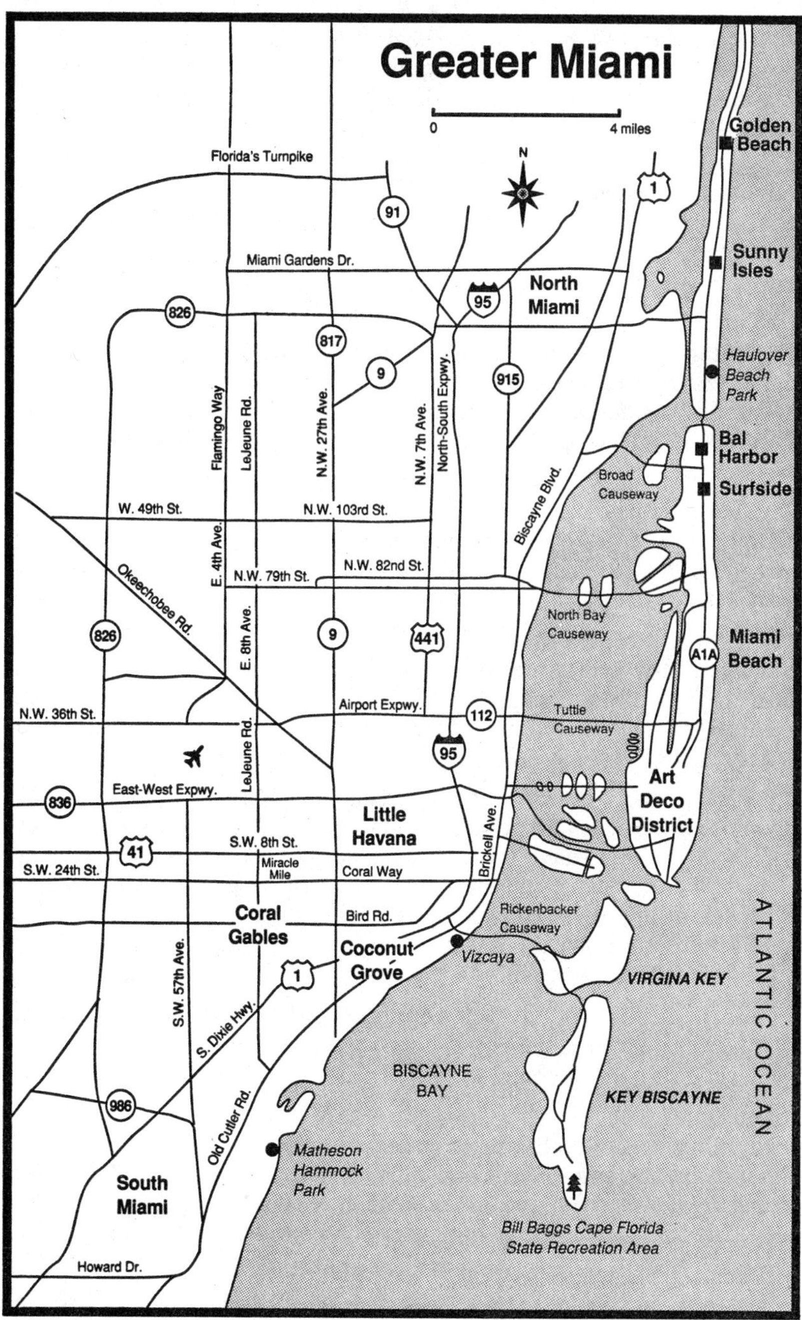
Greater Miami
0
4 miles
N
Florida's Turnpike
91
1
Golden Beach
Sunny Isles
Miami Gardens Dr.
95
North Miami
826
817
9
915
Haulover Beach Park
Flamingo Way
LeJeune Rd.
N.W. 27th Ave.
N.W. 7th Ave.
North-South Expwy.
Biscayne Blvd.
Broad Causeway
Bal Harbor
Surfside
W. 49th St.
N.W. 103rd St.
E. 4th Ave.
N.W. 79th St.
N.W. 82nd St.
Okeechobee Rd.
North Bay Causeway
826
E. 8th Ave.
9
441
A1A
Miami Beach
N.W. 36th St.
Airport Expwy.
112
Tuttle Causeway
LeJeune Rd.
95
836
East-West Expwy.
Art Deco District
Little Havana
Brickell Ave.
41
S.W. 8th St.
S.W. 24th St.
Miracle Mile
Coral Way
Coral Gables
Bird Rd.
Rickenbacker Causeway
Coconut Grove
Vizcaya
1
VIRGINA KEY
S.W. 57th Ave.
S. Dixie Hwy.
ATLANTIC OCEAN
BISCAYNE BAY
986
Old Cutler Rd.
KEY BISCAYNE
Matheson Hammock Park
South Miami
Bill Baggs Cape Florida State Recreation Area
Howard Dr.

having a major impact on the area. Previously an exclusive niche for the old-money elite, Miami Beach was beginning to attract many Jewish settlers escaping the cold northeastern states or looking for retirement havens. Despite elements of anti-Semitism, half the Miami Beach population was Jewish by 1947.

No doubt Miami's image as a land of promise was also partially responsible for drawing a new group of immigrants between 1960 and 1980. Sparked by Fidel Castro's Cuban revolution in 1959, more than half a million Cubans fled to Miami during subsequent years, searching for political sanctuary and a better life. Yet another large exodus occurred in 1980, when about 125,000 Cuban refugees arrived on Miami's shores by boat.

Eclipsing all previous changes in Miami's history, the arrival of these immigrants ignited a cultural metamorphosis that would dramatically alter this tropical realm. The Latin influence transformed every aspect of Miami's character: language, architecture, fashions, food, music and the media.

Today, Central and South Americans are also establishing new lives here. Together with the Cubans, they make up nearly half of Dade County's 1.8 million residents. Spanish billboards dot the metropolis, and sleek Latin financial institutions line the streets of downtown. Throughout the area, Spanish is spoken just as much as English.

As in no other major American city, Miami is dominated by Latin politics. Many key area government leaders are Hispanic, continuing to vie for their piece of political pie. Local elections often center around national and foreign issues dealing with Latin America rather than what's going on in Miami.

Like virtually every sprawling urban area, Miami is not without big city problems. Healthy crime statistics, racial strife and drug smuggling have not boded well for Miami's vacation image. The city has unique problems as well, like Hurricane Andrew, which struck the coast 25 miles southwest of Miami in August 1992. Packing winds that gusted through Coral Gables at 164 miles per hour, the storm left billions of dollars worth of damage from which the area is still recovering.

But the millions of travelers who come here each year have found much to write home about in the city's sophisticated art, architecture and entertainment, and lovely beaches and parks, as well as in the multifaceted communities that surround Miami in greater Dade County.

Within this culturally varied county lie 26 towns, all basking in a continuously breezy, subtropical climate. While the average temperature hovers splendidly between 70° and 80° Fahrenheit, visitors can expect a few dog-day afternoons when the thermometer climbs to 90° in the summer.

Ethnic diversity is a keynote in the neighborhoods scattered across these balmy environs, where the population includes Blacks, Asians, Jews and

Haitians, as well as numerous Hispanic cultures. Other groups have found their niches here, too, including gays, artists, trendsetters and aristocrats.

Among the many immigrants who have found permanent sanctuary in Miami are 65,000 Haitians. Fleeing poverty and political turmoil on their island, many settled north of downtown in one of Miami's oldest neighborhoods. There they painted the modest shops and bungalows crayon colors, and fused Caribbean creole flavor into the area. Signs of "Bienvenue!" (Welcome!) greet visitors of Little Haiti.

Miami the city is home to a mere 370,000 people. Its nucleus is a stunning downtown. At night, its skyscrapers form a brilliant skein with glowing bands of colored light twinkling against Biscayne Bay and winking at the Southern Cross so lucid in the sky. Nearby, ships ebb and flow through one of the nation's busiest ports.

Barely two miles across the water rests Miami Beach, a glittering chain of oceanside development that's now enjoying rejuvenation. Still a haven for both the elderly and millions of tourists each year, the area is being renovated by new Latin American settlers who are restoring dilapidated condominiums. Along the southern tip, the Art Deco District is emerging as Miami's shining star, where airy pastel enclaves with streamlined designs draw Europeans, artisans, musicians and actors.

Nestled on the west side of downtown is Little Havana, Miami's Cuban core, which centers around a bustling street flanked by Latin diners, small motels and glitzy nightclubs.

Southerly Virginia Key and Key Biscayne are heady little islands smothered in pine and palm trees and blessed with ribbons of billowy sand and demure waters. Movie stars and presidents have long taken refuge among these shores.

Nearby Coconut Grove is a former hippy harbor that turned trendy in the '80s. Swank shops and galleries, chic discos and eateries dot the busy streets here shrouded in towering oak trees.

Coral Gables, touted as the "Miami Riviera," is the area's Mediterranean mecca. Pristine country-club homes mingle with Moorish castles and rows of posh shops. Through the years, these preplanned surroundings have represented the world of Miami's high society.

Across Dade County's southern reaches, sprawling housing developments—aching for more space—creep through farmlands and back up to the Everglades. On the flip side, northern Dade has already grown beyond its means, a vast parcel of suburbia bursting to the Gold Coast.

Through it all, Miami remains a multifaceted city that continues to struggle for a clear identity, determined to retain its hold as a vacation center while evolving as a Latin American capital. For some, it is a glorious place in the sun, a sphere of heedless days and tropical nights. For others, it signifies a pulsing international center poised on the southeastern tip of the continent.

Art Deco District

During the post-Depression building boom of the late 1920s and early '30s, South Miami Beach became flush with an architectural rage called streamlined moderne. These geometric, artsy buildings popped up on every corner and were soon the neighborhood's mainstay. Now, 80 square blocks—bounded roughly by the ocean, Lenox Court, and 5th and 23rd streets—bulge with more than 800 historic buildings, making this the most concentrated historic district in the nation.

These days, the Art Deco District is experiencing a grand revival of the 1930s and '40s. Known locally as South Beach, this oceanside necklace of pastel-coated buildings, breezy alfresco cafés and palm-tree-studded sidewalks is foremost a traveler's fairy-tale world.

Tucked behind a 1937 storefront, the **Miami Design and Preservation League** (1244 Ocean Drive, in the Leslie Hotel; 305-672-2014) can supply maps, information and walking tours to get you started in the area.

To best absorb the deco ambience, stroll **Ocean Drive** between 6th and 23rd streets. Like a decorated candy store, this beachfront roadway brims with sherbet-colored hotels and cafés that snatch continuous ocean breezes.

True to deco style, the powder-blue-and-white **Park Central Hotel** (640 Ocean Drive; 305-538-1611) is a four-story study in geometrics. The 1937 beauty is adorned with fluted eaves, octagonal windows and dramatic vertical columns. For a peek at South Beach life in the '30s, check out the black-and-white photographs in the hotel lobby.

Down at the **Beacon Hotel** (720 Ocean Drive; 305-531-5891), parapets climb the facade and thin racing stripes slip around the sides of the 1936 building.

The monolithic date and temperature sign at 1001 Ocean Drive still spits out the numbers, as it has since the 1930s. Rooted firmly in the sand next to the **Beach Patrol Station,** the sign is a classic. While you're there, check out the funky lifeguard station, a nautical design that sent girls swooning in those days.

Is it a spaceship—or a nice big awning for the car? The "flying saucer sculptures" at the **Clevelander Hotel** (1020 Ocean Drive; 305-531-3485) look pretty hokey now, but back in 1938 they were the rage. Besides, guests still use them as sunshields. A shady situation, indeed.

Typical of the Mediterranean architecture sprinkled throughout the area, the majestic **Amsterdam Palace** (1114 Ocean Drive) is marked by a marble sculpture of "Kneeling Aphrodite." The three-story manor, now an apartment house, is fashioned after the Dominican Republic's Alcazar de Colón, which was home to the son of Christopher Columbus.

The pink-and-peach **Carlyle** (1250 Ocean Drive; 305-534-2135) forms an impressive series of curves, vertical columns and dramatic circular overhangs called "eyebrows." Built in 1941, the Carlyle was once a bustling hotel but is now a top-notch restaurant.

Next door, the **Cardozo Hotel** (1300 Ocean Drive; 305-534-2135) preens with symmetrical cantilevers and precise strokes of cream paint. Named after 1930s Supreme Court Justice Benjamin Cardozo, the hotel was featured in the 1959 film *A Hole in the Head*, starring Frank Sinatra, once a regular around South Beach.

These days, the Cardozo and other deco beauties frequently star in television commercials and shows. Camera crews set up camp along Ocean Drive, shooting scenes at all hours of the day and night. European modeling firms, also taking advantage of the artsy surroundings, fill up several hotels during the winter months while filming.

Another favorite of film crews is **Española Way** (between Washington and Drexel avenues). Walk this whimsical way and you will discover a Disneyesque vision of peach Mediterranean buildings, colorful striped canopies, arched windows and wrought-iron balconies, all framed by palm trees and gas lamps. Along the way are marvelous vintage clothing nooks, an alfresco café and galleries where you're apt to find artists at work.

Founded in 1922 by settlers who envisioned a Spanish-themed artists' colony, the area never really took off. Locals will tell you, though, how

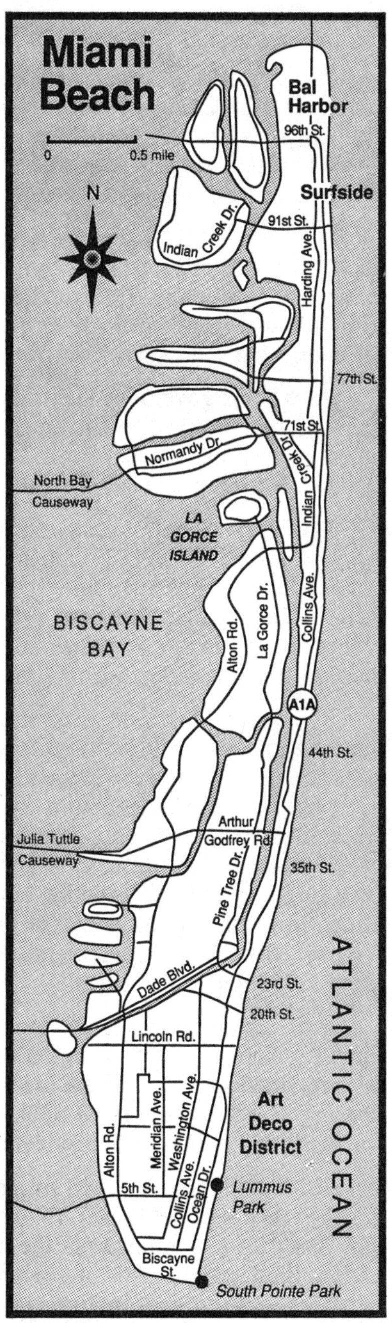

Desi Arnaz started the rumba craze on this very street. Recent restoration has lent a magical look to the street.

Just around the corner, eye-catching cameo embellishments adorn the entrance of the **Cameo Theatre** (1445 Washington Avenue; 305-532-0922). The district's premier theater drew jetsetters to international films when it opened in 1938. As fate would have it, the 1000-seat facility, now inundated inside with wild pink-and-green decor, is the setting for reggae, funk and modern rock concerts.

One of the grandest deco buildings, the 1928 **Main Post Office** (1300 Washington Avenue) is crowned by a marble and stained-glass lantern. Inside, light streams in through the glass, reflecting on rich murals and bronze grillwork that creep up a vast rotunda.

Also in the government district, **Old City Hall** (1130 Washington Avenue) asserts its presence with an eight-story neo-classical tower, one of the tallest in these parts. Mediterranean in style, this 1927 building has column-studded corridors that brood with history.

Farther south on Washington Avenue lies a strip that, the city will tell you, is "primed" for redevelopment. In other words, the shops here are run down and rows of frame homes haven't seen a coat of fresh paint in years. Still, this area offers a slice of local life. Crusty old Cuban men shoot the breeze on their front porches while dogs laze around the sidewalks. Friendly merchants chat in Spanish to shoppers, pushing specials of the day.

To see neighborhood restoration at its best, head east a block and navigate **Pennsylvania, Euclid** and **Jefferson avenues**. Quiet and very intimate, these roadways are rimmed with century-old oaks, massive banyan trees and flourishing sea grapes. The true colors, though, emanate from the charming deco homes and quaint apartment buildings. Distinct strokes of paint—namely, turquoise, pale yellow, salmon and seafoam green—have been carefully applied to cantilevers and parapets, creating a soothing visual effect. For example, drive by the **Milfred Apartments** (936 Pennsylvania Avenue), **Rosebloom Apartments** (820 Euclid Avenue) and **Murray Apartments** (750 Jefferson Avenue).

A bit farther north, you'll find the **Jackie Gleason Theater of the Performing Arts** (1700 Washington Avenue; 305-673-7300), where Miami's favorite entertainer broadcast his national television series. Another deco design, the 2705-seater has a sleek, rounded facade and serves as the venue for Broadway series performances and major ballet and symphony events.

If it's a cloudy day, you might stop off at the **Bass Museum of Art** (2121 Park Avenue; 305-673-7530; admission), the only art museum on Miami Beach. A streamlined marble motif, the two-story cultural house contains a limited collection of sculptures, period furniture, objets d'art and Old Master paintings, including a Peter Paul Rubens. More interesting, though, are the ever-changing contemporary European and American exhibits as well as historic art from around the world.

ART DECO DISTRICT HOTELS

Despite the decline of many Miami Beach highrise hotels, prices remain at a premium. The trick here is not so much where you stay but when. During the summer months, when temperatures soar, hotel rates plummet as much as 50 percent. One exception is the Art Deco District in South Miami Beach, where a revival of 1930s architecture has spawned small-scale hotels with real character and year-round moderate price tags to match.

The **Colony Hotel** (736 Ocean Drive; 305-673-0088) is easily the classiest resting place on the beachfront esplanade. After an 18-month restoration, the art deco gem reopened in 1991 with lovely results: a tiny lobby with marble floors and ethereal distressed walls, and 36 contemporary rooms with blonde oak furniture, valance draperies and soothing hues of mauve and pale green. A bustling bistro with a dramatic glass-framed fireplace welcomes guests out front. Deluxe.

The **Park Central Hotel** (640 Ocean Drive; 305-538-1611) evokes a real sense of the area's past. An art deco favorite, this 1937 moderne palace is chock full of wonderful black-and-white photos of old Miami. New life has been breathed into the terrazzo floors and mahogany ceiling fans throughout the lobby. Guest rooms—many with ocean views—are far from fancy, restored '30s furniture and spotless white walls display special care. Deluxe.

A no-frills inn on a congested street, the **Beachcomber Hotel** (1340 Collins Avenue; 305-531-3755) offers 32 clean but sparse rooms at budget-to-moderate prices. French doors and white ceiling fans give a breezy air to the small lobby of this family-owned establishment. There are no views here, but the beach awaits just a block away.

Beautiful European models frequently stay at the **Cavalier** (1320 Ocean Drive; 305-534-2135) while filming television commercials. This hostelry features a lobby with mirrored walls, green marble fireplace, dramatic ceilings and sassy rattan couches. The 44 oversized rooms and suites contain an interesting combination of period furnishings and high-tech portable phones and VCRs. Deluxe.

You'll find a chic crowd at the deluxe-priced **Cardozo** (1300 Ocean Drive; 305-534-2135), which is full of high gloss and modern decor. The 1939 U-shaped design snags the most ocean view possible, and three floors of sleek cantilevers and delicate strokes of paint spell streamlined heaven. Rooms are bathed in deco blue colors and have shiny lacquer furniture.

One of the country's busiest youth hostels has an art deco address and a pretty pink building to match. At the **Miami Beach International Hostel** (1438 Washington Avenue; 305-534-2988) wrought-iron balconies buzz with people-watchers, and the lobby is a flurry of activity. A 1920 amalgamation of painted cinderblock and dramatic cantilevers, the stopover is two blocks from the ocean and shares quarters with the **Clay Hotel**. The hotel offers 46 sparse but tidy rooms, while the hostel has separate dormitories for men and women. Kitchen facilities provided. Budget.

Situated five blocks from the beach on a pretty residential street, **Europe Guesthouse** (721 Michigan Avenue; 305-531-3099) is a tropical inn for gay men and women. Enveloped in palm trees and painted a sunny yellow, the 1923 wood plank house offers 12 modest rooms with eclectic but inviting decor: checkered floors, bahama fans, reproduction antique furniture and a queen or king size bed. There's plenty of privacy, particularly out back, where wood decks wind through a lush garden punctuated by a whirlpool. Moderate rates include full breakfast.

ART DECO DISTRICT RESTAURANTS

To dine in the Art Deco District is to relive the fabulous '30s and '40s. Artfully restored pastel buildings provide fairy-tale enclaves for breezy sidewalk cafés and intimate indoor eateries that stretch for 20 blocks along South Miami Beach.

When **Joe's Stone Crab** (227 Biscayne Street; 305-673-0365) opened in 1913, it cornered the market on stone crabs, and little has changed since. The local institution at the southern foot of Miami Beach has infamously long lines. Hungry diners allow bibs to be tied around their necks and subsequently feast on succulent Florida stone crabs dipped in mustard sauce and served with extra-large homemade fries. Miamians insist Joe's serves the best Key lime pie in the United States. Closed during the summer. Budget to deluxe.

For an evening of casual elegance, visit **Barocco** (Park Central Hotel, 640 Ocean Drive; 305-538-7700). Built in 1936, the art deco dining room features terrazzo floors and 1940s floral print drapes. The menu offers spaghetti, rigatoni, ravioli, pan-braised grouper and grilled loin of lamb chops. Enjoy your meal inside or out on the porch overlooking the ocean. Moderate to deluxe.

The sidewalk fare at **A Fish Called Avalon** (700 Ocean Drive; 305-532-1727) is fresh, imaginative and Floridaish. From its art deco perch in the restored Avalon Hotel, this sleek eatery offers locally caught fish and shellfish fused with tropical fruits and vegetables. There's something new every day, though you're apt to find grilled snapper with tomato-cucumber and avocado salsa or mahimahi with roasted potatoes, tropical fruit relish and passion fruit beurre blanc. Chicken and pasta dishes are also tops. White table linens and slip covers on the chairs create a minimalist mood that's appropriately beachy—and positively romantic on a windswept night. Deluxe.

Foremost among the sidewalk set is the **News Café** (800 Ocean Drive; 305-538-6397), where a rather bohemian crowd gathers to sip cappuccino and graze on deli sandwiches and flaky croissants. The small outdoor wooden tables and wrought-iron chairs create a perfect people-watching station. Inside, there's a great newsstand selling cigars, suntan lotions and the latest novels on Miami. Budget to moderate.

Remember bobby socks and pony tails? They'd fit right in at **The Palace** (1200 Ocean Drive; 305-531-9077), a streetside re-creation of a 1950s soda fountain. The curvaceous bar is adorned with bright blue penny rounds and antique black-and-chrome stools. Beachgoers with sand-covered feet munch on healthful fare such as pita pockets and veggie melts and drink chunky fruit smoothies. Moderate.

One of the most talked-about art deco restaurants, the **Carlyle Grill** (1250 Ocean Drive; 305-534-2135) has truly recaptured the grandeur of its heyday. Located in the old Carlyle Hotel, the elegant grill is swathed in hues of pink and peach and features a polished grand piano and crisp white tablecloths. Creative seafood, chicken and steaks are presented in an artful fashion. Try the grouper français and a special Carlyle salad. Deluxe to ultra-deluxe.

Miamians will point to **A Mano** and **The Stars and Stripes Café** (1440 Ocean Drive, in the Betsy Ross Hotel; 305-531-6266 and 305-531-3310, respectively) as prime examples of the area's new "tropical fusion" cuisine. Chef Norman Van Aken, who brought food fame to Louie's Backyard in Key West, works his culinary savvy at this duo situated (strangely) in a New England-style inn. Though A Mano is the most upscale—and serves the best food—both places merge tropical ingredients with local seafood, beef, pork, lamb and fowl. A Mano features pan-fried crab cakes with an orange béarnaise sauce, grilled swordfish with mango and black bean salsa, and other elaborate, to-die-for creations. At Stars and Stripes, you'll find specialties such as sautéed yellowtail with starfruit and Jamaican jerk chicken with papaya, plantains and avocado. Prices are ultra-deluxe at A Mano; deluxe at Stars and Stripes.

One of the district's most hip dining addresses, **The Strand** (671 Washington Avenue; 305-532-2340) caters to a mixed bag of artisans and nouveau riche. An arches-and-mirrors motif establishes a minimalist style, while the deluxe-priced menu offers nouvelle treatments of seafood, pasta and chicken. For those still waiting to make the big time, a budget section includes meatloaf and baked chicken.

In a city where Thai restaurants tend to be average at best, **Ruen Thai** (947 Washington Avenue; 305-534-1504) stands out. The little dining room is stunning with elaborate carved teak tables under glass while the servers are dressed in silk tunics. The menu is loaded with ginger and curry dishes (the grouper curry deserves high marks) as well as house specialties such as crispy duck and a delicious lobster chili paste. Best of all, everything can be ordered from mild to sizzling hot. Deluxe.

Lulu's (1053 Washington Avenue; 305-532-6147) is the area's tribute to southern dining, an upscale, down-home place that pushes chicken-fried steak, meatloaf, fried catfish and collard greens. Old hubcaps and gas station signs are parked on the walls downstairs, while the second floor is a shrine to Elvis Presley. Don't miss Elvis' fried peanut butter and banana sandwich. Moderate.

Gino's Italian Restaurant (1906 Collins Avenue; 305-532-6426) is one of those refreshing spots with cozy red booths, plastic grapes and kindly, attentive waiters. Basic Italian fare, such as lasagna, beef *bragiola* and chicken *francese*, comes with a glass of wine, minestrone soup and homemade Italian rum cake. Soft piano music makes you forget about the oceanside hubbub just outside the door. Moderate.

ART DECO DISTRICT SHOPPING

Throughout the Art Deco District, threads of spiffy moderne buildings shelter eclectic shops that are perfect for oceanside browsing. Without a doubt, shopping here is sheer entertainment.

Shake off the sand and stroll into **Chocolate** (119 5th Street; 305-674-1906), which bears not confections but chic beach paraphernalia. There are teeny bikinis, T-shirts and psychedelic painted jewelry.

The funky **Tommy at the Beach** (458 Ocean Drive; 305-538-5717) sports zebra-print bikinis, musclemen posters and deco T-shirts.

Get your art deco fix at **Decodence** (900 Ocean Drive; 305-672-4618), a cache of great gifts such as glass block telephones, tiffany lamps and adirondak chairs painted with tropical murals. One of the featured artists is a set designer for "Saturday Night Live."

Washington Avenue is quickly becoming the place to drop a buck. Vintage clothing and furniture shops and bohemian and ultra-hip boutiques line this noisy thoroughfare.

If you're looking to make an explosive entrance at a party, shop at **La Troya** (1419 Washington Avenue; 305-538-9445). Owners Frederico and Darrick design strictly outrageous "party dresses for party girls," ranging in price from $100 to $2000. A few of their customers: singer Glorida Estefan and Kate Pierson of the B-52s.

At the other end of the design spectrum, **Cha Cha** (1448 Washington Avenue; 305-532-1411) carries clothes for the bohemian look. Overalls, painted denims, metal studded belts and psychedelic caps are featured.

Flashbacks (1143 Washington Avenue; 305-674-1143) is the king of kitsch. The place is filled to the rafters with "20th century junk," marvelous items such as a Bee Gees lunch box, flower power mirrors and an "authentic" Beatles wig.

Discover some real gems at **One Hand Clapping** (432 Española Way; 305-532-0507), where there is a large collection of 1940s and 1950s art deco items with a tropical flair. You'll also find vintage fabrics and outrageous lamps from the 1950s.

Rubye's Treasures and Trappings (428 Española Way; 305-673-9226) is a costume fantasy world decorated to resemble a turn-of-the-century San Francisco dancehall, complete with purple ceiling. Here you can revel in vintage clothing as well as hats, gloves, bags and feather boas.

A pedestrian center running east and west, **Lincoln Road Mall** (Lincoln Road between Washington and Alton roads) was carved out of mangrove swamps back in 1913. For decades a chic mecca, the mall now lies nearly deserted much of the time but still possesses a few interesting shops and art galleries.

Immerse yourself in art at the increasingly popular **South Florida Art Center** (800, 900 and 1000 blocks of Lincoln Road Mall; 305-674-8278), a collection of galleries spanning three blocks along the mall. About 80 Miami area artists expend their creative energies here. The focus is on contemporary works in all media, although you'll encounter some impressive Renaissance, rococo, impressionist and even exotic Caribbean paintings and sculptures.

Pick up a good read at **Books & Books** (933 Lincoln Road; 305-532-3222), a well-stocked mart that's open until midnight on weekends.

Formality takes over at **House of Linen** (612 Lincoln Road Mall; 305-531-3902), where you'll find delicately embroidered linens and towels as well as oriental fans.

ART DECO DISTRICT NIGHTLIFE

For the hottest nighttime action, head straight to the Art Deco District. This beachside strand is quickly emerging as Miami's entertainment heart. Here a bohemian mood has spawned blocks of avant-garde clubs as well as breezy sidewalk cafés. Most of the action here is late-night, with many establishments staying open until dawn. The trend is toward alfresco jazz as well as the more unusual "progressive" clubs, which create a smaller rendition of New York City's avant-garde scene.

Everyone goes to **The Strand** (671 Washington Avenue; 305-532-2340) for a drink some time or other. The wavy glass block bar, which is part of a restaurant, is where you relax and soak up South Beach chicness.

Uncle Sam's Musicafe (1141 Washington Avenue; 305-532-0973) is a great idea. A combination record store/café/bar, this popular place headlines live jazz and alternative music and budget-priced sandwiches, burgers and pizza. Cover charge some nights.

Catering to a hip crowd, **5th Street** (429 Lenox Avenue; 305-531-2127) tenders reggae by local and national acts. Cover.

Nightly bands at the New York-style **Washington Square** (645 Washington Avenue; 305-534-1403) play rock-and-roll until 5 a.m. Cover on the weekends.

The **Island Club** (701 Washington Avenue; 305-538-1213) is a subdued corner bar with a restored warehouse atmosphere. Occasionally, live reggae and jazz are featured.

For loud acid and progressive music, head to **Club New** (245 22nd Street; 305-672-0068), which attracts an offbeat, hip-hop group. Cover.

Tired of trendiness? Then you'll love the frayed jeans crowd, bare bones decor, and down and dirty Tex-Mex food (served till 5 a.m.) at **Cactus Cantina Grill** (630 6th Street; 305-532-5095). The lineup of live rhythm-and-blues and rock-and-roll is top-notch.

The dusty juke box and worn pool tables at the **Irish House Pub** (1430 Alton Road; 305-534-5667) hint that this is one of a dying breed of genuine neighborhood taverns. You can bet the patrons are regulars here.

Over at the **Fairmont** (1000 Collins Avenue; 305-531-0050), there's live jazz and acoustic guitar music in a private, romantic garden setting.

Neon amoebas, peace signs and radical lingo adorn the black walls of the **Kitchen Club** (21st Street at the beach; 305-538-6631), a punk and funk habitat with a deejay who plays progressive and industrial music. Cover.

A hip, brick-and-glass fandango sprawled on the southern tip of Miami Beach, **Penrod's** (1 Ocean Drive; 305-538-1111) is a classy sports bar where reggae, jazz and rock-and-roll emanate from various rooms. With a dozen televisions and a hot tub, this place is hot. Cover.

Our Place Natural Foods Eatery (830 Washington Avenue; 305-674-1322) features folk music and jazz on the weekends. Mellow out at **Cafés des Arts** (918 Ocean Drive; 305-534-6267), where a classical guitarist performs in a formal, Parisian atmosphere.

An after-dinner crowd shows up at **Crawdaddy's** (1 Washington Avenue; 305-673-1708), where weekend jazz is played on a waterfront boardwalk.

For four years, Jackie Gleason broadcast his national television series from a Miami Beach theater. Reopened after an extensive facelift, the 2705-seat **Jackie Gleason Theater of the Performing Arts** (1700 Washington Avenue; 305-673-7300) offers a lineup of Broadway musicals, international and national orchestras, ballet, and Latin and Israeli dance.

Built in 1934 by Paramount Studios, the 465-seat **Colony Theater** (1040 Lincoln Road; 305-674-1026) is a restored art deco beauty that hosts major ballet and symphony performances as well as contemporary dance and theater.

To purchase tickets for major productions, call the theaters directly or check with **Ticketmaster** (305-358-5885) outlets.

GAY SCENE Nowhere has Miami's gay community become more of a cultural force than in South Beach. Here numerous nightclubs play mostly to an all-gay crowd, and range from neighborhood bars to elaborate ballrooms.

The small **Torpedo** (634 Collins Avenue; 305-538-2500) features high ceilings, drag competitions and an all-male crowd. Cover on Tuesdays for dancing.

For now at least, **Warsaw Ballroom** (1450 Collins Avenue; 305-531-4555) reigns supreme over Miami's gay nightlife. The giant dance club, which packs thousands of gay men in every weekend, hosts outrageous drag and comedy shows. In between, there's dancing and deejays. Cover.

There's no live entertainment at **Hombre** (925 Washington Avenue; 305-538-7883), but the videos of muscled men leave little to the imagination. A good neighborhood bar.

ART DECO DISTRICT BEACHES AND PARKS

South Pointe Park—Cloaking the tail of South Miami Beach is this 17-acre slice of close-cropped grass and meandering sidewalks. Situated near the Port of Miami, the park affords scenic views of cruise ship activity but unfortunately has a small beach that's strewn with seaweed, rocks and trash. The best section leads around a jutting ledge of boulders and a 300-foot pier, where snorkelers explore colorful exotic fish. To the north, the strand and highrises of Miami Beach provide an impressive panorama.

Facilities: Picnic pavilions, par course, restrooms, general store, outdoor amphitheater. *Fishing:* Good from the pier or rocks for yellowtail, barracuda and snapper. *Swimming:* Good, but be careful of strong currents. Also, cruise ship traffic stirs up the water sometimes.

Getting there: Located on the southern tip of Miami Beach, off of Washington Avenue.

1st Street Beach or **South Beach**—There's no official name for this beach, but it's the sand spot in the Miami area. In fact, more people jam onto this one block of southern beach than in the next five blocks combined. A sprawling sports bar spawns all the action, which spills out over a sandy crest and down into the ocean. Volleyball competitions go on continuously, and loud bar music permeates the salty air. Adding a classy touch, a modern boardwalk works its way down toward the ocean, where strong tradewinds and currents churn up great bodysurfing waves.

Facilities: Restaurant adjacent to the beach. *Swimming:* Good, but it's usually crowded. *Surfing:* The *only* place to surf in the Miami area, although it pales in comparison to the waves on Florida's central East Coast.

Getting there: At the southernmost block of Miami Beach.

Lummus Park—Not to be confused with the smaller Lummus Park in downtown Miami, this grassy palm tree plaza wanders along eight blocks of South Miami Beach. Fine white sand—stretching 300 glorious feet to the translucent aquamarine ocean—is dotted with neon umbrellas and wandering refreshment trucks. Young Europeans and kite flyers favor this beach. The best thing about the park is that the Art Deco District lies across the street, beckoning beachgoers to its pastel sidewalk cafés.

Facilities: Restrooms, lifeguards, playground, shady park benches, bandshell, bicycling and windsurfing rentals (call Penrod's at 305-538-2604), food and drink vendors; information, 305-673-7730. *Swimming:* Excellent. There's a sandbar extending about 50 yards out. *Windsurfing:* Good.

Getting there: On South Miami Beach, between 6th and 14th streets.

21st Street Beach—A one-block enclave of granulated sand wedged between highrises, this spot is frequented by gay men and women. The latter frequently shed their tops, making it the area's unofficial topless beach. The city's prized two-mile boardwalk, offering "unobstructed" ocean views behind skyscrapers, commences here and travels northward along a ridge of sand dunes.

Facilities: Lifeguards, food vendors; restaurants nearby; information, 305-673-7730. *Swimming:* Good.

Getting there: On South Miami Beach at 21st Street.

Central Miami Beach

This single stretch of beach—extending generally from 25th Street north to 87th Street—is what put Miami on the big resort map in the 20th century. A drive along the ocean here quickly reveals why. Still the nucleus of Miami's tourism, the area is concentrated with glistening highrise hotels, top-notch restaurants, an unusually wide swath of beach and miles of water on view everywhere.

Though parts of the area had declined during recent decades, a 1990s refurbishment has breathed new life into Central Miami Beach. Today it is quickly gentrifying into something that looks a lot like the Art Deco District. North of the district, Collins Avenue is a virtual wall of freshly painted pastels. Mid-rise buildings are washed with peach and pink, purple and plum. Streamline moderne eyebrows and balconies decorate their facades, and royal palms accent their feet.

One neighborhood that's seen little change over the years is the one on **La Gorce Drive**. This one-mile jag, north of Arthur Godfrey Road, serves as the primary address for Miami Beach's old money. Here you'll encounter crisp white palatial homes, Mediterranean estates and loads of big, wispy Australian pine trees.

Down the street lies **The Neighborhood**, seven blocks of beachy stores and apartments flanking Arthur Godfrey Road between Pine Tree Drive and Alton Road. This area also serves as a locus for the Hasidic Jewish community. More recently, young professionals have taken to this area, too, transforming many of the dilapidated buildings into quaint bungalows nestled along canals.

For an exceedingly strange experience, especially at night, stand on Collins Avenue, right around 42nd Street, and behold the mastodon before you. There, splashed ten stories high and 120 feet wide, is a mirror image of the **Fontainebleau Hilton** (4441 Collins Avenue; 305-538-2000). Behind this clever **Trompe l'Oeil Mural**, you'll find the real thing, a grandiose beachfront hotel with curving swimming pools and myriads of waterfalls. Though the hotel was built in 1954, the wall wasn't christened until 1986.

Queen of Miami Beach hotels, the Fontainebleau ruled the roost during the glitter days of the 1950s and '60s. With their backs to the street, the twin curved buildings have long promised exclusivity for those within their safe bounds. During the hotel's heyday, Bob Hope and Frank Sinatra frequently performed, and its impressive guest list included Joan Crawford, Joe DiMaggio, John F. Kennedy and Richard Nixon. But today much of that glamour is gone. Its legendary show club, in fact, is now a cabaret with Las Vegas-style shows. But there's still an edge of opulence and nostalgia that makes visiting the Fontainebleau a must.

One especially lovely stretch of Miami Beach, **Indian Creek Drive**, meanders along a spectacular waterway where luxury houseboats are moored. Get a different perspective of the La Gorce Drive homes across the waterway, their sweeping, well-tended estates flirting with passersby.

Things head downhill here, as "condomania" begins appearing on Collins Avenue along the ocean (but you can't see the water). Blame greedy developers and poor-sighted politicians for this mess along Miami's pristine beach. The reason behind the madness? It provides thousands of people an ocean view while shutting out the rest of the world.

THE CAUSEWAYS Dazzling by day and stunning at night, Miami's causeways, which connect the islands with the city, regularly dispense intoxicating views of Biscayne Bay. For beach inhabitants, these eight bridges are lifelines to the mainland, their link to the "real world." For those on the mainland, they act as gateways to pleasure centers of surf and sun.

MacArthur Causeway, which joins South Beach with downtown, offers a worthwhile side trip to **Watson Island**. Here you can watch luxury cruise ships inch their way to and fro in the **Port of Miami**.

In 1913, Miami pioneer John Collins completed the first bridge from downtown to Miami Beach. Now, the gleaming **Venetian Causeway** has taken its place and crosses six islands—**San Marino Island, Dilido Island, Biscayne Island, San Marco Island, Belle Isle** and **Rivo Alto Island**. Each with its place in the sun, they lie blanketed with plush residential areas.

The northern causeways, each with a different sumptuous view, are **Julia Tuttle, North Bay** (or John F. Kennedy), **Sunny Isles** and **Lehman.**

To the south, Rickenbacker Causeway is endowed with two natural spectacles: gorgeous turquoise waters and thin strips of sugary sand. At the end, two more pots of gold await—the smaller, less developed Virginia Key and larger Key Biscayne.

Along the way, you'll encounter seals, whales and Florida manatees—but only those living at **Miami Seaquarium** (4400 Rickenbacker Causeway; 305-361-5703; admission). The 35-acre attraction is flanked by water on three sides and affords a look at local marine and bird life, if you don't mind seeing it in cages and tanks. Get a hug from a sea lion, watch dolphins perform clever tricks and listen to the warbles and chirps of native birds such as anhingas, herons and ibis. The place is worth visiting, though overpriced.

CENTRAL MIAMI BEACH HOTELS

Towering hotels and condominiums create a virtual concrete wall eclipsing much of Miami's central coastline. If anyone intended to build a cozy motel along this stretch of beach, they never followed through.

A few blocks north of the Art Deco District, you'll find a good buy right on the beach. The **Traymore Hotel** (2445 Collins Avenue; 305-534-7111) delights with its cream-colored facade and rows of pink ledges that seem to race around the building. Like many area hostelries, the eight-story Traymore has been nicely restored. Shiny terrazzo floors and vast Greek columns grace the lobby, while formica furnishings and pastel schemes adorn the modern rooms. Near the beach, a broad clay-tiled loggia surrounds a Mediterranean-style swimming pool and bar. Moderate to deluxe.

For ocean views at moderate prices, it's tough to top the **Days Inn Oceanside** (4299 Collins Avenue; 305-673-1513). Although it's wedged next to a dingy building, the ten-story hotel saves face with its artsy pink-and-silver lobby and immaculate guest rooms. Amenities include an Olympic swimming pool and restaurant.

Wooden cabañas and miles of poolside concrete harken back to the days when Jackie Gleason was a familiar face at the **Eden Roc** (4525 Collins Avenue; 305-531-0000). Perched beachside, the T-shaped, 15-story hotel sports a rooftop fixture resembling a steamship visage. Underground fruit shops and a terrazzo lobby with Moorish columns create a time-worn, campy aura. Expect '50s-style furnishings and extra-large closets in each of 351 guest rooms, priced from deluxe to ultra-deluxe.

Leading the pack of luxury highrises is the **Fontainebleau Hilton** (4441 Collins Avenue; 305-538-2000), the signature address of Miami Beach. With 1206 rooms and nearly as many employees, this place is a city unto itself. Three curving, 14-story buildings hug a half-mile of beach, creating an alcove for a series of connecting pools with rushing water, hidden rocky caves and palm tree islands. The refurbished lobby, with floor-to-ceiling windows, gigantic crystal chandeliers and magnificent marble staircases, is more opulent than when the hotel opened in 1956. There are 13 restaurants and four bars, but who's counting? Guest rooms are furnished à la French provincial, but they're far from elaborate. The ultra-deluxe price tag is strictly for service and surroundings.

You can easily spot the **Doral Ocean Beach Resort** (4833 Collins Avenue; 305-532-3600) by its stark white tower set against a wide spread of sand. Built in 1962, the posh complex has kept pace by adding an extensive fitness center, and by refurbishing its 420 guestrooms in plush carpets and pastel colors. There's a heated Olympic-size swimming pool and—for those with bucks to burn—two 2500-square-foot suites with private butlers and helicopter transportation. Ultra-deluxe.

Another ultra-deluxe-priced beachfront establishment, **The Alexander** (5225 Collins Avenue; 305-865-6500) bears an edge of European refinement. Upon entering, guests receive champagne and register at beautiful teak desks. Set in a condo-turned-hotel, the 211 one- and two-bedroom suites are beautifully appointed with Renaissance furnishings, rich overlays of maroon and gold and full kitchens and wet bars. The private grounds are lush with swirling, boulder-lined pools and myriads of flowering plants.

Restorations worked wonders for the 1950s-era **Shawnee** (4343 Collins Avenue; 305-532-3311), a classic Miami Beach highrise with a pink-and-white veneer. Things here aren't luxurious, but they are contemporary. Follow the marble floors, clusters of comfy couches and water fountains through the lobby, then take the elevator to any of 477 cheery guest rooms, decorated with modern oak furniture, wall-to-wall carpets and seaside paintings. A concrete pool and two restaurants round out the amenities. Deluxe to ultra-deluxe in price.

CENTRAL MIAMI BEACH RESTAURANTS

Etched mirrors and art deco pinks and burgundies set an animated tone at **La Famiglia** (2445 Collins Avenue in the Traymore Hotel; 305-534-7111). This oceanfront eatery is heavy on Italian with added touches of French. Seafood, poultry, beef and pasta are all well-represented, with specialties like duck *à l'orange*, châteaubriand and medallions of veal in prosciutto. Prices are moderate.

A palatial Miami institution, **The Forge** (432 Arthur Godfrey Road; 305-538-8533) has long awed diners with its extravagant rococo designs and reverential American cuisine. Massive antique doors, polished brass statues, ten-foot chandeliers and carved wood mantels abound in the restaurant, converted from an actual forge in 1929. The vast wine cellar boasts some rare vintages indeed, with price tags in the five-figure range. Ultra-deluxe.

Sumptuous-looking health food is found at the colorful **Pineapples** (530 Arthur Godfrey Road; 305-532-9731), a cramped store/restaurant combination along shoppers row. Fresh fish, seafood and chicken are prepared with care and real imagination. Try the grilled salmon teriyaki and exotic fruit salads. Budget.

The **Mermaid Beach Bar** (4525 Collins Avenue at the Eden Roc hotel) doles out thick, seared burgers and greasy but addicting fries and pizza from its great beachside nook. There's an indoor section, but the best spot is outside where you can dine barefoot at plastic tables right over the sand. Swimsuit-clad servers double as bartenders. Budget.

Romantic candlelit tables overlooking gardens with rushing waterfalls await at **Dominique's** (5225 Collins Avenue in the Alexander Hotel; 305-861-5252). Local culinary aficionados celebrated when Dominique, owner of a popular Washington, D.C., bistro, brought his talents to this oceanfront address and began lavishing diners with nouvelle delicacies as well as exotics such as diamondback rattlesnake salad, sautéed alligator tail and wild boar sausage. Ultra-deluxe.

CENTRAL MIAMI BEACH NIGHTLIFE

Sit barside at **The Mermaid** (4525 Collins Avenue in the Eden Roc Hotel; 305-538-5803) and peer into a human aquarium. The lounge—actually built around a rooftop pool—is a great place to vegetate while listening to recorded reggae.

For a panoramic view of the city and beaches, check out **Alfredo's** (4833 Collins Avenue; 305-532-3600), an intimate piano bar on the 18th floor of the classy Doral Ocean Beach Resort.

The Waves (6551 Collins Avenue in the Howard Johnson Hotel; 305-861-7576) is an upscale singles club with Latin sounds and an art deco ambience. Cover.

You'll find a mix of Top-40, jazz and blues down the beach at **Brassie** (2201 Collins Avenue in the Holiday Inn; 305-534-1511), where an older crowd sips tropical drinks around a lush garden.

The dressy piano bar at **Dominique's** (5225 Collins Avenue, in The Alexander; 305-865-6500) is where you go for romancing. Calypso bands play on Sundays.

The **Hirschfield Theatre** (5445 Collins Avenue; 305-865-7529) is the setting for national touring musicals. The 850-seat facility, fashioned as an opera house, has played host to both original and well-established productions.

Miami's premier Latin cabaret, **Club Tropigala** (4441 Collins Avenue in the Fontainebleau Hilton; 305-672-7469) is a facsimile of a lavish Brazilian samba club. The 650-seat pink-and-purple showcase hosts extravagant Las Vegas-style revues as well as orchestra concerts.

CENTRAL MIAMI BEACH BEACHES AND PARKS

35th Street Beach—Another one-block respite between highrises, the beach here is narrower than those to the south, and the sand is somewhat shelly. Usually devoid of large crowds and quieter, this site is favored by older people who gather on covered benches along the boardwalk.

Facilities: Food vendors, lifeguards; many restaurants nearby. *Swimming:* Good, although seaweed sometimes collects near the shore.

Getting there: On Miami Beach at 35th Street.

46th Street Beach—Our favorite block of Miami Beach, this niche is strategically adjacent to the Eden Roc and Fontainebleau hotels, putting you in arm's reach of some hoppin' beachside activity. The slightly crested swath of white grains is a hot spot for paddleball players and kite flyers. A calm, shallow ocean shelf is ideal for swimming.

Facilities: Restrooms, lifeguards, jet ski and sailboat rentals; many restaurants and bars nearby. *Swimming:* Excellent.

Getting there: On Miami Beach at 46th Street.

74th Street Beach—You cross a busy roadway and go over a little ridge to reach this one-block recess on Miami Beach. A single row of palms and lush sea grapes flank the shell-studded sand, which stretches for 150 feet out to the ocean. The best part of being here, though, is the sweeping southern views of Miami Beach.

Facilities: Restrooms, showers, lifeguards, food vendors, playground area. *Swimming:* Good.

Getting there: On Miami Beach at 74th Street.

North Shore State Recreation Area—A slice of lush vegetation between skyscrapers, this eight-block locale flourishes with willowy Australian pines, oak trees and sea oats. Best of all, the ginger-colored sand is as clean as a pin. A boardwalk meanders through the foliage, while people laze in grassy coves adjacent to the beach.

Facilities: Restrooms, par course, pavilions; restaurants and stores within walking distance; information, 305-947-6357. *Swimming:* Very good.

Getting there: On Miami Beach between 79th and 87th streets.

North Miami Beach

Without a doubt, the oceanside towns north of Miami Beach are a separate entity. Set apart geographically but even more detached in spirit, these communities consider themselves a world away from the hustle of their southern neighbor.

Here, along this narrow island strand stretching to the Broward County line, celebrities and other well-to-do residents enjoy a quiet existence within their behind highly secured condominiums and estates. In fact, two towns—Bal Harbour and Golden Beach—offer no beach access and a minuscule amount of public parking for visitors.

A 1930s-era settling ground for French Canadians, **Surfside** is only five blocks long and seven blocks wide. You can pick up maps and information at the **Surfside Community Center** (9301 Collins Avenue; 305-864-0722), a wonderful place for catching up on all the small-town action. The rustic, low-slung complex borders a public swimming pool where old folks lounge under natty green umbrellas and play canasta. On the adjacent beach, you're apt to encounter topless sunbathing—a tradition among the French and German women who vacation here.

Cruise down **Harding Avenue**, the main drag where canopied shops and kosher delis nuzzle up to pink sidewalks. Teeming with swimsuit-clad people during the day, the place shuts down at night and resembles a ghost town.

A stone's throw away is the area's poshest point, a 250-acre enclave called **Bal Harbour**. Sculpted lawns, concrete condos and landscaped medians convey a sense of preserved elegance. Center attraction here is the **Bal Harbour Shops** (9700 Collins Avenue; 305-866-0311), an open-air collection of designer stores and manicured people.

Heading northward along the beach, you'll encounter a singular occurrence—a continuous stretch of sand and ocean with nary a building in sight. **Haulover Beach Park** (10800 Collins Avenue; 305-947-3525) lasts just one-and-a-half short miles but affords a peek at natural sand dunes, lush sea oats and unobstructed beach views.

Up the road stands the **Newport Beach Pier** (16701 Collins Avenue, Sunny Isles; 305-949-1300), built in 1936 and destroyed three times by hurricanes. Like its predecessors, this latest boardwalk is a hot spot for noisy pelicans and local anglers who ply the ocean waters for mackerel, bluefish and jacks.

Dade County's northernmost beach possesses one of Miami's true rarities, oceanfront homes. To see these endangered species, travel northward along Ocean Boulevard through **Golden Beach**, where two miles of palatial,

Venetian-style estates blanket the shoreline. The so-called "public" beach here welcomes only town residents.

NORTH MIAMI BEACH HOTELS

Catering primarily to a European clientele, **The Palms Resort on the Ocean** (9449 Collins Avenue, Surfside; 305-865-3551) is a pink-and-aqua anomaly that harkens back to the swinging '60s. Flashing lights, mirrored walls and pink elevator doors make up the lobby of this seven-story building. The 170 rooms offer clean but small accommodations swathed in yet more pink scenes. Locals like to frequent the beachside pool and chickee hut. Deluxe to ultra-deluxe.

If you can bear the garish floral designs and rude red carpeting in the lobby of the **Singapore** (9601 Collins Avenue, Bal Harbour; 305-865-9931), you'll love the ocean views. Largely a haven for an older Jewish crowd that returns every winter, the 240-unit beachfront tower offers clean rooms with Indian print designs and modest, 1950s-style furnishings. There's a swimming pool, restaurant and a hopping, big-band lounge. Deluxe.

Claiming a prime, ten-acre oceanside nest in posh Bal Harbour, the **Sheraton Bal Harbour** (9701 Collins Avenue; 305-865-7511) boasts a 300-foot beach and elaborate grounds with two freeform pools, rushing waterfalls, underground shops and four restaurants. In this 675-room showplace you'll also find an impressive lobby with a dramatic glass atrium and twirling mobile artwork. Guest rooms lend a tropical flavor, with rattan furniture, wood paneling and jungle prints. Ultra-deluxe.

The **Coronado Motel** (9501 Collins Avenue, Bal Harbour; 305-866-1625) is a rare Miami Beach species, on two accounts. First, it's only two stories tall, and second, the rooms are moderately priced and clean. The 41-unit hostelry has a heated pool and a quiet lobby with a pretty chandelier. Guest rooms have refrigerators and hot plates.

In an area sadly plagued by deteriorating highrise hotels, the **Golden Strand Ocean Villa Resort** (17901 Collins Avenue, Sunny Isles; 305-931-7000) is a real gem. The 152-unit resort, a time-share open to the public, is an oceanfront cluster of four- and five-story stucco buildings fashioned in a private, homelike setting. Guests can stroll the beachside boardwalk and tropical gardens that weave about a large pool and tiki hut. Apartments are decorated in contemporary styles with wicker furniture, kitchens and spacious balconies. Deluxe to ultra-deluxe.

NORTH MIAMI BEACH RESTAURANTS

When you're hankering for a thick, juicy, aged steak, go to **Palm Restaurant** (9650 East Bay Harbor Drive, Bay Harbor; 305-868-7256). This cozy speakeasy, a clone of the famed Manhattan steakhouse that opened in 1927, is furnished in wood and tin walls tacked with caricatures of local personalities. Besides delicious beef, Palm also excels in seafood such as jumbo Maine lobster. Ultra-deluxe. Closed in the summer.

More calorie-laden desserts await at **CoCo's Sidewalk Café** (9700 Collins Avenue in the Bal Harbour Shops; 305-864-2626). Here you can feast on "death by chocolate," an ultra-indulgent concoction of four chocolates. This American-style eatery sports terra cotta floors and wicker furnishings. Moderate in price.

Wolfie Cohen's Rascal House (17190 Collins Avenue, Sunny Isles; 305-947-4581) is a legend with the local Jewish community. Waitresses in white pinafores scurry about, delivering heaping plates of corned beef, chicken in the pot, *kreplaches* and stuffed cabbage to diners chatting in Yiddish. Gaudy aqua booths and scuffed terrazzo floors only add to the bustling atmosphere. A series of metal railings provides organized waiting for the perpetual lines of anxious patrons. Budget to moderate.

To get a good feel for South Florida's outdoors set, spend a weekend afternoon at **Salties** (10880 Collins Avenue, Sunny Isles; 305-945-5115). This fern bar is perched strategically on the Intracoastal Waterway and features dramatic wooden ceilings and spacious dockside dining. Boaters park their yachts three and four deep, vying for prime dock space. Scantily clad waitresses serve fresh seafood and hefty burgers and carry extra suntan lotion—just in case. Moderate to deluxe.

If you want to indulge—or over-indulge—consider **Prince Hamlet** (19115 Collins Avenue; 305-932-8488). This genteel establishment boasts a 62-foot buffet laden with Danish, Jewish and continental delights. There's salmon, Maine lobster, vegetables, cheeses, breads, fruits and salads. Or choose from a menu of duck *à l'orange*, prime rib, kosher sweetbreads and much more. Moderate to deluxe.

NORTH MIAMI BEACH SHOPPING

The designer capital of the area, **Bal Harbour Shops** (9700 Collins Avenue; 305-866-0311) houses such upscale caches as Gucci, Cartier, Fendi and Saks Fifth Avenue. Well-groomed crowds meander two levels of open-air alcoves festooned in tropical foliage, tall palms and waterfalls.

Just beyond the mall is Harding Avenue, where a two-block row of colorful canopied shops comprises the heart of tiny Surfside. The 1930s settling place for French Canadians, Harding Avenue mixes the old and new. At **Decor, Inc.** (9487 Harding Avenue; 305-866-0905) you'll find impressionist paintings framed in ornate brass and extravagant candelabra—just a few of the antiques for sale here.

Rafe Sweetheart Beauty Shop (9441 Harding Avenue, Surfside; 305-865-9179) is one of those wonderful classic salons where women still line up under long rows of hair dryers. Take a peek for old time's sake, or have a shampoo and manicure for the low price of $13.

Little people have fun at **Sugar 'n Spice** (9481 Harding Avenue, Surfside; 305-865-5265), a discount clothing store jammed with children's fashions and accessories.

NORTH MIAMI BEACH BEACHES AND PARKS

Surfside Beach—Wide sweeps of sand behind small hotels, this area offers a respite from the hustle of Miami Beach. French Canadians, who settled in Surfside during the 1930s and '40s, favor this beach and often shed their bikini tops, raising some local eyebrows. Ocean waves are calm, breaking far in the distance where a sandbar ledge begins. Most days, you'll see some card game action under the beach umbrellas.

Facilities: Lifeguards; numerous restaurants and stores nearby. *Swimming:* Excellent.

Getting there: Located on Collins Avenue in Surfside, between 88th and 96th streets.

Haulover Beach Park—A mile-and-a-half of tropical vegetation with skyscraperless views, this beach got its name in the early 1900s when residents had to "haul" their boats over surrounding swamplands to reach the ocean. Laden with thick carpets of grass, hilly sand dunes and chestnut-colored sand, Haulover is a real beauty. During the 1800s, the barefoot mailman traveled this firm-packed shoreline along his South Florida route. Now, the jetty is an angler's paradise and a great place to view the southern panorama called Miami Beach.

Facilities: Picnic tables, restrooms, lifeguards, concession stands, marina; information, 305-947-3525. *Fishing:* Not as good as it used to be, but it has its moments. Try from the jetty for snapper, grunt, mackerel and yellowtail. *Swimming:* Good.

Getting there: Along Collins Avenue in south Sunny Isles.

Sunny Isles Beach and **Newport Beach**—Extending for two miles in back of condominiums and hotels, these beaches are capped with rocky sand and dotted with small tiki huts. The rougher surf and perennial winds draw windsurfers and sailors to these shores. The hot spot is in front of the Holiday Inn, where wall-to-wall lounge chairs and pretty people line the beach. For picturesque southerly views, stroll the Newport Pier. Built in 1936, the boardwalk here was destroyed three times by hurricanes but has new life again.

Facilities: Food vendors, windsurfing, sailboat, parasailing and jet ski rentals near the pier. *Fishing:* Try from the pier. *Swimming:* Good, but the water is deep near shore.

Getting there: On Collins Avenue, between 163rd and 192nd streets.

Downtown Miami

More than anything, downtown Miami is an Americanized version of a Latin American city. Two decades of immigration have infused this great core with numerous powerful Latin business centers as well as a government in which the majority of top officials are Hispanic. Exploring the downtown area, you'll hear more Spanish spoken than English and see many Spanish billboards.

Constantly shaping and reshaping its skyline, downtown is a convolution of ultramodern skyscrapers reflecting against beautiful Biscayne Bay. An expansive yet quite conquerable area, the city is served by the Metromover monorail (305-638-6700), which travels the perimeter of the district, stopping at key points of interest.

Occupying the 27th floor of the sleek Barnett Bank Building, the **Greater Miami Visitors and Convention Bureau** (701 Brickell Avenue; 305-539-3000) will provide you with sightseeing information as well as a good view of the city.

Slicing through the heart of downtown, **Flagler Street** is the best place to capture urban life. Jammed with taxi cabs and Latin street vendors, this thoroughfare was first brought to life in the 1920s by some of the city's earliest merchants. Now, brick-lined moderne buildings house noisy electronics shops and discount jewelry centers.

One of the most beautiful buildings downtown, **Gusman Center for the Performing Arts** (174 East Flagler Street; 305-374-2444) is a Mediterranean dream world. Built in 1925 for Paramount Studios, the brick-faced theater is very ornate, resembling an Italian courtyard with twinkling ceiling lights and rolling cloud puffs. It's worth a trip just to experience the surroundings.

The **Dade County Courthouse** (73 West Flagler Street; 305-375-5775) is easily spotted from just about anywhere in the city. A slender building with a striking ziggurat roof, the courthouse is shaped like a rocket poised for lift-off. When it was assembled in 1925, the courthouse was the tallest building south of Washington, D.C., and remained Miami's loftiest structure until the 1970s. Inside, beautiful mosaics swirl across the ceiling and ornate brass designs embellish the doors and wall lamps. You can still see court in session at this granddaddy.

A couple of blocks to the east beats the cultural pulse of downtown. The three-building **Metro-Dade Cultural Center** (101 West Flagler Street) is a complex of Mediterranean modernism with broad checkered piazzas.

The most enthralling destination here, the **Historical Museum of Southern Florida** (305-375-1492; admission) offers a comprehensive, highly entertaining history of the region. Two floors of exhibits span 10,000 years, carrying you through Indian camps, boom or bust years and Miami's golden years as the nation's playground. Here you can sit in a 19th-century trolley car don period costumes or relax on the porch of an old cracker home. Better yet, peruse the thousands of snapshots of yesterday's Florida in the comprehensive photo library. If you love Florida, you'll adore this museum.

Across the piazza, the **Center for the Fine Arts** (305-375-1700; admission) is a showpiece of Mediterranean style and South Florida's major museum. The center has no permanent collection but hosts more than 15 national and international exhibits annually, including works by such notables as Pablo Picasso and Frank Lloyd Wright. Rounding out this cultural trio is the four-story **Miami-Dade Public Library** (305-375-2665).

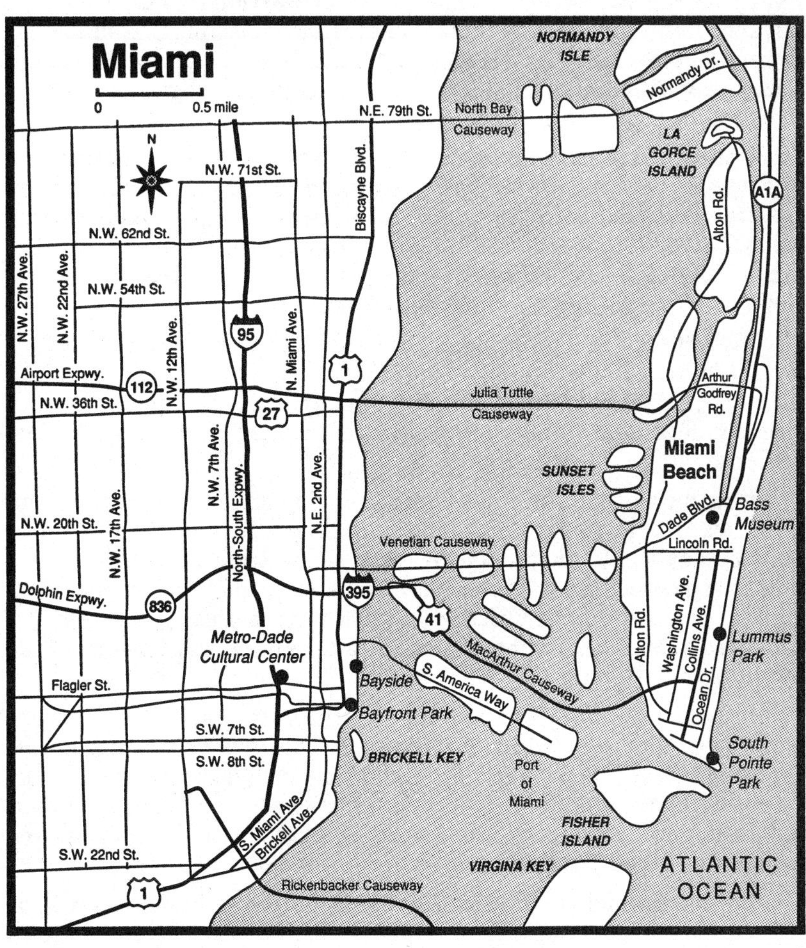

About four blocks northeast, the **United States Courthouse** (301 North Miami Avenue; 305-536-4548) is a place where you'll want to spend some time. This stately 1931 building is a masterful work of Spanish Mediterranean revival. Corinthian columns, glass arched doorways and miles of marble floor greet visitors. Around the vine-clad courtyard, artists have taken hold of the hallways, covering them with wild art murals.

For some more heady scenery, stroll around the corner to the **Ingraham Building** (25 Southeast 2nd Avenue), a 1927 study in Italian Renaissance architecture. Its compass arch entrances, heavy bronze doors and sweeping gold ceilings with hand-painted compartments are overwhelming. The building was named for J. E. Ingraham, Henry Flagler's right-hand man.

At the east end of 2nd Avenue, the savvy **Bayside Marketplace** (401 Biscayne Boulevard; 305-577-3344) rests primly along the bay, luring just as many sightseers as shoppers to its peach enclaves. The sprawling outdoor plaza is a great place to people watch while enjoying magicians, jugglers and strolling musicians.

Docked at the Bayside Marketplace is **The Heritage of Miami** (401 Biscayne Boulevard; 305-442-9697; admission), a coastal schooner that offers cruises around Biscayne Bay. The majestic tallship is modeled after the early 1900s schooners that traveled between Miami, Cuba and the Bahamas. Offered several times a day, the two-hour cruise provides excellent views of Vizcaya, Key Biscayne and Miami's skyline.

If you need some open space, head next door to **Bayfront Park** (301 North Biscayne Boulevard; 305-358-7550), 32 acres of rolling green hills and rock-studded palm tree gardens skirting the bay. This serene fleck of greenery, favored by after-work joggers, is frequently the site of outdoor concerts.

Your most historic stop downtown is several blocks south at the **Lummus Park District** (Northwest 4th Street and North River Drive). Here rests Dade County's oldest house, the **Wagner Homestead**. Built in 1858 by a struggling pioneer named William Wagner, the simple, four-room pine dwelling has hardily endured hurricanes, wars and the menace of progress. It's not a whole lot to look at, but it signifies a time when this concrete jungle was a mere wilderness.

Just south of downtown is Miami's version of Wall Street, a picturesque thoroughfare called **Brickell Avenue**. This impressive collection of ultramodern foreign (and a few domestic) bank buildings juts upward from the roadside, clinging to the skies that rim Biscayne Bay. Along the four-lane road, majestic palm trees and towering oaks create shade and natural sculptures for passing traffic.

Commercial highrises eventually merge with classy residential skyscrapers along this modern roadway. Here you'll spot the cleverly designed **Atlantis** apartment building (2025 Brickell Avenue). The architect built a large square gap into the middle of the building, punctuated the opening with a palm tree and an artsy spiral staircase, and then planted a single, rust-colored triangle atop the building. The Atlantis was completed in the early 1980s to great acclaim from Miami residents.

In the spirit of competition, owners of the neighboring **Villa Regina** apartments (15815 Brickell Avenue) splashed rainbow colors across their balconies, offsetting them with vertical racing stripes. From Biscayne Bay, the building looks like a painted accordion standing on end.

The enchantment of **Vizcaya Museum and Gardens** (3251 South Miami Avenue; 305-579-2813; admission) surpasses even all the hype passed out by local promoters. A vast Italian villa perched magnificently on Biscayne Bay, Vizcaya is the mastermind of farming magnate James Deering. A man infatuated with Renaissance styles, Deering hired 1000 people (one-tenth of Miami's population at the time) in 1914 to build the elaborate estate, a project that took two years and more than $15 million. Here you can wind your way through 34 rooms and halls lavishly adorned with priceless European antiques and paintings, oriental carpets, ornate moldings and spectacular architecture. Outside, stroll the botanical gardens, taking in the Great Stone Barge that rests brooding in the bay.

Across the street at the **Miami Museum of Science** (3280 South Miami Avenue; 305-854-4247; admission), engine parts whir, rainbows dance across a large soap bubble and chattering, wide-eyed children scurry about. This building boasts over 150 creative exhibits for children (and adults too), including an aviary and wildlife center. The adjacent **Space Transit Planetarium,** where you can "walk on Mars," hosts laser light and star shows (call the cosmic hotline at 305-854-2222).

"Miami Vice" gave you Hollywood's version of local crime-fighting techniques. To see the real stuff, turn in to the **American Police Hall of Fame and Museum** (3801 Biscayne Boulevard; 305-573-0700; admission). Distinguished by the patrol car parked across its facade, the museum offers over 10,000 absorbing exhibits that whisk you through the history of villain nabbing. There's a jail cell replica, a real gas chamber and guillotine, and a video crime clock with up-to-the-second statistics. If you're feeling sleuthy, visit the mock crime scene and solve a murder. Top detectives win certificates.

From Biscayne Boulevard, veer west to Northeast 2nd Avenue and head north. Like a Caribbean island scene, the street is edged with quaint frame buildings and bungalows washed in sunny yellows and sky blues, bright greens and soft pinks. Home to about 65,000 Haitian immigrants, **Little Haiti** (bounded by Biscayne Boulevard, Route 95, Northwest 46th Street and the 79th Street Causeway) is gentrifying into a colorful area rich in Creole cuisine and history.

DOWNTOWN MIAMI HOTELS

In downtown Miami, ultramodern corporate hotels continue to pop up, helping to shape and reshape the city's skyline. Rates here are deluxe and ultra-deluxe, and they don't fall in the off season. Inland, you'll find sprawling country club resorts and singularly chic addresses intermingled with a few chain motels and even fewer bed and breakfasts.

Conveniently located near the sprawling Bayside shops overlooking the port, the 1926 **Everglades Hotel** (244 Biscayne Boulevard; 305-379-5461) has kept pace with time. A restored lobby has attractive darkwood walls and marble floors, while 376 guest rooms are spotlessly decorated with wall-to-wall carpet and rattan furniture. An expansive rooftop pool and bar offer sweeping views. Moderate to deluxe.

The **Dupont Plaza** (300 Biscayne Boulevard Way; 305-358-2541) is one of those 1950s hotels with underground souvenir shops and pinball arcades. Dwarfed by neighboring highrises, the hotel rests along the Miami River and offers 12 floors of comfortable, spacious rooms with mauve and beige tones. Deluxe.

Rising 34 granite floors from Biscayne Bay, the **Hotel Intercontinental** (100 Chopin Plaza; 305-577-1000) takes on a stark look. Catering largely to a business crowd, the ultra-deluxe-priced hotel features a lobby with marble walls, a grand piano and a canopy of glass. Guest rooms are cushy, with black lacquer oriental armoires, floral print loveseats and granite tables.

A definite corporate hotel, the **Hyatt Regency** (400 Southeast 2nd Avenue; 305-358-1234) has a striking lobby with colorful, abstract artwork, huge potted palms and fluid glass and marble. The 24-story hostelry is conveniently connected to the Miami Convention Center and offers 615 modernly furnished rooms with contemporary art and good views of the city and river. Ultra-deluxe.

Perched nicely on the Miami River, the **Occidental Parc Suite Hotel** (100 Southeast 4th Street; 305-374-5100) is an elegant hotel with 16 floors of accommodations. Mahogany furnishings and subdued tones of plum and champagne persist throughout the guest rooms, many of which overlook the river. There's also a pool, jacuzzi and raw bar that rest waterside. Deluxe in price.

If it's charming, indigenous lodging you seek, look no further than the **Miami River Inn** (★) (118 Southwest South River Drive; 305-325-0045). Set in a courtyard of palms, the Victorian bed and breakfast exists in an unlikely area—a neighborhood of fishing companies. But its four early-1900s buildings have been splendidly restored, and its bedrooms individually decorated with antiques, carved wood beds and handmade drapes and quilts. Moderate to deluxe.

DOWNTOWN MIAMI RESTAURANTS

Sadly, there are but a few choice restaurants to be found in Miami's downtown. In a city where nearly half the people are Hispanic, the most frequently spotted eatery is the Cuban café. These narrow, oftentimes unkempt pit stops almost always have sidewalk takeout windows, where you can listen to Cuban radio stations while picking up some *sopa de pollo* (chicken soup), *papas fritas* (french fries), *morcillas* (blood sausage) and cold *cervezas* (beer). Stroll the bustling Flagler Street, where Latin street vendors offer *empanadas* (fried meat pies) and *batidos de frutas* (fruit milkshakes).

One sizzling lunch locale is **Granny Feelgood's** (190 Southeast 1st Avenue; 305-358-6233), where business types hobnob over clever health food creations. Granny's extensive menu features salads loaded with shrimp and chicken, inventive pastas, steamy vegetable soups and freshly squeezed fruit juices. Glass ceiling panes, oodles of hanging plants and great black-and-white photos of old Miami make for an airy atmosphere. Budget to moderate.

The stained paper sign at **The Big Fish** (★) (55 Southwest Miami Avenue Road; 305-372-3725) says it all: "No Shoes, No Shirt, No Suit . . . No Problem. Sit Down." This funky outdoor hideaway, tucked among Miami's drab dockside warehouses, has a tin roof and an array of mismatched wooden and aluminum tables. The menu, a total of five to six daily items posted on a piece of cardboard, consists of—you guessed it—fresh fish. A friendly owner introduces diners, a mishmash of crusty old folks and neatly dressed attorneys and financiers. Open for lunch only. Budget.

One of the city's smarter moves was to lease its 1923 firehouse to restaurateurs, who promptly returned **Firehouse Four** (1000 South Miami Avenue; 305-379-1923) to its original glory. A twentyish to thirtyish crowd mingles over chicken dishes in cozy booths surrounded by handsome mahogany floors. Central attractions are the 1920s fire hats and two shiny brass poles used by firefighters who slid from the second floor to the first. Budget to moderate.

Ever since *Esquire* magazine named **Las Tapas** (401 Biscayne Boulevard in Bayside Marketplace; 305-372-2737) one of the best new bars and restaurants of 1987, the Spanish-style eating house has been luring shoppers with its steamy concoctions of beef, chicken, seafood and pork. Glass walls enclose this two-story establishment, rimmed with black iron balconies and painted clay pots. Moderate.

Perched against the Miami River underneath a bridge, **East Coast Fisheries** (360 West Flagler Street; 305-373-5514) has been filling the local fish fix since 1933. The restaurant's fleet of 36 boats deliver fresh catches of the day, which might include grouper, snapper, bluefish, mackerel, kingfish, dolphin, flounder, lobster or stone crabs. For appetizers, the conch fritters are a must; for entrées, try the fried flounder with walnuts and grapes or garlic mahimahi. A casual, uproarious eatery located in a 1918 former shrimp packing house. Prices are moderate to deluxe.

If the overstuffed bagels and sandwiches at **Brickell Emporium** (1100 Brickell Plaza; 305-377-3354) don't strike any stomach chords, the menu will. The ten-page food directory contains entertaining "deli-talk," with a glossary of eatables. Selections, all at budget prices, include roast pork on garlic bread, cheese blintzes, pizza bagels and more than a dozen fresh salads.

Everyone loves **S & S Diner** (1757 Northeast 2nd Avenue, just north of downtown; 305-373-4291). The Miami institution, immortalized in Mel Kiser and Corky Irick's movie *Last Night at the S & S Diner*, packs 'em in daily with down-to-earth fare such as meatloaf, roast pork, stuffed cabbage, chopped steak with onions, turkey and dressing, and the best mashed potatoes around. After you've waited in line (and wait you will), you can take one of the 23 seats at the horseshoe counter. Save your appetite: Homespun vittles don't get much better than this. Budget.

To get a culinary taste of Little Haiti, drive along Northeast 54th Street between Biscayne Boulevard and Miami Avenue. Just west of Miami Avenue, you'll find a gem of a restaurant called **Chez Moy** (1 Northwest 54th Street; 305-757-5056). The small, immaculate eatery serves budget-priced creole delicacies (curried goat, spicy steamed fish) that truly makes you feel like you're in the French Caribbean.

DOWNTOWN MIAMI SHOPPING

Miami's premier shopping mecca, **Bayside Marketplace** (401 Biscayne Boulevard; 305-577-3344) is a $93-million study in cool aesthetics. A gay pink plaza hugging sparkling Biscayne Bay, the open-air mall is a labyrinth of giant ferns, palm trees and brick walkways dotted with white flower carts, strolling musicians and mimes. Though it brims with 145 novel stores and restaurants, Bayside is just as much a people-watching spot as a shopping address.

Venture over to **Mato** (305-577-8854) for futuristic gifts in eye-popping neon colors. There's a savvy pink telephone, minuscule calculators tucked in matchbook covers and clocks that look like compact discs.

At **Excess** (305-375-0393) casual women's wear takes on new meaning with shirts draped in pearls and denim minidresses. Just as exotic, **Atlantic Crossing** (305-381-7776) has hand-painted T-shirts with blue feathers and rhinestone-studded jackets depicting tropical locales.

Men can pick up their "Miami Vice" attire nearby at **Sartori Amici** (305-381-6168). The crisp white European suits and silk ties here carry hefty price tags, though. "Outrageous" is the key word at **Dapy** (305-374-3098), where novelties and high-priced designs include dancing Coke cans, neon stereos and bizarre salt and pepper shakers.

A flashy address, **Puttin' on the Ritz** (305-375-0375) is jammed with wild art sun visors, postcards, pink flamingos and other Miami-style objects. For a Brazilian flare, **Azteca de Oro** (305-375-0358) has jungle fashions, hand-loomed rugs and large painted parrots.

Top it off at **The Hat Collection** (305-381-6272), where you can don fedoras, safari caps, flapper hats and numerous other varieties of crown covers.

The mall's central breezy veranda is flanked by carts filled with objects from faraway places. **Passage to India** (305-375-9504) is where you can pick up fine Indian clothing and wooden jewelry.

Geronimo's Trail (305-577-3512) features Native American and Southwestern jewelry, candles and art. **Eels on Wheels** (305-252-4639) has colorful handbags made of (what else?) eelskin. **Button Up** (305-770-0313) sells nothing but imaginative buttons—jewels, pearls, ceramic sculptures—that you can clip-on over your boring buttons.

Your Jamaica connection is **Reggae Mania**, a cart stocked with crocheted dread hats, beads for dreadlocks, books on Bob Marley, and other Rastafarian goodies.

Formerly the place to shop downtown, **Omni Mall** (1601 Biscayne Boulevard; 305-374-6664) has been overshadowed by Bayside and has deteriorated somewhat during recent years. Clustered around the Omni Hotel, the enclosed dual-level center houses about 100 shops—mostly chain stores of all price levels and a few restaurants. The highlight here is not a store but a beautiful Italian carousel that makes kiddies squeal with delight.

A bustling urban thoroughfare cutting through the heart of downtown, **Flagler Street** is where some of the city's first merchants set up shop during the 1920s. Today, brick sidewalks are rimmed with Latin street vendors and fronted by noisy electronics marts and discount jewelry centers.

If diamonds are a girl's best friend, then the **Seybold Building** (39 East Flagler Street) is her dreamland. Herein lies ten floors of stores abounding with those twinkling jewels as well as gold and silver pieces. The name of the game is bargaining, and most merchants are anxious to strike a deal.

Don't miss **Burdines Department Store** (22 East Flagler Street; 305-835-5151), a landmark, 1936 streamlined moderne design that adds a touch of nostalgia to the area.

James Bond would have loved Miami. Here he could have shopped to his heart's content from a wide array of espionage toys: thumb-sized cameras for sneaking pictures, eyeglasses that let you see who's creeping up behind you, bugs for eavesdropping on your enemies. Spy shops are sprinkled across Miami, catering to an undercover and security-conscious clientele. In downtown Miami, **Spy Shops International** (350 Biscayne Boulevard; 305-374-4779) is like a small department store. On South Miami Beach, there's **Security Works** (715 5th Street; 305-534-4400). North of downtown, you'll espy **Miami Spy** (2695 Biscayne Boulevard; 305-573-9999).

DOWNTOWN MIAMI NIGHTLIFE

The Oak Room (100 Chopin Plaza in the Intercontinental Hotel; 305-577-4198) draws a large business clientele for after-work cocktails.

Good riverside views can be had at **Currents** (400 Southeast 2nd Avenue in the Hyatt Regency; 305-358-1234), an upbeat, lounge with an eclectic mix of recorded music: Top-40, pop, country, rhythm-and-blues and urban contemporary.

At **Firehouse Four** (1000 South Miami Avenue; 305-379-1923), a restored 1923 fire station, hundreds of downtowners clamor around happy-hour buffets and a cozy mahogany bar. A live band rocks outside Friday evenings.

One of the best bars around, **Tobacco Road** (626 South Miami Avenue; 305-374-1198) obtained the city's first liquor license back in 1912. An old speakeasy, "The Road" has a secret closet where illegal booze and roulette tables were once stashed. Upstairs, there's an impressive lineup of rhythm-and-blues bands. Cover on weekends.

The garden patio at **Coco Loco** (495 Brickell Avenue in the Sheraton Brickell Point; 305-373-6000) is an after-work roosting place for the suit-and-tie set. Later, you'll find a young Hispanic crowd dancing to recorded disco and Top-40 tunes.

Bayside Marketplace (401 Biscayne Boulevard; 305-577-3344) is the headquarters for outdoor entertainment. Afternoons and evenings, you'll find reggae, jazz and rhythm-and-blues bands playing center stage on the waterfront.

If you like that old time rock-and-roll, head over to **Dick Clark's American Bandstand Grill** (also at Bayside; 305-381-8800). Decorated with music memorabilia and checkered floors, the bayside grill has a small dancefloor and big burgers. The deejays are, as you'd expect, some of the best around.

THEATER, OPERA, SYMPHONY AND DANCE

The gorgeous **Gusman Center for the Performing Arts** (174 East Flagler Street; 305-374-2444), an ornate 1739-seat facility, is home to the Philharmonic Orchestra of Florida and the New World Symphony. The Gusman also hosts the popular Miami Film Festival.

Reminiscent of flashy pre-Castro Havana nightclubs, **Les Violins** (1751 Biscayne Boulevard; 305-371-8668) has strolling violinists and glittering, top-notch Latin floor shows. Cover.

The city's prized **Bayfront Park** (301 Biscayne Boulevard between Northeast 1st and 4th streets; 305-375-8480), which spans 32 acres of waterside palm trees and rolling hills, has a 17,600-person capacity amphitheater for outdoor musical concerts from symphony to rock.

The modern, cylindrical **James L. Knight International Center** (400 Southeast 2nd Avenue; 305-372-0929) is the 5000-seat address of jazz, rock-and-roll and pops concerts.

Larger concerts are held at the 16,500-seat **Miami Arena** (721 Northwest 1st Avenue; 305-530-4400), another ultramodern circular facility rimmed with palm trees.

Just north of downtown, the **Joseph Caleb Auditorium** (5400 Northwest 22nd Avenue in Liberty City; 305-636-2350) presents stellar drama by local Black artists. The 1001-seat facility is also the site of regional orchestra and Shakespearean performances.

Little Havana

Despite its name, Little Havana bears almost no resemblance to the Cuban capital, yet it serves as the core of Miami's Cuban population. The main drag is Southwest 8th Street, known locally as **Calle Ocho**, stretching just west of downtown from Route 95 to Southwest 35th Avenue. Calle Ocho is really just one long, noisy thoroughfare fringed with discount stores, flashing neon signs, gas stations and great Latin restaurants and nightclubs.

The best way to soak in the atmosphere here is to park and walk. The street signs, like the restaurant menus, are mainly in Spanish, but it's fairly easy to find someone who can translate. Old Cuban men in guayaberas socialize on street corners, while the younger set strolls the sidewalks with radios blasting Spanish music. You'll almost always find a crowd at **Domino Park** (Southwest 8th Street and Southwest 15th Avenue), a community center where locals gather for games of chess and dominoes.

On the roadways flanking Calle Ocho, tens of thousands of Cuban immigrants have settled in modest, well-kept neighborhoods. Many residents display the American flag or exhibit bright brass shrines of their favorite patron saint. Every March they hold the country's largest Hispanic festival, with fabulous food and music and a conga line that continues for blocks.

LITTLE HAVANA RESTAURANTS

Just west of downtown pulses another world. This haven for thousands of Cuban immigrants is also the settling ground for scores of Cuban eateries offering an abundance of food at incredibly cheap prices. A case in point is the **Casablanca Cafeteria** (2300 Southwest 8th Street; 305-642-2751), where diners belly-up to the long counter for heaping portions of *milanesa*, plantains and beef tongue creole.

You'll step back in time to the Old West when you enter **La Carreta** (3632 Southwest 8th Street; 305-444-7501). Leather-back chairs and heavy wooden chandeliers add a rustic feel to multiple dining rooms, where large color photos of Old Havana adorn the walls. Budget-to-moderate-priced selections feature traditional Cuban fare such as chicken and yellow rice, pork with black beans, and Spanish bean soup. With more than three dozen desserts to choose from, who could resist the final course?

As one of the more interesting buildings in Little Havana, **Casa Juancho** (2436 Southwest 8th Street; 305-642-2452) depicts Spanish Renaissance architecture. A barrel-tiled roof and tan stucco exterior match the brick pillars and wooden beam ceiling inside. Sacks of garlic and ham hocks hang around the open kitchen, where exceptional seafood, poultry and game dishes are whipped up. Deluxe.

There's an aura of disrepair, of time-worn seediness about **Malaga** (740 Southwest 8th Street; 305-858-4224). But no matter. This courtyard eatery, barely recognizable from the street, consistently offers some of Miami's foremost Cuban fare. Quaint wooden tables centered around a tangled mass of trees and vines set the stage for sumptuous pot roast simmered in sausages, spicy fried veal and pork and exceptional paella. Moderate.

President Ronald Reagan paid a visit to **La Esquina de Tejas** (101 Southwest 12th Avenue; 305-545-5341) in 1983 and turned the nondescript, streetcorner diner into an overnight success. What you'll find here is good standard Cuban food, namely *pollo asado* (baked chicken), *moros* (mixed black beans) and flan. The simple, Western-style decor features red brick floors, wooden paneling and ham hocks hanging in the front windows. Budget to moderate.

An anomaly in this Hispanic neighborhood, **Hy-Vong (★)** (3458 Southwest 8th Street; 305-446-3674) rightfully takes its place as Miami's best Vietnamese restaurant. With plain white walls and a few wilting plants, the atmosphere is nil. But the moderately priced food is prepared with great care by one of the owners, a Vietnamese woman who fled Saigon in 1975. The hearty fare includes *thi kho* (pork in coconut milk), *cari tom* (curried shrimp and crab), chicken with jicama and an interesting squid salad. Dinner only.

Your Nicaraguan connection can be found at **Guayacan Restaurant** (1933 Southwest 8th Street; 305-649-2015), a modest establishment with counter service and a few tables in the back. Here you can sample hen soup with meatballs, tripe and vegetables, *salpicón* (marinated beef) and other budget ethnic offerings.

LITTLE HAVANA SHOPPING

Miami's Cuban core offers one long street tagged with discount marts where you'll find not only good buys but an intriguing taste of local ethnic life. Concentrate on **Southwest 8th Street**, Little Havana's bustling main drag, between Route 95 West and 35th Street.

Designer leather goods await at **Cuchi** (1107 Southwest 8th Street; 305-285-0707), a quaint niche adorned with snazzy shoes and accessories for women and men. Over at **Lily's Records** (1260 Southwest 8th Street; 305-856-0536), you can find your favorite Latin tunes.

España Gift Importers (1615 Southwest 8th Street; 305-856-4844) is a cache of everything-Spanish, from frilly dolls and intricate porcelain to delicate fans.

You can pour over hundreds of historic Cuban coins and stamps at **Alvarez Stamp & Coin** (1735 Southwest 8th Street; 305-649-1176). A friendly owner will also show you his collection of pre-Castro documents.

Pick up a colorful, cool guayabera at **Cruise Casuals** (2700 Southwest 8th Street; 305-649-8621), a no-frills men's clothing store. Next door, **Kristian Flower Designs** (2706 Southwest 8th Street; 305-854-0019) stocks a vibrant array of unusual silk flower arrangements and beautiful, handwoven tapestries.

For books on international relations, stop by **Librería Universal** (3090 Southwest 8th Street; 305-642-3234), where topics range from Cuban-American and Afro-American issues to Caribbean politics.

LITTLE HAVANA NIGHTLIFE

Hispanic immigrants brought a whole new brand of nightlife to Miami, namely late-night supper clubs with lavish revues. Here on Little Havana's Southwest 8th Street you'll find some of the best.

Silk banana plants and murals of Colombia set the stage for Columbian music, salsa, Latin jazz and merengue at **La Tranquera** (971 Southwest 8th Street; 305-856-9476). Cover.

A cozy spot with long wooden tables and Spanish pottery, **Cacharrito's Place** (2235 Southwest 8th Street; 305-643-9626) features mariachi music and flamenco dancing. Cover.

Several excellent restaurants throw in some flamenco and strolling musicians with your meal. Try **Malaga** (740 Southwest 8th Street; 305-858-4224) and **Casa Juancho** (2436 Southwest 8th Street; 305-642-2452).

You'll see top-name Latin musical and comedy shows at the 255-seat **Teatro de Bellas Artes** (2173 Southwest 8th Street; 305-325-0515).

West of Little Havana, **Maxim's Supper Club** (76th Street and Southwest 8th Street; 305-264-9233) is an elegant affair with an orchestra and piano bar. Latin music is featured nightly.

Key Biscayne

Take the undulating Rickenbacker Causeway across the brilliant turquoise water of Biscayne Bay and you'll land on **Virginia Key,** a speck of an island smothered in immense Australian pines and quiescent beaches. Although the island has remained very much in its natural state, tourism is beginning to leave its mark here.

Farther down, the larger **Key Biscayne** is a lush flatland dotted with bushy sea grape trees and willowy pines. A historic crossroads, the barrier island was encountered by Ponce de León in 1513, when he dubbed it the Cape of Florida.

Crandon Boulevard is the key's main drag, cutting two miles through the length of the island. Quaint strip shopping centers, golf fairways and manicured condos line the boulevard, which is thankfully void of fast-food joints and intrusive highrises.

Tucked obscurely at the island's tip is the 1825 **Cape Florida Lighthouse** (1200 South Crandon Boulevard in Bill Baggs Cape Florida State Recreation Area; 305-361-5811; admission), Florida's oldest remaining lighthouse. Oblivious to noisy beachgoers, the red brick cylinder rises 95 feet from the beach and peers serenely across the Atlantic Ocean, remembering a time when it guided ships through the perilous coastal reefs. Its sturdy walls survived a severe Seminole Indian attack in 1836 as well as an onslaught by Confederate sympathizers during the Civil War. The lighthouse itself is closed to the, public but there is a tour of the lighthouse keeper's home—now a museum.

KEY BISCAYNE HOTELS

The island bears a mere trio of hotels, but thankfully each is nestled on a choice slice of beach. The **Silver Sands** (301 Ocean Drive; 305-361-5441), a traditional, L-shaped motel commanding fantastic views, is a departure from fancy oceanfront highrises. This homey, single-story hostelry surrounds a quiet courtyard with a pool and sandy path snaking its way to the beach. Guest rooms are clean but a little rugged, with exposed electrical cords and natty wall-to-wall carpets. Four wooden cottages are the best accommodations. Deluxe to ultra-deluxe.

The white, pyramid-shaped **Sonesta Beach Hotel** (350 Ocean Drive; 305-361-2021) sits crossways and purveys a sense of cool island elegance. The lobby is a mesh of Roman tile floors, glass tables and a waterfall plummeting down an abstract wall design. The Sonesta Beach has a palm tree-studded swimming pool and 301 rooms—all with ocean or island views—furnished with contemporary decor in pastel hues. An extensive children's program draws lots of families. Ultra-deluxe.

The **Sheraton Royal Biscayne** (555 Ocean Drive; 305-361-5775) is where you can really kick back and vegetate. A chickee-crowned courtyard surrounds two swimming pools and teems with tropical flowers and cackling exotic birds perched in bamboo cages. A maze of five low-slung pink-and-white buildings houses 192 guest rooms. Deluxe to ultra-deluxe.

KEY BISCAYNE RESTAURANTS

Eating out on Key Biscayne means trysting with cool blue Biscayne Bay. By far the best beachfront spot is **The Sand Bar** (301 Ocean Drive; 305-361-1049). Take in whiffs of coconut oil from nearby sunbathers while sipping rum drinks and feasting on burgers and fresh fish of the day. The Sand Bar is one of the few places where you actually dine on the beach, albeit on a wooden deck. Consistently slow service is the only drawback. Moderate.

Arguably, the **Rusty Pelican** (3201 Rickenbacker Causeway, Key Biscayne; 305-361-3818) has cornered the market on views. Poised on the edge of Key Biscayne and surrounded by water on three sides, the Pelican faces sweeping scenes of downtown and glistening Biscayne Bay. The two-story rustic wooden building is set amidst a sea of palm trees and flowering plants. Inside, you'll find brick floors, stone walls and huge fishing nets draped from the ceiling. Atmosphere is the obvious draw here, since the fare—which focuses on seafood—is good but overpriced. Try the coconut shrimp, grouper tempura or seafood pasta Alfredo. Moderate to ultra-deluxe.

If you crave oriental food, you'll love the **Two Dragons** (350 Ocean Drive in the Sonesta Beach Hotel; 305-361-2021). Sit in cozy wicker pagodas and sample traditional Chinese Mandarin and Szechuan cuisine, or stroll next door to the Japanese steakhouse, where a chef cooks right at your table. Black lacquered tables and ornate stained glass accented by palm fronds are found throughout the twin eateries. Dinner only; ultra-deluxe.

Bounded by palm trees and rolling fairways, **Ventana's On the Green** (6700 Crandon Boulevard; 305-361-0496) is a prime spot to lose an afternoon. The budget-priced summer menu features sandwiches and hamburgers while the moderate-priced winter offerings expand to include dinner entrées such as chicken marsala, roast beef and tortellini alfredo.

Deliciously fresh pasta keeps the island's chic crowd coming back to **Stefano's** (24 Crandon Boulevard; 305-361-7007). Winning entrées include linguine in lobster sauce, agnolotti, spinach *pappardelle* and snapper in fennel sauce. There's no glistening bay in sight, but pleasant garden surroundings are an acceptable substitute. Moderate to ultra-deluxe.

For the island's best steaks, try **La Choza** (971 Crandon Boulevard in L'Esplanade Shopping Center; 305-361-0113), a Nicaraguan-style eatery with rugged animal skins on the walls. Try the filets in jalapeño sauce, *pincho de lomitos* (shish kebabs) and baby tenderloin steak, served with heaps of rice and plantains. The white linen tablecloths and oversized potted plants add casual elegance to the leather-and-skin decor. Moderate to deluxe.

KEY BISCAYNE BEACHES AND PARKS

Hobie Beach—A ribbon of fluffy sand along a scenic causeway, this beach gets its name from the hundreds of sailboaters and windsurfers who whiz up and down the coast. Forever windy and spirited, Hobie Beach affords spectacular views of downtown while offering solace under canopies of Australian pines. It's crowded every day, especially on weekends, so get here early.

Facilities: Sailboard, sailboat, windsurfing and jet ski rentals, food vendors. *Swimming:* Okay if you stay very close to shore. Otherwise, you'll get plowed down by windsurfers and jet skiers. *Windsurfing:* The best.

Getting there: On the south side of Rickenbacker Causeway.

Virginia Key Beach—Sugar-fine sand rings most of this quiescent island that's smothered in tall pine trees and thick brush. At the eastern tip, where most people can be found, flocks of seagulls scurry about the placid shore, leaving their clawed imprints. But here's the real scoop: if you want seclusion, seek out the key's southwestern rim. Park in lot number one, then backtrack through the wooded areas until you find a series of natural coves. This was once a nude beach, and you'll still see a few birthday suits between these crevices. There's not much sand, but the water is crystal clear and shallow.

Facilities: Picnic tables, restrooms, lifeguards, concession stands, wooded trails. *Fishing:* Good from the shore. Sheepshead, snapper and occasionally lobster. *Swimming:* Exceptional.

Getting there: Off Rickenbacker Causeway.

Crandon Park Beach—Key Biscayne's most popular beach sports a very wide swath of tawny sand edged with clusters of palm trees and a sliver of grassy meadow. A concrete path and spacious grassy areas border the mile-long stretch, which is a popular spot for Hispanic families. Ocean waves purr gently against a knee-deep sand bar that extends nearly 300 yards out. Keep an eye out for dolphins and those lovable manatees, who travel the coastal waters.

Facilities: Picnic areas, restrooms, showers, lifeguards, concession stands, bicycle trails, botanical gardens; information, 305-361-5421. *Swimming:* Very good.

Getting there: Located midway down Key Biscayne off Rickenbacker Causeway.

Bill Baggs Cape Florida State Recreation Area—Situated at the pinnacle of Key Biscayne and masked in broad Australian pine trees, the 406-acre park offers scenic drives and broad beaches. Perched in the sand dunes, an 1825 lighthouse still peers across the horizon. In the distance, several stilt houses—built decades ago by fishermen—are clustered together in the

Atlantic Ocean, a peculiar spectacle for beachgoers. You'll also find nature trails and a tranquil little harbor that's perfect for swimming.

Facilities: Picnic tables, restrooms, showers, lifeguards, concession stands, nature trails, boardwalk; 305-361-5811. *Fishing:* Try from the seawall on the Biscayne Bay side. Snook, red snapper, yellow tail, jack and grouper may be biting. *Swimming:* Very good.

Getting there: At Key Biscayne's tip, off Rickenbacker Causeway.

Coconut Grove

South of Miami you'll find Coconut Grove, a turn-of-the-century village and the area's first real winter resort. Long a nest of quiet homes and quaint stores, "The Grove" attracted throngs of hippies during the 1960s and now dances to the trendiness of the 1990s. Although recent crime and deteriorating neighborhoods have caused a mild exodus, the village remains a hotbed of activity.

Your first sightseeing opportunity is **Silver Bluff**, an intriguing rock formation extending half a mile along Bayshore Drive between Crystal View and Emathia Street. Carved thousands of years ago by wave action, these knobby white constellations are made of oolitic limestone. Some of the area's first settlers, captured by the beauty of the bluff, built their homes around these rocks overlooking the bay.

Southward around a bend you'll encounter **Miami City Hall** (3500 Pan American Drive; 305-250-5300). A two-story gleaming white structure preening on Biscayne Bay, it looks more like a small hotel than a government center. But then, that's typical of Miami. Carvings of little world globes traipse across the facade, hinting that the 1930s building used to be a busy Pan American Airlines seaplane base.

The village core lies along **Main Highway** and **Commodore Plaza,** just south of City Hall. Miami's trendiness central, these streets are an experience in contrived aesthetics. Chic shops with bubbled canopies intermingle with towering oaks and nibble at the brick-lined roadways. Fashion-conscious women stroll the sidewalks, laden with perfume and shopping bags.

Coconut Grove founder Ralph Middleton Munroe, a true lover and protector of Florida's natural beauty, would have been heartbroken to see throngs of people and automobiles buzzing around what used to be the world's largest hardwood hammock. Quite aptly, the remaining smidgen of nature here is Munroe's **Barnacle** (3485 Main Highway; 305-448-9445; admission), a serene five-acre estate overlooking Biscayne Bay. An old horse-and-buggy trail meanders through a lush hammock to the house. This structure, built in stages between 1891 and 1928, is the oldest Dade County home still located on its original site. Reflecting Munroe's devotion to shipbuilding and the sea, the two-story frame building sports a barnacle-shaped roof and a large veranda to catch ocean breezes. Most of the 19th-century furnishings are intact, and Munroe's excellent collection of pioneer photographs adorn the walls. On the grounds is an ancient spring-fed well and a boathouse.

Another tribute to the area's earlier days, the **Coconut Grove Playhouse** (3500 Main Highway; 305-442-4000) is an inspiring, Spanish-style theater. Constructed in 1926, it was destroyed by the infamous hurricane that year and promptly rebuilt in 1927. Richly ornamented with parapets and twisted columns, the theater now hosts regional and major productions and continues to be a fashionable place to go.

Hidden away from the road in the middle of a private school, the **Pagoda of Ransom-Everglades School** (★) (3575 Main Highway; 305-460-8800) is a real find. The 1902 pine building was the entire school until the campus expanded in the 1940s. Now, strolling back to the pagoda is like taking a trip through time. All around, preppy students laze in the grass or play tennis, while inside the pagoda's dusty walls rest memories of days past: a 1919 typewriter, a 1929 school yearbook, a much-used limestone fireplace. Chances are, you'll be the only sightseer at this historic stop.

COCONUT GROVE HOTELS

One of the area's most opulent hotels, the **Mayfair House** (3000 Florida Avenue; 305-441-0000) is a work of art. Swirling hand-painted tiles, stained-glass panels and gorgeous mahogany and jade undulate throughout the lobby. A real reprieve from ultramodernism, the 181 suites—all very different—are simply romantic. Hinted with incense, each room has a Japanese hot tub, all-marble bathroom and striking hand-loomed linens. Amenities also include a rooftop pool and solarium and the classy Mayfair Shops just outside your door. The price tag is, needless to say, ultra-deluxe.

A terraced tower overlooking a large yacht basin, the **Doubletree** (2649 South Bayshore Drive; 305-858-2500) is a casual but stylish kind of place. White marble tiles, hand-hewn cedar paneling and contemporary works of art adorn the lobby, which spills out onto an airy pool deck overlooking a busy avenue. Some of the 190 guest rooms have wet bars and modern furnishings. Deluxe to ultra-deluxe.

Unlike most other regions of Florida, the Miami area has few bed and breakfasts. However, more than 40 families have opened their homes to travelers. The accommodations, most with budget and moderate prices, are sprinkled throughout Dade County and range from chic Coconut Grove homes to horse ranches. For reservations, contact **Bed and Breakfast Company for Florida and the Caribbean** (P.O. Box 439262, South Miami, FL 33243; 305-661-3270).

Beautiful jutting terraces brimming with flowering vines signify that you've reached the **Grand Bay Hotel** (2669 South Bayshore Drive; 305-858-9600), a very ritzy Miami address. Classical music is piped into a lobby styled with dramatic wood-trimmed glass walls, enormous crystal chandeliers and mirrored ceilings. Most of the 181 accommodations face the Grove's yacht basin and some are aesthetically furnished with period pieces and sunken

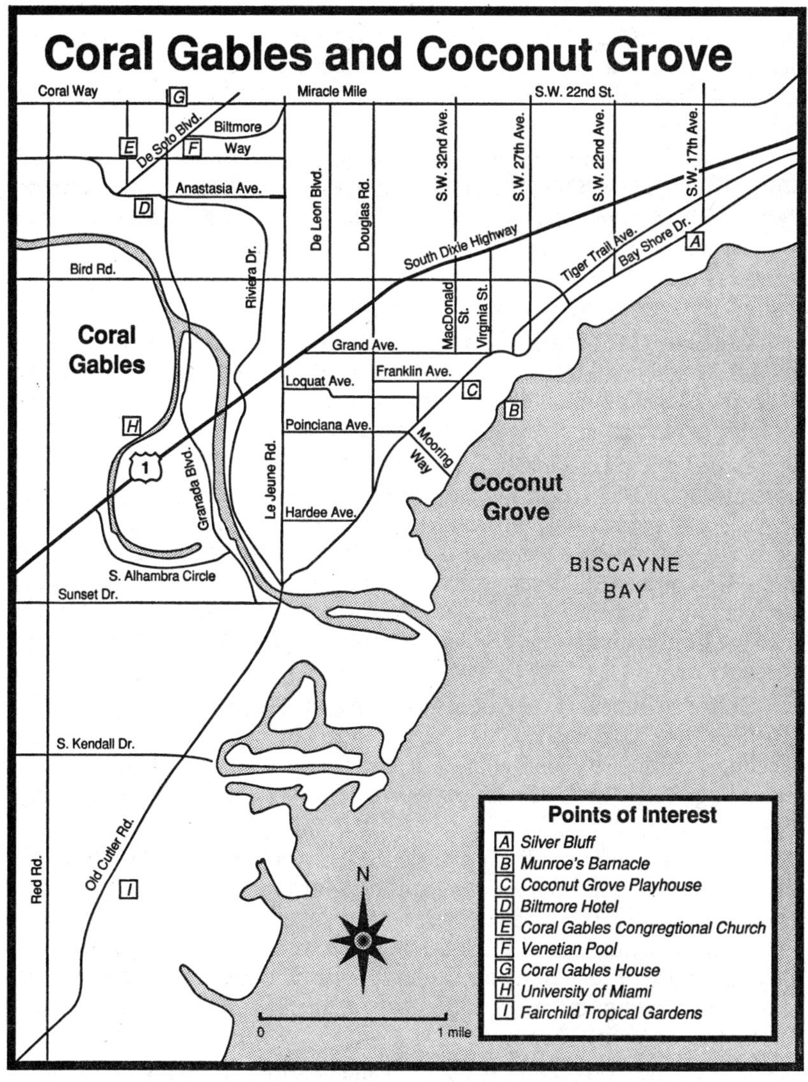

marble tubs. All units feature breakfast balconies, minibars and king-sized beds. A pool deck and restaurant are among the amenities. Unmatched for service, the Grand Bay even serves you a glass of bubbly while you check in. Ultra-deluxe.

COCONUT GROVE RESTAURANTS

Formerly an 1800s caretaker's cottage, **Tuscany's** (3484 Main Highway; 305-445-0022) now indulges a trendy clientele who convene on the outdoor red brick patio to gaze at a diverse group of passersby. The Italian-style cuisine includes the traditional selection of pastas, salads and fresh fruits. Moderate to deluxe.

The second-floor venue of **Kaleidoscope** (3112 Commodore Plaza; 305-446-5010) provides a bird's eye view of the street hubbub. This charming, glass-enclosed terrace has white patio furniture, ceiling fans and window box gardens. The cuisine may be American-style, but it's interesting all the same. Try the red snapper with glazed bananas or roast duckling with orange chutney and green peppercorns. Moderate to deluxe.

Zanzibar (3468 Main Highway; 305-444-0244) claims the prime people-watching corner and lavishes its outdoor patrons with tall frozen margaritas and red-and-yellow umbrellas to ward off the blazing sun. Budget-priced burgers, omelettes and salads are good for munching.

Café Tu Tu Tango (3015 Grand Avenue, in the CocoWalk entertainment plaza; 305-529-2222) is, quite simply, *the* place to nosh in Coconut Grove. Fashioned after an artist's loft in Barcelona, the wood-floored tapas bar is always crowded and always oh-so-good. Graze on an assortment of chips, dips, and fried tidbits such as calamari and alligator, or opt for a gourmet pizza that's brick oven baked. For fare more filling, try the chicken breast stuffed with *chorizo* (Spanish sausage), spinach and cheese. Budget to moderate.

Go for a Chinese fix at **Mandarin Gardens** (3268 Grand Avenue; 305-446-9999), the local headquarters for dependable Hunan, Mandarin and fiery Szechuan cuisine. Nestled along a tree-lined street, the diminutive eatery draws huge lunch crowds who pay homage to the sesame chicken, orange beef and crispy shrimp and broccoli. Budget to moderate.

Aptly named **Señor Frog's** (3008 Grand Avenue; 305-448-0999), this toad green stucco formation attracts a lively crowd who gulp huge margaritas and feast on gringo food as well as tasty traditional Mexican fare. Sepia photos of Mexican heroes, brick floors and a wooden bar set a casual tone. The extensive menu is quite entertaining, warning against a "boring!" consommé and listing an entrée called *arroa cabezón* but saying, "no translation, just order it!" Moderate.

One of the Grove's most distinguished addresses, the **Mayfair Grill** (3000 Florida Avenue, Coconut Grove; 305-441-0000) is situated in the dazzling Mayfair House hotel and purveys a real sense of grandeur. Embellishments of beautiful mahogany, marble and stained glass abound in a subdued, romantic setting. The menu offers such tempting gourmet delicacies as Everglades frogs' legs, seared ahi tuna and veal medallions with stone crab sauce. Dessert features chocolate-pecan crème brulée and croissant pudding with Wild Turkey sauce. Ultra-deluxe.

Monty Trainer's (2550 South Bayshore Drive; 305-858-1431) is a perfect place for a dog-day afternoon. This classic, palm-tree-crowned raw bar—a Grove legacy—plays host to swimsuit-clad locals and tourists who soak up the sun and calypso music. Outdoor picnic tables overlook an expansive marina. Excellent conch fritters, stone crab and those famous Florida oysters on the half shell are featured. Budget to moderate.

COCONUT GROVE SHOPPING

For more than a decade, the Grove's vogue shops have been patronized by trendsetters and those with money to burn. The best part of browsing these shady glass fronts is eyeing the other shoppers, who love to dress up for the occasion.

The heart of trendiness, **Mayfair Shops** (2911 Grand Avenue; 305-448-1700) is a glass-canopied atrium with savvy written all over it. Shoot up to the second and third floors in glass elevators, or laze around Mexican-tiled waterfalls and ornate marble sculptures. Many of the 50 stores—which include names such as Romanoff and Polo-Ralph Lauren—offer offbeat, outlandish styles with a Hispanic flair.

Carolyn Lamb (3015 Grand Avenue, Suite 173; 305-443-4631) keeps the "body conscious" woman in mind with sleek workout suits, lycra dresses and leggings, and other form-fitting getups.

Just outside the mall, **American Details** (3107 Grand Avenue; 305-448-6163) proffers an eye-pleasing scheme of handblown vases and perfumers, exotic wood jewelry boxes and kaleidoscopes.

Stroll down to Commodore Plaza, where posh shops peek out under brightly colored bubble canopies and tall oak trees. Behind a pretty white trellis you'll find the **Garden Gate** (3110 Commodore Plaza; 305-442-2789), a breezy spot overflowing with flowering bromeliads, begonias, African violets and other natural beauties.

If you don't like the crazy, 1960s-style fabrics and clothes at **Betsey Johnson** (3117 Commodore Plaza; 305-446-5478), you'll love the store's decor. Dramatic black staircases snake up from black-and-white checkered floors, accented by hot-pink walls with funky art murals.

Bask in the past at **Antiques in the Grove** (3168 Commodore Plaza; 305-448-7877), a marvelous shop where you can sort through flapper beads, jade statues, stunning crystal, antique jewelry, porcelain pieces, housewares and silver tea services.

The **Hendrix Collection** (3170 Commodore Plaza; 305-446-2182) houses an exceptional medley of Southwestern folk art, including painted wooden cacti, lifelike coyotes and snakes, gorgeous pine furniture and handcrafted jewelry.

For a Caribbean flavor, veer into **Carlos Art Gallery** (3162 Commodore Plaza; 305-445-3020), which carries a good variety of Haitian paintings, sculptures and ceramics.

Mom will find her string bikini at **Ritchie Swimwear** (3401 Main Highway; 305-443-7919), a colorful collage of neon, print and striped suits for men and women.

The place to be, **CocoWalk** (3015 Grand Avenue; 305-444-0777) is a perfect example of the area's trend toward yuppiness. The multi-level shopping and partying extravaganza, which opened in 1991, is a fanciful version of Spanish stucco and coral rock woven with fountains and balconies and walkways. Among the chic shops here, **The White House** (305-446-7747) caters to the woman who loves white. Suits, lingerie, parasols and picture frames are displayed. For the more daring shopper, **Studley's** (305-445-8829) features shirts strung with pearls and jeans painted with murals.

One of our favorite CocoWalk shops is **Animal Crackers** (305-445-1935). A toy store that feels like a jungle, it's hung with huge fabric vines and stuffed animals and filled with things that dance, sing and go bump in the night. If you're in a cactus kind of mood, duck into **Santa Fe Art** (305-442-4661). The spacious store carries painted vessels, windchimes, glassware, rugs, clothing and jewelry from the Southwest.

Nearby, watch your necklace being made at **Om Jewelry** (3070 Grand Avenue; 305-445-1865), a store and studio featuring gold and silver in freeform and angular designs.

COCONUT GROVE NIGHTLIFE

"The Grove" is a hub of nighttime activity. As dusk approaches, sidewalks teem with shoppers and bar hoppers and traffic crawls along the village streets.

A shorts-and-flip-flops crowd assembles at **Monty Trainer's** (2550 South Bayshore Drive; 305-858-1431), an outdoor, palm-crowned reggae and raw bar overlooking a marina. A live band plays nightly.

The town's best watering hole is **Tavern in the Grove** (3416 Main Highway; 305-447-3884), a nontrendy neighborhood spot with a long oak bar and framed Grove art. Pop, blues and folk music resound from a juke box.

Built in 1911 as an afternoon tea house, **Taurus** (3540 Main Highway; 305-448-0633) is now a habitat for trendsetters who mill around its shady pine porch. Live bands play Wednesday through Saturday, featuring blues, rock and jazz sounds.

The local laughline is **Mental Floss Theater** (3138 Commodore Plaza; 305-448-1011), an intimate forum that concentrates on high-quality improvisation. Popcorn and soft drinks, no alcohol. Cover.

The splendid **Coconut Grove Playhouse** (3500 Main Highway; 305-442-4000) offers major musical and drama productions as well as comedy acts. Built in 1927, the three-story, Spanish-style building is beautifully ornamented with twisted columns and parapets.

GAY SCENE Just outside Coconut Grove are several nightspots catering to the gay community. A subdued bar with pastel furnishings and a charming brick courtyard, **The World** (5922 South Dixie Highway, South Miami; 305-667-4753) attracts gay men and women with deejay-generated Top-40, disco, house and progressive rock. Cover on weekends.

The videos at **Uncle Charlie's** (3673 Bird Avenue; 305-442-8687) leave little to the imagination, the raucous crowd even less. But this wood-and-mirror disco is packed with gay men every night. Cover on weekends.

Cherry Grove (2490 Southwest 17th Avenue; 305-854-7262) is a neighborhood disco and dance bar frequented by lesbians. Cover.

Coral Gables

South of Coconut Grove off Route 1, you'll find **Coral Gables,** the dream-come-true city of one George Merrick. In the early 1900s, Merrick looked at these backwoods and envisioned grand things. He cleared citrus groves, laid streets and sidewalks, and brought in Mediterranean architecture, touting the spot as the "Miami Riviera." Those who visited Coral Gables, he promised, would find "endless golden sunlight and bronzed people."

Now this pristine, planned town boasts beautiful Spanish-style architecture and miles of country club living. Largely inhabited by wealthy Hispanics, the city is a labyrinth of winding streets that unfortunately can make life difficult for the first-time visitor. Refer to maps and even then, plan to spend some time backtracking.

Once you're in "The Gables," as locals call it, you'll spot the stately spire of the **Biltmore Hotel** (1200 Anastasia Avenue; 305-445-1926). Once the pinnacle of Coral Gables' elite community, the 1926 landmark now lies empty, a victim of bankruptcy. In its early days, the opulent Moorish-style castle was deemed "the last word in the evolution of civilization." Bing Crosby, Judy Garland and Al Capone were among those who took refuge behind these sturdy walls. The Biltmore is currently under renovation and will reopen late 1992.

Around the time the Biltmore was going up, Merrick donated the land across the street for the **Coral Gables Congregational Church** (3010 DeSoto Boulevard; 305-448-7421). An architectural gem, the city's first church is a Mediterranean revival design with barrel tiles and ornate baroque ornaments. Its bell tower, mirroring the Biltmore's, is nearly as stunning. During the 1920s, University of Miami students—protesting school policies—ran the school's first underground newspaper from the tower. More treasures await inside, where you'll encounter 16th-century furnishings, chandeliers and beautiful pews carved from native pecky cypress.

From here, twist your way northeast on DeSoto Boulevard to the **Venetian Pool** (2701 DeSoto Boulevard; 305-460-5356; admission). Born out of a rock pit, this Merrick-built retreat is a sprawling lagoon bordered by a Mediterranean villa and the mandatory Miami palm trees. Coral caves, Venetian lampposts and intermittent waterfalls canvas the place, which was the stomping grounds for William Jennings Bryan, Esther Williams, Johnny Weissmuller and other notables.

At the end of DeSoto lies Coral Way, the road where George Merrick spent his boyhood days. The **Coral Gables House** (907 Coral Way; 305-460-5361; admission), where Merrick grew up, has been enshrined by locals and is now a museum. Built around the turn of the century, the coral rock structure features a breezy veranda studded with Mediterranean columns and topped with barrel tiles.

Travel eastward on DeSoto and you'll uncover a gold mine known as Miracle Mile. This two-block address of swanky shops and brick-lined streets also houses **Coral Gables City Hall** (405 Biltmore Way; 305-446-6800), an imposing limestone structure that integrates circular and square design. Most impressive is a rounded wing with ornate columns and grotesque carvings true to the mannerist style. Stroll through the building and climb the worn, 1920s-era steps to the third and fourth floors. Along the way, you will see antiques and a brilliantly colored mural that spreads across a rotunda.

An easy place to find, the **University of Miami** (1306 Stanford Drive; 305-284-5500) is south of downtown Coral Gables. Miami's prestigious university has about 14,000 students and a 325-acre maze of low-slung buildings, twisting canals and shady plazas.

Center of activity here is the **Norman A. Whitten University Center** (1306 Stanford Drive; 305-284-5646), where crowds of international students mill around game rooms, cafeterias and a large swimming pool. Nearby, student thespians have developed an excellent reputation with performances at the 311-seat **Ring Theatre** (1380 Miller Drive; 305-284-3355).

Don't miss the **Lowe Art Museum** (1301 Stanford Drive; 305-284-3536; admission), which features a sizable collection of Renaissance and Baroque paintings, including several El Grecos and a Bellini.

Perhaps more than anything, Coral Gables is a residential village. Winding through its storybook streets, you'll find clusters of homes with specific architectural designs borrowed from various countries. Called **The Villages,** these 1920s neighborhoods are part of Merrick's scheme to bring in wealthy residents to his model city.

South of Route 1 on Riviera Drive and adjacent streets, **Chinese Village** consists of eight oriental homes styled with carved wooden balconies, curved tiled roofs and a great deal of lattice work. Animal sculptures perched atop some houses are meant to bring good luck to residents.

Just off Riviera on Hardee Road are the **French Country** and **French City Villages**. Country-style estates resemble châteaux, with rounded and square towers and wrought-iron balconies. The city version features snazzy French town homes surrounded by large walls.

The **Dutch South African Village**, on LeJeune Road, is not African at all but mirrors farmhouses of wealthy Dutch colonists. The quaint L-shaped and T-shaped homes are adorned with scroll work, high domed arches and spiraling chimneys.

In the midst of all this gentry is a point lost in time. Abandoned and all but forgotten, the **Pinewood Cemetery** (★) (47th Avenue just north of Sunset Road) rests in a deserted wooded lot between manicured lawns. Founded in 1855, Dade County's oldest cemetery is overgrown with palmettos and pine trees and sprinkled with pieces of broken headstones. In the center, a single memorial stone pays tribute to more than 200 Miami pioneers buried here. One tombstone that's still intact marks the grave of a Confederate soldier.

For a horticulture treat, travel south on Old Cutler Road to **Fairchild Tropical Garden** (10901 Old Cutler Road; 305-667-1651; admission). An 83-acre series of quiescent lakes, perfectly formed foliage and carpeted lawn, this place is a quiet reprieve from the surrounding hubbub. Here you get to look and touch.

Across the street and shrouded among shrubs is a historical marker in front of a **Sausage Tree** (★) (10400 Cutler Road). The tropical tree, born of a seed sent from Egypt in 1907, grows not sausages but rare fruit that looks like a cross between a mango and a papaya. Back in 1926, Miami homesteader Maud Black used the intriguing fruit to make jellies and jams, then sold them from a roadside stand underneath the massive tree.

CORAL GABLES HOTELS

A rare find in an urban area, **Place St. Michel** (★) (162 Alcazar Avenue; 305-444-1666) possesses all the charm of a French country inn. A mass of clinging ivy obscures the exterior from passing traffic, while inside awaits an unhurried world of carefully chosen antiques, tiled floors, potted flowers and personal service. Built in 1926, the hotel has 27 deluxe-priced bedrooms, warmly decorated with hand-loomed rugs, French shag lamps and high, detailed ceilings.

Granted, there's not much atmosphere at the **Holiday Inn Coral Gables** (1350 South Dixie Highway; 305-667-5611), located across the street from the University of Miami. But the clean, nicely decorated rooms, modern lobby and moderate price tag are drawing cards in this pricey town. The three-story, U-shaped building surrounds a standard motel swimming pool.

The quaint **David William Hotel** (700 Biltmore Way; 305-445-7821) is a good choice for deluxe-priced accommodations. Slightly camp, with a European flair, the 1965 hostelry has 13 floors of clean, carpeted rooms and a concrete rooftop pool. Continental breakfast included.

The **Hyatt Regency Coral Gables** (50 Alhambra Plaza; 305-441-1234) is one of those ultramodern establishments straining to imitate Old World elegance. Designed with a 14th-century Moorish castle in mind, the hotel features 242 rooms fashioned with flowing velvet draperies and impressive ten-foot windows. But the style just doesn't mesh with mini-bars and glass coffee tables. Built in 1988, the 14-story pink-and-white hotel takes up an entire city block and features a tiled pool terrace and a gourmet restaurant. Ultra-deluxe.

Another upscale downtown address, the **Colonnade Hotel** (180 Aragon Avenue; 305-441-2600) is an impressive tribute to Coral Gables' beginnings. In the lobby you'll find enchanting 1920s town photos and corridors of cathedral windows and pink-and-green marble. The 157 accommodations follow suit, providing formal surroundings with mahogany dressers, hand-blown candelabra and intricately painted vases. Ultra-deluxe.

CORAL GABLES RESTAURANTS

Dade County's most historic town also possesses the largest concentration of outstanding gourmet restaurants. Take, for instance, **Charade** (2900 Ponce de Leon Boulevard; 305-448-6077), a setting of Old World luxury in a 1925 mission-style building. High ceilings, European artwork, oriental dividers and striped chairs create a mood of understated elegance. The sun room and balcony are delightful places to dine. Fresh fish, beef and lamb star on the menu, a blend of new American and European cuisines. A few specialties: oven roasted salmon with a red chili honey glaze, grilled swordfish with dry roasted corn salsa, and medallions of veal Oscar. Deluxe.

A misfit along gourmet row, **House of India** (22 Merrick Way; 305-444-2348) promises two things: to provide some of the area's most exotic food, and to give you lots of it. You'll encounter large portions of dishes such as sweet coconut soup, *navrattan shai korma* (vegetables cooked with spices and cream), curried lamb and an intriguing clay-oven-baked bread.

Carved wooden dividers create private niches for diners, but the slightly tattered furnishings give a worn look. Budget to moderate.

In a city renowned for its abundance of French restaurants, **John Martin's** (253 Miracle Mile; 305-445-3777) is a welcome change of pace. Run by two Irish childhood buddies, the cultured eatery focuses on European cuisine with Gaelic accents. An enormous Waterford chandelier dominates the main dining room, a Queen Anne affair with high-back chairs and white linens. Try the lamb chops on a bed of spinach and goat cheese, oak-smoked salmon or Gaelic steak with whiskey-mushroom sauce. Moderate to deluxe.

You'd sort of expect to find **Restaurant St. Michel** (162 Alcazar Avenue; 305-444-1666) hidden along a hilly road in the French countryside. This splendid little restaurant, situated in a 1926 ivy-clad hotel of the same name, makes you wish the night would linger. Dramatic ceilings, beautiful antiques and elegant draperies punctuated with period furniture create tranquil environs. The New American cuisine is exceptional, with entrées such as grilled buffalo tenderloin with roasted corn and poblano chiles and hand-roasted breast of capon with smoked mustard and shiitake mushroom cream sauce. Deluxe to ultra-deluxe.

You can order any of the dishes at **Bangkok, Bangkok** (157 Giralda Avenue; 305-444-2397) with one to five stars, depending on how spicy you like it. Highly regarded by locals, the Thai eatery boasts a full range of fish, beef, seafood and poultry doused in savory and piquant sauces with fruits and vegetables. Two "American" dining rooms are rather plain, but an elaborate Thai balcony has scarlet carpets, redwood walls and carved wood tables with floor cushions. Moderate.

One of Coral Gables' most talked-about new restaurants is **Yuca** (177 Giralda Avenue; 305-444-4448). The name refers both to the tropical root vegetable and to the Young Upscale Cuban Americans who adore the restaurant's inventive cuisine. This mix of new American and Cuban cooking, or "nuevo Cubano," has produced inspiring dishes such as sweet plantains stuffed with cured beef, baby back ribs with spicy guava sauce and braised oxtail in a fiery burgundy sauce. Deluxe.

Just east of Coral Gables, a stretch of road called Coral Way offers a handful of reliable neighborhood restaurants. You'll find the same customers day after day at **Villa Italia** (3058 Coral Way; 305-444-0206), a simple yet intimate neighborhood café that serves Italian cuisine with gusto. This is food like grandma used to make—thick, hearty spaghetti sauces, bubbling cheesy lasagna, pizza loaded with meat and vegetables, and eggplant parmigiana, a house specialty. The prices, many less than $5, are incredible. A place not to miss!

Inhale that wonderful smoky aroma from **New Hickory Barbecue** (3170 Coral Way; 305-443-0842), where slabs of pork, beef and chicken are slow-cooked all day over a deep pit filled with hickory chips. The rough stone floors, redwood picnic tables and brick walls give this place a real Deep South feel. Not surprisingly, the New Hickory has been owned by the same family since 1954. Budget to moderate.

Scenes of Greek fishing ports are splashed on the walls of **Mykonos** (1201 Coral Way; 305-856-3140), aptly named for its savory Greek fare. A family-run eatery, this diner gets extra noisy when locals pile in for excellent *dolmadakia* (stuffed grape leaves), *moussaka* (layered beef and eggplant), *spanakopita* (spinach pie) and *pastitsio* (Greek lasagna). A Mediterranean treat, with budget prices.

CORAL GABLES SHOPPING

A ritzy Mediterranean-style city with country club pizzazz, Coral Gables boasts two blocks of posh shops dubbed **Miracle Mile** (between Douglas and LeJeune roads).

Coin and stamp collectors will adore **Gables Coin and Stamp** (259 Miracle Mile; 305-446-0032). Rows of rare coins and stamps line the shelves of this eclectic spot. In the back, **Albright Jewelers** (305-446-2986) carries interesting collectibles such as jewelry and porcelain.

Rudma Picture Co. (263 Miracle Mile; 305-443-6262) is where you'll find oils and lithographs from recognized Florida, South American and Cuban artists.

Coin and stamp collectors will adore **Gables Coin and Stamp** (259 Miracle Mile; 305-446-0032). Rows of rare coins and stamps line the shelves of this eclectic spot. In the back, **Albright Jewelers** (305-446-2986) carries interesting collectibles such as jewelry and porcelain.

Satin and lace abound at **Daisy & Tarsi** (311 Miracle Mile; 305-854-5557), an exclusive women's formal wear shop with racks of stunning cocktail gowns and bridal accessories.

The **Curio Shop** (349 Miracle Mile; 305-444-7234) is one of those places that's so jammed with objects, there's barely room to move. Still, the interesting porcelain, glass and early American and European furnishings will inspire any antique lover.

Looking for used and out-of-print books? Check out **Books & Books** (296 Aragon Avenue; 305-442-4408), which also has art and design literature, fiction and poetry.

There are more miracles on the east end of Coral Gables in the form of the **Miracle Center** (3301 Coral Way; 305-444-8890), a futuristic, 27-store mall. Designed as a shopper's fantasyland, the three-level emporium abounds with purple staircases, white pillars and freeform pools with multiple waterfalls. Step into the elevator, where piped-in fairy-tale music inspires that buying fever.

CORAL GABLES NIGHTLIFE

A local 1 a.m. bar curfew squelched much of the nighttime action in this posh, largely Hispanic city. However, sprinkled throughout these well-groomed lawns you'll discover some promising area theater.

Tucked behind a 1920s storefront, the **Minorca Playhouse** (232 Minorca Avenue; 305-446-1116) stages dramas, comedies and dance by several local troupes.

The 80-seat **New Theatre** (65 Almeria Avenue; 305-443-5909) hosts both experimental and traditional plays by a resident company.

The **University of Miami's Ring Theatre** (1380 Miller Drive; 305-284-3355) has cornered a loyal following with quality student-produced musicals, comedy and drama.

Southern Dade County

Across Dade County's southern reaches lie burgeoning residential developments that—aching for more space—creep through farmlands and citrus groves and back up to the Everglades. Meandering through this extensive spectrum you'll find miles of beautiful old and new homes nestled against pick-it-yourself spots and fruit fields.

The epitome of sprawling suburbia, Kendall is home to several hundred thousand yuppies who navigate the traffic-clogged roadways to downtown each workday. Nearby, Cutler Ridge and Perrine are 1950s neighborhoods originally christened "Big Hunting Ground" by the area's only real natives, the Seminole Indians. Farther south and seemingly worlds away, Homestead is a congenial farming town where the daily grind takes a back seat to enjoying life.

Dotted among these expanses are interesting museums along with pockets of historical sights and nature preserves. Kids won't want to miss the **Miami Youth Museum** (5701 Sunset Drive, South Miami; 305-661-3046; admission), a small but interesting niche in the 1926 Holsum Bakery Center. Exhibits, some of which change every six to seven months, offer plenty of activities for the youngsters, including drawing, counting, donning firefighters' uniforms and touching interesting plants.

More than 1000 beautiful but noisy birds reside at **Parrot Jungle and Gardens** (11000 Southwest 57th Avenue; 305-666-7834; admission), a classic Miami tourist attraction that opened in 1936. Here parrots fly free among 30 acres of tropical foliage and ponds, performing tricks and posing for curious sightseers.

Plan to spend some time at the **Charles Deering Estate** (16701 Southwest 72nd Avenue; 305-235-1668; admission). Open only on weekends, the sprawling bayfront estate offers a sublime look at the area's past. Deering, the brother of Vizcaya's James Deering, built the retreat in the 1920s to "escape the hubbub of downtown Miami." Next to a simple, three-story pine home, Deering constructed a spacious stone building to house his art collection. On the grounds is a magnificent stand of palm trees and more than 396 acres of virgin pineland and hammock, including a Tequesta Indian burial mound.

Scattered throughout the southwest reaches of Dade County lie modern subdivisions, pick-it-yourself produce fields and a few attractions worth the 45-minute drive from Miami.

Airplane fanatics will think they've reached heaven at **Weeks Air Museum** (14710 Southwest 128th Street in Tamiami Airport; 305-233-5197; admission). The brainchild of local aviation pioneer Kermit Weeks, the museum houses 35 antique aircraft. The brightly colored machines, poised for takeoff, include an all-plywood DeHavilland and the world's only flyable Grumman Duck, a reconnaissance aircraft used during World War II.

Metrozoo (12400 Southwest 152nd Street; 305-251-0403; admission) opened in 1981 and is one of the nation's largest zoos. More than 2000 animals wander about a 290-acre cageless habitat, separated from their spectators by watery moats. Don't miss the adorable Australian koalas and the white Bengal tiger. The top exhibit here is a jungle-style aviary where 300 Asian birds chirp, cackle and hop about on branches and clinging vines. Also check out the exhibit of Asian river life.

Next door is the interesting but often overlooked **Gold Coast Railroad Museum** (12450 Southwest 152nd Street; 305-253-0063; admission). Like a ghost town of train yards, the nearly deserted outpost possesses rows of historic trains. Climb through the fancy Ferdinand Magellan, a 1942 Pullman car built exclusively for U.S. presidents, or the streamlined Silver Crescent, built in 1948 for the California Zephyr. You can also cruise around 68 acres in a steam locomotive.

Go ape at **Monkey Jungle** (14805 Southwest 216th Street; 305-235-1611; admission), a partially cageless primate habitat situated in a lush South Florida hammock. Hundreds of chimpanzees, gorillas, baboons and orangutans swing through trees and perform tricks such as skindiving.

SOUTHERN DADE COUNTY HOTELS

Largely a corporate hotel, the **Miami Marriott Dadeland** (9090 South Dadeland Boulevard; 305-663-1035) is situated along a busy highway but affords picturesque views of downtown Miami and close proximity to one of the area's largest shopping malls. The 24-story building houses a spacious seventh-floor pool deck and guest rooms with large windows, contemporary artwork and mauve carpets. Marble floors and glass tables give the lobby a modern edge. The ultra-deluxe rates include a continental breakfast.

The usual chain motels line Route 1 in Homestead and Florida City. If you are looking for less expensive lodging, head into the downtown areas where you'll find rows of mom-and-pop motels along Krome Avenue. Some, like the **Super 8 Motel** (1202 North Krome Avenue, Florida City; 305-245-0311), have been remodeled, are near restaurants and offer plain but clean and roomy accommodations. Coconut palms and other tropical plants set this one somewhat apart. Budget.

SOUTHERN DADE COUNTY RESTAURANTS

Sumptuous portions of creative and traditional Japanese fare are in store at **Kampai** (8745 Sunset Drive, South Miami; 305-596-1551). This third-floor venue, which overlooks the inside of the historic Bakery Center, has clusters of shiny wooden tables, a wonderfully fresh sushi bar and an all-Japanese staff. Sample the sashimi, *sunomono*, crunchy chicken wings or intriguing grilled *unagi* (eel), all arranged decoratively in pretty wooden trays. Moderate to deluxe.

Valenti's (5775 Sunset Drive, South Miami; 305-667-0421) projects a soothing aura with swirling marble floors, curving staircase and Italian Renaissance paintings. The bill of fare is gourmet Italian, with delights such as gnocchi florentine, grilled dolphin sicilian, veal francese and saltimbocca. Don't pass up the chocolate beast, an engaging dessert with mounds of dark chocolate mousse. Moderate to deluxe.

For a taste of bonafide Florida Cracker cookin', head for **The Frog Pond** (17690 Southwest 8th Street, 305-553-2725). The no-frills, family-style eatery, stuck way out on Dade County's western horizon, pushes frogs' legs, catfish and alligator, all crisp-fried and served with hush puppies, cole slaw and fabulous french fries. Breakfast is big and, like lunch and dinner, budget to moderate priced.

Shorty's (9200 South Dixie Highway, Kendall; 305-665-5732) has long established a reputation as one of the best barbecue joints around. The log and brick cabin, which rests along a buzzing highway, is jammed with rustic wooden tables and decorated with neon beer signs. Folks come here to slurp on Shorty's scrumptious hickory sauce, which covers smoked ribs, chicken and beef. The service is extra friendly, but lines tend to be long during lunch. Budget to moderate.

Shibui (10141 Southwest 72nd Street; 305-274-5578) is a wonderful place to eat sushi. The shrimp, salmon and California rolls are outstanding, but best of all, they're served in a cozy upstairs sushi bar. Elsewhere, you can dine on cushions in a dimly lit loft or downstairs beneath a high wood ceiling. On the regular menu, you'll find delicious tempura, teriyaki, stir fry and sukiyaki. For dessert, try the unusual kiwi cheesecake. Moderate.

(Text continued on page 86.)

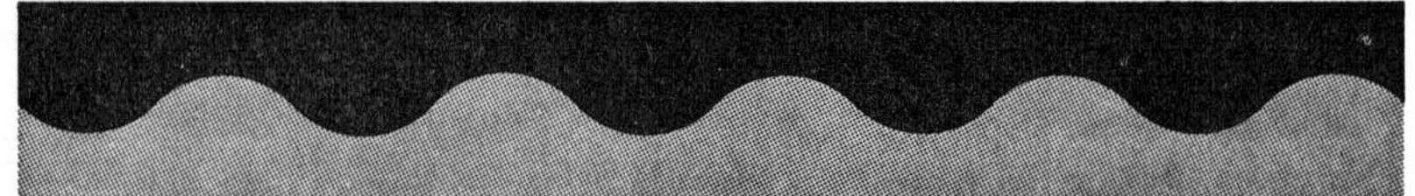

Horse Country

It's the most uncanny thing you ever imagined.

You're driving through suburban Miami sprawl when suddenly—for a few fleeting moments—you are enveloped by horse farms. Everywhere stretch beautiful, lush parcels of greenery punctuated with whitewashed wooden fences and horses of every color.

Welcome to **Horse Country** (★), Miami's last frontier and a place yet untouched by that rude intruder known as development. But ssshhhh! Don't tell anybody about this corner of the world. The friendly folks who live here would like to keep it that way, thank you. But then again, they'd also like to show you their little niche, because they think it's pretty special.

A rustic wooden sign greets curious drivers to Horse Country, a 2.5-square-mile sanctuary bounded roughly by Bird Road, Kendall Drive, Southwest 118th Avenue and Southwest 127th Avenue. About 12 miles west of downtown Miami, this tiny green stamp is home to about 2500 people and more than 7000 horses.

Amble along these quiescent roadways, dotted with produce vendors and "horse crossing" signs. Intermittently, you'll hear roosters crow and owls screech and see quaint ranches with red-roof barns. Appaloosas, pasofinos, Arabians and many other show horses graze peacefully or romp about the pasturelands.

Situated smack in the middle of Kendall—Dade County's fastest growing suburb—Horse Country has seen little change since peaceful farmers and ranchers settled here during the 1940s and '50s. The slow growth

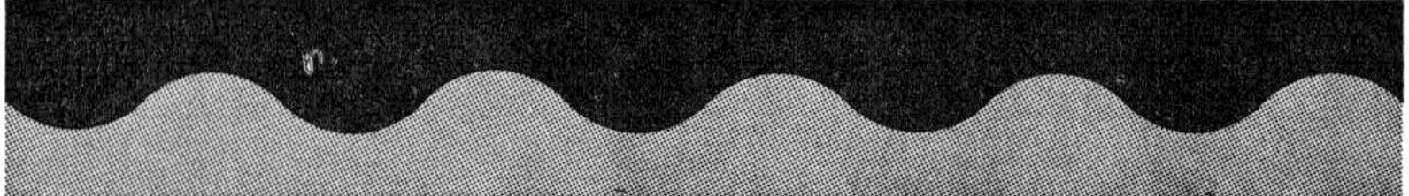

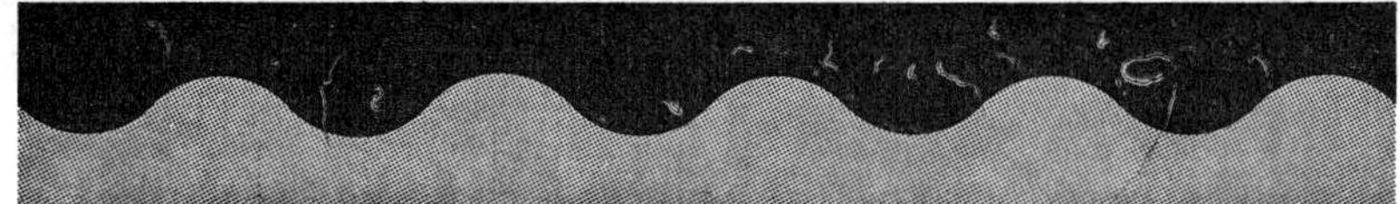

has been no accident. In fact, the seemingly quiet cranny has been the focus of frequent heated debates during the past decade, as residents repeatedly fought off new development. Everyone knows everyone around these parts. Many nights, neighbors get together to watch the blazing sun make its spectacular descent across the pastures.

This serene atmosphere is a perfect setting for horseback riding. On weekends, **Los Jimaguas Classy Carriages** (12201 Southwest 80th Street; 305-271-4289) offers eight horses for rent along with weekend hayrides. You might also try the equestrian center at **Tropical Park** (7900 Southwest 40th Street; 305-226-8315).

Several Horse Country families offer tours of their ranches, providing insight on horse raising and training. Most will arrange a riding or jumping demonstration if they're notified in advance. **Hunting Horn Stables** (6155 Southwest 123rd Avenue; 305-274-3133) offers riding lessons on its 40 hunter-jumper and Arabian horses.

Through the years, the reclusive area has spawned a variety of unusual sights. Within its bounds lie a fish and snail farm, two exotic bird farms, a bee farm and a wild animal retreat. You can catch glimpses of the latter by driving along 118th Avenue between 56th and 64th avenues. At any given time, you're apt to see camels, gangly giraffes, llamas or even elephants.

Certainly, this rural outpost in the midst of bustling urban Dade County is a real find.

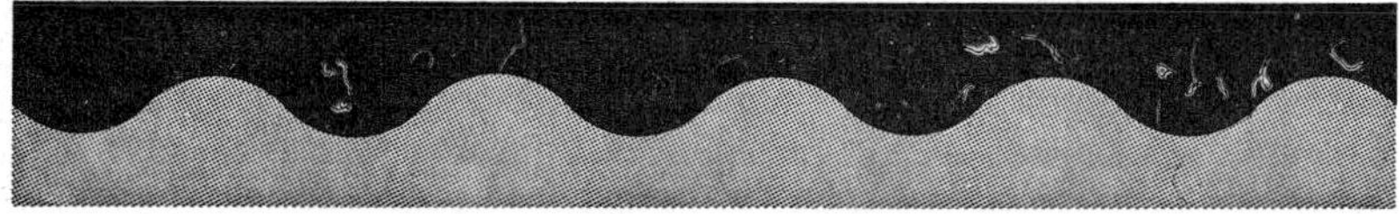

A rowdy college crowd frequently packs **Calico Jack's** (13503 South Dixie Highway; 305-378-0182), a beer-and-oyster pub with rock music, oak picnic tables and fishing nets that dance across the ceiling.

SOUTHERN DADE COUNTY SHOPPING

Although not generally recognized as a shopping destination, the town of South Miami offers a three-block stretch of eclectic stores that are worth perusing. You'll find these marts along Sunset Drive, between Southwest 57th and Southwest 59th avenues.

Keep an eye out for unusual and traditional antiques and jewelry at **Five Golden Rings** (5843 Sunset Drive; 305-667-3208). A solid gold cigar ash preserver, Italian cameos and intricate Victorian jewels are a few of the finds.

An anomaly in an urban area, **Robert's Western Wear** (5854 South Dixie Highway; 305-666-6647) has an ample stash of geddyup cowboy gear, Indian moccasins and woven blankets.

At **Alice's Day Off** (5900 Sunset Drive; 305-284-0301), you'll find skimpy neon bikinis, tropical painted earrings, rope anklets and other bright beachwear.

Brilliantly blooming azaleas, bromeliads and begonias beckon from inside **The Garden Gate** (5872 Sunset Drive; 305-661-0605). You can also pick up dainty wicker baskets at this fragrant stop.

Lamps in every shade are revealed at **Lightorama** (5832 Sunset Drive; 305-667-8941), where you'll discover art deco, tiffany and contemporary styles.

Tucked obscurely in a corner alleyway, **Joseph Rubini** (5794 Sunset Drive; 305-665-5070) has a marvelous cache of antique maps and charts. Some of the store's giant world maps date back to the 1500s.

If you love Florida's natural woods, you'll fancy the furniture at **Casa Floridiana** (4810 Southwest 72nd Avenue; 305-661-9947). Cypress loveseats and pine tables mingle with Early American chests of drawers and an extensive collection of contemporary Florida and Cuban art.

Along Route 1 near Kendall you'll discover two of the area's most talked-about malls. **Dadeland Mall** (Route 1 and Kendall Drive; 305-661-7582) is like a city unto itself, with 153 stores and restaurants in a sleek motif of white marble floors, glass atriums and palm trees. Several major department stores as well as chain shops offer everything from chic attire and furnishings to gourmet chocolate and nifty toys.

Cascading fountains, rock gardens, breezy gazebos and steep price tags await at **The Falls** (Route 1 and Southwest 136th Street; 305-255-4570), a ritzy collection of 65 unique shops and chain stores. This open-air setting is a popular strolling destination, even after the shops have closed at night.

SOUTHERN DADE COUNTY BEACHES AND PARKS

Matheson Hammock County Park—A coconut plantation in the early 1900s, Matheson Hammock is now the only real "local" beach park left in Dade County. Situated along the shoreline south of Coral Gables, the area is favored by families who picnic and fish. Winding trails crawl through more than 100 acres of thick mangrove hammock that blankets the area. There's not a lot of sand, but a shallow, manmade pond is ideal for shell hunting.

Facilities: Picnic tables, restrooms, lifeguards, concession stands, marina, nature and bike trails; information, 305-666-6979. *Swimming:* Good.

Getting there: Off old Cutler Road, just south of Coral Gables.

Larry and Penny Thompson Park—This nucleus of activity is set among the agricultural fields in southern Dade County and offers one of the few large campgrounds around Miami. Here you'll find a crystal clear lake dotted with swimmers, sailboats and skiffs, and 270 acres of criss-crossed jogging paths, a playground and rolling green grass.

Facilities: Picnic areas, restrooms, showers, playground, store, laundry facilities (for campers); *Fishing:* Freshwater fishing is good from lake banks or in boats. *Swimming:* Good year-round.

Camping: More than 200 campsites are available, offering hook-ups for RVs and vans as well as tent sites.

Getting there: At 12451 Southwest 184th Street near Metrozoo.

North Miami

This wide expanse of suburbia stretches above the head of downtown Miami and serves as the living quarters for more than 150,000 people. Most of the terrain here was developed during the 1940s and '50s and includes an amalgamation of posh estates, yacht-filled canals, gleaming strip shopping centers and crowded highways.

It seems ironic that the single true historic sight in northern Miami is indeed the oldest building in the Western Hemisphere. The **Ancient Spanish Monastery** (16711 West Dixie Highway, North Miami Beach; 305-945-1461; admission) was originally built for royalty in 1141 in Segovia, Spain. In 1925, William Randolph Hearst had the church disassembled and carted in more than 10,000 crates across the Atlantic Ocean to Miami. Interestingly, it remained in storage in Brooklyn until 1954, when local developers breathed life back into the grand monastery. Now its rough stone walls, ornate columns and buttressed ceilings rest quietly among palm trees and towering oaks. Carvings of crosses, crescents and stars dance across the stone walls, masons' marks etched by skilled craftsmen who originally constructed the building.

NORTH MIAMI HOTELS

Colonial architecture is rarer than snow in these parts, and that's why the **Bay Harbor Inn** (★) (9660 East Bay Harbor Drive; 305-868-4141) is such a wonderful find. Tucked away along the posh Bay Harbor waterways, this charming, restored 1948 hostelry is the pride of the neighborhood. In the main, two-story building, you'll find shiny wooden floors, high beam ceilings, leafy potted plants and turn-of-the century antiques throughout the lobby and suites. A second, 22-unit building offers more modern accommodations—all facing the water. Deluxe.

If you're wondering where members of Miami's upper crust while away their time, you'll find them at **Turnberry Isle Yacht and Country Club** (19999 West Country Club Drive; 305-932-6200), a 300-acre world of multimillion-dollar yachts, spa treatments, Jaguars and celebrities seeking solace. These heady environs consist of 24 tennis courts, two golf courses, five pools, and much more. Hotel suites are cleverly decorated with nouveau art, sleek Italian marble and huge sunken jacuzzis. The price, as you may imagine, is ultra-deluxe.

Inn On the Bay (1819 79th Street Causeway; 305-865-7100) has one very important thing going for it: water. The no-frills, family-style accommodations overlook beautiful Biscayne Bay and lie five minutes from the beach. A dramatic wooden ceiling and piano add character to the tiny lobby. Guest rooms are rather small, but offer clean, standard furnishings. The best news is, budget rates include a continental breakfast.

NORTH MIAMI RESTAURANTS

Few restaurants make dining more of an adventure than **Chef Allen's** (19088 Northeast 29th Avenue; 305-935-2900). Acclaimed South Florida chef Allen Susser, who hails from New York City's La Cirque, works his culinary wizardry amid classy art deco surroundings. Neon tubes trace lines around the dining room, washed in a cool gray. The ever-changing menu might feature such extravagances as blackened red snapper with chayote, plantains and orange sauce or boniato-crusted chicken breast with tamarind and gingered figs. The food is a tribute to Miami's new "tropical fusion" cuisine. Deluxe to ultra-deluxe.

Wonderfully imaginative food in a soft, pastel setting make **Mark's Place** (2286 Northeast 123rd Street; 305-893-6888) one of Miami's best American-style eateries. An open kitchen, loads of greenery and private clusters of tables and booths create intimate yet casual surroundings. Extensive lunch and dinner menus change daily. Innovative selections include potato fritters with caviar and a chive butter sauce, warm lamb salad, oak-grilled baby hen and pistachio-crusted grouper. Prices range from moderate to deluxe.

Need a health boost? Meander down the block to **Here Comes the Sun** (2188 Northeast 123rd Street; 305-893-5711). The health food store/restaurant has an ample selection of salads, sandwiches and hot eats for budget to moderate prices. Try the sunburger, chicken Roma and pasta served with a selection of sauces such as ginger-tamari, orange-sesame or lemon-spice. Heart-studded menu items are fat-, salt- and sugar-free.

Café Chauveron (9561 East Bay Harbor Drive; 305-866-8779) is one of those very elegant restaurants where hours seem to pass like minutes. The exquisite, ultra-deluxe establishment rests on the banks of the Intracoastal Waterway in the posh Bay Harbor Islands. Dependably superb French cuisine includes Maine lobster with sauterne and cream sauce, rack of lamb and imported Dover sole. Heavenly desserts. Closed late May through mid-October.

If you're tired of frills, hop over to Biscayne Boulevard and make a pit stop at one of the casual eateries along Miami's main eastern artery. **East Side Mario's** (19501 Biscayne Boulevard in the Adventura Mall; 305-935-3589) serves giant pizzas and quart-sized beers to hungry shoppers and a late-night local college crowd. High beam ceilings and polished oak floors give this southern-Italian-style bistro a real warehouse feeling. Fresh meats and cheeses dangle from above the step-up bar, and old license plates cover an entire wall. Budget to moderate.

On the outside, the **Gourmet Diner** (★) (13900 Biscayne Boulevard; 305-947-2255) has all the makings of a tiny truck stop. Sandwiched between the noisy highway and rickety train tracks, the nondescript frame building shivers every time a locomotive speeds by. But don't be deceived. Inside these humble surroundings awaits a wealth of splendid food, carefully prepared delicacies such as chicken chasseur, rack of lamb and seafood au gratin. Check the posted neon chalkboard for more than a dozen daily gastronomic delights. Budget to moderate.

Locals developed a craving for Philly steak sandwiches when **Woody's** (13105 Biscayne Boulevard; 305-891-1451) opened with curbside service in 1956. Now the open-air roadside stop has expanded into two rooms and serves twice as many of those budget-priced cheesy steaks on soft, buttery buns. The plastic tables combined with a view of a dirty gas station make for minimal atmosphere, but the place is usually packed.

Biscayne Wine Merchants (12953 Biscayne Boulevard; 305-899-1997) is a simple wine and cheese shop serving fresh, hefty sandwiches and salads to a large lunch time crowd. Pastel table tops, fresh flowers and courteous service greet diners. For dinner, try shrimp dijon, fettucine carbonara or a special chicken crustaces (stuffed with dill and crabmeat). Prices are in the moderate range.

Nestle into your own coral grotto at **Jama** (3363 Northeast 163rd Street; 305-949-4411), where fish aquariums and a ceiling dotted with tiny lights round out the decor at this Continental place. Tasty cuisine includes wienerschnitzel, Norwegian salmon with a dill sauce, flambéed dishes and *palacinke* crêpe desserts. Moderate.

Garnering our award for Miami's best greasy spoon is the **Dixie Diner** (★) (14821 West Dixie Highway; 305-945-1576), a seedy sort of joint where waitresses sport tattoos and muscle shirts. The down-home menu includes some mouth-watering fried chicken, liver and onions, meatloaf and southern-style breakfasts. Budget.

NORTH MIAMI SHOPPING

This area possesses two of Dade County's largest malls, which beckon beachgoers away from the sand and into their cool confines. Mall shopping—where some serious purchasing gets done—is frequently referred to by Floridians as "malling."

Adventura Mall (19501 Biscayne Boulevard; 305-935-4222), a modern, two-level enclosed plaza, boasts 186 shops running the gamut from chic boutiques and furniture stores to jewelry and book marts. Most shops are of the chain variety, and are anchored by several large department stores.

Just out of whistling distance, **The Mall at 163rd Street** (1421 Northeast 163rd Street; 305-947-9845) peeks out from underneath a bizarre Teflon-coated fiberglass roof, allowing plenty of light to stream in. More than 150 stores beckon from this location.

NORTH MIAMI NIGHTLIFE

A collection of umbrella-topped tables lining the Intracoastal Waterway, **Shooters** (3963 Northeast 163rd Street; 305-949-2855) is classic South Florida. People climb from their cushy yachts, parked dockside at the restaurant, to order food and drink.

There's a friendly local crowd at **Delaney Street** (7353 Fairway Drive, Miami Lakes; 305-823-7555), a small dance bar hosting Top-40 and oldies rock bands.

A sprawling warehouse slicked up in high-tech red and gray, **Studio One 83** (2860 Northwest 183rd Street, in the Carol City Shopping Plaza, Carol City; 305-621-7295) has jazz and disco rooms which feature either live music or deejays. Cover.

There's an overdose of hormones at **Facade** (3509 Northeast 163rd Street; 305-948-6868), a pulsating disco, Top-40 and house scene with scantily dressed women and overanxious men. A live band and deejays with female dancers plays nightly, but the cover charge is steep.

An after-work yuppie crowd gathers at **Charcoals** (15532 Northwest 77th Court; 305-362-6060), a mirror-and-chrome video bar with generous happy-hour food. Later at night, live groups play Top-40 music, Wednesday through Saturday.

The **Miamiway Theatre** (12615 West Dixie Highway; 305-893-0005), launched as a vehicle for local aspiring artists, is a 435-seat refurbished neighborhood cinema. It hosts a variety of events.

NORTH MIAMI BEACHES AND PARKS

Oleta River State Recreation Area—A real gem, this 855-acre park is nestled at the top of Biscayne Bay near the Intracoastal Waterway and the Oleta River. It bursts with wide open spaces yet shelters dense mangrove preserves. Opossum, raccoons and rabbits can be spotted frequently, along with native birds such as osprey and great blue heron. Though the 1200-foot beach is manmade, the sand consists of white crystals and borders a calm inlet that's ideal for swimming.

Facilities: Picnic areas, restrooms, bike trails, canoe rentals; information, 305-947-6357. *Fishing:* Great, from the seawall or dock. Snapper, shad and sheepshead. *Swimming:* Good.

Getting there: Located on Northeast 163rd Street (also State Road 826) and 34th Avenue in North Miami Beach.

The Sporting Life

SPORTFISHING

You can wrangle with a sailfish, marlin or even a barracuda when fishing Miami waters. To sign up, call **The Shark** (10800 Collins Avenue, Sunny Isles; 305-949-2948), **Therapy IV** (10800 Collins Avenue, Sunny Isles; 305-945-1578), **Carie Ann** (Crandon Park Marina, Key Biscayne; 305-361-0117), **Sandskipper** (4000 Crandon Boulevard, Key Biscayne; 305-361-9740) or **Thomas Flyer** (Bayside Marina, Miami; 305-374-4133).

SKINDIVING

You'll find plenty of scuba diving possibilities in the Miami area, especially around nearby coral reefs. For scuba equipment rentals and/or charters, contact **Aquanauts** (880 Southwest 8th Street, Miami; 305-859-8477), **Bubbles Dive Center** (2671 Southwest 27th Avenue, Coconut Grove; 305-856-0565), **The Diving Locker** (223 Sunny Isles Boulevard, Sunny Isles; 305-947-6025), **Diver's Paradise** (4000 Crandon Boulevard, Key Biscayne; 305-361-3483) or **Scuba Sports** (16604 Northeast 2nd Avenue, North Miami Beach; 305-940-0926).

WINDSURFING

It's a windsurfer's heaven around these parts, so grab a board from **Windsurfing Place** (3501 Rickenbacker Causeway, Key Biscayne; 305-361-1225) or **Sailboards Miami** (Rickenbacker Causeway; 305-361-7245). In North Miami Beach, look for windsurfing vendors in front of the **Holiday Inn Newport Pier** (16701 Collins Avenue; 305-949-1300) and the **Thunderbird Resort Motel** (18401 Collins Avenue; 305-931-7700).

SAILING

Let the wind guide you around Miami's scenic waters. For sailboat rentals and charters, check out **Florida Yacht Charters and Sales** (1290 5th Street, Miami Beach; 305-532-8600) and **O'Leary's Sailing School & Charters** (1819 79th Street Causeway, North Bay Village; 305-865-7245). Also along Miami Beach, look for the sailboat vendors at **46th Street Beach** (Collins Avenue and 46th Street). In Coconut Grove, try **Easy Sailing** (Dinner Key Marina; 305-858-4001), **Castle Harbor Sailboats** (Dinner Key Marina; 305-858-3212) or **Adventurers Yacht and Sailing** (20801 Biscayne Boulevard, North Miami Beach; 305-933-8285). In North Miami, there's **Gold Coast VIP Services** (1302 Northwest 188th Terrace; 305-653-0591).

JOGGING

Scenic jogging trails abound in the Miami area, including ones at **Haulover Beach Park** (10800 Collins Avenue, Sunny Isles; 305-947-3525), **Crandon Beach Park** (4000 Crandon Boulevard, Key Biscayne; 305-361-5421), **Matheson Hammock County Park** (9610 Old Cutler Road, South Dade County; 305-666-6979), **Larry and Penny Thompson Park** (12451 Southwest 184th Street, South Dade County; 305-232-1049) and **Greynolds Park** (17530 West Dixie Highway, North Miami; 305-945-3425).

GOLF

You can tee up at numerous public golf courses, including **Bayshore Golf Course** (2301 Alton Road, Miami Beach; 305-673-1580), **Haulover Beach Golf Course** (10800 Collins Avenue, Sunny Isles; 305-940-6719), **City of Miami Par Three Golf Course** (2785 Prairie Avenue, Miami; 305-674-0305), **Fontainebleau Golf Course** (9603 Fontainebleau Boulevard, Miami; 305-221-5181), **Key Biscayne Golf Course** (6700 Crandon Boulevard; 305-361-9129), **Palmetto Golf Course** (9300 Southwest 152nd Avenue, South Dade County; 305-238-2922), **Golf Club of Miami** (6801 Northwest 186th Street, North Miami; 305-821-0111) and **Greynolds Park** (17530 West Dixie Highway, North Miami; 305-949-1741).

TENNIS

Tennis is the rage around Miami, so not surprisingly there are many top spots for racquet addicts. Try **Flamingo Park Capital Bank Tennis Center** (corner of 11th Street and Jefferson Avenue, Miami; 305-673-7761), **North Shore Center** (350 73rd Street, Miami Beach; 305-993-2022), **Haulover Beach Park** (10800 Collins Avenue, Sunny Isles; 305-940-6719), **Morningside Park** (750 Northeast 55th Terrace, Miami; 305-754-1242), **Moore Park** (736 Northwest 36th Street, Miami; 305-635-7459), **Calusa Park** (Crandon Boulevard, Key Biscayne; 305-361-2215) or **Salvadore Park Tennis Center** (1120 Andalusia Avenue, Coral Gables; 305-460-5333).

BICYCLING

Traveling via bike offers a different perspective of the area, but be sure to steer clear of congested downtown. The best bicycle trails are found throughout the suburbs, parks and beaches.

If island cycling is your bag, you'll love Key Biscayne, where you can cruise through eight miles of shady pines, past sumptuous homes and hidden beach coves. Down in **Matheson Hammock County Park**, a 1.5-mile trail meanders through dense mangroves and along the beaches.

Along **South Miami Beach**, bicyclists take advantage of a wide sidewalk that stretches for more than 20 blocks in the Art Deco District. Farther north, **Haulover Beach** has a 1.5-mile trail along the billowy sand dunes. There are few designated bike paths or lanes on Central Miami Beach, making cycling a little tricky along the busy streets.

A 14-mile bike trail exists on **Old Cutler Road** from Coconut Grove southward to Cutler Ridge. Not recommended during rush hour, this route features paths and sidewalks that wind along Biscayne Bay and through the area's remaining agricultural communities.

For information on area bike routes, call the **Dade County Bicycle and Pedestrian Program** (305-375-4507).

BIKE RENTALS To rent a bike in the Miami area, try **Miami Beach Bicycle Center** (923 West 39th Street, Miami Beach; 305-531-4161), **Penrod's Patio** (1001 Ocean Drive, South Miami Beach; 305-538-2604), **Dade Cycle** (3216 Grand Avenue, Coconut Grove; 305-443-6075) or **Key Biscayne Mangrove Bicycle** (260 Crandon Boulevard; 305-361-5555).

HIKING

For information on walking tours, consult the "Sightseeing" sections in this chapter.

Transportation

BY CAR

If you arrive in Miami by car, you'll find the area laid out in a somewhat orderly fashion, with major highways easily navigated.

From the north, **Route 95** runs due south through the city and joins **Route 1**, which continues through Coconut Grove, Coral Gables and south Dade County. **Florida's Turnpike** and **Route 826**, better known as the Palmetto Expressway, head south along the western corridor.

Route 41, also called the Tamiami Trail, will bring you in from Florida's West Coast, and **Route 27** cuts in from Central Florida.

Your main east-west connections through Miami are **Route 836** and **Route 112/195**, which transport you to scenic causeways leading to Miami Beach. **Route A1A** runs north and south along the ocean throughout Miami Beach.

BY AIR

Miami International Airport (Wilcox Field), the nation's second busiest airport, brings visitors to the Miami area. Lying eight miles west of downtown, this megaport is served by many domestic/international carriers, including American Airlines, Continental Airlines, Delta Airlines, Northwest Airlines, Trans World Airlines, United Airlines and USAir. There are even more international carriers, including Aerolineas Argentinas, Aeromexico, AeroPeru, Air Canada, Air France, Air Jamaica, ALM-Antillean Airlines, Aviateca, Bahamasair, British Airways, BWIA International, Cayman Airways, Ecuatoriana Airlines, El Al Israel Airlines, Haiti Trans Air, Iberia, LAB-Bolivia, Lan Chile, Lufthansa, Mexicana, Taca, Varig Brazilian Airlines, Viasa and Virgin Atlantic Airways.

Taxis, limousines and buses wait to take passengers to points all over Dade County. **Super Shuttle** (305-871-2000) offers transportation via vans to downtown hotels and Miami Beach.

BY BUS

Two major bus companies that have teamed up as **Greyhound/Trailways Lines** bring passengers from all over the country to the Miami area. The main Miami terminal is at 4111 Northwest 27th Street (305-871-1810). Additional stations are located in Miami Beach (7101 Harding Avenue; 305-538-0381), North Miami Beach (16250 Biscayne Boulevard; 305-945-0801), Perrine (17344 Perrine Plaza; 305-251-2459) and Homestead (5 Northeast 3rd Road; 305-247-2040).

Astro Tours (2923 Northwest 7th Street; 305-643-6423) offers daily shuttles between Miami and New York, and **Omnibus La Cubana** (1101

Northwest 22nd Avenue; 305-541-1700) has daily service between Miami and Washington, D.C., New York and New Jersey.

BY TRAIN

Amtrak (Miami Station, 8303 Northwest 37th Avenue; 800-872-7245) will bring you into Miami from the northeastern states on its "Silver Star," "Silver Meteor" or "Palmetto." From the western United States, there are three trains to Miami by way of Chicago and Washington, D.C.

CAR RENTALS

It's wise to have a car in Miami, even though downtown parking is scarce and expensive.

Several major agencies can be found in the airport terminal, including **Avis Rent A Car** (305-637-4900), **Budget Rent A Car** (305-871-3053), **Dollar Rent A Car** (305-887-6000), **Hertz Rent A Car** (305-871-0300) and **National Inter Rent** (305-358-2334).

Companies with free airport pickup are **Alamo Rent A Car** (305-633-6076), **Biscayne Auto Rentals** (305-888-0721), **Enterprise Rent A Car** (305-576-1300), **General Rent A Car** (305-871-3573), **Interamerican Car Rental** (305-871-3030), **Racing Rent A Car** (305-871-5050), **Superior Rent A Car** (305-649-7012) and **Value Rent A Car** (305-871-6760).

PUBLIC TRANSPORTATION

Although public transportation in Miami is lethargic, you can still get around. The Metropolitan Dade County Transit Authority has 61 **Metrobus** routes covering about 2000 square miles.

The quickest way to get around is by Metrorail, a futuristic train that glides 21 miles along an elevated track between north and south Miami. Downtown, the Metromover monorail makes a two-mile radius around the city's perimeter, stopping at major centers and attractions.

For transit maps and a list of schedules, send for the "First Time Rider's Kit" (Metropolitan Dade County Transit Authority, 360 Northeast 185th Street, Miami Beach, FL 33162; 305-638-6700).

Tri-Rail (305-728-8445) is your link to the north, with double-decker trains traveling 67 miles into Dade and Palm Beach counties.

For an inexpensive, fun way to see the sights, check out **Old Town Trolley** (401 Biscayne Boulevard, Miami; 305-374-8687). These shiny trolleys meander through downtown, Coconut Grove and Coral Gables.

TAXIS

Numerous cab companies serve Miami International Airport, including **Yellow Cab** (305-444-4444) and **Central Cab** (305-532-5555).

GOLD

COAST

CHAPTER THREE

The Gold Coast

Its sparkling hotels, glittering jewels and golden sands would be reason enough to dub this section of southeast Florida "The Gold Coast." But, in fact, it was real gold salvaged from shipwrecks off the coast that earned the area its moniker, which remains applicable more than a century later.

Stretching from the top of Miami up to the Jupiter Inlet, the Gold Coast is anchored by two very different cities. Fort Lauderdale, famed for its inland waterways and fast-paced beach scene, provides the steam that drives the engine of development. Even now, Lauderdale's Broward County is still growing as if no one knew that the Florida land boom was supposed to have been over decades ago. Highway construction seems never-ending, with newer roads leading to residential communities that sprout from former swampland faster than coconuts grow on sandy beaches.

Roughly an hour's drive north, Palm Beach is as private as Fort Lauderdale is public. This island town turns its back on publicity, preferring to bask in its well-entrenched reputation as a playground for the well-to-do. So wealthy are Palm Beach's inhabitants that they occupy many of the town's legendary mansions—estates, really—only a fraction of the year, usually from January until Easter time. (Many shops and restaurants follow suit, closing at least during the summer months.) In the winter, life is a series of charity balls and other high-society gatherings.

Surrounding these two Gold Coast hubs is an enclave of beach towns and tennis and golf resorts. Today's visitor needs only an airline ticket to reach this paradise. But early 19th-century settlers veered into the unknown with little more than guns, machetes and verve.

Fort Lauderdale's beginnings can be traced to at least 1450 A.D., when the aboriginal Tequesta Indians are believed to have begun roaming the area around the New River. After the Spanish "discovered" northern Florida, increasing colonization forced the Seminole Indians south into the area.

It was during the Seminole Wars, in 1837, that one Major William Lauderdale was commissioned to establish the fort—long since crumbled into oblivion—for which the city would one day be named. Eventually, the fledgling settlement was enhanced by people of vision and skill such as Frank Stranahan. He arrived at the New River in 1893, established a ferry system and opened a trading post with the Indians. His home as well as those of other early citizens of prominence form the centerpiece of Fort Lauderdale's historic district today.

The Fort Lauderdale area was still mired in swampland when Henry Flagler extended his Florida East Coast Railway to present-day Palm Beach. This town, the legend goes, derived its name from a shipwreck in 1878. A Spanish ship with a full crew and 100 cases of wine aboard washed up on a virtually barren barrier island. They decided to sell their cargo, which included some 20,000 coconuts, to a visionary islander. He, in turn, unloaded the coconuts (at two for a nickel) to his neighbors, who planted them in the sand and created the groves that give Palm Beach its name.

Henry Flagler, who had co-founded Standard Oil with John D. Rockefeller, was apparently quite taken with the Palm Beach setting, so much so that he built the original Breakers Hotel here (it burned down and has since been rebuilt). On his heels came the self-taught architect Addison Mizner, who first visited south Florida for a health cure but soon became inspired to upgrade what he viewed as the inferior architecture of Palm Beach. Mizner's "touch" explains the pseudo-Spanish design of many older mansions in the area.

Yet Palm Beach was only a pit stop to Mizner, who had his sights set on an undeveloped stretch to the south, a place whose Spanish name—Boca Raton—is a vast improvement over the English translation, "rat's mouth." Here Mizner built the most expensive hotel of its time, the 100-room Cloisters Inn, the seed of the present-day Boca Raton Hotel and Club. Mizner worked hard to lure notables like Harold Vanderbilt and Irving Berlin to his paradise-in-the-making. A natural publicity hound, he is said to have declared: "Get the big snobs, and the little ones will follow."

By then, the Roaring '20s were in full swing, and Fort Lauderdale was about to boom. Henry Flagler had extended his railroad there in 1896, but it was a West Virginia developer named Charles Rodes who had the brilliant idea of increasing Fort Lauderdale's available square footage by "finger-islanding," a concept used to create Venice, Italy. He dredged a series of parallel canals from Las Olas to the New River, building up a group of peninsulas that offered waterfront locations to hotels and homes. From then

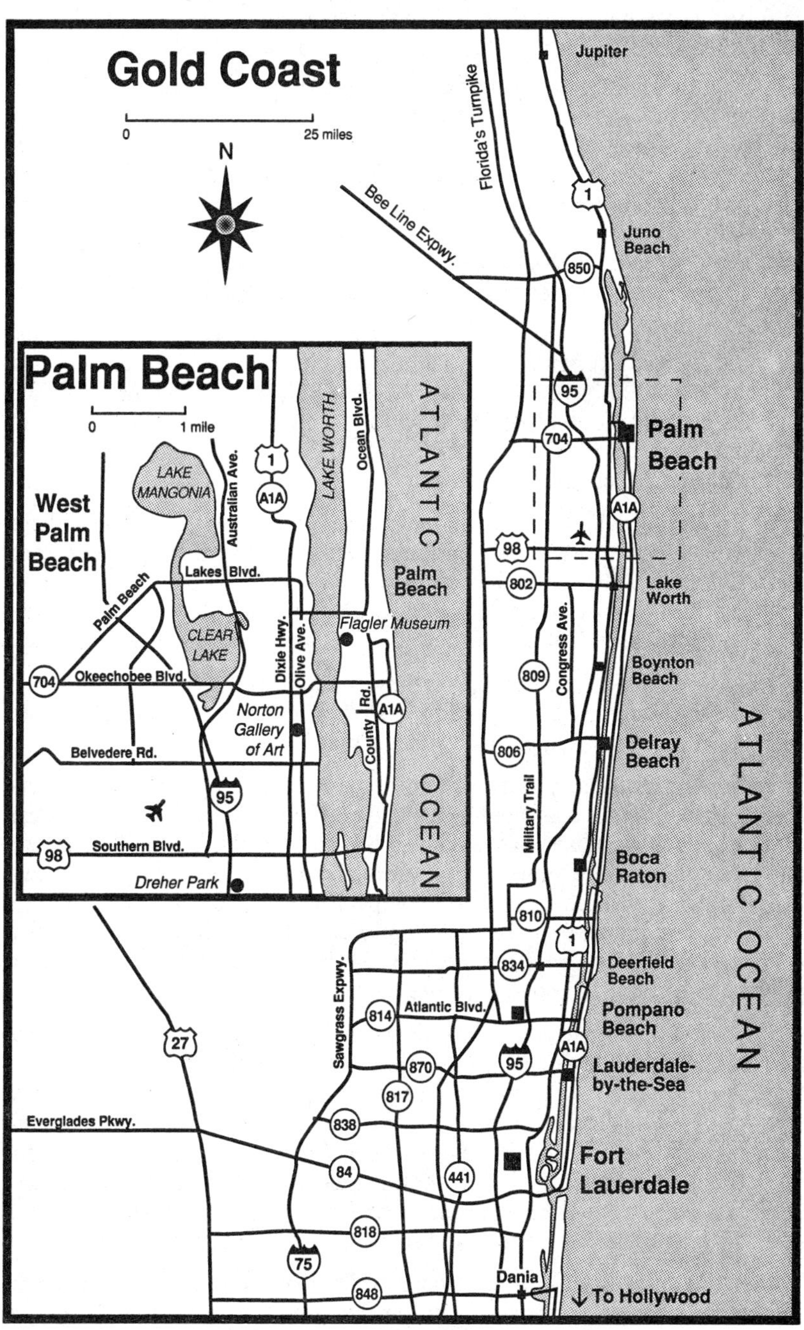

Gold Coast
0
25 miles
N
Jupiter
Florida's Turnpike
Bee Line Expwy.
1
Juno Beach
850
95
704
Palm Beach
A1A
98
802
Lake Worth
Congress Ave.
809
Boynton Beach
806
Delray Beach
Military Trail
Boca Raton
ATLANTIC OCEAN
810
1
834
Deerfield Beach
Sawgrass Expwy.
814
Atlantic Blvd.
Pompano Beach
27
95
A1A
870
Lauderdale-by-the-Sea
817
Everglades Pkwy.
838
84
441
Fort Lauerdale
818
75
Dania
848
To Hollywood
Palm Beach
0
1 mile
LAKE MANGONIA
Australian Ave.
1
A1A
LAKE WORTH
Ocean Blvd.
ATLANTIC
West Palm Beach
Lakes Blvd.
Palm Beach
Palm Beach
Flagler Museum
CLEAR LAKE
Dixie Hwy.
Olive Ave.
704
Okeechobee Blvd.
County Rd.
A1A
Norton Gallery of Art
Belvedere Rd.
95
OCEAN
98
Southern Blvd.
Dreher Park

on it was just a matter of time before the rest of the country learned about the "Venice of America" with its 250 miles of waterways.

Today, thousands of vacationers descend on the Gold Coast each year. In parts of Broward and Palm Beach counties, the population swells by as much as one-third during the winter season. In fact, the increase in traffic is almost the only way you can tell it's winter on the Gold Coast. The climate here is amazingly consistent, with a year-round average of about 75°. There are no hills and few lakes to distinguish one square mile of land from the next. Sand dunes, so well-preserved to the north, are rarely seen here. Slightly inland lie occasional mangrove swamps and hardwood hammocks.

The towns and small cities that have grown up since the 1920s around the hubs of Fort Lauderdale and Palm Beach have their own personalities. Hallandale and Hollywood, for instance, resemble nearby Miami, with their highrise oceanfront condominiums and low-priced motels. Davie, west of Fort Lauderdale, is Florida's version of the wild west, with farms and horse trails dotting the countryside.

Fort Lauderdale itself remains somewhat popular with college students heading south on spring break, a ritual that brought the city notoriety when portrayed in the 1960 film *Where the Boys Are*. Too much notoriety, it seems, for today the city has taken steps to discourage the hordes, to the delight of year-round residents. Meanwhile, the city's building boom continues unabated.

North of Fort Lauderdale, low-key communities like Lauderdale-by-the-Sea and Pompano Beach exhibit a slower pace, hemmed in by the sea and the Intracoastal Waterway, with no place to grow but up.

Crossing into Palm Beach County, the coast road travels through another series of towns, these with a distinctly different flavor than their cousins to the south. Boca Raton has become a tidy, extremely well-to-do community that attracts large numbers of retirees and golfers as well as an increasing abundance of high-technology companies. It is the site of the liveliest restaurant and nightlife activity in Palm Beach County. Delray Beach is a well-preserved oceanfront enclave for people who can afford Palm Beach prices but eschew the social requirements.

The coast is lined with tiny towns such as Boynton Beach, Lantana and the unsightly burg of Briny Breezes (where most homes are mobile and there is little beach access for visitors). Further north, Lake Worth shows signs of revitalization as an arts and antiques center. And then there's the queen herself, Palm Beach. Pristine and formal to the point of outright intimidation, the grande dame exudes wealth and confidence. Aside from public museums—and a smidgen of beach access—it seems to exist purely to serve itself, with its rows of mansions and abundance of fine shops and limousines.

A few miles north, Singer Island offers a sweep of beautiful beaches, oceanfront hotels and condos. And on the Gold Coast's northern tip lies

Jupiter, an underestimated locale favored by celebrities whose names will inevitably come up even during a brief visit.

Wherever visitors choose to go along the Gold Coast, they will find an increased awareness of the area's delicate ecology. Signs admonish speeding boats on waterways that harbor endangered manatees. Alligators, no longer endangered, thrive in the shrinking wilderness; shore birds of all kinds are abundant. The area seems devoted to unencumbered pleasurable pursuits, an idyllic getaway for the rest of the country. Deep-sea fishing and scuba diving are challenging tennis and golf as the most prevalent forms of recreation in the region.

Today, gold still washes up on the southeastern Florida beaches, figuratively at least. A stream of blue-sky days interrupted only by hurricane season (August to October), combined with endless recreational opportunities, ensures a gold-plated future for this stretch of the Florida coast.

Southern Broward County

From Flamingo gardens to jai alai, Southern Broward County offers another of the Sunshine State's intriguing destinations. Here you can find Native American villages and beachfront promenades, pythons and miniature golf courses, as well as Florida's Wild West. Cowboys in Florida? We'll get to that in a bit.

One of the best known towns in this region is Hollywood. This city, home to no movie studios, owes its moniker to one Joseph Young. During the 1920s, Young selected a swath of South Florida swamplands and—dreaming of his beloved Southern California—dubbed it Hollywood.

Today, Hollywood and its southern neighbor, Hallandale, are home to about 150,000 warm-weather loyalists and hard-core beach bums. Set apart from Fort Lauderdale both geographically and in personality, these twin cities exhibit a reserved style of living. The area's many retired residents while away their time on the beach or socializing downtown. Architecture harkens back to the 1950s, with rows of older, highrise condominiums taking front stage throughout the region.

Hollywood's subdued style, together with its colorful beach boardwalk, fine restaurants and quaint motels draw thousands of tourists seeking a pace slower than in Fort Lauderdale.

To get a feel for the area, travel on **Hollywood Boulevard** between Dixie Highway and the Atlantic Ocean. You'll pass through Hollywood's downtown, an area that's enjoying rejuvenation as dilapidated buildings slowly become rows of colorful canopied stores and restaurants. Stroll the brick sidewalks and lush, landscaped medians of this quiet city, then head east toward a scenic stretch of quiescent homes flanked by huge palm trees.

The height of activity takes place along the **Broadwalk**, which hugs the beach for over two miles between Simms and Georgia streets. Mom-and-pop motels, beer shacks and souvenir shops crowd along the promenade, creating a mood that's delightfully tacky. It was originally built of coral rock dredged from the Intracoastal Waterway. Long ago it was paved over with asphalt, and today it is peopled with bicyclists, joggers, senior citizens and women in itsy bitsy bikinis.

The **Art and Culture Center of Hollywood** (1650 Harrison Street; 305-921-3275; admission) houses an engaging collection of contemporary paintings and sculptures by South Florida artists. Most fascinating, though, are the ever-changing exhibits such as Florida Indian and Israeli art, avant-garde works and pre-revolutionary Russian abstract paintings. The single-story, airy building also displays an intriguing set of African artifacts.

If your entertainment tastes lean toward the dangerous, don't miss the alligator wrestling and snake shows at the **Seminole Native Village** (3551 North State Road 7, Hollywood; 305-961-4519; admission). Seminole Indians demonstrate their centuries-old technique of chasing and nabbing a man-size alligator. Ever want to pet a python? During the snake show, the Seminoles showcase pythons, rattlesnakes and other slithering creatures.

In between the shows, which are held throughout the day, you can tour a wildlife area that's home to bobcats, panthers, deer, crocodiles and otters. Children particularly enjoy the village museum, where they get to hold animal skeletons and skins.

You'll also find compelling paintings that trace the history, legends and lifestyles of the Seminoles. The artist, Guy LaBree, is a white man who as a child befriended the Indians and spent weekends on their reservation. He is known across Florida as the "barefoot artist" because—like those early Seminoles—he prefers to live shoeless.

The six-story **Hollywood Greyhound Track** (Route 1 and Pembroke Road, Hallandale; 305-454-9400; admission) is a Gold Coast landmark. During the season (December until April), an average crowd of 5000 racing fans turns out for the evening to watch greyhounds race around the oval track at speeds of up to 40 m.p.h.

Touted as the world's largest water theme park, **Atlantis: The Water Kingdom** (2700 Stirling Road, Hollywood; 305-926-1000; admission) is undeniably a fun place. The 68-acre attraction rests along Route 95, wooing harried drivers with its giant, snaking water slides, colorful kiddie rides, putt-putt golf courses and swimming pools. A great after-beach stop.

Speed comes in another form with the lightning-fast sport of jai alai, played at **Dania Jai Alai** (301 East Dania Beach Boulevard, Dania; 305-426-4330). Evolved from a version of handball played in ancient Basque

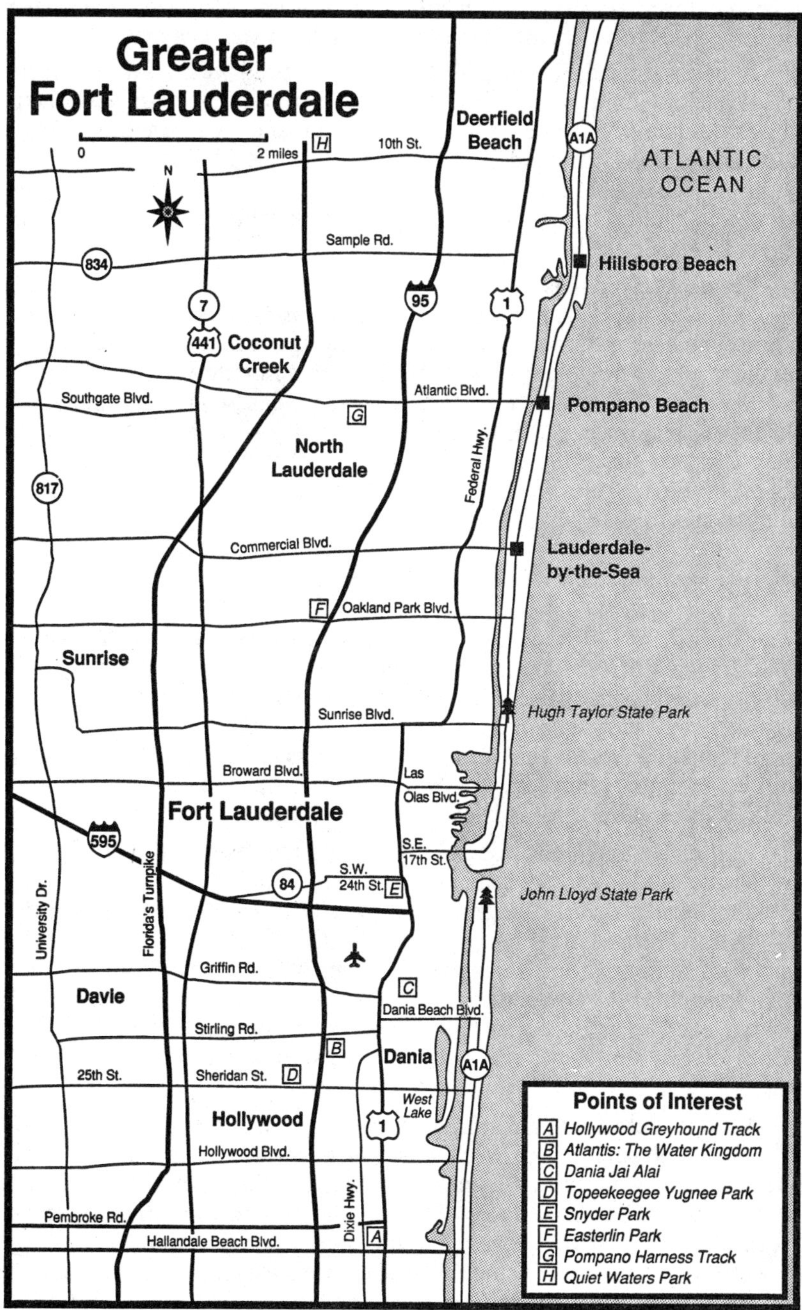
Greater
Fort Lauderdale
0
2 miles
N
ATLANTIC
OCEAN
Deerfield
Beach
10th St.
A1A
Sample Rd.
834
Hillsboro Beach
7
441
95
1
Coconut
Creek
Southgate Blvd.
Atlantic Blvd.
Pompano Beach
G
North
Lauderdale
Federal Hwy.
817
Commercial Blvd.
Lauderdale-
by-the-Sea
F
Oakland Park Blvd.
Sunrise
Sunrise Blvd.
Hugh Taylor State Park
Broward Blvd.
Las
Olas Blvd.
Fort Lauderdale
595
S.E.
17th St.
84
S.W.
24th St.
E
John Lloyd State Park
University Dr.
Florida's Turnpike
Griffin Rd.
C
Davie
Dania Beach Blvd.
Stirling Rd.
B
Dania
A1A
25th St.
Sheridan St.
D
West
Lake
Hollywood
1
Hollywood Blvd.
Dixie Hwy.
Pembroke Rd.
Hallandale Beach Blvd.
A
Points of Interest
A Hollywood Greyhound Track
B Atlantis: The Water Kingdom
C Dania Jai Alai
D Topeekeegee Yugnee Park
E Snyder Park
F Easterlin Park
G Pompano Harness Track
H Quiet Waters Park

hillside villages, jai alai is now played by professionals and offers legalized wagering (see "The Exotic Game of Jai Alai" in this chapter).

It's easy to find Florida's Wild West. Just head west 20 miles inland to **Davie.** This small town seems to have more in common with New Mexico's cattle country than it does with oranges and sandy beaches. Davie country is home to that rare and endangered species, the Florida cowboy, who works the area's cattle and horse ranches in the grand manner. Poking around this region, you'll swear you took a wrong turn somewhere and ended up on the Santa Fe trail.

Flamingo Gardens (3750 Flamingo Road, Davie; 305-473-0010; admission) is a slight misnomer. Small subtropical forest would be more accurate. The best way to get acclimated to the abundance of natural beauty here is to take the one-and-a-half-mile-long tram ride through citrus groves and hammocks of native plants. Bromeliads, orchids, heliconias and ginger plants—among the most beautiful in the country—can be easily spotted. Then there are the trees, especially the two dozen "Champion" trees, the largest of their species in Florida. Parrots, pheasants, flamingos and more wildlife add to the Fantasy Island feeling.

SOUTHERN BROWARD COUNTY HOTELS

The only Hollywood hotel on the Intracoastal Waterway is the **Hollywood Beach Hilton** (4000 South Ocean Drive; 305-458-1900). Most of the 306 oversized rooms have small balconies with views of a good stretch of the waterway and at least a sliver of ocean. The ambience is nothing to write home about, but the accommodations are spacious and comfortably appointed with contemporary furnishings. One of the best features of this Hilton is its lovely riverside pool and lounge area. Ultra-deluxe.

Hallandale and Hollywood are condominium towns, with few hotels; the few motels there and in Dania virtually all require a minimum seven-day booking. Going against the grain is the **Hollywood Beach Resort Hotel** (101 North Ocean Drive, Hollywood; 305-921-0990), a pale pink extravaganza of studios, rooms and suites. It looms over the beautiful beach and easily outshines the competition. The guest quarters are simply decorated, distinguished by art deco accents, brass track lighting and kitchen facilities. The resort has a pool and a bevy of boutiques, food outlets and movie theaters. Deluxe.

With its desert-colored stucco trimmed in brilliant teal awnings, **Sheldon Ocean Resort** (1000 North Surf Road, Hollywood Beach; 305-922-6020) stands out on the beach. Inside and out, the mid-rise hotel is decorated art deco funky. Terrazzo floors, '30s-style lamps and a kitschy wall mural accent the lobby, while 42 small but tidy guest rooms feature ceiling fans, popcorn ceilings and carpeting. Several efficiencies and one apartment are also offered at this oceanside spot. Budget.

Back in the 1930s, Hollywood founder Joseph Young used a slew of real estate agents to sell his new city. He put them up in a two-story villa that's now a gay guesthouse called **Maison Harrison** (1504 Harrison Street; 305-922-7319). Nestled on a palm-lined residential street, the tile-roofed home has been beautifully renovated with French doors, plush rugs, period furniture and polished wood floors. The owners used imagination and attention to detail in the five stylized bedrooms—four with canopy beds and private wood decks. A lush, secluded courtyard features a whirlpool and exercise room. Best of all, budget and moderate rates include a hearty continental breakfast.

SOUTHERN BROWARD COUNTY RESTAURANTS

La Concha Beach Club (900 North Broadwalk, Hollywood; 305-921-4190) is one of several open-air cafés on the inland side of Broadwalk, the long strip of pavement that runs in front of the beach. The best time to go is at breakfast, when you can enjoy eggs, bagels or pancakes while watching strollers and joggers warming up in the fresh light of day. La Concha is open throughout the day, serving budget-to-moderate-priced dishes such as a chicken salad platter, sandwiches and hamburgers.

Once you get past the ornate foyer, an overwrought fantasy based on the Roman bath concept, **Villa Perrone** (906 East Hallandale Beach Boulevard, Hollywood; 305-454-8878) gets down to business in two plant-filled, dimly lit dining rooms whose elegance is underscored by tuxedo-clad waiters. The menu is distinguished by several warm appetizers, and such main courses as veal, chicken, seafood, sausage and pasta dishes. Offering formal service and substantial portions at moderate to deluxe prices, Villa Perrone is a good value.

For an informal, inexpensive evening out, a good place to remember in Hollywood is **Mott Street** (★) (1295 East Hallandale Beach Boulevard; 305-456-7555), a friendly Chinese restaurant with low lights and high spirits. A laughing Buddha and a sleek lacquered screen dress up this long narrow room, but the point here is the variety of budget- and moderate-priced selections such as snapper steamed with ginger, scallions and black beans, orange-peel beef and salt-and-pepper squid.

One of the choicest spots around, **Hemmingway's** (219 North 21st Avenue, Hollywood; 305-926-5644) combines gorgeous ornate interiors, inventive cuisine and oodles of local history. Built in 1926 as Hollywood's first city hall, the building still harbors remnants of original jail cells. But the drab government walls have been replaced with embellishments of gold leaf, splendid stained glass and large Renaissance murals that skate across walls. Such extravagance is matched by fare like roast duck, garlic ribs and black forest bread topped with warm garlic cheese. Don't miss Hemmingway's salad, a virtual treasure hunt of whole fruits, exotic cheeses and veggies. Deluxe to ultra-deluxe.

Marcello's Restaurant (1822 South Young Circle, Hollywood; 305-923-1055) has a severe case of schizophrenia: the two dining rooms seem to belong to different restaurants. The one that fills up first is a high-ceilinged room with tables covered in marbleized cloth and an entire trompe l'oeil wall painted to look like Venetian housefronts. The other is the standard Italian restaurant cliché of red-and-white checkered tablecloths and travel posters. But they do share a menu of homemade gnocchi, tortellini and other pastas, as well as veal and seafood dishes. Budget to moderate.

Be sure to enter from the rear parking lot at **Marathon Greek Restaurant** (6 South Federal Highway, Dania; 305-920-5396). It's full of charm with its wrought-iron archway draped with vines and blossoms. Beyond this courtyard is a simple dining room with clothed tables and bentwood-style chairs with cane seats. Named for a battle site in ancient Greece, Marathon Greek is true to its roots with dishes such as moussaka, lemon chicken, spinach pie and some unusual listings, including stuffed cabbage leaves. Budget to moderate.

D'arcy's Grand Café (129 North Federal Highway, Dania; 305-923-1000) is an outpost of Continental cuisine housed in a converted two-story residence. Elaborate wallpaper, glass chandeliers and fringed fabric lightshades imbue the rooms with an unexpected 19th-century ambience. The menu contains such dishes as tortellini with sea scallops à la Provençal, rack of lamb with a mustard-herb-garlic crust, dover sole à la meunière and duck à l'orange. Moderate to deluxe.

One of the great pleasures of south Florida dining is doing it outdoors. **Bloody Mary's** (Sea Fair, Route A1A and Dania Beach Boulevard, Dania; 305-922-5600) has suited its menu to its open-air (sun or shade) setting. A half-pineapple stuffed with shrimp salad, grapes and strawberries or raw vegetables with smoked dolphin are cool combinations for super-hot days, while oysters on the half-shell, fish-and-chips, garlic chicken and a variety of hamburgers constitute heartier fare. Budget.

The Spiced Apple (3281 Griffin Road, Dania; 305-962-0772), an old roadside house, appears to have been lifted, rough-sawn cedar, pecky cypress and all, straight from the Blue Ridge Mountains. Country-fried steak, prime rib, roast sirloin with real gravy and Carolina delicacies such as skillet pork chops are among the specialties. Between courses, guests may stroll from room to room to check out the unique decor that ranges from antique trumpets to broom dolls to handmade baby cribs. Moderate to deluxe.

Armadillo Café (4630 Southwest 64th Avenue, Davie; 305-791-5104) will endear you to the earthy, seething flavors of the Southwest. Chef couple Eve Montella and Kevin McCarthy combine culinary passions to create delectable dishes spiked with chilis, salsas, pestos and other zesty flavors.

Choices might include lobster quesadillas, pan fried yellowtail with spicy pumpkinseed sauce, or a black and white soup that's a fiery combo of black bean and jalapeño jack soups. Moderate to deluxe.

The **Rustic Inn Crabhouse** (4331 Ravenswood Road, Fort Lauderdale; 305-584-1637) is located so far inland that first-time visitors are astonished to find a waterway right out back. It's famous locally for its garlic crab, best eaten over a table covered in newspapers. Fancier fare is also available, including Florida lobster, crab cakes, Key West shrimp and fresh fish. Moderate to deluxe.

SOUTHERN BROWARD COUNTY SHOPPING

Among the bevy of boutiques located on **Oceanwalk Mall** (Hollywood Beach Resort, 101 North Ocean Drive, Hollywood; 305-925-2955) are offbeat shops such as **Stone Love** (305-925-9374), offering minerals, gems, crystal balls, chimes and other "earthy" items. They also carry New Age books, tapes and videos. For inexpensive gifts and offbeat souvenirs, look into the **Pink Palm Company** (305-922-2900). Another tropical destination, **Palm Produce** (305-922-2900) carries the latest in beach attire, including colorful rayon dresses, straw hats, flip flops and Florida T-shirts that thankfully aren't tacky.

If you feel like slumming it, check out the divey shops along Hollywood's **Broadwalk** (along the ocean between Simms and Georgia streets). The neon-lit cubbyholes, which always advertise "big sales," have everything to satisfy the tourist in you.

Collectors, browsers and serious antique hunters will all find something to like about Antique Alley, a cluster of storefronts on Federal Highway (Route 1) in Dania. One of the best and friendliest of the lot is **Rose Antiques** (17 North Federal Highway; 305-921-0474), known for its crystal and china, notably an excellent assortment of demitasse cups and saucers by such manufacturers as Royal Doulton and Limoges.

The **Dania Antique Center** (3 North Federal Highway, Dania) houses more than a dozen dealers who operate in a line of cubbyholes selling mostly decorative pieces. Two deserve special mention: **Lee's Antiques** (305-925-7567), which has French deco and art nouveau items such as dresser top sets and perfume bottles, and **Royale Antiques** (305-922-5467), where you will find oil paintings and French furniture in excellent condition.

In north Dania, **Seafair** is a spacious beachside complex housing a handful of restaurants and shops. **The Captured Image** (101-18 North Beach Road; 305-922-8523) is an eclectic store with jewelry and beautiful collectibles made of pewter, porcelain, brass and lucite. It's also something of a New Age headquarters, selling crystals, incense and potpourri as well as 1960s and '70s memorabilia.

Classy Baskets (7383 Davie Road Extension, Davie; 305-433-4811) will custom-design a pretty basket with chocolates, gourmet foods, balloons and other decorative gifts.

SOUTHERN BROWARD COUNTY NIGHTLIFE

A live band rocks every night at **The Button South** (100 Ansin Boulevard, Hallandale; 305-454-0001), a spacious, warehouse-style habitat. A 6 a.m. closing time draws local bartenders. Cover.

It's a bit out of the way, but **Do Da's American Country Saloon and Dancehall** (700 State Road 7, Plantation; 305-792-6200) is one of the few country-and-western joints in this area. Fans have their choice of four different theme rooms, such as the Frontier Room, showcasing Nashville bands. Cover on weekends.

Subdued vibes permeate **Bloody Mary's at Seafair** (101 North Beach Road, Dania; 305-922-5600), a patio bar with live oldies music.

For top-notch jazz and contemporary tunes, check out the lounge at **Hemmingway's** (219 North 21st Avenue, Hollywood; 305-926-5644) restaurant. The ornate, rococo decor makes for a dressy environment.

SOUTHERN BROWARD COUNTY BEACHES AND PARKS

Hallandale Beach—The municipal beach at the northern edge of Hallandale is so small that it is easily overcrowded. Soft dark sand extends from a rock outcropping north to the border of Hollywood Beach, which is a short distance indeed. On a typical day, most visitors are teenagers and families with small children.

Facilities: Picnic areas, restrooms, showers, lifeguards, concession stands; restaurants and groceries nearby. *Swimming:* Good in areas where there are no submerged rocks.

Getting there: Located off Route A1A south of Route 824.

Hollywood Beach—This five-mile-plus swath of pale sand is larger than some islands. Sprinkled with palm trees, it is one of the most beautiful beaches on the entire Gold Coast. It is also one of the neatest, which, given its immense popularity, is a pleasant surprise. For much of its length, it is bordered by Broadwalk, a wide strip of pavement closed to automobile traffic and open to bicycles only at certain hours. The beach itself consists of medium-soft sand, good for walking but a little soft for jogging.

Facilities: Picnic areas, restrooms, showers, lifeguards, concession stands; restaurants and groceries on Oceanwalk. *Fishing:* Surf angling. *Swimming:* Excellent everywhere.

Getting there: There are dozens of access points off Route A1A, from Greenbriar Street to Sherman Street.

Hollywood North Beach Park (★)—It's easy to drive right past this 56-acre park sandwiched between Hollywood Beach and Dania Beach. Much of the park is a greensward planted with 500 species of vegetation, including oak trees and broad-leafed sea grapes. To protect the dunes, several crossovers have been built along the park's mile-long beach access area. You can jog or walk along Broadwalk, the 2.2-mile walkway that extends from Georgia Street to Simms Street, which lies within park territory. A pleasant change from most coastal parks, North Beach also operates a protection and relocation program for sea turtles, which can sometimes be observed in holding tanks.

Facilities: Picnic areas, play areas, restrooms, lifeguards, concession stands, 60-foot observation tower, bicycle and hiking paths, sports equipment rental, volleyball court; restaurants and groceries nearby; information, 305-926-2444. *Swimming:* Excellent.

Getting there: Located at Route A1A and Sheridan Street.

Dania Beach—This half-mile stretch of undeveloped oceanfront enjoys a very special phenomenon: When neighboring beaches erode, much of their sand ends up here. Hence Dania's soft sand has an unusual creamy-silver color. Less hectic than Hollywood Beach, this strand is nicely landscaped with palm trees and vegetation and rimmed with clear, almost-turquoise water. The pier here is scheduled to be torn down and re-built in 1992.

Facilities: Restrooms, showers; restaurant nearby.

Getting there: Off Route A1A via Oak Street.

Topeekeegee Yugnee Park—Scattered around a 40-acre lake are a number of attractions rarely found in a public park. T-Y Park, as it's called locally, is not the most beautiful recreation area on the Gold Coast, but it's one of the most unusual. The Falling Waters Swimming Lagoon offers slides and fountains to splash in; the Twisting Waters Flume Ride rises 50 feet, featuring 700 feet of turns, tunnels and drops. This 150-acre park is an ideal oasis for enjoying a variety of water sports on a hot south Florida day.

Facilities: Picnic areas, restrooms, concession stands, bicycle and other sports equipment rentals, windsurfing, sailing, paddleboat and canoe rentals, grocery store, softball and soccer fields, nature trails; information, 305-985-1980. *Fishing:* From a small fishing island in the lake. *Swimming:* In the lagoon.

Camping: There are 12 tent sites and 48 RV hookups; two-week limit. Fees are $16 per night for tents, $17 per night for RVs.

Getting there: The park is located at 3300 North Park Road, Hollywood.

Fort Lauderdale

Fort Lauderdale's reputation as a spring break haven has sadly led many visitors to overlook some of the splendid sights the city has to offer. Though it boasts 23 miles of balmy beaches, the city's beauty goes well beyond its shoreline. Traveling through the area, you'll quickly discover majestic estates lush with foliage, handsome commercial centers, hardwood hammocks, an impressive maze of clean waterways and a general feeling of the laid-back tropics.

Though much of its history barely trickles back 100 years, you'll still find plenty of historical intrigue. Tales of sunken treasure and pirates are interwoven into the architecture and the personalities that gave birth to this carefree locale. In fact, some of the city's original buildings were forged with wood culled from shipwrecks.

Most of Fort Lauderdale's sights are spread out, so it's essential to navigate by car. The good news is, the roadways are a near-perfect gridwork of east-west and north-south thoroughfares, so it's easy to get around.

Some of the Fort Lauderdale area's most unusual sights are not on any guide map. The **Manatee Viewing Area (★)** (Eisenhower Boulevard and Southeast 26th Street, Port Everglades) is one of the best places in south Florida to see these large, shy marine mammals.

It is a little easier to see marine mammals, however, when they are contained in a pool. **Ocean World** (Southeast 17th Street, Fort Lauderdale; 305-525-6611; admission) is a compact, spotless facility with a three-story underwater viewing tank and several outdoor entertainment areas. The number one attraction here is the series of dolphin shows. Incorporating the occasional sea lion, these tours de force are highly educational and entertaining. Ocean World also offers optional sightseeing excursions in glass-bottomed boats.

Meander along 17th Street Causeway east to the ocean and then wend your way north along Fort Lauderdale's infamous **Strip.** This five-mile stretch of road, which extends northward to Sunrise Boulevard, pulses with life, as the sidewalks and beach are a constant flurry of activity. Reminiscent of commercial areas along San Francisco's Fisherman's Wharf, the Strip is a series of T-shirt shops, fast-food joints, seedy pool bars and low-rise hotels. This byway seems devised for "cruising," and that's exactly what takes place 24 hours a day. Most nights, traffic is gridlocked along the beach.

This animated stretch of beach—bashed by locals ever since spring break brought it to life—is now nearly void of college vacationers and instead is peopled by a curious mix of families, gays and high school students. In an effort to attract an upscale crowd, city leaders have begun a massive revitalization of the area. Already, the beach has a sleek new look. Pretty brick promenades and gas lamps line the street and moorish pillars invite access to the beach. Brand new palm trees divide the roadway, and fresh paint covers several facades.

Fort Lauderdale's former image as Spring Break Capital of the Free World derived, oddly enough, from its popularity among college coaches, who began working out in the area back in the 1930s. Inevitably, word of excellent spring swimming conditions trickled down to underclassmen, who exploded on the scene in the early 1960s. This is one of numerous amazing-but-true facts divulged during a tour of the **International Swimming Hall of Fame** (1 Hall of Fame Drive; 305-462-6536; admission). After expanding and renovating, the museum is scheduled to reopen in early 1993 with computerized exhibits that let you pretend you're an Olympic diver, swimmer or judge. Also on display are artifacts such as wool, turn-of-the-century bathing costumes, sweatshirts that once belonged to such Olympic champions as Mark Spitz and Cynthia Potter, and swim-related works by artists from Honore Daumier to Norman Rockwell. International water buffs will want to tour the room of nations, where you can bone up on any swimmer or diver who won an Olympic metal.

For a peek at true Fort Lauderdale living, travel west on **Las Olas Boulevard** and explore the finger islands that protrude from the roadway. These tiny isles provide waterfront berths for thousands of residents and their extravagant yachts. Just west of this area is a row of posh downtown shops where pricey furs and priceless paintings peep from beneath bright awnings.

Rarely is a traveler able to explore a city on an old-fashioned trolley—without spending a dime. The free **Fort Lauderdale trolleys,** painted a brilliant cobalt blue, tool around downtown. Best of all, the trolleys are only ten minutes apart. Route maps and schedules (free, of course) are available on the trolleys, or the Downtown Development Authority (350 Southeast 2nd Street, Suite 500; 305-463-6574).

Several former private residences in this area are now open for touring. Built in the 1920s as an idyllic family retreat, the charming **Bonnet House** (★) (900 North Birch Road, Fort Lauderdale; 305-563-5393; admission) remains an oasis on 35 acres sheltered from all signs of modern-day urban life. Tours of the beautifully preserved two-story house and various nature trails are open to the public from May through November. The Shell Room, with its inlaid shells and an impressive collection of paired specimens, is worth a trip all by itself. Also not to be missed is the studio of Frederic Bartlett (who built the estate); many of his original paintings remain on display. White swans swim in a peaceful lake, and Brazilian squirrel monkeys cavort in a forest of trees in this enchanting enclave, which also fronts 700 feet of the Atlantic Ocean.

For additional information, maps and free brochures, stop by the **Greater Fort Lauderdale Convention and Visitors Bureau** (200 East Las Olas Boulevard, Suite 1500; 305-765-4466).

The **Museum of Art** (1 East Las Olas Boulevard, Fort Lauderdale; 305-763-6464; admission) houses pieces from the museum's permanent collection of 20th-century American and European paintings and sculpture by Dali, Andy Warhol, Matisse, Picasso and Henry Moore, as well as temporary shows. The museum is especially noted for having the largest collection in the United States of artwork from Copenhagen, Brussels and Amsterdam, and the largest collection in Florida of Primal, pre-Columbian and Native American art.

Downtown Fort Lauderdale's riverfront, abandoned over recent decades, is experiencing a revival. The city's **Riverwalk** (along the New River between Federal Highway and Southwest 7th Avenue) features meandering footpaths, manicured gardens and parks, and gazebos. A real highlight is the **Esplanade Park,** featuring a science exhibit complete with giant kaleidoscopes, a rain gauge and sextant, and plaques honoring the world's famous mathematicians and scientists. You'll find the park next to the gleaming **Broward Center for the Performing Arts** (624 Southwest 2nd Street; 305-462-0222), a cultural jewel that opened in 1991.

The **Fort Lauderdale Historical Society Museum** (219 Southwest 2nd Avenue, Fort Lauderdale; 305-463-4431; admission) is the best clearinghouse for information on the city's historic district, which extends roughly from the nearby railroad tracks east of here to 5th Avenue, and from the New River north to 2nd Street. The exhibits here are not extensive, though nicely done. They include scale models of historic structures and of a Seminole Indian village, complete with arts and crafts from the old days. The museum features an excellent selection of regional books.

A few blocks away is a complex with at least three reasons for visiting. You can bend a ray of light, crawl into a cave or play with other deceptively educational hands-on displays at the **Discovery Center** (401 Southwest 2nd Street, Fort Lauderdale; 305-462-4115; admission). The optical illusions hall, one of several diverse rooms in this old three-story house, is the kind of place where you could spend an entire rainy afternoon (with or without children along).

If you like old-fashioned things, the most attractive building in all of Fort Lauderdale may be the **Stranahan House** (Las Olas Boulevard at the New River Tunnel; 305-524-4736; admission). This two-story frame structure was built in 1901 by the city's first citizen, Frank Stranahan, who saw it evolve from a trading post to a family home. Constructed of Dade County pine, the house eventually sprouted bay windows, electric wiring and modern plumbing, all signs of the times as well as of the Stranahan family's prominence. The house is now restored to the 1906 period, furnished with appropriate examples of Victorian furniture, and open to guided tours.

The best way to see the most beautiful residential areas of Fort Lauderdale is via the city's intricate network of waterways. There are several ways to experience the waterways, but the easiest is, simply, to call a taxi.

A water taxi, that is. **Water Taxi of Fort Lauderdale** (1900 Southeast 15th Street; 305-565-5507) possesses a fleet of bright yellow skiffs that—for a moderate fare—shuttle passengers to points along the Intracoastal Waterway and New and Middle rivers.

If you prefer to travel en masse, try the **Jungle Queen** (Bahia Mar Yacht Center, 801 Seabreeze Boulevard; 305-462-5596), a 538-passenger riverboat that meanders through downtown and Port Everglades and stops at the **Seminole Indian Village** for a look at native trees and birds.

There's enough space in west Broward County for a number of "great outdoors" attractions, most notably **Everglades Holiday Park** (21940 Griffin Road, Fort Lauderdale; 305-434-8111). This privately owned facility offers the easiest close-by access point to the vast reaches of the Everglades, which stretches from the middle of the state to the western edge of greater Fort Lauderdale. The reason for driving all the way out here is to hop aboard an airboat that carries large groups out on 45-minute tours through tall saw grass and cattails and over low-lying waterplants. Coots, marsh hens and the occasional lone osprey can be easily photographed during frequent stops. Alligators pop up from time to time, sometimes becoming visible as they sun themselves on the banks at the feet of leafy pond apple trees. Included in the fare is a short layover at a small replica of a Seminole Indian village.

FORT LAUDERDALE HOTELS

From Hollywood up to Deerfield Beach, good hotels and quality inns are vastly outnumbered by nondescript motels. In Fort Lauderdale proper, you'll find a number of highrise hotels belonging to major chains, as well as some individually owned facilities on the south end of town. The "strip" of motels, bars and stores along Route A1A, across from the beach, is something of an eyesore, so most of our recommendations are located further afield. Thanks to a local ordinance, there is no construction whatsoever between Route A1A and the heart of the long beach. Since ocean views are thus a rarity, it's better to base your lodging selection on other factors.

Graced with a small lagoon on one side and a spectacularly wide semiprivate beach on the other, **Lago Mar** (1700 South Ocean Lane; 305-523-6511) offers a beautiful setting. In fact, with 180 rooms and suites, two swimming pools, tennis courts, a putting green, two restaurants and a lounge, Lago Mar could enter in the resort category. Currently undergoing some major renovations, a variety of accommodations are available in buildings designed to catch those gorgeous Gold Coast sunrises. A typical room has soft textured wallpaper, faux stone lamps, off-white furniture with brass handles, and accents of rose and forest green throughout. Ultra-deluxe.

Pier 66 Hotel and Marina (2301 Southeast 17th Street Causeway, Fort Lauderdale; 305-525-6666) looks like a cylindrical spaceship dreamed up by a 1960s sci-fi writer. Topped off with a 17th-floor revolving lounge, it dominates the coastal skyline and offers unsurpassed upper-level views. Spacious accommodations (388 rooms and suites) with subdued tropical color schemes sport small lanais that overlook the Intracoastal Waterway, the city, the ocean and 22 lushly landscaped acres. The top-notch amenities include restaurants, tennis courts, swimming pool and 40-person jacuzzi, spa and health club. Ultra-deluxe.

Located two blocks off the beach in a veritable motel ghetto, Fort Lauderdale-style of course, you'll find **Sea Château** (555 North Birch Road, Fort Lauderdale; 305-566-8331). Each room is decorated individually with an eclectic assortment of furniture. Efficiencies are available. Pool. Moderate.

Clean, quiet and centrally located, the **Sea View Resort Motel** (550 North Birch Road; 305-564-3151) rests only a football field's length away from the beach. Accommodations with two double beds are available at moderate to deluxe prices. Pastels are the color scheme and there's a pool right outside. Efficiencies available.

The gentility is almost palpable at the **Riverside Hotel** (620 East Las Olas Boulevard, Fort Lauderdale; 305-467-0671). Visitors here find a residential ambience: most of the 117 rooms have comfy beds covered with chenille spreads and solid oak furniture. The views are of tree-lined Las Olas Boulevard, the garden or the boat-bedecked waters of the New River. Coral fireplaces and terra cotta floors add a Spanish flavor. Dining rooms, bar and pool. Deluxe to ultra-deluxe.

One of the best values in the budget-priced category, the two-story **Friendship Inn** (2201 North Federal Highway, Fort Lauderdale; 305-564-9636) has large, well-ventilated, carpeted rooms furnished with two double beds. Ask for a second-floor room at the back of this motel court, away from Route 1 and the pool with its thatched-roof lounge areas.

As central Florida continues to be paved over, places like the **Bonaventure Resort and Spa** (250 Racquet Club Road, Fort Lauderdale; 305-389-3300) won't seem so far away. But right now the resort's 1250 acres still seem like they are in the middle of nowhere. The Bonaventure has a reputation for excellent golf and tennis as well as for its extensive spa facilities. Accommodations, spread among nine four-story buildings, do not live up to the quality of the recreational amenities, sad to say. Although large, tidy and more than serviceable, rooms and suites have none of the pizzazz you'd expect of such a resort. Pools. Ultra-deluxe.

Galt Ocean Mile is a well-known location in north Fort Lauderdale, consisting of one long phalanx of condominiums and other highrises. One of the few places open to the public is **Ocean Manor Resort** (4040 Galt Ocean Drive, Fort Lauderdale; 305-566-7500), an 11-story beachfront structure with a mix of shapes, sizes and styles from which to choose. Contemporary furnishings and views of either ocean or city add an extra dimension to otherwise unexciting accommodations. Suites with full kitchens available. Pool. Ultra-deluxe.

GAY LODGING Nestled on a finger island in one of Fort Lauderdale's most desirable neighborhoods, **Admiral's Court** (21 Hendricks Isle; 305-462-5072) is absolutely charming. The two-story, clay-tiled Mediterranean buildings hug a swimming pool and gardens dotted with sculptures and fountains. Out back, there's a second pool and a canal lined with yachts and sailboats. Eclecticism reigns in the 40 apartments, efficiencies and motel rooms. Some rooms have ceramic tile or cobblestone floors and formica furniture; others have carpeting and wicker. All units in this gay-friendly establishment are clean and comfortable. Motel rooms and efficiencies are moderately priced; apartments run in the deluxe to ultra-deluxe range.

Popular with lesbians, the **Mermaid Inn** (725 North Birch Road; 305-565-8437) rests in the prettiest of pink buildings just two blocks from the ocean. The congenial owners have nicely renovated every room of the U-shaped motel, adorning them with pale blue carpets, colorful bedspreads and modern appliances. One-bedroom apartments, efficiencies and spacious motel rooms are available. There's a heated swimming pool on the grounds, and grocery stores nearby for do-it-yourselfers. Prices fall in the moderate range.

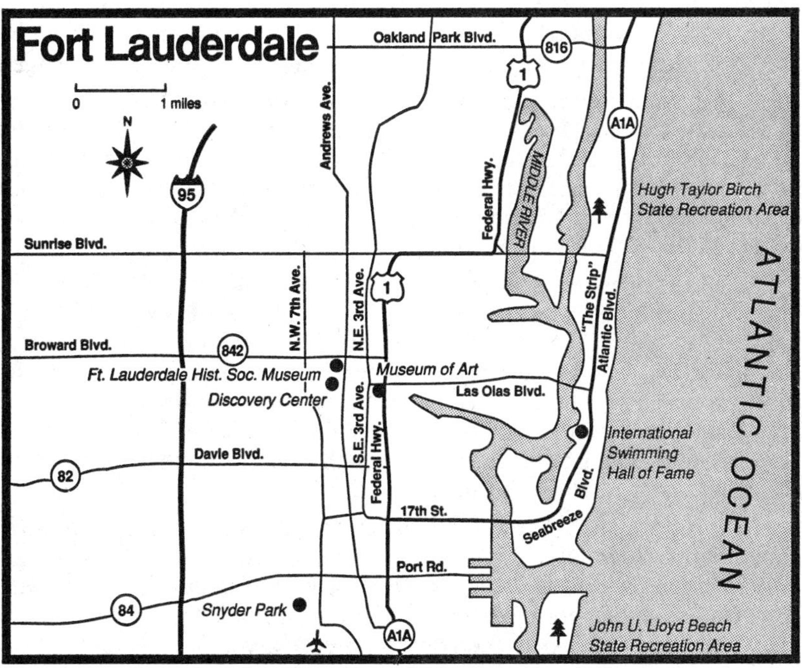

Fashioned in tropical Key West style, **Big Ruby's Guesthouse** (908 Northeast 15th Avenue; 305-523-7829) offers surroundings so private it's easy to miss the place. The ivory clapboard building is adorned with teal shutters, flower boxes and lacy gingerbread, and enveloped by jungle gardens. Eight comfortable guest rooms offer Bahamas fans, soft carpets, microwaves and refrigerators. Out front, there's a swimming pool, waterfall and spacious wood deck for sunning in the buff. A real retreat for gay men. Moderate.

FORT LAUDERDALE RESTAURANTS

Burt & Jack's (Berth 23, Port Everglades, Fort Lauderdale; 305-522-5225) stands alone on a point of land overlooking the Intracoastal Waterway. The setting and the star power of one owner—Burt Reynolds—may have something to do with the popularity of this place, which looks like a mission building imported from Mexico. The menu has a macho side—lots of lamb, steaks and prime rib—but also some popular seafood selections such as sea scallops and Maine lobster. Dinner only. Deluxe to ultra-deluxe.

Insiders know the place to go for succulent, explosively hot barbecue is **Ernie's Bar B Que and Lounge (★)** (1843 South Federal Highway, Fort Lauderdale; 305-523-8636). A plain building with few adornments in the one high-ceilinged dining room, Ernie's relies on a dynamite sauce for its draw. Meat choices include chicken, pork and ribs, each of which can be accompanied by corn on the cob, cole slaw and gallons of iced tea. Budget.

An upscale waterfront bistro in the California style, **Café 66 (★)** (at Pier 66 Resort and Marina, 2301 Southeast 17th Street, Fort Lauderdale; 305-525-6666) is an absolutely delightful spot. Everything on the short menu seems to be successful, from homemade pasta to delicate seafood dishes to spit-roasted meats. Spacious dining areas are staggered, affording views of the marina action beyond. Moderate to deluxe.

It's hard to get reservations at the **15th Street Fisheries** (1900 Southeast 15th Street, Fort Lauderdale; 305-763-2777), but locals swear it's always worth the trouble. This out-of-the-way waterfront restaurant offers excellent views and two levels of dining, both literally and figuratively. Go for the upstairs, where weathered wood walls are festooned with shrimp nets and small tables are covered with floral prints. Seafood is king here: blackened tuna, grouper, dolphin and snapper are usually available, but lamb and steak dishes are, too. Moderate to ultra-deluxe.

The hip way to arrive at the **Southport Raw Bar (★)** (1536 Cordova Road, Fort Lauderdale; 305-525-2526) is via private boat, but it's acceptable to come by land as well. This dockside joint is mighty lively, with loyal patrons sliding down oysters and clams, conch salad and excellent clam chowder, crisp crab cakes and fried shrimp. A great place to drop by for a snack in mid-afternoon. Budget.

Tucked away in the back of **The Chemist Shop** (★) (817 East Las Olas Boulevard, Fort Lauderdale; 305-463-8981) is a corner coffee shop worth investigating. Shopkeepers from the neighborhood flock to this little nook, with only a counter and a few tables, to enjoy good cheap food such as sirloin burgers and old-fashioned sandwiches like cream-cheese-and-olive and peanut butter-and-bacon. For dessert, there are soda-shop goodies concocted with an extra-rich ice cream especially made for The Chemist Shop. Budget.

In the heart of the Las Olas shopping district, **La Bonne Crêpe** (815 East Las Olas Boulevard, Fort Lauderdale; 305-761-1515) provides a refined oasis from the commercial bustle. A small restaurant with a slightly worn carpet and about a dozen tables clothed in lace, this is a local favorite famous for its authentic crêpes, cooked on a special grill imported from La Belle France. The repertoire includes some 50 crêpes, including ones made with sausage, ratatouille and Swiss cheese, as well as a variety of dessert crêpes. Open in winter only. Budget to moderate.

Across the New River from the Las Olas shopping district, **Shirttail Charlie's Restaurant** (400 Southwest 3rd Avenue, Fort Lauderdale; 305-463-3474) is a multilevel, multipurpose restaurant and bar. It's wonderful for an al fresco dockside luncheon of seafood salad, grilled fish or kebabs of steak, chicken, shrimp or fish, all budget-priced. At night, moderate-to-deluxe-priced dinners are served indoors in the upstairs dining room overlooking the river. A rather interesting menu lists a variety of fresh seafood, including scampi and conch, along with steaks, chicken and alligator.

One of downtown Fort Lauderdale's best-kept secrets is a delightful French café located in, of all places, the main library. **Charcuterie, Too** (100 South Andrews Avenue; 305-463-9578) is an artsy breakfast and lunch niche. Gastronomic delights such as chicken pommery, crab-stuffed potatoes, pasta primavera and torte rustica (flaky pastry rolled with ham, spinach and artichoke hearts) are displayed cafeteria-style, presenting a row of sheer visual delicacies. The surroundings are pure "Miami Vice," with pink ceramic palm trees, pastel placemats and white marble tabletops. Power lunchers know this is a prime place to nosh. Budget.

From the outside, **Siam Cuisine** (★) (2010 Wilton Drive, Wilton Manors; 305-564-3411) looks like little more than a roadside diner. Pity those who drive by and miss the sumptuous feast waiting inside. One of the better Thai restaurants to grace Broward County, Siam Cuisine offers sizzling fare such as *panang nua* (beef with coconut milk, curry and peanut sauce), *kanom gheeb* (steamed dumplings), *tom yum koong* (sour shrimp soup) and squid salad. Mirrored walls and only 15 wooden tables give a quaint, homey feel to the interior. Budget to moderate.

If there's ever an award for prettiest restaurant in Broward County, it should go to **Victoria Park Restaurant** (★) (900 Northeast 20th Avenue, Fort Lauderdale; 305-764-6868). The basic palette is sunrise-in-the-Caribbean—pink, white, yellow and blue; enchanting artwork underscores the concept. The food, however, is French Florida. On a typical night, the menu might list calf's liver Provençal, filet mignon in red wine, and fresh fish, either grilled or sautéed and perhaps embellished with a special spicy creole sauce. The choices are limited, but they change frequently in this upbeat setting. Seating is also limited, so reservations are advised. Dinner only. Moderate to deluxe.

Acclaimed for the best and biggest pizzas in town, **Big Louie's** (1990 East Sunrise Boulevard, Fort Lauderdale; 305-467-1166) lists 21 toppings, including Canadian bacon, fresh garlic, walnuts and spinach. Also popular are several versions of calzone, stuffed with cheeses, meats and vegetables. A wall of mirrors reflects Tiffany-style chandeliers and wooden tables trimmed in red and green in this friendly, casual pizzeria. Budget to moderate.

Croissan'Time (1201 North Federal Highway; 305-565-8555) is one of those wonderfully hidden eateries that depends on word-of-mouth advertising. Judging by the perpetual mobs, everyone's talking. The bright French café and bakery, decorated with checkerboard floors, mirrors and a handful of tiny tables, offers pâtés, quiches, french bread pizzas and croissants stuffed with meats and cheeses. For breakfast, there are gourmet omelettes and french toast; for dinner, chicken marsala and cannelloni. Desserts are the kind you can't pass up. Budget to moderate.

Now it can be told where those lovely older coffee shop waitresses get their start: as lovely younger coffee shop waitresses at **The Egg and You** (2621 North Federal Highway, Fort Lauderdale; 305-564-2045). This is a classic, where blue leatherette booths and counter stools are carefully coordinated with blue-and-tan wallpaper. The joint is jammed for weekend breakfasts because nearly everyone in town knows about the fresh ingredients and home-style cooking here. Open all day, The Egg and You serves deli-style sandwiches and homemade desserts from lunch time on. Typical dinner offerings are veal patties and dishes involving chicken or ground beef. Budget.

In all of Fort Lauderdale, **Mark 2100 Restaurant (★)** (2100 North Atlantic Boulevard; 305-566-8383) has to be one of the most difficult eateries to find. This breezy, oceanfront terrace is obscured behind several large buildings and gets no roadside advertisement. Locals love to gather here for great sunrise breakfast eats: eggs Benedict, crêpes, steak 'n eggs and warm sweet rolls. Lunch is not quite as special, offering basic fare such as chopped sirloin, club sandwiches and roast beef. The surroundings—a mix of plastic patio furniture topped by a canvas canopy—are ultra-casual. Budget.

Blue-and-white tiled floors set a fresh, seagoing tone at **Shooter's Restaurant** (3033 Northeast 32nd Avenue, Fort Lauderdale; 305-566-2855). At this extremely popular eatery, the tile leads through the indoor dining room out to the main attraction, the Intracoastal Waterway. Here several dozen umbrella-topped tables offer views of the passing flotilla of motorboats and luxury yachts. Appetizers (shrimp, nachos, fried cheese and conch fritters) by far outnumber entrées such as grilled fish, New York strip steak and pasta dishes. There is also lighter fare here, taco salads and sandwiches perfect for noshing outdoors. Budget to moderate.

One of the Fort Lauderdale area's best restaurants would seem to have two strikes against it. **By Word of Mouth (★)** (3200 Northeast 12th Avenue, Oakland Park; 305-564-3663) is very hard to find and does no advertising. But word of mouth has, indeed, worked very well. And no wonder, given the quality and variety of its California-style bistro cuisine. The setting is as fresh as the concept: ceiling fans cool the two airy rooms rimmed by windows and white lace curtains. A typical day's offerings include Key West lobster with artichokes, poblano-stuffed chicken and pasta roulade with spinach and pinenuts, to name only a few. Deluxe.

Down Under (3000 East Oakland Park Boulevard; 305-563-4123) may be Fort Lauderdale's best-known restaurant, famous for Continental cuisine in a semiformal setting facing the Intracoastal Waterway. The decor—dark wood, dimly lit—is not to my taste, but the food and service are virtually impeccable. Numerous seafood dishes include options from Maine lobster to Idaho trout to local snapper and pompano. Preparation is imaginative and consistent whether you're ordering chicken curry, beef Wellington or various veal or lamb dishes. Deluxe to ultra-deluxe.

Housed in a cavernous building at a busy intersection, **Who-Song & Larry's Restaurant and Cantina** (3100 North Federal Highway, Fort Lauderdale; 305-566-9771) is the kind of rollicking joint where everyone seems to be having a grand old time. A thoroughly south-of-the-border menu offers some twists on old standards, including lobster fajitas. Budget to moderate.

Fort Lauderdale's answer to Hawaii's most lavish restaurants, the **Mai-Kai** (3599 North Federal Highway, Fort Lauderdale; 305-563-3272) has gone one better and added an extensive garden out back, complete with walkways and waterfalls. For a romantic dinner à deux, reserve table number 185, which has a nook all its own in the gardens. Otherwise, join the fun-loving crowd inside for Peking duck, Cantonese dishes, scallops with oysters and ginger, or a variety of meats roasted in Chinese wood-burning ovens. The setting is a South Seas fantasy, complete with carved sculptures and grass skirts, but the effect is rather irresistible. Deluxe to ultra-deluxe.

FORT LAUDERDALE SHOPPING

Despite the advance of malls into seemingly every neighborhood on the Gold Coast, the best-known shopping address in Fort Lauderdale is **Las Olas Boulevard**. This tree-lined street in a residential area is home to a wide variety of stores, mostly one-of-a-kind boutiques.

Pyramid Treasures (1015 East Las Olas Boulevard; 305-525-4448) has an enchanting assortment of New Age-type goodies including crystals, special teas and an extensive stock of books on magic, self-development, the occult and creative dreaming.

Cleo (833 East Las Olas Boulevard; 305-462-7143), a mod women's boutique, draws customers such as Bianca Jagger and Jacqueline Stallone, better known as Sly's mom.

South by Southwest (831 East Las Olas Boulevard; 305-761-1196) is a visual delight. Handbags too beautiful to use and other wearable art are the mainstay. But true to its name, this boutique stocks string ties, elaborate leather belts, silver jewelry, framed southwestern artwork and fantasy sculpture like bandanna-clad coyotes howling in silence. There's even a neon cactus!

Audace (813 East Las Olas Boulevard; 305-522-7503) caters primarily to the gay man who likes his undergarments soft, clingy and pricey. T-shirts, belts and jewelry round out the accessories here.

Braided rugs, silky quilts and earthenware vessels are just some of the homespun handiworks you'll find at **Country Collection** (808 East Las Olas Boulevard; 305-462-6205). The sweet-smelling emporium also sells potpourri, candles and women's clothing.

Contemporary art lovers won't want to miss **Childers Gallery** (804 East Las Olas Boulevard; 305-463-9439), a refreshing collection of modern and post-modern oils, serigraphs and painted furniture. Particularly interesting is a chair encrusted in jewels.

One local attention-getter, **Apropos Art Gallery** (701 East Las Olas Boulevard; 305-524-2100), claims to be the country's only gallery carrying exclusively erotic art. Works here span a variety of media. You'll find paintings, sculptures and drawings as well as art by John Lennon and Pablo Picasso.

Within **The Galleria** (East Sunrise Boulevard between Ocean Boulevard and Federal Highway; 305-564-1015) are 150 shops and restaurants, anchored by several major department stores and dozens of chain outlets specializing in best sellers, polo shirts, safari clothing and imported soaps.

Sightseeing on the Gold Coast leads to some interesting finds such as the **Discovery Center Explore Store** (Discovery Center, 231 Southwest 2nd Avenue, Fort Lauderdale; 305-462-4115). A ground-floor room in this children's science museum spills over with kites, kaleidoscopes and treasures like inexpensive magnifying glasses, tops, books, games and playing cards depicting endangered species.

The Seminole Reservation in west Fort Lauderdale is home to a few shops with Indian crafts. At the **Anhinga Indian Museum and Art Gallery** (5791 South State Road 7; 305-581-0416) you'll find a large stock of clothing (much of it fringed), turquoise and silver jewelry, woven rugs, beaded dolls and potholders in traditional Seminole patchwork designs. In the same little complex, the **Flying Bird Gift Shop** (305-792-3445) sells jewelry, pottery, dolls and woven rugs.

Telephones fashioned from wooden ducks and Pepsi-Cola cans are among the odd devices displayed at the **Telephone Warehouse** (1978 East Sunrise Boulevard, Fort Lauderdale; 305-467-3600).

The 87-acre **Swap Shop Flea Market** (3291 West Sunrise Boulevard, Sunrise; 305-791-7927) is a great discount haven where more than 2000 vendors ply clothing, kitchen items, hardware, jewelry and much more.

It seems ironic that one of Broward County's biggest commercial centers was built next to its greatest natural treasure. **Sawgrass Mills** (crossroads of West Sunrise Boulevard and Flamingo Road, Sunrise; 305-846-2350), billed as the world's largest outlet mall, sprawls right on the edge of the Everglades, that fragile, mystical river of sawgrass. Opened in 1990, the retail extravaganza houses over 200 discount stores in a variety of architectural styles, including Mediterranean and Caribbean, contemporary and art deco. Many are brand-name and designer stores, including a discounted **Macy's** (305-846-8050) and the East Coast's only **Spiegel** (305-846-1276) outlet. The mall's real highlight, though, is the indoor lake filled with fake alligators and flamingos that talk.

FORT LAUDERDALE NIGHTLIFE

Riverwatch (Fort Lauderdale Marina Marriott, 1881 Southeast 17th Street; 305-463-4000) combines two restaurants with a dancefloor. Reflected in the club's glass-and-brass fixtures, patrons dance to Top-40 music provided by a disc jockey or to some of the area's most popular bands.

Broadway shows, including some performed by nationally known actors, are the main fare at the **Parker Playhouse** (707 Northeast 8th Street, Fort Lauderdale; 305-764-0700). Plan to reserve tickets well in advance.

The bars that best epitomize Fort Lauderdale's casual outdoor nightscene are clustered along the roadways flanking the Oakland Park Boulevard Bridge. Here half a dozen clubs and restaurant bars hug the Intracoastal Waterway, drawing lofty yachts that vie for prime dock space and give the area the nickname "Ego Alley."

With its stylish tropical motif and splendid dockside location, **Mombasa Bay** (3051 Northeast 32nd Avenue; 305-565-7441) is the place to kick back, Florida-style. Reggae bands play nightly except for Tuesday, which is blues night.

You'll find a super-casual crowd at **Shooters** (3033 Northeast 32nd Avenue; 305-566-2855), a popular indoor-outdoor spot with umbrella tables and dockside benches, and **Bootleggers** (3003 Northeast 32nd Avenue; 305-563-4337), another laid-back habitat where all the action centers around a swimming pool.

The topnotch house band at **September's** (2975 North Federal Highway; 305-563-4331), a fixture for several years, plays to a faithful local following that crowds the place Thursday through Saturday. The classy club, loaded with silk plants and lined with carpeted walls, caters to a crowd that's over 30. Cover on weekends.

The bi-level danceclub **Roxy** (4000 North Federal Highway; 305-565-3555) features two dancefloors and a huge wall of 30 televisions. Here you dance to a mix of current Top-40 and oldies.

The Gold Coast's newest cultural gem, **Broward Center for the Performing Arts** (624 Southwest 2nd Street, Fort Lauderdale; 305-462-0222) has an impressive lineup of Broadway plays, regional opera and drama, and Afro-Caribbean dance.

Squeeze (2 South New River Drive, Fort Lauderdale; 305-522-2068) has black walls, black lights and a new wave attitude. The music is progressive, the crowd strange but hip. Dance with someone, or even by yourself. Go ahead: Everybody else here does. Cover.

Just for laughs, check out the **Comic Strip** (1432 North Federal Highway; 305-565-8887) where well-known comedians come from as far away as New York and Los Angeles. Cover.

One of the most promising area theaters, **Brian C. Smith's Off Broadway at East 26th Street** (1444 Northeast 26th Street, Wilton Manors; 305-566-0554) stages a dependably excellent lineup of major drama and avant-garde productions in a 300-seat former film house.

Of course Fort Lauderdale would have a waterborne nightclub. **Discovery Cruises** (Port Everglades; 305-525-8400) offers a variety of evening cruises such as Salsa Night, with dancing to Latin bands. There's also the Captain's Club Gala Dinner cruise. Cover.

Jazz, reggae, rhythm-and-blues and even occasional rock-and-roll concerts are presented at the **Musician's Exchange** (729 West Sunrise Boulevard, Fort Lauderdale; 305-764-1912). This is the spot to hear both regional bands and nationally known artists in a comfortable lounge setting. Cover.

GAY SCENE Fort Lauderdale is a popular destination for gays. As more move into the area, more businesses, like those listed below, open to serve this growing segment of the visiting and resident populace. While there is no single gathering spot, certain beaches (such as the middle part of both John U. Lloyd State Beach Park in north Hollywood and Fort Lauderdale's strip), restaurants, hotels and nightclubs cater to a gay clientele.

For over a decade, **The Copa** (624 Southeast 28th Street; 305-463-1507) has been the city's most popular gay bar. Cool, clean and rambling, it features numerous rooms and a sprawling Key West-style patio bar strung with tiny lights. The extravagant entertainment runs till 6 a.m. Cover.

True to its name, **The Lodge** (211 Southwest 2nd Street; 305-525-1817) feels warm and cozy. Situated in downtown's historic district, the progressive club has wood floors and rafters, cushy chairs and couches.

Out near Route 95, **Tacky's Bar** (2509 West Broward Boulevard; 305-791-5092) caters to gay men who occasionally jam the dancefloor, dancing to the deejay's musical selection.

The classy **Pink Tails** (5460 North State Road 7; 305-730-7465) is a meeting place for lesbian women, hundreds of whom pack the place every weekend, dancing to Top-40 music on the giant dancefloor.

FORT LAUDERDALE BEACHES AND PARKS

John U. Lloyd Beach State Recreation Area (★)—As soon as we passed the guard station to this park, we could feel it was something special. A mile-long, tree-lined road leads past several beach access areas, each with its own personality. A narrow white sand beach extends 11,500 feet up to a jetty, the tip of which offers a sweeping view of the oceanfront to the south. Most beachgoers make a little nest between the high-water mark and the sea grass, which gives them a proprietary feeling that is one of the park's greatest appeals. Within these 244 acres is a self-guided nature trail meandering through a semitropical coastal hammock that takes about 45 minutes round trip. Bird life is abundant, and manatees can often be spotted in the shallows of Whiskey Creek.

Facilities: Picnic areas, restrooms, showers, barbecue grills, lifeguards, canoe rentals, concession stands; restaurants and grocery stores a short drive away; information, 305-923-2833. *Fishing:* Excellent off the jetty at the north end of the park; also try the Intracoastal Waterway. *Swimming:* Very gentle surf.

Getting there: It's located north of the intersection of Dania Beach Boulevard and North Ocean Drive.

Fort Lauderdale Beach—Many moviegoers of a certain age got their first impressions of Fort Lauderdale from the 1960 film *Where the Boys Are*, which prominently featured the glorious palm-fringed beach. The same film also started a trend among college students, who descended upon the beachfront every year for spring break. The city is discouraging these hordes, but Route A1A in Fort Lauderdale remains one of the most developed strips on the Gold Coast. Since hotel construction is limited to the inland side of the highway roughly from Las Olas Boulevard to Northeast 18th Street, most of the three-and-a half-mile beach of crushed shells and slightly coarse beige sand lies in full view. The least-crowded area is **South Beach Park** (★), located in front of the major hotels south of South Route A1A (Southeast 17th Street). It's not well-known, thus its relative peacefulness. To the north, the highrises along Galt Ocean Mile shade the narrow beach, which offers little public access anyway.

Facilities: Showers, lifeguards; restaurants and groceries across the highway. *Fishing:* Surf angling allowed when lifeguards are off-duty. *Swimming:* Terrific. *Surfing:* Occasionally good, restricted.

Getting there: Located on Route A1A. Major access street ends are Sunrise Avenue and Oakland Park Avenue.

Hugh Taylor Birch State Recreation Area—Within sight of highrise condominiums lie 180 protected acres of green trees and fresh water. The facility includes a coastal hammock, mangroves, freshwater lagoons and underground access to a pristine stretch of beach. The long, narrow park occupies an almost rectangular portion of barrier island between the Atlantic Ocean and the Intracoastal Waterway. Established in 1942, when Fort Lauderdale was still a small city, this peaceful sanctuary still offers visitors a glimpse of old Florida in its natural state.

Facilities: Picnic areas, restrooms, concession stand, nature trail, canoe rentals, exercise course; restaurants and groceries nearby; information, 305-564-4521. *Fishing:* Saltwater angling on the Intracoastal Waterway. *Swimming:* Wonderful at the beach, which is reached through a tunnel beneath Route A1A.

Getting there: At 3109 East Sunrise Boulevard, Fort Lauderdale.

North Broward County

No doubt North Broward County—particularly along the Atlantic Ocean—provides some of the most attractive scenery in the entire Fort Lauderdale area. The necklace of beach towns that extends to Palm Beach County are generally quiet and family-oriented, offering a reflective look at tropical living.

Along the north coast, towns such as tiny Lauderdale-by-the-Sea and Hillsboro Beach long ago developed to capacity and now continue to maintain and renovate what's already there. To the northwest, Coral Springs and Coconut Creek explode with new commercial centers and neighborhoods, providing housing for young professionals and a large retired population. It's here, out West, that you'll still find a few natural habitats and wonderfully dense hammocks.

We had never thought much about the lifespan of butterflies until we took the spellbinding tour at **Butterfly World** (Tradewinds Park South, 3600 West Sample Road, Coconut Creek; 305-977-4400; admission). Protected in this paradise for solar-powered flying insects, some of the 2000 specimens often survive here for as long as 14 days—twice their normal lifespan in the wild. The iridescent blue-banded eggfly, the Ecuadorian metalmark, the yellow-and-black Malay sulphur and more than 100 other types of butterflies and moths can be seen fluttering amid three acres landscaped with beautiful nectar-producing plants that are crucial to butterfly survival. Most peaceful of all is the Tropical Rain Forest, an 8000-square-foot screened structure housing specimens from all over the world. An extremely attractive gift shop sells souvenirs and dozens of items in butterfly shapes, from kites to kitchen magnets.

Pompano Beach is a small town with little in the way of formal sightseeing attractions. However, the **Pompano Harness Track** (1800 Southwest 3rd Street; 305-972-2000; admission) is the only place on the Gold Coast where you can see highly trained horses and their drivers in intense professional competition.

Perhaps the most scenic stretch of Broward County coastline lies from Deerfield Beach north to the Palm Beach County border. Here, a picturesque little town called **Hillsboro Beach** possesses a rare South Florida species: oceanfront estates. To take a peek (and that's as much as you'll ever get), drive along Route A1A north of Hillsboro Boulevard for about two miles. This thin strip of road is flanked on the west by the Intracoastal Waterway and on the east by majestic estates situated on manmade hills and shrouded by lush vegetation.

NORTH BROWARD COUNTY HOTELS

In South Florida, the word "villa" means a cluster of accommodations, not a grand estate in the Mediterranean tradition. A case in point is **Villas-by-the-Sea** (4456 El Mar Drive, Lauderdale-by-the-Sea; 305-772-3550). A total of 149 units are spread among a half-dozen buildings marching back from the beach. Every room was recently given a fresh look, with decorum that's light and contemporary: ceramic tile floors, wicker and formica furniture and modern amenities. The grounds are manicured and palmy, and feature heated swimming pools, a jacuzzi and barbecue grills. Efficiencies and large apartments available. Deluxe to ultra-deluxe.

Somewhat cozier than the average beach town motel, the **Sea Spray Inn** (4245 El Mar Drive, Lauderdale-by-the-Sea; 305-776-1311) has only six units on its two floors. This moderate-priced inn is decked out in cheerful color combinations such as yellow and white. Sparkling clean rooms all have kitchen facilities (tucked discreetly behind a partial wall) and breakfast tables. Across the street from the beach and within walking distance of shops and restaurants, the Sea Spray offers excellent value.

The decorating scheme at the **Reef Motel** (4312 El Mar Drive, Lauderdale-by-the-Sea; 305-776-1164) didn't break anybody's budget, but a few homey touches warm up these modest accommodations. This five-unit motel has a recessed patio area facing the beach and an upper-level sundeck protected from the constant ocean breezes. Efficiencies available. Moderate.

The **Pier Pointe Resort** (4324 El Mar Drive, Lauderdale-by-the-Sea; 305-776-5121) is a sleek and glossy complex, with 98 accommodations clustered in various villas. Pristine rooms are painted in pastels and carpeted in earthtones. With ceiling fans, rattan furniture and contemporary window coverings, this place evokes some of the better inns in the Caribbean. Masterful poolside landscaping and a beachfront location near the pier add up to very good value. Efficiencies available. Deluxe.

A brightly colored balcony rims the second story of **The Rainbow on the Ocean** (1231 Route A1A, Hillsboro Beach; 305-426-2525), an attractive motel fronting a narrow sand beach. The 25 units are well-kept and larger-than-average. Furniture is a hodgepodge of pseudo-French provincial and nondescript rattan. One efficiency available. Moderate to deluxe.

A cozy family resort, the beachfront **Sherwood Inn** (1460 South Ocean Boulevard, Pompano Beach; 305-941-6688) offers immaculate, contemporary-style rooms with a moderate price tag. The U-shaped motel hugs a landscaped courtyard with a pool and breezy patio bar, and houses 84 spacious rooms with white rattan furnishings, airy island prints and two queen beds. The best part is, most accommodations offer at least a peek at the ocean. A definite bargain.

In an area of interchangeable motels, **Hansel and Gretel's Tropical Guest House** (97 South Route A1A, Deerfield Beach; 305-427-4381) stands out as a congenial spot with an excellent location. The storybook motif is pretty much limited to lawn statuary in the shapes of dwarves and mushrooms, but who'd want to sleep in a gingerbread house anyway? Accommodations at this glorified motel court are quite modern, with quilted coverlets, contemporary wall art and several mirrors that give the illusion of additional space. Pool. Efficiencies available. Moderate.

Accommodations in the seven-story **Deerfield Beach Resort** (950 Southeast 20th Avenue, Deerfield Beach; 305-426-0478) are characteristic of this chain's reputation for spacious, well-appointed rooms. What's unusual here is the hotel's prime beachfront location (plus its being the only sizable facility in town). The design should win awards: rooms are well laid-out, beautifully decorated in pastels cool enough to soothe a sunburn, and furnished with comfortable beds, sofas and a slew of glass-and-brass tables. The elegant lobby and pool setting are reminiscent of better offshore resorts. Ultra-deluxe.

NORTH BROWARD COUNTY RESTAURANTS

If you fancy spectacular sunrises, don't miss the **Pier Restaurant** (Commercial Boulevard and Route A1A, Lauderdale-by-the-Sea; 305-776-1690). This no-frills coffee shop rests right on the Commercial Boulevard Pier, offering a few indoor tables and five outdoor booths suspended over the sand and peering across the ocean. The breakfast and lunch menus (no dinner) are scrawled on a rustic wooden sign. Choices are standard budget eats: bacon and eggs, pancakes, patty melts and frothy milkshakes.

The hours just prior to sundown are the most beautiful at **Sea Watch** (★) (6002 North Ocean Boulevard, Pompano Beach; 305-781-2200), one of the very few oceanfront restaurants on the Gold Coast. Hidden between condominium buildings, Sea Watch offers fabulous views of Jade Beach. You can stave off hunger pangs with seafood appetizers while you peruse a varied menu of fish, scampi, chicken and beef dishes. Rough wood and an expanse of glass add to the romantic atmosphere. Prices range from moderate to ultra-deluxe.

If you dine at only one Broward County restaurant, make it **Café Max** (2601 East Atlantic Boulevard, Pompano Beach; 305-782-0606). The little art deco gem, tucked in a strip shopping center, is widely known for its fabulous food artistry that tastes as good as it looks. Celebrated young chef Oliver Saucy, who cooks to rock-and-roll music in his open kitchen, uses the freshest ingredients to craft each day's menu. For appetizers, there might be caviar pie or "bumble bee" striped Florida lobster raviolis. For entrées, sweet onion-crusted yellowtail snapper or pistachio-crusted rack of lamb with raisin coconut couscous. Before dinner, visit the splendid wine bar. Deluxe to ultra-deluxe.

Cuban food is making inroads north of Miami these days, and one of the better places to sample it is at **La Corrida** (101 North Ocean Boulevard, Pompano Beach; 305-781-2323). Specialties include roast pork dishes (fat-free, amazingly enough), *ropa vieja* (shredded beef) and ham croquettes, but La Corrida also veers into Mexican and Spanish territory with enchiladas, burritos and a monster paella. Unfortunately, the Spanish art reproductions can't quite disguise that this was once a nondescript coffee shop. Budget to moderate.

It's easy to get lost on the way to **Cap's Place Island Restaurant and Bar** (Cap's Island off Lighthouse Point; 305-941-0418). First you have to find the right two-lane road. When that dead-ends at the water, you board a motorboat that is the sole means of transport to this unique destination. You will be following in the wake of Winston Churchill, John F. Kennedy and Marilyn Monroe, all of whom visited this local legend (though not at the same time, according to one chatty bartender). The food plays second fiddle to the rum-running, gambling-den atmosphere of this ramshackle restaurant. A highlight is stone crab, served warm or cold in season. Delicate snapper and other seafood round out a moderate-to-deluxe-priced menu that includes a sprinkling of chicken, pasta and steak dishes. Not to be missed is the salad made with fresh hearts of palm, still soft and sweet after the trip from a Lake Okeechobee palm farm. Since everything is cooked to order, you can take time to wander from room to room to view faded photographs and read old newspaper clippings about the area and the history of this one-of-a-kind gem. Call first for directions.

The Pelican Pub (2633 North Riverside Drive, Pompano Beach; 305-785-8550) would be wonderful if it were located on the Intracoastal Waterway, and not just near it. Still, it's comforting to be greeted by the sight of a fish case filled with pompano and snapper plucked from the sea that very morning. This casual, open-air restaurant casts a wide net, featuring lobster from Maine, scrod from Boston, crab from Alaska and conch from the Keys on its moderate-to-deluxe-priced menu.

The restaurant reputed to have the best French food in Deerfield Beach also has the most seats. In fact, with room for nearly 300 diners, **Brooks Restaurant** (500 South Federal Highway; 305-427-9302) seems almost too large, as the menu is better suited to an intimate setting. Still, the interior is a smooth medley of light pinks and blues, with candlelight reflected in mirrors and polished formal dining chairs. Appetizers, especially several with seafood, could constitute a meal. Among the main courses are Gulf shrimp, rack of lamb, duckling and fettucini, as well as half-a-dozen grilled meat choices. Dinner only. Deluxe to ultra-deluxe.

Formerly a hideaway casino for the cognoscenti, the **Riverview Restaurant** (1741 East Riverview Road, Deerfield Beach; 305-428-3463) has cleaned up its act. Diners in three low-ceilinged waterfront rooms can analyze a lengthy menu in the glow of miniature tabletop lighthouses. Even people who can't read in the dark will be safe with stone crabs, pompano, lobster or scallops. Or they may try "good things other than seafood," such as roast beef, veal, country ham or chicken. Artifacts from the days of illegal gambling include antique slot machines and ancient poker chips embedded into table tops. Moderate to deluxe.

NORTH BROWARD COUNTY SHOPPING

When it comes to inexpensive Florida souvenirs, an excellent source is **Bill's 5 & 10** (26 North Ocean Boulevard, Pompano Beach; 305-941-5994). If the object has oranges, palm trees or flamingos on it, you can find it at this well-stocked, old-fashioned dime store.

Instead of toting Florida fruit home with your luggage, you can have it shipped for you by **Dickinson's of Oceanside** (38 North Ocean Boulevard, Pompano Beach; 305-941-4219). In addition to fresh oranges and grapefruit, Dickinson's sells candied fruit, hand-dipped chocolates and small gift items such as coral and shell jewelry.

NORTH BROWARD COUNTY NIGHTLIFE

Reminiscent of a cozy, northern-style bar, **Raindancer** (3031 East Commercial Boulevard, Lauderdale-by-the-Sea; 305-772-0337) is adorned in dark woods and set off by a fireplace that never stops roaring. The recorded jazz and folk tunes and friendly bartender only add to the romance of this unexpected spot.

An overdose of hormones abounds at **Confetti** (2660 East Commercial Boulevard, Lauderdale-by-the-Sea; 305-776-4080), a sleek Top-40 dance establishment with a large dancefloor, colorful swirling lights and a dressed up, early-20s crowd. Cover.

Fisherman's Wharf Lounge (222 North Pompano Beach Boulevard, Pompano Beach; 305-941-5522) is one of those places where you can kick back under the stars. The beachfront patio stages live reggae and rock, and draws a curious mix of people.

Cool breezes flow with live mellow rock and Jamaican steel drum music at **The Cove** (1755 Southeast 3rd Court, Deerfield Beach; 305-421-9272), a casual but classy bar and restaurant perched along the Intracoastal Waterway.

NORTH BROWARD COUNTY BEACHES AND PARKS

Easterlin Park—Peacocks pose and strut in the shade of Royal Palms and pine trees, vying with squirrels and rabbits for handouts. This lovely grove, which includes 250-year-old cypress trees as well as ferns and wild coffee plants, is a family park with low-key facilities such as a playground, volleyball and shuffleboard courts and a small kidney-shaped lake. Pleasant, though not spectacular.

Facilities: Picnic areas, restroom, showers, nature trail; restaurants and grocery stores nearby; information, 305-938-0610.

Camping: There are 55 sites, 45 with RV hookups; $17 per night.

Getting there: At 1000 Northwest 38th Street, Oakland Park.

Markham Park—Sprawling over 665 acres west of Fort Lauderdale, Markham Park probably offers more recreational diversity than any other public facility on the Gold Coast. Trees and picnic shelters and canoe rides and greenswards offer relief from the heat. In cooler weather, there's plenty of room for kite flying and football. To the east is a model-airplane field, and to the north two target ranges. In short, something for just about everyone.

Facilities: Picnic areas, restrooms, showers, boat ramp, concession stand, volleyball courts, observatory tower; information, 305-389-2000. *Fishing:* License required for freshwater angling in a lake and a lagoon.

Camping: There are 86 sites, eight with RV hookups; $17 per night.

Getting there: Located at 16001 West State Road 84 in Sunrise.

Lauderdale-by-the-Sea Beach—Less glamorous than its namesake to the south, this is more of a community beach. The shoreline stretches about one mile in front of motels and private residences. Fringed by palm trees, the sand is the same coarse mixture as that on Fort Lauderdale Beach.

Facilities: Showers; restaurants and groceries nearby. *Fishing:* Very good off Anglin's Pier. *Swimming:* Excellent. *Surfing:* Fair, north of the pier.

Getting there: Located between Flamingo and Pine avenues off Route A1A.

Pompano Beach—Another segment of the beach that extends nearly the entire length of Broward County, Pompano has 3000 feet of coarse sand on which to romp. It lacks some of the allure of Fort Lauderdale Beach because most of it is obscured by concrete buildings between the ocean and Route A1A. The pier has been extended to more than 1000 feet, making it the longest one on the Gold Coast.

Facilities: Picnic areas, restrooms, showers, lifeguards, concession stand; groceries and restaurants nearby. *Fishing:* Excellent off the pier. *Swimming:* Very good.

Getting there: The beach is located in Pompano Beach off Route A1A between Southeast 14th Street and the Hillsboro Inlet, with numerous access points.

Quiet Waters Park—The lake waters in this 427-acre park are indeed quiet, even though water skiing is allowed. That's because no power boats are involved; skiers are towed around the lake via cable. Bike paths and wide paved roads give this park an open feel. It is quite popular with families, especially on weekends and holidays.

Facilities: Picnic areas, restrooms, playground, lifeguards, concession stand, miniature golf, boat rental, bike rental, waterskiing; restaurants and grocery stores are nearby; information, 305-360-1315. *Fishing:* Bass, bream and catfish angling allowed everywhere except in the swimming and waterskiing areas. *Swimming:* In designated lake areas.

Camping: There are 23 sites; $16 per night.

Getting there: Located at 6601 North Powerline Road in Pompano Beach.

Deerfield Beach—This 5700-foot undeveloped beach is one of the few places on the Gold Coast where shells can be collected. The sand is soft and deep and studded with boulders at the low-water mark. The southern part is more serene than the other sections, though farther away from shops and restaurants.

Facilities: Picnic areas, restrooms, showers, lifeguards, pier; restaurants and groceries nearby. *Fishing:* Surf angling. *Swimming:* Best at North Beach.

Getting there: Located in Deerfield Beach between Southeast 10th Street and Northeast 4th Street off Route A1A.

Deerfield Island Park (★)—Accessible only by water, this 55-acre park is a remarkable wilderness area with two fascinating trails. Mangrove

Trail is a 1500-foot raised boardwalk leading through eight acres of red, white and black mangroves, a stunning swamp where light trickles through the leaves and shorebirds can be seen cruising above the Royal Palm Waterway and the Hillsboro Canal. On the other side of the island, Coquina Trail proceeds toward the Intracoastal Waterway, where there is a rocky overlook. Keep an eye out for grey fox, raccoons and armadillos. Allow at least two hours to enjoy this unique wonderland.

Facilities: Picnic areas, restrooms; information, 305-360-1320.

Getting there: Access is by private boat or via the free boat transportation provided Wednesday and Saturday mornings from the dock on Riverview Road, Deerfield Beach.

Boca Raton and Delray Beach

Driving north on Route A1A from Deerfield Beach into Boca Raton—and from Broward County into Palm Beach County—lends credence to the adage that "the grass is always greener on the other side." A sense of order, of serenity, of the wherewithal to hire full-time gardeners is unmistakable as one crosses the county line. The well-kept condominiums one hasn't seen since Hallandale appear once again, this time with bright green manicured lawns.

Boca Raton has become a tidy, extremely well-to-do community that attracts large numbers of retirees and golfers as well as an increasing abundance of high-technology companies. It is the site of the liveliest restaurant and nightlife activity in Palm Beach County. Delray Beach is a well-preserved oceanfront enclave for people who can afford Palm Beach prices but eschew the social requirements.

The bustle that characterizes the areas to the south is largely absent here; serenity has been preserved—or established—in a number of places. The **Gumbo-Limbo Nature Center** (1801 North Ocean Boulevard, Boca Raton; 407-338-1473), for example, has been set up to protect the area's West Indian hardwood hammocks. The free educational facility, run by the county school system, features an ocean research center, biology lab, and naturalist exhibits that allow visitors to touch the skin of a snake or the pelts of small animals. Four saltwater aquariums, scheduled to open in late 1992, will showcase brilliant fish, stingrays, crabs, shrimp and other ocean wonders. Visitors can poke their hand into one tank and pet a live conch, sea urchin or horseshoe crab. From here, a wide boardwalk leads through a shady glen to an observation tower where you can scan much of the 67-acre park as well as the beach nearby.

Part of the fun of touring Boca Raton is the chance to look at the Spanish influence in architecture that distinguishes many homes as well as shopping centers. Stop by the **Historical Society** (71 North Federal Highway; 407-395-6766) to pick up their brochure highlighting the town's historic buildings.

Boca Raton's first museum also boasts the most endearing name: the **Singing Pines Children's Museum** (498 Crawford Boulevard; 407-368-6875; admission). Tucked away behind city hall, it was named for the sound made by pine trees blowing in the breeze. The house itself, said to be the oldest unaltered woodframe building in the city, is as interesting as the exhibits inside. A "Florida cracker cottage" constructed, in part, of Dade County pine floors and timber found on the beach, it was moved in 1976 to its present hideaway location. The museum focuses on Victoriana and pioneer Florida memorabilia, including a kitchen equipped with an ancient stove, a vintage Singer sewing machine and an old-fashioned telephone. Creative exhibits for children include marvelous antique toys and other displays.

The **Boca Raton Museum of Art** (801 West Palmetto Park Road, Boca Raton; 407-392-2500) has three galleries displaying the permanent collection of late 19th and early 20th century works by such artists as Picasso, Degas and Matisse. Temporary exhibits range from one-person shows of oil paintings to collections of photography to annual presentations of African artworks.

In recent years, Palm Beach County and polo have become inextricably linked. The winter season lasts from January through April at the **Royal Palm Polo Sports Club** (6300 Old Clint Moore Road, Boca Raton; 407-994-1876; admission). Polo is a difficult game to grasp, what with thundering hooves and swinging mallets. But the game's speed and complicated rules make this a fascinating sport to watch, and a rewarding one to master.

As you follow Route A1A out of Boca Raton toward Delray Beach, the ocean disappears behind trimmed hedges that border beachfront mansions one can only imagine visiting. **Delray Beach** is a vital town, with a real "Main Street" (Atlantic Avenue) and a sense of life-beyond-tourism.

One of the most appealing sites to visit is located nearly an hour from the beach. An atmosphere of peace envelops the **Morikami Museum and Japanese Gardens** (4000 Morikami Park Road, Delray Beach; 407-495-0233). The centerpiece of this 200-acre pine forest preserve is the museum, which is devoted to the Japanese folk arts and stands in tribute to the Japanese Yamato colony that existed here early in this century. On the grounds is a two-acre garden, done in the Japanese style with a koi pond and a bonsai garden in the back. The museum houses a Shinto sanctuary, its harmonious proportions typical of 16th- and 17th-century architecture. There are displays on Japanese baths and tea ceremonies and hands-on exhibits of obi tying, origami and musical instruments.

BOCA RATON AND DELRAY BEACH HOTELS

The ambience at **The Bridge Hotel** (999 East Camino Real, Boca Raton; 407-368-9500) evokes the serenity of the unruffled 1950s. The style and decor of the 121 accommodations is in keeping, with a contemporary palette of pastel colors throughout the rooms. Private balconies, especially on the upper floors, offer stupendous views of the Intracoastal Waterway. Health spa and pool. Ultra-deluxe.

One of the most famous, most beautiful and—at the time it was constructed—most expensive hotels on the Gold Coast is the **Boca Raton Resort and Club** (501 East Camino Real, Boca Raton; 407-395-3000). Designed in 1926 as the Cloister Inn by eccentric architect Addison Mizner, the property today has become an extensive world-class resort. The original hotel, which exudes Old World charm, has been expanded to 327 rooms, all exquisitely decorated with floral print fabrics and lustrous mahogany furniture. Another 775 accommodations have been added; they range from golf villas to contemporary hotel rooms in a 27-story tower and in the nearby, more casual Beach Club. The hotel, located on the Intracoastal Waterway, has a full-service marina. Golf, tennis, restaurants, pools. Ultra-deluxe.

You could bounce a quarter off the neat-as-a-pin beds at the **Shore Edge Motel** (425 North Route A1A, Boca Raton; 407-395-4491), a low-slung structure surrounding a little pool and manicured courtyard. Rooms are on the small side, though chrome-framed artwork and attractive patterned curtains add a fillip of freshness. Spanking clean bathrooms are tiled in festive south Florida colors such as aqua and pink. A few dollars more nets a large efficiency unit, with a separate dining area. Moderate to deluxe.

An impressive colonial facade distinguishes **Wright-by-the-Sea** (1901 South Ocean Boulevard, Delray Beach; 407-278-3355), one of the more agreeable oceanfront inns in southern Palm Beach County. Within, 28 sizable units are arranged in two two-story structures facing a neatly landscaped lawn that has a heated pool as its centerpiece. Ultra-deluxe-priced studios as well as one- and two-bedroom apartments have full kitchens and plenty of windows for cross-ventilation. Typical decor includes elegant window valances and high-quality cane furniture that underscores the residential tone. Croquet and shuffleboard courts.

Royal palms soar to the second story of the 15-unit **Huntingdon Resort** (82 Gleason Street, Delray Beach; 407-278-1700). Moderate-to-deluxe-priced one-bedroom accommodations are vast affairs, with all-electric kitchens and fairly attractive furnishings, though nothing matches. One block from the beach. Small, budget-priced efficiencies available. Pool.

The **Seagate Hotel and Beach Club** (400 South Ocean Boulevard, Delray Beach; 407-276-2421) is a nice combination of motel and resort with an excellent location midway between Fort Lauderdale and Palm Beach. Two buildings house 70 accommodations that face either a garden or one of two pools. A typical room has peach-colored furnishings with blue accents in the floral chintz upholstery, ceiling fans and wall-to-wall carpeting. Beach club with private beach. Efficiencies available. Ultra-deluxe.

One of the prettiest seaside inns on the central Gold Coast is **Dover House** (110 South Ocean Boulevard, Delray Beach; 407-276-0309). In the off season, rates begin in the moderate range but skyrocket to ultra-deluxe in the winter. Accommodations are spacious, sporting attractive wallpaper, contemporary furnishings, ceiling fans and full kitchens. Dover House comprises 41 units spread over two floors in three buildings, all sporting snappy awning-shaded, furnished semi-private balconies.

Pastel colors, ceiling fans and blond furniture suit the oceanview location of the **Bermuda Inn** (64 South Ocean Boulevard, Delray Beach; 407-276-5288). Wall-to-wall carpeting and a dining table compensate for the small size of the accommodations at this two-story motel across the street from a public beach. Pool. Efficiencies available. Moderate to deluxe.

BOCA RATON AND DELRAY BEACH RESTAURANTS

Top of the Bridge (Bridge Hotel, 999 East Camino Real, Boca Raton; 407-368-9500) is the kind of standby supported by locals and tourists alike. Adorned in a classic color scheme of forest green and salmon and furnished with sturdy club chairs and high-backed banquettes, the huge room manages to be interesting but not stimulating. So it is with the menu, a collection of local seafood, veal, beef, lobster and pasta dishes. It's a comforting choice for people who can afford to pay deluxe to ultra-deluxe prices and are not in the mood to sample exotic culinary trends, thank you very much.

The Morada Bar and Grill (5100 Town Center Circle, Suite 100, in the Crocker Center, Boca Raton; 407-395-0805) features cuisine so contemporary it's almost avant-garde, especially for southeastern Florida. Lobster tortellini, duck ravioli, grilled salmon and even chicken and filet mignon receive imaginative, distinctive treatment. The dining room is a place of dazzling beauty, with glossy teakwood tables, brass railings, balconies draped with plants and glass walls that soar two stories high. Bypassers can witness the kitchen wizardry through another glass wall that fronts the mall. Moderate to deluxe.

Certain restaurants tend to show up on everyone's Top Ten list. A case in point is **La Vielle Maison** (770 East Palmetto Park Road, Boca Raton; 407-391-6701). The people who founded this restaurant used a formula they developed in Fort Lauderdale: an old house, lots of antiques, dark floral carpeting and an expensive menu devoted almost exclusively to continental cuisine. La Vielle Maison features an eye-catching entrance through wrought-iron gates and a jungle of a garden. Florida seafood gets French treatment in dishes such as pompano aux pecans and a terrine of local lobster. Other specials include quail, lamb, veal and venison. Dining is a leisurely affair here, and the earlier of two nightly seatings is recommended. Deluxe to ultra-deluxe.

It's cash only at **Tom's Place** (7251 North Federal Highway, Boca Raton; 407-997-0920), a local favorite secure in its niche as the king of the barbecue hill. This is no place to linger; you come here when you want good food and you want it fast. There's beef stew, fried chicken, generous "fixin's" and, of course, ribs, chicken and pork swimming in a legendary secret sauce. Budget to moderate.

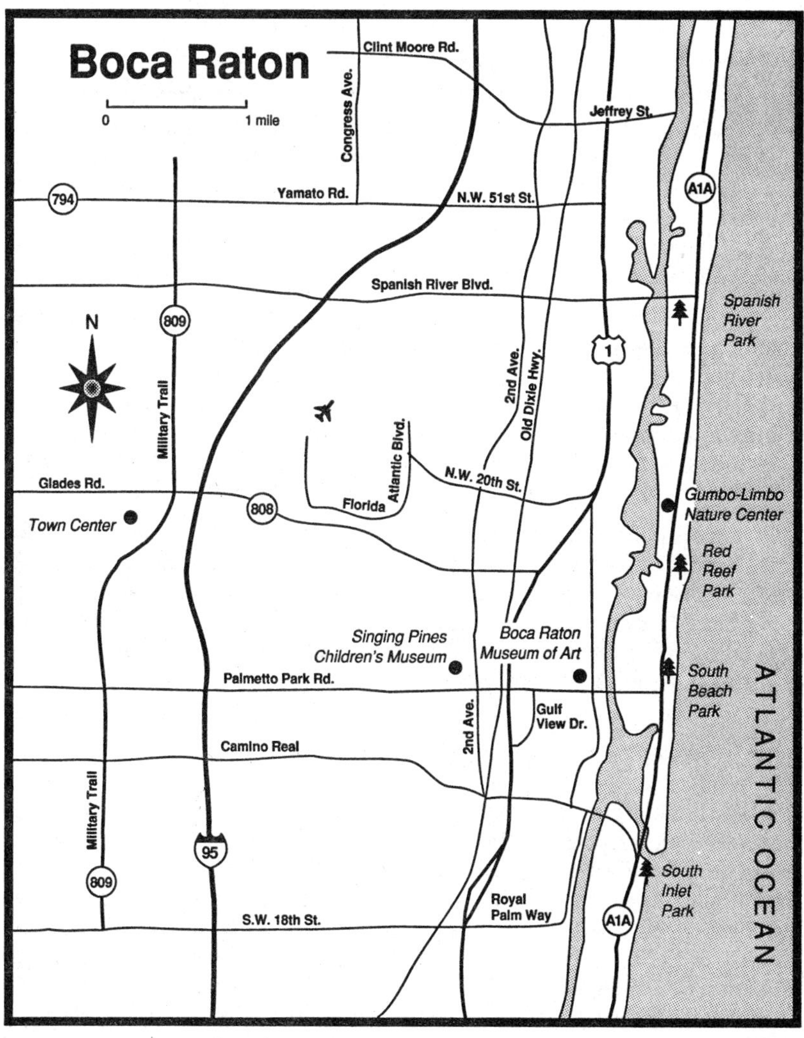

They named this tiny roadside eatery **Basil Garden** (5837 North Federal Highway, Boca Raton; 407-994-2554), but the place is so redolent of garlic they should call it the "stinking rose" garden. Yet this is the kind of restaurant to which patrons return time and again for seafood and such Italian dishes as pasta and veal specialties including saltimbocca and osso bucco. Prices are moderate to deluxe at this warm, neighborhood ristorante.

The **Seafood Connection Restaurant** (6998 North Federal Highway, Boca Raton; 407-997-5562) is where locals come when they want to eat well in an attractive setting without breaking the family budget. Lots of plants, ceiling fans and rattan light fixtures enliven two separate dining rooms. Dozens of kinds of seafood are prepared in many ways, from unusual combination platters to more elegant dishes such as salmon Wellington. Budget to moderate.

For food and service that's superbly orchestrated, **Roberto** (402 Plaza Real, Mizner Park, Boca Raton; 407-276-4411) is difficult to surpass. Outstanding veal chops, rack of lamb and salmon headline the Continental prix-fixe menu, but the restaurant is known for its Wisconsin duck accented with *cassis*. Lovely tapestries, painted fans and ornate mirrors provide a sophisticated ambience. Deluxe to ultra-deluxe.

Displaced Bostonians aren't the only travelers who'll feel at ease at **Boston's on the Beach** (40 South Route A1A, Delray Beach; 407-278-3364). There's an anything-goes atmosphere at this beach town eatery just across the highway from the surf. Go for a table on the covered porch, as indoor seating is nothing special. Hot entrées include sole, shrimp, oysters and a Massachusetts "clambake dinner" starring the requisite lobster, clams, clam chowder and corn on the cob. Moderate to ultra-deluxe.

A shining example of the casual dockside hangout, the convivial **Banana Boat Restaurant** (739 East Ocean Avenue, Boynton Beach; 407-732-9400) has a wooden deck with tables so close to the water that diners can recognize friends cruising the Intracoastal Waterway. The food is good and the setting ideal for a late lunch or hot entrées such as fresh fish, shrimp or teriyaki steak. Moderate.

BOCA RATON AND DELRAY BEACH SHOPPING

The bubble-gum pink facade and red tile roofs of the **Royal Palm Plaza** make this landmark Boca Raton shopping center easy to spot from Route 1. Located between Palmetto Park Road and Camino Real, shops such as **Royal Palm Antiques** (407-391-8780) are familiar to regular customers seeking chandeliers, serious furniture and large objets d'art with an Oriental flavor. **Heidi's** (407-391-5454) is the place for cocktail party fashions. **Maus & Hoffman** (407-368-9983), a branch of the well-known menswear shop, features a large selection of suits, sportshirts, shoes, ties (many by Hermès) and lightweight hats ideal for the Gold Coast climate.

This Spanish-style plaza also houses gift boutiques such as the **Crystal Bowl** (407-391-3678), filled to the brim with decanters, vases, bowls and candlesticks. For dozens, if not hundreds, of brand-name fragrances, follow your nose to **Gay's Perfumerie** (407-391-8099), which stocks classics as well as plenty of perfumes and colognes for experimenting.

Just north of Royal Palm Plaza is the city's newest shopping gem. Fashioned like a little Mediterranean village, **Mizner Park** (Route 1, two blocks north of Palmetto Park Road; 407-362-0606) is a delightful place. Here you'll find palm-lined stone streets, fountains and tiny pools, as well as peach sandstone buildings decorated with curved balconies, vivid awnings and dozens of clever shops and eateries. There's everything from jewelry stores and high-fashion swimwear to an Israeli art gallery and a terrific gourmet mart. But even if you don't buy, strolling here is sheer entertainment. Two notable stores are **Swim 'n' Sport** (407-391-3990), featuring contemporary swimwear and **Christy Taylor Gallery** (407-750-7302), carrying delicate blown-glass sculptures of modern design.

The **Town Center at Boca Raton** (6000 West Glades Road; 407-368-6000) is home to a variety of fine shops as well as chain stores. The people who turn out collectibles they call "tomorrow's heirlooms" have a retail outlet at **The Franklin Mint Gallery** (407-392-4144). In this jewelry-store setting you will find an array of specialty items such as sterling silver jewelry, wildlife prints, porcelain figurines and Rolls Royce models.

Town Center is also the locale for **Maraolo** (407-391-7001), purveyors of elegant shoes and glamorous accessories in leather and exotic fabrics. **Bentley's Luggage** (407-395-2380) stocks national-brand suitcases as well as leather goods, travel accessories and gift items. Up-to-the-minute fashions for the younger man are the stock-in-trade at **Attivo** (407-395-4240). Town Center also has a place in its heart for larger-size women's fashions: **August Max** (407-392-7494) has casual clothes as well as career ensembles.

Browsing the handful of shops at **Crocker Center** (5050 Town Center Circle, Boca Raton) provides a pleasant change from shopping in a full-scale mall. Decorating your home? Stop in **Lois Collection** (407-750-1288) and scan the murals, silk flower arrangements, wood furnishings and china.

The local branch of Maine's **Snappy Turtle of Kennebunkport** (1038 East Atlantic Avenue, Delray Beach; 407-276-8088) brims with clever clothes and accessories for women and children. In downtown Delray Beach, **Penelope's Breads and Threads** (520 East Atlantic Avenue; 407-272-1000) is a one-of-a-kind mix of handicrafts (mostly woven) and fresh-from-the-oven baked goods.

Located at the intersection of South Ocean Boulevard and Ocean Avenue in Manalapan, the **Plaza del Mar Shopping Center** looks like a bit of Cape Cod with its low-rise, gray-shingled facade. One of the best shops here is **Straw and Substance** (407-585-3311). Distinctive gift items include offbeat walking canes (some topped with duck heads, etc.), crystal objets d'art and potpourri. **Rhoda's Gentlemen's Apparel** (407-585-7378) stocks menswear ranging from bathrobes and hats to sportshirts and fashions fit for an evening out in Palm Beach.

BOCA RATON NIGHTLIFE

Atop a six-story hotel, the **Top of the Bridge Lounge** (999 Camino Real, Boca Raton; 407-368-9500) offers romantic views of the Intracoastal Waterway. A four-piece band plays big band standards on weekends.

Wildflower (551 East Palmetto Park Road; 407-391-0000), like many clubs in Boca Raton, is a combination restaurant and lounge. Odd-shaped windows, papier-mâché tropical birds and disco lights add to the confusion in this Spanish-style two-story building. Satellite bars upstairs offer views of patrons dancing below to Top-40 music.

Club Boca (7000 West Palmetto Park Road, Boca Raton; 407-368-3333) is a high-decibel nightclub with a central bar and a dancefloor in back. A big hit with young urban professionals, it offers patio seating in the rear for cooling off between the latest progressive dance music. Cover.

Zelda's (705 West Palmetto Park Road, Boca Raton; 407-391-6601) is reminiscent of a European café. Featuring live Brazilian jazz, Zelda's is open until 5 a.m.

A large replica of a three-masted schooner makes an unusual centerpiece at the **Bounty Lounge** (Holiday Inn, 1950 Glades Road, Boca Raton; 407-368-5200). Few people over 40 seem to venture here for dancing to first-rate Top-40 bands that perform in front of a huge video screen. A second-floor balcony bar provides a safe retreat if the music gets too intense. Cover.

Broadway reproductions, occasionally with guest stars, are the main fare at the **Royal Palm Dinner Theatre** (303 Southeast Mizner Boulevard, Boca Raton; 407-392-3755).

The **Caldwell Theatre Company** (7873 North Federal Highway, Boca Raton; 407-241-7432) offers a mix of popular comedy and dramatic stage productions during their summer and winter seasons.

BOCA RATON AND DELRAY BEACH BEACHES AND PARKS

South Inlet Park (★)—The least-known beach in Boca Raton, South Inlet Park has 850 feet of soft clean sand. Since it is so small, it is often less crowded than its neighbors to the north and is an especially good choice on weekdays.

Facilities: Picnic areas, restrooms, showers, lifeguards, pier; information, 407-964-4420; restaurants and groceries a short drive away. *Fishing:* Surf angling. *Swimming:* Very good.

Getting there: Located off South Route A1A, at 1298 South Ocean Boulevard, directly south of Boca Inlet.

South Beach Park—The dense tropical growth that characterizes Boca Raton's sand dunes is one of South Beach's greatest charms. In fact, one almost despairs of finding the beach at all, but rest assured, it lies on the other side, accessible via three walkways. This pristine—if rather narrow—swath of semicoarse sand disappears beyond curve after curve of coastline.

Facilities: Restrooms, showers, lifeguards; restaurants and groceries a short drive away. *Swimming:* Good. *Snorkeling:* Fair.

Getting there: Located at 400 North State Road A1A, Boca Raton.

Red Reef Park—Touted as a local favorite, the developed beach at Red Reef Park is nearly a mile long. A very long boardwalk leads through a veritable forest of sea grapes, palmettos, Australian pine and palm trees before descending to the pristine beach itself, which is composed of pale, loosely packed sand. Red Reef Park, roughly 80 acres in size, straddles Route A1A and extends all the way to the Intracoastal Waterway. On the inland side is a nature center and another boardwalk, a wonderful place to spot the wide variety of small birds that make their homes in the lush foliage.

Facilities: Picnic areas, restrooms, showers, lifeguards, golf course; restaurants and grocery stores a short drive away; information, 407-393-7974. *Fishing*: Excellent surf angling in designated areas. *Swimming:* Very good. *Snorkeling:* Good in spots.

Getting there: Located at 1400 North State Road A1A, Boca Raton.

Spanish River Park—This is really Boca Raton's crowning glory, offering forest shade, sunswept beach and more facilities than any other local park. Perhaps there is a well-enforced city ordinance declaring that all Boca beaches be kept sparkling clean; that would explain the almost primitive look of this wide, oyster-shell-white apron of sand. Within the 93-acre park are dozens of spots for picnicking, including a sheltered area on a lagoon off the Intracoastal Waterway. It's worth climbing the 72 steps to the top of an observation tower for the marvelous view of the park, ocean and city.

Facilities: Picnic areas, restrooms, showers, lifeguards, boat lagoon, playground, nature trail, bicycle trails; information, 407-393-7810. *Fishing:* On the Intracoastal Waterway. *Swimming:* Excellent on the beach.

Getting there: Located at 3001 North State Road A1A, Boca Raton.

Atlantic Dunes Park (★)—Only the eagle-eyed traveler will spot the sign for Atlantic Dunes Park on the first pass. The entrance is nearly invisible, thanks to stands of Australian pines. The soft pale sand beach is so small—the park is only seven acres in all—that it has almost a clubby feel. The beach is fairly narrow and the waves do not break right for bodysurfing, but it's wonderful for strolling and sunbathing away from urban development.

Facilities: Picnic areas, restrooms, showers, lifeguard. *Swimming:* Fair.

Getting there: Located off South Route A1A, one mile south of Delray Municipal Beach across from Azalea Avenue.

Delray Municipal Beach—Some 7000 feet of very soft light-brown sand fronts the city of Delray Beach. There's something irresistible about a beautiful beach, strewn with shells, that's easy to find, easy to reach and easy to love. Low dunes covered with sea grapes are interspersed with foot paths leading down from the parking area. On crystal-clear days, the Gulf Stream, less than five miles offshore, is visible as a strip of darker blue, often with some wave action to distinguish it.

Facilities: Restrooms, showers, lifeguards, concession stands for cabanas and umbrellas; restaurants and groceries nearby. *Swimming:* Outstanding; also good bodysurfing.

Getting there: Located on Route A1A, with numerous access points from Casuarina Road up to Vista del Mar.

Gulf Stream County Park—Since beach access is highly restricted in the posh enclave of Gulf Stream, it's especially satisfying to find this little gem. It's a public park that looks like a private resort landscaped with palmettos, Australian pines and tall sea grapes. A long boardwalk leads to a 600-foot ribbon of white sand. The sole drawback to this beach is some rocks that are submerged at high tide.

Facilities: Picnic areas, restrooms, showers, lifeguard; restaurants and groceries nearby. *Swimming:* Good at low tide.

Getting there: At 4489 North Ocean Boulevard south of Briny Breezes.

Boynton Public Beach—A 1000-foot wooden boardwalk extends the length of the beautifully landscaped park fronting Boynton Beach. From there, dune walkovers lead to a narrow beach, where medium-hard sand slopes deeply to the water's edge. Parking is at a premium so early—or late—arrival is recommended.

Facilities: Picnic areas, restrooms, showers, concession stands; restaurants and grocery stores a short drive away. *Swimming:* Good.

Getting there: Off Route A1A two miles north of Route 804.

Lantana Municipal Beach—Distinguished by abundant shrubbery, including sea grapes as high as palm trees, the approach to Lantana Beach is as attractive as the beach itself. Several boardwalks lead over tall sand dunes to a 746-foot-long strip of dark sand that narrows to as little as ten feet at high tide. Accordingly, the beach has a secluded feel with none of the grandeur of wider, more open stretches of coastline.

Facilities: Picnic areas, restrooms, showers, lifeguards; restaurants and grocery stores a short drive away. *Swimming:* Good. *Surfing:* Fair.

Getting there: Located at Ocean Avenue and Route A1A, Lantana.

Palm Beach and West Palm Beach

Palm Beach is a town imbued with sheer extravagance and social formalities—daily spa treatments, elegant balls, winsome polo matches—not to mention a certain magic that emanates from all this prosperity. By contrast, West Palm Beach exists as the area's major metropolitan center, a stretch of flat, tropical earth with a sizable downtown area and sprawling residential developments.

Downtown West Palm Beach has two completely different faces. Skirting its eastern boundary is Flagler Street, a three-mile strip of picturesque roadways flanked by rows of massive palm trees and estates. But on the west side of town lies a poorer economic stratum and buildings in need of repair. Around the city are breezy tropical neighborhoods inhabited largely by young professionals who are renovating older homes, as well as retirement centers for wealthy northeasterners.

Lying in the southern shadow of these two communities is Lake Worth, a turn-of-the-century town situated around a beautiful lake. Its historic beachfront is a hot spot for locals and tourists alike.

Unlike southern Miami and Fort Lauderdale, the West Palm Beach area virtually shuts down during the summer months. Hotels offer rates that are 50 to 70 percent off winter prices, and many restaurants and shops close completely. That means the beaches are less crowded (yes, you might even find yourself alone on a long stretch of sand) and the universal mood is quite placid.

As visitors approach the city of Palm Beach, they usually keep an eye out for the **elegant homes** the town is noted for. Along Route A1A south of the city, many mansions are hidden behind tall hedges and looming walls. You'll have better luck in two other places: the blocks between Route A1A and Lake Worth (the Intracoastal Waterway) south of town, and along Ocean Boulevard north of the Breakers Hotel.

No visit to Palm Beach is complete without at least a window-shopping stroll down **Worth Avenue,** which runs from the ocean inland for several blocks of merchandising paradise. Of particular interest are the small "vias" tucked away beyond archways leading from Worth Avenue into tiny courtyards lined with fine boutiques and chic restaurants.

The **Church of Bethesda By the Sea** (★) (141 South County Road at Barton Avenue, Palm Beach; 407-655-4554) makes for a refreshing pause between more intense sightseeing stops. The walls of the clerestory have stained-glass windows representing the saints of various Christian countries such as St. George of England and St. Joan of France. Hidden behind the church, beyond the flagstone courtyard, is a lovely formal setting known as **Cluett Gardens.** Fountains, benches and unusual botanical species combine with a tiled pond to create a serene retreat.

The **Society of Four Arts Garden** (off Royal Palm Way one block east of the Intracoastal Waterway, Palm Beach; 407-655-7226) is a beautifully kept landscape with high walls, decorative fencing and myriad details such as a lichen-covered stone bench. Tiny walkways lead past ponds filled with gold fish to clusters of trees and flowering shrubs and, finally, to an expansive lawned area. Here in the **Philip Hulitar Sculpture Garden** stands a variety of outdoor pieces, ranging from some classic animal forms to whimsical items such as a six-foot-tall curve of black steel sculpted to form a question mark and bearing a humorous inscription.

The **Palm Beach Chamber of Commerce** (45 Cocoanut Row; 407-655-3282), the **Chamber of Commerce of West Palm Beach** (401 North Flagler Drive, West Palm Beach; 407-833-3711) and the **Palm Beach County Convention and Visitors Bureau** (1555 Palm Beach Lakes Boulevard, West Palm Beach; 407-471-3995) can each provide additional sightseeing information.

Also in Palm Beach are some very unusual points of interest. The **Hibel Museum of Art** (150 Royal Poinciana Plaza, Palm Beach; 407-833-6870) is a love-it-or-hate-it kind of place devoted to the works of Edna Hibel. As such, it claims to be the only nonprofit art museum in the United States consisting solely of the works of a living female artist. There are ten rooms of paintings, lithographs and drawings, all lovingly displayed in good light. The guides here will tell you all you ever wanted to know, perhaps even more, about Edna Hibel.

For an instructive lesson on how to spend lots of money, and spend it well, visit the **Henry M. Flagler Museum** (Cocoanut Row and Whitehall Way, Palm Beach; 407-655-0868; admission). Commanding a close-up view of Lake Worth (the Intracoastal Waterway), Whitehall was built in 1901 by Flagler, the king of the Florida East Coast Railroad and the man credited with putting Palm Beach on the map. The 55-room mansion is a monument to the Gilded Age: period rooms, vast collections of porcelains, paintings and silver. There is so much to see that it's advisable to sign up with a tour guide who knows which furniture actually belonged to Flagler and which decorative pieces were added later. Allow time to tour The Rambler, the rail car that Flagler himself used. Built in 1886, it was restored with carefully reproduced carpeting, upholstery and window coverings. Looking at the papered ceiling, inlaid wood, tulip chandeliers and brass flourishes, one wonders if things get any better than this on the Orient Express.

West Palm Beach is a hodgepodge of one-way streets and resuscitated downtown neighborhoods. But there are some gems for the determined visitor. Especially in light of its relatively small size, the **Norton Gallery of Art** (1451 South Olive Avenue, West Palm Beach; 407-832-5194) has an extraordinarily impressive collection. Buddhist sculptures, jade carvings and ceramics can be found in the Chinese collection, paintings by Bonnard, Picasso, Dufy, Monet, Pissarro, Gauguin and Renoir in the French section. The Norton is famed for its 20th-century American art holdings as well.

Far west of the glittering arcades of Palm Beach lies another manmade wonder, the 500-acre wildlife enclave at **Lion Country Safari** (Lion Country Road off Route 80, West Palm Beach; 407-793-1084; admission). Here, some 63 species of animals roam almost free, while humans, caged in their automobiles with windows rolled up for security, tour the park on paved roads. When Lion Country Safari opened in 1967, it was the first attempt at "cageless zoos" in the United States. While it is a far cry from the Serengeti Plain in Africa, the park is unsurpassed in affording Florida travelers a chance to go eyeball to eyeball with exotic animals—lions, zebras, ostriches, elephants—which they can photograph in a seminatural setting. The attraction also offers a petting zoo, featuring both domestic species and a variety of animals of African and Asian stock. The driving tour takes anywhere from 45 to 60 minutes and can be followed with amusement rides, paddleboat excursions or other diversions.

The **Dreher Park Zoo** (1301 Summit Boulevard, West Palm Beach; 407-533-0887; admission) may not be the world's finest, but it has some distinctive features. There is a petting zoo and a special place for South American animals such as the capybara (at about four feet and 100 pounds, the world's largest rodent) and the common rhea, a two-legged feather duster that closely resembles an ostrich.

Dreher Park is also home to the **Science Museum and Planetarium** (4801 Dreher Trail North, West Palm Beach; 407-832-1348; admission), an outstanding facility with compelling experimental exhibits that teach visitors about optical illusions and other scientific phenomena. The **Aldrin Planetarium** has a regular schedule of entertainment, including laser light shows on Saturday nights, while the **Gibson Observatory** is open for stargazing on Friday evenings when skies are clear.

The season in Palm Beach would not be complete without attending a polo match. The most prestigious place to watch the ponies in action is the **Palm Beach Polo and Country Club Stadium** (13420 South Shore Boulevard, West Palm Beach; 407-793-1440; admission), not only because of its world-class facilities but because its name is linked with that of England's Prince Charles, who has played a few chukkers here. Matches are scheduled every Sunday afternoon from early January until mid-April.

There are two other places to enjoy major spectator sports in Palm Beach County. Anyone who's watched horse races will likely be intrigued by greyhound racing. These high-bred dogs run around the track at speeds of up to 40 miles per hour. The place in Palm Beach County to see the action is the **Palm Beach Kennel Club** (Belvedere Road and Congress Avenue, West Palm Beach; 407-683-2222; admission). There are both day and night races and, of course, plenty of wagering windows.

The heaviest concentration of jai alai frontóns—large indoor stadiums—in the country is in south Florida. The world's fastest ball game is played at **Palm Beach Jai Alai** (1415 45th Street, West Palm Beach; 407-844-2444) from September until July. (See "The Exotic Game of Jai Alai" in this chapter for further information.)

Palm Beach County has its own point of access to the Everglades, located off a grim stretch of state road far to the west of frontóns and polo fields: the **Arthur R. Marshall Loxahatchee Wildlife Refuge** (Route 441 and Lee Road, West Palm Beach; 407-734-8303; admission). This 145,000-acre refuge is home to a wide variety of reptiles, mammals and waterfowl. The highly endangered Everglade kite feeds here, along with various snakes such as the Everglade indigo snake and yellow rat snake.

A haven for wildlife, it is less hospitable to humans, who must hike two trails to explore the refuge's sawgrass ridges, sloughs, wet prairies and tree islands. Before venturing into the region, check out the visitors center located at the park's entrance.

PALM BEACH AND WEST PALM BEACH HOTELS

This is the land of grande dame hotels, dignified resorts of the old school that attract the same well-heeled clientele year in and year out. But smaller, less expensive facilities here also offer access to the same fine beaches, marvelous shopping and myriad restaurants.

There's not much besides palm trees and salt air to remind one of the islands at the **Palm Beach Hawaiian Ocean Inn** (3550 South Ocean Boulevard, Palm Beach; 407-582-5631). A long two-story building contains a variety of accommodations, from standards rooms (each with two double beds) to oceanfront suites. Accordingly, rates range from deluxe to ultra-deluxe. Pool, restaurant and bar.

Several one and two-story buildings are scattered between Ocean Boulevard and the water at the **Beachcomber Sea Cay Motor Apartments** (3024 South Ocean Boulevard, Palm Beach; 407-585-4646). Furniture in the 50 mid-sized accommodations is distinctive, if a little worn. Fabric vertical blinds and pastel-tiled baths help spiff things up. Pool. Efficiencies available. Moderate to ultra-deluxe.

The **Plaza Inn** (215 Brazilian Avenue; 407-832-8666) calls itself Palm Beach's only bed and breakfast, but it feels more like a charming hotel. Washed a pale pink, the three-story art deco house has been restored so that its wood floors and carved ceilings positively gleam. Each of the 50 rooms offer cozy touches such as handmade comforters, lace draperies, poster beds and myriads of fresh carnations. Amenities include a heated swimming pool and jacuzzi and bountiful breakfasts served in a cypress dining room. The ocean is just one block away. Deluxe to ultra-deluxe.

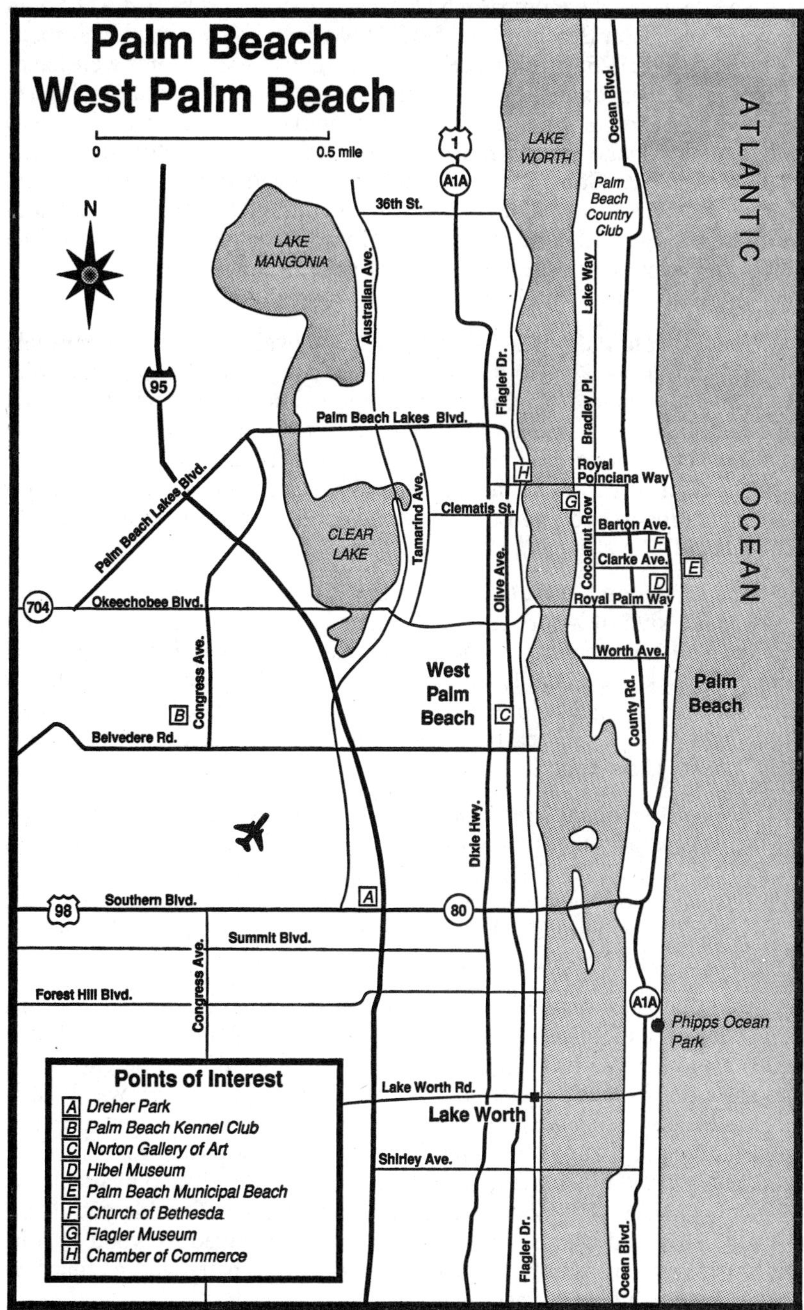
Palm Beach
West Palm Beach
0
0.5 mile
N
LAKE MANGONIA
CLEAR LAKE
LAKE WORTH
ATLANTIC
OCEAN
36th St.
Australian Ave.
Palm Beach Lakes Blvd.
Tamarind Ave.
Clematis St.
Okeechobee Blvd.
Congress Ave.
Belvedere Rd.
Southern Blvd.
Summit Blvd.
Forest Hill Blvd.
Lake Worth Rd.
Shirley Ave.
Flagler Dr.
Olive Ave.
Dixie Hwy.
Ocean Blvd.
Lake Way
Bradley Pl.
Royal Poinciana Way
Cocoanut Row
Barton Ave.
Clarke Ave.
Royal Palm Way
Worth Ave.
County Rd.
Palm Beach Country Club
West Palm Beach
Palm Beach
Lake Worth
Phipps Ocean Park
1
A1A
95
704
98
80
Points of Interest
A Dreher Park
B Palm Beach Kennel Club
C Norton Gallery of Art
D Hibel Museum
E Palm Beach Municipal Beach
F Church of Bethesda
G Flagler Museum
H Chamber of Commerce

The queen of the Palm Beach landscape, the **Breakers Hotel** (1 South County Road, Palm Beach; 407-655-6611) has been holding court high above the ocean since 1926, when the ceilings of its great public rooms were hand-painted by European artists. Fifteenth-century Flemish tapestries, bronze and crystal chandeliers, and 20-foot-high windows facing courtyard gardens and fountains make this palatial resort one of the most distinctive hotels on the Gold Coast. Some 1100 staff members—that's roughly two per guest room—knock themselves out to keep things running smoothly. Accommodations are large and done mostly in seafoam green and sunrise pink. The hotel offers a variety of restaurants, golf courses, tennis courts and an extensive beach club. Ultra-deluxe.

The **Heart of Palm Beach Hotel** (★) (160 Royal Palm Way, Palm Beach; 407-655-5600) manages to be charming and congenial almost to the point of intimacy, in spite of having 88 accommodations. Rooms are decked out simply in light colors, glass-topped tables and summer-cottage fabrics. Some have tiny lanais near the heated pool out back. In a town that can turn a cold shoulder to travelers, this is that rarity: a home away from home (in a great location to boot, midway between Worth Avenue shops and the public beach). Deluxe to ultra-deluxe.

The **Brazilian Court** (301 Australian Avenue, Palm Beach; 407-655-7740) is the kind of luxury residential-style hotel that appeals to long-term visitors. The 134 accommodations, located in several buildings interspersed with courtyards, are liberally decorated in sunny colors. The Brazilian Court has enjoyed a reputation for excellent service and European ambience since the days it hosted such dashing guests as Errol Flynn, Gary Cooper and Cary Grant. Ultra-deluxe.

Two of the island's most popular activities—shopping and beaching-it—are easy to pursue from the **Colony Hotel** (155 Hammon Avenue, Palm Beach; 407-655-5430). Only one-half block from the ocean and a short stroll to posh boutiques, the six-story white complex hugs a pool and tiki huts. Cool cream tones permeate the 119 guestrooms, tropically styled with print draperies and bedspreads. Ultra-deluxe.

Bed and breakfasts are a rare commodity in South Florida, and that makes **Hibiscus House** (★) (501 30th Street, West Palm Beach; 407-863-5633) an incredible find. Tucked discreetly in a manicured neighborhood and shrouded in lush vegetation, the charming frame hostelry was built in 1921 as the home of a West Palm Beach mayor. Distinctive period furniture, hand-loomed rugs and glossy pine floors decorate the sitting rooms and six moderately priced bedrooms of the two-story building. Also available are a balconied suite and poolside cottage at deluxe rates. Outside you'll find a quaint courtyard where a swimming pool is surrounded by wood decking and vine-covered trellises. All rooms have private baths and ceiling fans and include a full breakfast.

Far from the madding crowd at the beach, sequestered on 2200 acres, the **Palm Beach Polo and Country Club** (13198 Forest Hill Boulevard, West Palm Beach; 407-798-7000) is a world unto itself. This sports mecca attracts tennis buffs and golf and polo players (from Prince Charles down to rank beginners) to some of the finest facilities in Florida. Decor in the one- and two-story condominiums is typically a refined blend of pale colors, fine furnishings and handsome artwork. Pools. Ultra-deluxe.

PALM BEACH AND WEST PALM BEACH RESTAURANTS

It's hard to miss **John G's** (10 South Ocean Boulevard, Lake Worth Beach; 407-585-9860)—just look for the perpetual lines of customers that stretch around the corner. Revered by locals, who pack the place for succulent fresh fish, John G's is a nautical-style diner that serves hearty portions. For breakfast, try the cinnamon nut french toast or stuffed croissant; lunch and dinner specialties include rainbow trout, cobia (a Florida cracker specialty) and an assortment of sandwiches and salads. Budget to moderate.

No sign even hints at the presence of **Le Monagasque (★)** (2505 South Ocean Boulevard, Palm Beach; 407-585-0071), tucked away on the ground floor of the President Condominiums. A touch of Monaco can be found in this intimate dining room, where pink linens, smooth white leather banquettes and murals of the tiny principality give the impression of permanent spring-time on the Mediterranean. The cuisine at this delightful hideaway relies on traditional French preparations: pâté, bouillabaisse, frogs' legs, duckling and filet mignon béarnaise. Dinner only. Deluxe to ultra-deluxe.

Only in Palm Beach. Where else would you find women dressed to the hilt in a cheap burger joint? Of course, **Hamburger Heaven** (314 South County Road; 407-655-5277) isn't just any burger dive. Since 1945, the local coffee shop has been dealing out famously delicious hamburgers oozing with juice and cheese. Terrazzo floors, a U-shaped bar and the constant clang of dishes create a friendly, unpretentious mood. But if you're feeling slightly pretentious, go for the steak tartar or roast leg of lamb. Budget to moderate.

No socialite worth his or her caviar would consider a visit to Palm Beach complete without a meal at **Café L'Europe** (150 Worth Avenue; 407-655-4020). Sequestered on the upper floor of The Esplanade shopping arcade, this is a very formal restaurant in the continental style, with acres of polished wood floors and yards of pink linen tablecloths topped with diminutive lamps. Typical entrées include pecan-crusted salmon, roast duckling and sautéed veal, all at ultra-deluxe prices. To one side is a "caviar bar" for light seafood dishes and gourmet coffees.

French and Italian are the dominant culinary influences at **Renato's** (87 Via Mizner, Palm Beach; 407-655-9752). Specialties range from pâté and escargot to veal and grilled fish. The setting is French country, with lots of glass and rich Provençal fabrics. Patio seating available during the high season. Deluxe to ultra-deluxe.

For a luncheon on the move, try **Piccolo Mondo** (12 Via Mizner, Palm Beach; 407-655-9752), an Italian-style food boutique off Worth Avenue. Tomato and mozzarella salad, cold pasta primavera and hamburgers are among the budget-priced offerings at this hole-in-the-wall.

It's almost impossible to visit Palm Beach without being referred to **Chuck & Harold's Café** (207 Royal Poinciana Way; 407-659-1440). Unfortunately, securing one of the sidewalk tables requires expert timing (or a friendship with the staff). If the bar is noisy, head for the rear of the restaurant, where tables are arranged around the rim of a circular room with a tropical motif. The extensive menu can be confusing; stick to seafood, house-made pastas or barbecued anything and you'll probably be happy. Moderate to deluxe.

Several Palm Beach restaurants inspire unswerving loyalty; a prime example is **Toojay's (★)** (313 Poinciana Plaza; 407-659-7232). The deli section up front is usually crowded with people in tennis togs ordering take-out; beyond that is a large room opening onto a courtyard. Toojay's is particularly notable for its elaborate salads, but the dinner menu also includes such hot entrées as crab cakes, lasagna and meat loaf. Budget.

E. R. Bradley's Saloon (111 Bradley Place, Palm Beach; 407-833-3520) started life in the 1920s as a casino and has now evolved into a watering-hole-cum-kitchen especially beloved by the younger crowd. A limited menu relies heavily on salads, steaks, pastas and enormous hamburgers, which can be enjoyed in either of two small dining rooms or on a side patio. Bradley's is at peak form at brunch, when the chef turns out offbeat dishes such as Cajun eggs and sausage with hollandaise sauce. Moderate.

One of the few budget-to-moderate-priced Thai restaurants on the Gold Coast is **Wattana Thai** (7201 South Dixie Highway, West Palm Beach; 407-588-9383). Curried sea scallops, crisp-fried frogs' legs and "Volcano Jumbo Shrimp" are among the intriguing listings. Mirrored walls and glass-topped tables reflect the few oriental-red wall decorations in this small restaurant.

"Cooked in sight, must be right," declares the sign outside **Howley's** (4700 South Dixie Highway, West Palm Beach; 407-833-5691), a landmark coffee shop outfitted with formica tables, spindly houseplants and windows overlooking the busy street. This is the place to go for homecooked stomach warmers such as deep fried chicken, meat loaf with brown gravy, and roast pork with dressing. Burgers are big, as are the breakfasts. Budget.

The **Rhythm Café (★)** (3238 South Dixie Highway, West Palm Beach; 407-833-3406) is a pit stop with real soul. Lingering unobtrusively along a busy highway, the funky eatery sports dusty black-and-white checkered floors, '50s and '60s antiques and a bar top that looks like a piano keyboard.

Not the kind of place you'd expect to dine on gourmet cuisine such as *assiente* of smoked Norwegian salmon, *bistecca fiorentina* (grilled steak with fresh lime and garlic) or wild rum truffles. The one-page menu, which changes daily, spells pure gastronomic delight. Dinner only. Prices are moderate to deluxe.

Glass block, oriental screens and well-spaced, linen-topped tables make **Café Prospect** (3111 South Dixie Highway, West Palm Beach; 407-832-5952) a stylish place to dine. The gay-owned restaurant caters to loyal gay and straight patrons who adore the chef's dressy American dishes. Baby back ribs, roasted duck, chicken breast dijon and shrimp coconut are a few specialties. Moderate.

PALM BEACH AND WEST PALM BEACH SHOPPING

Not many people view Lake Worth as a mecca of merchandise, but in fact Lake Avenue is becoming known for its antique shops, among other things. **Antiques and Uniques** (811 Lake Avenue; 407-582-8922) is a sliver of a store specializing in country and primitive pieces—as well as items for children. At **Carousel Antique Center** (815 Lake Avenue; 407-533-0678), a group of small dealers has joined forces to offer a wide variety of oldies but goodies.

A fine literary alcove, **Two On A Shelf** (2521 North Dixie Highway, Lake Worth; 407-582-0067) stocks 50,000-plus books on art, Florida architecture and history and much more.

A stone's throw from Lake Avenue, top-notch paintings and sculptures by local artists grace the walls of **Lake Avenue Gallery** (709 Lucerne Avenue just off of Lake Avenue; 407-585-0003), which specializes in contemporary American craftwork, including some Southwestern adobe artworks.

West of Lake Worth and worth a special trip is **Hoffman's** (5190 Lake Worth Road, Greenacres; 407-967-2213), a chocolate "shoppe" with a dizzying assortment of fruits and handmade chocolates (some sugar-free) that can be boxed on the spot or shipped anywhere. While you're trying to make up your mind, you can watch chocolate-making through big glass windows or stroll the small but lovely gardens outside.

The best-known shopping street on the Gold Coast—if not in all of Florida—is **Worth Avenue** in Palm Beach, a boulevard of chic boutiques that qualifies as a tourist attraction in its own right. A mere few blocks are lined with some 200 stores, ranging from homegrown enterprises to the royalty of internationally known merchant princes.

You will come across many familiar names of designer stores—Cartier, Hermès, Chanel and Sara Fredericks, to name a few—but you can also stop at unique places such as **The Meissen Shop** (★) (329 Worth Avenue; 407-832-2504), which offers an outstanding collection of antique porcelain Meissen figures and dinnerware from the 18th, 19th and early 20th century. You'll also find rare collectors' items by the great Meissen masters. The only store of its kind in the United States, this exquisite shop qualifies as a small museum.

On a corner of Worth Avenue, **Cloud 10** (450 South County Road; 407-835-9110) will dress little girls in dreamy thousand-dollar dresses—and more affordable ones as well. For little boys, there are handmade sneakers, designer jeans and snazzy three-piece suits.

Veer off onto the sidestreets to check out some smaller outlets such as **Melangerie** (60 Via Mizner; 407-659-5119), with its tailored European linens, porcelain dolls, china and silver, and **Jack Davidson** (4 Via Parigi; 407-655-0906), an eclectic blend of English pine, Victorian bamboo, glassware and painted earthenware.

One bizarre "via" sidetrip is **Gallery Via Veneto** (250 Worth Avenue, Suite 1; 407-835-1399), where a courtyard is sprinkled with bigger-than-life bronze and onyx sculptures.

On the south side of Worth Avenue, between branches of world-class shops you will find less-ubiquitous merchants. Lovers of linen will be elated to discover **Pratesi** (324 Worth Avenue; 407-655-4414), renowned for its luxurious bedsheets, and **Kassatly's, Inc.** (250 Worth Avenue; 407-655-5655), which has been a local favorite for linens (including a marvelous array of handkerchiefs), lingerie and selected sportswear for men and women since 1923.

During the winter, gourmet belgian chocolates are flown in daily for customers of **White Swan Chocolate** (240 Worth Avenue; 407-833-2511). The dreamy chocolate shop carries the most imaginative line of truffles, including Key lime, chambord raspberry and bananas foster.

Falling somewhere between an art gallery and a clothing store, **Salvatore Ferragamo** (200 Worth Avenue; 407-659-0602) displays its signature silk scarves as if they were valuable paintings. Also on hand are stunning evening bags, dresses, suits and shoes for women, as well as clothing and luggage for men.

Naturally Palm Beach provides prime hunting grounds for second-hand goods at shops such as **Tally Ho Antiques** (250 Worth Avenue; 407-832-2800), a tiny source for kid-sized furniture and other miniature antiques, divvied up between two postage-stamp spaces. Open in winter only.

Within the confines of the two-story **Esplanade** (150 Worth Avenue) you'll find a bevy of famous designer stores as well as one-of-a-kind shops. If time is tight, make a beeline for the **Purple Turtle** (407-655-1625), which stocks a high-fashion line of children's clothes with an emphasis on European manufacturers.

PALM BEACH AND WEST PALM BEACH NIGHTLIFE

In an elegant supper-club setting appropriate for Palm Beach, the lounge at the **Colony Hotel** (155 Hammon Avenue; 407-655-5430) features sophisticated nightcaps and weekend dancing to big-band sounds 'til the wee hours.

With its big and brassy bar, corinthian columns and pink balloon draperies, **Au Bar** (336 Royal Ponciana Way, Palm Beach; 407-832-4800) looks like a place for celebrities. Little wonder, since the bar made big the night William Kennedy Smith and his uncle, Senator Ted Kennedy, met a young woman here. (The woman left with Smith and later charged him with rape.) Ever since, curious tourists have been pouring in to Au Bar—which responded by charging a $10 weekend cover. Dance music, spun by a deejay, ranges from heavy metal to Viennese waltzes.

A funky habitat with a warehouse feel, **Respectable Street Café** (518 Clematis Street, West Palm Beach; 407-832-9999) is smack in the middle of downtown but incredibly easy to miss. A late-night local crowd mingles in cozy wooden booths and listens to live reggae. Also featured is a deejay playing progressive and house music. Cover for live shows.

A throwback to Greenwich Village coffeehouses, **Artsbar** (302 South Dixie Highway, West Palm Beach; 407-832-0944) features tiny tables in a black backdrop. This is the hot spot for great live jazz, gourmet coffees and munchies. Occasionally, there's quality improvisation. Cover.

One of the hottest area nighttime destinations is **Waterway Café** (2360 PGA Boulevard, West Palm Beach; 407-694-1700), an expansive reggae club that rests waterside. Crowds jam the inside bars and spill across a bridge to a floating tiki bar festooned with life preservers.

The **Kravis Center for Performing Arts** (701 Okeechobee Boulevard, West Palm Beach; 407-833-8300) is the venue for a variety of programs, including symphony concerts, musicals, classical concerts and ballet performances. This is also the site of productions by the **Palm Beach Opera** (407-833-7888), which stages performances of major operas between December and March.

GAY SCENE With its black lights, black bar and blinking video screens, **Casbar** (4619 Okeechobee Boulevard, West Palm Beach; 407-684-9300) is one swanky scene. The gay men who pack this "cruise bar" come to dance and mingle.

HeartBreaker (2677 Forest Hill Boulevard, West Palm Beach; 407-966-1590), decorated in gray and mauve and glass block, has the look of a small palladium. Laser lights and recorded house music get feet moving in this popular weekend club for gay men and women.

H.G. Rooster's (823 Belvedere Road, West Palm Beach; 407-832-9119) is a prime example of a friendly, high-class bar. Ceramic tile, faux finished walls and soft lights give it a stylized ambience, while videos, Top-40 music and weekly male strippers provide the entertainment.

PALM BEACH BEACHES AND PARKS

Lake Worth Municipal Beach—A forbidding jumble of squat concrete buildings diminishes the charm of this 1200-foot-long public beach. Intended as a casino, the main structure houses an office and a couple of shops. Next door is a large freshwater public pool. Soft cream-colored sand and substantial surf action nevertheless make this one of the prettiest beaches in the area. For a good view of the beach, walk out onto the long fishing pier.

Facilities: Picnic areas, barbecue grills, playground, restrooms, showers, lifeguards, concession stands; information, 407-533-7367. *Fishing:* Pier and surf angling. *Swimming:* First-rate. *Surfing:* Very good south of the pier.

Getting there: Located at Routes 802 and A1A (South Ocean Boulevard).

John Prince Park—Located on the shores of Lake Osborne, John Prince Park devotes more than 600 acres of its 1000 acres to recreational facilities. Graced with grassy picnic areas and lake views and dotted with trees, the park is a very relaxing place to spend an entire day.

Facilities: Picnic areas, boat rentals, restrooms, nature trail, softball field, boat ramps, bicycle path, par course, tennis courts; restaurants and grocery stores nearby; information, 407-964-4420. *Fishing:* Freshwater angling.

Camping: There are 266 sites for tents and RVs; hookups available. Fees are $15 per night; information, 407-582-7992.

Getting there: Located at 2700 6th Avenue South, Lake Worth.

Phipps Ocean Park—One of the few public beaches in the vicinity of Palm Beach, this low-profile park is easily overlooked. The sand is soft and pale on this 1300-foot beach. Otherwise, it is unremarkable. Swimmers should note that there is quite a drop-off just beyond the high-water mark.

Facilities: Picnic areas, restrooms, showers, lifeguards; restaurants and grocery stores nearby; information, 407-585-9203. *Swimming:* Very good.

Getting there: Located in Palm Beach, one and a half miles north of Lake Worth Pier.

Palm Beach Municipal Beach—Though mostly invisible from the highway, there are six miles of public beach on the other side of the seawall along South Route A1A. The pale, pink-tinged sand virtually disappears at points, but a good place to set up camp is at **Clarke Beach** at the foot of Clarke Avenue. The lifeguards can warn you against places where obstructions lie beneath the mint-green seawater. Given how much of Palm Beach is strictly private property, one gets an almost giddy feeling about enjoying this long stretch of public beach, which extends about three miles both north and south of Royal Palm Way.

Facilities: Showers, lifeguards; restaurants are nearby. *Swimming:* Very good. *Surfing:* Very good at the end of Hammon Avenue.

Getting there: Major access points between Hammon Avenue and Barton Avenue.

Northern Palm Beach County

This northern ledge of the Gold Coast is arguably one of its most scenic. The frenetic development that blankets Fort Lauderdale and much of Palm Beach County has barely brushed these windswept shores. In an effort to preserve what nature has bestowed upon them, Jupiter residents have long restricted new construction and thus protected their beaches from highrise buildings. Life is still quiet in these reaches, unhindered by the fast-paced social set of Palm Beach and void of any real industry except tourism.

A boat ride on the Intracoastal Waterway is a stressless way to tour northern Palm Beach County. The *Star of Palm Beach*, a replica of a Mississippi River paddlewheeler, cruises out of **Star Landing** (Phil Foster Park, under the Blue Heron Bridge, Riviera Beach; 407-842-0882; admission). The boat accommodates 300 passengers on an enclosed lower main deck and an open promenade deck above. The captain will undoubtedly deliver a spiel laced with gossip, tall tales and some actual facts as you putt-putt past the glorious mansions lining the Intracoastal Waterway between Singer Island and Palm Beach. Luncheon, brunch and dinner-dance cruises are currently available.

Heading north from Palm Beach, Route A1A merges occasionally with Route 1 as its heads toward Juno Beach. There's not much traditional sightseeing in this town, but what's here tends to be outdoors-oriented. The **Marinelife Center of Juno Beach** (1200 Route 1; 407-627-8280) forms the centerpiece of Loggerhead Park. A small but enthusiastic and knowledgeable staff explains the ecology of sea turtles and shows specimens. Various marine organisms and other small displays fill the remainder of this small but engaging science museum. During the summer, the museum conducts "turtle walks" along a nearby beach.

Be forewarned: the complex waterways around Jupiter pose a challenge to the driving visitor. You may have to make several passes before finding a particular attraction. One worth the trouble is the picturesque **Dubois House** (Dubois Park, Jupiter; 407-747-6639), built in the late 1890s by Harry Dubois. His new bride wanted a water view, and she apparently got it: the house is set atop a 20-foot-high, 90-foot-long Indian shell mound (bits of which the family allegedly sold over the years). Aside from a coat of paint over previously plain cypress walls and the construction of a coquina rock fireplace, the house is said to look much as it did in the early part of the century. Period furnishings include the old Dubois dining set and a piano, and other objects donated later such as a treadle sewing machine and a food safe. Open on Sunday afternoons only.

The **Loxahatchee Historical Museum** (Burt Reynolds Park, 805 North Route 1, Jupiter; 407-747-6639, admission), housed in a re-created Florida cracker-style building, is a one-room exhibit hall that tracks local history for the past 10,000 years. In addition to pre-historic Indian displays, you'll find artifacts galore, all packed wall-to-wall in this tiny but intriguing showplace.

The oldest existing structure in Palm Beach County is the **Jupiter Inlet Lighthouse** (Jupiter Inlet; 407-747-6639). This red brick landmark, constructed by the U.S. Lighthouse Service in 1860, has a small museum at its base featuring historical artifacts and other memorabilia related to the area. Open Sunday afternoons only.

NORTHERN PALM BEACH COUNTY HOTELS

The **Tahiti Motel Apartments** (3920 North Ocean Drive, Riviera Beach; 407-848-9767) is a two-story structure that stretches from the highway all the way to the sands of Singer Island. Moderately priced motel rooms have two double beds and fully tiled baths, but not much in the way of frills. Furnishings are a mixture of dark veneer and provincial designs. On site are two pools, a croquet court and a putting green. Efficiencies available at deluxe rates.

Exceptional value lies beyond the unassuming exterior of **Bellatrix (★)** (1000 East Blue Heron Boulevard, Singer Island; 407-848-4815). It looks like just another roadside motel, but a typical room features high ceilings, one entire wall made of mirrors, and queen-sized sleeper sofas. This 14-unit motel, with efficiencies and one-bedroom apartments, offers dockage at the back door on the Intracoastal Waterway. Pool. Moderate.

Four stories of accommodations are available on the beach at the **Ocean Club Resort** (3100 North Ocean Drive, Singer Island; 407-848-3441). Rattan furniture and pastel upholstery that echoes the beige and turquoise of the seascape outside create very pleasant rooms, each of which has a private balcony. Pool. Efficiencies available. Ultra-deluxe.

The place to stay in Jupiter is the **Jupiter Beach Hilton** (Route A1A and Indiantown Road; 407-746-2511). The rooms are so endearingly decorated with rattan and wicker and floral fabrics that most guests would never guess the hotel's size—193 rooms. Standard rooms with two double beds are a little cramped, but there is a balcony with a view of the splendid beach. This is surely one of the most attractive, most personalized Hiltons in the country. Pool. Ultra-deluxe.

NORTHERN PALM BEACH COUNTY RESTAURANTS

Tucked under the Blue Heron Bridge like some genial troll, the **Crab Pot** (★) (386 East Blue Heron Boulevard, Riviera Beach; 407-844-2722) doubles as a time machine taking patrons back to simpler, lazier days on the river. Start with a cool drink at the chickee bar (chickee being Seminole for thatched roof) while you adjust to the easy-does-it ambience. Then try something from the raw bar or a full seafood dinner of stone crab claws, stuffed flounder, scallops, shrimp, or the trademark platter of three different versions of fresh crab. Somehow everything tastes better when eaten on newspaper-topped tables in an open-air waterfront setting. Moderate to deluxe.

Sinclair's American Grill (Jupiter Beach Hilton, Indiantown Road and Route A1A, Jupiter; 407-746-2511) benefits from its sophisticated tropical decor, a blend of light woods, luxuriant foliage and muted color combinations. The kitchen seems to do best with grilled meats; seafood dishes and more elaborate concoctions can be a disappointment. But with restrained expectations, Sinclair's can offer an extremely pleasant experience. Budget to deluxe.

At the top of our list of reasons for visiting the Gold Coast is the opportunity to dine outdoors on balmy evenings. A fabulous place to indulge in this sensuous experience is **Harpoon Louie's** (★) (1065 North Route A1A, Jupiter; 407-744-1300). Some regulars do prefer the large, contemporary dining room with its bare wood, ceiling fans and tropical foliage, but nothing compares with the outside tables, in full view of the scenic Jupiter Inlet and the lighthouse across the way. (If you're going for breakfast, try to arrive in time to watch the sunrise.) The menu is among the most innovative of any waterfront restaurant on the coast, listing shrimp Bombay, seafood Wellington, pompano with crab, sea scallops and several beef-and-reef combinations. Each entrée arrives with a little something extra; the waiters seem to get a big kick out of watching eyes light up with surprise. Moderate to deluxe.

The **Log Cabin** (631 North A1A, Jupiter; 407-746-6877) looks as though it should be nestled against some hazy Carolina mountain. This true find is a real log cabin, wonderfully furnished with country antiques and permeated with rough hewn oak floors, cedar paneling and vaulted beam ceilings. The hearty fare is strictly Southern, with specialties such as baby back ribs, fried Okeechobee catfish (yum!), brunswick stew and flapjacks blanketed in hot syrup. With such a scrumptious lineup, who could resist this place? Budget to moderate.

For a quick, budget-priced breakfast or lunch, keep an eye out for **Café Copenhagen** (287 Route A1A, Tequesta; 407-746-8947). There are only six booths and six tables in this bakery-cum-restaurant, which keeps things cozy. The home-country inspiration is evident in specials like Danish open-faced sandwiches, but you'll also find omelettes, waffles, chicken-stuffed patty shells and a serving of "eight of the nicest shrimp." Closed in the summer.

NORTHERN PALM BEACH COUNTY SHOPPING

The outstanding shopping possibilities dwindle north of Palm Beach itself. For a last-ditch effort at toting back souvenirs, comb through **Sea Shell City** (2100 Broadway, Riviera Beach; 407-844-2576), noted for its assortment of shells, collected from all over the world.

Singer Island's Ocean Mall, a cluster of low-slung beachfront buildings and modules, does offer some interesting window shopping as well as unusual stores.

Brightly painted wooden birds peek out from **Brenda's Boutique** (2419 Ocean Avenue, Ocean Mall, Singer Island; 407-842-7177), a beachy shop filled with unique and handpainted clothes as well as unusual gifts.

Nestled out in the rural part of Jupiter, **Burt Reynolds Gift Store** (16133 Jupiter Farms Road; 407-746-0393) is the best spot to stock up on Burt paraphernalia. A kiddie petting zoo, with emus, goats and horses, is a side attraction.

NORTHERN PALM BEACH COUNTY NIGHTLIFE

Walking into **Club Safari** (8000 RCA Boulevard, in the Marriott hotel, Palm Beach Gardens) is like stepping into an Indiana Jones film. Webbed with vines and spidery trees, this faux jungle has idols, bulls and other Disneylike characters that sing and blow smoke. Bring your dancing shoes—everyone jams to energized music, spun by a deejay. Cover on weekends.

You're apt to catch Burt Reynolds at his **Backstage** (1061 East Indiantown Road, Jupiter; 407-747-9533) lounge, a classy club with pink walls and black lacquer accents that hosts live jazz bands.

Jox Sports Club (200 North Route 1, Jupiter; 407-744-6600) is guaranteed to satisfy the "upscale jock" in the crowd. Shoot a game of hoops or pool, or jam on the big dancefloor, mesmerized by 50 video monitors. Top-40 music is compliments of a deejay.

NORTHERN PALM BEACH COUNTY BEACHES AND PARKS

Riviera Beach Municipal Beach—This is a picture-postcard beach, replete with hard-packed powder-white sand. Backed by highrise hotels and condominiums, it is still wide enough to remain in full sun most of the day. It is an outstanding beach for strolling or jogging.

Facilities: Restrooms, showers, lifeguards; restaurants and groceries nearby. *Swimming:* Very good in mild surf.

Getting there: Located due east of the Blue Heron Boulevard Bridge off Route A1A, Singer Island.

Ocean Reef Park—Sandwiched between hotels, Ocean Reef Park is landscaped with Australian pines, sea grapes and numerous palm trees. With grey squirrels darting through the underbrush and picnic areas scattered far apart, it is a very pleasant place for a midday stop. Wooden dune crossovers lead to a wide dark-sand beach. Scuba divers make beach dives off this part of the coast.

Facilities: Picnic areas, playground, restrooms, showers, lifeguards; restaurants and grocery stores nearby. *Swimming:* Good.

Getting there: Located about three-fourths of a mile north of the Blue Heron Boulevard Bridge off North Route A1A.

John D. MacArthur Beach State Park (★)—When you want to get away from it all, head up Route A1A on Singer Island. To find this beach, you have to park by the side of the road and follow a foot path through a coastal hammock and a mangrove swamp. On the other side of a tall sand dune is a completely undeveloped beach of soft mocha-colored sand. If you walk north, you'll soon be completely out of sight of the oceanfront hotels. It's a Robinson Crusoe kind of place, where you have to take everything you need. The surf is mild here.

Facilities: Picnic areas, restrooms, showers, nature center; information, 407-624-6950. *Swimming:* Excellent at the first beach. *Skindiving:* One of the best shoreside limestone reefs in this part of Florida.

Getting there: Located at 10900 South Route A1A, Singer Island, North Palm Beach.

Juno Beach (★)—This unmarked stretch of oceanfront lies nearly out of sight of the bluff-top highway. A narrow band of soft dark sand extends some 2600 feet on this underpopulated part of the coast. Roadside parking is at a minimum, and it takes a bit of ingenuity to find your way down to the beach.

Facilities: Picnic area, restrooms, showers, playground. *Fishing:* Surf angling. *Swimming:* Excellent.

Getting there: Located in Juno Beach off Route A1A approximately three-fourths of a mile north of Donald Ross Road.

Loggerhead Park—Extending from Route 1 east and encompassing some 900 feet of beach, this public park contains an observatory tower, recreational offices and the Marinelife Center of Juno Beach.

Facilities: Restrooms, picnic areas, playground, tennis courts, nature trail, lifeguard; information, 407-627-8280. *Swimming:* Permitted.

Getting there: Located at 1200 Route 1, Juno Beach.

Carlin Park—This developed park fronts 3000 feet of rock-strewn beach, accessible via boardwalk. Rimmed with Australian pines and sea grapes, the dark, soft sand beach is rather narrow. Across the street is a softball diamond, six tennis courts lit for night play, a parcourse and a duck pond.

Facilities: Picnic areas, restrooms, showers, lifeguards, concession stands. *Fishing:* Surf angling. *Swimming:* Very good.

Getting there: Off Route A1A in Jupiter, south of Indiantown Road.

Jupiter Beach Park—This developed beach extends 1700 feet south of the Jupiter Inlet. The sand is grainy and chocolate-colored, and rocky outcroppings lie near the high-water mark. It's a good beach for walking and for watching boats cruise in and out of Jupiter Inlet.

Facilities: Picnic areas, restrooms, showers, lifeguards, concession stands; restaurants and groceries a short drive away. *Fishing:* Surf angling. *Swimming:* Excellent.

Getting there: On Jupiter Beach Road off Route A1A, Jupiter.

Blowing Rocks Preserve (★)—This wild area of coastline would look more appropriate in the Galapagos Islands than in Florida. What makes it intriguing are the extensive rock formations that comprise most of the beach. Only 4000 feet long, Blowing Rocks has a wild, windswept appearance, though much salt-tolerant vegetation manages to survive on the dunes. Try to arrive at high tide, when the surf occasionally blows water through holes in the outcroppings.

Facilities: Nature trails. *Swimming:* Poor.

Getting there: Off Route A1A, a mile south of the Martin County line.

The Sporting Life

SPORTFISHING

Deep-sea fishing for marlin, shark, dolphin and sailfish is one of the most popular sports on the Gold Coast, and there seems to be no end of charter outfits in the area. Among them are **Flamingo Fishing** (801 Seabreeze Boulevard in the Bahia Mar Yacht Basin, Fort Lauderdale; 305-462-9194) and **Captain Bill's** (Bahia Mar Yacht Basin, Fort Lauderdale; 305-467-3855).

In Palm Beach County, try your luck with the **Blue Heron Fishing Fleet** (Blue Heron Bridge, Riviera Beach; 407-844-3573) or **Drift Boat Two Georges** (728 Casa Loma Boulevard, Boynton Beach; 407-732-4411).

The most economical approach, clearly, is to pay the nominal fee to fish off **Anglin's Fishing Pier** (2 Commercial Boulevard, Lauderdale-by-the-Sea; 305-491-9403). You can rent equipment, buy bait and fish to your heart's content 24 hours a day.

BOATING

Fort Lauderdale, dubbed "The Venice of America" for its extensive canal system, is a boater's paradise. The Intracoastal Waterway, which extends the length of the Gold Coast, can be explored via sailboat or motorboat.

Ski boats, sightseeing boats and power boats are available at **American Boat Rental** (1005 Seabreeze Boulevard, Fort Lauderdale; 305-761-8845). The ubiquitous **Club Nautico** has several locations for renting jet skis and powerboats: in Fort Lauderdale (Pier 66; 305-523-0033) or Pompano Beach (101 North Riverside Drive, in the Sand's Harbor Resort Marina; 305-942-3270). If you can handle a hobie cat, contact **Radical Surf & Sail** (615 Ocean Drive, Pompano Beach; 305-781-0033).

Singer Island Sailboat Rental (Phil Foster Park, off Blue Heron Boulevard, Riviera Beach; 407-848-2628) teaches sailing lessons and rents boats by the hour.

Renting a boat in Jupiter provides easy access to both Palm Beach county waters and the intriguing waterways of the Treasure Coast to the north. **Jupiter Hills Marine** (18261 Route 1; 407-744-0727) rents pontoon boats and can provide a ski boat with driver.

SKINDIVING

The clear waters along the Gold Coast create sensational conditions for a variety of water sports. Coral reefs, sunken wrecks and abundant marine life off the 23-mile coastline of Broward County, in particular, afford almost limitless scuba diving and snorkeling opportunities.

One of the most highly respected dive shops is **Pro Dive** (Bahia Mar Yachting Center, Fort Lauderdale; 305-761-3413), which offers daily reef and wreck dives as well as basic, open-water and advanced certification classes. Similar services are available through **Lauderdale Diver** (1334 Southeast 17th Street, Fort Lauderdale; 305-467-2822), **Divers Unlimited** (6023 Hollywood Boulevard, Hollywood; 305-981-0156) and **Force E**, which has outlets in Fort Lauderdale (2104 West Oakland Park Boulevard; 305-735-6227), Pompano Beach (2700 East Atlantic Boulevard; 305-943-3483) and Boca Raton (877 East Palmetto Park Road; 407-368-0555). In Boynton Beach, try **Dive Shop II** (700 Casa Loma Boulevard; 407-278-9111). For dive rentals and charters in West Palm Beach, contact **Dixie Divers** (1401 South Military Trail; 407-969-6688).

SURFING AND WINDSURFING

Surfers and windsurfers find an endless summer on the Fort Lauderdale waters. In Fort Lauderdale, surfboards and related equipment can be rented from **Island Water Sports** (115 Commercial Boulevard; 305-491-6229) and **BC Surf & Sport** (1495 North Federal Highway; 305-564-0202).

You can rent windsurf boards from **Windsurfing Madness** (1804 East Sunrise Avenue, Fort Lauderdale; 305-525-9463), **Radical Surf & Sail** (615 Ocean Drive, Pompano Beach; 305-781-0033), **Fun Boards** (500 South Ocean Boulevard, Delray; 407-272-3036) and **Singer Island Sailboard Rental** (Phil Foster Park, off Blue Heron Boulevard, Riviera Beach; 407-848-2628).

WATERSKIING

In Fort Lauderdale, you can rent boats, as well as wave runners, at **Watersports** (2025 East Sunrise Boulevard; 305-761-1672). They offer professional instruction. Wave runners—which are like two-person jet skis, only more stable—are also available in Fort Lauderdale at **Surf Water Sports** (on the beach in front of the Marriott Harbor Beach Hotel; 305-462-7245) and **Watersports Unlimited** (301 Seabreeze Boulevard; 305-467-1316). **McGinnis Ski School** (2421 Southwest 46th Avenue, Fort Lauderdale; 305-584-9007) and **Lyle Lee's Ski School** (3701 Northwest 9th Avenue, Pompano Beach; 305-943-7766) offer lake skiing. An unusual twist is waterskiing without a boat, something you can try at **Quiet Waters Park** (6601 North Powerline Road, Pompano Beach; 305-429-0215). A contraption known as Ski Rixen involves a cable that pulls skiers around a lake.

PARASAILING

On a clear day, one of the loveliest sights in Fort Lauderdale is the image of parasailors soaring above the ocean. For rentals in Fort Lauderdale try **Watersports Unlimited** (301 Seabreeze Boulevard; 305-467-1316) or **Surf Water Sports** (on the beach in front of the Marriott Harbor Beach Hotel; 305-462-7245).

GOLF

The Gold Coast climate is ideal for such sports as golf. Dozens of courses dot the Greater Fort Lauderdale area, including many semiprivate clubs that welcome nonmembers. Robert Trent Jones designed the 18-hole course at the **American Golfers Club** (3850 North Federal Highway, Fort Lauderdale; 305-564-8760). Other challenging courses include the **Deer Creek Golf and Tennis Club** (2801 Deer Creek Country Club Boulevard, Deerfield Beach; 305-421-5550), **Bonaventure Country Club** (200 Bonaventure Boulevard, Fort Lauderdale; 305-389-2100), **Grand Palms Golf Country Club** (110 Grand Palms Drive, Pembroke Pines; 305-431-8800) and the **City of Lauderhill Municipal Golf Course** (4141 Northwest 16th Street; 305-730-2990). In Delray Beach, visitors may play at **Delray Beach Municipal Golf Course** (2200 Highland Avenue; 407-243-7380) or **Kings Point Atlantic Par Three** (7000 West Atlantic Avenue; 407-499-0140). In Boynton Beach, there is the **Cypress Creek Country Club** (9400 South Military Trail; 407-732-4202) as well as the **Boynton Beach Municipal Golf Course** (8020

The Exotic Game of Jai Alai

They call it the fastest game on two feet, and it's one of the oldest ball games in the world, yet jai alai remains a mystery to most Americans. That's probably because there are only 11 places to play the game in the United States. Of those, ten are located in Florida. On the Gold Coast, there are *frontóns*—large arenas with indoor courts built especially for jai alai—at **Dania Jai Alai** (301 East Dania Beach Boulevard, Dania; 305-426-4330) and **Palm Beach Jai Alai** (1415 45th Street, West Palm Beach; 407-844-2444).

The best way to learn how jai alai is played is to observe a few games. But it does help to know a little bit about how the sport developed and what is happening on the court. Since the ball frequently travels at 150 miles per hour, there is a great deal of action.

Jai alai (pronounced hi-li) originated in the Pyrenees Mountains of northern Spain during the 15th century. Basque villagers decided the game of handball would be considerably enhanced if they used a bread-basket to catch and sling the ball. Eventually, the basket evolved into the curved *cesta* used today. The *pelota* developed into a ball smaller than a baseball but as hard as a golf ball.

In many ways, jai alai resembles the game of handball. The game is played on a three-walled court called a *cancha*, normally 175 feet long. A wire fence on the fourth side of the court protects spectators from the action. To their right is the *frontis* (front wall), usually made of granite to resist the force of the *pelota*. In both singles and doubles, the point is to hurl the ball against the front wall with such finesse that it cannot be hit by the opposition. The agility of professional jai alai players is astounding to watch, especially since it's nearly impossible for spectators to anticipate where the ball is going to rebound from the wall.

A typical evening of jai alai (a Basque term meaning "merry festival") includes 14 games, each lasting approximately 15 minutes with 10-minute intermissions. Spectators are allowed to place a wide variety of bets: win, place, show, daily doubles, quiniela doubles, quienielas, perfectas, superfectas, trifectas and Pick 6.

It takes a while to get the hang of it, but the more you know the particulars (or the more money you have riding on the outcome), the more exciting you will find this fast-paced sport.

Jog Road; 407-969-2200). There are many courses in Palm Beach County open to the public, including the **Boca Raton Municipal Golf Course** (8111 Golf Road, Boca Raton; 407-483-6100), **Red Reef Executive Golf Course** (1111 North Ocean Boulevard, Boca Raton; 407-391-5014), **North Palm Beach Country Club** (951 Route 1, North Palm Beach; 407-626-4343) and **West Palm Beach Country Club** (7001 Parker Avenue; 407-582-2019).

TENNIS

The tennis courts of south Florida have produced such champions as Chris Evert Lloyd. We can't guarantee your backhand will improve, but we can guarantee enough courts to go around. Courts and instruction are available through the **City of Fort Lauderdale Parks and Recreation Department** (305-761-5346). You can play at **George English Park** (1101 Bayview Drive, Fort Lauderdale; 305-566-0622), **Holiday Park** (701 Northeast 12th Avenue, Fort Lauderdale; 305-761-5378) or **West Lake Park** (1200 Sheridan Street, Hollywood; 305-926-2410). The City of Boca Raton offers instruction at **Memorial Park** (271 Northwest 2nd Avenue; 407-393-7978). The **Palm Beach Parks and Recreation** (407-964-4420) can direct out-of-towners to courts in their vicinity. In Lake Worth, there are courts in **John Prince Park** (2700 Sixth Avenue South; 407-964-4420) and at the **Lake Worth Racquet and Swim Club** (4090 Coconut Road; 407-967-3900).

BICYCLING

Since southeast Florida is almost entirely level, bicycling is an easy way to get around. The best places to ride in the Fort Lauderdale area are along the wide paved roads on the west side of the city, such as **Nob Hill Road** north of Broward Boulevard and **Atlantic Boulevard** (which parallels Route A1A on the east side). In Dania, the smooth road inside **John U. Lloyd State Park** is a good cycling route (four miles round trip). In this area, group rides are organized by **Mike's Cyclery** (5429 North Federal Highway, Fort Lauderdale; 305-493-5277) and **Big Wheel** (6847 Taft Street, Hollywood; 305-962-7857).

For scenic routes, it's hard to beat the one that parallels the **Intracoastal Waterway** on the west side of Palm Beach. The paved trail begins just north of the Flagler Bridge and runs nearly to the tip of the island. Cycling is also the best way (short of a personal invitation) to see the mansions in Palm Beach, on both the narrow interior streets and the wider avenues such as **Ocean Boulevard**, which runs north of Royal Poinciana Way to the northern tip of the island.

A trail runs along the west side of **Route A1A** between Deerfield Beach and Boca Raton, adjacent towns on the Broward/Palm Beach county line.

To join the Saturday morning 38-mile group ride from Boca Raton to the Lake Worth pier and back, call **Boca Schwinn** (3150 North Federal Highway, Boca Raton; 407-391-0800).

BIKE RENTALS You can rent bicycles in Fort Lauderdale from **International Bike Shop** (1900 East Sunrise Boulevard; 305-764-8800) or **Florida Bicycle** (515 West Sunrise Boulevard; 305-763-6974). In Delray Beach, **Bike America** (119 Northeast 5th Avenue; 407-278-0053) rents bicycles. Other rental outlets include **Bicycle World Inc.** (2990 Jog Road, Greenacres; 407-439-5020) and **Palm Beach Bicycle Trail Shop** (223 Sunrise Avenue, Palm Beach; 407-659-4583).

HIKING

Thanks to its completely flat landscape and year-round high temperatures, the Gold Coast is not known for its hiking trails. The best places to hike range from the beaches—where the pack is hard enough—to various parks and nature preserves. Few places allow overnight camping.

SOUTHERN BROWARD COUNTY TRAILS Though not really a hiking trail, a good walk uninterrupted by traffic lights can be enjoyed at **Broadwalk,** (2.2 miles) the paved path, closed to automobiles, that runs beside Hollywood Beach.

FORT LAUDERDALE TRAILS In **Hugh Taylor Birch State Recreation Area** there is a paved hiking trail through much of the 180 acres of coastal hammock and other plant communities.

Two trails lead through different parts of the Secret Woods Nature Center (305-791-1030) in Fort Lauderdale. **Laurel Oaks** is a short, 1216-foot trail where you may spot birds and squirrels rustling among fall leaves. This makes a good combination walk with **New River Trail**, a 3200-foot-long boardwalk through various habitats: a raised portion leads to a stand of pond apple and mangrove trees along the south fork of the New River.

NORTH BROWARD COUNTY TRAILS The Fern Forest Nature Center (305-970-0150) in Pompano Beach has three trails. **Cypress Creek Trail** (.5 mile) is a boardwalk excursion; ask for a self-guiding trail booklet. **Prairie Overlook Trail** (1 mile) loops past an open prairie, providing eye-level views of oak-cabbage palm communities. **Maple Walk** (.3 mile) runs through a red maple swamp that is often quite wet during the late summer rainy season.

A good hike is available on Saturday mornings at Deerfield Island Park (Deerfield Beach), accessible by boat only from the dock on Riverview Road, near the Riverview Restaurant. The 1500-foot **Mangrove Trail** boardwalk is an entrancing exploration through eight acres of red, white and black mangrove. **Coquina Trail** is a slightly rocky path that leads to a lookout over the Intracoastal Waterway. Guided nature tours offer information on the varied plant life of this secluded island.

DELRAY BEACH TRAILS Within Delray Beach's **Morikami Japanese Park** is a path (1.5 miles) through a peaceful pine forest.

PALM BEACH AND WEST PALM BEACH TRAILS A bike path (5 miles) in **John Prince Park** in Lake Worth provides lakeside hiking opportunities. There are also nature trails in this urban park.

NORTHERN PALM BEACH COUNTY TRAILS Within **Jonathan Dickinson State Park** is a trail (9.3 miles) that leads to primitive backpacking sites. Several nature trails can be found in this 10,328-acre Hobe Sound park, which consists of mangrove, river swamp, sand pine scrub, pine flatwoods and a portion of the Loxahatchee River. Ranger-guided tours are available year-round.

Transportation

BY CAR

Route 95 is the major north-south artery on the Gold Coast. Closer to the ocean, **Route 1** (Federal Highway) is used largely for local traffic. On the coast itself, **Route A1A** parallels the Atlantic almost the entire distance from Hollywood to Jupiter.

BY AIR

Two airports are located on the Gold Coast: Fort Lauderdale Airport and Palm Beach International Airport. Also convenient is Miami International Airport, about an hour's drive southwest of Fort Lauderdale (see the "Transportation" section in Chapter Two).

The **Fort Lauderdale Airport** has regularly scheduled service by Air Canada, American Airlines, Continental Airlines, Delta Airlines, Northwest Airlines, Trans World Airlines, United Airlines and USAir.

Located in West Palm Beach, the **Palm Beach International Airport** is served by American Airlines, Continental Airlines, Delta Airlines, Northwest Airlines, Trans World Airlines, United Airlines and USAir.

In Fort Lauderdale, **Broward County Transit** (305-357-8400) has bus service between the airport and its main terminal at Northwest 1st Avenue and Broward Boulevard.

For van service to and from Fort Lauderdale Airport call **Atlantic Airport Service** (305-566-9794) or **Broward Transportation Airport Services** (305-561-3525).

Palm Beach Transportation (407-684-9900) services the Palm Beach International Airport. **Shuttle Tran, Inc.** (407-683-6603) provides shuttle service to any location in Palm Beach, Broward or Dade counties. Transportation between Boca Raton and the Palm Beach International Airport is provided by **Boyce-Transportation, Inc.** (407-391-4762).

BY BUS

Greyhound Bus Lines has extensive service throughout the Gold Coast. In addition to bus stops, there are terminals in the Fort Lauderdale area at 1707 Tyler Street, Hollywood (305-922-8228) and 513 Northeast 3rd Street, Fort Lauderdale (305-764-6551).

In the Palm Beach area, Greyhound has terminals at 402 Southeast 6th Avenue, Delray Beach (407-272-6447) and 100 1st Street, West Palm Beach (407-833-8534). The bus also stops in Boca Raton at 141 Northwest 20th Street, though there is no station.

BY TRAIN

For train aficionados, **Amtrak** (800-872-7245) offers service to the West Palm Beach station (201 South Tamarind Avenue) via the "Palmetto," "Silver Star" and "Silver Meteor."

CAR RENTALS

Among the major firms located in or near the terminal at Fort Lauderdale Airport are **Alamo Rent A Car** (305-525-4713), **Avis Rent A Car** (305-359-3250), **Budget Rent A Car** (305-359-4747), **Dollar Rent A Car** (305-359-7800), **General Rent A Car** (305-524-4635) and **Hertz Rent A Car** (305-359-5281).

Car rental agencies at the Palm Beach International Airport include **Avis Rent A Car** (407-233-6400), **Budget Rent A Car** (407-683-2401), **Dollar Rent A Car** (407-686-3301) and **National Inter Rent** (407-233-7368).

PUBLIC TRANSPORTATION

Bus service throughout Broward County is provided by **Broward County Transit** (305-357-8400). Public libraries, chamber of commerce offices and many beachfront hotels and motels sell weekly Transpasses, which entitle the buyer to unlimited use of the bus system for seven days.

In the Palm Beach area, **Co Tran** (407-233-1111) offers regularly scheduled bus service on a variety of routes.

TRI-RAIL (305-728-8445) is a commuter rail system operating throughout the Gold Coast, with 66 miles of track between Miami International Airport and Palm Beach.

TAXIS

Service at the Fort Lauderdale airport is available through **Friendly Checker** (305-923-2302) and **Yellow Cab** (305-565-5400). In Palm Beach, **Yellow Cab** (407-689-4222) provides both taxi and limousine service.

EAST

COAST

CHAPTER FOUR

East Coast

Florida's East Coast stretches more than 300 miles, from the glittering edge of the Gold Coast up to the genteel environs bordering the Georgia state line. For that entire distance, the Atlantic Ocean alternately laps and crashes against a seemingly endless stretch of beach.

Those who rush through the state along the fast-moving inland interstates rarely realize that virtually all of this coast is separated from the ocean by a series of lovely barrier islands. Between these islands and the mainland is the Intracoastal Waterway (called a river in some locales), where calmer inland waters provide safe passage for pleasure craft everywhere on the coast. Most of the fun, a lot of the area's history, and even a glimpse into the future can be found on the islands.

This chapter leads the Florida visitor from south to north, but the state, and its East Coast, was originally developed north to south. The first known visitor to Florida was the Spanish explorer Ponce de León, who landed in 1513 near present-day St. Augustine. By 1562, the French were making inroads near the mouth of the St. Johns River. While the land itself was not considered particularly valuable—no precious metals and little fertile land had been found—the peninsula was deemed strategic for the safe passage of Spanish ships, laden with treasure from the south and bound for the mother country. King Philip II's determination to rout the French from northeast Florida led to a series of encounters so brutal that the bay at St. Augustine (now Matanzas Bay) became known as "The Bay of Slaughter."

There were more struggles in the early 1600s against the British, and later against English colonists from the north who succeeded in establishing Florida's northern boundary at the St. Marys River in 1742. Still to come were lengthy wars with the Seminoles, the native Indians who resisted displacement by American settlers, and the American Civil War, which divided Florida between Union and Confederate control.

By the late 19th century, however, the smoke had cleared and guidebooks to the state were drawing visitors eager to escape the northern winters. In the 1880s Florida lured its most important tourist since Ponce de León. His name was Henry Flagler, and he had a vision of Florida's East Coast as one long stretch of luxury resorts. Frustrated by the lack of transportation, the former Standard Oil executive established the Florida East Coast Railway and extended it from Jacksonville all the way to Miami. Thus began the state's big boom. With each few miles of railway, another wintertime playground was established, frequently by Flagler himself, who built such legendary resorts as the Flagler Hotel in St. Augustine and the Breakers in Palm Beach.

Flagler also built the Ormond Hotel in Ormond Beach, paving the way for scores of prosperous families from the Northeast (the Astors, Rockefellers and Vanderbilts among them) to discover the pleasures of Daytona Beach. When the beach was found suitable for automobile traffic, the race was on, assuring this city its place in world land-speed record books.

Over the years, various settlers arrived on the East Coast for varied reasons. The French Huguenots, for instance, driven from the North by the Spanish, were the first Europeans to invade what had been the territory of the Tomoka Indians. Indigo and sugar plantations and orange groves were established around Daytona Beach, but, as elsewhere on the coast, the population explosion ultimately arrived via Flagler's train cars. As a result, the East Coast has a hodge-podge history, as outposts were built years before an adequate transportation system that would assure stability.

Today, no single focal point highlights the region, but it is united by one sensibility—an overwhelming consciousness of the ocean's proximity. The salt air, the casual atmosphere, the emphasis on water sports and the abundance of exquisite seafood provide constant reminders.

If a common thread can be identified, it is the threat of overdevelopment along the coast. The ocean, which as late as 1980 was visible for miles at a stretch, has been disappearing behind a phalanx of condominiums and, in Daytona Beach especially, has largely become the exclusive visual domain of oceanfront hotel guests. The good news is that virtually every square foot of East Coast beach is open to the public.

The geography in this region is fairly consistent: flat sandy beaches fringed with palm trees and imported Australian pines (not true pines, by the way). The climate is another matter. Winter can be quite chilly in the north, for instance, and sweaters are often necessary in January as far south as Cocoa Beach. But the climate is on the whole temperate. On the central East Coast, temperatures range from an average low of 50° in January to

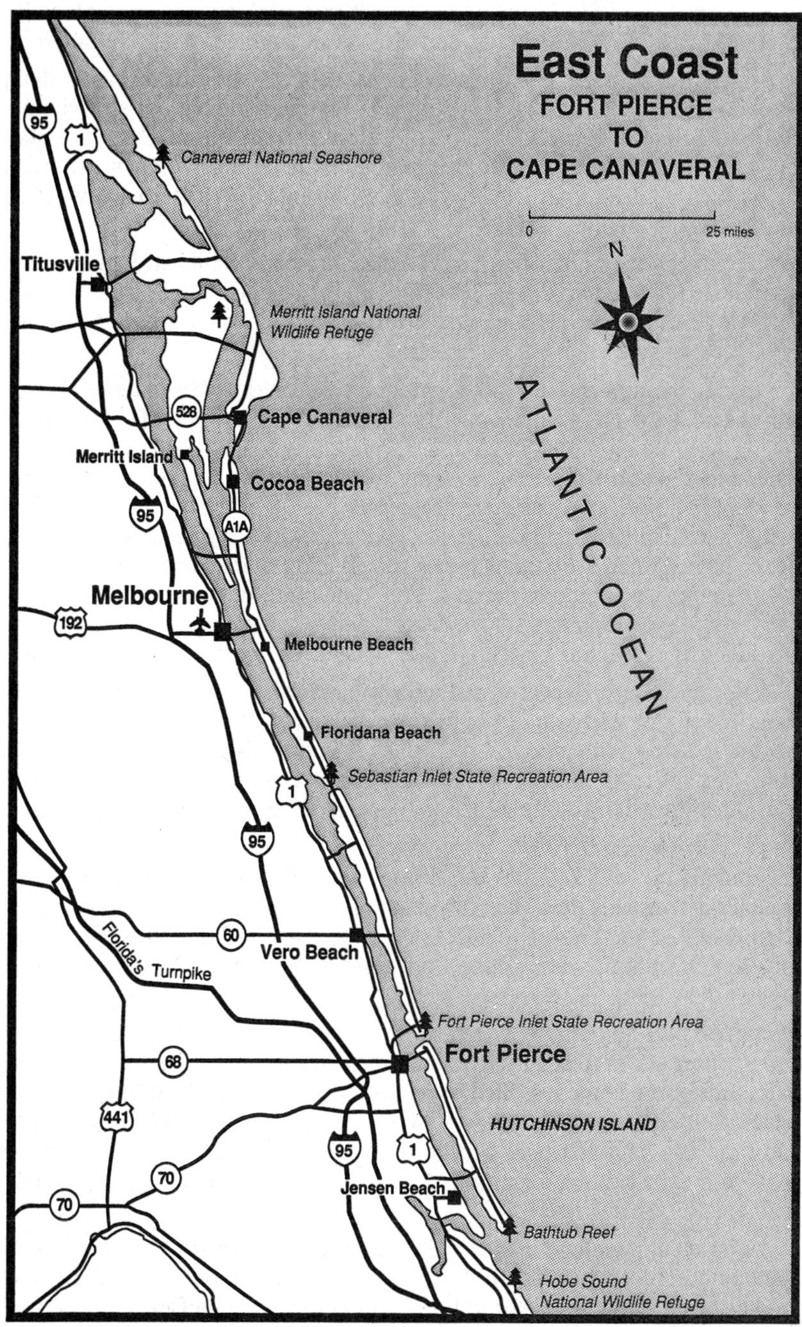
East Coast
FORT PIERCE
TO
CAPE CANAVERAL
0
25 miles
N
ATLANTIC OCEAN
95
1
Canaveral National Seashore
Titusville
Merritt Island National
Wildlife Refuge
528
Cape Canaveral
Merritt Island
Cocoa Beach
95
A1A
Melbourne
192
Melbourne Beach
Floridana Beach
Sebastian Inlet State Recreation Area
1
95
60
Vero Beach
Florida's Turnpike
Fort Pierce Inlet State Recreation Area
68
Fort Pierce
441
HUTCHINSON ISLAND
95
1
70
Jensen Beach
70
Bathtub Reef
Hobe Sound
National Wildlife Refuge

an average high of 89° in July. In the northeast, nighttime temperatures dip to an average of 47° in winter and rise to an average of 89° in summer.

Oddly enough, the best sightseeing route in eastern Florida has evolved into almost "hidden" status. It is possible—and recommended—for visitors to drive the entire East Coast along Route A1A. This beach-hugging road lopes through resort towns and retirement enclaves and villages not much bigger than intersections. Route A1A runs through the barrier islands, often within earshot of the surf.

Except in the bigger towns, A1A has a sleepy quality to it, especially when it narrows to two lanes. This route runs through "Old Florida," a land of fishing camps, marinas and waterfront shanties with some of the freshest, most inexpensive seafood in the state.

Along the way is a string of towns and cities, many of them quite distinct. Fort Pierce, for example, more closely resembles a 19th-century fishing village than it does the glossy brochure image of Florida beach resort towns. Established in 1838 as a United States Army post to fend off the Seminole Indians, the fort developed as a distribution center for beef, citrus and vegetables raised in the surrounding agricultural areas. The waterways from Stuart up to Vero Beach have gained acclaim as prime sportfishing ports, yet there is no trace of self-importance among natives. This casual attitude apparently has carried over to development, for there are relatively few condominiums or hotels along the beaches of Hutchinson Island, on which these towns lie.

North of Vero Beach, Fort Pierce's fancier neighbor, is a particularly beautiful stretch of road; at points, you can see the ocean on one side and the Intracoastal Waterway on the other. It is off this part of the coast that many Spanish cargo ships were wrecked in past centuries. To this day, pieces of eight still wash up on the beaches after major storms. Hence the nickname of the region, the Treasure Coast.

Indialantic and Satellite Beach are so small that they could be missed were it not for roadside signs. The next real city up the road is Cocoa Beach. Established at the end of the 19th century, the town is said to be named for the coco plum, which once flourished here along with citrus groves.

Since NASA established a space center here in the 1960s, the town has turned into something of a bedroom community for scientists, astronauts and support staff. A beautiful stretch of beach offers sensational viewing points for space launches. Sharing nearby Merritt Island with the Kennedy Space Center is the 140,000-acre Merritt Island National Wildlife Refuge and the Canaveral National Seashore, expanses of pristine wilderness that provide a safe habitat for hundreds of species of mammals, reptiles, amphibians, birds and fish.

The most developed of east Florida's resort towns is Daytona Beach. Here automobile traffic is still tolerated on the beach, but professional racing has been removed inland to the tracks at the Daytona Beach Speedway.

In fact all beach driving is hotly disputed and may end soon, as environmentalists argue that the cars interfere with Mother Nature, especially the sea turtles who come up to lay their eggs on Florida's beaches in the early summer.

St. Augustine has attracted visitors ever since Ponce de León stepped ashore, allegedly in search of the mythical Fountain of Youth. Established in 1565 by Pedro Menéndez de Aviles for the king of Spain, it is the oldest city in the country, a fact pounded home at virtually every old house and tourist attraction. This is a quaint city of narrow streets and considerable charm. It was envisioned by Henry Flagler as the first in a string of resort towns. But as the railroad took more and more tourists and settlers to the south, St. Augustine faded from prominence. Thus, its downtown area looks much the way it has for centuries.

Forty miles north of St. Augustine, Jacksonville is more a working-class city, a sprawling megalopolis that may one day rival Atlanta as the industrial hub of the South. Only lately has this city begun reviving its downtown area and rehabilitating some of the lovely old neighborhoods. Nearby lie the towns of Atlantic Beach and Jacksonville Beach, which, although they have their share of motels, still remain largely residential and far more low-key than Daytona Beach.

Tucked away in the northeast corner of the state, within sight of Georgia's coast, Amelia Island is virtually a hidden destination in itself. The south end of the island has largely been appropriated for golf courses and condominiums, while Fernandina Beach, on the north end, has the monopoly on historic sites. While there is not as much to see here as in St. Augustine, Amelia Island has an even more complex military history, having existed under eight different flags since 1562: French, Spanish, English, Spanish again, Patriots (a local group that overthrew the Spaniards), the Green Cross of Florida, Mexican, American, Confederate and then American again.

From Spanish conquerors to time-share condominiums, the East Coast of Florida has remained one of the most enticing destinations in the country.

Fort Pierce Area

If anything could be said to unify the disparate communities from Jensen Beach to Sebastian Inlet, it would be the sleepy quality of this string of small riverfront cities and little beach towns. Vero Beach is something of an exception, with its posh shops and chic restaurants, but for the most part it seems the 20th century has yet to make its presence known. Route 1 serves as the major inland artery, while Route A1A zigzags from mainland to oceanside, over bridges connecting the Intracoastal Waterway to the slim barrier islands of South Hutchinson and North Hutchinson.

The same temperate climate that has made Indian River citrus famous for quality has also made the Fort Pierce area a mecca for sports lovers. The calm inland waterways provide bountiful opportunities for fishing, as do offshore currents. But in centuries past, the ocean also spelled doom for Spanish galleons and other ships caught in storms or unexpectedly rough waters, and the bounty salvaged from these wrecks inspired a new nomenclature for the region. Sandwiched between the Gold Coast and the Space Coast (as the Cape Canaveral area has been dubbed), this part of the world now calls itself the Treasure Coast.

This area's approach to tourism is so low key that travelers must use some initiative to spot several points of interest. The **Environmental Studies Center** (2900 Northeast Indian River Drive, Jensen Beach; 407-334-1262), for instance, looks like a small-town elementary school. But this 1930s-era WPA building houses an intriguing array of natural science exhibits, including a display of manatee and dolphin skeletons and a wet lab where you can observe captive loggerheads, sharks and other marine life.

Gilbert's Bar House of Refuge (★) (301 Southeast MacArthur Boulevard, Stuart; 407-225-1875; admission) was built in the 1870s as a haven for sailors shipwrecked in nearby waters. Standing on a slim strand only yards from the ocean, the white clapboard house, said to be the oldest structure in the area, has several ground floor rooms furnished much as they were when stranded sailors stayed here, plus a small museum of marine artifacts and antiquated lifesaving equipment. Also on view is a small aquarium with seasonal fish.

Dominating a curve of road north of Gilbert's Bar, the **Elliott Museum** (North East Ocean Boulevard, Stuart Beach; 407-225-1961; admission) is easily recognized by its gracious white columns. The museum, named after American inventor Sterling Elliott, houses collections of almost Smithsonian scope. Most curious is an old-fashioned apothecary shop that re-creates a turn-of-the-century commercial establishment. You'll also find local history displays, including Indian artifacts, as well as a hodgepodge that ranges from antique photographic equipment to an old-fashioned Victorian parlor. The museum's crowning glory is its lineup of classic automobiles, motorcycles and bicycles, a fantasy garage that illustrates the history of automotive engineering.

From here north to Fort Pierce and beyond, some of the best sightseeing can be done from a car, driving either on Route A1A or on **Indian River Drive** (★), the narrow winding road that parallels the west bank of the Indian River. Shaded, peaceful and traveled mostly by locals, the drive passes between the river and gracious homes, some so large they have names instead of numbers.

Be sure to stop by **Heathcote Botanical Gardens** (★) (Savannah Road, one-and-a-half blocks east of Route 1, Fort Pierce; 407-464-4672), a three-acre reserve thick with mature trees, blooming flowers and radiant foliage. Don't miss the Japanese bonsai exhibit.

Indian River Drive leads north into Fort Pierce, where you can find South Route A1A (Seaway Drive) and cross the causeway heading east. You can stop at the **St. Lucie County Historical Museum** (414 Seaway Drive; 407-468-1795; admission), which specializes in artifacts from the 1715 wreck of a Spanish treasure fleet bound from Havana. A glass-encased exhibit shows how divers locate the many wreck sites off this stretch of coastline. Also educational are a reconstructed Seminole encampment and the 1907 Gardner House next door. The **St. Lucie County Chamber of Commerce** (2200 Virginia Avenue, Fort Pierce; 407-461-2700) can provide more information on the historic sights.

Fort Pierce Jai Alai (1750 South King's Highway; 407-464-7500; admission) is a huge frontón where you can watch the fast-action sport of jai alai, originally developed by Basque peasants in the Pyrenees Mountains.

Even non-divers will find much of interest at the circular little **UDT-SEAL Museum** (3300 North Route A1A at Pepper Park, Fort Pierce; 407-489-3597). Located near a World War II beach training site, the museum honors the Underwater Demolition Teams (UDTs) and Sea, Air and Land Teams (SEALs) with military exhibits, documents, photographs and paintings from several wars. The small weapons and other artifacts collected from North Vietnamese soldiers alone warrant a visit.

The **McLarty State Museum** (Route A1A, 14 miles north of Vero Beach; 407-589-2147; admission) displays relics salvaged from 18th-century ships wrecked off the nearby coast. A narrated slide show illustrates the development of a barrier island, and rangers are often on hand to answer questions about marine topics like sand dunes, coral reefs and sea turtles.

FORT PIERCE AREA HOTELS

The coast from Stuart to Vero Beach is better known for citrus and sailfishing than for its posh accommodations. Condominiums outnumber hotel rooms; the best motels are along the inlet in Fort Pierce itself and near the ocean in Vero Beach.

The **Indian River Plantation** (555 Northeast Ocean Boulevard, Stuart Beach; 407-225-3700) makes a stunning first impression when approached via Route A1A from the west. The 200-acre resort stretches from the Indian River Intracoastal Waterway to the Atlantic Ocean, with 325 guest accommodations ranging from condominium suites to luxurious hotel rooms decorated in soft colors and outfitted with handsome, well-made contemporary furnishings. The plantation is a sports-lover's dream: golf courses meandering beside waterways, tennis courts, a swimming pool and access to myriad water sports. Deluxe to ultra-deluxe.

River's Edge (2625 Northeast Indian River Drive, Jensen Beach; 407-334-4759) seems to be the only motel in this entire area located directly on the Indian River. The accommodations are spacious at this tan-and-brown two-story complex, where the 18 two-room suites can be had for a moderate price. The decor, however, is almost nonexistent, and kitchenettes seem to have been squeezed in as an afterthought.

The **Harbor Light Inn** (1160 Seaway Drive, Fort Pierce; 407-468-3555) is by far the smartest of the little lodging spots along Seaway, the southern route to the beaches. Painted a cheery Mediterranean blue and white, with flourishing tropical plants flanking a blue-tiled pool (complete with built-in spa and a gazebo), this 20-room inn proves that accommodations don't have to be rustic to fit right in with the relaxing pace of riverside life. Rooms are spacious, well lit and equipped with a refrigerator and wet bar. The best ones have furnished balconies where guests can view sea birds and fishing boats. And when the sun begins to set, the place to appreciate it is on one of the inn's private docks. Moderate to deluxe.

One of the most laid-back places to lodge in Fort Pierce, the **Holiday Beach Motel and Apartments** (1750 Seaway Drive; 407-461-1540) has two floors of rooms and efficiencies. Rooms tend to be small, but the ones with water views are at least a bit brighter than the rest. This is the kind of place where you can settle down on the dock with a rod and reel and a bucket of bait and not stir for an entire afternoon. Budget to moderate.

The **Caribbean Apartments and Motel** (1502 Seaway Drive, Fort Pierce; 407-461-5628) offers 12 spacious ground-floor rooms hugging a large waterfront courtyard. Kitchenettes available. Budget to moderate.

The rooms are shipshape at the three-story **Mariner's Lodge** (222 Hernando Street, Fort Pierce; 407-466-5724), located about a block and a half from the beach. Ask for an upper-floor oceanview room; it will be decked out in pale blue patterns, solid blond wood furniture and prints of sailing ships. Moderate.

If you don't mind slightly mismatched carpets and bedspreads, the accommodations at the **Surf and Sand Resort Motel** (1516 South Ocean Drive, Vero Beach; 407-231-5700) are quite a deal. There's lots of light from two sides, a small pool and proximity to the beach, shops and restaurants. Moderate.

True to its name, the **Aquarius Oceanfront Resort** (1526 South Ocean Drive, Vero Beach; 407-231-5218) sits right on the beach. Fringed with palm trees, sea oats and tiki huts, the two-story complex features a heated pool and shuffleboard courts. Most of the 27 guest rooms have kitchenettes, and all offer wall-to-wall carpets and tropical decor. Moderate.

The **Driftwood Resort** (3150 Ocean Drive, Vero Beach; 407-231-0550) achieved notoriety in the 1930s by virtue of its amateurish architecture and offbeat decor, both the work of entrepreneur/raconteur Waldo Sexton. Finds from flea markets, antique stores and the sea itself are strewn about the property, with ships' bells and driftwood predominating. Rooms are modern and clean but not as interesting as the public areas at this colorful inn. Moderate to deluxe.

FORT PIERCE AREA RESTAURANTS

The poshest restaurant on Hutchinson Island is **Scalawags** (555 Northeast Ocean Boulevard in the Indian River Plantation Resort, Stuart; 407-225-3700). French country furniture, fine linens and a tasteful color scheme of green and apricot warm up this 140-seat restaurant. Two walls of glass provide an expansive view of the marina and the Intracoastal Waterway. Seafood and beef receive imaginative treatment here, as do pasta dishes such as one with roast duck. Dinner only. Moderate to deluxe.

Conchy Joe's Seafood Restaurant (★) (3945 North Indian River Drive, Jensen Beach; 407-334-1130) sports a thatched roof and an island-inspired decor that make it look suspiciously like a tourist trap, yet it's anything but. You'll almost always find a crowd of regulars in the delightful open-air dining room perched over the Indian River. At lunch, they'll usually be snacking on conch meat in some guise (fritters, burgers, etc.), or something from the raw bar. But there's also a full menu featuring specialties such as soft-shell crab and seafood pasta dishes. Moderate to deluxe.

Every beach town should have a dining place as cheery and casual as **BJ's Breakfast Café** (10545 South Route A1A, Jensen Beach; 407-229-5504). Located right across the highway from the beach, BJ's features an extensive breakfast menu from ham and cheese omelettes to french toast. Sandwiches, salads and hamburgers are served at lunch. Budget.

Few restaurants make as much of their setting as does **Mangrove Mattie's** (1640 Seaway Drive, Fort Pierce; 407-466-1044), where bare wood and tropical prints look wonderful against the backdrop of Fort Pierce Inlet. Ask to be seated on the veranda and order a cup of conch chowder, a throat-warming concoction with tomatoes and spices. Also recommended are almost any dishes made with the sweet local shrimp. The Sunday brunch buffet is extensive and delicious. Moderate to deluxe.

Cooled off by pastel walls and plenty of fans suspended from high ceilings, the **Captain's Galley** (825 North Indian River Drive, Fort Pierce; 407-466-8495) is the place to go for an imaginative breakfast: pigs in a blanket, pork chops with eggs, pecan pancakes or granola. You can order breakfast any time of day, but then you'd miss the conch chowder, seafood salads, chicken dishes and the catch-of-the-day. Moderate.

It's worth going out of your way to find **Out of Bounds** (★) (604 Atlantic Avenue, Fort Pierce; 407-464-1052), an odd combination of good, creative food served in a spacious dining room festooned with tennis racquets and hockey sticks. The sports-inspired list of dishes includes the "Jack

Nicklaus" (battered and pan-fried fish topped with hollandaise sauce) and the "Indianapolis 500" (snails with spinach). But the chef turns serious in the kitchen, creating such daily specials as lobster and beef tenderloin sautéed with garlic, mushrooms, onions and macadamia nuts then flambéed with Jack Daniels. Moderate.

A small, nine-booth café festooned with piñatas and sombreros, **Enriqos Mexican Restaurant** (3215 South Route 1, Fort Pierce; 407-465-1608) is known for its fresh approach to south-of-the-border standbys such as *chile rellenos*, fajitas and *pollo asada*. Budget.

Route 1 is blessed with a number of ethnic restaurants that offer budget-priced specials. Located right on the highway, **Panda Panda Restaurant** (3211 South Route 1, Fort Pierce; 407-465-0570) has the short, squat look of a fast-food joint. In fact, it's a hospitable place with an impressively long menu. Pork and seafood predominate at this Szechuan-style restaurant. Prices are moderate.

One of the many ethnic restaurants located in shopping centers, **Italia in Bocca** (2509 South Route 1, Fort Pierce; 407-461-0065) pays homage to the mother country with ceiling lamps in the green, white and red color scheme of the Italian national flag. So much for decor. In addition to pizzas, this modest place features veal, shrimp and pasta dishes. Moderate.

The station wagons with Florida license tags that fill the large parking lot at **Norris's Famous Place for Ribs** (3080 North Route 1, North Fort Pierce; 407-464-4000) provide evidence that locals often patronize this lively family-style restaurant. Big tables are set for big appetites. Beef is the major draw here—everything from barbecued ribs to french dip to old-fashioned hamburgers. Then there's chicken, seafood and side dishes like corn on the cob and Texas-style chili. Budget to moderate.

P. V. Martin's Beach Café (5150 North Route A1A, Fort Pierce; 407-465-7300) is a large, single-story clapboard structure in a beautiful oceanfront location where sea oats graze the windows. Far from being ramshackle, the dimly lit dining rooms are graced with elegant touches such as tables topped with Mexican blue tiles. The deluxe-priced menu includes alligator tails and soft-shell crab as well as more conventional beef and chicken dishes. And local connoisseurs consistently recommend P. V. Martin's Sunday brunch.

It's a little disconcerting to find a pool at the front door of **Chez Yannick** (1601 South Ocean Drive, Vero Beach; 407-234-4115), but that's only one distinguishing feature of this interesting restaurant. Understated in its decor and ingeniously designed with freestanding room dividers, Chez Yannick offers a *très Français* menu highlighting duck à l'orange, filet mignon béarnaise and other sophisticated fare. Moderate to deluxe.

Easily overlooked by travelers, the **Village South Restaurant and Lounge** (2900 Ocean Drive, Vero Beach; 407-231-6727) is a brick-fronted hangout for an older set who look as if they could afford to eat anywhere they choose. Maybe it's the spinach salad, the soups, the pasta dishes, the elegant chilled seafood platter or the veal specialties that keep this place busy even for weekday lunch. Whatever, this is a pleasant, refined little enclave. Moderate to deluxe.

The **Beachside Restaurant** (3125 Ocean Drive, Vero Beach; 407-234-4477) is a welcome respite from the pricier establishments in this oceanfront neighborhood. Breakfasts, salads, sandwiches and delicacies like crabmeat quiche are served at neat tables covered with blue floral fabric and topped with glass. No greasy spoons at this budget-priced find.

It's easy to guess that Waldo Sexton, the local legend behind the nearby Driftwood Resort, had a hand in creating the **Ocean Grill** (1050 Sexton Plaza, Vero Beach; 407-231-5409), a weathered-wood wonder that appears ready to fall into the sea with the next big wave. The basic surf 'n' turf menu is spiced with *coquilles St. Jacques*, crab au gratin and Florida oysters. Moderate to deluxe.

The most compelling feature of **Lepire's** (4700 North Route A1A, Vero Beach; 407-231-1600) is its atrium setting overlooking a pool. The moderately priced menu is nothing to write home about; it's a mélange of chicken, veal and gumbo. But the island-inspired furnishings and waterside setting give it an enchanting atmosphere. Dinner only.

Black Pearl (1409 Route A1A, Vero Beach; 407-234-4426) is not on the ocean, but it does ride the wave of haute cuisine sweeping the area. A comely little restaurant with a spiffy awning, it has come up with offerings such as cheese-and-spinach fritters, local fish in parchment and Cajun pasta dishes. Dinner only. Moderate to deluxe.

FORT PIERCE AREA SHOPPING

Not surprisingly, in light of the fierce sun and heat, the preferred habitat of the southeast Florida shopper is the fully air-conditioned mall. In second place is one of the many shopping centers and strips that line Route 1 from Stuart all the way to Vero Beach. High-priced boutiques are a dime a dozen in the finer hotels, but other than those, there isn't much retail action at the beach.

When it's time to tee off, it's time to visit **Nevada Bob's** (705 North Route 1, Stuart; 407-692-9700). Located in Riverside Shoppes, this 4000-square-foot emporium is discount headquarters for name-brand equipment and accessories ranging from head covers and shoes to practice videotapes and distance-finders. Customers are welcome to try out a set of clubs on the in-store putting green.

Sequestered in a semi-forested setting, **Treasure Coast Square** (Route 1 and Jensen Beach Boulevard, Jensen Beach; 407-692-0100) exudes sleek elegance in and out. Marble-clad lobbies decorated with fancy trees and skylights enhance the fantasy image of this stunning structure. Nationally and internationally known chains such as **Waldenbooks** (407-692-9615) make this their address in Jensen Beach. You'll find a variety of Florida jams and jellies, salad dressings, local cookbooks and gourmet coffees at **Kitchen Gifts and Gadgets** (407-692-3007). This kitchen shop also offers wreaths, dried flower arrangements and baskets, as well as a wide range of utensils, bakeware and cookware. A contemporary shop offering traditional and stylish European suits and jackets, **Park Avenue Menswear** (407-692-2704) is also a good place to look for accessories.

Chocoholics unite, and untie a gift box of hand-dipped chocolates (dietetic or regular strength) from **Bruno's House of Chocolates** (2650 North Route 1, North Fort Pierce; 407-461-3229). The people at Bruno's give tours of the "factory" (really a candy kitchen), where they create candies and novelties using loving hands and no preservatives.

A four-block stretch along Ocean Drive in Vero Beach is a trove of delightful discoveries. The biggest sparkler is **Bottalico Gallery (★)** (2908 Ocean Drive; 407-231-0414), a gallery/studio for the highly original work of Glen Bottalico. Colorful trompe l'oeil scenes cover screens, boxes and canvases. Whimsical shells, butterflies and flowers are painted on baskets and candlesticks. The prices seem quite moderate when you consider these are collector's items.

In the airy bleached stucco **Portales de Vero Shopping Arcade** (2855 Ocean Drive, Vero Beach), ground-floor merchants include **The Art Works** (407-231-4688), a contemporary gallery; and **Harry L. Buck Jewelers** (407-231-0808), specializing in jade, lapis lazuli and fresh-water pearls. Toward the back, **Roundabout** (407-231-3323) overflows with small gifts and stationery items. What a selection: Italian-designed desk pens; sophisticated wrapping paper and festive bags; children's writing materials; and oodles of small items at dime-store prices.

The **Hawaiian Shop** (3117 Ocean Drive; 407-231-5818), here since the '50s, racks up casual island wear including muumuus, sandals and men's Hawaiian shirts in slightly subdued patterns.

A must-see, especially for women looking for that special something to wear to a nice Vero Beach restaurant, is **Orchid Island Trading Co.** (3143 Ocean Drive; 407-231-0620). Here you'll find fine dresses, beach wear and accessories that make excellent gifts.

FORT PIERCE AREA NIGHTLIFE

Crabby's (2075 Northeast Indian River Drive, Jensen Beach; 407-334-2500) is a funny name for a restaurant-cum-lounge housed in a rather elegant building on the river. Instead of going in the main door, take the side entrance that leads to a small lounge and a terrace beyond. There's a reggae band Sunday nights.

You don't have to dress up to go dancing at **Frankie and Johnny's** (414 South Atlantic Avenue, Fort Pierce; 407-464-5467), though you'll fit in better if you wear a ten-gallon hat. The country-and-western bands are the real thing at this big corner nightclub. Cover.

At the stroke of five, office workers begin to congregate at **P. J. Clark's** (122 North 2nd Street, Fort Pierce, 407-468-9090). With a biplane suspended from the ceiling and peanut shells on the floor, P. J.'s is the kind of place that knows how to help people unwind.

One week it's rhythm-and-blues, the next week music from the '60s and '70s at **Marvin Gardens** (3030 North Route 1, Vero Beach; 407-567-3939).

The 633-seat **Riverside Theatre** (3250 Riverside Park Drive, Vero Beach; 407-231-6990) presents half-a-dozen performances by the Acting Company of Riverside each year, such as Broadway musicals, comedies and dramas.

FORT PIERCE AREA BEACHES AND PARKS

Hobe Sound National Wildlife Refuge—One of the most successful sea turtle nesting areas in the country, Hobe Sound Refuge consists of more than three miles of beach, sand dunes, and mangroves plus a sand-pine scrub forest. So abundant is the wildlife in this refuge that an appealing sign has been posted admonishing visitors not to "aggravate, harass, irritate, molest, bother, beleaguer" or otherwise annoy the animals. Thus protected, scrub jays and other songbirds survive in peace in the mainland forest, and several varieties of sea turtles struggle to shore to lay their eggs on the island portion of the park.

Facilities: Restrooms, interpretive museum, nature trail; information, 407-546-6141. *Fishing:* Saltwater fishing off the beach and along the Intracoastal Waterway. *Swimming:* There is ocean swimming off of North Beach Road.

Getting there: Located off Route 1 several miles north of Jupiter.

Jonathan Dickinson State Park—This inland park undulates through some 10,000 acres topped by Hobe Mountain, at 86 feet the closest thing to a real mountain in south Florida. A variety of plant communities including sand pine scrub, mangrove and river swamp support a great deal of animal life. Deer and rabbit are common sights, but there are also otter, snakes, fish and birds. The park is a refuge for nearly extinct species such as southern bald eagles, Florida scrubjays and manatees, which live in the portions of the Loxahatchee River where salt water has made an intrusion.

Facilities: Picnic area, bicycle and boat rental, concession stand, nature and bike trails. Guided tours up the wild Loxahatchee. Information, 407-546-2771. *Fishing:* Salt and freshwater angling. *Swimming:* Good near the shore.

Camping: There are 135 sites, most with RV hookups; $17-19 per night. Moderately priced cabins are also available (reservations required); information, 407-746-1466.

Getting there: Located five miles north of Jupiter off Route 1.

Bathtub Reef Park—An offshore reef near the southern tip of Hutchinson Island forms a bathtub-calm shallow area that attracts snorkelers. This sandy, undeveloped beach extends for 1100 feet just north of St. Lucie Inlet.

Facilities: Restrooms, showers, lifeguards; groceries and restaurants are found nearby. *Fishing:* Very good. *Swimming:* Highly recommended. *Snorkeling:* Excellent.

Getting there: Follow Route A1A south to the end of Hutchinson Island.

Stuart Beach (★)—The oceanfront stretch of five-acre **Martin County Park** is one of the loveliest developed beaches around Fort Pierce. Stuart Beach is accessible via a boardwalk shaded by several stands of Australian pines. Dune crossovers lead to a smooth, light-brown beach, extremely popular with locals. There are undeveloped beaches both north and south of this park.

Facilities: Picnic areas, restrooms, showers, lifeguards, playground, volleyball courts, basketball courts, concession stand; nearby are restaurants and grocery stores. For information, 407-288-5690. *Fishing:* Surf fishing directly in front of boardwalk. *Swimming:* Good, but waves break close to beach. *Surfing:* Fair.

Getting there: On MacArthur Boulevard, Hutchinson Island.

Savannas Recreation Area—Fort Pierce has the distinction of having a 550-acre wilderness park located within its city limits. A fragile ecosystem of marsh and uplands, the park features fresh-water lagoons and creeks banked with lily pads and soft marsh grasses, home to a number of waterfowl and wading birds.

Facilities: Picnic areas, restrooms, showers, concession stand, boat rentals; information, 407-464-7855. *Fishing:* Bass and compatible freshwater game fish.

Camping: There are 65 sites, all with RV hookups; $10-16 per night.

Getting there: Located off Route 707-A between Route 1 and the Indian River.

Frederick Douglass Memorial Park (★)—Of the ten or so public access points on Hutchinson Island, this minimally developed park is one of the most stunning. A narrow strip of clean, creamy sand stretches for more than 1000 feet. Fringed by delicate Australian pines, the beach is one of the prettiest in this area.

Facilities: Picnic area, restrooms, showers, lifeguards; grocery and restaurants are nearby; information, 407-468-1521. *Swimming:* Excellent.

Getting there: On Route A1A four miles south of Fort Pierce Inlet.

Fort Pierce Inlet State Recreation Area—Covering 340 acres directly north of the inlet, the park includes a coastal hammock, dunes and a pristine swath of hard sand known as North Jetty Beach. This beach and others to the north have better waves than those on the south side of the inlet, thanks to the creation of a rock jetty that affects the wave patterns. Dynamite Point, on the inlet, is the best place in the area for observing the shorebirds that feed and nest along the waterfront. There is also some beachfront along the inlet itself.

Facilities: Picnic areas, restrooms, showers, lifeguards in the summer; groceries and restaurants nearby. Information, 407-468-3985. *Fishing:* The most popular spot is off the jetty. *Swimming:* Excellent at North Jetty Beach. *Surfing:* Some of the county's best waves. *Snorkeling:* Pretty good near the rocks.

Getting there: Located in Fort Pierce at 905 Shore Winds Drive.

Pepper Beach—Wooden walkways cross tall sand dunes dotted with sea grapes to a 2000-foot stretch of hard sand beach. This simple and pristine spot is ideal for picnicking.

Facilities: Restrooms, showers, lifeguards; restaurants and grocery stores are located nearby; information, 407-468-1521. *Swimming:* Excellent. *Surfing:* Not the best.

Getting there: Located on North Route A1A north of Fort Pierce Inlet, Fort Pierce.

Jack Island State Preserve (★)—Even people who have heard of Jack Island have trouble finding it and may drive past the narrow access road several times before making the correct turn. At the end of a glorified driveway, invisible from the highway, a footbridge leads across the water to a 631-acre mangrove island. Nature trails lead visitors to several excellent vantage points for observing the waterfowl and other birds that flourish in this sanctuary. Mangroves, seagrapes and a coastal hammock add to the allure.

Facilities: None. *Fishing:* Good.

Getting there: Located two-and-a-half miles north of Fort Pierce Inlet off Route A1A.

Sebastian Inlet State Recreation Area—Sebastian is a name well known to surfers who love to ride the six-foot waves that pound the northside beach. But the beautiful 576-acre recreation area also attracts swimmers, walkers, anglers, bird watchers and boaters. The park, less than a mile across at its widest point, is divided by a manmade inlet. Pristine white sand beaches on either side of the inlet stretch off into the horizon. On the north side of the inlet, a good-sized lagoon offers calm, warm, shallow waters. Beachcombing is excellent here; pieces of eight from offshore wrecks are occasionally washed on shore by storms.

Facilities: Picnic areas, restrooms, showers, lifeguards, concession stands, visitor center; for information, 407-984-4852. *Fishing:* Fishing and shrimping are good off the catwalks under the inlet bridge. Surf angling north of the jetty. *Swimming:* Excellent north of the fishing and surfing beaches near the jetty. *Surfing:* Tops on this part of the coast; an area just north of the jetty is set aside for surfers.

Camping: There are 51 sites with RV hookups; $15 per night; information, 407-589-9659. Reservations recommended in the winter.

Getting there: Located 16 miles north of Vero Beach on Route A1A.

Cape Canaveral Area

Scenic Route A1A hugs the shoreline on its way north from the Fort Pierce area to Cape Canaveral. Except for a few condominium complexes, virtually nothing lies between the roadway and the beach as the two-lane highway cuts through small residential communities such as Indialantic and Melbourne Beach. The biggest city in the region is Melbourne, a landlocked harbor on the Intracoastal Waterway, but Cocoa Beach, basically a company town for NASA and the Kennedy Space Center, is better located for sightseeing.

Melbourne boasts several art galleries and one major museum devoted to the arts. Located in a beautifully landscaped setting overlooking the Intracoastal Waterway, the **Brevard Art Center and Museum** (1463 North Highland Avenue, Melbourne; 407-242-0737; admission) rotates displays of its permanent collection of modern art, African primitive works and pre-Columbian art. This sleek, contemporary museum also hosts touring art exhibitions from around the country.

Mother Nature and the trappings of the space age exist side by side in the Cape Canaveral area. Every time a space shuttle blasts off in a cloud of steam and smoke, the waterfowl and other wildlife on surrounding Merritt Island are momentarily disturbed before returning to the peaceful routine established by their kind over the centuries.

You can recapture the history of America's space exploration—plus glimpse its future—at the Kennedy Space Center's **Spaceport USA** (Route 405, Merritt Island; 407-452-2121). This fascinating complex is an absolute must-see and one of the greatest values in Florida, especially since most of the attractions are free. You should either hook up with a guide for an introductory half-hour tour or begin on your own with a walk in the *Rocket Garden*, where you can find rockets from each stage of America's space program. Established in 1958, NASA centered many of its early, manned operations at nearby Cape Canaveral, still the site of weather and communications satellite launchings. By 1964, what had become known as the NASA Kennedy Space Center was relocated to adjacent Merritt Island.

Inside the *Gallery of Space Flight* are full-sized models of a lunar rover and the Viking Mars Lander, along with actual spacecraft. One of the most eye-opening displays is the one-tenth scale model of the rocket that sent the Apollo 11 astronauts to the moon; it's amazing to see how small the capsule was compared with the size of the entire spacecraft.

The *Galaxy Center* houses an exhibit of space-related art and two theaters. The Galaxy Theater screens multimedia presentations on various space topics. But for sheer exhilaration, you simply cannot top the 37-minute film shown on a 70-foot-wide screen in the IMAX Theater (admission). The sound system is so extraordinary that the entire theater shudders when a shuttle is launched into space. The rest of the film consists of spectacular footage shot by astronauts in the course of various missions. You will feel almost as if you, too, are looking down on the planet earth from outer space, practicing emergency evacuations and conducting experiments in weightlessness.

You should make reservations as soon as you arrive for this show as well as for the two-hour **Bus Tour** (admission) of outlying attractions inaccessible by private vehicle. Double-decker buses depart from the visitor center every 15 minutes all day long and take visitors to the 52-story Vehicle

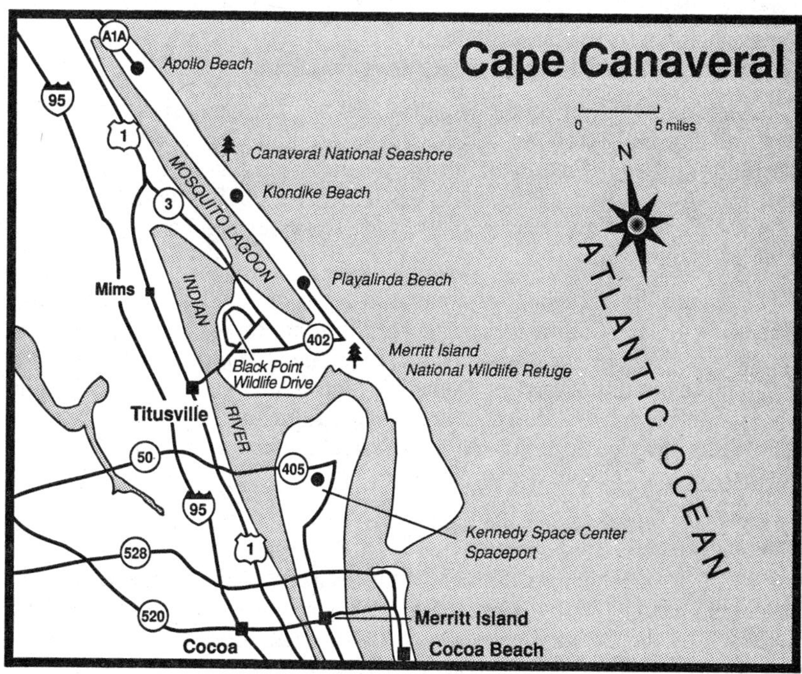

Assembly Building, a replica of a control room that lies within good snapshot distance of one of the two launch pads near the ocean.

Also on Merritt Island are the offices of the **Cocoa Beach Tourism and Convention Council** (400 Fortenberry Road; 407-452-4390), a good place to pick up free maps and brochures.

Near the Cape Canaveral Air Force Station, Florida's greatest natural resource, sunshine, is the main attraction at an unusual site. The **Florida Solar Energy Center** (300 Route 401, Cape Canaveral; 407-783-0300) offers a self-guided tour of its research, development and testing facilities, including several houses equipped to produce solar electricity.

The remainder of Merritt Island, north of the Kennedy Space Center, is largely devoted to the **Merritt Island National Wildlife Refuge** and the Canaveral National Seashore (see the "Cape Canaveral Area Beaches and Parks" section below). Within Merritt Island Refuge (407-861-0667), two auto tour routes guide visitors to prime viewing sites. One road, **Black Point Wildlife Drive** (★), leads into habitats for such unusual species as the anhinga, a bird that swims in the canals with only its snakelike head visible above the water.

The **Brevard Community College Planetarium** (1519 Clearlake Road, Cocoa; 407-631-7889; admission) offers several perspectives on natural history and the space age. The comfortable theater here screens a changing roster of educational skyscape shows and full-dome motion pictures. The planetarium boasts the largest telescope available to the public in the entire state, and a lobby filled with space memorabilia.

A short drive away on the same campus, the **Brevard Museum of History and Natural Science** (2201 Michigan Avenue, Cocoa; 407-632-1830; admission) takes visitors back in time through exhibits of Victorian furniture, Indian tools and pottery, and the remains of extinct animals. As for natural history, the museum maintains an extensive shell collection and 22 acres of nature trails.

The wildlife that inhabits the upper reaches of the St. Johns River (one of the few North American rivers that runs south to north) is best viewed from a boat. Half-hour airboat rides at the **Lone Cabbage Fish Camp** (★) (Route 520, six miles west of Route 95, Cocoa; 407-632-4199) cruise the inland marshes for a close-up look at exotic flora and fauna. (See "On the Wild Side: Sea Turtles and Alligators" in this chapter.)

CAPE CANAVERAL AREA HOTELS

Most of the accommodations in the area are near the ocean, and the better ones can be found in Cocoa Beach. The city of Cocoa, separated from the beach by the Banana River, Merritt Island and the Intracoastal Waterway, is a few miles closer to the Kennedy Space Center.

The **Brevard Hotel** (112 Riverside Drive, Cocoa; 407-636-1411) must have been terrific in its glory days, unfortunately long past. This pale, two-story inn was built in 1923; today, it has the tone of a very quiet but totally respectable rest home. Entering the large, mustard-yellow lobby, seeing the french doors on the far side facing out onto the Indian River, we could almost hear the echoes of lively yesterdays. Upstairs, too much wood makes the rooms look dark. But you should have no trouble booking one overlooking the river, and you'll be within easy walking distance of the blocks of shops and sophisticated restaurants of Cocoa Village. Budget.

The **Inn at Cocoa Beach** (4300 Ocean Beach Boulevard, Cocoa Beach; 407-799-3460) offers the best of everything. All the rooms in this four-story, T-shaped inn are beautifully decorated with fine furniture, plush carpeting and little touches like throw pillows, stools and framed artwork. Attractive drapes cover sliding glass doors that open onto private patios. There are gorgeous views of the ocean right out front, and it's possible to witness space launches from the second-floor rooms. This place has a residential charm all too rare in an area dominated by chain hotels. Deluxe to ultra-deluxe.

One of the biggest surprises in Cocoa Beach is the **Howard Johnson Plaza-Hotel** (2080 North Atlantic Avenue; 407-783-9222). Forget the image of screaming orange and blue so familiar to highway travelers—this is a different Howard Johnson's. Take the lobby, for instance, a gleam of marble and sparkling tile with wicker settees and a high ceiling. Upstairs, luxurious rooms are sleekly furnished in pale woods and come in peaches-and-cream or aqua-and-turquoise colors. Deluxe to ultra-deluxe.

Within easy walking distance of the Canaveral Pier, the **Ocean Suite Hotel** (5500 Ocean Beach Boulevard, Cocoa Beach; 407-784-4343) makes up in room size what it lacks in proximity to the ocean. Variations of beige and rose give these rooms a streamlined look that compensates for the rather bulky appearance of the building itself. Moderate.

The **Days Inn Oceanfront** (5600 North Atlantic Avenue, Cocoa Beach; 407-783-7621) is a bargain only if you insist on a second-story room facing the courtyard. Otherwise, your door will open onto either a pathway to the ocean or an unattractive parking lot. Peach and seafoam green decor is contemporary in a bare-bones kind of way. Eight units equipped with modest cooking facilities are tabbed in the moderate range.

CAPE CANAVERAL AREA RESTAURANTS

Nannie Lee's Strawberry Mansion (1218 East New Haven Avenue, Melbourne; 407-724-8078) is just about impossible to miss. Inside this pink Victorian confection, tables are set in practically every room, upstairs and down, within a homey setting of stained glass and floral wallpaper. The menu lists elaborate dishes such as fish Oscar along with veal, pasta dishes, chicken dinners and steaks considered the best in town. Dinner only. Moderate.

Cheek-by-jowl with the decorous Nannie Lee's, **Mister Beaujeans (★)** (1218 East New Haven Avenue, Melbourne; 407-984-3121) shares its brick courtyard entry but not much else. Waffles, omelettes and unusual breakfast offerings like eggs and cheese in a pita pocket are served all day in a small L-shaped room gleaming with polished wood. After the sun warms the courtyard, it's fun to enjoy luncheon offerings such as BLTs, cheeseburgers with guacamole, grouper sandwich or conch fritters at one of the glass-topped tables outside. Budget.

Most towns have one restaurant revered as a local institution. On the Space Coast, that place is **Bernard's Surf** (2 South Atlantic Avenue, Cocoa Beach; 407-783-2401). It's been on the same corner since the 1940s, boasting the freshest crab, lobster and fish in the county. Bernard's is divided into three parts: a raw bar, a formal, dimly lit dining room and a lounge rimmed by red leatherette booths. An oversized menu is required to list the steak, rib and chicken offerings as well as dozens of seafood dishes, all in a variety of combinations. You'll also find such delicacies as Cajun-fried alligator tail, caviar and escargot. Moderate to deluxe.

The most interesting restaurant in Cocoa Beach is **The Mango Tree** (118 North Atlantic Avenue; 407-799-0513). Food doesn't get much better than this, nor does interior design. The restaurant is an artist's concept of Caribbean dining, with orchids and trees growing through the ceiling. An added greenhouse dining area enhances the tropical ambience. A spirited and obviously well-to-do crowd patronizes The Mango Tree for unusual appetizers such as seafood *en croûte* and dinner entrées developed from classic Continental cuisine: Dover sole, veal piccata, sweetbreads in bordelaise sauce, steak au poivre. Deluxe to ultra-deluxe.

Alma's Italian Restaurant (306 North Orlando Avenue, Cocoa Beach; 407-783-1981) offers a moderately priced menu ranging from veal to pizza and boasts a wine cellar of 200 vintages. A maze of small rooms makes this old-fashioned Italian eatery warm and inviting.

Desperadoes (301 North Atlantic Avenue, Cocoa Beach; 407-784-3363) serves up south-of-the-border fare like tostadas, *quesadillas* and *sopapillas* in a casual, rough-wood setting. Budget.

Budget-priced dishes dominate the menu at **Herbie K's Diner** (2080 North Atlantic Boulevard, Cocoa Beach; 407-783-6740). An exterior of glass brick and neon announces that this is an updated version of the all-American '50s diner; inside, black-and-white tiles, counter seating and table-top jukeboxes provide an appropriate setting for burgers, fries, shakes, malts, sandwiches and much more. Open 24 hours a day on the weekends.

The urge to splurge can be satisfied at **Carlyle's** (2080 North Atlantic Avenue in the Howard Johnson Plaza-Hotel, Cocoa Beach; 407-783-9222), a formal, airy restaurant open for lunch, dinner and Sunday brunch. Seated on hand-carved chairs upholstered in tapestry fabric, diners peruse a diverse menu that includes shrimp parfait, Cajun popcorn (crayfish), gourmet pizza topped with seafood, a fruit-and-vegetable platter and an oriental combination of baby-back ribs, crab wontons, sesame stir-fry and rice. The lunch menu also lists hamburgers and sandwiches, but they seem out of place in such an elegant setting. Moderate.

Route 520, the major artery connecting the mainland, Merritt Island and Cocoa Beach, is home to a number of fast-food outlets as well as some moderately priced ethnic restaurants. Also along this stretch is **Gatsby's Dockside** (500 West Cocoa Beach Causeway, Cocoa Beach; 407-783-2380), an informal waterside restaurant with seating both indoors and out. Grab a patio table. Gatsby's menu is ideal for sharing: you can order baskets of finger foods like baby-back ribs with cole slaw, nachos or a sampler of cheese sticks and potato skins. Soups, burgers and full-scale seafood entrées are available, as are filling combinations such as a huge spinach salad accompanied by hot, spicy Buffalo-style chicken wings. Moderate.

Coconuts on the Beach (2 Minuteman Causeway, Cocoa Beach; 407-784-1422) has a gray, weathered wood exterior that belies its laid-back ambience. Although you can order full seafood entrées and dine indoors, most of the action is outside, where tables are filled with casually dressed beachgoers enjoying appetizers such as nachos or sweet-potato fries. Budget to moderate.

Peking Garden (155 East Route 520, Merritt Island; 407-459-2999) is an attractive establishment with dark Chinese-red furnishings and lace-curtained booths. Among the two dozen chef's specialties are hot-and-spicy pork and beef dishes, crabmeat rangoon and versions of sweet-and-sour chicken and pork that appeal to children's palates. Budget.

It's a good idea to tuck a meal under your belt before setting out for the Kennedy Space Center. Cheap and convenient is the **Kountry Kitchen** (★) (1115 North Courtenay Parkway, Merritt Island; 407-459-3457). In this big, friendly joint, an honest country breakfast of bacon, eggs, grits and biscuits is laid out as early as 5 a.m. Or on the way back, stop in for homestyle dinners: spareribs, salmon patties, chicken and dumplings, chicken-fried steaks and other hearty meals. Budget.

On the main thoroughfare leading to the Kennedy Space Center is **Victoria's Family Restaurant** (370 North Courtenay Parkway, Merritt Island; 407-459-1656). The exterior won't remind you much of Greece, but within the brick-and-wood interior you will find *moussaka* and its country cousins, as well as seafood and chops. Budget to moderate.

On the mainland, lunch in quaint little Cocoa Village can be as fancy as a meal in a French restaurant or as simple as a homemade sandwich and an ice cream cone at the **Village Ice Cream and Sandwich Shop** (120-B Harrison Street; 407-632-2311), a hole-in-the-wall located near some of the best boutiques in the neighborhood. Budget.

The best-known spot to eat in Cocoa Village is the **Black Tulip** (207 Brevard Avenue; 407-631-1133). First courses like quiche or crab cakes are substantial enough for a filling meal, but this is an excellent place to take advantage of local seafood dishes: grouper with shrimp in hollandaise or the catch-of-the-day with bananas in lemon butter. Service is formal in this cozy spot. Moderate to deluxe.

For an intimate dinner amid New Orleans-style decor, stop in at **Café Margeaux** (220 Brevard Avenue, Cocoa; 407-639-8343). The moderately priced menu offers entrées such as Caribbean duckling in coconut sauce, filet mignon and Dover sole.

Between Cocoa and the Merritt Island Wildlife Refuge, a delightful mainland stop near Route 1 is **Dixie Crossroads** (★) (1475 Garden Street, Titusville; 407-268-5000). Despite its size (350 seats), this family-style favorite makes you feel right at home, with waitresses refilling your glass of iced tea every time they pass by the table. And everything edible that swims in nearby waters can be found here, in plentiful helpings. Don't miss the rock shrimp, succulent and tasty thumb-sized delicacies that go well with a little red rice. Shellfish can be ordered in servings of one dozen, two dozen or all-you-can-eat. Moderate-priced dinners include soup, salad, a side dish and light, bite-sized corn fritters.

CAPE CANAVERAL AREA SHOPPING

In the city of Melbourne, **East New Haven Avenue** is a quaint neighborhood of antique stores and art galleries with a smattering of clothing shops. But the best reason to visit is **City News Books** (901 East New Haven Avenue; 407-725-0330). This store offers racks of regional publications, maps and travel guides along with a fair selection of fiction, including comic books.

Brick walkways, cobblestone patios and an abundance of shade trees play up the historic atmosphere of **Cocoa Village** (bounded by Riveredge Boulevard, King Street, Florida Avenue and Derby Street) in downtown Cocoa. Some 50 shops are interspersed with restaurants and service establishments over approximately 15 city blocks. Mostly housed in restored lowrise buildings dating from the turn of the century, the retail shops range from hardware stores to purveyors of antique jewelry.

You can watch artist Greg Wooten in progress at **Indian River Pottery** (116-B Harrison Street; 407-636-4160), a charming one-room outlet accessible through a tiny palm-fringed courtyard. In this tropical oasis, handmade mugs, bowls and vases in a variety of designs are created.

Promenade (11 Harrison Street; 407-631-3700) specializes in contemporary women's fashions, mostly in soft crushable natural fabrics that travel well. Somehow there is space in this narrow little shop for an extraordinary collection of large handmade earrings tagged at surprisingly low prices.

The Wine Experience (316 Brevard Avenue; 636-5480) devotes its large corner location to kitchenware, Australian and California wines (relatively hard to find in this part of the world) and accessories such as baskets and gourmet foods.

Gay's Toys (405 Brevard Avenue; 407-632-5890) offers a good selection of dolls and old-fashioned wooden train sets.

Glassware and china are the mainstays at **Village Antiques** (401 Brevard Avenue; 407-639-8902). **Forget-Me-Not** (404-A Brevard Avenue; 407-632-4700) is an amalgamation of women's fashions and accessories and antique and estate jewelry.

Typical of the homey atmosphere in Cocoa Village, **Handwerk House** (407 Brevard Avenue; 407-631-6367) features a cuddly collection of stuffed animals and cloth dolls, among other merchandise that begs to be chucked under the chin.

You wouldn't dare eat off the dinnerware at **Village Plate Collector** (120 Forest Avenue, Cocoa; 407-636-6914), which carries beautifully etched china, miniatures, bells and figurines as well as lithographs and dolls.

Not many travelers are in the market for hardware, but that's no reason to bypass **S. F. Travis Company** (★) (300 Delannoy Avenue; 407-636-1441). Established in 1885, ten years before Cocoa made the map, this is the kind of place where you can buy a single nail or screw. Or simply tour the 35,000-square-foot premises, where barges used to dock out back before the space was landfilled. This low-key legend has the most authentically historic atmosphere in all of Cocoa Village.

On the rim of Cocoa Village, **SunRay T-Shirts** (105 Brevard Avenue; 407-632-6666) could be mistaken for a loading dock, but it's actually the place that manufactures specialty T-shirts, notably ones for the Kennedy Space Center. You can get good deals in seconds emblazoned with space shuttle logos and in overruns from other clients—that is, if you're in the market for a knit shirt sporting a breast pocket that says "Bill, Southern Wall Systems." Just the thing for your next bowling date.

Ron Jon Surf Shop (4151 North Route A1A, Cocoa Beach; 407-799-8888) almost qualifies as a tourist destination. Calling itself the world's largest surf shop, this warehouse-size store consists of two floors awash with swim wear, beach gear and equipment for all manner of watersports (including an extensive rental department).

CAPE CANAVERAL AREA NIGHTLIFE

Weekends are the best time to drop by **Desperadoes** (301 North Atlantic Avenue, Cocoa Beach; 407-784-3363), a casual, rough-hewn spot that features live soloists.

A flashing neon flamingo marks the spot at **The Tropicana** (900 North Atlantic Avenue, Cocoa Beach; 407-799-3800). It's not just a disco but an entire entertainment complex, with a bar featuring a monster television screen, a big dancefloor with mirrors and a pool room. Cover.

Coco's (1550 North Route A1A in the Hilton Hotel, Cocoa Beach; 407-799-0003) is a small lobby-level disco lounge where you're likely to find a middle-aged crowd. Typical entertainment is a three-piece band playing Top-40 tunes.

Thanks to a few bright strips of neon, it's possible to spot **Brassy's Take II** (501 North Orlando Avenue, Cocoa Beach; 407-784-1277) from the street. Inside, the dancefloor seems to stretch into infinity, especially before 10 p.m. After that, a sizable crowd of young locals usually fills it up. Cover.

Cocoa Beach nightlife isn't all rock-and-roll; it just seems that way. A dependable spot to relax after dark is **Dino's Jazz Piano Bar** (315 West Route 520, Cocoa Beach; 407-784-5470). In this dark room lined with bookshelves and furnished with a bevy of cocktail tables, there's usually a combo playing on a small platform, or at the very least some mellow taped music.

"Your dime, my time" is how folks at **Bumper's Dance Bar** (2080 North Atlantic Avenue in Herbie K's Diner, Cocoa Beach; 407-783-6740) answer the phone. Besides peppy employees, the bebopping, skirt-swirling joint features '50s and '60s decor and music to match.

Gatsby's Sports Emporium (West Route 520 near Route A1A, Cocoa Beach; 407-784-4514) usually has a live Top-40 band and a faithful gang of regulars in attendance. Cover on weekends.

GAY SCENE Popular with the gay and lesbian crowd, **Saturday's** (4060 West New Haven Avenue, Melbourne; 305-724-1510) is a 4000-square-foot dance bar located in a pastel-colored building. Inside are two bars, mirrors, ceiling fans and prints of handsome men. Female impersonators perform twice a week.

Located in the Bayview Plaza shopping center, **Country Gents** (5675 North Atlantic Avenue, Cocoa Beach; 407-784-6626) is a country-and-western gay cruise bar. A rough-sawn wood interior features rodeo posters, saddles and boots. Dance to recorded music.

CAPE CANAVERAL AREA BEACHES AND PARKS

Canaveral National Seashore—It took an act of Congress to set aside the last 25-mile stretch of undeveloped beach in eastern Florida. In 1975, the government acted to preserve some 68,000 acres of water and wilderness stretching north from the Kennedy Space Center. In this pristine setting, alligators, turtles and manatees can be seen in some of the shallow lagoons; some 300 species of birds have been observed at the seashore, including endangered ones such as the brown pelican and the bald eagle. The barrier island, consisting mostly of pure quartz sand, was formed more than a million years ago. Evidence of ancient residents has been found stacked into a number of mounds, most notably Turtle Mound, a 35-foot-tall pile of oyster shells assembled by the Surreque Indians sometime between 600 and 1200 A.D. Vegetation has covered the mound, but it's still possible to climb up for a view of the surrounding terrain.

Klondike Beach—This is the central of three distinct beaches at Canaveral National Seashore. Klondike is a totally undeveloped area at the end of a hike through saw palmettos and Spanish bayonets. Angel wings, sand dollars, and smooth rounded moon snails are among the shells found on all three beaches. (The other beaches, Playalinda and Apollo, are described below.)

Playalinda Beach—Though primitive, Playalinda is Cape Canaveral's most developed beach and its most accessible. Five miles of pristine white sand form a narrow ribbon between the high-water line and the delicate sand dunes. Within sight of NASA's launch pads, Playalinda is usually closed for weeks prior to a launch.

Facilities: Portable toilets; information, 407-267-1110. *Fishing:* Surf angling. *Swimming:* Excellent. *Surfing:* Waves are big enough, but currents can be strong.

Getting there: Located east of Titusville off Route 402.

Apollo Beach—Located at the north end of Cape Canaveral Seashore, this beach is accessible by dune walkovers. Like Playalinda, it is a long strip of white quartz sand.

Facilities: Restrooms; information, 407-267-1110. *Fishing:* Surf and pier angling. *Swimming:* Excellent. *Surfing:* Good.

Getting there: Take Route A1A south from New Smyrna Beach.

Merritt Island National Wildlife Refuge—Egrets, herons, gulls and terns form a welcoming committee on this 140,000-acre preserve north of the John F. Kennedy Space Center. A diverse habitat includes salty estuaries, dense marshes, pine flatwoods and hammocks of hardwood where armadillos are as common as gray squirrels. The portions of the refuge that are not marsh consist of dense vegetation that helps protect such exotic species as air plants and indigo snakes. The best times to visit are spring, fall and winter. Several species of migratory waterfowl retreat here during the coldest months of the year, making this one of Florida's prime birdwatching areas.

Facilities: Restrooms, marked walking trails and auto tour routes; visitor center, 407-861-0667. *Fishing:* Fresh and saltwater angling.

Getting there: On Merritt Island along Route 402, east of Titusville.

Daytona Beach Area

The best-known resort town on the central East Coast, Daytona Beach is famous for its 23-mile-long beach, a marvel of sparkling sand packed so hard you can easily drive a car on it. And that's what people started doing in the early 1900s, gradually developing the beach into a natural race track where speed records were set as early as 1903.

Today, automobile racing and sunshine are still the paramount attractions up and down the strip of sand that stretches from Ponce Inlet north to Flagler Beach. There is history here, too, in archaeological remains and the ruins of old plantations.

The marshlands around Turnbull Creek provide a serene setting for the **Atlantic Center for the Arts** (1414 Art Center Avenue, New Smyrna Beach; 904-427-6975), an unusual facility devoted to literature and the graphic arts. Single-story gray wooden buildings scattered over some 67 acres give the property the appearance of a low-key resort. In fact, they are used as galleries, performance spaces and lodging for resident artists.

Poised near the inlet separating New Smyrna Beach from Daytona Beach, the second-tallest lighthouse in the United States, the 175-foot-tall **Ponce de León Inlet Lighthouse** (South Peninsula Drive, Ponce Inlet; 904-761-1821; admission) affords a breathtaking view of the inlet as well as the surrounding communities. Built in 1887, the so-called "Light Station at Mosquito Inlet" is no longer in service, but the entire facility, including the keeper's cottages, is open to the public.

Appropriately, **Destination Daytona** (126 East Orange Avenue, Daytona Beach; 904-255-0415) is centrally located, the better to offer guidance and tips to visitors.

Another way to get your bearings in Daytona Beach is by leaving the driving to someone else. Such as a riverboat captain. The **Dixie Queen II Riverboat** (841 Ballough Road, Daytona Beach; 904-255-1997; admission) runs sightseeing cruises up and down the Halifax River. You have a choice of three balconied decks from which to view the passing sights: huge homes along Riverside Drive, waterfront parks, fast-moving windsurfers and the occasional surfacing manatee.

Housed in a former bank that is Daytona Beach's finest example of Beaux-Arts design, the **Halifax Historical Museum** (252 South Beach Street; 904-255-6976) is best known for the six murals depicting local attractions such as the Ponce de León Inlet Lighthouse. But more fascinating is a highly detailed wood-carved model of the Boardwalk area circa 1938, with hundreds of thumb-sized people filling the bandshell. This elegant museum's historical displays range from artifacts retrieved from nearby plantation ruins to a smattering of memorabilia from the early days of car racing.

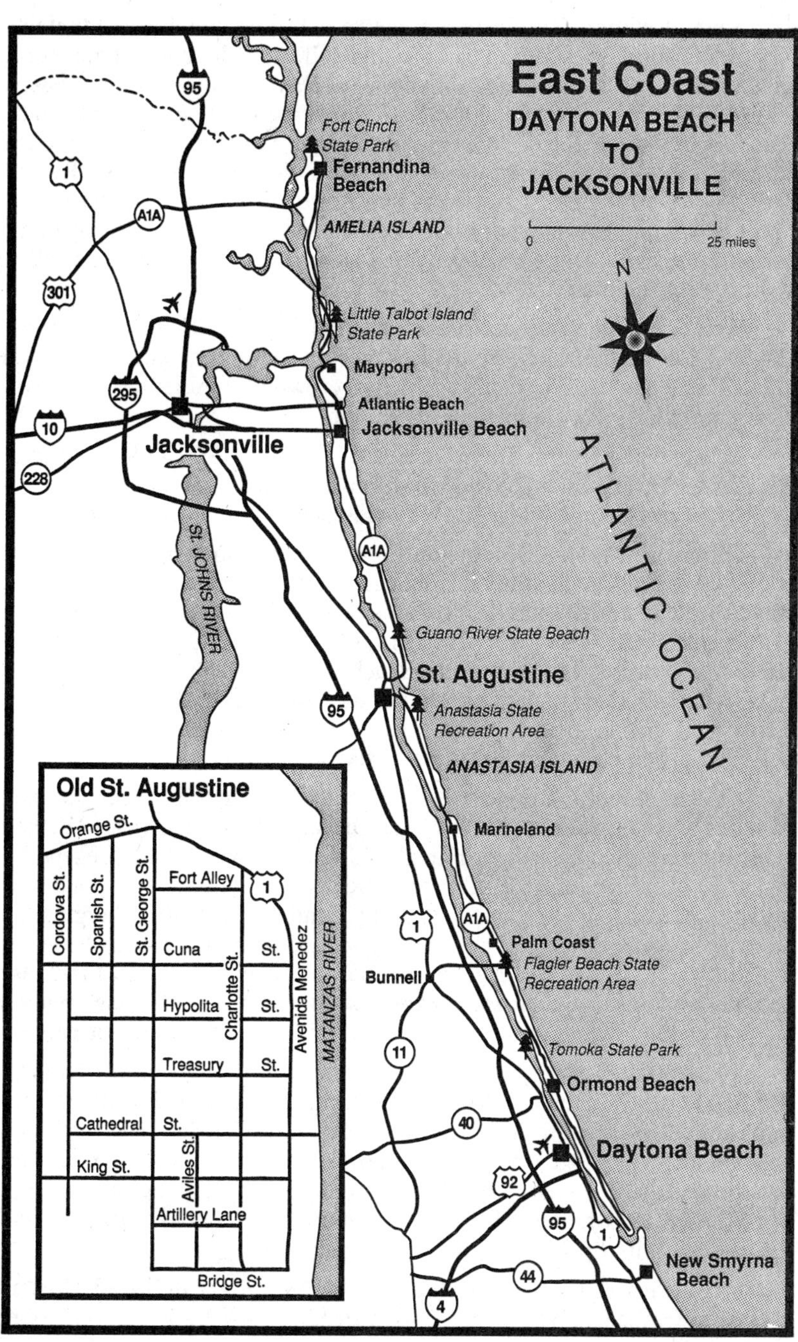
East Coast
DAYTONA BEACH
TO
JACKSONVILLE
0
25 miles
N
ATLANTIC OCEAN
Fort Clinch
State Park
Fernandina
Beach
AMELIA ISLAND
Little Talbot Island
State Park
Mayport
Atlantic Beach
Jacksonville Beach
Jacksonville
ST. JOHNS RIVER
Guano River State Beach
St. Augustine
Anastasia State
Recreation Area
ANASTASIA ISLAND
Marineland
Palm Coast
Flagler Beach State
Recreation Area
Bunnell
Tomoka State Park
Ormond Beach
Daytona Beach
New Smyrna
Beach
95
1
A1A
301
295
10
228
11
40
92
44
4
Old St. Augustine
Orange St.
Cordova St.
Spanish St.
St. George St.
Fort Alley
Cuna
St.
Charlotte St.
Hypolita
St.
Treasury
St.
Avenida Menedez
MATANZAS RIVER
Cathedral
St.
King St.
Aviles St.
Artillery Lane
Bridge St.

A single stretch of Volusia Avenue near the Daytona Beach Municipal Airport constitutes a sporting paradise in itself, with three major attractions within sight of each other. Most famous is the **Daytona International Speedway** (1801 Volusia Avenue; 904-253-7223; admission), which replaced the beach as the prime racing locale in 1959. You too can travel the banked, 2.5-mile tri-oval race track that drivers like Cale Yarborough and Richard Petty helped put on the map. Unless you're a qualified racer, however, you won't be driving, but riding in a tour bus. The most renowned of many events hosted here is the Daytona 500, which attracts hundreds of thousands of visitors each February.

Next door at the **Daytona Beach Kennel Club** (2201 Volusia Avenue; 904-252-6484; admission) you can wager on the greyhounds circling the track. This clean, well-lit facility attracts a crowd of families and older couples, particularly for its matinee races.

Across the street, the **Daytona Beach Jai Alai** (1900 Volusia Avenue; 904-255-0222; admission) provides fast-moving action. Jai alai, a game created by Basque peasants, is played as a round-robin game in the United States.

Things in Daytona Beach didn't always move so fast, as you can see at one of the city's most interesting museums, where a giant sloth is displayed next to contemporary Florida artworks. Far from the beaten track, in a forested setting in Tuscawilla Park, the **Museum of Arts and Science** (1040 Museum Boulevard, Daytona Beach; 904-255-0285; admission) boasts an eclectic collection including 19th-century drawings and one of the largest displays of Cuban artwork in the United States. In the same facility you will find a planetarium and a natural science exhibit.

Among the more impressive riverfront sights in neighboring Ormond Beach is **The Casements** (25 Riverside Drive; 904-676-3216), a 1912 mansion that was once the winter retreat of John D. Rockefeller. (Legend has it that Rockefeller, in a fit of spite, purchased the eight-acre estate for a pittance after discovering that the nearby Ormond Hotel was charging him more than another guest for the same accommodations.) Exhibits of Hungarian folklore and Boy Scout memorabilia are displayed within the house; regional and national artwork is exhibited in galleries and in the great octagonal atrium. There are tours of the building and two acres of gardens.

The setting is as appealing as the artwork at the **Ormond Memorial Art Museum** (78 Granada Avenue, Ormond Beach; 904-677-1857). Lush tropical gardens filled with palms, shrubbery, flowers, fish ponds, walkways, benches and a small gazebo provide an oasis only steps away from Granada Avenue traffic. Founded to display the highly symbolic religious paintings of Malcolm Fraser, the five-room museum also serves as a gallery, with visiting exhibits by Florida artists and sculptors.

Racing artifacts can also be found at the **Birthplace of Speed Museum** (160 East Granada Boulevard, Ormond Beach; 904-672-5657; admission), which covers the years 1902 to 1958. Only aficionados of the sport, however, will find much of interest in this small museum, where the main exhibits are photographs of cars and drivers.

For a step into the more recent past, drive north of Ormond Beach to **Bulow Plantation Ruins State Historic Site** (★) (off King's Road north of the Old Dixie Highway, Bunnell; 904-439-2219). A mile-long unpaved road leads through dense undergrowth to a picnic area; the ruins lie another quarter-mile away to the left. Looming out of the jungle like a movie prop from *Raiders of the Lost Ark* is a series of crumbling coquina shell ruins, all that remains of an 18th-century sugar mill. An interpretive center nearby tells the story of the plantation's development by slave labor, its prosperous production of sugar cane, cotton, rice and indigo, and its ultimate destruction by the Seminole Indians who burned plantations in anger over being displaced by settlers.

Nearly midway between Daytona Beach and St. Augustine is one of the coast's best-kept secrets, **Washington Oaks State Gardens** (★) (Route A1A, Palm Coast; 904-445-3161; admission). This 390-acre park provides a sublime sanctuary where nature has been largely left alone. A half-mile trail leads through a coastal hammock of magnolia, hickory, oak and shore juniper along the Matanzas River. Equally lovely are the manmade gardens, a delightful arrangement of flowering plants and shrubs such as azaleas and camellias interspersed with small reflecting ponds and enhanced by the sounds of songbirds.

About 40 miles north of Daytona, Route A1A runs right through **Marineland** (904-471-1111, Marineland; admission), a roadside attraction since it was built in 1938 to facilitate underwater filming. Newer oceanariums have since surpassed it in scope, but there's something endearing about this seaside complex, despite fading paint and a somewhat confusing layout. The most enduring feature is the porpoise show, performed several times a day by well-trained sea mammals in an oceanview amphitheater. There is almost always entertainment of some kind, whether it's a special-effects film called *Sea Dream* or divers hand-feeding sharks in a huge tank sporting hundreds of portholes for underwater viewing. Marineland also boasts a 35,000-gallon recreation of a Florida fresh-water spring.

DAYTONA BEACH AREA HOTELS

Its temperate climate and 23-mile-long beach have made this area among the hottest destinations in Florida. Route A1A is one long canyon of hotels and motels that try to differentiate themselves with decorative themes ranging from Polynesian to Mayan. In fact, many of them are very much alike on the inside, and almost all are equidistant from the beach. The places below have been selected for value, individuality and location.

South of Daytona Beach, the town of New Smyrna Beach is so sleepy as to be nearly yawn-inducing. The perfect place to take advantage of this back-to-the-19th-century feeling is the **Riverview Hotel** (103 Flagler Avenue, 904-428-5858). You truly can't miss this place. It presides over the Intracoastal Waterway in a sparkling coat of cream-colored paint, its cheery white balconies gleaming in the sun. Built as a two-story house, this former bridge tender's residence grew into a three-story hotel in the early 1900s. The rooms are decorated with reproduction antiques, including four-poster beds. Louvered french doors lead to a balcony, a patio or the pool deck. Continental breakfast is included in the deluxe to ultra-deluxe rates.

A few stoplights south of the frantic midtown action, the beach has the same sun, the same clean sand, but fewer people. In front of the **Day Star Motel** (3811 South Route A1A, Daytona Beach; 904-767-3780), you can at least find a square of sand to call your own. For budget prices, you get two double beds and a pool open 24 hours a day. For a little more, you can get a large oceanfront efficiency. These accommodations aren't beautiful, but they are clean and well maintained.

The aroma of potpourri greets the visitor at **Captain's Quarters Inn** (3711 South Route A1A, Daytona Beach; 904-767-3119), a five-story all-suite inn. Country provincial patterns, oak dressers and plump pillows piled up on the sofa give these suites a homey touch. The country style extends to private balconies furnished with rocking chairs. Prices range from deluxe to ultra-deluxe.

One of the most unusual hotel configurations I've ever seen belongs to **Perry's Ocean-Edge** (2209 South Atlantic Avenue, Daytona Beach; 904-255-0581), a complex of 206 units. Once you make up your mind whether to rent an oceanfront motel room, enclosed garden room, apartment suite or garden efficiency, you then must decide which of three pools to enjoy. The huge solar-heated one is sheltered from the fierce Florida sun by soaring shade trees, plus a retractable roof. There's plenty of room poolside for lounge chairs, tables and a whirlpool. Moderate-priced rooms; deluxe-priced efficiencies.

Its prime beach location, the generous size of its rooms and the tasteful decor make the highrise **Nautilus Inn** (1515 South Atlantic Avenue, Daytona Beach; 904-254-8600) a good stopping place. Pastel patterns blend in perfectly with the beach palette visible from every private balcony. Evening cocktails and a continental breakfast are served in a bright oceanfront room. An outdoor spa bubbles away between pool and beach. Kitchenettes available. Deluxe.

The **Sea Gate Motel** (39 South Ocean Avenue, Daytona Beach; 904-238-0054) offers a good location and moderately priced motel rooms in typical color combinations of blue and brown. Amenities here include only cable television and kitchenettes.

It's hard to beat a hostel for low prices, and the **Daytona Beach International Youth Hostel** (140 South Atlantic Avenue, Daytona Beach; 904-258-6937) is no exception. Odds are you'll find long-haired youngsters watching television or playing pool in the lobby. If you don't mind sharing a room and sleeping in a bunk bed (lockers are available for a fee), this centrally located, 180-bed hostel is a deal. Budget.

You might rub your eyes in disbelief when you come across the **St. Regis Hotel (★)** (509 Seabreeze Boulevard, Daytona Beach; 904-252-8743). Set back from the bustle of a busy, upscale commercial street by a small green lawn, this historic inn is painted white and fronted by a wide porch. Upstairs, five renovated rooms, each with its own bath, are decorated in antiques, though nothing fussy. The St. Regis provides a calming change of pace from the big, sterile oceanfront hotels and is closer to boutiques and nightclubs. Moderate.

Anyone who has ever wanted to sleep in a room named for Christopher Columbus, Queen Isabella or Marco Polo can do so at **The Villa** (801 North Peninsula Drive, Daytona Beach; 904-248-2020). This gay-friendly, Spanish-style mansion is set on three acres with a pool. It's only one block from the Halifax River and four blocks from the beach. Guests sleep in a four-poster bed or in a nautically themed room where Columbus would feel right at home. Baroque furniture, a library and formal dining room make it a best buy. Moderate.

The gay-friendly **Buccaneer Motel** (2301 North Atlantic Avenue, Daytona Beach; 904-253-9678) offers 15 quiet, '50s-style rooms as well as five suites in an adjacent Spanish-style home with a tile roof. Across the street from the beach, this complex has seven kitchenettes and a pool. Carpeted rooms have a blue bamboo motif and ceiling fans. Second floor units offer an ocean view. Budget to moderate.

Indigo Lakes Resort (2620 Volusia Avenue, Daytona Beach; 904-258-6333) is an oasis of velvet green fairways, grounds sprinkled with lakes, ponds and trees, all-weather tennis courts and an Olympic-size pool, all capturing the subdued ambience of a country club. This self-contained resort also harbors a fitness trail and shuffleboard and volleyball courts. The focus here is on the outdoors; the rooms are spacious, very comfortable and equipped with a private patio or balcony. Guests will have to drive about 15 minutes to the beach. Deluxe to ultra-deluxe.

Directly north of Daytona Beach is Ormond Beach, a quieter, more residential neighborhood. Here the **Mainsail Motel** (281 South Atlantic Avenue; 904-677-2131) lives up to its name; everything is done in bright whites and sky blues. Rooms are sparkling and spacious, with a railed balcony and a view of palm trees and the oceanside pool. There is also a sauna and exercise room. Moderate.

South of St. Augustine in Marineland, there's only one game in town, and that's the **Quality Marineland Inn** (9507 Ocean Shore Boulevard; 904-471-1222), an unprepossessing set of concrete blocks that separate Route A1A from the beach. The best thing to be said about the 122 clean, no-frills rooms is that they all have some kind of ocean view. The vistas from the upstairs balconies in the older building make rooms in that section preferable. Moderate.

DAYTONA BEACH AREA RESTAURANTS

A brick courtyard embellished with wrought iron makes a lovely entrance to **Riverview Charlie's** (Riverview Inn, 101 Flagler Avenue, New Smyrna Beach; 904-428-1865). True to its waterfront location, this glass-walled restaurant does best with its seafood, including local shellfish as well as Boston scrod and mahimahi. Chicken and sirloin are also available at moderate prices.

The **Asian Inn Chinese Restaurant and Cocktail Lounge** (2516 South Route A1A, Daytona Beach Shores; 904-788-6269) is something of a generic oriental restaurant with only a few handsome screens for decor. Occupying a tiny corner of a shopping strip, this family-style establishment serves spicy Szechuan dishes and Mongolian barbecue as well as blander Cantonese cuisine. Budget to moderate.

The question at one spot is not so much *if* you want catfish, but *how* you want it: blackened, fried, garlicky, Cajun-style, baked or broiled with lemon. But **Aunt Catfish's (★)** (4009 Halifax Drive, Port Orange; 904-767-4768) also dishes up flounder and plenty of other seafood. In this rustic riverfront restaurant, entrées come with "country fixin's" like cole slaw and hushpuppies, just the kind of full meal you'd expect in such a friendly place. Moderate.

Ship's lanterns and etched glass create a nautical theme at **Blackbeard's Inn** (4200 South Atlantic Avenue, Daytona Beach; 904-788-9640). Located closer to Ponce Inlet than to central Daytona Beach, this cozy restaurant features steak and prime rib as well as seafood. Moderate.

The **St. Regis Hotel and Restaurant** (509 Seabreeze Boulevard, Daytona Beach; 904-252-8743) stands out as one of the most elegant dining rooms in town. Hardwood floors, mirrors and attractive paintings create an exquisite dining spot within this historic hotel. Frogs' legs, scallops, crab, shrimp and other seafood courses are executed with the same flair as the veal and beef dishes. Service is cordial but professional. Deluxe.

It seems that every beach town has a restaurant called the **Chart House** (645 South Beach Street, Daytona Beach; 904-255-9022), but this one is grander than most. Tables are grouped for intimacy and arranged in semicircular tiers; lots of bare wood, glass and foliage give the place a distinctly pleasant personality. Steaks are big, juicy and properly cooked to order, but the fresh fish dishes are the real stars. Deluxe.

A popular family-style eatery, **Delta Restaurant** (790 South Atlantic Avenue, Ormond Beach; 904-672-3140) rest across from the ocean and supplies fine views from its glass-enclosed atrium. Prime rib, seafood, gyros and *souvlaki* are a few of the American and Greek-style offerings. Moderate.

Easily identifiable by its deeply pitched roof, **Julian's Dining Room and Lounge** (88 South Route A1A, Ormond Beach; 904-677-6767) is a spacious, dimly lit restaurant specializing in charbroiled steaks, chops, chicken and seafood. Moderate.

If you want some of the best food in the area, you'll have to work hard at finding **La Crêpe en Haut** (142 East Granada Boulevard, Ormond Beach; 904-673-1999). Located on the upper floor of a courtyard mall called Fountain Square, it has an atmosphere akin to a rather swank living room decorated with fine furniture and serene colors. It comes as no surprise that you'll be paying deluxe to ultra-deluxe prices for lamb, seafood, sweetbreads and elegant beef dishes, only a few of the items on a serious, multi-course menu.

International but still generic, **Bennigan's** (890 South Route A1A, Ormond Beach; 904-673-3691) lists Italian snacks and Mexican munchies for starters, some quiches and warm salads, and entrées categorized as southwestern, oriental, country and Cajun. A huge sand-colored structure with green-and-white awnings, Bennigan's is easy to find and popular with the beach crowd, especially for Sunday brunch. Moderate.

DAYTONA BEACH AREA SHOPPING

You could fill a book with a list of Florida's shopping malls, but the **Daytona Beach Outlet Mall** (2400 South Route 1, South Daytona; 904-756-8700) warrants singling out. Forget to pack a particular item of clothing? You could outfit the entire family at some of the 40 factory outlets here and pay maybe one-half what you would in a department store. **Bargain Box Lingerie** (904-767-1255) is a boutique specializing in loungewear, lingerie and sleepwear. A little larger than a boutique, **Bon Worth** (904-760-4794) manufactures its own line of upscale women's sportswear, from trendy slacks and shorts to blazers and skirts.

Discount shopping is something of a specialty in Daytona Beach. Women's clothing can be bought direct from the factory at **Frayne Fashions** (2136 South Route A1A; 904-252-3878). **Polly Flinders** (2417 North Route A1A; 904-672-2644) sells adorable handsmocked dresses and other clothing for little girls.

In Daytona Beach, **Seabreeze Boulevard** makes good strolling for windowshoppers. One eye-catcher is **Deja Vu** (226 Seabreeze Boulevard, Daytona Beach; 904-253-7061), a shop specializing in antiques with a Florida look, rattan, mid-20th century pottery and glass, and period furniture from the 1930s. You'll definitely want to give this store the twice over. Also worth a look is **Touché** (310 Seabreeze Boulevard; 904-252-2365), a shop that imports clothing items from Europe, Israel, California and New York and sells them at boutique prices.

Take your credit cards along to **The Lucille Leigh Collection (★)** (142 East Granada Boulevard, Ormond Beach; 904-673-2042), the most beautiful store on this part of the coast. The merchandise here is somewhere between museum and department store quality. Essentially high-fashion accessories for the home, the selection includes exquisite candle holders, silk tassel pulls, cloisonné vases and glass objets d'art.

DAYTONA BEACH AREA NIGHTLIFE

The pulse of this resort area's nightlife throbs, naturally enough, close to the heart of the beach: namely, within surfing distance of Atlantic Avenue and Seabreeze Boulevard. A few rock-and-roll spots are further flung, such as **The Other Place** (642 South Atlantic Avenue, Ormond Beach; 904-672-2461), usually referred to as OP, which has game rooms and pool tables. Also near the intersection of Route A1A and Seabreeze Boulevard, a variety of clubs cater to nearly every nightlifer's tastes.

A good place to start the evening, before going on to the dance palaces, is the **Oyster Pub** (555 Seabreeze Boulevard, Daytona Beach; 904-255-6348). All comers to this convivial corner saloon are greeted with a powerful aroma of salt—that's from the raw oysters. A sea of cocktail tables surrounds an enormous horseshoe bar; the music is loud, the vibes very, very casual.

Razzles (611 Seabreeze Boulevard, Daytona Beach; 904-257-6236), a relative newcomer to the scene, features the latest light, video and sound equipment. Once the crowd—a mix of sizes, shapes and ages, but all trying to be cool—deigns to step onto one of the two dancefloors, this cavernous disco can be the liveliest place in town, and it's tops for people-watching. Cover.

Finky's (640 North Grandview Avenue, Daytona Beach; 904-255-5059) features live country music every night. Between sets a deejay spins platters. Cover.

You can 'ave a beer with a bloke at **Great Barrier Reef** (600 North Atlantic Avenue in the Howard Johnson Hotel, Daytona Beach; 904-255-4471), an Aussie-style do-drop-in with wooden kangaroos and contemporary dance music. Or, take a short walkabout to **600 North** (also in the hotel) for a pumped-up, disco atmosphere.

Finally, if you simply must dance to "Louie, Louie" one more time, get on down to the **Ocean Deck** (127 South Ocean Avenue, Daytona Beach; 904-253-5224), the local favorite for late-night raw bar snacking. You'll recognize it by the booming sound system that always seems as if it's about to raise the roof.

The **Seaside Music Theater** (904-252-6200) has a somewhat split personality. In the summer months, the repertory company of performers and musicians stage light opera, Broadway fare and other productions at the **Daytona Beach Community College Theater Center** (1200 Volusia Avenue, Daytona Beach). Winter finds them performing dinner theater in the Treasure Island Inn (2025 South Route A1A, Daytona Beach).

The **Daytona Playhouse** (100 Jessamine Boulevard, Daytona Beach; 904-255-2431) hosts various theater productions from September through June.

GAY SCENE **Beachside Club** (415 Main Street, Daytona Beach; 904-252-5465) is known for its live entertainment and drink specials and features a 34-foot bar. The interior is decorated with posters of men, hanging flowers and mirrors. A disc jockey plays danceable music and a little jazz.

Located to the rear of a topless nightclub, **Boulevard Station** (542 Seabreeze Boulevard, Daytona Beach; 904-258-3827) is the largest gay venue in Volusia County. A New York-style nightclub, it features 50 video monitors, neon lighting, a contemporary stage, pool tables and wall mirrors perfect for checking out yourself and others. There's dancing nightly to a wide

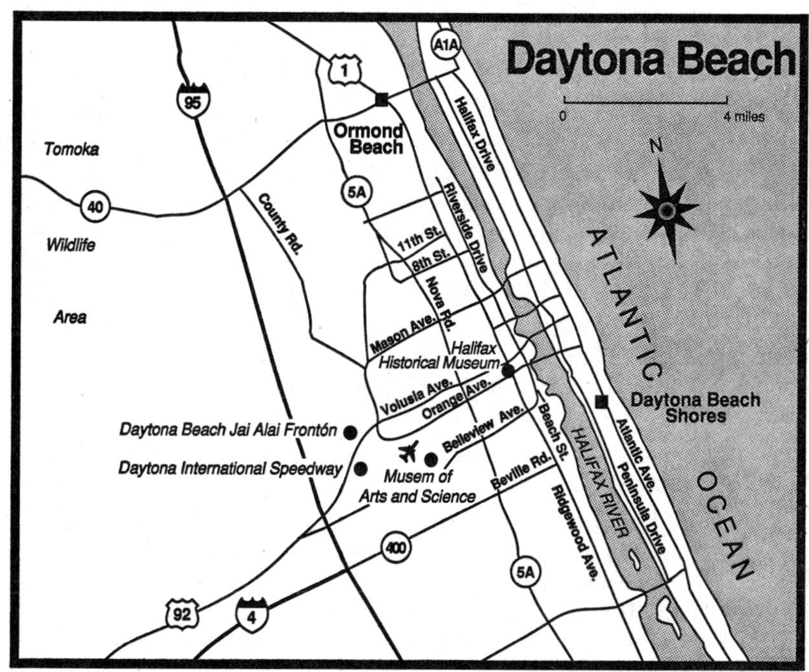

variety of music played by a disc jockey. Female impersonators entertain Wednesday night.

Located in a teal-and-peach brick building, **769 Club Restaurant and Lounge** (769 Alabama Street, Daytona Beach; 904-253-4361) is a popular women's club that features American cuisine. Modern art and paintings of lions decorate the walls of this establishment where you can relax at the U-shaped bar. A jukebox, pool tables and outdoor volleyball court add to the fun. While the crowd is predominantly lesbian, men are also welcome.

DAYTONA BEACH AREA BEACHES AND PARKS

Lighthouse Point Park (★)—When the locals tire of the crowds in central Daytona Beach, they head south to a less well-known beach. Bypassed by Route A1A, Ponce Inlet Park is often overlooked except by travelers in search of the Ponce de León Inlet Lighthouse. The southern portion of the park is a tree-shaded greensward with a children's playground. You can picnic while watching the fishing boats in the marina. To the east is a particularly beautiful stretch of pale sandy beach where it's possible to take long walks in relative peace and quiet.

Facilities: Picnic area, restrooms; grocery stores and restaurants are nearby. *Fishing:* Surf fishing. *Swimming:* Good.

Getting there: At the end of Atlantic Avenue south of Daytona Beach.

Daytona Beach—The promotional brochures proclaim 23 miles of hard sand beach, but technically only four miles of that lie within the city limits of Daytona Beach. To the south is Daytona Beach Shores, to the north, Ormond Beach, both virtually indistinguishable from Daytona Beach. Aside from the expanse of clean beige sand (500 feet wide at low tide), the most striking aspect of the beach is the presence of automobiles. Motorists are required to park perpendicular to the ocean, in single file, and to restrict their beach driving to poorly marked "lanes." A speed limit of 10 mph is enforced, but it is still distracting to have to look both ways before proceeding into the surf.

Facilities: Picnic areas, restrooms, showers, lifeguards; grocery stores and restaurants are nearby. *Fishing:* Surf and pier angling. *Swimming:* Excellent everywhere. *Surfing:* At the north end.

Getting there: Located between Ocean Dunes Road and Plaza Boulevard off Route A1A.

Tomoka State Park (★)—The approach to this 949-acre preserve is along a driveway worthy of an antebellum plantation (which it once was), with magnolia trees and moss-draped oaks threatening to overtake the road. Flanked by the Halifax and Tomoka rivers, Tomoka State Park has lush coastal hammocks dense with shrubs and trees. Raised boardwalks allow visitors to explore the moist low-lying swamps and marshes.

Facilities: Picnic areas, canoe rental, restrooms, showers; grocery stores and restaurants are nearby. Interpretive center, 904-676-4050. *Fishing:* Saltwater angling.

Camping: There are 100 sites with RV hookups; $17–19 per night.

Getting there: At 2099 North Beach Street in Ormond Beach.

Flagler Beach State Recreation Area—With frontage on the ocean as well as on the Intracoastal Waterway, this windswept park offers close encounters with a variety of wildlife. A short nature trail winds through taller sand dunes, where scrub oaks and shrubs make an excellent habitat for the Florida scrub jay. On the inland side of the park, fiddler crabs and wading birds wander through the marsh grasses and shallow waters near the boat basin. On the ocean side, sea turtles lay their eggs (in early summer) in the rough coquina-shell sand above the high water mark on this narrow, undeveloped beach.

Facilities: Restrooms, showers, picnic areas; grocery stores and restaurants and are located nearby; information, 904-439-2474. *Fishing:* Pompano and whiting are common surf-casting fish. Flounder and speckled trout can be caught in the Intracoastal Waterway. *Swimming:* Excellent.

Camping: There are 34 sites with RV hookups; $17–19 per night.

Getting there: Located at 3100 South Route A1A, Flagler Beach.

St. Augustine

The oldest city in the United States is a singular blend of narrow lanes and wide sweeping beaches, overhanging balconies and grand old homes. Founded in 1565 by Pedro Menéndez de Aviles, the Spanish settlement was looted in 1586 by Sir Francis Drake and eventually taken by the British two centuries later. Over the centuries it has been the jewel in the crown of Florida, a prize for which several nations have fought.

With more than 400 years of history behind it, St. Augustine today offers more sightseeing spots than any other city on Florida's east coast, especially along the narrow streets in the heart of the old town.

The picturesque Bridge of Lions spans the Intracoastal Waterway to link Anastasia Island with St. Augustine. Here, since many of the city's numerous attractions charge nominal admission fees, the economical and efficient way to tour is via **Sightseeing Trains** (170 San Marco Avenue; 904-829-6545), which offer narrated seven-mile excursions with stop-off privileges at major points of interest. Passengers may disembark at will and take any later train they wish.

It is at **Fort Matanzas National Monument** (southern end of Anastasia Island; 904-471-0116) that visitors get their first glimpse of St. Augustine's history. Actually, the crumbling fort, built in 1742 on the site of a bloody 16th-century battle between the French and Spanish, sits across the Matanzas River on Rattlesnake Island and is accessible by a small ferry that docks at the visitors center.

The candy-striped tower visible from twenty miles away makes it easy to find the **Lighthouse Museum of St. Augustine** (81 Lighthouse Avenue, Anastasia Island; 904-829-0745; admission). Florida's first lighthouse is still used, and off-limits, but the partially burned out, two-story Victorian lighthouse keeper's home has been restored as a coastal museum with exhibits on the area's history, a period room and a theater that screens a half-hour video on lightkeepers.

The most imposing structure in old St. Augustine is **Castillo de San Marcos** (1 Castillo Drive; 904-829-6506; admission), a massive, symmetrical 17th-century structure built by the Spanish from coquina shell rock. Visitors enter near the **Old City Gate** via a drawbridge across the moat and proceed into a grassy courtyard. Some of the surrounding ground-floor rooms have been furnished to reflect various aspects of garrison life throughout the fort's extensive history; others serve as museums with exhibits on military history. Visitors should appreciate the view from atop the 35-foot-high ramparts. And make sure to take a walk around the outside grounds, a setting so pastoral it's hard to envision the carnage that took place beyond the gates of this never-conquered fort.

The **St. Augustine Visitor Information Center** (10 Castillo Drive; 904-825-1000) offers brochures, maps of the historic district and even an introductory video for visitors.

Close to the center of town, **St. George Street** is closed to automobile traffic from Orange Street south to Cathedral Place. This district, restored to evoke a late 18th-century atmosphere, is lined with coquina stone houses converted into shops. Among these buildings are such interesting attractions as **St. Augustine's Spanish Quarter** (29 St. George Street, 904-825-6830; admission), a reconstructed Spanish village, where craftspeople in period costumes demonstrate blacksmithing, potting, weaving and candle dipping.

Through a door off the main thoroughfare, persistent visitors will find the **St. Photios Chapel** (★) (41 St. George Street; 904-829-8205), a tiny building with an altar surrounded by stunning frescoes, religious icons painted directly onto the walls and domes. Also here is an enlightening display relating to Greek-American history, plus a small gift shop with exquisite postcards of the chapel interiors as well as souvenirs and Greek-made clothing.

Another impressive landmark, the **Cathedral of St. Augustine** (35 Treasury Street; 904-824-2806) dates to 1797. Built to replace a church that was destroyed when the area was under British rule, it is open for daily tours.

For further glimpses into Florida's past, stop by the **Dr. Peck House** (143 St. George Street; 904-829-5064), a 1750-era home decorated in early territorial style. Nearby, the **Oldest Wooden Schoolhouse** (14 St. George Street; 904-824-0192) was used by the Spanish during the 18th century. Today it exhibits educational artifacts from that period.

Elsewhere in the historic part of town is the **Oldest House** (14 St. Francis Street; 904-824-2872; admission), occupied as early as 1727 and now headquarters for the local historical society. On the property are both the **Webb Museum,** devoted to St. Augustine's past, and the **Tovar House,** which houses an army museum.

Diverting but of dubious authenticity is the **Oldest Store Museum** (4 Artillery Lane; 904-829-9729; admission), where the atmosphere of a 19th-century general store is somewhat diluted by the inclusion of a 1927 Model T Ford truck and the like.

In a city of so many "oldests," it comes as no surprise that **Potter's Wax Museum** (17 King Street; 904-829-9056; admission) claims to be the first of its genre in the United States. Guides lead groups on informative tours past more than 170 exceptionally well-crafted likenesses of such notables as John F. Kennedy, plus composers, artists, noblemen and other historic figures.

The very impressive **Lightner Museum** (City Hall Complex, King and Cordova streets; 904-824-2874; admission) packs a double wallop. First, it occupies the site of the former Alcazar Hotel, part of Henry Flagler's legacy of elegant Florida resorts. Second, the museum comprises three floors of exquisite possessions displayed with matching good taste. The Lightners' collection of cut glass, Victorian art glass and the stained-glass creations of Louis Tiffany could serve as a graduate course in the history of this painstaking craft. Other decorative arts, furnishings and costumes evoke America's Gilded Age, but the best spot is the Music Box Room, where tour guides occasionally demonstrate the features of these delicate antiques.

Venturing out along San Marco Avenue, you will happen upon the **Old Jail** (167 San Marco Avenue; 904-829-3800) and the **Old Sugar Mill** (254 San Marco Avenue; 904-829-2244), which houses a museum displaying 19th-century milling tools.

Ripley's Believe It Or Not Museum (19 San Marco Avenue; 904-824-1606; admission) is one of several similar exhibits in the country. Here are a dizzying three floors filled with testimony to the weird, odd, compulsive, inventive and misshapen people and things of this world, from a miniature railroad bridge fashioned from some 31,000 toothpicks to the stuffed body of a two-headed calf, complete with exclamation points following every description!

Although it seems kind of hokey, the **Fountain of Youth Discovery Park** (155 Magnolia Avenue; 904-829-3168; admission) is as irresistible to most tourists as the concept of youth-giving waters must have been to Ponce de León, who is believed to have set foot near here in 1513. You might skip sampling from the fountain and go straight to the Historical Discovery Globe, representing a view of earth from outer space, and the planetarium, where the skies are set to look as they would have from the deck of Ponce de León's galleon. Take note of Magnolia Avenue, a glorious archway formed by oak trees.

Nearby, the **Mission of Nombre de Dios** (27 Ocean Avenue; 904-824-2809) is easily sighted by the Great Cross that soars 208 feet above the easternmost point of the mission, believed to be the site of the first Roman Catholic mass ever celebrated in the United States.

ST. AUGUSTINE HOTELS

Small inns are not everyone's cup of afternoon tea, yet they are most simpatico with the intimate atmosphere of historic St. Augustine. Other than these, the most prevalent type of lodging is the moderate-priced motel, both in town and near the beach.

Absolutely free for the taking is one of St. Augustine's finest attractions: the sweeping view of Matanzas Bay. This bonanza can be easily appreciated from one of the three porches that embellish the **Westcott House** (146 Avenida Menéndez; 904-824-4301). A Victorian concoction of pale peach and blue with carved white trim, this bed and breakfast inn is resplendent with antiques, lush carpeting and lustrous pine floors. All eight rooms have private baths, some with clawfoot tubs, and a distinctive color scheme; almost every inch of the ground-floor Menéndez Suite, for instance, is painted eggshell blue. Some might object to the Westcott's overstylized decor; everything is just too-too. However, that's easy to overlook when you consider the pluses: verandas furnished with perfect white wicker and a brick courtyard for enjoying breakfast alfresco. Deluxe.

The Mediterranean-revival-style **Casa de la Paz** (22 Avenida Menéndez; 904-829-2915) makes a nice counterpoint to St. Augustine's Victorian bed and breakfast inns. The smooth stucco exterior would be austere were it not for the barrel-tile roofing and molded sills. Here the best views of Matanzas Bay belong to a suite that occupies the entire third floor. The other rooms also have their charms, and each its own bath, but for extra privacy book one of the veranda rooms, which have their own entrances. Every guest can enjoy the seclusion of a Spanish walled courtyard and sunporch. Moderate to deluxe.

No one is going to turn down your bed at the **Monson Motor Lodge** (32 Avenida Menéndez; 904-829-2277), a pseudo-Spanish-style motel that delivers surprising value. Rooms are spacious enough to accommodate a couple of imitation-leather reading chairs and louvered dividers between bedroom and dressing room. The tiled baths are also nice. Moderate.

Unlike some of the more formal bed and breakfasts in this quaint town, the **Kenwood Inn (★)** (38 Marine Street; 904-824-2116) has that definite lived-in feeling. In 14 one-of-a-kind guest rooms, the Kenwood mixes antiques and lace curtains with fresh touches such as hand-stenciled walls. The large parlor, a comfortable gathering place for guests, is transformed into a dining room for breakfast. The graceful pecan tree partially shading the brick-lined patio may well have been planted when this house was built more than a century ago. But the pool—a rare amenity in St. Augustine—is contemporary. Moderate.

The **St. Francis Inn** (279 St. George Street; 904-824-6068), a public guest house since 1845, is a comfortable three-story warren of individually decorated accommodations ranging from single rooms to three-room suites with kitchenettes. Original fireplaces and attractive wainscoting imbue this cozy plank-and-stucco inn with much charm, as do the courtyard and tropical gardens. Budget to moderate.

In the heart of the well-preserved historic district, two very different bed and breakfasts sit cattycornered. **The Victorian House** (11 Cadiz Street; 904-824-5214) offers moderate-priced accommodations in the main house and a four-room carriage house. Both are painted a soft vanilla with pewter-blue trim and are connected with a spiffy white picket fence. Built as a boarding house in 1890, the renovated version plays up its past with canopied beds, handwoven coverlets and hand-hooked rugs on heartpine floors.

The **Casa de Solana** (21 Aviles Street; 904-824-3555) is geared toward travelers who like everything just so and don't mind adhering to a rigid timetable. For example, breakfast is served at a ten-foot-long mahogany table in the formal dining room at 8:30 on the dot. Of course, the reward is a classic southern breakfast. Four suites are decorated with antiques; each has either a fireplace, a view of Matanzas Bay or a balcony overlooking a large garden. Deluxe.

North of the historic district, moderately priced accommodations are available at the **Ramada Inn** (116 San Marco Avenue; 904-824-4352). This five-story motel has clean, decent rooms with views of the pool or the parking lot, but we wouldn't recommend staying here except for the convenient location.

Across Matanzas Bay on Anastasia Island, the **Conch House Marina Resort** (57 Comares Avenue; 904-829-8646) looks as if it had been lifted, thatched roof and all, directly from a South Seas island. Most rooms are spacious—even the studio apartments have two double beds—and have wallpaper, contemporary furnishings and drapes covering sliding glass doors. The best views, however, are not from the rooms but from the pool, the small riverside beach and a number of multilevel outdoor bars that help give this resort its extremely relaxed ambience. Moderate to deluxe.

ST. AUGUSTINE RESTAURANTS

Bunches of plastic grapes droop from the ceiling of **The Monk's Vineyard** (56 St. George Street; 904-824-5888), a funky, stained-glass grotto where waiters pad around in monk's robes and sandals. Loaded sandwiches are the highlight, with specials like "the Abbott" (roast beef, mushrooms and horseradish sauce). Budget.

With its stucco facade, archways, tiled walls and fountains, **The Columbia Restaurant** (98 St. George Street; 904-824-3341) looks as though it might have been shipped over from Spain. The cuisine is in keeping: paella, chicken with yellow rice, *boliche* (Cuban rump roast with chorizo sausage). Moderate.

Scarlett O'Hara's (70 Hypolita Street; 904-824-6535) is a convivial restaurant used as a watering hole by hordes of locals. Located in a renovated residence on a shady side street, it is a convenient spot for budget-priced lunches of soup, salad and sandwiches. In the evenings, finger food such as steamed Louisiana crayfish and raw oysters can be enjoyed inside the lounge or out on the front porch where you can watch the passing scene. Budget.

As if St. Augustine didn't claim enough "oldests" and "firsts," it also has what could be the world's only café located in a (now-empty) swimming pool. The **Café Alcazar** (★) (25 Granada Street; 904-824-7813), hidden away in the mall of antique shops behind the Lightner Museum, is well worth the effort required to find it. Crêpes, "croissandwiches," beef in cauliflower sauce and imaginative salads combine to create one of the most innovative menus in town. Lunch only except for dinner Friday nights. Budget.

One look at **Raintree Restaurant** (102 San Marco Avenue; 904-824-7211) tells you this place must have been a private home, and indeed it was. Built in 1879, it features a formal dining room with antiques and huge historic paintings, a garden terrace and upstairs seating on weekends. The fare is elaborate: veal Oscar, rack of lamb, seafood, and various duck, chicken and beef dishes. Moderate to deluxe.

Le Pavillon (45 San Marco Avenue; 904-824-6202) serves hearty European food like roast rack of lamb, duckling, schnitzel and bouillabaisse in a small turn-of-the-century house with French country decor. Moderate.

The **San Marco Grille** (123 San Marco Avenue; 904-824-2788) enjoys a steady clientele of locals, who can depend on this well-appointed restaurant for consistency and variety. Grilled chicken, seafood pasta dishes, deviled crab and several substantial salads are among its mainstays. Ask for a table facing the plant-filled patio, where tiny lights twinkle in the shrubbery at night. Moderate.

For no-nonsense food at any time of day, check out the **Seaport Café** (116 San Marco Avenue in the Ramada Inn; 904-824-8388). In this cozy coffee shop you can enjoy a dinner of fried shrimp, prime rib or fish at budget prices.

The **Gypsy Cab Company** (828 Route A1A, Anastasia Island; 904-824-8244) has a casual, café atmosphere that transcends bare floors and a view of the highway. The standard menu of fresh fish and steaks is spiced up with such offbeat selections as chicken stuffed with herbs and tomatoes, and shrimp sautéed with hot sausage. Moderate.

Located in a refurbished storefront **35 Houston** (415 Anastasia Boulevard, Anastasia Island; 904-829-6513) confines itself to a short menu executed with flair in a small kitchen. A friendly but professional staff presents such specials as rack of lamb, crab cabs with crawfish etouffée and sesame-seared yellowfish tuna. Deluxe.

ST. AUGUSTINE SHOPPING

Souvenir buying is a snap in St. Augustine; most of the 40-plus attractions in the country's oldest city stock all manner of mementos. The best shopping is along historic **St. George Street**, where pubs and points of interest rub shoulders with an intriguing medley of shops.

The Museum Store (53 St. George Street, 904-825-5040) is great fun to tour. Blue Zoo ceramics from Chile, Peruvian Christmas ornaments and Mexican "worry stones" are a few of the items imported from around the world.

Among the handmade goods at **San Agustin Imports** (46 St. George Street; 904-829-0032) are Panama hats, the real thing from Ecuador. The cozy **Colonial Shop** (8 St. George Street; 904-824-8974) specializes in early Americana and country wares, including lots of pewter figurines and wooden knickknacks. Finding seashells in Florida is like shooting fish in a barrel, but **The Shell Shop** (140 St. George Street; 904-824-8778) is known for its good-looking glass-bottomed lamps filled with beautiful specimens.

A block from St. George Street, **Casa Italia** (12 Cathedral Place; 904-824-1961) stocks hundreds of colorful porcelain dolls and clowns. Collectors will discover both common and rare dolls measuring from a tiny two inches to three feet in size.

In a city as old as St. Augustine, you'd expect to find antiques. The place to go is the **Lightner Antique Mall** (King and Granada streets, behind the Lightner Museum; 904-824-2874), where you'll find a wide range of collectibles, including antique linens and moderately priced pieces of china.

ST. AUGUSTINE NIGHTLIFE

St. Augustine will never be ranked with the great nightlife cities of the world. This is a day-time town but, true to its tradition of southern hospitality, it does offer a little bit for almost every visitor with energy left over from a full day of sightseeing.

Right in the historic district, the **Monson Bayfront Dinner Theatre** (in the Monson Lodge, 32 Avenida Menéndez; 904-829-2277) presents a variety of Broadway comedy hits in a casual dining room that seats 92 patrons. Reservations are encouraged whether you plan to have a full dinner or merely show up in time for the curtain.

After dark, **Scarlett O'Hara's** (70 Hypolita Street; 904-824-6535) undergoes a subtle metamorphosis from restaurant to Happy Hour hangout to dance bar. It features rock-and-roll bands, usually with a country flavor, most evenings. Cover on weekends.

The **Conch House Marina Lounge** (57 Comares Avenue; 904-829-8646) is a convivial spot where the atmosphere is enhanced by the riverfront setting and the plucking of a lone guitarist.

For dancing into the wee hours, it's **Reflections** (Holiday Inn, 1060 Route A1A South; 904-471-2555), where a disc jockey spins Top-40 hits.

ST. AUGUSTINE BEACHES AND PARKS

St. Augustine Beach—This is a simple beach, just a few thousand square feet of hard sand topped with a little powder and nudged by an endless series of small waves. The only drawback to this paradise is that automobile traffic is allowed on the beach.

Facilities: Picnic areas, restrooms, lifeguards; restaurants and grocery stores are nearby. *Fishing:* Off the pier. *Swimming:* Excellent.

Getting there: There are eight access points between St. Augustine-by-the-Sea and Pope Road, off Route A1A, south of St. Augustine.

Anastasia State Recreation Area—Within this 1722-acre park are four distinct plant communities: sand dunes, salt marsh, coastal scrub and coastal hammock. Gulls, pelicans and sandpipers swoop along the broad beach, while the lagoon and tidal marshes to the west harbor herons, egrets and other wading birds. Salt Run Lagoon offers shelter from the waves, high winds, and large crowds that spill onto this two-mile swath of white sand south of the St. Augustine Inlet.

Facilities: Restrooms, showers, picnic areas, boating facilities, lifeguards, concession stand; information, 904-461-2033. *Fishing:* Surf and lagoon fishing. *Swimming:* Excellent. *Surfing:* Fair. *Windsurfing:* Excellent at Salt Run Lagoon.

Getting there: Located at 5 Anastasia Park Drive, St. Augustine.

Jacksonville Area

The military fortifications that played such a strategic role in Florida's early history add a special dimension to sightseeing in the northeast corner of the state, especially on Amelia Island. In Jacksonville, the presence of several fine arts museums and renovated old neighborhoods reflect that city's increasing sophistication.

The largest city by area in the United States, Jacksonville also represents one of the oldest cities in Florida. Resting along the St. Johns River it combines a high-rise cityscape with the lazy ambience of the old South.

Just off Route A1A, the **Beaches of Jacksonville Chamber of Commerce** (413 Pablo Avenue; 904-249-3868) provides brochures and maps indicating points of interest in the area.

The **Fort Caroline National Memorial** (12713 Fort Caroline Road, near the junction with Monument Road, Jacksonville; 904-641-7155) covers 134 acres along the St. Johns River. A reconstructed version of the original 16th-century fort is located at the end of a quarter-mile path beyond the visitor center, where displays help interpret the conflicts between the original French settlers and the Spanish soldiers who followed.

The Koger Collection of Oriental porcelains highlights the extensive endowment at the **Jacksonville Art Museum** (4160 Boulevard Center Drive; 904-398-8336), the oldest museum in the city. In addition to pre-Columbian artifacts and contemporary works of art, the museum also offers classes, concerts and lectures.

The **Jacksonville Museum of Science and History** (1025 Museum Drive; 904-396-7061; admission) has both permanent and changing exhibits on natural history, Indian cultures and ancient Egypt as well as shows on physical science. The planetarium in this vast building is known for its powerful projector, capable of showing the night sky as it would be seen from any location in the world.

In front of the museum, the spectacular **Friendship Fountain** sprays 17,000 gallons of water per minute 120 feet into the air. The fountain is lit at night, providing a beautiful focal point for nearby **Riverwalk**, a 20-foot wide cement boardwalk bordering the south bank of the St. Johns River. Several pavilions feature daytime entertainment for joggers, walkers and office workers taking a break to enjoy the view of north Jacksonville from the comfort of a park bench. Built of weathered wood to resemble an old-fashioned pier, Riverwalk features arching lampposts that echo the form of the bridges at either end.

Before you leave downtown, drop by the **Jacksonville Chamber of Commerce** (3 Independent Drive; 904-366-6600) or the **Jacksonville and**

Its Beaches Convention and Visitors Bureau (413 Pablo Avenue; 904-249-3868) for additional tourism information.

The **Cummer Gallery of Art** (829 Riverside Avenue, Jacksonville; 904-356-6857) is known for its displays of decorative and fine art, notably its collection of Japanese *netsuke* (small carved figurines of jade, ivory and wood) and Chinese snuff bottles fashioned from semi-precious stones or porcelain. An entire room is devoted to 18th-century Meissen porcelain tableware, believed to be the largest collection in the world open to the public. A formal Florentine-style garden, a series of plants, trees, brick walkways and reflecting pools, extends from the mansion down to the river's edge.

The **Jacksonville Zoo** (one mile east of Heckscher Drive; 904-757-4462; admission) features some unusual innovations, such as separating some of its 700 animals by moats rather than cage bars. The Birds of Prey Aviary has tall trees and even a waterfall; the Wetlands Discovery features an elevated walkway above a natural swamp. Children as well as adults may take a ride on an elephant.

Guided and self-guided tours are offered at the **Anheuser-Busch Brewery** (111 Busch Drive near the airport; 904-751-8116). Enveloped in a constant aroma of brewing beers, this enormous facility features huge windows overlooking the floor where the long brewing process is conducted. There is also a tasting room.

There's almost always a greyhound race to be found somewhere in greater Jacksonville, but the track closest to downtown is the **Jacksonville Kennel Club** (1440 North McDuff Avenue; 904-646-0001).

In sleepy little Mayport, an old schoolhouse has been transformed into the low-key, highly informative **Marine Science Education Center** (1347 Palmer Street; 904-246-2733). Essentially a facility for local school-children, it also welcomes curious visitors. There is an outstanding display of regional shells, exhibits on the formation of beaches and specimens of marine life ranging from shark jaws to live turtles and alligators.

North of the ferry docks on Fort George Island, the **Kingsley Plantation (★)** (Route A1A; 904-251-3537) affords an unsettling glimpse into history. One of the oldest plantations in the state, it was purchased in 1817 by Zephaniah Kingsley, who operated a worldwide slave-trading business here on Spanish land. A two-mile oyster-shell road, under the canopy of subtropical forest, leads to the riverfront buildings where Kingsley and his African princess wife once lived. There are guided tours of her house.

The history of northeastern Florida—which existed under eight different flags over four centuries—is a story of confrontations, military skirmishes and fleeting triumphs on a par with the more Byzantine plots concocted by Hollywood adventure-movie writers. The carefully arranged maps, charts, pictures and memorabilia at the **Amelia Island Museum of History** (233 South 3rd Street, Fernandina Beach; 904-261-7378; admission) are, for the most part, self-explanatory. But you should call ahead if you'd like one of the excellent guided tours (by reservation only) of the museum and/or of the historic district.

JACKSONVILLE AREA HOTELS

For a city of its mind-boggling size, Jacksonville has surprisingly few non-chain hotels, especially in the downtown area. The most notable exception is the elegant **Omni Hotel** (245 Water Street; 904-355-6664). Pale, polished wood columns and walls swathed in rose and beige fabrics seem the epitome of refinement compared to the concrete jungle outside. Expect to pay ultra-deluxe prices for beautiful rooms and fine service, and for amenities such as a gorgeous restaurant and lounge.

On the river, **House on Cherry Street** (184 Cherry Street, Jacksonville; 904-384-1999) offers southern comfort at moderate prices. This four-room Georgian Colonial home features beautiful Pennsylvania antiques, a big screen porch and large yard reaching down to the water's edge. Spend the night in a canopy bed and wake up to a full breakfast featuring homemade muffins. Be sure to check out the duck decoy collection.

The **Sea Turtle Inn** (1 Ocean Boulevard, Atlantic Beach; 904-249-7402) is built so that every room has a view of at least a slice of ocean, so close you can almost smell it. But not quite: all the room windows are sealed. Other than that, the place is delightful, with comfortable dual double beds and endless vistas of the sand stretching into the horizon. Deluxe.

If you want to stay in a one- or two-bedroom condominium on the water, consider the **Beachcomber** (411 South 1st Street, Jacksonville Beach; 904-249-2663). Decorated with bamboo furniture, this white stucco condo provides full kitchens and private balconies. At the low end of the deluxe range, units are rented for a minimum of two nights.

On Amelia Island, the best-known destination is the **Amelia Island Plantation** (Route A1A; 904-261-6161), a first-rate resort that sprawls over 1240 acres between pristine beach and carefully preserved tidal marshlands. The plantation (a word commonly used on Florida's East Coast to describe residential resort communities) is known for the quality and quantity of its villas, available in one- to three-bedroom sizes. Fashioned of pale stucco and built in clusters around swimming pools, these luxurious accommodations are nestled in the semishade of ancient oak trees and graceful palmettos. The decor is sophisticated: top-quality chairs and sofas, sparkling kitchens, attractive drapes. In addition to 45 holes of golf, 25 tennis courts and a full-service health center, recreational opportunities include bicycle and horseback riding, boating, fishing and nature trails that curve along the golden marshes. Not to mention four miles of beachfront so clean that the shells look as if they had been polished by hand. Ultra-deluxe.

An oceanfront inn right out of a 1940s romantic movie provides most visitors with their first glimpse of Fernandina Beach's charm. Clapboard-covered and unpretentious, the **Seaside Inn** (1998 South Fletcher Avenue; 904-261-0954) is a wayfarer's delight, a renovated hotel, restaurant and lounge on the very lip of the Atlantic. Second-floor oceanside rooms are decorated in the simple fashion of a well-worn summer home, with pastel walls, ceiling fans and double beds topped with fluffy comforters. Moderate.

Ever fantasized about your very own lighthouse? A uniquely romantic conception, the **Lighthouse** (748 South Fletcher Avenue, Fernandina Beach; 904-261-5878) never really served as one, but feels as if it did. Four circular rooms are stacked one on top of another, with sea oats brushing against the shuttered windows and the surf only feet away. Old lacquered charts cover the walls of the circular stairway. In the kitchen, tables and seats are suspended from the beamed ceiling. The top floor of this two-bedroom delight is an empty room surrounded by a railed deck with a 360° view. For a deluxe price you get the entire complex and breakfast delivered in a basket.

The cozy **1735 House** (584 South Fletcher Avenue, Fernandina Beach; 904-261-5878), built of tongue-and-groove Georgia pine in 1928, has five rooms whose names (Patriots, Captain's Cabin, etc.) refer to Amelia Island's seagoing history. In fact, ten more yards to the east and the inn itself would be seagoing. All oceanview rooms are outfitted with a dining table, rather funky baths, small refrigerators (some have efficiency kitchens) and sitting areas decorated in rattan with rose fabrics that complement the patterned bedcovers. Continental breakfast is included in the moderate price.

The **Captain's House** (268 South Fletcher Avenue, Fernandina Beach; 904-261-5878) would fit right in on old Cape Cod, with its pale gray clapboard exterior trimmed in white. Nine comfortably furnished apartments extend along the length of this three-story building, fronted by sliding glass doors that open onto a patio. Deluxe.

Off the beach in downtown Fernandina Beach, the spacious **Williams House Bed and Breakfast Inn (★)** (103 South 9th Avenue; 904-277-2328) makes you wonder what it would have been like to grow up amid 4000 square feet of floor space—and another 1300 square feet of covered porch. This pre-Civil War, two-story pale gray bed and breakfast has four remodeled rooms upstairs, one sporting a balcony underlooking a centuries-old oak tree. Even Scarlett O'Hara would've loosened her corset at the sight of breakfast choices such as french toast with cream cheese and nuts, or country fresh eggs baked inside cheese dough. Moderate.

The **Bailey House** (28 South 7th Street, Fernandina Beach; 904-261-5390) is a traditional Victorian building with turrets, gables, peaks and bay windows, a wide staircase and spacious parlors decorated with assorted antiques, including an old organ in working condition. Four spacious guest rooms are furnished in brass beds, clawfoot tubs and fringed lamp shades. Moderate.

JACKSONVILLE AREA RESTAURANTS

Pale pink walls, pink napkins, fresh flowers, lace curtains and moss green carpet set the tone for **Sterling's Café** (3551 St. Johns Avenue, Jacksonville; 904-387-0700). European specialties include wild mushroom pasta, grilled swordfish and salmon baked with ginger and fresh ground pepper served on a celeryroot purée bed with a cabernet buerre rouge. Deluxe.

The **Silver Spoon** (Jacksonville Landing, 2 East Independent Drive, Jacksonville; 904-353-4503) commands a sweeping view of the St. Johns River from its deck tables. Inside, a long narrow room is festooned with rows of hanging woven baskets and brass planter pots reflected in a wall of glass. The moderately priced menu features steaks, ribs and seafood, plus a lot of small dishes suitable for a late lunch or early dinner. Chicken appetizers come barbecued, herbed or Cajun-level spicy and go well with creamy potato-cheese soup, deep-dish quiche or a hearty salad.

Juliette's (245 Water Street in the Omni Hotel, Jacksonville; 904-355-6664) is an expansive, elegant restaurant. You can enjoy fresh fish cooked to order, roast Long Island duckling, bouillabaisse, châteaubriand or other steak dishes in the formal dining room with its low lighting and tapestried booths, or at tables set in the plant-rimmed atrium. Deluxe.

When we finally spotted **Crawdaddy's** (1643 Prudential Drive, Jacksonville; 904-396-3546) behind a phalanx of office towers, we thought the building had burned; but no, that's the way it's supposed to look, sort of like an abandoned warehouse. The interior is equally distinctive: several whimsically decorated rooms scattered over numerous levels, where nothing matches except a handful of carved wooden chairs. In this one-of-a-kind setting, specialties range from alligator and Cajun dishes to seafood, chicken and prime rib. Moderate to deluxe.

The restaurants in the revitalized San Marco district attract a lot of young people who have discovered the European flavor of the neighborhood. **The Café Carmon** (1986 San Marco Boulevard, Jacksonville; 904-399-4488) exudes cosmopolitan intimacy, with a choice of seating at café tables out front, near the open kitchen, or along a brick wall hung with impressionist prints. An imaginative mix of daily specials like roast loin of lamb with a pesto cream sauce augment a standing lineup of tortes, salads, quiches and charcuterie items. It's an excellent choice for late-night dining at moderate prices.

With its gazebo-like interior and white trellises, the **Yum Yum Tree** (3566 St. Johns Avenue, Jacksonville; 904-388-9007) is well suited to its upscale Avondale surroundings. This is where shoppers stop for gourmet sandwiches, quiches, crêpes and other light luncheon items. Budget.

The beachfront **Crab Pot Restaurant** (12 North Oceanfront Drive, Jacksonville Beach; 904-241-4188) is a landmark located across from the Flag Pavilion. Cavernous and kind of corny with its plastic bibs and a flashy

T-shirt display in the lobby, the Crab Pot prints a long menu of local and imported fresh bounty from the sea: shrimp, scampi, steamed blue crabs, tuna salad, conch fritters, seafood creole, catfish parmesan, peel 'em yourself shrimp and a variety of mixed platters. Moderate.

An all-you-care-to-eat barbecue buffet makes **Chiang's Mongolian Bar-B-Q** (1504 North 3rd Street, Jacksonville Beach; 904-241-3075) a terrific value, especially since the moderate price includes beef, pork, chicken and vegetables. Other than that, Chiang's is standard shopping-strip oriental, a big, brightly lit room with typical red and gold decor. You can also order à la carte from a sizable list of such standbys as lemon chicken, wonton soup, chow mein and teriyaki chicken. Service is prompt and friendly and portions are large at this family-oriented restaurant. Budget to moderate.

G'day. At the tin-roofed **Outback Steakhouse** (3760 South 3rd Street, Jacksonville Beach; 904-237-7888) you'll find boomerangs and kangaroo pictures on the wall, safari clad waitpeople and some of the zestiest food in town. This down under theme, designed to make any Australian feel at home, is an ideal steak house setting. If you're not hungry for prime rib, filet or porterhouse, try the ribs, chicken, shrimp, pork or fish of the day. Even the appetizers have a kick. Moderate.

A tiered dining room on the ocean, **First Street Grille** (807 North 1st Street, Jacksonville Beach; 904-246-6555) is a picture window perfect place to enjoy fresh seafood and steaks. Done in Key West style with flowers and painted birds on the walls, the dining room is complemented by a spacious deck complete with a tiki bar where you can enjoy steel drum and jazz bands. Moderate.

Sprouting huge awnings and a spiffy picket fence, the **Homestead** (1712 Beach Boulevard, Jacksonville Beach; 904-249-5240) has long been a roadside favorite for deep South home-style cooking. The atmosphere is cozy despite plastic tablecloths and wrought-iron chairs. Who cares, when they can be eating all kinds of seafood and chicken dishes, including a special called "lizards"—a combination of chicken liver and gizzards served with rice. Moderate.

The brick, glass and brass exterior promises conviviality, and boy, does the **Ragtime Tavern and Seafood Grill** (207 Atlantic Boulevard, Atlantic Beach; 904-241-7877) deliver. Three levels of seating allow for intimate dining or group get-togethers. Specialties include gumbo, shrimp, mesquite-grilled catch-of-the-day and a curried spinach salad. A lunch of salad, wine, coffee and a plate of Ragtime's signature *beignets* falls well within the moderate range; dinner prices run from moderate to deluxe.

Salud! (★) (207 Atlantic Boulevard, Atlantic Beach; 904-241-7877) is Florida's answer to Spain's tapas bars, cafés that serve a wide variety of "little dishes." Salud! is particularly fun with a group interested in sharing orders of deep-fried crab wonton, baked feta cheese, tuna sesame or conch fritters. Moderate.

Head to Amelia Island and you will find restaurants serving everything from flounder to fettucine. **Southern Tip** (★) (4802 Route A1A, Amelia Island; 904-261-6184), located at the rear of a shopping/dining complex called Palmetto Walk, could easily be mistaken for a French country home. Paintings, mirrors and flowers appoint this gracious two-story dining room featuring a Continental menu. Specialties include veal, lamb, pasta, beef and the catch of the day. Among the popular appetizers are black-eyed pea cakes, escargot and stuffed artichoke hearts. Also here are dessert and espresso bars. Moderate to deluxe.

The Sandbar (Forest Drive, Fernandina Beach; 904-261-4185) is an out-of-the-way institution on the west side of Amelia Island. Billboards with large red arrows lead diners to this marshfront family-style restaurant, where dark wood and low ceilings enhance the hideaway feeling. Half the items on the menu—oysters, shrimp and crab served fried, broiled, fresh or raw in the shell—probably were caught within half-a-mile of the Sandbar. Chicken and steaks are also available. Moderate.

The prettiest restaurant in the town of Fernandina Beach is unquestionably **Brett's Waterway Café** (1 South Front Street; 904-261-2660). With an elegant feel, this waterfront eatery offers both indoor and outdoor dining. The menu is equally sumptuous, a mix of continental cuisine, fresh seafood and beef dishes. Deluxe.

If you're looking for fried or boiled seafood dishes, consider the **Surf Restaurant** (3199 Fletcher Avenue, Fernandina Beach; 904-261-5711). Across the street from the beach, this unpretentious establishment with blue carpet, mauve walls, overhead fans and plants is known for its fried shrimp and clams, as well as charcoal grilled fish and steaks. The wine list is excellent. Moderate.

A small bistro with a big menu, **Loaf and Ladle** (5 South 2nd Street, Fernandina Beach; 904-277-1879) is the place to go for egg dishes and grits, soups and salads and dinner entrées like grouper in a white-wine sauce covered with crabmeat. Checkered tablecloths, black and white parquet floors and paintings by local artists add to the charm of this cozy spot. Moderate.

The **1878 Steak House** (12 North 2nd Street, Fernandina Beach; 904-261-4049) specializes in local seafood and steak sold by the ounce. The decor is rather florid, giving this second-floor restaurant the atmosphere of a Wild West hotel. Dinner only. Moderate to deluxe.

The **Marina Restaurant** (101 Centre Street, Fernandina Beach; 904-261-5310) is so close to the docks that fishermen could probably toss their catches from the boat decks into the frying pan. Except for a few nautical artifacts like a miniature lighthouse, the decor is plain, letting the fresh lobster, fantail shrimp and plump flounder carry the day. Large portions at moderate prices.

Slider's Restaurant (1998 South Fletcher Avenue, Fernandina Beach; 904-261-0954), named after the Louisiana slang word for oysters, is the quintessential beach town hangout. No table linens, no decoration, no pretensions, just a short, simple, moderately priced menu dominated by raw oysters, fried shrimp and broiled fish.

Snug Harbor (201 Alachua Street, Fernandina Beach; 904-261-8031) is one of half-a-dozen restaurants clustered around Centre Street, the main shopping artery. The back porch here is often occupied with locals waiting in line for some soft-shell crabs, baked grouper or fresh Florida lobster. Prices are moderate except for budget-priced lunch specials large enough to keep a fisherman going all day.

JACKSONVILLE AREA SHOPPING

Sprawling over 841 square miles, the city of Jacksonville has plenty of room for vast suburban malls such as **Regency Square** (9501 Arlington Expressway, 904-725-1220), where stores range from **Dillard's** (904-721-9166), a department store, to local branches of a lingerie shop called **Victoria's Secret** (904-721-2161).

Something of a magnet for the credit-card-carrying public, the two-story **Jacksonville Landing** (2 Independent Drive, Jacksonville; 904-353-1188) dominates the north bank of the St. Johns River just west of the Main Street Bridge. You could easily spend a day here, stopping for nourishment at any of half-a-dozen restaurants or sipping espresso while watching the passing parade of river traffic.

Instead of the giant department stores and hole-in-the-wall T-shirt shops found in so many malls, most of the retailers here are medium-sized concerns specializing in quality goods. At **Laura Ashley** (904-358-7548) you'll find an array of dresses and fabrics sporting floral prints inspired by the English countryside. Unique baskets woven from palm fronds and wicker are offered at **The Straw Market** (904-356-8524). Also featured are woven cotton throw pillows, colorful rugs, antique glassware and Coke bottles.

Neighborhoods like Five Points and San Marco offer an eclectic mix of boutiques, but the grande dame of residential retailing is unquestionably Avondale. It's easy to see why this neighborhood has been dubbed "antique alley." Good places to browse for somebody's heirlooms include **Avenue Antiques** (3564 St. Johns Avenue; 904-388-1995), which specializes in Oriental porcelains and paintings, and **Canterbury House Antiques** (1776 Canterbury Street; 904-387-1776).

For contemporary gifts, one of the best shops in all of Jacksonville is **The Jade Tree** (3600 St. Johns Avenue; 904-384-7287). Elegant picture frames, glass and crystal objets d'art, chic coffee mugs and picnic baskets are available in almost every price range.

Shops such as **Miz Lucy** (3637 St. Johns Avenue; 904-387-1231) reflect the tax bracket of the surrounding neighborhood of mansions and sweeping lawns. This small store is known for its tasteful fashions for women. Check at **The Hobby Horse** (3550 St. Johns Avenue; 904-389-7992) or nearby **Khakis** (3643 St. Johns Avenue; 904-384-2712) for a good selection of clothing for children.

Dubbed "Little Landing" by locals making a comparison to the much bigger Jacksonville Landing, **St. Johns Village** (4000 St. Johns Avenue) is located down the road from the Avondale shops. **White's Bookstore** (904-387-9288), which has a number of outlets in the area, is represented here with a large, well-lit room full of fiction, non-fiction, magazines and book-related gifts.

In the Jacksonville Beach area, **Costa Verde Shopping Center** (2405 South 3rd Street, Jacksonville Beach) is one of the smaller and nicer clusters of shops to be found on or near Route A1A. China and crystal vases galore sparkle in the windows at the **Pineapple Post** (2403 South 3rd Street, Jacksonville Beach; 904-249-7477). Next door, the latest fashions from Milan and Paris are the stock-in-trade at **Barton/Sligh's** (904-246-9436), a name known to career women, who frequent the downtown location of this upscale boutique.

Get a feel for Florida's northern neighbor at **The China Cat** (226 4th Avenue South, Jacksonville Beach; 904-241-0344), where old Georgia pine and pecan furnishings are among the lovely antiques.

Your seashell connection is **The Corner Store** (200 North 1st Street, Jacksonville Beach; 904-249-2494), a treasure trove of island jewelry and T-shirts as well as Hummels, David Winter cottages and other collectibles.

Several shops can be found near the intersection of Route A1A and the ocean. **The Crabapple Tree** (40 Ocean Boulevard, Atlantic Beach; 904-249-5182) is a sweetheart of a store laden with teddy bears, Christmas ornaments, fudge and Crabtree & Evelyn toiletries. For a look at some original local artwork, try **Sunshine Frames** (1315 North 3rd Street, Jacksonville Beach; 904-246-7133). This small gallery also sells engravings and lithographs.

If you just have to take a gift home and can't think of anything, you'll get help at both **Shorelines** (115½ 1st Street, Neptune Beach; 904-246-9133), which has inexpensive casual jewelry, T-shirts and gifts.

On Amelia Island a couple of miles north of the Amelia Island Plantation, **Palmetto Walk** (4800 Route A1A) consists of several residential-type buildings that house a number of boutiques and restaurants. The sportswear for men and women at **Heron's Sportswear Inc.** (904-261-3677) wears labels such as Polo/Ralph Lauren and is eminently suitable for resort life. For casual dressing, T-shirts and sweatshirts are available at **Cotton Tops** (904-277-4426). **Carol's Collection** (904-261-5241) encompasses perfumes, accessories and other gifts. Exquisite antique furniture, silver frames and needlepoint pillows make **The Plantation Shop** (904-261-2030) look like someone's lovingly decorated parlor.

The pride and joy of Fernandina Beach's restored district is **Centre Street,** which extends inland several blocks from the City Docks. The slow pace of island life can be felt here even in the busiest shops that share the street with restaurants and service establishments catering to locals.

For material on the state's history and tourist attractions, as well as a good assortment of Florida-based fiction, check out the **Book Loft** (214 Centre Street; 904-261-8991). The best of several women's clothing shops is **Personalities** (118 Centre Street; 904-277-3319). This comfortably chic boutique sells beach togs, walking shorts, T-shirts and some fancy handbags.

If you want to take a little bit of Dixie home with you, you should dawdle in **Southern Touch** (301 Centre Street; 904-261-5377), purveyors of basketry and other country handcrafts.

A couple of blocks off Centre Street, **Helen D'Agnese** (14½ North 4th Street, Fernandina Beach; 904-261-0433) sells works of art in a variety of media (and claims former president Jimmy Carter as a collector). Her specialties are limestone sculpture and oil paintings in the Latin American primitive style.

If shopping centers had existed at the turn of the century, they would have looked like **C House Colony** (South 9th and Beach streets, Fernandina Beach), a ramshackle string of clapboard buildings. **J. Max Homeplace** (904-277-2431) is a hodgepodge of baskets, china boxes and other decorative items. At **Jeff Steel Jewelers** (904-277-3830), artisans can often be seen at work fashioning pieces of jewelry out of gold.

JACKSONVILLE AREA NIGHTLIFE

For an evening of easy-listening music in plush surroundings, **Juliette's** (245 Water Street in the Omni Hotel, Jacksonville; 904-355-6664) is the place to go in downtown Jacksonville. A handsome room with comfortable chairs and spacious cocktail tables, Juliette's features a combo Thursday and Friday evenings.

With outdoor and indoor dancefloors, **The Warehouse** (2309 Beach Boulevard, Jacksonville Beach; 904-249-2050) offers numerous possibilities. Inside you can rock to Top-40 deejay music. Outdoors you'll enjoy live bands playing rock, reggae and progressive music. There is also a full bar, as well as a game room with video machines and pool tables. Cover.

The lounge at **Crawdaddy's** (1643 Prudential Drive, Jacksonville; 904-396-3546) is one of the area's more unusual nightclubs. A sizable bar and dancefloor are the focal points of a barnlike main room where the decor is half the fun. The musical fare is high-velocity Top-40 tunes.

Popular with the over-30 crowd, **Pappa's** (10940 Beach Boulevard, Jacksonville; 904-641-0321) is a spacious spot to bend an elbow, toss back a cold brew and tune in to Top-40 hits spun by a deejay.

An outpost of restaurants and clubs makes Baymeadows Road, between downtown Jacksonville and the beaches, something of an after-dark mecca. For laughs, listen in at **The Punch Line** (9911 Old Baymeadows Road, Suite 101, Jacksonville; 904-641-4444). Cover.

There's usually a sizable crowd at **Bombay Bicycle Club** (8909 Baymeadows Road, Jacksonville; 904-737-9555). This high-profile restaurant/lounge complex rocks to Top-40 tunes nightly until the wee hours.

Broadway musicals and comedies are the stock in trade at the **Alhambra Dinner Theatre** (12000 Beach Boulevard, Jacksonville; 904-641-1212). Buffet dinners are available before evening performances.

Jacksonville's oldest theater company, **Theatre Jacksonville** (2032 San Marco Boulevard, Jacksonville; 904-396-4425), also claims to have been entertaining audiences longer than any other community theater in the country.

The **Florida Ballet** (123 East Forsyth Street, Jacksonville; 904-353-7518) offers an array of programs from classical ballet to contemporary works.

The **Jacksonville Symphony** (33 South Hogan Street, Suite 400, Jacksonville; 904-354-5547) schedules more than 100 performances each year. The sizable regional orchestra and its various ensembles play in the Civic Auditorium, in pops concerts at the Florida Theater, and elsewhere.

As you might expect, **Einstein-A-GoGo** (327 North 1st Street, Jacksonville Beach; 904-249-4646) attracts a collegiate crowd, but you'll also find a mix of much older and somewhat younger fans dancing to live and deejay music at this easygoing nightclub. Cover.

The music isn't live, but the patrons certainly are at **Bukkets Baha** (222 Ocean Front, Jacksonville Beach; 904-246-7701). Disc jockeys spin Top-40 platters nightly until after midnight.

Aside from jazz groups playing at **Salud!** (207 Atlantic Boulevard, Atlantic Beach; 904-241-7877), nightlife at the beaches runs heavily to rock-and-roll. The southern music tradition is alive at **57 Heaven** (8136 Atlantic Boulevard, Jacksonville; 904-721-5757). This roadside joint is a sentimentalist's dream, with dance music from the '50s and '60s. Cover on weekends.

Out in the Amelia Island area you'll find several prime night spots. **The Palace Saloon** (113 Centre Street, Fernandina Beach; 904-261-6320), built in 1878 and believed to be the oldest bar in Florida, should be on your must-see list. A large, high-ceilinged room with memorabilia from the early days, it's the prime local gathering spot from happy hour into the wee hours. Cover on weekends.

Downstairs at the 1878 Steak House, the brick-walled **Brass Rail Bar** (North 2nd Street, Fernandina Beach; 904-261-4049) has live entertainment Friday evenings.

The liveliest spot on Amelia Island is **Slider's Lounge** (1998 South Fletcher Avenue at the Seaside Inn, Fernandina Beach; 904-261-0954), an easygoing nightclub that features a changing line-up of both homegrown and visiting bands.

GAY SCENE The only gay bar and nightclub on the beach, **Bo's Coral Reef** (201 5th Avenue North, Jacksonville Beach; 904-246-9874) is a mauve cinderblock building accommodating crowds up to 1000. This mirrored club has a big dancefloor, video monitors and pool tables. Bands play progressive, high-energy music Wednesday through Sunday. On Thursday nights you can join the $5 beer bust.

A red-brick building decorated with a train motif, **Junction** (1261 King Street, Jacksonville; 904-388-3434) is a popular gay bar.

Phoenix (1216 Kings Avenue, Jacksonville; 904-398-0101) features two gay bars separated by a glass wall. Progressive music sets the tone in the high-tech video bar. In the country-and-western bar you'll find rustic decor, natural wood and terra cotta floors. A monthly full moon party is a major attraction.

JACKSONVILLE AREA BEACHES AND PARKS

Guano River State Park (★)—Of four beaches between St. Augustine and Jacksonville, this one is the most special and the hardest to find. There is a wild, untamed feeling to this grainy sand beach laden with thousands of shells. Hidden from the highway by private residences and two-story sand dunes, it is hard to reach—you must make your way along poorly marked paths through underbrush and over the hills of sand—but is far less crowded than nearby beaches. Your reward for the adventure: a breathtaking expanse of oceanfront beauty.

Facilities: None; information, 904-825-5071. *Fishing:* Surf fishing only. *Swimming*: A big dropoff at certain tide levels means that swimming varies from fair to very good.

Getting there: About five miles north of St. Augustine on Route A1A.

Jacksonville Beach—The southernmost of the three urban beaches east of downtown, Jacksonville Beach encompasses some 2400 feet of hard sand. It is extremely popular with locals and tends to be more crowded on the weekends than either Neptune or Atlantic beaches to the north.

Facilities: Concession stands, lifeguards; restaurants and groceries are nearby. *Fishing:* Off the pier. *Swimming:* Very good everywhere.

Getting there: Located near Route A1A between J. Turner Butler and Beach boulevards; can be reached at the end of any of 64 streets that cross North 1st Street in Jacksonville.

Hanna Park—One of the best-marked and best-maintained parks in northern Florida, this spot has 450 variegated acres, with fresh-water lakes, hiking trails, a nature preserve, well-preserved sand dunes and more than a mile of clean hard-sand beach.

Facilities: Picnic areas, restrooms, showers, concession stands, lifeguards; information, 904-249-4700; restaurants are in nearby Mayport and Atlantic Beach. *Fishing:* Surf and freshwater angling. *Swimming:* Fine along the entire beachfront; most popular is the stretch in front of Pelican Plaza. *Surfing:* Best waves are at the north end off Dolphin Plaza.

Camping: There are 300 sites, all with RV hookups; $10 per night for tent campers, $13.25 for hookups.

Getting there: At 500 Wonderwood Drive in Atlantic Beach.

Little Talbot Island State Park—Actually an entire 2500-acre barrier island north of the mouth of the Fort George River, this long, narrow strip of land offers a diverse landscape that changes continually from the effects of wind and water. In this nearly pristine environment, it's possible to see what Florida looked like before the coming of condominiums. A series of seaward dunes, interspersed with low-lying troughs, are in many places lush with low-growing plants such as flowering morning-glories and held in place with taller sea oats. Five miles of glistening white sand beach are accessible by dune crossovers, one at the south end of the island and one near the middle. Inland estuaries support abundant marsh life; oysters, crab, fish, turtles and migrating seabirds are common sights. The central portion of this wild island harbors a hammock of oak, holly and magnolia trees.

Facilities: Picnic areas, restrooms, showers; information, 904-251-2320. *Fishing:* Speckled trout, striped bass, bluefish, redfish, flounder, mullet, sheepshead and whiting can be caught in the Atlantic, the Fort George River or Myrtle and Simpson creeks. *Swimming:* Good waves for bodysurfing. *Surfing:* Good all along the coast.

Camping: There are 40 sites, all with RV hookups; $17–19 per night.

Getting there: Located northeast of Jacksonville on Route A1A.

Amelia Island Beach (★)—The southernmost beach on this barrier island is arguably the most beautiful in east Florida. The sand is fine, dark and firmly packed; small, perfectly formed shells appear to have been arranged by hand in orderly patterns. A secondary ridge of sand dunes, behind the eroded line of beachfront dunes, forms a pretty backdrop with sea oats and other salt-resistant plants. Much of the beach fronts Amelia Island Plantation, which the public may not walk through, but there is easy public access north of the resort.

Facilities: Restrooms, picnic areas, lifeguards. *Fishing:* Surf fishing. *Swimming:* Excellent.

Getting there: The beach is located north of Nassau Sound off Route A1A.

Amelia City Beach and **Fernandina Beach**—These beaches are contiguous stretches of pale sand beach, mostly within yards of Route A1A. Amelia City Beach is a little cleaner and less crowded than its neighbor to the north.

Facilities: Restrooms, lifeguards; concession stand at Fernandina Beach only. *Fishing:* Surf angling. *Swimming:* Excellent. *Surfing:* Fair.

Getting there: Located off Route A1A north of Amelia City. Major access points at Peters Point, South Fletcher Avenue, Scott Road and Sadler Road.

Fort Clinch State Park—Located at the northern tip of Amelia Island, this 1086-acre park has both natural and historic attractions. Bounded by the Amelia River on the west, Cumberland Sound on the north, and the Atlantic on the east, the park's many natural features include a coastal hardwood hammock, huge sand dunes, a sandy beach and a salt marsh. Alligators, wading birds and small animals can be sighted along a nature trail.

Facilities: Picnic area, restrooms, showers, lifeguards; restaurants and grocery stores are nearby; information, 904-277-7274. *Fishing:* Striped bass and speckled trout are plentiful off the long pier on the east side of the park. *Swimming:* Excellent on the ocean side.

Camping: There are 62 sites, all with RV hookups; $17-19 per night.

Getting there: The park is located at 2601 Atlantic Avenue in Fernandina Beach.

The Sporting Life

SPORTFISHING

For a deep-sea fishing excursion in the Fort Pierce area, contact **Charter Boats** (219 Fisherman's Wharf, Fort Pierce; 407-489-2180) or **A Simbar Fishing** (806 Indian River Drive, Sebastian; 407-589-4868). Among the other boats that cruise for shark, sailfish, marlin, dolphin, king and barracuda is **The Lady Stuart** (Bailey's Boat Company, Jensen Beach; 407-286-1860).

Most of the charter fishing boats in the Cape Canaveral area are docked at Port Canaveral for easy access to an ocean teeming with snapper, grouper and shark, to name a few of the common fish. **Miss Cape Canaveral** (407-

783-5274) is an 83-foot party boat that takes day as well as nighttime excursions. At 95 feet, the **Pelican Princess** (407-784-3474) is said to be the largest fiberglass party boat in the country; at least it's large enough to contain both a sundeck and a galley.

Full-day or half-day fishing excursions are among the most popular sports in the Daytona Beach area; some boats take anglers as far out as the Gulf Stream. A number of charter outfits are located within a short drive from major Daytona Beach hotels including **Sea Love Marina** (4884 Front Street, Ponce Inlet; 904-767-3406).

Tarpon, king fish and shark are common in the waters off St. Augustine. Fishing boats can be chartered at **Conch House Marina Resort** (57 Comares Avenue, Anastasia Island; 904-824-4347) and **Sea Love Charters** (250 Vilano Road, St. Augustine; 904-824-3328).

There are myriad opportunities to fish in the surf or off piers along the East Coast of Florida, but offshore angling is a completely different experience. Charter boats can be hired at **King Neptune Deep-Sea Fishing** (Monty's Marina, 4378 Ocean Street, Mayport; 904-246-0104), a short drive north from Atlantic Beach. On Amelia Island, you can sign on for either fishing or sightseeing aboard a boat from **Tradewinds** (1 South Front Street, Fernandina Beach; 904-261-9486) or the **Amelia Angler** (Amelia Island Plantation, Route A1A on Amelia Island; 904-261-2870).

BOATING

To cruise the Intracoastal Waterway in the Fort Pierce area under your own power, you can rent a variety of craft and waterskis from **Taylor Creek Marina** (1600 North 2nd Street, Fort Pierce; 407-465-2663) or from **Rosemeyer's Boat Rental** (3281 Northeast Indian River Drive, Jensen Beach; 407-334-1000). **Days Inn Driftwood** (3150 Ocean Drive, Vero Beach; 407-231-0206) rents waterskis, jetskis, windsurfers and kayaks.

If it moves on water, chances are you can rent it at **The Water Works** (1891 Route 520, Merritt Island; 407-452-2007). Sailboats, power boats and jetskis.

Canoes, kayaks, paddle boats, pontoons and ski boats can be rented at **Daytona Recreational Sales and Rentals** (1001 North Route 1, Ormond Beach; 904-672-5631). **Club Nautico** (3050 Harbor Drive, St. Augustine; 904-825-4848) has power boats for rent. Sailboats are the specialty at **Marina Port Orange** (3537 Halifax Drive, Port Orange; 904-767-6408).

SURFING AND WINDSURFING

To rent the right stuff for surfing the big waves around Sebastian Inlet, try the **North Jetty Surf Shop** (1018 Shorewinds Drive, Fort Pierce; 407-

(Text continued on page 228.)

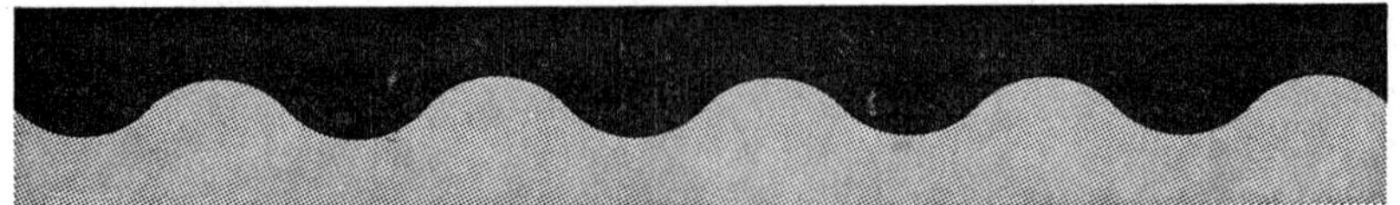

On the Wild Side: Sea Turtles and Alligators

An odd ritual can be observed on summer nights along Florida's barrier islands. A group of people, usually dressed in raincoats to protect against a gentle rainfall, walk slowly in front of the sand dunes, peering down at the ground in the moonlight. Occasionally, they will spot huge tracks, like something a tractor might make, leading from the water's edge to the dunes and back again. These are the tracks of sea turtles, which come out of the water to lay their precious eggs in the sand above the high-water mark. The people are there to help protect the eggs from poachers and other animals of prey. When the eggs—perhaps 120 or more per female—do hatch, the tiny turtles will make their precarious way to the ocean, where more predators, such as sharks, reduce the survival rate to as little as one in 1000.

For more than 100 million years, sea turtles have been roaming the earth's waters, though relatively few people ever get a chance to see them. For a few weeks each year, however, it is possible along Florida's East Coast to spot one of these enormous creatures, which often grow as long as five feet and weigh 500 pounds or more. Depending on the locale, loggerhead and greenback turtles can be spotted sometime between June and October.

Sea turtles, hunted for centuries for their meat, are now protected by the Endangered Species Act. To ensure their survival, regulatory agencies carefully oversee their habitat, which includes the beaches. From Jensen Beach to Amelia Island, however, park rangers and other authorized groups sponsor "Turtle Watches" that allow people to witness the giant reptiles laboring to crawl the 40 or 50 yards from the sea to the safety of the sand dunes and using their flippers to dig out a nest. Some turtle eggs may be scooped up by rangers, to be released later. The rest are guarded until the hatchlings appear and begin their instinctive but treacherous journey to the open water. No one knows where the turtles spend their first year or how they navigate the oceans, but the females will ultimately return to the original beach to build their own nests.

Turtle walks are sponsored at the Sebastian Inlet State Park and at Jensen Beach. Call the appropriate chambers of commerce for information about reservations.

Turtles, of course, are not the stuff of legends, which are spun about Florida's other big reptiles. Some people call them alligators, some call

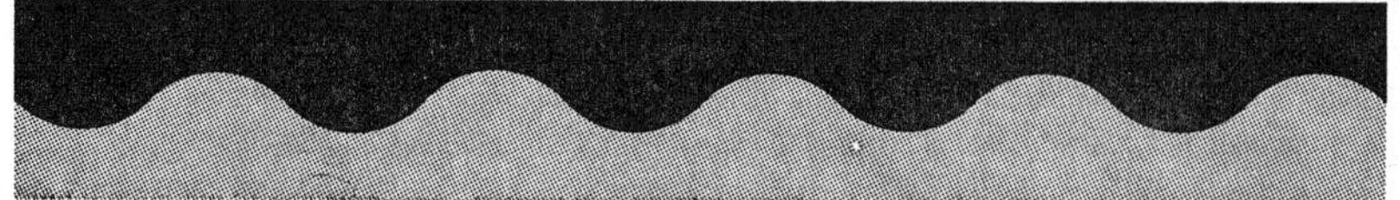

them crocodiles, but Floridians refer to those long, scary-looking creatures with big teeth and equally big appetites simply as 'gators. (Actually, American alligators are technically one family of Crocodilia; they share ancestors with the dinosaur.) Like sharks, alligators have remained relatively unchanged over millions of years and, also like sharks, they are among the most feared marine predators in the world. So feared, in fact, and so valued for their meat and leatherlike hides that they were placed on the Endangered Species List until recently. Now, as any visitor to Florida can tell you, there seems to be no shortage.

Mangrove swamps such as those on Merritt Island are favorite habitats of the alligator, as are the marshes along rivers such as the St. John's, which runs north from around Melbourne all the way to Jacksonville. Alligators, which are typically seven- to eight-feet long, are cold-blooded predators that often seize their prey under water. They can and do, however, also seize small animals from the banks of ponds.

In places such as the Merritt Island National Wildlife Refuge, the best vantage point for observing alligators is from an automobile. It is also possible to see alligators from an airboat such as the one operated by the **Lone Cabbage Fish Camp** (★) (407-632-4199) west of Cocoa. These and similar craft cruise the shallow waterways, often passing 'gators sunning themselves on the banks or slithering in the tall grass. The alligator's eyes and nostrils jut above its head so that it can swim with little of its scaly body exposed yet still breathe and see its surroundings. This quirk makes it easy to spot alligators in the water; just look for a pair of protruding eyes.

The best place to see alligators is at the **St. Augustine Alligator Farm** (Route A1A, two miles south of the Bridge of Lions, Anastasia Island; 904-824-3337), where the 'gator has been the star attraction for nearly a century. Here is the oldest collection of alligators existing in a controlled environment, a natural center for continuing research on this still-mysterious species. Wooden decks spanning the habitats create ideal viewing conditions while offering total safety for the curious public. Carved out of 30 acres of forest, this clean and well-run facility provides a chillingly close, open-air encounter with enough of these forbidding creatures to populate several nightmares. To round things out, there are raccoons, ostriches, tortoises, turtles and, for children to pet and feed, sheep, goats and deer.

466-7873) or **Deep 6 Watersports** (416 Miracle Mile Extension, Vero Beach; 407-562-2883). Windsurfing can be ventured either in the surf or on the smoother waters of the Intracoastal Waterway. Lessons and rentals are available at **Treasure Coast Windsurfing** (2659 Northeast Dixie Highway, Jensen Beach; 407-334-6722) and at the **Sailboard Center** (9125 Route 1, Vero Beach; 407-589-2671).

For the widest array of surfing equipment and accessories in the Cape Canaveral area, and possibly on the entire East Coast, surfers pay their respects to the **Ron Jon Surf Shop** (4151 North Route A1A, Cocoa Beach; 407-799-8888). This warehouse-size store also stocks clothing and equipment for a wide variety of other watersports. The smooth waters of the Banana River are at the doorstep of **Calema Boardsailing** (2755 North Banana River Drive, Cocoa Beach; 407-453-3223).

Several shops in the Daytona Beach area rent surfboards and offer lessons including **Daytona Beach Surf Shops** (520 Seabreeze Boulevard, Daytona Beach; 904-253-3366). For windsurfing rentals and lessons, **Sandy Point Sailboards** (1114 Riverside Drive, Holly Hill; 904-255-4977) is conveniently located on the Intracoastal Waterway.

Certain stretches of the beaches around St. Augustine are specially designated for surfers and windsurfers. If you left your board at home, you can rent one at **Blue Sky Surf Shop** (517 Anastasia Boulevard, St. Augustine; 904-824-2734), **Surf Station** (1020 Anastasia Boulevard, St. Augustine; 904-471-9463) or **Surf Station II** (6880 Route A1A South, St. Augustine; 904-471-8823).

The long expanse of uncluttered beaches east of Jacksonville have become very popular with surfers and windsurfers. Several outfits in the area rent surfboards, sailboards, boogie boards and even skates and wetsuits. Try calling these shops to see what they have available: **Aqua East Surf Shop** (696 Atlantic Boulevard, Neptune Beach; 904-246-2550), which also maintains a hotline with recorded information on surfing and sailing conditions (904-246-9744).

SKINDIVING

A variety of reefs and wrecks make the waters off the Treasure Coast exceptional for diving. For trips or lessons, contact **Dixie Divers** (1717 South Route 1, Fort Pierce; 407-461-4488) or the **Deep 6 Dive Shop** (416 Miracle Mile Extension, 407-562-2883). To hook up with other divers and snorkelers, and to rent gear, try **American Divers International** (691 North Courtenay Parkway, Merritt Island; 407-453-0600).

HORSEBACK RIDING

One of the most romantic activities is horseback riding on the beach, but there are very few places on Florida's East Coast where this is possible.

A notable exception is on Amelia Island, where **Sea Horse Stable** (7500 First Coast Highway, Amelia Island; 904-261-4878) has horses and guides available to the public.

GOLF

Several semiprivate clubs in Fort Pierce offer golfing privileges to the public. Among them are **Indian Hills Country Club** (1600 South 3rd Street; 407-461-9620) and **Gator Trace** (4260 Gator Trace Avenue; 407-464-0303). The 18-hole championship course at **Dodger Pines Country Club** (4600 26th Avenue, Vero Beach; 407-569-9606) is also open to the public, as are the links at the **Sebastian Municipal Golf Course** (101 East Airport Drive, Sebastian; 407-589-6800).

Though not as popular here as elsewhere, golf is a growing sport in the Cape Canaveral area. Among the courses open to the public are **Cocoa Beach Municipal** (Tom Warriner Boulevard, Cocoa Beach; 407-868-3351) and **Turtle Creek** (1278 Admiralty Boulevard, Rockledge; 407-632-2520).

The best-known courses in the Daytona Beach area are probably those at **Indigo Lakes** (Route 92 at Route 95, Daytona Beach; 904-254-3607), which is rated the eighth best in Florida. Other choices include **Daytona Beach Golf and Country Club** (600 Wilder Boulevard, Daytona Beach; 904-258-3119), **Daytona Par 3 Golf Club and Driving Range** (2500 Volusia Avenue, Daytona Beach; 904-252-3983), **New Smyrna Beach Municipal Golf Course** (1000 Wayne Avenue, New Smyrna Beach; 904-427-3437) and the **Tomoka Oaks Country Club** (Route 1 and Nova Road, Ormond Beach; 904-677-7117).

Golf courses are sprinkled around Jacksonville from the airport to the beach. Public links include **The Dunes** (11751 McCormick Road, Jacksonville; 904-641-8444), **Pine Lakes Golf Club** (Main Street near Pecan Park Road, Jacksonville; 904-757-0318) and **Jacksonville Beach Golf Club** (Penman Road, Jacksonville Beach; 904-249-8600).

Most of the courses on Amelia Island are open only to resort guests. An exception is the **City of Fernandina Golf Course** (2800 Bill Melton Road, Fernandina Beach; 904-277-7370).

TENNIS

The best places to play are the courts protected from strong ocean winds. In Fort Pierce, try the **Lawnwood Recreation Complex** (1302 Virginia Avenue; 407-468-1521). You can make reservations in Vero Beach at the **Riverside Courts** (east of the Barber Bridge; 407-231-4787).

If you're staying in the Cape Canaveral area, one of these sets of courts should be nearby: **Cape Canaveral Recreation Complex** (7500 North Atlantic Avenue, Cape Canaveral; 407-868-1226), **Cocoa Beach Recreation**

Complex (Tom Warriner Boulevard, Cocoa Beach; 407-868-3333) or **Kiwanis Island Park** (Route 520 on Merritt Island; 407-455-1380).

The year-round moderate climate of Daytona Beach makes it ideal for tennis at places such as **Cypress Courts** (925 Cypress Street; 904-258-9198), **Derbyshire Courts** (849 Derbyshire Road; 904-253-4622) and **Seabreeze Courts** (1101 North Route A1A; 904-255-6202).

Just north of Daytona Beach in Ormond Beach, there are courts at the **Ormond Beach Tennis Center** (300 North Nova Road; 904-677-0311); the semiprivate **Tomoka Oaks Country Club** (20 Tomoka Oaks Boulevard; 904-672-3397); and at the beautifully landscaped **Ormond Beach Racquet Club** (38 East Granada Boulevard; 904-676-3285), which accepts reservations.

You can play tennis comfortably almost all year round in northern Florida, with the exception of the dead of winter. The Jacksonville area has a number of public tennis courts including **Boone Park** (3730 Park Street; 904-384-8687), **Hendricks Avenue Courts** (1541 Hendricks Avenue; 904-399-1761) and **Huguenot Park** (200 16th Avenue South, Jacksonville Beach; 904-249-9407).

BICYCLING

Bicycling in Florida means never having to pedal uphill. In the Fort Pierce area, a good north-south route is along **Route A1A**, which is often in sight of either the ocean or the Intracoastal Waterway. **Indian River Drive** is another scenic two-lane road that parallels the Intracoastal Waterway on its west bank from Jensen Beach north to Fort Pierce. The views include the river as well as the lovely waterfront homes.

In the Cape Canaveral area, a bicycle path runs along **Route A1A** from 5th Avenue in Indialantic north to Patrick Air Force Base, a distance of about ten miles. Another option lies slightly inland. To reach **South Tropical Trail**, head west from Indian Harbor Beach over the Mathias Bridge; there is no bike path, but many cyclists ride the road all the way up to the intersection with Route 520 on Merritt Island.

Cyclists in the Daytona Beach area recommend riding up and down **John Anderson Drive**, which runs north of Ormond Bridge along the east bank of the Intracoastal Waterway. On the west side of the water is **Beach Street**, which leads through residential areas up to Tomoka State Park.

St. Augustine's historic district is an excellent place to bicycle, the better to appreciate the old homes, gardens and other sights.

In Jacksonville, the people at **Champion Schwinn** (1025 Arlington Road; 904-724-4922) conduct guided 15-mile bicycle tours. Some of the smoothest cycling is at the beach, or on it. First Street is good for bicycling and is close to the ocean. On Amelia Island, the 30-block historic district in downtown Fernandina Beach is a good place to sightsee from a bicycle seat.

BIKE RENTALS **Macs Bike Shop** (3472 Northeast Savannah Road, Jensen Beach; 407-334-4343) rents children's and adult's bicycles as well as baby seats and bike carriers for the car. **Pedal Power** (1676 Southeast Port St. Lucie Boulevard, Port St. Lucie; 407-335-1310) also rents bicycles. In Vero Beach, try **Euler's Schwinn Cyclery** (1865 14th Avenue; 407-562-2781) for parts, service and rentals.

Beach bikes can be rented from **Ron Jon's Surf Shop** (4151 North Route A1A, Cocoa Beach; 407-799-8888).

In the Daytona Beach area, **Ormond Schwinn** (205 South Yonge Street, Ormond Beach; 904-677-2425) and **Volusia Schwinn South** (3132 South Ridgewood Street, South Daytona; 904-756-0008) rent bicycles.

Bicycles are available for rent at **American Bicycle Company** (1404 South 3rd Street, Jacksonville Beach; 904-246-4433). The store also conducts evening and weekend morning group rides.

On Amelia Island, try the **Village Store** (Amelia Island Plantation; 904-261-4428) or **Fernandina Beach Schwinn Cyclery** (11 South 8th Street, Fernandina Beach; 904-277-3227) for temporary wheels.

HIKING

FORT PIERCE AREA TRAILS Designated hiking trails are few and far between along the Treasure Coast, unless you count the vast stretches of beach that make up 22-mile-long Hutchinson Island. Three suggested trails can be found on protected state property:

The **Sand Pine Scrub Nature Trail** (.5 mile) winds over a sandy ridge bordering the Intracoastal Waterway. Sand pine trees, scrub oak, wild rosemary and wildlife such as opossum, raccoon and the occasional armadillo provide a changing landscape.

Unless you go by boat, reaching **St. Lucie Inlet State Park** requires a six-mile hike from the U.S. Department of the Interior Wildlife Refuge at the north end of Jupiter Island. Additional trails lie within the 36,000-acre park.

Within the 600-acre refuge that comprises Jack Island, the **Marsh Rabbit Run Trail** (4 miles) is named for the dark-brown, short-eared animal often visible in the shrubs or even in the water. Walkways lead through red, white and black mangroves, into a tropical beach hammock.

CAPE CANAVERAL AREA HIKING The best-known trails in the region lie on Merritt Island, whose northern portion is dominated by a vast wilderness refuge, though shorter nature trails can be found on the mainland.

The fully paved **Dent Smith Trail** (1 mile) makes a convenient tour through 35 acres on the campus of the Florida Institute of Technology in Melbourne. Some 300 varieties of ferns, palms and other lush flora flourish within this shade-filled botanical garden.

The **Brevard Museum Nature Center** (25 acres) has three short trails (one paved) that meander through three distinct ecosystems: a pine sandhill community, a hardwood hammock and a freshwater marsh.

Within the Merritt Island National Wildlife Refuge are several trails. The **Black Point Wildlife Drive** (7 miles) is so poorly paved that it's better to hike it. The path borders coastal salt marshes harboring abundant wildlife—mammals, amphibians, reptiles and fish. Hundreds of species of birds nest in or near the refuge; the best times for birdwatching are early morning and early evening.

The **Allan Cruickshank Memorial Trail** (5 miles) begins at Point 8 on the Black Point Wildlife Drive and loops around a shallow saltwater marsh. There is an observation tower overlooking the marsh as well as a photo blind, located near the parking lot.

Southeast of these two trails is the **Oak Hammock Trail** (.5 mile), which runs through a subtropical forest where the ecology of the hammock plant community is explained in interpretive signs. The **Palm Hammock Trail** (2.5 miles), which shares a parking lot with the Oak Hammock Trail, leads through cabbage palm hammocks, hardwood forest and open marsh.

One of the most unusual trails on Florida's East Coast is the **Sand Road Trail** (13 miles), which runs north from Playalinda Beach to Apollo Beach. Actually a two-rut road, it offers a close encounter with the vegetation that grows on and behind the coastal dunes. The path also runs directly beneath the Atlantic Flyway, where hundreds of thousands of migratory birds fly back and forth on their annual journeys.

The **Beach Trail** (24 miles) is a beachcomber's dream, starting at Playalinda Beach and ending up at Apollo Beach. The Canaveral National Seashore is virtually unmatched as a long stretch of publicly owned beach in Florida, and this trail is completely undeveloped.

DAYTONA BEACH AREA TRAILS Few marked trails exist on this part of the coast, though the hard sand beach is excellent for hiking.

The trailhead for the **Bulow Woods Hiking Trail** (4 miles) is located deep in the woods near the Bulow Plantation Ruins. It leads into an ancient hammock of live oak and hardwood trees, following the former plantation road across a stream to an island before looping back. Since the land floods easily along Bulow Creek, hikers should beware of alligators on these waterside paths.

The **Washington Oaks State Gardens Nature Trail** (.5 mile) borders the scenic tidal marshes of the Matanzas River. An excellent habitat for wading birds and waterfowl, the trail is especially recommended at sunset.

JACKSONVILLE AREA TRAILS Although there are short nature trails within a couple of parks, the best hiking in the area can be found north of the Jacksonville city limits.

The **Island Hiking Trail** (4.1 miles) is laid out on the northern portion of Little Talbot Island. It leads north from near the entrance station through a maritime hammock believed to be the oldest part of the island. Besides the extensive barrier island vegetation, the best feature of this trail is the number of shorebirds and migrating waterfowl that can be viewed. The well-marked trail passes near huge sand dunes before emerging at the beach. From this point, it is a 1.4-mile hike south toward the trailhead.

Transportation

BY CAR

Route 1, which runs from Stuart to Jacksonville, is the main highway on the East Coast. To the east of Route 1, **Route A1A** runs along the Atlantic Ocean wherever possible, crossing bridges between barrier islands or curling slightly inland, often dovetailing with Route 1. To the west of Route 1 is **Route 95,** the interstate that extends the length of Florida.

BY AIR

Three major airports serve this part of Florida: Melbourne Regional Airport, Daytona Beach Regional Airport and Jacksonville International Airport. In addition, it is possible to reach the southern portion of the East Coast via Palm Beach International Airport, the closest major airport to Fort Pierce. (See Chapter Three, "Gold Coast," for information pertaining to Palm Beach International Airport.)

The **Melbourne Regional Airport** has regular service by American Airlines, Continental Airlines, Delta Airlines and USAir.

A number of major airlines provide scheduled service into **Daytona Beach Regional Airport**. Among them are American Airlines, Continental Airlines, Delta Airlines and USAir.

Jacksonville International Airport is presently served by most national carriers. There is regularly scheduled service via American Airlines, Continental Airlines, Delta Airlines, TWA, United Airlines and USAir.

In addition to taxis, there is scheduled service to and from the Daytona Beach airport via the **Daytona Orlando Transit Service** (904-257-5411), or DOTS, with home and hotel pick-ups available. At Jacksonville International Airport, **Gator City Taxi** (904-355-8294) provides service to and from Amelia Island.

BY BUS

Greyhound Bus Lines has several locations on the East Coast: Vero Beach (905 Route 1; 407-562-6588), Cocoa (302 Main Street; 407-636-6531), Melbourne (460 South Harbor City; 407-723-4323), Daytona Beach (138 South Ridgewood Avenue; 904-253-6576), St. Augustine (100 Malaga Street; 904-829-6401) and Jacksonville (10 North Pearl Street; 904-356-5521).

BY TRAIN

Jacksonville is a busy hub for both interstate and intrastate service by **Amtrak** (3570 Clifford Lane; 904-766-5110). Amtrak also stops in West Palm Beach, the closest station to Fort Pierce.

CAR RENTALS

Arriving at the Melbourne Regional Airport, you will find well-known car rental agencies such as **Avis Rent A Car** (407-723-7755), **Alamo Rent A Car** (800-327-9633), **Hertz Rent A Car** (407-723-3414) and **Budget Rent A Car** (407-725-7737).

Car rental agencies providing service to the Daytona Beach Regional Airport include **Avis Rent A Car** (904-253-8183), **Alamo Rent A Car** (800-327-9633), **Hertz Rent A Car** (904-255-3681) and **Budget Rent A Car** (904-255-2249).

Alamo Rent A Car (800-327-9633), **Avis Rent A Car** (800-331-1212), **Hertz Rent A Car** (904-741-2151), **National Inter Rent** (800-328-4567), **Thrifty Car Rental** (904-757-3366) and **Value Rent A Car** (904-757-1710) all have rental agencies in the vicinity of Jacksonville International Airport.

PUBLIC TRANSPORTATION

Getting around the East Coast without a car is not easy, but it is possible. In the Cape Canaveral area, limited bus service is available via **Space Coast Area Transit** (407-633-1878).

The **Volusia County Transit Authority** (904-761-7700), or VOTRANS, provides extensive bus service throughout the Daytona Beach area. VOTRANS also operates a trolley that runs up and down Route A1A near the beach.

Jacksonville Transit Authority (904-630-3100) has bus service both within the city and between downtown Jacksonville and the beaches.

TAXIS

From the Melbourne Regional Airport, taxi service into Cocoa Beach and other Space Coast locales is available through **Anthony Ross' Cocoa Beach Cab** (407-783-7200).

Yellow Cab (904-354-5511) and **Checker Cabs** (904-764-2472) both service the Jacksonville International Airport.

CENTRAL

FLORIDA

CHAPTER FIVE

Central Florida

Central Florida is a land of many faces. At last count, at least five separate personalities could be spotted in its crazy-quilt character. One minute you might notice the youthful spirit of its green, rolling hills. Then, in a flash, you're dealing with sophisticated six-lane interstates buzzing between roller coasters, mouse ears, acrobatic whales and discount outlet malls. The next minute, a soft jolt returns you to a quieter time when steamboats puffed along lazy rivers toward destinations studded with Victorian mansions.

One enchanting aspect of central Florida was around long before the steamboats—the area's countless springs, lakes and rivers. This part of the state boasts waters of crystal-ball clarity, waters that gush and gurgle and teem with fish, waters that have given life to fertile agricultural lands. Those acres have produced still another side of central Florida—rows of citrus trees that lie like neatly plaited hair, as well as farms of winter vegetables and miles of cattle scrub.

Central Florida's past is as multifaceted as its landscape. The mouse-eared character now most associated with the area lives only in the short-term memory of central Florida history. Evidence found at mid-Florida archeological sites reveal an era of prehistoric Indian tribes and, deeper still into the memory banks, of ancient seas covering the land.

Recorded history here begins with the invasion of the Spanish in the 16th century. Oddly enough, their greatest contribution to central Florida's future was the herd of cattle they brought to the New World. The conquistadors eventually left, but the cows remained. The herds adapted to scrubland pasture, multiplied and became the foundation of lucrative ranches.

During the early ranching era, the word *cracker* first came into use to describe this region's inhabitants. The word got its origin from the whips used on cattle drives through the Florida scrubland. In later years, cracker came to describe the common lifestyle of inland Floridians. Although it sometimes carries a negative tone today, the term actually defined earthy, hard-working folks who strove to make a living off the ocali, as they called the scrubland. Much of this cracker scrubland later became the Ocala National Forest, named after the old Indian word borrowed by the crackers.

Citrus fruit, one of the crackers' earliest commercial crops, eventually helped give birth to Florida's tourist trade. Union soldiers returning from Florida after the Civil War told great tales of the land where oranges flourished, and where water clear as gin bubbled from the bowels of the earth.

Soon the dawning of Florida's golden age of steamboats fueled both tourism and agricultural enterprise. Rumors that a fountain of youth lay at DeLeon Springs near DeLand, and word of the incredibly warm and colorful waters at Silver Springs, kept river traffic at a full head of steam. Glamorous steamers, carrying produce and freight below, often boasted fabulous staterooms and salons on upper decks. They carried the wealthy and powerful on sightseeing tours of Florida's interior. In 1882, one such steamer, the *DeBary*, took President Chester Arthur up the St. Johns River.

Today remnants of that era can be found in the glorious mansions these rich visitors left in their wake, in styles ranging from spiffed-up cracker to Victorian Gothic. By the 1800s, railroads had replaced steamships as the principal mode of transportation, and tourism flourished.

Life in this area during the 20th century generally rolled along at a steamboat pace. Then, in 1971, central Florida was given a solid shake. That's the year a quiet little town named Orlando had its environs invaded by a mouse, the year Walt Disney World was born. The Orlando area has never been the same since.

The 27,400-acre park actually lies in a community called Lake Buena Vista. But both Kissimmee and Orlando have been set ablaze by Disney's precedent-setting attraction. All the hoopla has metamorphosed sleepy little Orlando into the world's number one tourist destination. This gives the entire area a cosmopolitan flavor. Shops, restaurants and attractions have responded with imported wares, international cuisine and multilingual service.

Fortunately the city has handled its newfound fame well. While other Florida resort areas have fallen victim to haphazard development, Orlando and Kissimmee have retained their natural beauty and have held fast to their cowtown roots.

Away from Orlando, farther into Florida's interior, you'll find the area's history hiding. Northeast of the city, the towns of Sanford and DeLand remember the steamship era with architectural monuments and river-boat attractions. Sand pine forest and spring waters still refresh travelers tired of

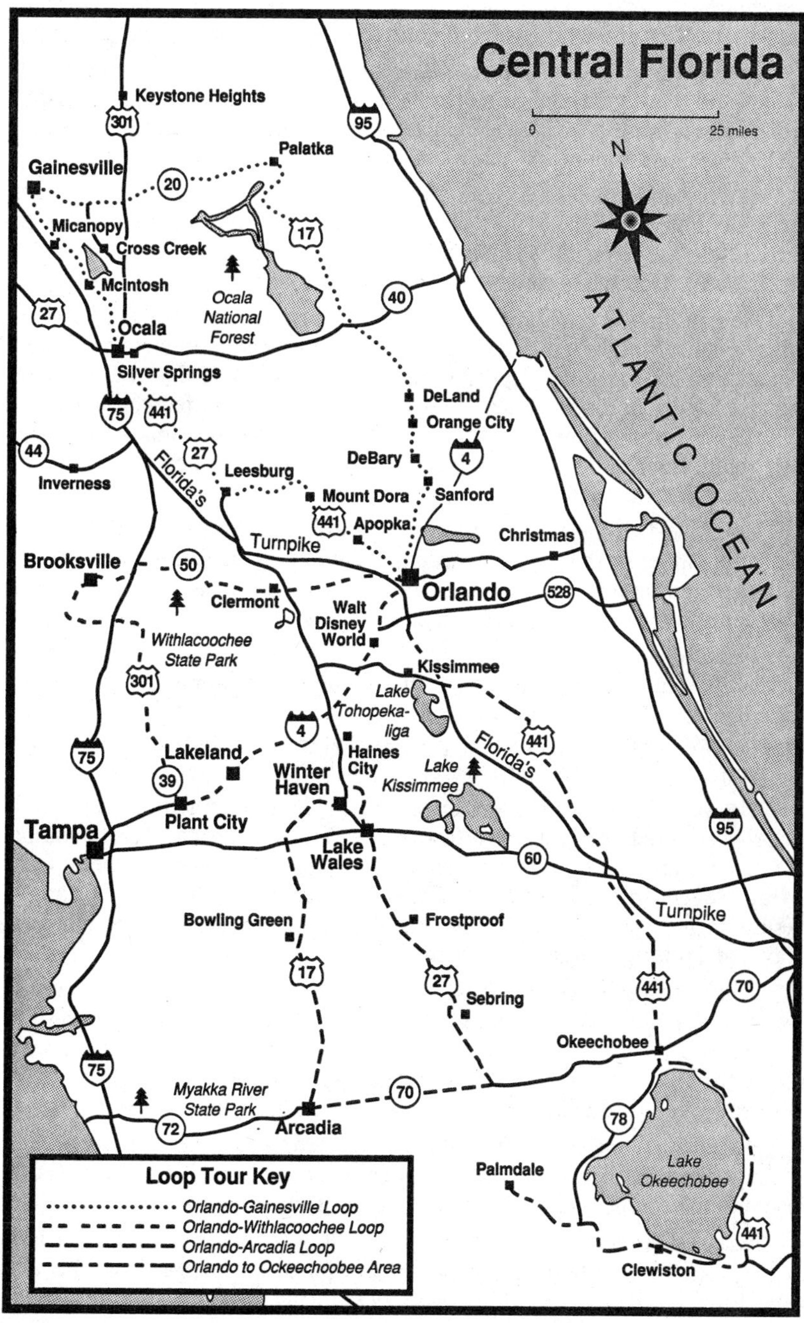
Central Florida
0
25 miles
N
ATLANTIC OCEAN
Keystone Heights
301
95
Palatka
Gainesville
20
Micanopy
17
Cross Creek
McIntosh
Ocala National Forest
40
27
Ocala
Silver Springs
DeLand
75
441
Orange City
44
27
DeBary
4
Inverness
Florida's
Leesburg
Mount Dora
Sanford
441
Apopka
Christmas
Turnpike
Brooksville
50
Orlando
528
Clermont
Walt Disney World
Withlacoochee State Park
Kissimmee
301
Lake Tohopekaliga
4
441
Florida's
75
Lakeland
Haines City
Lake Kissimmee
39
Winter Haven
Plant City
95
Tampa
Lake Wales
60
Turnpike
Bowling Green
Frostproof
17
27
441
70
Sebring
Okeechobee
75
Myakka River State Park
70
78
72
Arcadia
Palmdale
Lake Okeechobee
441
Clewiston
Loop Tour Key
Orlando-Gainesville Loop
Orlando-Withlacoochee Loop
Orlando-Arcadia Loop
Orlando to Ockeechoobee Area

resort hubbub. The magic number 72 is the temperature these springs maintain, as well as the average temperature of upper central Florida.

State parks and national forests in this area also offer refuge to the crowd-weary, and to alligators, Florida panthers, deer, wild turkeys and migratory birds. Here fishing camps take the place of towering hotels, and fried catfish pushes steak au poivre off the plate.

At the northern reaches of central Florida, the city of Gainesville remains relatively untouched by tourism. The University of Florida here focuses on horticulture and veterinary sciences and has gained fame for developing the sports drink Gatorade, named for the school mascot.

Neighboring Cross Creek is best known for a former resident, Pulitzer-Prize-winner Margaret Kinnan Rawlings, who named a collection of short stories and a cookbook after the town. Sadly, the film *Cross Creek* has brought hordes of tourist to the town, disrupting its rural lifestyle. The nearby villages of Micanopy and McIntosh have had no such misfortune, and they retain their quiet ways, enlivened somewhat by art and antique shopping districts.

Southwest of the Gainesville area, Ocala borders a national forest of the same name. In the past few decades, the city has become synonymous with thoroughbred horse breeding. Here, sleek Arabians and Morgans adorn the scenery as they graze beneath trees heavy with Spanish moss.

Numerous springs surround the Ocala National Forest. Among them, Silver Springs, which produces a billion gallons of water a day, is thought to be the world's largest formation of artesian springs. One of Florida's oldest destinations for travelers, Silver Springs attracted such luminaries as writers William Cullen Bryant and Harriet Beecher Stowe in the 1880s.

Between Ocala and the western coastline, Florida remains mostly rural. The Withlacoochee River winds toward the Gulf above a state forest bearing the same name. Nearby in Brooksville, a historic marker commemorates a tragic event in Florida history. On December 28, 1835, a tribe of angry Seminole Indians massacred 139 U.S. soldiers, reopening a barely healed scar and igniting the second Seminole War.

Citrus still reigns in the hills south of Orlando. Here temperatures average in the high 70s and the climate is generally rainier than along the coast. Blossom-scented tranquility settles in between pretty little towns named either for the many nearby lakes or for the escape from cold they offer: Winter Haven, Lakeland, Lake Alfred, Frostproof, Lake Wales.

Arcadia's name comes from the Greek word for bucolic pleasures. Once an important railroad stop, today it is known mainly for its rural riverside orientation, cowboy population and annual rodeo.

Lake Okeechobee, whose name means "big water" in the Seminole language, forms a thumbhole in the palette of Florida landscape. After the lake overflowed during a 1928 hurricane, destroying crops and costing lives,

President Herbert Hoover mandated that it be dammed. The resulting dikes created rich soils where crops could flourish. The lake and its waterways, which lead to both coasts as well as the Everglades, were once an important transportation route for Indians and early settlers. Today it serves as an agricultural center surrounded by Indian reservations, sugar cane fields and small towns whose population changes with the seasons of crop harvesting. It is the most hidden of central Florida's personalities, the last face visitors usually get to know.

In the inner areas of central Florida, visitors can find the state's true character, hidden behind Florida's sparkling mask of sand and sophistication. By unraveling the different personalities of this area, you can come to understand the real depth of that character.

To explore multifaceted central Florida, we have divided the area into several loops (see map at the beginning of this chapter). The listings begin with the **Orlando and Disney World** area—the first destination for most visitors who arrive in central Florida. From there you'll find several sidetrips looping between Orlando and outlying areas: The **Orlando–Gainesville Loop** heads north and encompasses the Ocala region. The **Orlando–Withlacoochee Loop** leads north and west of Orlando, to the Withlacoochee State Forest and back through the Lakeland area. The **Orlando–Arcadia Loop** heads south and west of Orlando and includes Myakka River State Park near the West Coast. The final route out of the city is a straight shot south and is labeled **Orlando to Okeechobee Area.**

Walt Disney World Area

Here you are in amusement park heaven. This rollicking tour must begin where the history of Florida theme parks took its first Peter Pan-like leap: **Walt Disney World** (Lake Buena Vista; 407-934-7639; admission). Before you visit, it's wise to plan ahead how you will spend your time among attractions too numerous to see in a week. For comprehensive information on all the theme parks of Orlando you can pick up a copy of *Disney World and Beyond: The Ultimate Family Guidebook* or a pack of *Disney World and Beyond: Family Fun Cards* (see "Also Available from Ulysses Press" at the end of this book).

Almost everyone, no matter how reclusive, regardless of age, creed or religion, inevitably visits this colossal theme park. Cynics—who snicker at its fantasy formula, orderliness, ultra-cleanliness, cornball humor and conservative overtones—nevertheless seem to be swept away by the pure joy of Uncle Walt's fertile imagination.

If at all possible, plan your Disney World visit to avoid holidays and peak seasons. Huge crowds mean long waiting lines. In any case, it's a good idea to arrive as the park opens so you can be among the first wave of visitors fanning out into the park's many theme lands.

The wonderful world of Disney à la Florida encompasses 27,400 acres that include the Magic Kingdom, EPCOT Center, Disney World Village, Disney-MGM Studios, resorts, playgrounds and camping facilities. First here was the **Magic Kingdom,** claiming almost 100 of those acres. You board this trip to never-never land right on Main Street in the Town Square, which sports turn-of-the-century shops and other buildings. But this is no ordinary main street, you soon discover. Hedges are trimmed to look like mouse ears and animals, and not a speck of litter is to be seen.

And then, straight ahead, you spot a sight that makes even adult hearts leap: Cinderella's Castle rising in the distance. You expect Tinkerbell to sprinkle stardust any minute now—some sort of magic must be used, for this place transforms even the most cynical theme-park critic into a kid.

Several subkingdoms lie within the Magic Kingdom. *Mickey's Starland* opened on the mouse's 60th birthday in 1988. Mickey and friends greet visitors to this playground/petting farm. In *Adventureland,* "Pirates of the Caribbean" is one of the most popular animated exhibits. As with the other favorites, it is best to schedule this swashbuckling boat trip late in the afternoon or into the evening hours to avoid crowds.

In *Fantasyland,* amusement park rides with the Mad Hatter and Dumbo themes are best enjoyed before too much cotton candy, soda pop and hot dogs are ingested. Lines form continuously for the well-loved "20,000 Leagues Under the Sea" submarine voyage and the terminally cute "It's A Small World."

In *Frontierland,* all the world's a raucous gold-rush town. The big draw here is "Big Thunder Mountain," a roller coaster that previews things to come in *Tomorrowland.* There, "Space Mountain" builds up suspense with sound effects, signs warning heart patients against undue excitement, and long lines. You are then wheeled into the dark and whizzed through galaxies with no idea when the bottom is going to drop out. You do know for sure that it will happen—and it eventually does, to the thrill of strong-stomached joy-riders.

Also in Tomorrowland, "American Journeys" and "Carousel of Progress" are corporation displays that require no ticket. For some reason this deters crowds from entering these fine tributes to American scenery and industry. Liberty Square's crowd-pleasers are the "Haunted Mansion," with its stretching room and hitchhiking ghosts, and the "Hall of Presidents," with its audio-animatronic heads of state.

In the Experimental Prototype Community of Tomorrow, better known as **EPCOT**, the world is divided merely in two: Future World and World Showcase. As you enter, you'll pass beneath the spherical trademark of EPCOT, rising 17 stories high and known as "Spaceship Earth." If you plan to eat dinner at one of the international theme restaurants in World Showcase, your first stop ought to be the "Earth Station," where computer video screens take your reservations. The more popular restaurants fill as early as 10 a.m. in the winter season, so take care of this piece of business first.

Because Future World is the more popular of the two, I recommend visiting the *World Showcase* first and leaving the future for later. Besides, I prefer this part of EPCOT. Perhaps it's not a realistic tour of the 11 nations it visits, and it undoubtedly lacks the animated sophistication of Future World and the Magic Kingdom, but it nonetheless adds culture and class to the world of Disney. The different countries are represented in this circular tour by films and live street shows as well as structures, wares and foods demonstrating heritage and customs.

For instance, a CircleVision film takes you on a dizzying tour of Canada. The United Kingdom exhibit features a pub and food shops. In France, the focus is on cuisine and the Eiffel Tower model, re-created from original blueprints. Moroccan streets are lined with aromatic shops while pagodas and bonsai welcome you to Japan.

For a World Showcase tour of the United States, "American Adventure" presents a 30-minute audio-animatronics show tracing the history of the nation in a colonial theater setting. Your hosts: Ben Franklin and Mark Twain. Then you can visit the bridges and gondolas of Venice, followed by a continent-wide step to a Bavarian village. The CircleVision film in the China exhibit whisks you away on an impressive journey beyond the Great Wall. From Norway take an adventure sail into the land of the midnight sun aboard the *Maelstrom*. Last stop, Mexico, for a boat ride, some animated theatrics and a quick burrito.

Who said you couldn't make it around the world in 80 minutes?

In *Future World*, my favorite exhibit is one sponsored by Kodak called "The Image Works," where big kids as well as little ones are invited to play a series of games involving art, music, electronics and filmmaking.

The most popular EPCOT attractions include "Journey Into Imagination," an audio-animatronics tour through the creative process hosted by a character named Figment; "Captain EO," starring a 3-D Michael Jackson; and "The Living Seas," with its six-million-gallon marine life aquarium.

Disney World visitors can also play Swiss Family Robinson on a tropical island at **Typhoon Lagoon** (separate admission). At this aquatic park you can also snorkel among creatures of the Caribbean, such as baby sharks and parrotfish. Or you can get wet on any of the many water slides and rapids, or float a tube down a 100-foot artificial mountains.

Another water theme park, **River Country** (separate admission), is laid out in a woodsy setting at the Fort Wilderness Campground Resort. Heated swimming pool, water slides and whitewater tubing provide wet fun.

Also at Disney World, **Discovery Island** (separate admission) takes a nonanimated look at nature. The island zoo features more than 90 animal and 250 plant species, including exotic animals such as the Galapagos tortoise.

Another attraction on these 27,400 acres is the **Disney-MGM Studios** (separate admission). Here visitors can dabble at acting and tour animation production facilities, sound stages and street scenes where Disney and Touchstone films will be shot. One highlight is "Catastrophe Canyon," where special effects create flash floods, earthquakes and other film disasters right before your eyes.

When you've experienced enough disasters, go a round with a big ape —King Kong, that is—at **Universal Studios** (1000 Universal Studios Plaza, Orlando; 407-363-8000; admission). Located about 20 miles north of Disney World, the Florida rendition of California's Universal Studios Tour whisks you through "Jaws" shark attacks, "Ghostbuster" raids, "Psycho" shower scenes and other memorable movie encounters.

Back to reality? Route 192 leads you into downtown Kissimmee along a trail of flashing billboards and high-tech signs with ten-foot letters, all trying to persuade you to feed an alligator, watch a medieval joust, get wet, ride an airboat, buy oranges or T-shirts and eat seafood. This is "Tourist Trap Trail," also known as Irlo Bronson Memorial Highway or Spacecoast Parkway.

One of the first super attractions you will encounter is **Old Town** (5770 West Route 192, Kissimmee; 407-396-4888), a nostalgic extravaganza of shops and restaurants, with a ferris wheel, fountains and cobbled streets. A few museums are also tucked away here and there.

Next comes **Xanadu** (4800 West Route 192, Kissimmee; 407-396-1992; admission): here, in the 21st century, computers select the menu according to your dietary needs and preferences, then prepare the meal in proper proportions, and—the best part—clean up. This 15-room home of the future also features climate control, a waterfall spa and a spaceship design.

Near Xanadu, one attraction uses alligator appeal to draw visitors. At **Alligatorland Safari Zoo** (4580 West Route 192; 407-396-1012; admission) over 1000 exotic animals keep the Florida natives company.

Despite its whirlwind tourist reputation, **Kissimmee** manages to maintain the flavor of its humble cattle town beginnings. When you reach this town at the end of the road, you will find a total change from the maelstrom behind you. Little has changed in the heart of the city since its founding in 1878. Many original buildings remain, including the courthouse and **Makinson's Hardware Store** (308 East Broadway; 407-847-2100), purported to be the state's first hardware store.

A weekly event recalls the town's beef and dairy industry roots: every Wednesday visitors can sit in on the town's cattle auction at the **Kissimmee Livestock Market** (805 East Donegan Avenue, Kissimmee; 407-847-3521).

Located near the lakefront in downtown Kissimmee, the **Monument of States** (Monument Avenue, Lake Front Park; 407-847-3174) is built of stones from every state in the nation, plus 21 foreign countries. Built in 1943 by the townspeople, it stands as a 70-foot monument to tourism. Somewhat disheveled in appearance, it appeals to rock-hounds with its impressive gathering of flint, alabaster, coquina, meteors, stalagmites, marble, petrified teeth, lava and other specimens.

Lake Front Park lies at the end of Monument Avenue. This city park skirts Tohopekaliga Lake (called Lake Toho for short), where fishing, canoeing and bicycling are popular sports.

Another hint of Kissimmee's noncontrived lifestyle can be found in the 50-mile-long **Kissimmee Chain-of-Lakes** (★) resort area. This string of lakes, of which Lake Toho is the largest, provides seclusion to its visitors. Houseboating, motorboating, sailing, bass fishing and bird watching are among the water activities offered here. Follow Route 525 out of Kissimmee for a scenic oak-tunnel drive around the big lake.

For more information on the area, stop in at or call the **Kissimmee-St. Cloud Convention and Visitors Bureau** (1925 Route 192, Kissimmee; 407-847-5000).

North of Kissimmee on Route 441, you will find a pair of giant alligator jaws beckoning you to enter **Gatorland** (Route 441, Orlando; 407-855-5496; admission). Here over 5000 Florida alligators and crocodiles can be viewed, along with exotic snakes, birds and monkeys. Not as much a tourist trap as it sounds, this refuge maintains a natural cypress swamp setting, carpeted with ferns and brightened with orchids. Scenes from *Indiana Jones and the Temple of Doom* were filmed in this jungle atmosphere.

WALT DISNEY WORLD AREA HOTELS

With the dawning of Walt Disney World, hotels began to bud more profusely than orange blossoms in the area. It has taken a while for the demand to catch up with the supply of slapped-up chain lodgings. Consequently, you can find some deals here, especially in the off-season (from May 1 until December 15).

Lodging at Walt Disney World is not your least expensive option, but if personality is important to you, you'll find plenty of it here. Room rates reflect the glamour and convenience of staying in fantasyland. The properties are family-oriented and provide free transportation to and from the Magic Kingdom and EPCOT. In season, booking a year in advance is not considered overpreparation. Accommodations at all Disney properties can be booked through the **Walt Disney World Central Reservations Office** (Box 10100, Lake Buena Vista 32830; 407-824-8000).

Contemporary Resort Hotel (World Drive, Lake Buena Vista; 407-824-1000) has the least amount of personality of the Disney properties.

Meant to look futuristic with a monorail through the lobby, lots of glass and a 15-story atrium housing shops and restaurants, the place actually comes off as stark and sterile. Of its 1052 spacious, ultra-deluxe-priced rooms, those facing the Magic Kingdom offer the best view.

The **Grand Floridian Beach Resort** (Walt Disney World, Lake Buena Vista; 407-824-8000) is the grande dame of the Disney resort area. Though new, it has a look and feel of old elegance that recalls the privileged style of Florida's 19th-century railroad tycoons. Victorian verandas, red gabled roofs and brick chimneys lend the exterior its grand appearance. Inside, Florida's belle epoch is re-created using fine detail work: stained-glass domes, crystal chandeliers, ornate balustrades. The 905 rooms rent at ultra-deluxe rates.

More remote from the Mickey Mouse rat race, **Disney Inn** (1950 Magnolia Palm Drive, Lake Buena Vista; 407-824-2200) is favored by golfers and those looking for seclusion. It sits between two golf courses and features two pools, a health club and all the other Disney amenities in its 288-room facility. Ultra-deluxe.

Polynesian Village (1500 Seven Seas Drive, Lake Buena Vista; 407-824-2000) creates a South Pacific ambience. The two-story longhouses lie on South Seas Lagoon and its sandy, tropical beaches. In typical Disney fashion, the common areas feature a bit of manufactured Polynesia, complete with volcanic rock fountains and rain forests. The 855 ultra-deluxe rooms accommodate up to five people each.

The new accommodations at **The Caribbean Beach Resort** (900 Cayman Way, Lake Buena Vista; 407-934-3400) are named and color-coded for the different islands: peach for Barbados, hot-pink for Martinique, etc. A centrally located street market with Caribbean food and wares contributes to the theme. The 2100 units surround a 42-acre lake, with a marina and beach. Each "island" has its own pool. Deluxe.

Other resorts in the mega-park, although called "official" Disney hotels, are not owned by Disney World, which means slightly lower rates. Most offer free transportation and EPCOT restaurant reservation privileges. You can also reserve rooms at these hotels through the Walt Disney World Central Reservations Office.

For a taste of old England, try **Grosvenor Resort** (1850 Hotel Plaza Boulevard, Lake Buena Vista; 407-828-4444). Its 620 rooms are pleasantly decorated in a modern style with British flair and are equipped with a refrigerator and VCR. Guests have access to a game room, tennis courts, two pools, and volleyball and basketball courts. Deluxe to ultra-deluxe.

The **Hotel Royal Plaza** (1905 Hotel Plaza Boulevard, Lake Buena Vista; 407-828-2828) plays the other side of the street. Modern with Spanish highlights, this 400-room facility is decorated in contemporary style and offers its guests a restaurant, two lounges, tennis courts, a sauna, swimming pool and putting green. The hotel's boast is its celebrity rooms: one two-bedroom suite with memorabilia from Burt Reynolds, the other with Barbara Mandrell's personal belongings and family portrait. Ultra-deluxe.

To top that, the **Buena Vista Palace** (1900 Buena Vista Drive, Lake Buena Vista; 407-827-2727), the Royal Plaza's sister hotel, houses 1028 rooms and even trendier decor. The interior is lavish and sleek, featuring a sky-high atrium topped with stained glass and streaming with water. The rooms are modern affairs with private balconies. Ultra-deluxe.

Another group of hotels, named "Maingate Hotels" for their location at Disney World's northern entrance, are of the generic chain variety and offer lower rates than on-property hotels. A few stand out:

Tennis players with generous vacationing budgets might like **Vistana Resort** (8800 Vistana Center Drive, Lake Buena Vista; 407-239-3100). With more than 800 units available, the resort can accommodate large groups in their spacious designer villas and town houses, all with full kitchens. Fourteen tennis courts are framed in 50 acres of lush landscaping. A swimming pool and health club are other extras. Ultra-deluxe.

For the most reasonable prices near Disney World, head to the string of chains on Route 192. The two-story brickfront **Golden Link Motel** (4914 Route 192, Kissimmee; 407-396-0555) sits on Lake Cecile. A swimming pool and fishing pier come with 84 clean and adequate rooms. Prices are budget.

Arches and red brick trim lend **Gemini Motel** (4624 Route 192, Kissimmee; 407-396-2151) a touch of Mediterranean flavor. Eighty large, modern rooms are complemented by a restaurant next door and a swimming pool. Budget.

One hotel that deserves mention along this route is the **Casa Rosa Inn** (4600 West Route 192, Kissimmee; 407-396-2020). The 54 moderate-priced rooms offer quiet rest and a small pool. The motel itself shows a little character with its blushing Iberian facade. The rooms are thankfully clean and not gimmicky.

Fresh as a hibiscus, **Hawaiian Village Inn** (4559 Route 192, Kissimmee; 407-396-1212) decorates its 114 rooms in tropic tones and offers family convenience. Some rooms include kitchenettes, and the inn also has a restaurant. Swimming pool and playground are kid-pleasers. Moderate.

In a historic neighborhood of downtown Kissimmee, near the lake, **The Unicorn Inn** (8 South Orlando Avenue; 407-846-1200) is an English style bed and breakfast with eight guest rooms. Breakfast is served in a beige and green dining room furnished with antiques. Frilly curtains offer an old-time touch to the renovated rooms at this double-decker, tin-roofed historic home. Moderate.

WALT DISNEY WORLD AREA RESTAURANTS

Critics have acclaimed the restaurants at **EPCOT's "World Showcase"** in Walt Disney World for some of the finest ethnic and continental cuisine in the state. During the winter season, the most popular ones are difficult to get into. Same-day reservations can be made at one of EPCOT's World Key Information Centers; if you are staying at a Disney resort you can book further in advance by calling 407-824-8800.

At EPCOT's **Rose and Crown,** serving wenches deliver simple English pub fare such as fish and chips, Scotch eggs or steak-and-kidney pie. You can dine indoors or on the patio at the edge of the lagoon. Moderate to deluxe.

The most talked-about of EPCOT's restaurants, **Les Chefs de France,** boasts superb cuisine, with French classics such as steak au poivre, grouper and salmon-vegetable mousse en croûte, and roast duck with prune sauce. Some find the imported French service staff a bit snobby, but that was never my experience. The only problem I found was overcrowding. Moderate to deluxe.

Alfredo's comes a close second to the French restaurant in popularity at EPCOT. Fine Italian dishes such as fettucine Alfredo, whose inventor the restaurant is named for, veal piccata and plenty of pasta are featured. Moderate to deluxe.

For Mexican food, try EPCOT's candlelit, romantic **San Angel Inn.** Mexican-American courses include stuffed Baja lobster, chicken mole, red snapper in peppers and onions, and the incredible margaritas and chocolate Kahlua mousse pie. Moderate to deluxe.

Couscous and *bastila* are some of the exotic-sounding dishes served at the **Marakesh** restaurant in EPCOT. The first consists of tiny seminola grains served with a vegetable stew; the second is spicy pork, almonds, saffron and cinnamon layered with filo. The atmosphere is properly North African, featuring belly dancers and a three-piece band. Prices are moderate to deluxe.

Away from EPCOT, Walt Disney World has even more to offer diners. Moored at Disney World Shopping Village, the **Empress Lilly** (407-828-3900) is a popular showboat dining experience, which nonetheless does not feature outstanding cuisine. Three different theme rooms offer varied menus and degrees of formality. The polished but casual "Fisherman's Deck," features seafood at moderate-to-deluxe prices. In the intimate "Steerman's Quarters," steak, lamb and chicken entrées are tabbed in the deluxe range. For deluxe-to-ultra-deluxe-priced French cuisine in a plush, lace-and-velvet setting, dine in the "Empress Room."

Because of keen competition between hotels, many of the area's best restaurants can be found in its resorts. At the new Grand Floridian Beach Resort, **Victoria & Albert's** (Disney World Village, Lake Buena Vista;

407-824-2383) does a fixed-price menu served by folks dressed as maids and butlers. The restaurant offers fish, fowl, veal, beef and lamb dinners, often followed by their famous dessert soufflés. Dress code. Prices are ultra-deluxe.

The Outback (1900 Buena Vista Drive, Lake Buena Vista; 407-827-3430), located in Disney's Buena Vista Palace Hotel, takes its guests down under. Australian-style food is prepared on grills in the middle of the dining room. Rack of lamb, lobster tail and 99 brands of beer are served by waiters in safari suits. To arrive at the restaurant, guests ride a glass elevator car through a waterfall. Moderate.

In the same hotel, the elegant **Arthur's 27** (407-827-3450) dazzles with primo cuisine and breathtaking views of the Magic Kingdom in lights. Caviar and Gulf shrimp brochette head up imaginative specialties including catch of the day in Key lime sauce and duck breast smothered in a cilantro-black bean sauce. Prices are fixed at ultra-deluxe for a four- or six-course meal.

Nearby, in the Hilton Hotel, **American Vineyards** (1751 Hotel Plaza Boulevard, Lake Buena Vista; 407-827-4000) pays homage to the grape. Decor, posters, wine labels and paraphernalia define the theme. Entrées include roasted veal steak in mozzarella sauce, rack of lamb and Gulf shrimp sautéed in garlic butter. Deluxe.

An old island atmosphere is created with wooden fanback chairs painted in pastels, a stuffed marlin on the wall and casual attitudes at **Key Largo Steaks & Seafood** (5770 West Route 192, Kissimmee; 407-396-6244). A moderately priced menu mixes steak with grouper, calamari and lobster entrées.

WALT DISNEY WORLD AREA SHOPPING

At **Walt Disney World** (Lake Buena Vista; 407-824-4321), you will find many ways to spend your shopping dollars. Within the Magic Kingdom and EPCOT, shops offering exotic and fantasy souvenirs abound. **Walt Disney World Village Marketplace** (407-828-3058) is a gathering of more shops, in case you have any money left. You will find unique gifts and souvenirs in all of these shops, but you are better off concentrating on rides and shows while at Disney World, and looking around the Orlando area for gifts. Many of the nearby shopping centers carry the same merchandise at better prices.

If you are intent upon an authentic Disney World memento, however, here are a few places to check out:

Sea chest goodies are buried in **House of Treasure** (Adventureland, Magic Kingdom). Buy your pirate souvenirs here. **Frontierland Trading Post** (Frontierland, Magic Kingdom) excels in gifts and leather goods in a western, Indian and Mexican vein.

Pringle of Scotland (United Kingdom, World Showcase, EPCOT) deals in wools, tartan, kilts and other Scottish wear. Indian and Eskimo crafts, moccasins and such are stocked at **Northwest Mercantile** (Canada, World Showcase, EPCOT). **Tangier Traders** (Morocco, World Showcase, EPCOT) carries genuine goods from Morocco—clothing, leather goods and accessories. German giftware, such as clocks, beer steins and wood carvings, can be found at **Volkskunst** (Germany, World Showcase, EPCOT). **Fjording and the Puffin's Roost** (Norway, World Showcase, EPCOT) sells authentic Norwegian souvenirs made of glass, pewter and wood.

Old Town (5770 West Route 192, Kissimmee; 407-396-4888) is a tourist-belt shopping center offering specialty wares and trendy items in an old-fashioned ambience. Brick-lined streets re-create a nostalgic atmosphere of nickel cokes, merry-go-rounds, ice cream parlors and city squares.

In Old Town, **Swinging Things** (407-396-7238) carries a line of imported hammocks, hammock chairs and wind chimes. At the same location, **Mango Republic** (407-239-6012) deals in T-shirts, cotton fashions, straw hats and other items with Caribbean soul. Old Town's **The Rolls** (407-396-1037) is a car-lover's mecca, carrying mugs, T-shirts and even toilet paper emblazoned with car names. **Old Town Magic Shop** (407-396-6884) carries an enticing collection of tricks and magic books, with a free lesson for every trick purchase.

WALT DISNEY WORLD AREA NIGHTLIFE

The Disney area, so resplendent with sightseeing gimmickry, has debuted its own brand of dining entertainment. Area restaurants take dinner theater a step further, to "dinner arena." The entertainment is usually more noteworthy than the food at these extravaganzas. Most require advance reservations, especially on weekends. I have included most of the major dinner attractions here, along with a sampling of more low-key gathering spots and watering holes.

This new wave of dinner theater was no doubt born at Disney World, where revue theater abounds. Most popular is **Hoop-Dee-Doo-Revue** (Fort Wilderness Resort, Walt Disney World, Lake Buena Vista; 407-824-8000), where the Pioneer Hall Players crack corn in an Old West setting with appropriate chow.

At **Polynesian Revue and Mickey's Tropical Revue** (Polynesian Village Resort, Disney World, Lake Buena Vista; 407-824-8000) two different shows appeal to children and adults with an outdoor South Seas motif. Hula dancers and fire jugglers entertain while diners enjoy barbecue fare.

The show at **Top of the World** (Contemporary Resort, Walt Disney World, Lake Buena Vista; 407-824-8000) features Broadway's greatest hits performed by a troupe of dancers and singers.

Aside from the revues, Walt Disney World offers a few other forms of lively evening entertainment. The **Biergarten** at EPCOT inspires good times with a Bavarian beer garden atmosphere. An oom-pah-pah band and yodelers entertain.

The **IllumiNations Laser Show** at EPCOT Center is a must-see. This grand finale could easily be the highlight of your Disney visit. Staged at 9 p.m. nightly over the lagoon at World Showcase, the program features laser projections choreographed with classical and modern music. The il-

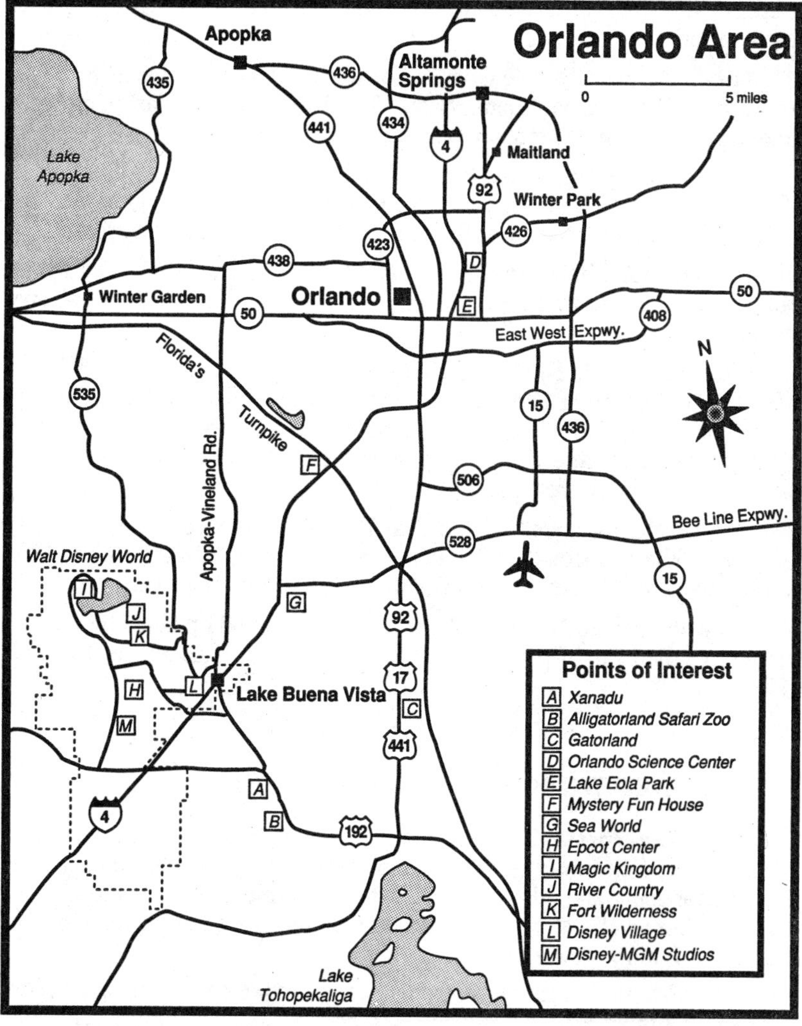

luminations go much further than most laser shows, creating powerful images across shooting streams of water, the Spaceship Earth globe and EPCOT's international buildings.

The *Empress Lilly* showboat's **Baton Rouge Lounge** (Walt Disney World Village, Lake Buena Vista; 407-828-3900) features comedy entertainment with music.

With typical Disney extravagance, **Pleasure Island** combines, in a single complex, six themed nightclubs catering to every musical taste, a comedy club, a teen dance club, restaurants, lounges and a ten-screen movie house. A single cover charge allows entrance into all this nightlife palace has to offer.

Also in the vicinity, The **Giraffe Lounge** (Hotel Royal Plaza, Walt Disney World Village, Lake Buena Vista; 407-828-2828) is a splashy, crowded dance spot featuring video screens and Top-40 music.

Nearby, **Laughing Kookaburra Good Time Bar** (Buena Vista Palace, Walt Disney World Village, Lake Buena Vista; 407-827-2727) lists 99 varieties of beer and features live dance music in an Australian-theme setting.

The **Arabian Nights** (6225 West Route 192; 407-239-9223) dinner attraction features chariot races, Arabian horse dancing and white Lippizaner shows.

Wolfman Jack's Rock n' Roll Palace (5770 West Route 192, Kissimmee; 407-396-6499) in Old Town boasts the spectacular showmanship typical of this area's attractions. In a grandiose palace, rock-and-roll takes a trip down memory lane. A house band performs nightly, often followed by old touring rock-and-roll bands of fame. Cover.

Another dining novelty, **Medieval Times Dinner Tournament** (4510 Route 192, Kissimmee; 407-396-1518), brings back the Middle Ages. Here you eat fowl with your fingers and watch jousting tableside.

Fried chicken and cowboy shenanigans are served up at another dinner attraction called **Fort Liberty** (5260 East Route 192, Kissimmee; 407-351-5151).

WALT DISNEY WORLD AREA BEACHES AND PARKS

Fort Wilderness—This 730-acre woodland area lies along Bay Lake at the northern extremity of Walt Disney World. Streams and smaller lakes facilitate canoeing and other water activities. Overnight campers are afforded the added bonus of free bus transportation to and from the Magic Kingdom and EPCOT amusement areas.

Facilities: Restrooms, showers, lifeguards, canoe rentals; groceries and restaurants nearby; information, 407-824-2900. *Swimming:* Good.

Camping: There are 704 sites, all with RV hookups, $38-49 per night; information, 407-934-7639.

Getting there: Located on Vista Drive in Walt Disney World.

Southport Park (★)—A natural recreational refuge on Lake Tohopekaliga's south shore, this facility is years away from metro mania. The difficult-to-find spot is maintained by the regional park district as a prime fishing area and secluded park. Carpets of grass and live oak hammocks make the grounds comfortable and attractive. Open from October through April.

Facilities: Picnic area, restrooms, showers, groceries; restaurants are several miles away in Kissimmee; information, 407-933-5822. *Fishing:* Good.

Camping: There are 53 sites, most with RV hookups; $8-11.50 per night.

Getting there: Located on Southport Road, east of Route 531 and about 20 miles south of Kissimmee.

Downtown and North Orlando

There was, once upon a time, a snoozing, full-of-character little town known as Orlando. Today the character we associate with Orlando wears mouse ears. The city woke up with a jolt and became one of the fastest-growing centers of tourism in the world. But away from the theme parks that bring travelers to Orlando's door still beats the heart of a real city. Downtown Orlando boasts character even today: museums, galleries, renovated shops and restaurants, turn-of-the-century architecture, science centers, tropical gardens and parks.

The city's mix of historic and modern architecture finds a pretty reflection in the many lakes of downtown Orlando. In the town's center is Lake Eola, whose **Centennial Fountain** was built to commemorate the city's 100th anniversary in 1975. It features a modern-sculpture design and a rainbow of lights at night. When the fountain was dedicated, waters were added from fountains in Spain, England, the Confederacy, France and the U.S.—all nations that have ruled Florida. A lovely lakeside park, with moss-covered oaks and an Oriental pagoda, provides a spectacular view of the fountain.

An appropriate attraction close to Disney's celluloid world is the **Cartoon Museum** (4300 South Semoran Boulevard #109-110, Orlando; 407-273-0141). The owner's collection of funnies predates film cartoons, however, featuring vintage comic books and magazines, and rare editorial and cartoon art.

On a more serious note, the Orlando neighborhood known as Loch Haven Park offers three fine museums. The **Orlando Museum of Art** (2416 North Mills Avenue, Orlando; 407-896-4231) spotlights 20th-century American works, pre-Columbian artifacts, African art and rotating exhibits from around the world. The **Orange County Historical Museum** (812 East Rollins Street, Orlando; 407-898-8320; admission) travels back 10,000 years with the display of a Timucuan Indian canoe, then takes visitors to the Big Freeze of 1894, which devastated the area's citrus crop, and finally rolls into the early 20th-century era of boom and depression. An old firehouse station at the museum's back door recalls the days of bucket brigade firefighting.

Facts are flavored with fun at the **Orlando Science Center** (810 East Rollins Street, Orlando; 407-896-7151; admission). Here you can find out your moon weight, learn to produce electricity with your own energy or explore a simulated space craft. Daily planetarium shows run in an adjoining facility.

Sightseeing takes a natural turn at **Leu Gardens** (1730 North Forest Avenue, Orlando; 407-246-2620; admission). Bordering one of the many lakes that turned Orlando into a wet and wild playground, the gardens include over 50 acres of trees, orchids, roses, camellias and other flowering flora. A home on the property showcases the lifestyle of a wealthy turn-of-the-century family.

If you're interested in touring Orlando from the clouds, you might try one of the ballooning enterprises in the area. Try **Rise & Float Balloon Tours** (5767 Major Boulevard, Orlando; 407-352-8191) for an overview of this colorful city. **Aerial Adventures** (3529 Edgewater Drive, Orlando; 407-841-8757) includes a champagne brunch at Lili Marlene's Restaurant in its flight pattern.

Right outside Orlando on Route 426, the town of **Winter Park** delights visitors with its tree-lined avenues and a lovely oldtime **Central Park** complete with benches, fountains and a stage. In recent years, a sinkhole that gobbled up a few buildings has gained the town notice.

Rollins College (Holt Avenue, Winter Park; 407-646-2000), with its Mediterranean design, is the cultural center of Winter Park. At the entrance of the lakeside campus, the Walk of Fame is lined by 800 inscribed stones from the homes of luminaries such as Charles Dickens and Mary Queen of Scots.

At the **Morse Museum of American Art** (133 East Welbourne Avenue, Winter Park; 407-644-3686; admission), turn-of-the-century functional and decorative art is featured. Furniture, blown glass, pottery and paintings make up the collection. Most impressive is the priceless display of Tiffany stained glass.

Scenic Boat Tours (★) (312 East Morse Boulevard, Winter Park; 407-644-4056) takes you on a peaceful one-hour tour of Winter Park's extensive lakes and canals. Here you can relax amid the migratory birds and waterfowl—Florida nature at its undisturbed best.

The work of internationally acclaimed realist artist Albin Polasek is preserved at the **Polasek Foundation** (★) (633 Osceola Avenue, Winter Park; 407-647-6294). The facility served as home to the sculptor/painter for his final 16 years, and many of his original works, as well as replicas, are kept there for public viewing.

The **Maitland Art Center** (231 West Packwood Avenue, Maitland; 407-539-2181) displays contemporary art in an Indian-motif complex of buildings and tranquil gardens designed as a retreat for avant-garde artists. The lovely Garden Chapel on the grounds has become a popular spot for weddings.

The **Florida Audubon Society State Headquarters** (1101 Audubon Way, Maitland; 407-645-3826) concentrates, as one would suspect, on bird life. It includes a gift shop and a huge aviary.

DOWNTOWN AND NORTH ORLANDO HOTELS

Overlooking Lake Eola Park from across the street, the **Orlando International Youth Hostel** (227 North Eola Drive; 407-843-8888) provides uncommon hostel accommodations. Housed in an old stucco, Mediterranean-style home in an upscale downtown neighborhood, the Plantation Manor features a lobby fireplace and piano and a generous, breezy front porch with a view of the lake. There are 33 rooms in the historic building, plus 11 more in a motel building behind it, all renting at budget rates.

The **Courtyard Inn at Lake Lucerne** (211 North Lucerne Circle East, 407-648-5188) offers 22 moderate-to-deluxe-priced suites in three lovely homes. One building, the Norment-Parry Inn, is the oldest existing home in Orlando. Sitting on Lake Lucerne, it offers guests loveliness indoors and out. Ornate Victorian embellishments are complemented with American and English antiques throughout the seven character-filled guest suites, parlor and other rooms.

Parliament House (410 North Orange Blossom Trail, Orlando; 407-843-6671) offers 120 carpeted rooms and efficiencies at budget prices. The pink, grey and white motel has a pleasant beach on Roc Lake, but guests don't get near the water unless they want to risk a one-on-one with an alligator or two. The good news is that the Olympic-sized pool is open 24 hours, as is the restaurant. Rooms in this gay-friendly motel feature Florida scenes and balconies with views of the lake, pool or pecan grove.

A find for the crowd-escapee is **Park Plaza Hotel** (307 Park Avenue, Winter Park; 407-647-1072). This 27-room hotel oozes old-fashioned southern charm. Wicker and antique furniture, fern-decked balconies, brass accents and seclusion are the perfect antidotes to a whirlwind trip through the Orlando area. Amenities include a restaurant and bar. Moderate to deluxe.

Just off Park Avenue, the **Langford Resort Hotel** (300 East New England Avenue, Winter Park; 407-644-3400) offers 226 guest rooms, dressed up simply and offering a hint of hotel days gone by. The lobby boasts a Seminole Indian decor with art, cypress tables, terra-cotta floors and jungle vegetation. A sauna, whirlpool, swimming pool and restaurant with live entertainment complete a one-of-a-kind lodging package. Moderate.

DOWNTOWN AND NORTH ORLANDO RESTAURANTS

For fresh and reasonable seafood, try **Gary's Duck Inn** (3974 South Orange Blossom Trail, Orlando; 407-843-0270). It's housed in a flat red building. The walls are done in knotty pine with typical nautical trappings. The specialty of the house is red snapper. Moderate.

Lili Marlene's Aviator Pub (129 West Church Street, Orlando; 407-422-2434) in Church Street Station serves steaks and seafood in an atmosphere of an English pub with an antique airplane theme. Prices for lunch and dinner fall into the moderate category.

Número Uno (2499 South Orange Avenue, Orlando; 407-841-3840) holds high regard among Orlando residents for its Cuban cuisine. The facility offers simple decor and a menu of standard Cuban specialties such as rice and beans, roast pork and bean soup. Budget.

Unpretentious surroundings and dependably fine French fare draw the locals to **Coq au Vin** (4800 South Orange Avenue, Orlando; 407-851-6980). The menu features such favorites as chicken liver pâté, fresh rainbow trout splashed with champagne, and roast duck with figs, pecans and apples. Moderate to deluxe.

Plush and panoramic, **Lee's Lakeside** (431 East Central Boulevard, Orlando; 407-841-1565) overlooks Lake Eola and the Centennial Fountain downtown. The deluxe menu does surf and turf superbly, with such specialties as châteaubriand bouquetière, tournedos, King crab and lobster. A crock of cheese with breadsticks and wonderful piña colada muffins accompany each entrée.

It's called **La Cantina** (4721 East Colonial Drive, Orlando; 407-894-4491), but it serves steaks, not tacos, and they come with side dishes of spaghetti, not refried beans. Despite the possible confusion, La Cantina serves some of the best steaks to be found in this beef capital. The surroundings are as comfortable as the food is good. Moderate.

Haute cuisine graces the tables at **La Normandie** (2021 East Colonial Drive, Orlando; 407-896-9976). In six different rooms, handmade Norman chairs and other French furniture and tableware bestow an air of elegance. Delicacies such as veal scallopini in Calvados sauce, tripe, salmon and rack of lamb with garlic sauce please the palate. Deluxe.

Chinese food is served by waiters pushing carts at **4-5-6** (657 North Primrose Drive, Orlando; 407-898-1899). Entrées such as steamed sea bass and chicken with snow peas are well-prepared in an atmosphere that couldn't be less formal. Budget to moderate.

A firm fixture in the ever-changing world of restaurants is **House of Beef** (801 John Young Parkway, Orlando; 407-295-1931). Since 1957, this purveyor of perfectly aged steaks has fed meat lovers, who are allowed to choose their cuts from a glass showcase. There's also a selection of seafood and vegetarian platters on the moderate-priced menu, plus a catalog of over 400 wines and an ample salad bar.

If you're hankering to quietly eat a steak away from tourist crowds, **Cattle Ranch** (6129 Old Winter Garden Road, Orlando; 407-298-7334) is your place. Thick cuts are tossed onto a blazing orangewood fire for extraordinary flavor. Cowpoke elegance describes the ambience; down-home good describes the moderately priced eats.

The place to go in ritzy Winter Park is **Park Plaza Gardens** (319 Park Avenue South; 407-898-1899). Here lunch consists of salads and quiche; dinner emphasis is on seafood and veal. The charmingly elegant dining room is filled with plants and lit with candles for romance. Deluxe to ultra-deluxe.

The stylish **Park Avenue Grille** (358 North Park Avenue, Winter Park; 407-647-4556) is decorated with marble tables, maroon-and-gray trappings, rows of tall cross-hatched windows and—the Avenue's trademark—lots of plants. Seafood—with a few landlubber specialties thrown in—is served broiled, blackened, fried, steamed—you choose the method. Moderate.

Ask any local where to go for fun as well as haute cuisine and they'll likely direct you to **Pebbles** (2516 Aloma Avenue, Winter Park; 407-678-7001). Here imaginative food is served in a trendy but warm setting: glass-dome ceilings, snug booths, and tables topped with mini potted palms and pepper mills. Try the goat cheese tomato concassé, nutty cheesy salad or honey-roasted spareribs. Moderate to deluxe.

If authentic Mexican food in a packed casa is your style, try the homemade guacamole and refried beans, burritos, etc. at **Paco's** (1801 West Fairbanks Avenue, Winter Park; 407-629-0149). Budget.

The British Tearoom (1917 Aloma Avenue, Winter Park; 407-677-0121) is a humble shopping center eatery that serves budget breakfasts and lunches. Featured English specialties include rarebit, lamb pie and Cornish pastie.

Housed in a turn-of-the-century home set back among the oaks, **Jordan's Grove** (1300 South Orlando Avenue, Maitland; 407-628-0020) is a find. The ever-changing menu here features lamb, poultry, seafood and pasta. The tab is ultra-deluxe for a four-course meal enjoyed in gracious surroundings.

Maison & Jardin (430 South Wymore Road, Altamonte Springs; 407-862-4410) is named for its homey, garden atmosphere. Highly accomplished in local gourmet cuisine, the dressy restaurant features a variable continental menu that includes dishes as traditional as veal Oscar and as innovative as veal steak with lobster, avocado and green peppercorn sauce. Outside, showy flower beds frame Mediterranean villa architecture. Inside, windows and a glassed gazebo give diners a view of the seven-acre grounds. Deluxe to ultra-deluxe.

DOWNTOWN AND NORTH ORLANDO SHOPPING

Church Street Station (129 West Church Street, Orlando; 407-422-2434) is a cobblestone and wrought-iron complex of saloons, restaurants and shops.

Within Church Street Station, the **Church Street Exchange** is filled with specialty shops, with an immense game room comprising one floor.

In Church Street Station's Bumby Building, the **Buffalo Trading Co.** (407-841-8472) sells western and Indian antiques, in keeping with the shoot-'em-up theme of the mall. In the same building, The **Bumby Emporium** (407-422-2434) deals in gift items and Church Street souvenirs.

A few blocks from Church Street Station, **Caribbean Records & Variety Store** (539 West Church Street; 407-423-7552) offers Jamaican music, artwork and jewelry.

For the chic, **Park Avenue** (Winter Park) lines up designer-name shops, antique boutiques and restaurants. Here, fern bar trendiness is taken to the streets, where rows of greenery hang from wrought-iron balconies.

In a French country-type store right off Park Avenue, **Vieille Provence** (122 Park Avenue North, Winter Park; 407-628-3858) sells European antiques, pine furniture, imported fabrics and miscellaneous gift items.

Also on the Avenue, **The Black Sheep** (114-B Park Avenue South, Winter Park; 407-644-0122) specializes in hand-painted needlepoint canvases, imported wools, silks, fabrics and accessories.

Winter Park Stamps (340 Park Avenue North; 407-628-1120) stocks stamps from every European country. The store's United States stamps alone number several hundred thousand and date back to the 1840s.

DOWNTOWN AND NORTH ORLANDO NIGHTLIFE

Country-and-western dancing to live music happens at the down-home **Sullivan's Trailways Lounge** (1108 South Orange Blossom Trail; 407-843-2934). Cover.

Church Street Station (129 West Church Street, Orlando; 407-422-2434) houses several clubs. The most famous is **Rosie O'Grady's,** which features bawdy Dixieland entertainment: cancan dancers, Dixie bands, tap dancers and vaudeville acts.

On the quieter side at Church Street Station, **Apple Annie's Courtyard** guests are entertained by live bluegrass and folk tunes. For disco fanatics, **Phineas Phogg's Balloon Works** blares out contemporary tunes. At **Cheyenne Saloon,** a lot of strummin', pickin' and foot stompin' goes on in a huge former opera house. Here you'll have a chance to see some Florida-style clogging, a dance tradition borrowed from the mountains.

Dramatic ceilings, beautiful artwork and mellow music make **Pebbles Downtown** (17 West Church Street, Orlando; 407-839-0892) a classy spot for a drink.

For a cozy pub atmosphere, go to **Bull & Bush** (★) (2408 Robinson Street, Orlando; 407-896-7546), have a Guinness and play some darts.

Popular with the trendy, after-work set, **Mulvaney's Irish Pub** (27 Church Street, Orlando; 407-872-3296) has an acoustic lineup.

For a taste of culture, check out what's happening on stage at the **Bob Carr Performing Arts Center** (401 Livingston Street, Orlando; 407-849-2577). This community theater produces a different play each month.

J. J. Whispers (5100 Adamson Street, Orlando; 407-629-4779) is a hot spot that attracts the young to its high-tech disco, and a thirtyish crowd to its club featuring music of the '40s, '50s and '60s. Live stage acts appear in the restaurant-lounge. Cover.

The place to be seen in Orlando is **Shooter's** (4315 North Orange Blossom Trail; 407-298-2855), a sprawling lakefront complex with occasional live bands. With multiple bars, beaches and a swimming pool, the place jams.

Deejay-spun Top 40 tops the charts at **Frat House** (11599 East Colonial Drive, Orlando; 407-273-9600).

The crowd at the **Crocodile Club** (118 West Fairbanks Avenue in Bailey's Restaurant, Winter Park; 407-647-8501) is ultra-toney; the music, compliments of a deejay, is Top-40.

Rollins College's **Annie Russell Theatre** (Holt Avenue, Winter Park; 407-646-2501) hosts year-round theater performances.

The Mill (330 West Fairbanks Avenue, Winter Park; 407-644-1544) serves up just-brewed beer, relaxing jazz and acoustic guitar.

Harper's Tavern (537 West Fairbanks Avenue, Winter Park; 407-647-7858) is a popular local watering hole with dependably good Top-40 bands. Cover.

GAY SCENE **Parliament House Nightclub** (410 North Orange Blossom Trail, Orlando; 407-425-7571) offers five venues popular with the gay crowd. In the show bar there are female impersonators and a variety of reviews and contests. Another possibility is the horseshoe-shaped piano bar.

The parquet floor in the nicely lit disco is ideal for dancing. The vast lounge bar includes a variety of video games.

A popular women's club, **Key Largo Lounge** (6900 North Orange Blossom Trail; 407-291-0686) features three bars, a pool, game room and disco dancing. This eclectic, two-story establishment is decorated with mirrors, neon art and paintings. Upstairs and downstairs dancefloors rock to disco sounds. Men are invited to join the action.

DOWNTOWN AND NORTH ORLANDO BEACHES AND PARKS

Tosohatchee State Reserve—Here woodlands and wetlands comprise 28,800 acres of eastern Orange County along the St. Johns River. This spacious park boasts two natural wonders: a rare virgin cypress swamp and Florida's largest stand of virgin slash pine. Activity is kept low key here. Hiking trails are extensive and fishing is popular.

Facilities: Hiking trails; groceries and restaurants nearby; information, 407-568-5893. *Fishing:* Good for crappie, catfish and bass.

Camping: For backpackers and horseback trail riders only; $3 per night.

Getting there: Located off Route 50 near Christmas.

South Orlando

Let the theme parks begin again as you move to the city's southern outskirts, where a nearness to Disney World seems to spark contagion. International Drive and its offshoots are the center of activity here, with their jumble of hotels, restaurants, outlet stores, souvenir shops and amusement parks.

Lying just north of International Drive, **Mystery Fun House** (5767 Major Boulevard, Orlando; 407-351-3355; admission) is a glorified combination of a house of mirrors and spook house. They've thrown in moving floors and other special effects, as well as a shooting arcade, miniature golf course and Enchanted Forest.

With so much waterfront in Florida, the current wave of manmade water parks seems redundant. They remain popular, nonetheless. One in this area, **Wet 'n Wild** (6200 International Drive, Orlando; 407-351-3200; admission), includes the typical aquatic adventures of these places—water slides, flumes, tubing chutes and wave pools.

Fun 'n Wheels (6739 Sand Lake Road at International Drive; 407-351-5651; admission) is a small park by Orlando's standards. Its yellow-and-white striped awnings herald kiddy automotive fun in the form of bumper cars, go-carts and other carnival rides such as a wet slide and ferris wheel.

Second only to the Disney attractions in popularity is **Sea World** (7007 Sea World Drive, Orlando; 407-351-3600; admission). Here the famous killer whale Shamu is the star of the sea show. Sea lions, otters, a walrus, the Famous People Players and dolphins perform. Going to a polar extreme at Sea World, the Penguin Encounter has created a natural environment for over 250 of the tuxedoed birds. The 160,000-gallon Tropical Reef, a water-ski show and the "Terror of the Deep" tunnel are added attractions at this splashy park.

Covering 135 acres and spotlighting seven shows and seven major exhibits, Sea World literally provides a world of experiences. There are botanical gardens, a Hawaiian village, a Japanese village and a playground for the kids. When you're ready to depart terra firma you can enter the 400-foot sky tower and survey the world's most popular marine-life theme park.

For more information on Orlando's sights, visit the **Orlando/Orange County Convention & Visitors Bureau, Inc.** (8445 International Drive, Orlando; 407-363-5871).

SOUTH ORLANDO HOTELS

Lodging on or near International Drive in southern Orlando offers proximity to the area's attractions, plus a solid dose of character. These hotels are generally more upscale than the ones found on Route 192 near Disney World.

MIC Lakefront Inn (6500 International Drive, Orlando; 407-345-5340) is a modern 164-room facility sitting on the edge of a small lake across from the Wet 'n Wild theme park. Large and inviting rooms, a polished lobby, lovely pool area and trendy bar can be had at moderate-to-deluxe rates.

Key West ambience reigns at **The Floridian of Orlando** (7299 Republic Drive, Orlando; 407-351-5009). A forest of potted tropical plants sets the mood in the lobby. The 300 rooms convey a casual air with their pastel tones. A restaurant, lounge, outdoor bar and swimming pool complete the picture. Moderate to deluxe.

For a luxury Orlando vacation no one can touch, experience the **Hyatt Regency Grand Cypress** (1 Grand Cypress Boulevard; 407-239-1234). This full-service resort trolleys you to all the many available activities: jogging trails, a 45-acre Audubon nature preserve, golf courses, a tri-level fantasy swimming pool cascading with waterfalls and spanned by a suspension bridge, horseback riding, tennis courts, boat rentals, bicycling trails, sand beach, racquetball courts—there's not much you can't do at Grand Cypress. Inside the hotel, the lobby exalts in flowing streams and flourishing tropical flora.

The guest rooms are furnished with special touches such as wicker settees, love seats and pastel color schemes. Ultra-deluxe.

Ducks are the unique attraction at **The Peabody** (9801 International Drive, Orlando; 407-352-4000). They parade through the soaring lobby, across a red carpet especially laid for their daily procession to the pond. There's a Dux Restaurant and a Mallard Lounge. The hotel's 891 rooms are as elegant as its lobby. On the fourth floor you'll find a recreation center complete with four tennis courts and an Olympic-sized pool. Ultra-deluxe.

The personality of **Orlando Heritage Inn** (9861 International Drive, Orlando; 407-352-0008) is southern Victorian. Its 279 guest rooms are done up in lacy curtains, quilted bed covers and paddle fans. The lobby is a vision of wainscot, floral wallpaper, stretch windows and antique chandeliers. Food and dinner theater entertainment are provided in this open yet intimate spot. Moderate to deluxe.

SOUTH ORLANDO RESTAURANTS

Local couples and families are the main patrons of **Donato's** (5159 International Drive, Orlando; 407-363-5959), located near Universal Studios. The wood-floored Italian deli and eatery, stashed away in a strip shopping center, serves huge portions of delicious veal, chicken, spaghetti and other saucy pasta dishes. There's also pizza and fresh seafood. Best of all, its boisterous, homestyle atmosphere make it an anomaly in this gimmicky theme park area. Budget to moderate.

The Stouffer Resort's **Atlantis** (6677 Sea Harbor Drive, Orlando; 407-351-5555) serves elegant French-Mediterranean cuisine on tables surrounded by nicely appointed furnishings and art. The deluxe-to-ultra-deluxe-priced menu contains such pleasures as grilled swordfish with port wine sauce, rack of lamb with mushroom and sun-dried tomato sauce and Maine lobster. The resort's less formal **Tradewinds** offers fancy sandwiches and salads as well as nouvelle preparations such as rainbow trout with pine nuts, dill and lime meunière. Moderate to deluxe.

The Grand Cypress' **La Coquina** (1 Grand Cypress Boulevard, Orlando; 407-239-1234) does it all with perfection, from the spotless table linen and glimmering chandeliers, to the nouvelle Continental cuisine and artistic pastries, to the single rose for the lady upon departure. The deluxe to ultra-deluxe menu dabbles in seafood, poultry, lamb and delightful sauces.

For budget-priced meals with an exotic flair, check out the international food pavilion at **Mercado Shopping Village** (8445 South International Drive, Orlando; 407-345-9337). You'll have a choice of fast foods from Greece, Latin America, Mexico, Italy and the United States. I tried **The Greek Place** (407-352-6930) and enjoyed Greek salad and lemon soup that rated well above the average mall food. The counter menu also offers *moussaka*, gyro sandwiches, dolmades and other authentically prepared Greek specialties.

Orlandoites will point to **Ran-Getsu** (8400 International Drive, Orlando; 407-345-0044) as your best bet for authentic Japanese food. The sushi bar whips around like a dragon's tail, and floor tables overlook a bonsai garden and pond. Besides sushi, the restaurant offers sukiyaki, kushiyaki, deep-fried alligator tail and other Japanese-Florida crossbreeds at deluxe prices.

Creativity is the main ingredient at the Peabody Hotel's **Dux Restaurant** (9801 International Drive, Orlando; 407-352-4000). Madeira raisin sauce tops pheasant; steamed salmon and sole are braided together; grilled veal loin is served with a sage corn sauce. The marble and crystal grandeur is as impressive as the ultra-deluxe menu.

At **Capriccio** (9801 International Drive, Orlando; 407-352-4000), also in the Peabody, Italian goes to California. Besides innovative dishes of Italian descent, pizza is the pièce de résistance here. No ordinary pizza, mind you, these are topped with such ingredients as sun-dried tomatoes, deli cheeses and fresh herbs, then cooked in wood-burning ovens. Other delicacies include swordfish with a caper-anchovy-scallion butter sauce and angelhair with tiger shrimp. Prices are deluxe in an atmosphere of polished black marble.

In almost every Florida city, one finds a restaurant named for Ernest Hemingway, and Orlando is no exception. This **Hemingway's** (Grand Cypress Resort; 407-239-1234) conforms to the Key West style preferred by most of these restaurants, with a casual atmosphere and seafood cuisine. Orlando's version also offers an elevated poolside location and a woodsy ambience. The menu swims with grouper, pompano, squid, conch, shrimp and other salty creatures, plus a steak or two. Ultra-deluxe.

For Indian cuisine, **Darbar Restaurant** (7600 Dr. Phillips Boulevard, Orlando; 407-345-8128) specializes in tandoori cooking. Lamb, chicken and vegetables are marinated and grilled in a clay oven or over mesquite charcoal, and served with pilafs, curried side dishes and chutney. The dining room reflects the Indian motif with lavish overstatement: heavy chandeliers, crimson-and-gold walls and lots of marble. Moderate.

In a simple setting, **Christini's** (7600 Dr. Phillips Boulevard, Orlando; 407-345-8770) creates a formal atmosphere and imaginative Italian cuisine. The pasta is made fresh on the premises and served with fish, shrimp, lamb, lobster, clam and veal specialties, seasoned with herbs from the owner's garden. Deluxe.

SOUTH ORLANDO SHOPPING

One of the largest gatherings of factory outlets is **Belz Factory Outlet Mall** (5401 West Oakridge Road, Orlando; 407-352-9611). Over 170 stores sell discounted books, jewelry, electronics, clothing and dinnerware. One shop at Belz called **Everything But Water** (407-363-9752) sells swimwear and accessories.

At **Mercado** (8445 International Drive, Orlando; 407-345-9337) shopping village, shoppers are entertained while they browse the brick streets and Mediterranean-style storefronts full of ethnic shops. Here you'll find **Exclusively East Gallery** (407-351-2626), which sells very expensive Oriental vases, statues and wallhangings. **The Conch Republic** (407-363-0227) in Mercado sells Key West aloe lotions and singer Jimmy Buffet's line of tropical clothing and jewelry.

Also in the Mercado, **Coral Reef** (407-351-0100) carries unique artwork including Oriental *chokin* items and some remarkable pieces by a Gainesville artist working with crushed pecan shell and powder. In **Hello Dolly** (407-352-7344) collectible dolls are sold. Spiffy clothing and gifts for the car enthusiast await at **One For the Road** (407-345-0120).

Pick up your MGM and Universal Studios movie paraphernalia and T-shirts at **Once Upon A Star** (407-363-4449).

If the cowboy bug bites, mosey on over to **Great West Boot Outlet** (5597 International Drive, Orlando; 407-345-8103) to get outfitted in one of their 5000 pairs of boots.

Florida Mall (8001 South Orange Blossom Trail, Orlando; 407-851-6255), while conventional, stands out because of its size. Housing over 175 retailers, its anchors include several department stores.

SOUTH ORLANDO NIGHTLIFE

Bloopers Sports Bar (5715 Major Boulevard; 407-351-3340) is an Orlando favorite offering a big-screen television and karaoke nights. Occasional live music is featured.

At the **Mardi Gras** (8445 International Drive, Orlando; 407-351-5151) dinner attraction, as you might imagine, the show has a New Orleans theme. Brightly painted papier-mâché masks, clowns and balloons create a carnival atmosphere. Entertainment comes from a jazz band and cabaret performers.

More medieval dinner entertainment is offered at **King Henry's Feast** (8984 International Drive, Orlando; 407-351-5151). Magicians, acrobats and King Henry himself come to the stage. The outside looks like a castle, complete with moat and notched turrets. Inside, swords, shields, heavy pewter wine and ale tankards, and grand chandeliers create a Middle Age ambience.

The Plantation Dinner Theatre (9861 International Drive, Orlando; 407-352-0008) sits in the lobby of the Heritage Inn. Open yet intimate, it features light drama in Victorian surroundings.

The entertainment at **Mark Two** (3376 Edgewater Drive, Orlando; 407-843-6275) is more traditional dinner theater. Local troupes perform Broadway classics.

SOUTH ORLANDO BEACHES AND PARKS

Turkey Lake Park—A large, natural city park that centers around a lake known as the headwaters of the Everglades. Designed for family pleasure, the park features two sandy beaches, a swimming pool, bike trails and natural flora that thrive here in the midst of the metropolis. Children will enjoy the re-created cracker farm and the petting zoo.

Facilities: Picnic areas, restrooms, showers, playground, bike rentals, observation deck, nature trails; groceries and restaurants are nearby; information, 407-299-5594. *Swimming:* Good. *Fishing:* Good for panfish off the pier or from a boat.

Camping: There are 32 sites, all with RV hookups, and a primitive campground; $6.50-16.40 per night.

Getting there: Located at 3401 South Hiawassee Road in Orlando.

Moss Park (★)—A 1500-acre county park sandwiched between two lovely lakes. Shadiness and a nice sand beach give this metropolitan fringe park its oasis feel. Much of its acreage remains in a natural, undeveloped state. It's not well-advertised, but the locals know it well.

Facilities: Picnic areas, restrooms, pavilions, playground, tennis courts, horseshoe pits, nature trails; groceries and restaurants nearby; information, 407-273-2327. *Swimming:* Good. *Fishing:* Good for perch, bass and other local freshwater fish.

Camping: There are 20 sites, all with RV hookups, and a primitive campground; $11-14 per night.

Getting there: Located off Route 15A on Moss Park Road, southeast of Orlando's Route 528.

Orlando–Gainesville Loop

Since most central Florida vacations begin in Orlando, we will take you on a series of loops to outlying areas, tours that can be accomplished in a day or two. The first loop heads west toward Gainesville, via DeLand and Palatka—a tour featuring the riverside vistas and lively springs of central Florida. We return through Ocala, known for its thoroughbreds and the nearby Silver Springs and Ocala National Forest.

Right outside Orlando, the **Bradlee-McIntyre House** (150 West Warren Street, Longwood; 407-332-6920) exemplifies the mansions that heralded the golden days of steamships. Built in 1885 in Altamonte Springs, it was moved to its present location in the early 1970s. The architecture and appointments have been restored to its Queen Anne style.

At **Big Tree Park** (General Hutchinson Parkway, north of Longwood; 407-323-9615), a 126-foot-high knobby growth marks the largest bald cypress tree in the nation. With a diameter of over 17 feet, the "Senator" has been estimated to be 3000 years old.

The old steamboat town of **Sanford** is today known as the "Celery Capital of the World." Still retaining its riverside personality, Sanford also blends agricultural, historic and metropolitan characteristics.

The **Seminole County Historical Museum** (300 Bush Boulevard, Sanford; 407-321-2489) depicts the town's diversity with exhibits covering the citrus industry, cattle ranching and vegetable farming. Railroad and steamboat memorabilia and furnished rooms of a typical steamboat-era mansion are also featured.

For a narrated tour of St. Johns River wildlife and a peek at its great steamboat days, ride aboard **St. John's River Cruises** (Sanford Boat Works, Route 415, Sanford; 407-330-1612; admission). Alligators, osprey, manatees and bald eagles will greet your passage as they did a century ago.

Rivership Romance (433 North Palmetto Avenue, Sanford; 407-321-5091; admission) leaves out of Monroe Harbor Marina on a popular day or evening river sightseeing trip aboard an old-time paddlewheeler. The Friday and Saturday evening cruise includes dinner and dancing.

More information on Sanford awaits at the **Greater Sanford Chamber of Commerce** (400 East First Street; 407-322-2212).

As you follow Route 17-92 out of Sanford, along glistening Lake Monroe, you will come to the **Central Florida Zoological Park** (Route 17-92, Lake Monroe; 407-323-4450; admission), a 110-acre zoo and picnic area with thatched-roof shelters. Llamas, ostriches and 400 other exotic animals are on display here.

An interesting sidetrip en route to DeLand takes you into the city of **Cassadaga** (★), a community begun by spiritualists. Psychics meet here in the winter months, and palm readers abound year-round in this shady, eccentric little village.

DeLand once was an important steamboat stop on the St. Johns River. Today, it is home to Florida's oldest private university, named for the cowboy hat that funded it: Stetson University (Woodland Boulevard). On campus, you will find the **Gillespie Museum of Minerals** (Michigan and Amelia avenues, DeLand; 904-822-7000). This collection of over 25,000 specimens includes Florida coral rock, fluorescents and meteorites.

Even if you're reluctant to try it, you may want to watch folks skydiving, a sport popular in the DeLand area. Both lessons and shows are offered at **Skydive DeLand** (★) (1600 Flight Line Boulevard, DeLand; 904-738-3539).

For more information, and a self-guided tour of the DeLand area, see the folks at the **DeLand Area Chamber of Commerce and Visitors Center** (336 North Woodland Boulevard; 904-734-4331).

At Barberville, you can visit a folk museum for demonstrations of the lifestyles of early settlers. The **Pioneer Settlement for the Creative Arts** (Route 40 and Route 17, Barberville; 904-749-2959; admission) features a bridge house, log cabin, country store, caboose and train depot as they appeared at the turn of the century.

Up Palatka way, the St. Johns River thickens, scoring deep folds in the hills in its way. The **Ravine State Gardens** (1600 Twigg Street, Palatka; 904-329-3721) takes you down into the lush world of moss, ferns, palms, jasmine, mimosa and banana trees. Two deep ravines create a cool refuge and a dreamy mood filled with butterflies and song birds.

The area of central Florida west of Palatka was made famous by writer Marjorie Kinnan Rawlings. Best known for her Pulitzer-Prize-winning novel, *The Yearling*, Rawlings moved to this part of cracker Florida to write and manage a citrus grove. The **Marjorie Kinnan Rawlings State Historic Site** (Hawthorne; 904-466-3672; admission) preserves the author's rambling cracker home as it appeared when she lived there. An antique typewriter sits on a screened-in porch, tinned goods and dried herbs stock kitchen shelves, and bottles of Appleton Rum and a carton of Lucky Strikes sit by the parlor fireplace. All this tells the story of a woman who called herself "part man," and who endured the hardship of bare-bones backwoods living. Tours are given to a limited number of visitors (it's best to go early or late in the day) by a woman who dresses and plays the part of Rawlings.

Southwest of Hawthorne lies the town of **Cross Creek**, which is also the title of Rawlings autobiography. In *Cross Creek* Rawlings recorded the simple lifestyles of her central Florida neighbors. In *Cross Creek Cookery* she compiled recipes and food lore of the region.

Our tour next leads to **Gainesville**, known primarily as a university town. Away from big-city contact, life in this town remains quiet, arty and liberal. These qualities are immediately evident in the downtown area, where sidewalk cafés, restored storefronts and cobblestoned plazas add character.

The **Gainesville Area Chamber of Commerce** (300 East University Avenue; 904-336-7100) distributes information nearby.

Gainesville's premier attraction re-creates the area's rich prehistory. The **Florida Museum of Natural History** (University of Florida, Newell Drive and Museum Road; 904-392-1721) displays a Mayan palace, Florida cave, Sioux Indian exhibit, fossil study center, and a superb collection of rare seashells.

You can step back even further in time at **Devil's Millhopper State Geological Site** (4732 Millhopper Road, Gainesville; 904-336-2008; admission), where the discovery of fossilized sharks' teeth and other artifacts proved that the state was once covered by the sea. Here a five-acre sinkhole plunges 120 feet deep and shelters wildlife peculiar to the area. The temperature seems to drop ten degrees as you follow the boardwalk from pines to splashy waterfalls and furry ferns.

Jungle and safari life have come to Gainesville at the unusual **Fred Bear Museum** (★) (Fred Bear Drive at Archer Road; 904-376-2411; admission). Bear founded the museum with artifacts from his worldwide career hunting with a bow, which he touts as good sportsmanship. Along with the buffalo, wolves, caribou and elephant Bear has felled, visitors can view archery exhibits and relics from Indian, Eskimo and African civilizations.

After Gainesville, this looping tour heads back south on its return to Orlando. Along the way via Route 441, you encounter the town of **Micanopy**, listed on the National Register of Historic Districts. It is the picturesque headquarters of artisans and antiquarians in the Gainesville area.

Farther along, **McIntosh** sits as content as a purring cat on the shores of Orange Lake. The quiet village is half Victorian homes of the early 1900s, half RV fish camp of midcentury making. One would not be surprised to meet a horse-drawn carriage traipsing McIntosh streets, one of which was designed to run on either side of an old tree, rather than plowing it down.

Parimutuel betters will enjoy following the fast-paced game of jai alai at the **Ocala Jai Alai Frontón** (Route 318, Orange Lake; 904-591-2345; admission).

Ocala is known for its thoroughbreds and stately homes. The city has worked hard to re-establish an old-fashioned flavor. At its center sits the **town square park** (Northeast 8th Avenue and Silver Springs Boulevard), with its reproduced, domed Victorian gazebo. The downtown area is called "Brick City" because it was rebuilt with red brick following a devastating fire in 1883.

A few blocks away, another **historic district** stretches along Fort King Avenue between 3rd and 13th streets. Here the era of early tourism and steamboat mansions is remembered in over 200 homes built in styles ranging from Gothic to colonial Italianate to Queen Anne revival.

The **Appleton Museum of Art** (4333 East Silver Springs Boulevard, Ocala; 904-236-5050; admission) houses exotic and unusual treasures collected by Arthur Appleton, Chicago industrialist and local thoroughbred trainer. Within this marble palace you'll find earthenware from 12th-century Persia, Oriental vases, 1st-century Peruvian art, a Mexican effigy vessel, a Napoleonic sword and 19th-century paintings. In short, it's a varied and rich collection of art spanning 5000 years of culture.

Ocala's outlying area is a land of gurgling springs, oaks covered with hanging moss, pine scents, white-fenced ranches and muscular thoroughbreds sleek with sweat. A few decades ago, breeders discovered that Ocala's healthful combination of sunshine, mineral spring water and fertile soil was as good for race horses as it was for the visitors who had discovered the area's many fountains of youth a century before.

Today, this lush area of coastal backyards is dotted with **thoroughbred farms** that make you think you've arrived in Kentucky, but for the occasional sabal palm towering above low-slung ranch homes. Many of these bluegrass farms can be seen off routes 441 and 301; the greatest concentration roll along Route 200. Some of the ranches welcome visitors. The best way to arrange a tour is through the **Ocala/Marion Chamber of Commerce** (110 East Silver Springs Boulevard, Ocala; 904-629-8051).

A different sort of racing is the focus at **Don Garlits' Museum of Drag Racing** (13700 Southwest 16th Avenue, Ocala; 904-245-8661; admission). Displays here trace the history of the sport back to its California infancy in the 1950s. Vehicles raced by the museum's founder and namesake, King of Speed "Big Daddy" Don Garlits, are exhibited along with other unusual four-wheel forms of transportation.

One of the best known bubbling spring fountains in the state is **Silver Springs** (Silver Springs Boulevard, Silver Springs; 904-236-2121; admission), which has attracted touring nature lovers since first lady Mary Todd Lincoln and author Harriet Beecher Stowe came here in the 1880s. It's the largest limestone artesian spring formation in the world, with an average output of 800 million gallons of water a day. The teeming life visible through the springs' pure waters inspired the invention of the glass bottom boat by a Silver Springs resident. This is still a favored mode of seeing what lies above and below the waters here.

Within the 360 acres, those who can take their eyes off what lies underwater will spot giraffes, ostrich, monkeys, llamas and other exotic animals. If you feel as though you're in a Tarzan movie, you're not far from the truth. The jungle setting of Silver Springs was often used for making these jungle films. There's also a petting zoo and daily animal shows.

Continuing on Route 40, you will travel into the extensive wild lands of **Ocala National Forest** (see the "Orlando-Gainesville Loop Beaches and Parks" section below). A good route for exploring this area is a loop that begins north on Route 314, then south on Route 19 out of the forest toward Mount Dora. Or, you can follow Route 42 west to Route 27-441 for an unpopulated inspection of the forest and the cracker way of life it once bred. Along this twisty road you'll see a hidden cross-section of Central Florida: cracker shacks, horse and cattle farms, rolling hills, spring waters and citrus groves.

One of the prettiest towns in Florida, **Mount Dora** is a storybook village of gingerbread mansions, lakeside inns and 19th-century ambience. The downtown sector boasts brick and wrought-iron structures, New England touches, one of the state's proudest antique store districts, and a mountainous Florida elevation of 184 feet. Stop in at the **Mount Dora Chamber**

of Commerce (341 Alexander Street; 904-383-2165), housed in a restored railroad station, for a guide to the area's antique shops and historic homes.

Among the showiest of these regally preserved mansions is the **Donnelly House** (Donnelly Street between 5th and 6th avenues), an ornate fantasy castle in Steamboat Gothic style, accented with stained glass and hand-carved trim. Built in 1893 for one of the city's founders, it is now used as a Masonic Lodge. Across the street, shady Donnelly Park provides shuffleboard and tennis courts.

Housed downtown in the old city firehouse and jailblock, **Royellou Museum** (between 5th and 4th avenues off Baker Street, Mount Dora; 904-383-0006) features the largest collection of bayonets this side of West Point and historic photographs as well as temporary exhibits.

The **Miss Dora** (Route 441, Tavares; 904-343-0200; admission) takes tours out of Gator Inlet Marina into the Dora Canal, the channel that runs between Lake Dora and Lake Eustis. These lovely cypress-studded waters have been preserved from logging to provide refuge for various waterfowl and migratory birds.

Florida Cactus, Inc. (★) (2542 South Peterson Road, Plymouth; 407-886-1833) will change any preconceived notions about cactus being merely green prickly plants that grow in desert wastelands. Visitors here can see the amazing plants growing across the United States—a 24-by-12-foot map of the country is made of cacti, a different variety representing each state. Red, yellow and pink cacti, cacti that form a 75-foot-circumference electric clock, small cacti, gigantic cacti: Florida Cactus does more with cacti than you ever cared to imagine.

ORLANDO-GAINESVILLE LOOP HOTELS

A cute little row motel, **DeBary Motel** (101 Route 17-92, DeBary; 407-668-5230) rents ten units with kitchenettes. Clunky wooden chairs and potted plants in front of each room give this unfancy place a cozy feel. Budget.

The historic **Sprague House Inn** (125 Central Avenue, Crescent City; 904-698-2430) houses a collection of stained-glass windows that trace the history of the area's steamboat days. This restored facility offers bed-and-breakfast hospitality in a turn-of-the-century building. The six guest rooms each include a sitting room and private bath. The one offering a lake view is irresistible. Moderate.

For a smidgen of New England hospitality, stay at **Cape Cod Inn** (3820 Southwest 13th Street, Gainesville; 904-371-2500), a 40-room facility at the southern end of town. The ambience here is colonial with a tropical flavor. Broyhill furniture and pastel shell bedspreads decorate the rooms. Exterior architectural design makes this roadside motel look like a country inn. Budget.

Outside Gainesville, you can enter the 19th century at **Orange Springs Historic Country Inn** (1 Main Street, Orange Springs; 904-546-2052). Not far from author Margaret Kinnan Rawlings' home, it embodies the type of backwoods peacefulness reflected in the author's writings. The inn combines history and sport, with oak mantels and quilted antique beds in the four rooms and canoeing on the inn's own spring. Moderate.

Sitting among a row of impressive old Florida homes and renovated store fronts, the **Herlong Mansion** (★) (402 Northeast Cholakka Boulevard, Micanopy; 904-466-3322) is a stately affair in Greek revival style. Set in a historic village, this old-fashioned bed and breakfast has six guest rooms. Ten fireplaces warm the 15-room mansion, which once was a humble home. Now a three-story palace, it boasts 12-foot ceilings, carefully reworked wood and antiques of many periods. Moderate to deluxe.

Merrily Bed & Breakfast (★) (Avenue G and 6th Street, McIntosh; 904-591-1180) is a perfectly charming place to stay. Oak-shaded grounds, a home the color of butter, tin peaked roofs, a porch swing, banana muffins at the breakfast table and afternoon tea instill the proper ingredients into this experience. Built in 1888, the inn houses three guest rooms with shared baths. Moderate.

A handful of cinderblock cabins with full kitchens dot the lake shores at **Orange Lake Fish Camp** (Lake Road, Orange Lake; 904-591-1870). You can rent boats at this peaceful haven fringed with cypress. Budget.

Seven Sisters Inn (820 Southeast Fort King Street, Ocala; 904-867-1170) takes you back to the 19th century with style and good taste. The seven restored guest rooms are lavishly furnished with antiques, king-sized beds, hand-stitched linen and private baths. Victorian grace is remembered in the architecture of the three-story mansion with its wrap-around porch. Breakfast, served in the garden room, includes lavish dishes such as fresh fruit in cream and baked eggs with caviar. Moderate to deluxe.

The **Raddison Inn Ocala** (3620 West Silver Springs Boulevard, Ocala; 904-629-0091) is a gracious 100-room facility with boastful grounds. The guest rooms are touched with luxury, each with either a balcony or patio. Units are reasonably priced in the budget-to-moderate range. There's also a pool, lounge, and a restaurant.

In the Victorian city of Mount Dora, **Lakeside Inn** (100 South Alexander Street; 904-383-4101) preserves a feeling of old-fashioned hospitality graced with natural outdoor beauty and perfect period appointments. Like a clutch of southern belles, the inn's trio of buildings, pale and pretty, sit shaded in plantation ambience and vegetation. Modern amenities complementing the natural beauty include a swimming pool, tennis courts, lawn bowling, gourmet restaurant and lounge. A boardwalk leads to a wildlife picnic island, and a sandy beach fringes the lake. The 87 restored rooms are done à la Laura Ashley, and heavy on the romance. Deluxe.

Lake Ola Beach Motel (Route 441 South, Mount Dora; 904-383-4713) spreads its 16 rooms before a lovely lake panorama and claims its own private beach. Each unit comes with a kitchenette and unembellished comfort. Budget.

ORLANDO-GAINESVILLE LOOP RESTAURANTS

Old whiskey stills, washing machines and studio cameras—all copper of course—establish the theme at **Copper Cove** (201 Cassadaga Road, Lake Helen; 904-228-3400). Set against a wooded glen, the budget-priced eatery dishes up home-cooked vittles like grilled ham steak and fried chicken, biscuits and gravy, and french toast.

Pondo's (1915 Old New York Avenue, DeLand; 904-734-1995) serves continental versions of pasta, prime rib, steak, duckling and veal in the gracious, comfortable setting of a two-story 1920s home. The place has an air of old elegance, dressed up in crisp white tablecloths when every other restaurant in the country seems to be in peach and mauve. A beautiful fireplace and oak antiques greet guests at the restaurant's entrance. Moderate.

The homestyle cooking at **Original Holiday House** (704 North Woodland, DeLand; 904-734-6319) has drawn crowds since the late 1950s. Guests serve themselves buffet style in this well-preserved old home. Choices include leg of lamb, fish, roast beef and salad. Budget to moderate.

Amid Far East trappings, **Won Lee** (1329 North Woodland Boulevard, DeLand; 904-734-0904) specializes in Cantonese cooking and also offers the usual Chinese dishes. Budget.

One of the most interesting breakfast spots you'll come across is **Old Spanish Sugar Mill Restaurant** (Ponce de León Boulevard, DeLeon Springs; 904-985-5644), inside DeLeon Springs State Recreation Area. Here, the tables have built-in griddles so you can create you own flapjacks with various batters and toppings. Budget.

Continental goes from Old World to nouvelle at **Karlings Inn** (4640 North Route 17, DeLeon Springs; 904-985-5535). In a converted home, wienerschnitzel and pasta meet lobster tails with Scotch cream sauce. Moderate to deluxe.

The **Sprague House Inn** (125 Central Avenue, Crescent City; 904-698-2430) serves lunch and dinner in its Victorian steamboat-age dining room. The moderate menu covers prime rib, shrimp, fresh fish and chicken specialties.

The **Wine and Cheese Gallery** (113 North Main Street, Gainesville; 904-372-8446) serves hefty, cheesy sandwiches and imaginative salads in an umbrellaed courtyard behind a deli and wine shop. The Big Cheese, for example, stacks Havarti, Jarlsberg and Danish Caraway cheeses on homemade French bread. The menu offers over 100 brands of import beers as well as a wide selection of wine. Budget.

If you enter **Sovereign Restaurant** (12 Southeast 2nd Avenue, Gainesville; 904-378-6307) on the garden side, you will walk down a narrow alley that feels like New Orleans' French Quarter. White-painted brick walls hung with carriage lanterns lead to a glassed-encased patio fringed in greenery. Inside, the restaurant sits in an old, high-ceilinged warehouse, where an extensive menu offers rack of lamb, seafood Newburg, duckling, saltimbocca and other dishes of European descent. Deluxe.

Along Gainesville's downtown streets, lovely sidewalk cafés add a European charm. One such place is **Emiliano's Café and Bakery** (7 Southeast 1st Avenue; 904-375-7381). Named for a master baker whose grandchildren revived his Puerto Rican fame in America, Emiliano's specializes in Caribbean pleasures. Chicken breasts in a sauce of triple sec and oranges, swordfish escovitch and Caribbean pork roast star here. Seating is both indoors and out. Moderate.

Toby's Corner (101 Southeast 2nd Place, Gainesville; 904-375-7620) departs from the avant-garde college scene with its conservative elegance and traditional Continental cuisine featuring dishes such as prime rib, duckling à l'orange and grouper *en papillote*. Deluxe.

Joe's Deli (1802 West University Avenue, Gainesville; 904-373-4026) may be the most perpetually mobbed eatery for miles around. It's *the* place to be before and after college football games, late at night, and almost any other time. Expect generous, meaty subs, tasty pizzas and great people-watching. Budget.

If hunger strikes on your way out of town, stop at a big stone building bearing a sign that says **Brown Derby** (5220 Southwest 13th Street, Gainesville; 904-373-0088). A warm interior with a huge fireplace invites lingering over a cover-all-bases menu. Steak and seafood dishes of every type are available for moderate tabs. Pasta, poultry and sandwiches are also represented.

Intimate and diminutive, **Petite Jardin** (2209 East Silver Springs Boulevard, Ocala; 904-351-4140) resides in an airy storefront setting of white linens and fresh flowers. The bill of fare is Continental-American, with goodies like lobster Newburg, prime sirloin au poivre flambé and sautéed soft-shell crab. The wine list includes 80 labels, most from California. Moderate to deluxe.

The hot spot for lunch in Ocala is **Peter Dinkel's** (725 East Silver Springs Boulevard; 904-732-8003). Set in a Victorian home decorated with a horse-racing theme, the restaurant serves sandwiches, steaks and seafood. The porch dining area provides the best ambience when weather allows. Moderate.

The accent is on Florida at the Ocala Hilton's **Arthur's** (3600 Southwest 36th Avenue, Ocala; 904-854-1400). Pastel colors complement an atmosphere both open and intimate. The regional cuisine favors hometown favorites such as conch chowder, plus other American dishes like prime rib, snapper and filet mignon. Moderate to deluxe.

A bit of New Orleans sits amid the New England-style architecture in downtown Mount Dora at **The Lamp Post** (523 Donnelly Street; 904-383-6118). This showcase of wrought-iron balconies and columned esplanades, features continental-style meals prepared with care and imagination. Moderate to deluxe.

Rocking chairs sit on the wide front porch of Lakeside Inn's **Beauclair Dining Room** (100 South Alexander Street, Mount Dora; 904-383-4101). Formal elegance reigns inside, where heavy valanced curtains are tied back around windows overlooking the pastoral inn grounds. The moderate-to-deluxe-priced menu offers nouvelle entrées such as duckling and filet mignon glazed with an orange-pineapple sauce.

Behind a picket fence, **The Gables** (322 Alexander Street, Mount Dora; 904-383-8993) serves moderately priced meals in a quaint but elegant setting. Specialties include chicken cordon bleu, prime rib, aged beef and seafood.

Perched on a rising hill outside Orlando, **Townsend Plantation** (604 East Main Street, Apopka; 407-880-1313) enables diners to view grazing horses, white picket fences, restored Queen Anne buildings, a pond and floral gardens from the main dining room. The three-story building has several other dining areas—a room of white wicker and bentwood chairs, one dominated by a fireplace, and a third whose theme is a child's rumpus room. Southern-style food is served by the bowlful at moderate prices. A sampling of the house specialties: frogs' legs and pasta, Cajun alligator tail, country ham with redeye gravy and chicken with garden herbs (grown right outside the door).

"Catfish is king" proclaims the menu at the locally favored **Wekiwa Marina Restaurant** (★) (1000 Miami Springs Road, Longwood; 407-862-9640). You can find them in the clear spring waters right outside the restaurant. Inside they're fried and all-you-can-eat. In proper cracker style, barbecue ribs, frogs' legs, hushpuppies and cheese grits can also be enjoyed in the spartan riverside setting. Moderate.

ORLANDO–GAINESVILLE LOOP SHOPPING

In Sanford, the **Magnolia Mall** (1st Street and Magnolia Avenue) is an outdoor downtown renewal project that adds a little flash to this rural community. In the mall, **Delightful Finds** (407-323-3995) gathers antiques, Wedgwood china, Depression-era glass and other collectibles and gifts.

Flea World (433 North Palmetto Avenue, Sanford; 407-321-1792) peddles everything from oranges to automobiles within a 100-acre enclosed flea market. It also features an amusement park for the kids.

Jabberwocky (113 West Rich Avenue, DeLand; 904-738-3210) sells unusual old-fashioned gifts and children's games.

Gainesville reflects the sort of downtown shopping our cities used to offer before urban sprawl and mega-malls took over. Behind restored storefronts lie the boutiques, natural food restaurants and quirky shops typical of older university villages.

Modern sculpture sits in walkways at a downtown cobblestoned minimall called **Sun Center** (101 Southeast 2nd Place, Gainesville). There you'll find an interesting little costume shop called **Persona** (904-372-0455) that rents and sells masks, costumes and antique clothes, hats and jewelry.

Gainesville is known for its artists and craftsmen. A collection of their creations can be found at **Gainesville's Artisans' Guild** (806 West University Avenue; 904-378-1383).

For mall-lovers, **Gainesville Mall** (2552 Northwest 13th Street, Gainesville; 904-372-9615) features big and small shops alike.

The small gift shop at **Fred Bear Museum** (Fred Bear Drive at Archer Road, Gainesville; 904-376-2411) carries big treasure. Rare Indian and Eskimo art, archery equipment and articles of gold, jade and ivory reflect the museum's emphasis on bow-hunting and safari life.

North of Gainesville, **Wisteria Corner** (225 North Main Street, High Springs; 904-454-3555) is a treasure trove of antique objects such as furniture, vintage clothing, linens, teddy bears and farm tools. Check the old barns out back for great bargains.

For the adventurer, **The Great Outdoors Trading Co.** (65 North Main Street; 904-454-2900) supplies kayaks, backpacks, sleeping bags and other roughing-it necessities.

Paddock Mall (3100 College Road, Ocala; 904-237-1221) is the area's largest enclosed shopping center. Taking its name from Ocala's horse-farming tradition, it features a striking equestrian sculpture at the mall's center, around which cluster some 84 specialty and department stores.

Antique shops are scattered throughout the antique-looking downtown area, and found en masse at **Renningers Twin Markets** (South Route 441, Mount Dora; 904-383-8393).

The Silver Oyster (418 Donnelly Street, Mount Dora; 904-383-5556) sheds a more recent light on things with brand new china, silver and collectibles.

Schwab's Antiques (426 Donnelly Street, Mount Dora; 904-383-6030) specializes in clocks, Oriental rugs and Victorian and empire furniture.

Carol's Donnelly Shoppe (120 East 4th Avenue, Mount Dora; 904-735-0660) sells gifts of distinction: antique picture frames, jewelry and decorative lamps.

ORLANDO–GAINESVILLE LOOP NIGHTLIFE

In Sanford, listen to country music at **The Barn** (1200 South French Avenue; 407-330-4978).

Cultural entertainment can be found at **Seminole Community College** (100 Weldon Boulevard, Sanford; 407-323-1450), where concerts, plays and poetry readings are staged.

Western entertainment is presented at **Platters Lounge** (350 International Speedway Boulevard, DeLand; 904-738-5200) at the Holiday Inn. A live country band plays nightly.

Reggae music finds an enthusiastic audience in Gainesville. Try **Central City** (201 West University Avenue; 904-374-8002) for live reggae and other types of music. Cover.

Lillian's Music Store (112 Southeast 1st Street, Gainesville; 904-372-1010) is a jazzed-up urban saloon where live bands play Top-40 and '60s music.

You will find nickel beer Thursday nights and pool tables at **Players Billiards & Sports Club** (1611 Southwest 13th Street, Gainesville; 904-378-1599).

The collegiate crowd frequents **Danny's Eating and Drinking Establishment** (University Avenue and Main Street, Gainesville; 904-373-0115), a sports pub with recorded contemporary vibes.

The old, impressively preserved **Hippodrome State Theater** (25 Southeast 2nd Place, Gainesville; 904-375-4477) stars a professional cast of thespians performing classic theater.

The city's Civic Ballet dances at the **Florida Theater** (233 West University Avenue, Gainesville; 904-375-7361).

The **Ocala Civic Center** (4337 East Silver Springs Boulevard, Ocala; 904-236-2851) hosts a variety of touring musical and dramatic productions, as well as the Marion County Performing Ballet.

The Icehouse Players (11th and Unser streets, Mount Dora; 904-383-4616) stage theatrical performances throughout the year.

Tommy's Tavern (604 East Main Street, Apopka; 407-880-1313), site of a former clinic and doctor's home, now is a bar whose walls are adorned with a collection of old medicine bottles.

ORLANDO–GAINESVILLE LOOP BEACHES AND PARKS

With the exception of the Everglades, this segment of Florida gives the best view of what the state looked like before the Europeans arrived. It also contains one of the state's largest concentrations of outdoor recreational areas. Springs, lakes, forests and rolling hills provide an endless playground for sportsfolk.

Lake Monroe Park—At the spot where the St. Johns River bulges into a lake, this county park maintains unsophisticated charm beneath tunnels of spreading oak. Used mostly for boating and fishing by locals, it is quiet and secluded.

Facilities: Picnic area, restrooms, showers; groceries and restaurants nearby in Lake Monroe or DeBary; information, 407-668-6522. *Fishing:* Good.

Camping: There are 44 sites with RV hookups (ten accommodate tents); $8-$10 per night.

Getting there: Located on Route 17-92 between Sanford and DeBary.

Blue Spring State Park—Winter home of Florida's cherished manatee, this park's river shores once served as a steamboat landing. The year-round 72° waters offer refuge for St. Johns River's population of lovable one-ton sea mammals. The manatees can be seen from observation platforms built along Blue Spring Run. At certain times during the manatees' winter stay, the waters actually become crowded with the huge mammals. A tour boat, guided by a park ranger, affords more opportunity to observe them. A visitor center is located at the park's entrance.

Facilities: Picnic area, restrooms, showers, lifeguards, hiking trails, canoe rentals (904-775-6888), snack bar; limited groceries sold in park, restaurants a few miles away in DeLand or Orange City; information, 904-775-3663. *Swimming:* Good. *Fishing:* Good for large-mouth bass, bream, blue gill, crappie. *Skindiving:* Good clear waters for viewing rock formations and manatees.

Camping: There are 31 sites, 25 with RV hookups; $15.40-17.40 per night. A hike-in camp is also available for backpackers; $3 per night.

Getting there: Located at 2100 West French Avenue in Orange City.

Hontoon Island State Park—At this facility you'll see Indian mounds, bald eagles and cypress trees—all viewable from an 80-foot observation tower—and a replica of a Timucuan Indian totem that was found here. But no cars or motorcycles: this 1650-acre spit of land lies in the middle of St. Johns River and requires boat transportation to reach. A ferry comes here daily.

Facilities: Picnic area, restrooms, playground, hiking trail; groceries and restaurants several miles away in DeLand; information, 904-736-5309. *Fishing:* Good for bass, crappie and other freshwater panfish.

Camping: There are 12 tent sites; $8 per night. Also available are six rustic cabins, each accommodating up to six people; $20 per night. Reservations required.

Getting there: The ferry landing is located at 2309 Riverridge Road near DeLand.

(Text continued on page 280.)

Central Florida's Grapefruit League

In Florida, spring fever arrives early. And it hits at a fever pitch—the speed of a sizzling fastball. For this is the site of the Grapefruit League, where baseball pros turn the flab of winter into the muscle of spring. Across the Sunshine State, the month of March means hot dogs, line drives and the crack of a bat. It means baseball training season.

Grapefruit League training is serious business. Over a million fans attend the Florida games each year, bringing millions of dollars into local economies. Cities and counties vie to be chosen as spring training sites, each pitching fancy enticements to team owners. And few areas pursue the sport more aggressively than central Florida.

The most grandiose temptation was Polk County's creation of an entire city for the Kansas City Royals, which had played for years in Fort Myers. Orlando-based publishing giant Harcourt Brace Jovanovich wooed the team by building the magnificent 7000-seat **Baseball City Stadium** (Route 27 at Route 4, Baseball City; 813-424-7130) which opened in time for the 1988 season. Then, to sweeten the deal, the company built a $15-million, 43-acre baseball complex with six full-size fields, indoor batting tunnels, a minor league clubhouse and a player dorm.

The Houston Astros are kept happy in Kissimmee at the **Osceola County Stadium and Sports Complex** (1000 Bill Beck Boulevard; 407-933-5400). This top-of-the-line facility boasts four practice fields and a two-story clubhouse with conference rooms, kitchen and locker rooms.

Lakeland has managed to keep the Detroit Tigers on home turf for more than 50 years at **Joker Marchant Stadium** (North Lakeland Hills Boulevard; 813-682-1401). Little Plant City staged a ninth-inning coup when it stole the Cincinnati Reds from urban Tampa, just 15 miles to the west. Now, thousands of fans show up for practice and exhibition games at the **Cincinnati Reds Spring Training Complex** (1900 South Park Road; 813-752-1878).

Not to be stuck out in left field, Fort Myers lured the Minnesota Twins from Orlando with promises of a state-of-the-art facility. The $15 million **Lee County Sports Complex** (corner of Six Mile Parkway and

Daniels Parkway; 813-335-2342) features a 7500-seat stadium for the Twins as well as several training and community fields.

A southern agricultural neighbor of Miami, Homestead has built a premier $20 million, 6500-seat complex. The spring training site of the Cleveland Indians, this field of dreams has 14 skyboxes, an electronic press box, a restaurant and parking for 3000.

Northward on the Gold Coast, the New York Yankees call **Fort Lauderdale Stadium** (5301 Northwest 12th Avenue; 305-776-1921) home during the spring, while the Atlanta Braves and Montreal Expos share the **West Palm Beach Municipal Stadium** (715 Hank Aaron Drive; 407-683-6100 for the Braves; 407-684-6801 for the Expos).

Along Florida's East Coast, catch the New York Mets at the **St. Lucie County Sports Complex** (525 Northwest Peacock Boulevard, Port St. Lucie; 407-871-2100) or the Los Angeles Dodgers at **Holman Stadium** (4101 26th Street; 407-569-4900) in Vero Beach. The Florida Marlins, baseball's newest team, will warm up at the **Cocoa Expo** (500 Friday Road, Cocoa; 407-639-3976) until the completion of their Brevard County training site.

Over on the West Coast the Texas Rangers play at **Charlotte County Stadium** (2300 El Jobean Road, Port Charlotte; 813-625-9500), while Sarasota has the Chicago White Sox at **Ed Smith Stadium** (2700 12th Street; 813-954-4101). The Pittsburg Pirates wind up at Bradenton's **McKechnie Field** (17th Avenue and 9th Street West; 813-747-3031), the St. Louis Cardinals play ball at St. Petersburg's **Al Lang Stadium** (180 2nd Avenue Southeast; 813-822-3384), and the Philadelphia Phillies show up at **Jack Russell Stadium** (800 Phillies Drive; 813-441-8638) in Clearwater. A short pitch north, **Dunedin Stadium at Grant Field** (373 Douglas Avenue, Dunedin; 813-733-9302) is home to the Toronto Blue Jays.

Catch Florida's brand of spring fever. If you're like most fans, you'll find spring training action more intimate and even more exciting than regular season games. Call well in advance for tickets or plan to arrive around 10 a.m. for practice time. Most parks feature amateur baseball games when the big leaguers aren't around.

DeLeon Springs State Recreation Area—This park promised a fountain of youth to wintering visitors as far back as the 1890s and was named for the original seeker of anti-aging waters. A great deal of wildlife can be spotted along the nature trails here. Remains of an old Spanish sugar mill stand near the spring, a favorite local swimming hole.

Facilities: Picnic areas, restrooms, pool, restaurant; groceries are a few miles away; information, 904-985-4212. *Swimming:* Good. *Fishing:* Good.

Getting there: It's off of Route 17, seven miles north of DeLand.

Gold Head Branch State Park—This 1561-acre park claims diverse terrains, including a dramatic ravine where waters gush and the rare needle palm grows. Remains of a dam and cotton gin are visible along a nature trail. Four lakes and a marsh habitat support fox, gophers, squirrels and the rare black bear. The ravine is cool and lush, with a verdant carpet of ferns growing beneath turkey oaks and other hardwoods.

Facilities: Picnic area, restrooms, showers, backpack trails, canoe and bicycle rentals; restaurants and grocery stores are about six miles away in Keystone Heights; information, 904-473-4701. *Swimming:* Good. *Fishing:* Good for bass, crappie and bream.

Camping: There are 74 sites, 37 with RV hookups; $10-12 per night. Primitive, hike-in camping allowed at $3 per night. Also available are 12 fully equipped cabins; $50 per night. Reservations required.

Getting there: Located off Route 21, about six miles northeast of Keystone Heights.

San Felasco Hammock State Preserve—A mosaic of hilly, woodsy, swampy terrain covered with sinkholes, caves, lakes, ponds, ravines and Indian sites. This preserve provides an excellent example of Florida's precarious honeycombed underground. Along the nature trail you'll see springs being sucked out of sight, only to bubble up to the surface here and there, and disappear again. The park is named for its outstanding groves of trees, representing over 150 species.

Facilities: Nature trail; information, 904-336-2008.

Getting there: The preserve is on Route 232, four miles northwest of Gainesville.

Payne's Prairie State Preserve—A park that combines history and recreation. A visitor center unreels the area's past from 10,000 B.C., the date of its oldest Indian artifacts, through the 1600s, when the land served as the largest Spanish cattle ranch in Florida. Flora here consists mostly of the sort of spooky marshes that recall horror movies. Visitors can see the park from an observation tower or on guided tours. A swimming area is roped off in lovely Lake Wauberg, edged by a grassy beach. Bird life of all sorts abounds.

Facilities: Picnic areas, restrooms, showers, playground, hiking trail, boat ramp; groceries and restaurants nearby in Micanopy; information, 904-466-3397. *Fishing:* Good.

Camping: There are 50 sites, all with RV hookups, $10-12 per night.

Getting there: The entrance is located on Route 441 near Micanopy.

O'Leno State Park—A riverside park encompassing a variety of Florida landscapes. The Santa Fe River goes underground at a pool and then returns to the surface three miles downstream. Sinkholes, hardwood hammocks, a river swamp and sandhill communities provide diversified sightseeing along nature and canoe trails.

Facilities: Picnic areas, restrooms, showers; grocery stores and restaurants are located five miles away in High Springs; information, 904-454-1853. *Swimming:* Good. *Fishing:* Good.

Camping: There are 64 sites, all with RV hookups; $10-12 per night. A backpacking campground is also available; $3 per night.

Getting there: The park is located on Route 441 near the junction of Route 27.

Ocala National Forest—The southernmost national forest in the continental United States, this 400,000-acre, pristine terrain combines the invigorating scent of pine woods with the exotic warmth of clean spring waters. The terrain most associated with Ocala is the hot, dry lands known as The Big Scrub, which was made famous by Margaret Kinnan Rawlings in *The Yearling*. The forest's recreation areas invite bass fishermen, scuba divers, sunbathers, hikers, swimmers, campers, wildlife lovers, hunters and canoers. Deer, squirrels, raccoons and alligators dwell among the sand pine. Within the forest, several different recreational areas cluster around separate springs. For more information on the area, stop in at the Visitor Information Center (Route 40; 904-625-7470).

Camping: There are many primitive and developed campgrounds throughout the forests; prices range from no charge (backpacking camps) to $14 per night (RV hookups). Some of the developed areas include Juniper Springs, Alexander Springs and Salt Springs.

Getting there: Located on Route 40, east of Ocala.

Alexander Springs—The springs here maintain a perfectly swimmable 72° year round and are among the largest in the area. A clean, sandy beach skirts these fertile springs, which produce over 75 million gallons of fresh water daily. One of the largest deer herds in the state also headquarters among the sand pine. Nature trails and canoe runs take visitors back to unspoiled Florida.

Facilities: Picnic areas, restrooms, showers, canoe rentals, hiking trail; groceries and snack bar in park; information, 904-669-3522. *Swimming:* Excellent in spring waters. *Fishing:* Great for bass and other freshwater fish. *Skindiving:* So good, many instructors certify students here. If you're on your own, you must show a certification card to the official on duty.

Camping: There are 66 sites; $9 per night.

Getting there: Located in Ocala National Forest off Route 445.

Juniper Springs—Another natural bubbler, Juniper Springs pumps out 20 million gallons of water a day and provides recreational facilities for the outdoorsperson. This particularly lovely spot features an old wheel-powered stone mill that sits at the edge of the springs. The waters are so clear you can photograph fish darting among the lily pads. The park includes a spring-fed cement pool, edged in sandy beach.

Facilities: Picnic areas, restrooms, showers, canoe rentals; groceries and snack bars in park; information, 904-625-3147. *Swimming:* Very good; permitted in Juniper Springs pool only.

Camping: There are 79 sites; $12 per night.

Getting there: Located in Ocala National Forest on Route 40.

Salt Springs Campground—The springs here flow into Lake George, Florida's second largest lake. The warm springs have helped to create the most tropical environment in the Ocala area, with lots of palms and vibrant, blossoming flora.

Facilities: Picnic areas, restrooms, showers, groceries, canoe and boat rentals; information, 904-685-2048. *Swimming:* Good. *Fishing:* Good for striped and largemouth bass, catfish, bream, mullet and crappie.

Camping: There are 208 sites, 135 with RV hookups; primitive camping is available; $10-13 per night.

Getting there: Located in Ocala National Forest on Route 19.

Farles Prairie (★)—Visitors who want to escape the crowds at the major Ocala campgrounds should check this one out. It is one of several lightly developed sites designed for more primitive camping. The area, sheltered in pines and cleared for easy access, makes an ideal spot for campers who like to rough it a bit.

Facilities: Pit toilets; groceries and restaurants several miles away; information, 904-625-7470.

Camping: Permitted, no fee.

Getting there: Located in Ocala National Forest on Route F95.

Big Scrub (★)—A true cracker experience for hardcore escapists, this campsite is even more remote than Farles Prairie. Rolling dunes of sand provide the only shade from the scrub's aridity. Midday, you'll find even the lizards snuggled below ground, away from the desert-like heat.

Facilities: Restrooms; groceries and restaurants several miles away; information, 903-625-7470.

Camping: Permitted, no fee.

Getting there: Located in Ocala National Forest at the intersection of Routes F88 and F79.

Lake Griffin State Recreation Area—A natural boating and fishing haven on the shores of a large lake. Much of the park is marshy and not good for swimming. Locals will tell you this is the place to see "floating islands," a phenomenon caused by chunks of shoreline breaking away into the lake.

Facilities: Picnic area, restrooms, nature trail; groceries and restaurants nearby in Fruitland Park; information, 904-787-7402. *Fishing:* Good for bass and bream.

Camping: There are 40 sites, all with hookups; $15-17 per night.

Getting there: Located on Route 27 about four miles south of Fruitland Park.

Trimble Park (★)—This bird sanctuary and county recreational area lies on a peninsula jutting into Lake Beauclair. The lake, known principally to locals, is huge and beautifully trimmed in mossy oaks and cypress. You'll have to watch closely for one inconspicuous sign on Route 441 that signals the turnoff for the park, which takes you down a winding scenic road. Mainly a fishermen's mecca, this park is also a satisfying find for privacy-seeking campers.

Facilities: Picnic area, restrooms, showers, pavilions, playground, nature trails; groceries and restaurants several miles away in Mount Dora; information, 904-383-1993. *Fishing:* Good.

Camping: There are 15 sites, all with RV hookups; $11-14 per night.

Getting there: The park is located at 5802 Trimble Park Road off Earlwood Road near Mount Dora.

Kelly Park—This 200-acre county park features the highly productive clear-water Rock Spring, which has created a large swimming pool. The park shows off some of the area's loveliest natural attire of oaks and palm trees. Boardwalks have been built on some of the nature trails.

Facilities: Picnic area, restrooms, playground, nature trails; grocery stores and restaurants a few miles away; information 407-889-4179. *Swimming:* Excellent.

Camping: There are 21 sites, all with RV hookups; $11-14 per night.

Getting there: Located on Kelly Park Drive, one-half mile off Route 435 near Apopka.

Wekiwa Springs State Park—Here you'll find sand pine forest and wetlands on an extensive springs system. These spring-warmed waters have created a popular swimming spot for Orlando refugees. The area around the spring swimming pool is cemented, with wooden bridges that cross the crystalline waters and lead to a sandy beach. Trails take you through wet forests along the springs, and to various other plant communities.

Facilities: Picnic area, restrooms, showers, lifeguards, playground, hiking trails, canoe rental, snack bar; groceries and restaurants a few miles away (one nearby restaurant can be reached by canoe); information, 407-884-2009. *Swimming:* Good. *Fishing:* Good for catfish and other freshwater fish. Because of the marshes, you must fish from a boat.

Camping: There are 60 sites, all with RV hookups; $15-17 per night. Primitive camping allowed; $3 per night.

Getting there: Located off Wekiva Springs Road between Apopka and Route 4.

Orlando–Withlacoochee Loop

To explore the section of inland Florida west of Orlando, head out of town northbound, to begin a looping route that skirts the West Coast and Tampa, and returns to Orlando from the southwest. This area is known as the Green Swamp and is an important underground aquifer system in Central Florida. Typical Green Swamp terrain includes cypress marshes, sand-hills, pine forests and hardwood hammocks.

The loop tour begins at the **Florida Citrus Tower** (141 North Route 27, Clermont; 904-394-8585; admission), which offers a sweeping view of miles of fruit groves. A tram tour keeps acrophobics closer to the ground to view the same area. There's also a citrus packing plant, ice-cream shop, candy kitchen and gift shops.

View one of Florida's most recent enterprises—winemaking—at **Lakeridge Winery & Vineyards** (★) (19239 Route 27 North, Clermont; 904-394-8627). The winery opened in 1989 and uses all Florida-grown grapes. Over 40 acres of grapes have been planted for future use. Tours and samplings are offered daily.

If you go west to Bushnell, you can view the site where the Second Seminole War began at the **Dade Battlefield State Historic Site** (off State Road 476; 904-793-4781). The museum and nature trail here commemorate December 28, 1835, when a tribe of Indians ambushed troops under Major Francis L. Dade. The Dade Massacre began seven more years of bloody and costly battles in Florida.

From there you can explore the **Withlacoochee State Forest,** which lies between Inverness and Brooksville (see the "Orlando-Withlacoochee Loop Beaches and Parks" section below). Stop at the **Hernando County**

Chamber of Commerce (101 East Fort Dade Avenue, Brooksville; 904-796-2420) to find out more about the area.

Many towns in central Florida's garden belt claim a crop for their identity. In **Plant City**, the strawberry is king, with its own mid-winter Strawberry Festival. Plant City, named for Florida developer Henry Plant, is also home to the Cincinnati Reds baseball training camp (see "Central Florida's Grapefruit League" in this chapter).

Nearby, the city of Lakeland is most famous for the Frank Lloyd Wright architecture at **Florida Southern College** (11 Lake Hollingsworth Drive; 813-680-4116). The campus sits on one of the town's 13 lakes and is open to the public. Twelve buildings here were designed by Wright, including a chapel with a unique steeple and the spectacular science building with its planetarium. This is the largest concentration of Wright's architecture in the world. The renowned architect built the structures of steel, sand, glass with an eye for blending his structures into the grove and lake surroundings. For a self-guided tour map of the campus, stop at the administration building.

On Lake Morton in Lakeland, the **Polk Museum of Art** (800 East Palmetto Street; 813-688-7743) presents and ever-changing world of contemporary and classic art. The **Lakeland Area Chamber of Commerce** (35 Lake Morton Drive; 813-688-8551) distributes information on the city and its environs.

ORLANDO-WITHLACOOCHEE LOOP HOTELS

Mission Inn Golf and Tennis Resort (Howey-in-the-Hills; 904-324-3101) offers modern-day amenities with a taste of Florida's heritage. The architecture of the 189-room facility is Spanish, the vintage of the golf course is Roaring '20s, the river yacht's design is the '30s, and the concept behind the jacuzzi, marina, tennis courts and exercise room is definitely the '80s. The resort is especially known for its hilly (in Florida!) golf course. You'll also hear boasts about the multitude of bass in Lake Harris. Ultra-deluxe.

To find the most inexpensive lodging in central Florida, try one of the down-to-earth fish camps that dot nearly every lake. Some offer only RV accommodations, but many rent cabins or cottages. One such place is **Riverside Lodge** (12561 East Gulf to Lake Highway, Inverness; 904-726-2002), east of town on the Withlacoochee River. Nine cinderblock cabins are equipped with full kitchens and screened porches. Three-day minimum; budget.

The Crown Hotel (109 North Seminole Avenue, Inverness; 904-344-5555) gets its name from the collection of replicated British crown jewels it displays in its resplendent lobby of brass, wood and gold-edged mirrors. To complete the regal spell, a sword collection sits against a blue velvet background, and royalty portraiture decorates the wall of the sweeping staircase. The Crown houses 34 rooms, an English pub and restaurant, and a pool in the backyard. The cozy rooms are small but lavishly decorated with tasseled drapery and carriage lamp accents. Moderate.

Lakeland has its share of chain motels and roadhouses. One you will find tidy and pleasant is the **Bradley Motel** (3208 Route 92 East; 813-665-4065). Each of its 18 rooms comes with a kitchenette and a budget price tag.

ORLANDO–WITHLACOOCHEE LOOP RESTAURANTS

El Conquistador (Howey-in-the-Hills; 904-324-3101) matches the Spanish flavor of the Mission Inn resort, where it is located. The menu is as simple as the surroundings are elegant. The featured dishes include fettucine with shrimp in white-wine sauce, chicken marsala and veal Oscar. Moderate to deluxe.

Complete elegance graces the atmosphere at **Churchill's** (109 North Seminole Avenue, Inverness; 904-344-5555) in the fabulous Crown Hotel. Classic French fare is served in British surroundings. Regal carpeting and heavy drapery in rust and tan tones are set off with brass fixtures and crystal chandeliers. The seasonal menu features seafood, meat and poultry dishes. Deluxe.

The best deal around is found at a little cornflower blue cottage with white trim known as **The Blueberry Patch Tea Room** (414 East Liberty Street, Brooksville; 904-796-6005). Inside, the color scheme continues, complemented with white wicker, an antique stove, grandfather clock, old phonograph and other unusual pieces. For budget prices you get deluxe homemade dinners with a gourmet flair. Crab soufflés, quiches, seafood creole, salads and diet-breaking desserts such as silk and Kentucky Derby pies are some of the specialties. As for the name: you get blueberry muffins with every meal, and a different vintage tea pot sits upon each table.

One of the joys of visiting this part of Florida is taking a trip to **Buddy Freddy's** (★) (1101 Goldfinch Drive, Plant City; 813-754-5120). Here you'll happily discover the foods of home: fried chicken with volcanoes of whipped potatoes, thick-sauced chicken and dumplings, gooey macaroni and cheese and stewed lima beans. Thank Freddy for the wonderful eats, and brother Buddy (who plays host) for the friendly, neighborly ambience. Prices fall in the moderate range.

If you love steak—or even sort of like it—head for **The Red Barn** (★) (6150 New Tampa Highway, Lakeland; 813-686-2754). Still hidden to many locals, this down-home gem has earned a reputation as one of Florida's premier steakhouses. Lodged in a no-frills, 1930s dairy barn, it features a cold case piled with just-cut beef. Order from here, or from the menu that also lists chicken, seafood and ham (what else?) steak. Prices are moderate.

ORLANDO–WITHLACOOCHEE LOOP SHOPPING

Only those completely lacking in curiosity can pass up **Chez Funk** (10431 Howell Avenue, Brooksville; 904-799-8658). Sitting in a complex of curiosity shops along Route 41, it attracts customers with outrageous signs advertising "world famous 'tourist trap' art." Inside you'll find an array of used and antique glad rags.

Brooke Pottery Inc. (223 North Kentucky Avenue, Lakeland; 813-688-6844) provides an ample selection of personalized pieces.

Lakeland Square (3800 Route 98 North, Lakeland; 813-859-5411) is the area's largest enclosed mall. Among its 120 stores and shops are counted several major department stores.

ORLANDO–WITHLACOOCHEE LOOP NIGHTLIFE

There's live country music entertainment three nights a week at **Brass Rail Saloon** (1065 South Vineland Road, Winter Garden; 407-656-8300).

In quiet lakeside Inverness, nightlife begins and ends at the town hub, the Crown Hotel. **The Fox and Hounds Pub** (109 North Seminole Avenue; 904-344-5555) within provides warm surroundings for a glass of ale or a nightcap.

The Saw Mill (3425 New Jersey Road South, Lakeland; 813-647-1788) features a piano bar for easy listening music.

Looking for **Kokomo** (6606 South Florida Avenue, Lakeland; 813-644-6392)? You'll find a variety of live entertainment featured every evening here, including an all-male revue. Cover.

The cultural center of Lakeland is **Florida Southern College** (Ingraham Avenue; 813-680-4116). Call the school to find out about upcoming concerts and dance performances. The on-campus **Loca Lee Buckner Theatre** (813-680-4214) also stages a season of plays and shows.

The **Polk Museum of Art** (800 East Palmetto Street, Lakeland; 813-688-7743) hosts orchestras and performing artists.

ORLANDO–WITHLACOOCHEE LOOP BEACHES AND PARKS

Lake Louisa State Park—A preserved segment of Green Swamp, this area is an important underground aquifer system in central Florida. The park lies on the shores of Lake Louisa and also encompasses Bear Lake. Typical Green Swamp terrain is found here: cypress marshes, sandhills, pine forests and hardwood hammocks.

Facilities: Picnic area, restrooms; grocery stores and restaurants a few miles away in Clermont; information, 904-394-2280. *Swimming:* Good. *Fishing:* Good.

Getting there: Located off Route 561 south of Clermont on Lake Nellie Road.

Withlacoochee State Forest—This is the second largest state forest in Florida. Within its 113,000-plus acres, four separate tracts are designated: Forest Headquarters Tract, Croom Tract, Richloam Tract and Citrus Tract. These are subdivided into various recreation areas and forestry stations. The park focuses on the Withlacoochee and Little Withlacoochee rivers, which flow through a variety of indigenous Florida landscapes. Hiking trails penetrate the forest in several areas, allowing visitors a look at the region's diverse flora and fauna.

Facilities: Picnic areas, restrooms; grocery stores and restaurants in Inverness and Brooksville; information, 904-796-5650. *Swimming:* Good. *Fishing:* Good.

Camping: There are three main campgrounds (hookups available); $8-10 per night. Primitive camping is allowed off of the hiking trails.

Getting there: The park, which spreads through four counties, has its main entrance off Route 75 near Brooksville.

Fort Cooper State Park—This is the site of a destroyed Seminole War fort. The sandy lake beach here may not be the kind you see touted in Florida vacation brochures, but it is one of the nicest freshwater beaches of central Florida. Old Military Trail on the edge of Lake Holathlikaha leads you down the path of history, where wounded soldiers once recuperated at a hastily built fort during the Seminole wars. Vegetation includes sweet-gums, hickories and magnolias among the area's typical oak and longleaf pines.

Facilities: Picnic area, restrooms, showers, canoe and boat rentals, playground, volleyball courts, nature trail; groceries and restaurants a few miles away in Inverness; information, 904-726-0315. *Swimming:* Good. *Fishing:* Good.

Getting there: Located at 3100 South Old Floral City Road, south of Inverness.

Saddle Creek Park—A county park with a sand beach bordering the creek, Saddle Creek contains 734 acres of well-maintained camping and picnicking facilities. But because of development there's little left of nature here, nor much seclusion.

Facilities: Picnic area, restrooms, playground, nature trail; groceries and restaurants a few miles away; information, 813-665-2283. *Swimming:* Good.

Camping: There are 40 sites, half with RV hookups; $9-11 per night.

Getting there: Located on Fish Hatchery Road off Route 92 between Lakeland and Auburndale.

Orlando–Arcadia Loop

For a pleasant drive into rural Central Florida, take alternate Route 27, which veers off Route 4 south of Orlando. Here in the heartland, citrus scents the air with its blossoms in spring, its ripe juices in winter. Known as the Highlands area, this section lies along Florida's central ridge.

The quirkiness of **Lake Wales** can be seen by its main attractions: an eccentric dollhouse-like country inn, a singing tower and a "spooked" hill. Start exploring the area north of town at the first of these, **Chalet Suzanne Inn Village (★)** (Chalet Suzanne Road, Lake Wales; 813-676-6011), and have a peek at the quaint Old World restaurant, inn, gift shops and ceramic studio. Tours can be arranged through the soup cannery, where the restaurant's trademark dishes are canned. Its signature romaine soup was sent to space with Apollo 16. In the tiny ceramic studio in the midst of the meandering cobblestone village, you can watch craftspeople making dishware and personalized gifts.

A trip to **Bok Tower Gardens (★)** (Route 17A, Lake Wales; 813-676-1408; admission) is a treat for the senses: exotic blossoms scent leaf-paved paths, and squirrels chatter atop towering oaks. Here, in 1928 Dutch immigrant Edward Bok built a 200-foot carillon tower of Georgia marble and St. Augustine coquina stone to show his appreciation for the beauty he felt America had brought into his life. He planted the 128 acres around the "singing tower" in magnolias, azaleas and plants from the Orient to create an atmosphere of peace. The carillon, a registered historic structure, rings out classic harmonies every half hour to add a special magic to this place.

The thing we found spookiest about **Spook Hill** (North Avenue and 5th Street, Lake Wales) was the convoluted route you must take to get there if you follow the signs. To make it simpler, take a left on North Avenue when returning to town from Bok Gardens. At the bottom of the hill, you must turn around to experience the mystery here: "spooks" power your car back up the hill. A legend accompanies the mystery.

Lake Wales itself is a pretty little town that lassoes a lake. For a scenic view of the water and its lakeside mansions and park, follow **Lakeshore Boulevard**. The history of the area, including the building of the railroad that settled inland Florida, can be seen at **Lake Wales Museum** (325 South Scenic Highway, Lake Wales; 813-676-5443). The museum, housed in the city's first structure, sits next to a historic railroad car.

Also surrounded by lovely lakes, Avon Park offers a single formal attraction, the **Avon Park Museum** (3 North Museum Avenue; 813-453-3525). An old Seaboard Coast Lines railroad depot houses a homely little museum containing memorabilia of the area's development.

Sebring is best known for its **Sebring International Raceway** (813-655-1442), where the 12-Hour Endurance Race is held each March. Aside from the roar of engines, this is a pretty lake-mottled town blending a sense of heritage, a touch of sophistication and an outdoors orientation. For more information, stop at the **Greater Sebring Chamber of Commerce** (309 South Circle, Sebring; 813-385-8448).

At the crossroads of Routes 27 and 70, head west toward Arcadia. As you approach the city, you'll probably notice an increase in pickup trucks. This town is the center for area ranchers. The state's oldest rodeo, the **All-Florida Championship Rodeo** (813-494-2014), has been held in Arcadia since 1929.

Downtown Arcadia has been restored to its railroad days. **The Depot** (4 West Oak Street) was redone to house museum items, photos and train paraphernalia. Stop in and ask for a tour.

For a lovely sidetrip into Florida's deeper past, visit **Myakka River State Park** (13207 Route 72, east of Sarasota; 813-361-6511), which remains virtually the same as it did before the state was settled. To tour this massive region of pristine lakes, rivers, marshes and forest, **Myakka Wildlife Tours** (813-365-0100) takes tram safaris and airboat tours into the woods and swamps.

Following Route 17 back north out of Arcadia, you will catch glimpses of the aptly named Peace River. This shallow waterway offers an off-the-civilized-path view of backwoods Florida as the Indians knew it, via canoe. **Canoe Outpost–Peace River** (Arcadia; 813-494-1215) will arrange equipment and transportation for any length trip you have in mind, all the way up to Bartow. The river trip reveals nature in the raw. Cypress knees and alligator snouts break the surface of the calm waters. Armadillos and deer scurry alongside the banks, while cranes and herons pick minnows from the shallows. Live oaks tower, supporting their own mini-forests of air plants, epiphytes, mistletoe and Spanish moss.

Pioneer Park (Routes 64 and 17, Zolfo Springs; 813-735-0330) is a modest preservation-recreational area that features board-and-batten structures from the area's frontier days. Located on the Peace River, it is also a popular canoeing and fishing spot.

For an entirely unusual sidetrip to a bizarre kingdom, visit **King Solomon's Castle** (Solomon's Road, Lily; 813-494-6077), west of Zolfo Springs off Route 665. It's hard to say which entertains more, the three-story castle built of offset-press plates and other articles scavenged from the junk yard, the creekside natural trail, or artist Howard Solomon—the self-proclaimed ruler in this world removed from reality. Once dubbed the "DaVinci of Debris," Solomon has created imaginative stained-glass and second-life works that are truly inspired.

One of Florida's oldest and most popular destinations for travelers is **Cypress Gardens** (Route 540, Winter Haven; 813-324-2111; admission), with its lush scenery and water sports. The gardens are peopled with hoop-skirted southern belles, human pyramids on skis and air dancing on the high wire with "Captain Robins Flying Circus." Kodak's "Island in the Sky" takes you on a ride to a world towering 16 stories above the botanical gardens. On the grounds you'll also find an old Southern town that harks back to the antebellum era, and Lake Eloise where a world-famous waterski revue is staged. This precursor of modern amusement parks offers at least a day's worth of entertainment: visitors can stroll through the gardens or board canal boats.

An unusual museum found in Winter Haven is the **Water Ski Museum and Hall of Fame (★)** (799 Overlook Drive; 813-324-2472). The memorabilia, photos and literature here trace the development of waterskiing from 1922, when the sport was born at Lake Pepin, Minnesota, to modern times.

ORLANDO–ARCADIA LOOP HOTELS

The prestigious **Grenelefe Resort** (3200 State Road 546, Grenelefe; 813-422-7511) offers an entire vacation on its grounds. Hidden among Florida highland hills, its woodsy 1000 acres cling to the shores of ample Lake Marion. The resort takes its Robin Hood theme from the lake's name, with roads dubbed Nottingham Way and Robyn Lane and a café called Camelot's Patio. Three golf courses, 20 tennis courts, four swimming pools, nature trails, two restaurants, a lounge, a marina stocked with rental boats and fishing guides keep guests active. The resort holds 950 modern, roomy suites and villas. Ultra-deluxe.

Old World eclecticism reigns at quirky **Chalet Suzanne Country Inn** (Lake Wales; 813-676-6011). Squeezed in among hills of citrus groves, the inn features 30 rooms personalized with a mix of Scandinavian and Mediterranean styles. Red brick and wrought iron architecture is accented by cobblestone walkways in the courtyard. A swimming pool, specialty shops and private lake are added attractions. Deluxe to ultra-deluxe.

Guests can have a Western-style vacation at **River Ranch** (Route 60, Lake Wales; 813-692-1321). Dude ranch activities include a bridle path and carriage rides, and the facility features tennis, horseshoes, badminton, golf and a health club. Accommodations include RV sites, efficiencies, suites and luxury cottages. Outdoor barbecues, wild west saloons and rodeo shows complete this new concept in Florida vacationing. Moderate to deluxe.

For something less ostentatious, try the **Big Oak Motel** (3618 Alternate Route 27 North, Lake Wales; 813-676-7427). This eight-unit row motel puts its back to Lake Starr; the end room has a view of the lake. The budget-priced rooms are neat, with friendly little touches here and there. All have kitchenettes.

You don't even have to sleep to feel rested at **Lake Brentwood Motel** (2060 Route 27 North, Avon Park; 813-453-4358). A calm and clear lake laps at the property's back door, and rowboats sit in waiting for guests to use free-of-charge. The 14 units double up two to a cinderblock cottage and go for budget rates. Generous trees shade lawn chairs that induce an immediate drop in blood pressure.

Back again by popular demand, the **Kenilworth Lodge** (836 Southeast Lakeview Drive, Sebring; 813-385-0111) is a restored Sebring landmark. This time around it's been reincarnated as an imposing bed and breakfast of 137 rooms. Its distinctive double-towered face overlooks Lake Jackson across the street. The enormous lobby shows its age with a grand blackened-brick fireplace, a majestic staircase and a potbelly stove. Modern touches include rattan and floral furnishings and dhurrie rugs. Room decor also blends old and new. A swimming pool, restaurant and an old-time sitting porch complete the amenities of this historic inn. Budget to moderate.

Safari Inn (1406 Route 27 North, Sebring; 813-382-1148) tries to simulate a lot of character with witch-capped buildings and a lobby full of jungle skins and statues. Somehow the place just comes off as a glorified motor lodge. Rates for the 37 units dwell in the moderate range. There's a swimming pool for all guests to use.

Lake Roy Motor Lodge (1823 Cypress Gardens, Winter Haven; 813-324-6320) is not only down the street from its hometown attraction, Cypress Gardens, it also has a white sand beach to brag about. The rooms are carpeted and paneled in dark, less-than-modern shades and textures. But you can't beat the view of the lake. Most of the 34 units are apartments with full kitchens and rent in the moderate range. Watercraft of every variety can be rented on the premises to take full advantage of the chain of lakes the lodge borders.

ORLANDO-ARCADIA LOOP RESTAURANTS

Chalet Suzanne Restaurant (Chalet Suzanne Road, Lake Wales; 813-676-6011) is legendary for its fine cuisine, served in a Swiss-style chalet. Its signature romaine soup is canned on the premises as are other soups bearing the Chalet Suzanne label. The tables, set with fine European china, offer either a stunning overlook of the lake or seclusion behind stained-glass walls. Chicken Suzanne, curried shrimp, shad roe and lobster Newburg are among the proffered entrées. Ultra-deluxe.

One of the loveliest places to eat in all of Florida is on the patio of the **Garden Café** (Route 17A, Lake Wales; 813-676-1408) at Bok Tower Gardens. Here, with a view of the chiming pink monument and its surrounding green-and-floral al fresco decor, you feel cut off from modern tempos. The fare is nothing more than counter-service sandwiches, soup and hot dogs, but the pastoral ambience and serenades from Bok Tower can't be beat by the swankiest restaurant. Budget.

A spot of great local repute, the **Olympic Restaurant** (504 Route 27 North, Avon Park; 813-452-2700) seems to serve the entire town at lunchtime. The dining area is a couple of sprawling rooms with some Greek pictures on the wall. The food is plain good eating: budget-priced country-fried chicken, fried seafood platter, barbecue spare ribs, spaghetti and sandwiches.

To eat where the locals do in Arcadia, get over to **Wheeler's Goody Café** (13 South Monroe Avenue, 813-494-3909). This side-street spot features typical diner decor—a formica counter with wooden stools, and china plates on the walls. The budget-priced menu is covered with denim and offers cracker dishes such as country-fried steak, baked sausage and rice, hot roast beef sandwiches and ten different varieties of homemade pies.

While visiting Myakka State Park, you may want to make the short trip to an unusual backroads haunt known as **Snook Haven** (★) (off River Road, Venice; 813-485-7221). Sitting right on the Myakka River, this local secret is known for its Sunday barbecue picnics, Friday night fish fries and legend of the Killer Turtles: local lore has it that a rare species of tree-climbing turtle inhabits nearby woods, and that they can fall on people, with fatal results. Regardless, exploring the grounds is part of the experience here. Simple fare such as fish, burgers and chicken wings is available all week. Budget.

Tasty seafood and prime steaks have given **Christy's Sundown** (Route 17 South, Winter Haven; 813-293-0069) its top billing with locals and critics. Antiques and works of art combine to create a Mediterranean mood. Lobster, stone crab, shish kebab, Kansas City steaks and Alaskan King crab run in the moderate price range.

ORLANDO–ARCADIA LOOP SHOPPING

In Chalet Suzanne Restaurant's **Gift Shop** (Chalet Suzanne Road, Lake Wales; 813-676-9003), you can buy gift packages of assorted Chalet Suzanne soups, homemade bottled sauces and sets of the restaurant's special dishware. Also within the village at Chalet Suzanne, the **Antique Chapel** sells elegant antique glass and dishware.

The **Bok Tower Gardens Gift Shop** (Route 17A, Lake Wales; 813-676-1408) offers a unique selection of giftware relating to the singing tower and its gardens: recorded carillon and classical music, bells and chimes, nature books, floral and Scandinavian rosemaling crafts.

Among the barrage of citrus and souvenir shops in central Florida, the **Fruitree** (Highway 27 South at Route 542, Dundee; 813-439-1396) is king of the heap. In one stop you can buy all the bagged oranges, bottled jellies, cypress clocks and "I was here" gifts you could possibly need.

In Arcadia, buy your cowboy boots at the **American Shoe Shop** (112 West Oak Street; 813-494-3911). One of Arcadia's many antique dealers is **Townsend Antiques** (5 East Oak Street; 813-494-2137).

Phyl's Lemonade Stand (132 West Oak Street, Arcadia; 813-494-3606) sells greeting cards with a cowboy theme and an extensive selection of collectibles and modern glassware. **The Grapevine** (104 West Oak Street, Arcadia; 813-494-3598) sells boutique fashions for children and adults.

The Christmas spirit lives year-round at **Tis The Season** (602 Route 1792 North, Haines City; 813-421-2363), which features wreaths, garlands and additional festive goodies.

ORLANDO–ARCADIA LOOP NIGHTLIFE

Lake Wales Little Theater (411 3rd Street North, Lake Wales; 813-676-1266) stages community theater performances.

Afternoon cultural events are regularly hosted at **Bok Tower Gardens** (Route 17A, Lake Wales; 813-676-1408), including recitals and special gala events that celebrate the blossoming of certain flowers.

ORLANDO-ARCADIA LOOP BEACHES AND PARKS

Lake Kissimmee State Park—A 5000-acre lakeland that features a reconstructed cow camp of the 1870s. Two other lakes named Tiger and Rosalie keep the great Kissimmee company in this out-of-the-way wildlife haven. A trail along the park's scrubland features scenes and exhibitions of life in the year 1876, when cowboys herded scrub cows here. History comes alive as cattle herders re-enact their 19th-century ways. The park also features hiking trails and an observation deck overlooking Lake Kissimmee, and it's a good place to spot the area's rich wildlife. Bald eagles are relatively common here, keeping company with squirrels, quail, ospreys, sandhill cranes, alligators and white-tailed deer.

Facilities: Picnic areas, restrooms, showers, hiking trails; restaurants and grocery stores are several miles away in Lake Wales; information, 813-696-1112. *Fishing:* Good for bream, bass, etc.

Camping: There are 60 sites, half with RV hookups; $12-14 per night.

Getting there: Located at 14248 Camp Mack Road, 15 miles east of Lake Wales.

Lake Arbuckle Park (★)—A secluded, rustic fishing and camping haven sitting on Lake Arbuckle. The park's seven acres feature cypress- and oak-studded grounds.

Facilities: Picnic area, restrooms; groceries and restaurants several miles away; information, 813-635-2811. *Fishing:* Good for crappie, bass, bream, etc.

Camping: There are 58 sites, 38 with RV hookups; $7-9 per night.

Getting there: Located eight miles off Lake Reedy Boulevard east of Frostproof.

Highlands Hammock State Park—Alligators and orchids can be seen from a "trackless train" that tours the cypress swamps and semitropical jungles in this popular park. Hiking trails also travel some of its 3800 acres, and a paved bicycling loop traverses the hammock. The park is named for the high, forested terrain found on Florida's central ridge. White-tailed deer herd here, and otters, Florida scrub jays plus an occasional bald eagle and Florida panther can be found.

Facilities: Picnic areas, restrooms, playgrounds, bike rentals, nature trails; information, 813-385-0011.

Camping: There are 138 sites, 113 with RV hookups; $13-15 per night.

Getting there: Located west of Sebring off Route 27 at the end of Hammock Road.

Myakka River State Park—A large recreational and wildlife refuge area bordering both river and lake. This beautiful, pristine park of 28,875 acres includes mossy laurel oaks along the river, butterfly orchids, saw palmettos and pop ash. Log cabin structures serve as picnic pavilions. Deer, turkey, wood storks, sandhill cranes, owls and sapsuckers populate the forest. A wilderness preserve of 7500 acres restricts the number of visitors who enter this area of pure old Florida panoramas.

Facilities: Picnic area, interpretative center, pavilions, excursion airboat and tram tours (813-365-0100), canoe and boat rentals, bicycle rentals, nature trails, snack bar and grocery concessions; information, 813-361-6511. *Fishing:* Good for bass, bream and catfish.

Camping: There are 76 sites, half with Rv hookups; $14-16 per night.

Getting there: The main entrance is located at 13207 Route 72, about 17 miles east of Sarasota. A north entrance on Route 780 is open only on weekends and holidays.

Orlando to Okeechobee Area

This final route leaving Orlando takes you to Florida's most secluded areas, south toward the Everglades and the southwest Gulf Coast.

Heading south out of Orlando, Route 441 is part of The Florida Cracker Trail. The names of towns along the way sound cowboy-inspired: Holopaw and Yeehaw Junction. The name **Lake Okeechobee** is of Indian invention and means "big water," an apt title for the state's largest inland body of water. The town that borrows its name, Okeechobee, is known as the speckled perch (more commonly known as crappie) capital of the world.

The lake itself, the second largest freshwater lake within United States boundaries, covers 750 square miles. With most of the region's waterways flowing into it, Lake Okeechobee in turn serves as a major source of water for southern Florida.

The city of **Clewiston** perches on the southwest edge of Lake Okeechobee like a fisherman on the high seat of a bass boat—something you see much of in this famous fishing mecca. Surrounding the lake is a skirt of fertile mucklands, which Clewiston puts to use sweetening its economy with sugar cane. The city pays homage to the crop that has lifted it above the poverty of neighboring towns. Besides the Sugarland Highway and a football arena called Cane Field, there are local shops selling stalks of cane and other sweet souvenirs.

West of Clewiston a fork in the road gives you a choice between staying on Route 27 to explore the wildlife and unusual attractions of Fisheating Creek, or heading to the town of **LaBelle,** known for its annual Swamp Cabbage Festival. This mid-winter event honors the state tree, the sabal palm, whose insides are now known at trendy delis as hearts of palm, but which old crackers simply called swamp cabbage. The festival features displays of Seminole Indian arts and food, clogging shows and stewed swamp cabbage.

If you opt to head north, near the little town of Palmdale you'll find two unusual attractions that represent the endurance of cracker life. The **Cypress Knee Museum** (Routes 27 and 29, Palmdale; 813-675-2951) displays nature's best sculptured masterpieces. Given such titles as "Mother and Child," "FDR" and "Flipper," cypress knees are the knobby protuberances that allow the submerged roots of the cypress tree to breathe. In the center of the museum grows the world's largest transplanted cypress. A cypress swamp and an oak and palm hammock lie along a boardwalk.

Gatorama (Route 27, Palmdale; 813-675-0623; admission) celebrates one of Florida's oldest natives in the way they did it before the big parks came along. Looking like so many other exploitive roadside attractions, this one is low-key, soft-sell. You see 'gators, of course, and crocodiles, wild cats, flamingos and peacocks. That's all. No ferris wheels. No animation.

Also near Palmdale, you can find **Babcock Wilderness Adventures** (Route 31, Babcock; 813-656-6104; admission). This spot combines a nature tour with a history lesson aboard a swamp buggy. Visitors penetrate secluded cypress swamp and hear about the area's bygone ranching days. The starring attraction is a new group of panthers.

ORLANDO TO OKEECHOBEE AREA HOTEL

The town of Clewiston actually defines itself by the colonial, pillared **Clewiston Inn Hotel** (109 Royal Palm Avenue; 813-983-8151), rebuilt in 1937 after fire destroyed it. Painted sugar white and sporting wildlife murals, the inn on Lake Okeechobee tells the town's history—where once the

Everglades encroached, now sugarcane fields flourish. The 53 rooms are simple and comfortable. A restaurant and bar are located within. Moderate.

ORLANDO TO OKEECHOBEE AREA RESTAURANTS

The **Old South Room** (109 Royal Palm Avenue, Clewiston; 813-983-8151) in the Clewiston Inn is set back in the hotel's sugarcane heyday of 1926. Shuttered windows, sugar-white linen and ladderback chairs create a Southern ambience. The moderately priced menu includes 'gator tail, catfish, steaks and chicken.

You can't miss **Old South Bar-B-Q** (Route 27, Clewiston; 813-983-7756). The forest of wooden Burma-Shave-style signs promise the type of good food one expects from a barbecue joint. As much a tourist attraction as a food service, the restaurant is a veritable museum of frontier Florida artifacts. For budget-to-moderate tabs you can get your fill of barbecued vittles, catfish, hushpuppies and hot apple pie.

ORLANDO TO OKEECHOBEE AREA SHOPPING

Touch of Country (202 Sugarland Highway, Clewiston; 813-983-5050) carries baskets, potpourri, stuffed animals and other pretty gifts.

The **Cypress Knee Museum** (Routes 27 and 29, Palmdale; 813-675-2951) includes a gift shop where you can purchase peeled cypress knees (an early Florida art form), a glass table with a cypress base or other related articles.

ORLANDO TO OKEECHOBEE AREA NIGHTLIFE

The Everglades Lounge (108 Royal Palm Avenue, Clewiston; 813-983-8151) in the Clewiston Inn features a wildlife mural and old-fashioned socializing.

Another good place for a cold brew in Clewiston is **The Pub** (210 West Sugarland Highway; 813-983-9511).

ORLANDO TO OKEECHOBEE AREA BEACHES AND PARKS

Prairie Lakes Refuge (★)—Eight thousand acres of well-protected wet forest and grasslands that shelter diverse animal species. The endangered sandhill crane favors the area's habitat, as do alligators, deer and a variety of migratory birds. Three lakes border the park: Kissimmee, Jackson and Marian. The preserve's principal purpose is protecting animal life; facilities for people are purposely sparse and geared toward the backpacker.

Facilities: Picnic areas, pit toilets, nature trails; groceries and restaurants several miles away; information, 904-732-1225 *Fishing:* Good.

Camping: Permitted in three primitive campgrounds; no fee. Permit and two-week advance reservation are required. Bring potable water.

Getting there: The refuge is located on Route 523, 11 miles northwest of Kenansville.

Okee-Tantee Recreation Area—Basically an RV park on Lake Okeechobee, the state's largest inland body of water, known for its large fish population. The lake is the big attraction here; the rest of the terrain is virtually arid grasslands. A security fence fails to add much to the ambience.

Facilities: Picnic area, restrooms, showers, boat rental, groceries and restaurants; information, 813-763-2622. *Fishing:* Good.

Camping: There are 215 sites, most with RV hookups; $15.90-21.20 per night.

*Getting there:*Okee-Tantee is located at 10430 Route 78 West, south of Okeechobee.

Pahokee Marina and Campground—A small preserve on a strip of shoreline at Florida's mammoth Lake Okeechobee, the geological center of a fertile agricultural area. Camping sites fall along the lake's shoreline, which has been dammed to prevent flooding. The marina provides a good fishing spot for the area's boast—speckled perch. Vegetation is mostly Australian pines.

Facilities: Restrooms; groceries and restaurants nearby; information, 407-924-7832. *Swimming:* Good. *Fishing:* Good.

Camping: There are 103 sites, 64 with RV hookups; $10-12 per night.

Getting there: Located on Route 441 at Pahokee.

Loxahatchee National Wildlife Refuge—The northernmost introduction to Everglades territory and its unique ecosystem. Airboats are your magic carpet through this alligator and panther homeland that comprises 146,000 acres. Visitors will learn about the fragile world that thrives within the life-giving swamp waters of the Everglades. Mangroves, sawgrass, cattails and some cypress grow in this animal refuge. The highly endangered Everglade kite nests here, along with various snakes, such as the Everglades racer and yellow rat snake.

Facilities: Restrooms, interpretative center, walking tours, nature trails, boat and canoe rentals; groceries and restaurants several miles from the entrances; information, 407-734-8303. *Fishing:* Good, especially for bass.

Getting there: There are two entrances. Park headquarters lie off Route 441 near the town of Loxahatchee. The southern end can be reached from Lox Road north of Hillsboro Boulevard near Delray Beach.

The Sporting Life

SPORTFISHING

Visitors staying near Disney World can hook up with a fishing charter through **Fort Wilderness Campground** (407-824-2900). Also in the Orlando area, **Bass Bustin' Guide** (5935 Swoffield Drive, Orlando; 407-281-0845) guarantees fish.

Chuck Matthews (5280 Haywood Ruffin Road, St. Cloud; 407-892-7184) takes bass fishing charters into the Kissimmee-area Chain of Lakes. A long-time fishing guide on Lake Okeechobee, **Eddie Clay** (Okeechobee; 813-763-2785) specializes in catching bass.

BOATING

See the "real" Florida as pilot of your own airboat at **Airboat Rentals U-Drives** (4266 Vine Street, Kissimmee; 407-847-3672). **Sanford Boat Rentals** (Sanford; 407-321-5906) rents houseboats and pontoons. **Rusty Anchor** (Mount Dora; 904-383-3933) also rents motorboats.

HOUSEBOATING

Along the St. Johns River, houseboating is a popular pastime that combines sightseeing with lodging. Houseboat arrangements can be made at **Sanford Boat Rentals** (4370 Carraway Place, Sanford; 407-321-5906) or **Hontoon Landing Marina** (2317 River Ridge Road, DeLand; 904-734-2474).

WATERSKIING, WINDSURFING AND PARASAILING

Orange Lake Watersports (8505 West Route 192, Kissimmee; 407-239-4444) takes you waterskiing and rents jet skis in Florida's land of lakes. You can rent a small boat or be schooled in windsurfing, parasailing, waterskiing and jet skiing at **Splash-N-Ski** (10000 Turkey Lake Road, Orlando; 407-352-1494).

CANOEING

Central Florida waterways provide prime canoeing.

In the Disney area, canoes can be rented at **Fort Wilderness Campground** (Vista Drive, Walt Disney World, Lake Buena Vista; 407-824-2900).

Northwest of Orlando, there's **King's Landing** (5714 Baptist Camp Road, Apopka; 407-886-0859).

Near Sanford, **Katie's Wekiva River Landing** (190 Katie's Cove, Sanford; 407-322-4470) provides livery and equipment service for canoeing trips. **Santa Fe Canoe Outpost** (High Springs; 904-454-2050) outfits canoers for trips on the Santa Fe River.

Over 45 miles of canoe runs have been established in **Ocala National Forest** (Route 40, Ocala). Canoes can be rented at **Alexander Springs Recreation Area** (904-669-3522), **Juniper Springs Recreation Area** (904-625-2808) and **Salt Springs Recreation Area** (904-685-2185).

Oklawaha Outpost (off Route 316, Fort McCoy; 904-236-4606) rents canoes, kayaks and equipment and provides livery service for trips on the Oklawaha River in Ocala National Forest.

The **Withlacoochee River RV Park** (State Road 575, Withlacoochee; 904-583-4778) rents canoes for paddling trips in the area. The **Nobleton Canoe Outpost** (Route 476, Nobleton; 904-796-4343) arranges trips on the Withlacoochee River ranging from two hours to one week in length.

Canoe Outpost–Peace River (Route 661, Arcadia; 813-494-1215) is an excellent canoe outfitter. You can choose from a number of trips on the shallow Peace River, ranging from day trips to overnighters requiring up to 30 hours of paddling.

You can rent canoes at **Myakka River State Park** (13207 State Road 72, east of Sarasota; 813-361-6511), famous for the great canoeing possibilities along the river and in its lakes.

HORSEBACK RIDING

Horseback riding provides a unique and popular mode for experiencing inland forests. Many state parks in this area have blazed bridle paths, but you must bring your own mount. Following are some places you can rent horses.

Poinciana Horse World (3705 Poinciana Boulevard, Kissimmee; 407-847-4343) rents horses.

In Ocala's fertile horse farming country, you can jump into the saddle at **Oakview Stable** (Southwest 27th Avenue, Ocala; 904-237-8844).

Myakka Valley Campground and Stables, Inc. (7220 Myakka Valley Trail, east of Sarasota; 813-924-8435) rents horses to ride on its trails and provides tent sites and showers for equestrian campers.

GOLF

Walt Disney World (Lake Buena Vista; 407-824-2270) boasts three championship courses. Nearby **Poinciana Golf & Racquet Club** (500 Cypress Parkway, Kissimmee; 407-933-5300) allows public play.

In Orlando, the **Alhambra Golf Club** (4700 South Texas Avenue; 407-851-6250) is open to the public.

In Sanford, you can golf at the **Mayfair Country Club** (Highway 46A; 407-322-2531).

Golden Ocala Golf Course (7300 Highway 27, Ocala; 904-622-0198) is famous for its replication of eight internationally known holes, including the St. Andrew's 1, the first hole ever played.

In Lakeland, **Skyview Golf Course** (1100 Skyview Boulevard; 813-665-4005) has 18 holes.

Sebring Shore Golf and Country Club (603 Lake Sebring Drive; 813-385-1923) is open to the public.

Haine City's **Sun Air Golf and Country Club** (50 Sun Air Boulevard East; 813-439-1576) welcomes area golfers.

In the Lake Okeechobee area, tee off at **Clewiston Golf Course** (1200 San Luiz, Clewiston; 813-983-7064).

TENNIS

In the Orlando area, try the **Orange Lake Country Club Resort** (8505 Route 192, Kissimmee; 407-239-0000).

The courts at **Oak Street Park** (Oak Street, Kissimmee) feature tennis, racquetball and lighted facilities.

In Mount Dora, you will find public courts at 6th and Donnelly streets, and at 11th and Unser streets.

Public tennis courts lie within **Dade Battlefield State Historic Site** (off County Road 476, Bushnell; 904-793-4781). In Lakeland, eight courts are open to the public at **Scott Kelly Recreation Complex** (404 Imperial Boulevard; 813-644-2467).

BICYCLING

The best biking in the Orlando area is at **Walt Disney World.** There are no bike paths, but the roads are safe for scenic rides along lakes and forests outside the bustle of Magic Kingdom and EPCOT.

Bike paths weave around many of Orlando's lakes, such as at **Turkey Lake Park** (3401 Hiawassee Road; 407-299-5594). Bike paths also circle many of the lakes and parks in the Kissimmee area, and in Winter Park, Sanford and Lake Wales.

The university area of Gainesville provides special lanes and paths for bicyclers. **Highlands Hammock State Park** (Hammock Road, Sebring; 813-385-0011) has bike trails and rentals. **Myakka River State Park** (13207 Route 72, east of Sarasota; 813-361-6511) allows biking on its many backwoods roads.

BIKE RENTALS The **Fort Wilderness Bike Barn** (Walt Disney World, Lake Buena Vista; 407-824-2742) at the Disney campground rents bikes.

In Orlando, try the bicycle rental concession stand at **Turkey Lake Park** (3401 Hiawassee Road; 407-299-5594).

Bikes and More (2133 Northwest 6th Street; 904-373-6574) services bike renters in the Gainesville area.

Highlands Hammock State Park (Hammock Road, Sebring; 813-385-0011) and **Myakka River State Park** (13207 Route 72, Sarasota; 813-361-6511) also rent bicycles.

HIKING

Florida hiking approaches its finest here in the land of lakes, springs and forests. Over 200 miles of the statewide **Florida Trail** zigzag through this primeval belt, augmented by a smorgasbord of short jaunts in the area's many state, county and city parks.

DOWNTOWN AND NORTH ORLANDO TRAILS **Tosohatchee State Reserve Trails** (27 miles) provide an easy to moderate tour of the St. Johns River in total seclusion. Hikers can see diverse wildlife, as the gray fox, hawk, bobcat, owl and turkey all call the preserve home.

SOUTH ORLANDO TRAILS **Turkey Lake Park** (7 miles) provides a moderate hike inside Orlando. The system of nature trails here borders Turkey Lake with its live oak hammocks and cattail marshes.

ORLANDO-GAINESVILLE LOOP TRAILS **Blue Spring State Park Trail** (4 miles) winds gently through hardwood hammocks, swamp marsh, sand pine scrub and flatwoods, ending at the park's primitive campground. The easy trail views mostly vegetation, although an occasional squirrel or raccoon can be seen.

Gold Head Branch State Park (3 miles) comprises a section of the Florida Trail. The habitat is much the same as at Blue Spring, except for the park's outstanding ravine, which allows 1.4 miles of cool respite. The trail also skirts the swimming area on Lake Johnson.

The **Natural Bridge Hiking Trail** (13 miles) winds through O'Leno State Park north of High Springs. It crosses the natural land bridge known as River Sink, where the Sante Fe river flows subterraneously, and the River Rise, where it reappears. A portion of the trail takes historic paths, such as the one along Wire Road where the first telegraph lines were strung. The whole gamut of northern Florida wildlife lies along this path.

The **Ocala Trail** (66 miles), a portion of the 1300-mile-long Florida Trail, travels the length of the Ocala National Forest. It is the largest continuous trail on public property in the state. White-tailed deer are the stars of the animal show here, appearing in abundance. The forest is also home to the endangered red-cockaded woodpecker.

Hikers are also allowed to use the **Ocala One-Hundred Mile Horse Trail,** which is divided into three sections: the 40-mile Prairie Trail, the 40-mile Flatwoods Trail and the 20-mile Baptist Lake Trail. These are all loop trails for which the trailheads are located off Route 19, about two miles north of Altoona.

The **Timucuan Indian Trail** (1.8 miles), in Ocala Forest's Alexander Springs Recreation Area, takes you on a self-guided tour of the lives of Florida's ancient Indian tribes. The trail skirts the springs pool, then loops back through marsh and hardwood vegetation.

The **Wekiwa Springs** section of the Florida Trail (13.5 miles) traverses the state park located along the springs. Hikers can enjoy the wet world of limestone cavern springs; they can also spot cranes, herons and owls as well as the endangered gopher tortoise and indigo snake.

ORLANDO-WITHLACOOCHEE LOOP TRAILS The **Croom Hiking Trail** (29 miles) in the Withlacoochee State Forest traverses abandoned rock mines, prairies and ravines. The easy terrain follows the Withlacoochee River and then loops off into three different paths.

At **Richloam Tract** (31 miles) a looping trail takes you through a low-lying, more densely timbered section of Withlacoochee. The moderately difficult trail runs along the Withlacoochee River and its little brother and crosses various streams and creeks.

McKethan Lake Nature Trail (2 miles) is a less ambitious Withlacoochee hike that circles a small fishing lake. It lies within the Forest Headquarters Tract of the state forest, between Brooksville and Inverness. Don't be fooled by its shortness. Hikers still get an eyeful of various lovely terrains as this path explores bottomlands, hardwood hammocks and pinelands brightened by wildflowers and magnolias.

ORLANDO-ARCADIA LOOP TRAILS **Lake Kissimmee State Park**'s (12.5 miles) contribution to the Florida Trail consists of double loops. The first travels through the pine and scrubby flatwoods of Buster Island. Along the north loop, hikers can view the remains of an old cemetery and turpentine-producing operation.

The **Caloosa Nature Trail** at Babson Park Audubon Center, north of Babson Park, is a self-guided hike that points out different species of indigenous plant life, such as the papaw, golden rod and muscadine grape. Abundant animal life includes fox, rabbits, gopher tortoises and various birds.

In **Myakka State Park** (38 miles), the Florida Trail Association has developed a network of scenic footpaths divided into four loops. The landscape ranges from high and dry to low and marshy, the trail difficulty from easy to moderate. Many native species find refuge here, including alligators, otters, bald eagles and sandhill cranes.

ORLANDO TO OKEECHOBEE AREA TRAILS The lightly traveled trail at **Prairie Lakes State Preserve (★)** (12 miles) affords unequalled opportunity for wildlife observation along its easy-to-hike path. Sandhill cranes, red-cockaded woodpeckers, turkey and deer enjoy the preserve's three lakes and 8000 acres of wetlands and prairie.

Transportation

BY CAR

Orlando is the Rome of central Florida. Since the majority of Florida vacations begin here, all roads seem to lead to Orlando, and away from it to coastal lands or heartland lake resorts and parks.

Route 4, which runs from Daytona Beach to Tampa, is the major artery through Orlando. Forming an X with Route 4, the **Florida Turnpike** traverses mid-Florida from Miami in the southeast to Route 75 northwest of Orlando. **Route 75** and parallel **Route 441** skewer Ocala and Gainesville.

Bisecting all of central Florida and running west of Orlando is **Route 27**, which threads its way south of Gainesville, through Ocala, Lake Wales and Sebring, to Lake Okeechobee and the Everglades. **Route 17** shoots off 27 at Haines City to reach the quiet towns of Bartow, Wauchula and Arcadia.

BY AIR

The **Orlando International Airport** receives direct flights from over 50 cities in the United States. Major domestic airlines serving the area include American Airlines, Continental Airlines, Delta Air Lines, Northwest Airlines, Ozark Air Lines, Trans World Airlines, United Airlines and USAir. International service is provided by Air Canada, British Airways, Icelandair and KLM Royal Dutch Airlines.

Inexpensive ground transportation to the Disney World area is provided by **Mears Motor Shuttle** (407-423-5566). Other alternatives for ground transportation in the Orlando area include **Airport Limousine Service of Orlando** (407-422-4561), and **Kissimmee Cab** (407-847-4867).

Airport Passenger Express (904-622-2292) provides scheduled service between the Orlando airport and Ocala daily.

The **Gainesville Airport** is serviced by Delta Air Lines and Piedmont Airlines.

Embassy Limousine (904-373-3280) and **Gainesville Cab Company** (904-371-1515) provide ground transportation in and out of the airport.

BY BUS

In Orlando, there is a **Greyhound/Trailways** station (555 North Magruder Street; 407-843-7720).

Greyhound/Trailways has stations in Ocala (512 North Magnolia Avenue; 904-732-2677) and DeLand (224 East Ohio Avenue; 904-734-2747).

BY TRAIN

In central Florida, **Amtrak** (800-872-7245) makes stops at Orlando (1400 Sligh Boulevard), Kissimmee (416 Pleasant Street), DeLand (2491 Old New York Avenue) and Palatka (12th and Reid streets). If you are traveling to the Orlando area from the vicinity of New York City, you may wish to consider Amtrak's **Auto-train.** You can board your car at Lorton, Virginia, four hours from New York, and drive it off at Sanford (600 Persimmon Avenue), less than 25 miles east of Orlando.

CAR RENTALS

Car rental companies located at the Orlando airport include **Avis Rent A Car** (407-851-7600), **Budget Rent A Car** (407-850-6700), **Dollar Rent A Car** (407-859-4250), **Hertz Rent A Car** (407-859-8400) and **National Car Rental** (407-855-4170). Companies that provide free airport pickup service include **Agency Rent A Car** (407-381-3290) and **Enterprise Rent A Car** (407-859-2296).

Ugly Duckling Rent A Car (407-847-5599) supplies used rental cars.

At the Gainesville Airport you can rent from **Avis Rent A Car** (904-376-8115), **Hertz Rent A Car** (904-373-8444) or **National Car Rental** (904-377-7005); **Enterprise Rent A Car** (904-371-6599) offers free pickup service.

PUBLIC TRANSPORTATION

Limited city bus service covers the main drags in Kissimmee and Orlando. For schedules in Orange and Seminole counties, call the **Tri-County Transit Authority** information office (407-841-8240).

For traveling to and from tourist attractions in the Orlando area, try the **Rabbit Bus** (407-291-2424). It picks up passengers off International Drive in Orlando, and makes stops at Walt Disney World, Sea World and the Disney Village.

Regional Transit System (904-334-2600) runs throughout Gainesville.

EVERGLADES

AND KEYS

CHAPTER SIX

The Everglades and the Keys

At the tip of Florida lie two of the state's greatest treasures, the Everglades and the Florida Keys. Technically, the former is a great, broad and shallow life-giving river flowing from Lake Okeechobee through thousands of acres of marshland. The latter are a chain of lush subtropical islands floating like an emerald necklace that marks the meeting of the Atlantic Ocean and the Gulf of Mexico.

To last century's dreamers and speculators, the Everglades loomed as a useless, mosquito-ridden swamp that might one day be drained and tamed and put to good use. The Keys harbored tales of pirate treasure and fortunes gleaned from ships tossed to bits on the shallow coral reefs that lay to the east in the Atlantic Ocean. At least one man envisioned these islands as a playground for wealthy sportsmen and a natural gateway to Cuba and Central America.

An understanding and appreciation of the Everglades has come only in recent decades, far too long after the waters that spilled out of Lake Okeechobee and gently fed this region were diked and rechanneled. Developers and farmers were both unaware and unconcerned about the devastating effects of so drastically changing the natural world of South Florida.

Then, in 1947, Marjorie Stoneman Douglas wrote a book that acclaimed the unique value of this subtropical wilderness, once inhabited by Indians and now home to myriad creatures and plants found nowhere else in the United States. She also struck at the conscience of those who had disregarded the irreparable damage being done to this important natural region whose existence contributes to the ecological life of the whole peninsula. "There are no other Everglades in the world," she began in *The Everglades: River of Grass.* Her words held both truth and warning.

The year that remarkable book was published, President Truman dedicated 2000 square miles of the southernmost Everglades as a national park. UNESCO declared the region a World Heritage Site in recognition of its value as a critical natural wonder of the world. In this preserved area visitors can begin to experience what Douglas described almost half a century ago. Here they can admire the hidden beauty and learn of the fragility of the *pa-hay-okee* or "grassy water," as the Indians called this vast, beautiful region that is really a river running 50 miles wide and a few inches deep. A close look deep into the tall sawgrass reveals the area's true nature.

Each entrance to the park shows a different side of the Everglades' rich character. In the northeastern region, Shark Valley offers a tour into sawgrass prairie, rich in birdlife and alligators. The northwest gateway is at Everglades City, jumping-off place to the Ten Thousand Islands, a Gulf Coast mangrove archipelago popular with fisherfolk and vacationers. The main entrance, southwest of Homestead, leads visitors along a 38-mile park road that meanders through sawgrass prairie, hardwood hammock, cypress swamps and lake regions, ending at Flamingo on the edge of Florida Bay.

Winter is the time to visit the Everglades, the only season when mosquitoes won't eat you alive. In winter you can leave your car, walk the trails, canoe the streams and contemplate the subtle beauty of the place. There are no breathtaking panoramas in this region, where the altitude seldom rises above three feet, but rich rewards await those who take the time to explore. Slumbering alligators lie like half-sunken logs in shallow ponds. Comical anhingas gather on low branches, hanging their wings out to dry after fishing forays. Bird populations are spectacular and diverse, including such easily recognized favorites as roseate spoonbills, osprey, brown pelicans and bald eagles. Endangered and rare animals such as the shy manatee, the Florida panther and the American crocodile, though seldom seen, reside deep within the watery world of the Everglades.

Though the signs explain where to go and how to get there, the Everglades is a region of hidden treasures waiting to be discovered by those who quietly search, wait and watch. And everywhere within the park rings the message that the Everglades is still a fragile region whose water supply is controlled from the outside by those who turn the valves and try to balance the needs of humans with those of this crucial, life-giving place.

In 1912, developer Henry Flagler completed his greatest project, a railroad from Florida City to Key West. He was spurred by dreams of carrying sportsmen to luxurious fishing camps and freight to ships sailing from Key West to Cuba and Central America. The remarkable rail line crossed three dozen islands and spanned bridges from less than 50 feet in length to one seven miles long. The state's worst recorded hurricane destroyed the railroad in 1935, but the sturdy bridges and trestles became the links for what would become the Overseas Highway, which still follows or parallels the original rail route.

Some of the Keys are so narrow that you can watch the sunrise over the Atlantic and see it set into the Gulf of Mexico only by strolling across the road. To the east lie the continental United States' only living coral reefs, popular with divers, snorkelers and passengers in glass-bottom boats. Because of these protective reefs, there is little surf and hence few sandy beaches in the Keys, a surprise to most visitors.

Time, folks claim, means little in the Keys. Visitors quickly discover that slowing down is both easy and essential, especially when the weather

is too good to pass up, which it is most of the time. Winters are wonderfully mild, with average highs around 77° and lows around 60°. Summer highs average about 89°, but sea breezes help keep life pleasant.

The Keys are basically vacation and retirement havens these days, now that wrecked sailing ships no longer yield up their booty on the rocky reefs, the sponge beds are gone and the commercial fishing industry has greatly dwindled. Romantics call these spots "America's Caribbean islands" or "the islands you can drive to." Accommodations run from crowded RV and trailer parks to motels with a boat dock for each room to luxurious resorts. Dining runs the gamut from shrimp-boils on a pier to gourmet feasting in sedate surroundings. The basic fare, of course, is seafood.

Fishing, boating and diving are the main sports of the Keys. Marinas lie on both sides of many of the islands; game fishing can be accomplished from rickety bridges as well as from classy yachts. Each of the centers of population claim to be "the best" of something, whether it be fishing, diving, relaxing, eating or partying.

Note: Addresses and directions throughout the Florida Keys are usually given in "Mile Markers" (MM). Each mile along Route 1 is marked on a small green sign with white numbers, beginning with MM 126, one mile south of Florida City, and ending with MM 0 in Key West.

Largest of all the islands, Key Largo is the gateway to the Keys and the beginning of the 113-mile journey to Key West. As Route 1 meanders out to sea, it passes through populated areas that could be anywhere in the country, with chain motels, restaurants, little shopping centers and ever-increasing development. But that's where the similarity ends, for this is a water-borne highway heading into magnificent sunsets, bordered by sea or mangroves or marinas and even bits of surviving jungle-like hammocks. Alongside it runs the vital viaduct, a huge pipe carrying water from the mainland to sustain the residents and visitors to these dependent islands that, though surrounded by the sea, offer nothing but rainwater for drinking.

As the closest key to John Pennekamp Coral Reef State Park, Key Largo is the area's premier diving site. Less than 20 miles farther along, Islamorada, on Upper Matecumbe Key, is the centerpiece of a group known as the "purple isles," thanks to an explorer who probably named them for the violet sea snails that thrived there. The region is famous for sportfishing and was once the prosperous headquarters for wreckers and salvagers. The next good-sized center of population is the town of Marathon on Vaca Key. The whole area is a popular winter resort and choice fishing spot.

Crossing the famous Seven Mile Bridge, Route 1 enters the Lower Keys, whose population center is Big Pine Key. The flora and fauna are different here from much of the rest of the Keys, and one of the few fine beaches is found in the Lower Keys. Big Pine is also home to the endangered tiny Key deer. From here on, the population thins out considerably until one approaches Key West, the nation's southernmost city and nearly the outermost region of the state. Only the Dry Tortugas, 68 miles out to sea, lie beyond.

Key West offers visitors just about everything the rest of the Keys do, and much, much more. The main tourist center, Old Town, swings with nightlife, sightseeing trips, diving, fishing, arts events, festivals and a nightly sunset celebration. Following in the footsteps of former residents Ernest Hemingway and Tennessee Williams, artists and writers have gathered in Key West for decades. It's also the site of a large gay community. There is history here, too, evidenced especially in the grand collection of historic old Victorian and Bahamian-style houses and the tales of famous folk who have lived and visited here. Key West has become one of the nation's chief traveler destinations. Some claim it is the only city in the United States that has never had a frost.

One might suspect that the Keys, being such a narrow chain of islands, could not provide any "hidden" sites to explore. But the hidden spots are there for the finding, little pockets of natural wilderness, small restaurants away from the highway, quiet lodgings on out-of-the-way islands, bits of history and treasure out to sea. Since winter is the chief tourist season in the Keys, rates are considerably lower in the summer.

Last century's dreamers and speculators might be surprised at what Florida has made of or, some might say, done to its southernmost treasures, the Everglades and the Florida Keys. For travelers, the area is rich indeed.

Everglades Area

The Everglades region is so vast it would take many weeks to experience its many subtle, hidden offerings. At first glance, much of it appears to be an endless prairie, dotted here and there with bits of forest. But first glances are misleading. The "prairie" is actually a slowly flowing river, its "forests" often island hammocks or little stands of dwarf cypress. Travelers who take time to search out the Everglades' treasures will be rewarded with views of exotic wildlife and plant life, from the abundant alligator to jewel-like snails, from gumbo-limbo trees to delicately blooming marsh grasses.

The auto traveler has several options; for a broad introduction to the Everglades, consider trying both the routes suggested here. We have included wilderness regions as well as coastal sights.

WESTWARD FROM MIAMI Heading westward from Miami, Route 41, known as the Tamiami Trail, provides an almost straight shot from the Atlantic to the Gulf Coast. It plunges through the heart of the Everglades, skirting the northern edge of **Everglades National Park** and cutting through the southern portion of the **Big Cypress National Preserve**. Though not wildly scenic, it is an intriguing road, traveling through miles and miles of what the Indians called *pa-hay-okee*, or "grassy water." Sometimes the narrow highway is paralleled by canals, their banks busy with people fishing with cane poles. In other places Australian pines grow so tall and full that they have been repeatedly trimmed to form a half-roof over the road. But mostly the landscape is sawgrass prairie, with the great, wide, almost hidden, life-giving river running imperceptibly through it. Drivers are instructed to travel this road with lights on at all times, a safeguard against possible tedium and the strange effect the region seems to have on one's depth perception when contemplating passing.

Although the Miccosukee Indians trace their ancestry back to centuries before the United States became a nation, they were not recognized as a tribe by the federal government until 1962. About 500 of them now live on a reservation along Route 1. They are descendants of a group which successfully hid in the Everglades during the period when Florida's Indians were being rounded up and sent west. You can visit the designed-for-tourists **Miccosukee Indian Village** (Route 41, about 25 miles west of Florida's Turnpike; 305-223-8388; admission) for a guided or self-guided tour that includes a museum, cooking and living chickees (palm-thatched native houses), a nature walk, craft areas, a shooting gallery and an arena where you can watch alligator wrestling. Nearby, the **Miccosukee Airboat Rides** offer noisy, environmentally questionable trips over the sawgrass deeper into the Everglades; the longer rides include a stop at an old hammock-style Indian camp.

The 15-mile, two-hour tram tours offered in the **Shark Valley** (Route 41, about 25 miles west of Florida's Turnpike; 305-221-8455) section of the Everglades National Park acquaints visitors with the heart of the sawgrass region. Stops are made along the way to spot birds or alligators, and for lessons on the park's hydrology, geology, vegetation and wildlife. Time is also allowed for climbing the 65-foot observation tower, which provides excellent views of the vast wetlands. Sightseers may also travel the tram road on foot or bicycles, which are rented at the entrance.

Where Route 41 veers northwestward, you can head straight and take a scenic detour on **Route 94,** which heads deep into cypress and pineland backcountry on its way toward Pinecrest. This is called the "loop road," but unless you have a four-wheel drive vehicle, you would do best to turn back when the road begins to deteriorate, about eight miles in, near an interpretive center.

Back on Route 41, northwest of Shark Valley, you will enter **Big Cypress National Preserve,** 716,000 acres of subtropical Florida swampland vital to the preservation of the Everglades. To get an idea of Big Cypress' importance and beauty, stop at the **Oasis Ranger Station** (813-695-4111) and see the excellent audiovisual introduction to this crucial region.

Though not encouraged by the National Park folks because of their noise and impact on the fragile environment, airboats and swamp buggies are popular with tourists. **Wooten's** (Route 41, Ochopee; 813-695-2781; admission) offers these rides all day long, every day, carrying visitors away from the highway into the deeper regions of the Everglades. A number of private individuals also offer rides; you'll see their signs along the road.

Slow down as you come up to the microscopic community of Ochopee, or you might miss "the smallest and most photographed post office in North America." You'll know it by the American flag, the blue letter box, the sign that reads **Post Office, Ochopee, FL** and all the tour buses disgorging passengers so that they can go into the tiny frame building and get their letters stamped.

By turning south on Route 29, you can reach the entrance to the western edge of the Everglades National Park, at Everglades City. Stop at the **Everglades City Chamber of Commerce** (Routes 41 and 29; 813-695-3941) to pick up information about this little town and the neighboring region.

At the privately owned **Eden of the Everglades** (Route 29, two miles south of Route 41, Everglades City; 813-695-2800; admission) you can ride a quiet jungle boat or airboat to observe some of the flora and fauna of the area in a natural setting.

Continue south to the **Everglades National Park Visitor Center** (Route 29, south of Everglades City; 813-695-3311). Here you can obtain information about the western regions of the park, including the **Ten Thousand Islands** area. The **Everglades National Park Boat Tours** (Visitor Center; 813-695-2591) cover portions of this territory on the Gulf of Mexico, informing visitors how the mangrove islands are formed and acquainting them with the resident wildlife, especially shore and wading birds. Endangered American bald eagles, gentle manatees and playful dolphins often reward the sharp-eyed explorer. Some of the tours make stops on a small Gulf island for shelling and a guided walk.

Nature trips by boat into the Ten Thousand Islands area are offered by **Captain Dan** (Chokoloskee Island; 813-695-4573). **Island Charters** (Chokoloskee Island; 813-695-2286) offers nature trips especially geared to photographers and birdwatchers.

Chokoloskee (Route 29, across the causeway south of Everglades City), a small island filled with motor homes, cottages and little motels, is a popular spot for visitors wishing to fish the Ten Thousand Islands region. It also has the distinction of being built on a gigantic shell mound created by early Indians.

To see the Everglades from the air, you can hop a plane at **Air Tours of South Florida** (28720 Southwest 217th Avenue, Homestead General Airport; 305-248-1100). You'll discover that, despite its tremendous size, the national park is only a portion of the Everglades. From the air, too, you'll realize what a watery and remote area this really is. Air Tours also offers 50-minute rides over the Upper Keys and Miami area, the latter trip scanning miles of beaches and picturesque islands. Ecological and historical narratives accompany the flights.

After you leave the park's western area, you can travel seven miles east of Route 29 on Route 41 to get to **Fakahatchee Strand State Preserve** (813-695-4593), the major drainage slough of the Big Cypress Swamp (see the "Beaches and Parks" section in this chapter). You can walk the boardwalk through the tall, dense, swamp forest of royal palm and bald cypress and admire some of the numerous orchidlike air plants that are said to grow only here. Rangers conduct weekend "wet" walks into the swamp to see other rare plant life.

SOUTHWARD FROM MIAMI The Florida City/Homestead communities serve as a gateway to both the Everglades and the Florida Keys. For information on this area, you might begin at the very fine **Visitor Center** at Florida City (160 Route 1; 305-245-9180). Here you can obtain information about the main public portion of Everglades National Park as well as a number of other places to see and things to do in the Florida City/Homestead area.

There is a lot to be seen off the Atlantic coast east of Florida City in **Biscayne National Park**, most of it underwater (see the "Everglades Area Beaches and Parks" section below). But even if you are not a snorkeler or scuba diver, you can get an excellent view of the nearby coral reef from the **glass-bottom boat** that departs from park headquarters at Convoy Point. Daily trips to the reef, as well as island cruises in the winter, are offered by **Biscayne Aqua Center** (Biscayne National Park Headquarters, end of 328th Street, east of Florida City; 305-247-2400).

Florida City is the hub of the most southern farming area in the continental United States. A drive northward on Krome Avenue or along any side road in the area will take you through vast **truck gardens** where you may see, and even pick from, great fields of tomatoes, corn, strawberries, okra, peppers and other fruits and vegetables. Large acreages are also devoted to avocados, limes, mangos and papayas. For an extensive, entertaining and informative tour of this farm region, join an **Agricultural Guided Tour** (#32 Gateway Estates, north of Route 27, Florida City; 305-248-6798; admission).

You can get an idea of how the early settlers lived in this fertile, challenging region between the eastern edge of the Everglades and the sea by visiting the **Pioneer Museum** (★) (826 North Krome Avenue, Florida City; 305-246-9531; admission). The down-home collection consists mainly of fine old photographs and items from Florida family attics, and is housed in a caboose, a reconstructed railway station and an agent's house, left over from the days of Henry Flagler's "railroad that went to the sea." (Open October through April.)

The **Coral Castle** (28655 Route 1, Homestead; 305-248-6344; admission) is a strange place; some claim it's almost mystical. According to legend, this curious limestone mansion was built, between 1923 and 1940, because of an unrequited love. Its creator, a Latvian immigrant, claimed to know the secret of the construction of the pyramids. Perhaps he did, for he was able to move multi-ton pieces of local coral rock to the site and construct towers, massive stone furnishings, a nine-ton gate that swings open to the touch, a 5000-pound valentine heart and myriad other strange symbols of devotion to his mysterious lost love. Supposedly, no one has ever figured out the builder's secret, but you can go and give it a try, and marvel at this historic curiosity.

Lovers of orchids and all things beautiful should not miss **Fennell's Orchid Jungle** (26715 Southwest 157th Avenue, Homestead; 305-247-4824; admission). Over 100 different orchids are native to Florida, and they make up only a small portion of the over 12,000 varieties you'll find in this wonderful jungle hammock.

North of Homestead, the **Preston B. Bird & Mary Heinlein Fruit & Spice Park** (24801 Southwest 187th Avenue, Homestead; 305-247-5727; admission) is a 20-acre random grove planted with over 500 varieties of fruit, spices and herbs from around the world. Visitors are invited to stroll among the citrus, banana, lychee, mango, starfruit and other tropical trees. On the grounds of this living museum stands the **Bauer-Mitchell House,** the oldest known house in the area. An excellent example of pine pioneer construction, with crude beams, tongue-and-groove ceiling and generous porch, this old home hints at the challenging life led by South Dade County homesteaders.

EVERGLADES NATIONAL PARK South of Homestead, the cultivation suddenly stops, and Everglades National Park begins, almost like a boundary of uneasy truce between man and nature. You quickly forget that Miami is just up the road a piece or that tended gardens lie behind you. Before you lies the mysterious world of what some call "the real Florida," the home of the alligator, the panther, the royal palm and the flamingo.

There are a number of ways to tackle this area of the park. For help in designing your plan, stop at the **Main Visitor Center** (11 miles southwest of Homestead; 305-242-7700) just before entering the gate. Here park staff members will provide you with all sorts of helpful information, including weather, trail and insect conditions and listings of the season's varied and informative ranger-guided tours. A fine audiovisual presentation and a wide assortment of books provide good introductions to the area.

Once you have paid your admission and entered the park, you are on the single park road that will eventually arrive at Flamingo, 38 miles away, at the tip of the state on the edge of Florida Bay. This winding, lonely road traverses the heart of the park, meandering among tall pines, through seemingly endless expanses of sawgrass prairie and alongside mysterious dark ponds. Off this road lie a number of paths, trails, boardwalks and waterways designed to give the visitor as wide an Everglades experience as possible.

Some of the trails require only short strolls of half-a-mile or less, but they reward with close-up views of a great range of environments and inhabitants. Because so much of the terrain is submerged in water, it is wise to stick to the paths provided unless you go exploring with a park ranger.

Right inside the park entrance, watch for signs to the **Royal Palm Visitor Center** on your left. Even if you have already spent a good amount of time at the main center, you would do well to take a stroll down each of the two half-mile trails that begin here. Close together but very different, each plunges into a distinctive Everglades environment. Interpretive signs help you notice things you might otherwise miss, such as how the strangler fig got its name or why alligators are so vital to the survival of the region.

The **Anhinga Trail** travels a boardwalk across Taylor Slough, a marshy pool that attracts winter birds and other wildlife that assemble with apparent unconcern for the season's thousands of visitors with cameras and zoom lenses. This is a perfect spot for viewing alligators and numerous water birds. Here, too, you can gaze across broad vistas of sawgrass prairie.

Nearby, the **Gumbo-Limbo Trail** leads through a jungly tropical hardwood hammock rich in gumbo-limbo, strangler fig, wild coffee, royal palms and other tropical trees as well as numerous orchids and ferns. Air plants and butterflies often add to the beauty of this spot; interpretive signs help visitors get acquainted with tropical flora that will occur again and again throughout the park.

About six miles from the main entrance, the half-mile **Pineland Trail,** near a camping area at Long Pine Key, circles through a section of slash pine forest. Here the ground is dry; occasional fires keep undergrowth in check so the pines can thrive without competition. This is a good place to get a look at the rock and solution holes formed in the shallow bed of limestone that lies under South Florida. Or just to picnic beside a quiet lake. For a view of pinelands closer to the park road, stop at the **Pinelands** sign about a mile farther on.

As you continue down the park road and gaze across the sawgrass prairie, you will notice stands of stunted trees that, during winter, appear dead or dying, since they are hung with moss from ghostlike gray branches. These are bald cypress, which thrive in watery terrain but remain dwarfed due to the peculiar conditions of the Everglades. In spring they put out lovely green needles. Some that you see, although dwarfed, have been growing here for over a century.

About six miles beyond the Pinelands, you come to the **Pa-hay-okee Overlook,** named for the Indian word for Everglades, meaning "grassy waters." Walk the short boardwalk and climb the observation tower for a wonderful panorama of the sawgrass prairie dotted with collections of ancient dwarf cypress and small island hammocks of hardwoods. This is one of the best overviews in the park; it's a great place for birdwatching.

Some park rangers refer to hammocks as the "bedrooms of the Everglades," the places where so many wild creatures, large and small, find dry ground and shade from the tropical sun. About seven miles from Pa-hay-okee, you can explore one of these magnificent "highlands" that thrive just above the waterlines. The half-mile **Mahogany Hammock Trail** enters the cool, dark, jungly environment of a typical hardwood hammock, where you'll find rare paurotis palms and large mahogany trees, including one said to be the largest mahogany in the United States. Look and listen closely—barred owls, golden orb spiders, colorful *Liguus* tree snails and many other creatures make their homes in this humid "bedroom."

From Mahogany Hammock the park road heads due south through stands of pine and cypress and across more sawgrass prairie. You are now nearing the coast and will begin to see the first mangrove trees, evidence of the mixing of salt water from Florida Bay with the freshwater that flows from the north. You will pass several canoe-access spots along the road here, including the one at West Lake, about 11 miles from Mahogany Hammock.

Stop at the **West Lake Trail** for a good close-up look at mangroves. You can walk among the four species that thrive here along the half-mile boardwalk trail. With a little practice you will be able to identify them all—the predominant red mangroves with their arched, spidery prop roofs, black mangroves sending up fingerlike breathing tubes called "pneumatophores" from the mud and white mangroves and buttonwood on the higher, dryer shores of the swampy areas. The West Lake shoreline is one of many important spawning grounds for fish and shellfish that in turn attract raccoons and other wildlife who come to feed. You may see a gourmet diner or two if you walk quietly and keep your eyes open.

As you near the end of the park road, you will pass **Mzarek Pond,** another lovely birdwatching spot, especially rewarding during the winter months. Roseate spoonbills often come to this quiet, glassy pond to feed, along with many other common and exotic waterfowl.

The road ends at the **Flamingo Visitor Center** (38 miles from the main entrance; 813-695-3101, ext. 182), where a remote fishing village once stood. Early settlers could reach the area only by boat, and all sorts of activity, legal and not, went on here. Along with fishing and farming and the making of charcoal, businesses at various times included production of moonshine whiskey and the gathering of bird plumes for ladies fashionwear. The town is gone now, replaced by a marina, concessions, a motel and cabins, and a shop and visitor center. At Flamingo you can select from a variety of sightseeing opportunities, such as ranger-guided walks, wilderness canoe trips, tram rides, campfire programs and hands-on activities. Offerings vary with the seasons; check at the visitor center for a schedule.

Sightseeing by boat is particularly enjoyable. Most boat tours in this region, including some backcountry explorations, are available year-round. Sunset cruises are a delight, offering views of spectacular skies as well as allowing close-ups of a wide variety of birds winging their way to shore. In winter, pelicans ride the gentle waves, and gulls soar up and around the boat. Some boat trips will take you to **Cape Sable (★)**, the farthest-out point of southwestern Florida, where the Gulf of Mexico laps a broad, sandy beach.

For more birdwatching, especially in winter, take a short stroll from the visitor center to nearby **Eco Pond**. At dusk you may see ibis, egrets and other water birds winging in for the night to nest in nearby trees.

EVERGLADES AREA HOTELS

If you prefer to stay close to the western park area, try the **Captain's Table Lodge and Villas** (Route 29, Everglades City; 813-695-4211). This large resort offers hotel rooms and suites in its main lodge and one- and two-bedroom villas, some featuring screened decks. There is a large pool and complete marina. Boat tours of the Ten Thousand Islands are available; good beaches are only five miles away—by boat. Moderate.

The **Rod and Gun Lodge** (200 Riverside Drive, Everglades City; 813-695-2101), a 1920s-era hunting and fishing club, no longer rents rooms in the lodge itself. You *can* sit on its airy screened porch or admire the mounted game fish and red cypress paneling of the massive old lobby. And you can stay in the rather ordinary cottages on the grounds, swim in the screened-in heated pool, play shuffleboard and feast in the lodge's huge dining room. Complete docking facilities alongside attract some pretty impressive boats. Moderate.

Ivey House (107 Camellia Street, Everglades City; 813-695-3299) is a shot-gun style residence built in 1929 with twin- or double-bedded rooms furnished in southern pine. Take your continental breakfast on one of the comfortable porches. Moderate.

A good place to stay and convenient to the eastern edge of Everglades National Park is the **Park Royal Inn** (100 U.S. 1, Florida City; 305-247-3200), an attractive gray motel with white trim whose 160 rooms are pretty generic but very neat and clean and carpeted. There is a heated pool. Budget to moderate.

Despite the hokey stenciled signs tacked to posts, **Grandma Newton's Bed & Breakfast** (★) (40 Northwest 5th Avenue, Florida City; 305-247-4413) remains pretty hidden to the average traveler, but it's worth finding just to meet Grandma Newton. She is a real grandma, and her tin-roofed frame house with beaded walls and ceilings and a big yard feels like a real old-fashioned Florida dwelling. The four pleasant bedrooms are furnished in what Grandma calls "mostly country junk," and the breakfasts of grits, eggs, meats, potatoes and fresh-baked biscuits make you wish you could visit every weekend. Budget to moderate.

To really experience the Everglades, stay at least a couple of nights in the **Flamingo Lodge** (1 Flamingo Road, Flamingo; 813-695-3101). This, the only accommodation in the park, is a plain old motel with window air conditioners and jalousies that can be opened to let in the intriguing watery smells of the 'glades and the shallow bay. Far from city lights and surrounded by jungle sounds, Flamingo Lodge lies in the heart of the Everglades. It offers a beautiful pool circled by tropical plants. Flamingo also offers rustic cottages with fully equipped kitchens and all motel amenities. Moderate.

EVERGLADES AREA RESTAURANTS

The **Miccosukee Restaurant** (Route 41, Miccosukee Indian Village; 305-223-8388) is a typical roadside restaurant with strip-steak/fried-fish fare. But the local Indians who own and operate this place add their own special dishes to the menu—good things such as pumpkin bread, fry bread, Miccosukee burgers and tacos, and catfish caught in the Everglades. It's the best place to eat while traveling the Tamiami Trail. Moderate.

Along with the usual fried and broiled seafood, you can try such delicacies as 'gator tail, cooter (freshwater soft shell terrapin) and lobster tail at the **Oyster House** (Route 29, Everglades City; 813-695-2073). Ships' wheels and other nautical paraphernalia create a very pleasant, informal seaside atmosphere. Moderate.

The menu at the **Rod and Gun Club** (200 Riverside Drive, Everglades City; 813-695-2101) like so many area eateries, features frogs' legs, stone crab claws and native fish in season, but the ambience is unlike any other in far South Florida. You may dine in the massive, dark, cypress-paneled dining hall of this once-elegant old hunting and fishing lodge or be seated on the airy porch where you can have a splendid view of the yachts and other fine boats that dock a stone's throw away. The selection of seafood, steak and chicken is small, but well prepared. Moderate to deluxe.

If you wonder what happens to all those good vegetables that grow around Homestead, you'll find bunches of them in hefty servings at **Potlikker** (591 Washington Avenue, Homestead; 305-248-0835). A barbecue pit smokes away on the premises, preparing succulent ribs that are part of the down-home southern assortment of items such as steak, chicken pot pie and Cajun breaded catfish. The place boasts at least 11 vegetables daily, ranging from mustard greens to okra-and-tomatoes. The frame country-style building and mostly budget prices make this a friendly family-type eatery.

Donzanti's (255 Northeast 3rd Drive, Homestead; 305-248-5281) pays homage to the basic Italian cooking that leaves you fat and happy. Sit at a red-clothed table and watch waitresses toting platters loaded with hand-rolled pasta, thick sauce and meat, chicken cacciatore and veal parmigian. If you're super hungry, go for Mamma D.'s special: lasagna, spaghetti, manicotti, sausage and meatballs, all blanketed in melted mozzarella. Budget to moderate.

It's amazing to think that a scalloped awning, some pretty lace curtains and a few prints of Paris scenes could turn a storefront strip center unit into a charming French restaurant, but that's just what has been done at **Le Kir** (1532 Northeast 8th Street, Homestead; 305-247-6414). Such specialties as *médaillon de veau à la crème* and duck with grand marnier sauce contribute to the authenticity. The prix-fixe dinner is ultra-deluxe.

The Mexican fare at **Casita Tejas** (10 South Krome Avenue, Homestead; 305-248-8224) includes such Tex-Mex favorites as fajitas and chimichangas but also features genuine south-of-the-border dishes like *carne guisada* (spicy stewed beef and potatoes). The setting is fun and cheery, styled with wood dividers, woven blankets and glass tables.

Although it's the only place to dine in the Everglades National Park, the **Flamingo Lodge Restaurant** (Flamingo; 813-695-3101) is surprisingly good. The small but satisfactory menu features chicken and beef dishes. There's also a lunch and dinner buffet available. Located on the second floor of a small complex, the multilevel restaurant presents pretty views of Florida Bay. Tropical plants within and the dark night without remind you that while the moderate menu is routine, the setting is quite exotic.

EVERGLADES AREA SHOPPING

Along with the usual souvenirs, you will find handcrafted baskets, jewelry and the intricate, colorful patchwork clothing for which the Miccosukee Indian women are famous, at the **Miccosukee Indian Village Gift Shop** (Route 41, 25 miles west of Florida's Turnpike; 305-223-8388.)

If you are a souvenir hound, stop at **Wooten's** (Ochopee; 813-695-2781) and you'll never have to go anywhere else for those plastic flamingos and vinyl alligators.

Cauley Square (22400 Old Dixie Highway; 305-258-3543) has a Miami address, but Homestead claims it, too. This restored area of historic homes and buildings encompasses a variety of shops, including a tea room, craft stores, clothing boutiques and antique shops.

The **Redland Gourmet & Fruit Store** is located on the grounds of the Preston B. Bird & Mary Heinlein Fruit & Spice Park (24801 Southwest 187th Avenue, Homestead; 305-247-5727). Here you can browse among shelves of imported and domestic dried and canned exotic fruits, unusual spices and seeds, and out-of-the-ordinary juices, jellies and jams. There is a good selection of cookbooks and reference books on tropical fruits.

On your drive to the main entrance of Everglades National Park, you'll pass a large, tacky, ramshackle produce stand known as **Robert Is Here** (19200 Southwest 344th Street, Homestead; 305-246-1592). Not only does Robert have fresh treats such as mangos, lychees, monstra, tamarind, star fruit and whatever citrus is in season, he serves up Key lime milkshakes and sells jellies and preserves "made by his own mother."

While the **Gift Shop at Flamingo Resort** (end of park road; 305-253-2241) has lots of the usual Florida souvenirs, they also have some interesting books on the Everglades, along with high-quality shirts and stationery.

EVERGLADES AREA NIGHTLIFE

Folks in search of serious nightlife in the Everglades City area go to Naples; from the Florida City/Homestead area it is less than an hour's drive to the bright lights of Miami and Miami Beach.

"The Glassroom" at the **Oyster House** (Route 29, Everglades City; 813-695-2073) does have a bar and juke box.

In Homestead and Florida City, there is an assortment of roadside taverns, and some of the motels keep their lounges open and provide occasional entertainment for late-night socializers, but most folks will tell you that the sidewalks roll up early around here.

If you spend any nights at Flamingo, deep in the Everglades, take time to walk outside (providing it's not mosquito time) away from the lights of the lodge and marina. On a moonless night, you'll experience a darkness that is ultimate, and hear sounds made nowhere else in the United States, as the subtropical jungle creatures begin their night-long serenades.

EVERGLADES AREA BEACHES AND PARKS

Everglades National Park—With an area of 1.5 million acres, this protected section of Florida's Everglades covers the southwestern end of the state and a vast section of shallow Florida Bay dotted with tiny keys. There is no other park like it in the world. Geologically and climatically unique, the Everglades is a 50-mile-wide subtropical "river of grass" flowing almost imperceptibly from Lake Okeechobee to the sea. To fully appreciate it, one needs to spend time, for it does not overwhelm with spectacular scenery. Rather, its gently waving grasses dotted with stunted bald cypress, its clear ponds, its hardwood hammocks and pinelands are home to plant and animal life native to both the Caribbean Islands and the temperate United States. Inhabitants such as roseate spoonbills, wood storks, crocodiles and alligators, green sea turtles, southern bald eagles and manatees can be discovered by walking the trails, canoeing the waters and exploring with park rangers. Winter is the most comfortable time to visit, unless one is well-equipped to do battle with mosquitoes. Some of the facilities are closed from May 1 to October 31.

There are three main accesses to Everglades National Park. On the northern boundary, Shark Valley is a day-use area; Everglades City, on the western side, offers access to the Ten Thousand Islands region. The main park area for visitors encompasses the southern tip of the Florida mainland.

Facilities: Main area (FLAMINGO): Picnic areas, restrooms, restaurant, motel, cabins, grocery, marina, interpretive trails, boat tours and boat rentals, canoe rentals, bike rentals; information, 305-242-7700. SHARK VALLEY: Restrooms, hiking and biking trail, bicycle rentals, tram rides; information, 305-221-8776. EVERGLADES CITY: Restrooms, visitor center, boat tours, canoe rentals; information, 813-695-3311. *Swimming:* Not recommended except on certain island locations accessible only by boat. *Fishing:* Excellent in inland waters, especially for largemouth bass, and in coastal waters for snapper, redfish and trout.

Camping: There are two campgrounds with numerous sites; $8 per night for tent/RV sites, $4 per night for walk-in sites. Wilderness camping is allowed, with a permit, in the Main area and Everglades City area; no fee. There are also many privately owned campgrounds throughout the park.

Getting there: Main visitor center entrance on Route 9336, ten miles southwest of Florida City. Northern Shark Valley entrance off Route 41, 35 miles west of downtown Miami. Everglades City entrance on Route 29 off Route 41.

Big Cypress National Preserve—A 716,000 acre area of subtropical Florida known as Big Cypress Swamp makes up this preserve. Its establishment reflected a serious concern for the state's dwindling wetlands and watersheds, especially those affecting the Everglades National Park. Established in 1974, this preserved wilderness area of wet and dry prairies, coastal plains, marshes, mangrove forests, sandy pine woods and mixed hardwood hammocks has few facilities for visitors. It exists to protect the abundant wildlife living here and the watershed, which will be needed by future South Florida generations.

Facilities: Picnic tables at several roadside parks, restrooms at the Oasis Visitor Center, hiking trail; information, 813-695-2000 or 813-695-4111.

Camping: Primitive camping allowed; no fee.

Getting there: On Route 41 between Shark Valley and Everglades City.

Fakahatchee Strand State Preserve—This strand, the drainage slough for the Big Cypress Swamp, is the largest and most interesting of these natural channels cut by the flow of water into the limestone plain. The slough's tall, dense, swamp forest stands out on the horizon in contrast to the open terrain and sawgrass plain around it. Its forest of royal palms, bald-cypress trees and air plants is said to be unique on earth. Approximately 20 miles long and three to five miles wide, the preserve offers visitors views of some of its rare plant life, including a wide variety of orchids. From November through April, rangers conduct weekend "wet" walks into the swamp to see other unusual plant life.

Facilities: Interpretive trail, boardwalk; information, 813-695-4593.

Getting there: On Route 29, six miles northwest of Everglades City.

Chekika State Recreation Area—This 640-acre park allows easy exploration of some of the many Everglades terrains, including a tropical hammock, tree islands and the grassy waters flowing over honeycombed limestone surface rock. The small campground is located in the hardwood hammock, providing a pleasant and protected wilderness experience within an easy drive of Miami. Alligators make their home in the park and are to be respected.

Facilities: Picnic area, restrooms, showers, nature trail, boardwalk; groceries and restaurants in Homestead; information, 305-251-0371 or 305-242-7700. *Swimming:* Pleasant artesian-water swimming in a natural depression in the hammock.

Camping: There are 20 sites; $8 per night.

Getting there: Off 177th (Krome) Avenue, 15 miles from Homestead.

Biscayne National Park—This 181,500-acre marine park is one of the largest of its kind in the National Park system, but most of it is hidden from the average traveler since it lies under the waters of Biscayne Bay and the Atlantic Ocean. The park includes a small area of mangrove shoreline, part of the bay, a line of narrow islands of the northern Florida Keys, and the northern part of John Pennekamp Coral Reef. Brown pelicans, little blue herons, snowy egrets and a few exotic fish can be seen by even the most casual stroller from the mainland jetty, but to fully appreciate the beauty of this unusual park you should take a glass-bottom boat tour or go snorkeling or scuba diving around the colorful reef. The little mangrove-fringed keys allow discovery of such tropical flora as gumbo-limbo trees, strangler fig and devil's potato. Birdlife abounds.

Facilities: Picnic areas, restrooms, boat tours; information, 305-247-7275. *Fishing:* Excellent saltwater fishing in open waters; prohibited in harbors. Lobster may be taken east of the islands in season. *Swimming:* Not recommended except on the tiny beaches of Elliott and Sands keys where care must be taken to avoid sharp coral rock and spiny sea urchins.

Camping: Primitive camping allowed on Boca Chica Key and Elliott Key, no fee, but you must obtain a permit for camping on Elliott Key. Prepare for mosquitoes.

Getting there: Park headquarters are at Convoy Point, nine miles east of Homestead. The rest of the park is accessible by boat from Convoy Point.

Homestead Bayfront Park—This is a next-door neighbor to the mainland part of Biscayne National Park (see above). It's a very popular spot enhanced by a small manmade beach, grassy areas and some shade offered by pines and palms. Entrance to the park is through a dense grove of mangroves, allowing a close look at these amazing island-building trees.

Facilities: Picnic areas, restrooms, showers, marina; information, 305-247-1543. *Fishing:* Good shore fishing for snapper. *Swimming:* Pleasant, off a small manmade beach.

Getting there: Follow signs at Biscayne National Park (see above).

Key Largo Area

Key Largo is the first of the Keys you will reach along the Great Overseas Highway, Route 1, when you head south from Florida City. Motels, resorts and campgrounds abound through much of this, the largest of the Keys. The center of population is the town of Key Largo, where you'll pass dozens of dive shops, for directly to the east of this long key lies the only living coral reef in the continental United States. This underwater paradise is rich in both marine life and interesting shipwrecks, some centuries-old.

Humphrey Bogart and Lauren Bacall made the town famous in their spell-binding movie *Key Largo*, about crime and a hurricane. You'll still hear about the film today; a few places claim to have had a part in its making. For lots of good information on the Key Largo area, stop at the **Chamber of Commerce** (MM 106; 305-451-1414).

Slow down as you approach the short bridge that crosses the **Marvin D. Adams Waterway** (MM 103), a manmade cut that creates a channel all the way across a narrow section of Key Largo. The banks on either side of the cut are the one place you can really get a good look at the geological makeup of the Upper Keys. There are fine examples of petrified stag horn coral, coral heads and other materials of the ancient coral reef on which the islands are built.

To observe treasures recovered from Florida's reefs, visit **Kimbell's Caribbean Shipwreck Museum** (MM 102.6, Key Largo; 305-451-6444; admission). Resembling a 15th-century castle, the structure contains historical exhibits and glittering riches. The spoils on display include a jewel-studded gold medallion, Chinese "blue and white" porcelain, ancient rupees and a collection of sea-salvaged coins.

Whether or not you're a snorkeler or scuba diver, **John Pennekamp Coral Reef State Park** (Route 1, MM 102.5, Key Largo; 305-451-1202; admission) offers many ways to enjoy this underwater treasure (see the "Key Largo Area Beaches and Parks" section below). An excellent visitor center features a giant reconstruction of a living patch reef in a circular aquarium and other exhibits of the undersea world, mangrove swamps and hardwood hammocks. Glass-bottom boat tours, as well as scuba and snorkeling tours, are offered daily (305-451-1621).

Glass-bottom boat cruises to the reef are also available on the **Key Largo Princess** (MM 100, Holiday Inn docks, Key Largo; 305-451-4655). Choose from daily public cruises as well as sunset cruises with underwater lights.

If you want a very small bit of nostalgia, you can usually see the original **African Queen**, the little boat in which Humphrey Bogart and Katharine Hepburn battled the jungle and found romance, on display at the Holiday Inn docks (MM 100). If the ship's gone for the day, you can have a look at the *Thayer IV*, the boat seen in the Hepburn film *On Golden Pond*.

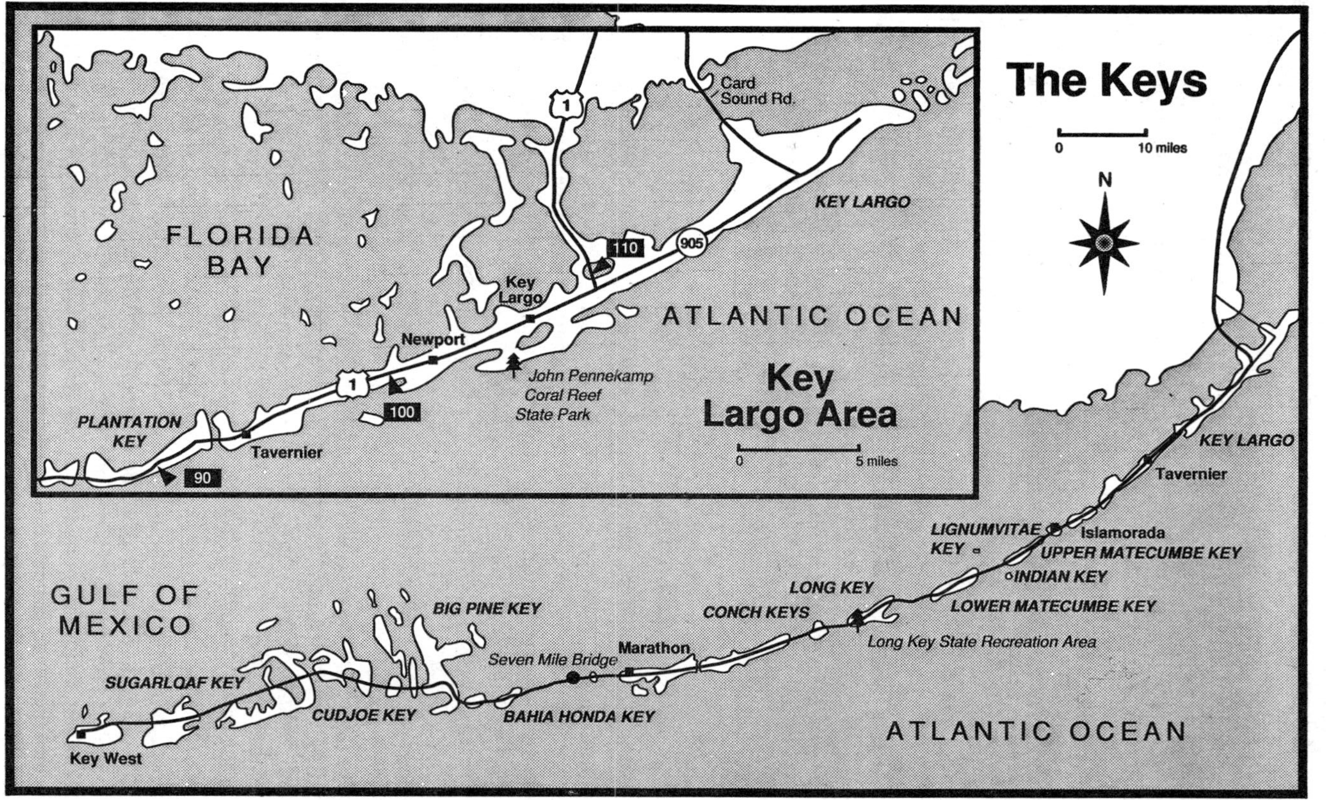
The Keys
0
10 miles
N
FLORIDA BAY
Card Sound Rd.
1
110
905
KEY LARGO
Key Largo
ATLANTIC OCEAN
Newport
John Pennekamp Coral Reef State Park
1
100
Key Largo Area
0
5 miles
PLANTATION KEY
Tavernier
90
KEY LARGO
Tavernier
LIGNUMVITAE KEY
Islamorada
UPPER MATECUMBE KEY
INDIAN KEY
LONG KEY
LOWER MATECUMBE KEY
CONCH KEYS
Long Key State Recreation Area
GULF OF MEXICO
BIG PINE KEY
Seven Mile Bridge
Marathon
SUGARLOAF KEY
CUDJOE KEY
BAHIA HONDA KEY
ATLANTIC OCEAN
Key West

Atlantic bottlenose dolphins can often be spotted swimming and cavorting in Key Largo area waters, especially on the bay side. For a closer experience with these delightful and intelligent sea mammals, make an appointment to visit **Dolphins Plus** (MM 100, Key Largo; 305-451-1993; admission), one of several places in the Keys where you can swim with dolphins. Basically a research center, Dolphins Plus studies how dolphins relate to human beings and is researching the dolphin's role in "zoo-therapy" with handicapped and disabled individuals.

The little town of **Tavernier** (around MM 92) boasts a bit of history that local folks are hanging onto as best they can. Along with the Old Methodist Church on Route 1, a few **old frame houses** (★) with big shutters for protection against hurricanes remain, mementos of the farming days before pizza parlors and gas stations. You can see them if you wander the few side streets and peer among the dense tropical trees.

For Everglades airboat rides and sightseeing tours of the Florida Bay backcountry (as well as fishing, hunting and nighttime frogging trips), contact **Captain Ray Cramer** (305-852-5339), said to be one of the best authorities on the region, an excellent guide and spinner of regional tales. He operates out of his home and will make arrangements to meet you.

KEY LARGO AREA HOTELS

Accommodations are numerous in the Keys, from small motels to condominiums to chain hotels and motels to luxurious resorts. Almost all offer something special, from a dock for snorkeling to extensive dive and fishing charters. Lodging information may be obtained from the **Florida Keys Visitors Bureau** (Key West; 800-352-5397).

Jules' Undersea Lodge (★) (51 Shoreland Drive, near MM 103.2, Key Largo; 305-451-2353) is so hidden that you can't even see it when you get there—because it's 22 feet below the surface of a tropical lagoon. You don't have to be a scuba diver to get into your ultra-deluxe air-conditioned quarters (there are two rooms for guests and an entertainment room); the staff will give you lessons. The reward is a unique underwater experience, with fish swimming by your 42-inch windows, no noise except the comforting reminder of the air support system, and the knowledge that you are staying in a one-of-a-kind lodging.

Tropical trees, dense foliage, ibis in the yard and a nice little bayside beach reinforce the claim at **Largo Lodge** (MM 101.5, Key Largo; 305-451-0424) that "paradise can be reasonable." The price is actually moderate to deluxe, but for it you get one of six very nice, roomy apartments with a kitchen, living room and big screened porch with space for lots of diving gear. The place is beautifully maintained, and the owner is delightful. Do ask for a unit away from busy Route 1.

Marina del Mar Resort (MM 100, Key Largo; 305-451-4107) is one of those places with everything—lodging, water sports, marina, restaurant and nightclub, tennis courts, fitness center, pool and diving services. On the oceanside of the island, it is convenient to the popular nearby diving waters. The units are spacious and airy with tile floors and whirlpool tubs; there are also suites with full kitchens. Deluxe.

The **Sunset Cove Motel** (south of MM 100; 305-451-0705) is really a complex of small, old-time, plain but neat apartments. This modest spot has a real old Keys feel. It's set among life-sized carved panthers and pelicans and enhanced with talking parrots and wonderful, relaxing Jamaican swings in the shade of thatched "chickees." The hosts obviously love being here and treat their guests to occasional jukebox parties and free use of their glass-bottom paddleboat and other small craft. You can help with the feeding of their friendly flock of pelicans, many of whom have been restored to health from fishhook wounds and other injuries. Prices fall in the moderate to deluxe range.

At the **Stone Ledge Resort** (MM 95.3, Key Largo; 305-852-8114) you'll have access to a nice dock, a small bayside beach, a shady yard and a pleasant motel room, efficiency or studio apartment in the long, low cream-colored stucco building. Typical of many of the area's mom-and-pop motels, this one is quite pleasant. Ask for a unit away from the highway. Moderate in price.

KEY LARGO AREA RESTAURANTS

You'll meet both locals and returning divers at **Dave's Rasta Pasta** (★) (45 Garden Cove Drive, oceanside off MM 106.5; 305-451-8022), a pasta and seafood spot serving appetizers of well-fried fish, conch fritters, shrimp and such, enhanced by lots of draft and imported brews. Moderately priced dinner entrées include seafood linguine and ravioli, as well as mesquite-grilled and Jamaican-jerk-grilled meats and fish.

For a beautiful, wide-open, classy place to sample Sicilian treatments of local seafood, try the **Italian Fisherman** (MM 104, Key Largo; 305-451-4471). On nice days they throw open all the doors along a broad expanse of bay; but even if it's chilly you can see a fine sunset through the wide windows. The decor is a mass of white wicker and blue upholstery; outside the dining deck is shaded by tropical trees. The *linguine marechiaro*, an assortment of shrimp, scallops, clams and the day's fresh catch all cooked in a marinara or garlic butter sauce and served on a bed of linguini, is a popular favorite. Moderate.

An intimate fine-dining restaurant is **Snook's Bayside Club** (★) (off Route 1, MM 99.9, Key Largo; 305-451-3847). Very popular with local folks, this moderate-to-deluxe-priced establishment overlooking Florida Bay offers fine treatments of seafood and splendid sunsets. A tablecloth-and-crystal restaurant, Snook's is a nice change from the dozens of roadside fish places.

If you get tired of seafood or want a little down-home mainland food, stop at **Mrs. Mac's Kitchen** (MM 99.4, Key Largo; 305-451-3722). This shack-style eatery has about the best chili east of Texas and pita bread concoctions almost too fat to bite down on. The chefs broil delicious steaks and feature different theme specials (Italian, meat, seafood, etc.) for dinner each night. The place is small, with more varieties of beers than seats, so it's noisy and fun. Moderate.

KEY LARGO AREA SHOPPING

Key Largo is the main spot for Upper Keys shoppers, so there are shopping centers, groceries and all the functional kinds of stores you might need, as well as tacky souvenir and T-shirt shops.

A well-known underwater photographer offers all the necessary equipment, for sale or rent, for capturing your diving and snorkeling adventures on still or video film at **Stephen Frink Photographic** (MM 102.5, Key Largo; 305-451-3737).

The Book Nook (MM 100, Waldorf Plaza, Key Largo; 305-451-1468) has a large selection of books about the area and Florida in general, as well as maps and charts for divers. They also keep a good selection of classics and have plenty of recent bestsellers to keep you occupied when you've had too much sun.

Several places in the Keys specialize in embossed and handpainted handbags, some ready-made, many with nautical designs, and others done to suit your own special wishes. You can find them at the **Florida Keys Handbag Factory** (MM 91.5, Tavernier; 305-852-8690), where they also sell T-shirts and "island" clothing.

KEY LARGO AREA NIGHTLIFE

If you're willing to experience a raunchy sort of bikers' beach bar in exchange for some possible nostalgia, stop at the **Caribbean Club** (MM 104, Key Largo; 305-451-9970). It is claimed that some parts of the movie *Key Largo* were filmed here, and it just may be true. Even if it's not, the sunsets from the deck are terrific. The joint is open from 7 a.m. to 4 a.m.

Coconuts (MM 100 at Marina del Mar, Key Largo; 305-451-4107) is a waterfront spot with live entertainment every night ranging from Top-40 to reggae. Inside, the huge dancefloor has a classy light show and a fog machine; outside, you can enjoy a drink on the canopied deck overlooking a canal with boats. Cover.

Woody's (MM 82; 305-664-4335), a late-night restaurant and lounge with a raucous bar crowd and dancing to a live band specializing in "Southern rock," boasts pool and other such frivolities. If you're only hungry, they offer take-out food until 3:30 a.m.

KEY LARGO AREA BEACHES AND PARKS

John Pennekamp Coral Reef State Park—This remarkable place is the first underwater state park in the United States. Together with the adjacent **Key Largo Coral Reef National Marine Sanctuary**, the park encompasses an area of about 178 nautical square miles, most of which lies out in the Atlantic Ocean north and east of Key Largo. Most visitors come to see the coral formations, seagrass beds and spectacular marine life of the reefs, either by scuba diving, snorkeling or taking a glass-bottom boat tour. The land section of the park acquaints visitors with mangrove swamps, a tropical hammock with many varieties of indigenous plant life, and numerous shore birds. An excellent visitor center, featuring an underwater marine life garden, a touch tank and other interpretive exhibits allow even those who prefer staying on dry land to experience a bit of the underwater world.

Facilities: Picnic areas, restrooms, bathhouse, showers, visitor center, nature trail, observation tower, snack bar, gift shop, dive shop, boat rental, marina, docks; information, 305-451-1202. *Fishing:* Both among the mangroves (for mangrove snapper, trout, sheepshead, snook) and in the Atlantic (for gamefish such as kingfish, mackerel, yellowtail). Tropical fish are protected. *Swimming:* Calm waters in three small swimming beaches.

Camping: There are 43 sites, some with hookups, at the state park; $23 per night for tent sites, $25 per night for hookups. Private RV and tent campgrounds are nearby, including **Key Largo Kampground and Marina** (MM 101.5, Key Largo; 305-451-1431) and **Calusa Camp Resort** (MM 101.5, Key Largo; 305-451-0232), which tend to be cramped but offer functional places for divers to stay.

Getting there: Entrance at MM 102.5 on Route 1, in Key Largo. Much of the park is accessible only by boat.

Harry Harris Park—This county park is one of the few public parks in the area for spending a day beside the ocean. It is spacious, with broad grassy areas and scattered trees. The beach isn't much, but the water is clear and full of fish.

Facilities: Picnic areas, restrooms, playgrounds, shuffleboard, boat ramps. *Swimming:* Possible, in clear water. *Fishing:* Off the jetties.

Getting there: Take Burton Drive at MM 92.5 in Tavernier; it's about a quarter of a mile to the park.

Islamorada Area

Islamorada (pronounced *eye-lah-mor-ah-dah*) was named by Spanish explorers and means "purple isles," perhaps for the way the land appeared on the horizon, perhaps for the abundant violet snail shells or the brilliant flowering plants found there when the islands were wild.

The Islamorada area begins at Windley Key (MM 85) and runs through Long Key (below MM 68). The community of Islamorada, on Upper Matecumbe Key, is its center of population. The area's brief ventures have included shipbuilding, tropical fruit and vegetable farming, turtling, sponging and the immensely prosperous business of salvaging shipwrecks. Fishing has always been especially fine in this area, and today tourism is the chief enterprise here.

The town is a collection of businesses that provide local folk with essentials while inviting visitors to "stay here," "eat here," "party here," "buy here." Holiday Isle, a gigantic resort and entertainment complex, dominates Windley Key with the latest in youthful party hype.

As with the other parts of the Keys, much of what Islamorada has to offer is out to sea. You'll see signs along Route 1 for boat rentals, diving cruises and fishing charters. Stop at the red caboose that houses the **Islamorada Chamber of Commerce** (MM 82.5; 305-664-4503) for information about both land and sea areas.

If you are traveling with your boat, you'll like knowing about **Bud N' Mary's Marina and Dive Center** (MM 79.8; 305-664-2211), especially if you enjoy being in the middle of such sea-related activities as snorkeling, fishing and diving charters, party boats, glass-bottom boat tours, backcountry fishing trips and sunset and sightseeing tours. Even without your own vessel you can still enjoy Bud N' Mary's glass-bottom boat cruises to Alligator Reef. Along the way you'll have a chance to do a little snorkeling (at Alligator Reef!).

For a nice, friendly marine show where, if you're lucky, you might get to hold a hoop for a jumping dolphin or get a kiss from a seal, stop at **Theatre of the Sea** (MM 84.5, Islamorada; 305-664-2431; admission), one of the oldest marine parks in the world. It may now have fancier, more sophisticated competitors, but this place is still fun and quite personal. There are sea creatures that can be touched, dolphins who join visitors for a "bottomless boat" trip and pretty tropical grounds to explore. Visitors can also swim with dolphins here by reservation.

Stop for a minute at the **Hurricane Monument** (MM 81.5, Islamorada) to meditate on the terrible storm of Labor Day, 1935. Before the anemometer blew away, winds were recorded at 200 mph; the barometer fell to 26.35, one of the lowest pressures ever recorded in the Western Hemisphere. This slightly neglected but nevertheless moving monument was dedicated in 1937 to the memory of the 423 people who died in that storm.

The three-hour trip to **Indian Key State Historic Site** (★) (boat leaves from MM 78.5, Indian Key Fill between Upper and Lower Matecumbe Keys; 305-664-4815; admission) presents the remarkable story of a ten-acre island that was once the prosperous seat of Dade County. Beneath the nearby, usually calm waters of the Atlantic lie the most treacherous reefs off the Florida coast, source of income first for Indians, and then for Americans who turned "salvaging" wrecked ships into profitable businesses. The bustling island town was destroyed in a grisly Indian attack in 1840. Today, rangers guide visitors down reconstructed village "streets" among the tall century plants and other tropical growth.

Another three-hour trip takes visitors to **Lignumvitae Key State Botanical Site** (★) (boat leaves from MM 78.5, Indian Key Fill between Upper and Lower Matecumbe Keys; 305-664-4815; admission) and shows how an island was formed. This key encompasses 280 acres; its virgin tropical forest is a reminder of how all the Keys probably appeared before people came in numbers. Ranger-guided walks through this rare environment introduce such unusual trees as the gumbo-limbo, mastic and poisonwood. The restored **Matheson House**, built in 1919, has survived hurricane and time; it demonstrates how island dwellers managed in the early days of Keys settlement, dependent on wind power, rainwater and food from the sea.

Near MM 66 lies the entrance to the **Layton Nature Trail** (★), an almost-hidden loop trail from highway to bay, winding through a dense hammock of carefully marked tropical plants, such as pigeon plum, wild coffee and gumbo-limbo, that are unique to the Keys. For travelers in a hurry, the

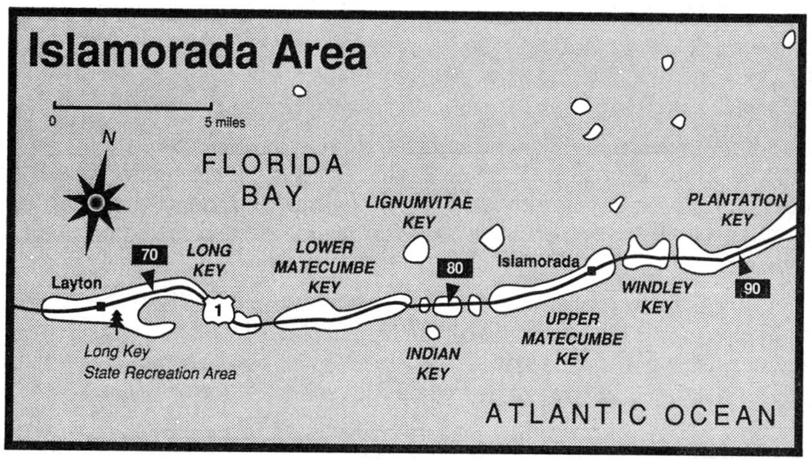

20-minute walk provides a good introduction to the flora that once covered most of the Keys.

Located 18 feet below the surface of the Atlantic Ocean, the **San Pedro Underwater Archaeological Preserve** (★) (1.3 nautical miles south of Indian Key; P.O. Box 776, Long Key 33001; 305-664-4815) welcomes divers, snorkelers and observers in glass-bottom boats. The *San Pedro* was a 287-ton, Dutch-built galleon in the New Spain fleet that left Havana harbor on a July day in 1733 and met its doom when hurricane winds drove it onto the reefs. The shipwreck park, dedicated in 1989, features an underwater nature trail where one can view varied populations of fish, crustaceans, mollusks and corals. Original anchors, ballast stones, bricks from the ship's galley and concrete cannon replicas enhance the park.

An **historical marker** west of Layton (near MM 66) marks the site of Long Key Fishing Club, established in 1906 by Flagler's East Coast Hotel Company. One aim of the group was to stop the wholesale destruction of gamefish in this mecca for saltwater anglers. The president of the club, which fell victim to the 1935 hurricane, was American author Zane Grey.

ISLAMORADA AREA HOTELS

The Islamorada business area includes another piece of Route 1 lined with mom-and-pop and various chain motels. If you prefer renting a home, condo or townhouse for a week, or even months, contact **Freewheeler Vacations** (Islamorada; 305-664-2075).

Folks who enjoy being where the action is choose to stay at **Holiday Isle Resorts and Marina** (MM 84, Islamorada; 305-664-2321), a great complex of lodgings, swimming pools, bars, restaurants and shops strung out along a stretch of Atlantic beach. The five-story main hotel and its three-story neighbor offer oceanfront rooms, efficiencies, apartments and suites. Some are ordinary motel-type rooms; others are luxury apartments with kitchens, bars and wrap-around balconies overlooking the ocean. Deluxe to ultra-deluxe.

If you want the glitz and fervor of Holiday Isle for lower rates, go a mile back up the road to **Harbor Lights** (MM 85, Islamorada; 305-664-3611) for moderate motel rooms and deluxe-priced efficiencies. Owned by Holiday Isle, this place operates a free trolley to take guests to the bustling center of things.

At **The Islander Motel** (MM 82.1, Islamorada; 305-664-2031) you can snorkel in the clear ocean water off the fishing pier or swim in the freshwater and saltwater pools. The Islander offers pleasant hotel rooms (some with kitchenettes) and fully equipped villas with screened porches. The 25-acre oceanside resort is rich in tropical plants and features shuffleboard. This is a popular place for families. Moderate.

Vacationers in search of sheer luxury have been coming to **Cheeca Lodge** (MM 82, Islamorada; 305-664-4651) for over half a century. Perched on the edge of the Atlantic Ocean, this four-story hotel has received a massive facelift. Much of the original wood remains in the updated lodge, which has classy lobby areas, spacious rooms, freshwater and saltwater pools, indoor and outdoor dining, tennis courts and a small golf course. Villas are scattered around grounds shaded by a variety of tropical trees. A fine, long pier invites fishing and serves as a take-off point for scuba divers and snorkelers. Ultra-deluxe.

For moderate rates, you can stay at the quiet, unadorned, oldish **Gamefish Resort** (MM 75.5; 305-664-5568), which offers motel rooms, efficiency apartments or combinations for families needing suites. The place is very plain, with tropical plantings and a clear tidal salt pool complete with lobsters in the rocks. It's very popular with families and retired folk who like the quiet and easy access to fishing and who feel comfortable with the aging but neatly kept furnishings.

ISLAMORADA AREA RESTAURANTS

The restaurant with the reputation is **Marker 88** (MM 88, Islamorada; 305-852-9315), whose continental cuisine has rated raves from some of the nation's top culinary magazines. Entrées include fish du jour topped with tomato concassé, and rice colonial Bombay, a magic mélange of beef and veal slices, curry, shrimp, scallops, pineapple, banana, pimento and scallions. Nestled beside Florida Bay and shaded by waving palms, Marker 88 is informally elegant and intimate with a rich tropical ambience. The wine list is as impressive as the creative menu. Deluxe to ultra-deluxe.

Of the many places to eat at Holiday Isle Resort, the classiest is the **Horizon Restaurant** (MM 84, Islamorada; 305-664-2321) atop the five-story main hotel. You can get fine views of the bay and the ocean while enjoying Keys seafood prepared in a variety of fashions including traditional broiled or fried, and meunière or almandine styles. The chef also does a variety of things with Caribbean queen conch, an old-time Keys shellfish now protected locally. Deluxe to ultra-deluxe.

You have two choices at the red-and-white-awninged **Coral Grill** (MM 83.5, Islamorada; 305-664-4803). You can gorge at the sumptuous moderately priced buffet upstairs, which features country staples like fried fish and roast turkey, or you can stay downstairs and control your intake. Native fish are treated several ways; especially tasty is the "Matecumbe" style, sautéed with scallions, black olives, pimento, butter and lime. Except for all the sparkling lights in the trees out front, the place appears undistinguished, but the moderate-priced menu makes it good for families.

The shimmering mermaid on the wall of the **Lorelei** (MM 82, Islamorada; 305-664-4656) may catch your eye, but it's the trellises, ceiling fans and handblown light fixtures that give this yacht-basin restaurant a nice "early Keys" feel. They do all sorts of things with the catch of the day here—broil, blacken, coconut-fry and serve it with Creole or meunière sauces. There are traditional conch chowder and fritters, too, and a devastating chocolate-chip Kahlua cheesecake for dessert. Moderate to deluxe.

Just before President George Bush was inaugurated in 1989, he went bonefishing in Islamorada and had dinner at Cheeca Lodge's **Atlantic's Edge Restaurant** (MM 82, Islamorada; 305-664-4651). The appetizer was stone-crab pie with scallions and tomatoes, a sublime sample of the excellent gourmet dining available in this elegant restaurant. Baked grouper is prepared in a plantain crust, Florida lobster with balsamic vinaigrette and grilled baby vegetables, and chicken with glazed onions and cabbage. There is a fine wine list, too. Deluxe to ultra-deluxe.

Manny and Isa's Kitchen (MM 81.6, Islamorada; 305-664-5019) is a very delightful, very plain little place where chatter among the staff is Spanish and food is tops. A number of authentic Cuban dishes such as *picadillo* and *palomilla* steak with black beans and rice make a very ample budget meal. Regular Keys seafood and other American items extend into the moderate range. With 24 hours notice, Manny and Isa will prepare a special Spanish paella dinner for two or more.

The Green Turtle Inn (MM 81.5, Islamorada; 305-664-9031) has been around since 1947, serving conch and turtle chowders, turtle or alligator steak and home-baked breads along with all sorts of traditional seafood dishes and prime rib. The walls are papered with photos, and hundreds of dollar bills hang above the bar. It's a noisy, slightly frantic place when full, which is often. Moderate to deluxe.

Paradise Café (MM 68.5, Islamorada; 305-664-4900) is a pink-and-green little place that deserves a medal for bravery for locating next door to another popular Italian eatery. Sam's small menu specializes in such olfactory-tantalizing items as red *bragiola*, rolled and braised beef stuffed with seasonings and served with red sauce, or *calamari marinara fra diavolo*, a squid entrée you can have spicy hot if you are up to it. If you can't make up your mind, try the "Three Muskateers," a multiple-item entrée. Moderate.

ISLAMORADA AREA SHOPPING

The Rain Barrel (MM 86.7, Plantation Key, 305-852-3084) is a store full of top-quality crafts, and much more. Many of the craftspeople create their wares right in this tropical setting that resembles a village more than a store. There are potters, jewelers, leather workers, fine artists and a maker of incredible silk flowers.

For a wide assortment of hand-crafted pottery, park under the trees and browse through **Village Pottery** (MM 86.5, behind Rain Barrel, Islamorada; 305-852-5976). Sometimes you can see the potters at work.

You can buy all sorts of beachwear, straw hats, funky T-shirts and souvenirs at the **Bimini Town Shops** alongside the docks at Holiday Isle Resorts (MM 84, Islamorada; 305-664-2321).

For trendy sporting goods and clothing, as well as fishing tackle that includes handmade rods, gaffs, flies and trolling lures and reels, stop at **H. T. Chittum & Co. General Mercantile** (MM 82.7, Islamorada; 305-664-4421).

ISLAMORADA AREA NIGHTLIFE

There's live entertainment every night in the restaurant/lounge at **Plantation Yacht Harbor Resort** (MM 87, Islamorada; 305-852-2381), a pleasant spot overlooking Florida Bay. It's mostly mellow, sometimes country-western, sometimes classic rock, usually featuring a single performer but occasionally a top touring band.

Nightlife begins in the daytime at **Holiday Isles Resort** (MM 84, Islamorada; 305-664-2321) with a host of party areas sporting such names as Jaws Raw Bar, Bilge Bar and the World Famous Tiki Bar. Signs also point you to "Kokomo," a beach bar named after the fact for the Beach Boys' famous song. There's canned and live music to suit a variety of tastes throughout the days and nights. Up in **The Horizon Restaurant**, atop the five-story main hotel with fine views of the ocean, there's quieter live entertainment for listening and dancing.

Next to the "all-you-can-eat" restaurant at Whale Harbor, the **Harbor Bar** (MM 83.5, Islamorada; 305-664-9888) features live rock music and a raw bar. Come early enough to watch the fishing boats come in. Some consider this place to be a mellow alternative to the area's late-night teen haunts.

You can enjoy a quiet drink at a table overlooking the Atlantic in Cheeca Lodge's elegant **Light Tackle Lounge** (MM 82, Islamorada; 305-664-4651). There's also deck seating available.

In 1960, Hurricane Donna blew what is now the **Cabaña Bar** (MM 82, Islamorada; 305-664-4338) out to sea. After it was towed back, the place became a mellow bayside lounge. Live musicians perform reggae and easy listening "sunset music" nightly.

ISLAMORADA AREA BEACHES AND PARKS

Long Key State Recreation Area—Like the key on which it is located, this park is long and narrow, its shoreline of shallow flats, thin beaches and mangrove lagoons all shaped by the usually gentle Atlantic waters. Mahogany, Jamaica dogwood, gumbo-limbo and other tropical trees inhabit the tangled hammocks that, along with the mangrove swamps, can be crossed on boardwalks and viewed from an observation tower. Even though the traffic of Route 1 is closer than you might wish, you can actually camp right next to the ocean, shaded by tall Australian pines.

Facilities: Picnic areas, restrooms, nature trail, showers, observation tower, groceries in nearby Layton; information, 305-664-4815. *Fishing:* Excellent saltwater fishing adjacent to the park and in deep Gulf Stream waters of the Atlantic. *Swimming:* Good.

Camping: There are 66 sites, including 30 with RV hookups, and six primitive sites. Fees are $24 per night ($26 per night for hookups).

Getting there: The recreation area is located on the ocean side of Route 1 at MM 67.5.

Marathon Area

The Marathon area actually encompasses a collection of islands from Conch Key (below MM 65) to the beginning of the Seven Mile Bridge (MM 47) and includes far more than the bustling, traffic-filled, friendly metropolis and its occasional suburbs and resorts. Just before the outskirts of the city lies the oceanfront community of Key Colony Beach, a designed village where even the smallest houses seem to have their own individual boat docks. And here and there among these islands and from their bridges you'll encounter open spaces and fine views of the ocean and Gulf.

One of those views hits visitors immediately upon entering the Marathon area via **Long Key bridge**. If you have not yet been overwhelmed by the realization that when you travel the Keys you're really heading out to sea, get ready. You'll certainly feel the impact after you leave Layton and cross the beautiful bridge over the point where the Atlantic Ocean meets the Gulf of Mexico between Long Key and the first little Conch Key. On most days, this meeting is calm and gentle. The horizon stretches blue on all sides as sea and sky meld. Travelers often stop at the little pull-offs on either end of this bridge—the second longest in the Keys—to take in the vastness of the water and the handsome bridge. Because the shore is sandy here, you will see people wading out in the shallow water or trying out their snorkeling and scuba gear.

After leaving the beautiful scenes at the Long Key bridge, Route 1 continues through several small Keys, including Duck Key, once site of a salt-making enterprise and now inhabited by showy homes and a large resort, Hawk's Cay. Nearby Grassy Key is home of the **Dolphin Research Center** (MM 59; 305-289-1121), where a tax-deductible contribution will allow you to play and swim with the friendly creatures (reservations required). Your money goes, in part, to the center's program of providing rest and recreation for dolphins who have become stressed-out from long years of performance and the overcrowded conditions of captivity. (Like humans, dolphins can suffer ulcers and loss of appetite.)

Continuing on Route 1, you will encounter population pockets and empty spaces, skirt the residential and vacation village of Key Colony Beach, and arrive finally at Marathon, the last good-sized town before the famous Seven Mile Bridge. Stop at the **Greater Marathon Chamber of Commerce** (MM 48.7; 305-743-5417) for information on this bustling area, which boasts shopping malls, a modern airport, commercial boat yards and lots of facilities for travelers.

Hidden from the casual observer, though actually located in the heart of Marathon, is **Crane Point Hammock** (★) (headquarters of Florida Keys Land and Sea Trust, MM 50; 305-743-3900). Considered by many to be the most environmentally and historically significant piece of property in the Keys, this bayside 63-acre nature preserve of tropical hardwoods and mangrove wetlands contains many exotic tree specimens, archaeological sites and an historic conch-style house.

Crane Point Hammock is also home of the **Museum of Natural History of the Florida Keys** (305-743-9100; admission) and the **Florida Keys Children's Museum** (305-743-9100; admission). The former features a re-created coral reef, Indian and shipwreck artifacts, and displays on pirate life. Ideal for the entire family, the latter museum's exhibits include a tropical Caribbean lagoon, marine touch tank, historic sailing vessel and native American hut built with palm fronds.

If you head toward the ocean at MM 47.5 (11th Street), you will end up around the **commercial fishing docks,** where you can watch the comings and goings of shrimp boats and other craft of the Marathon fleet.

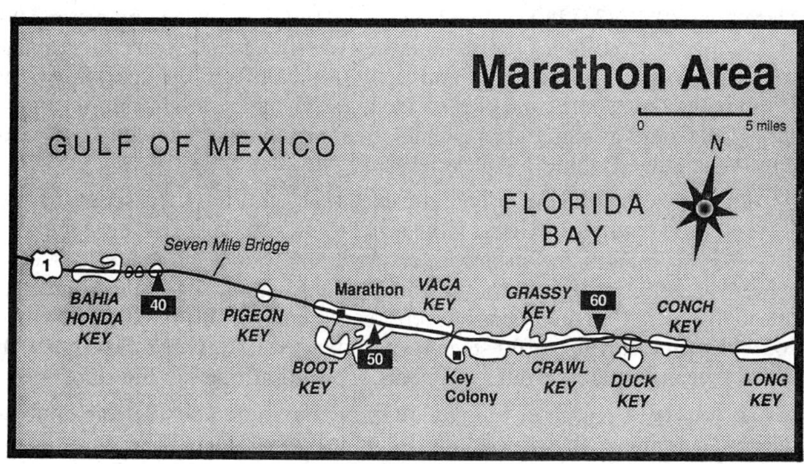

MARATHON AREA HOTELS

If you like a resort where everything is at your fingertips, the 60-acre **Hawk's Cay Resort and Marina** (MM 61 at Duck Key; 305-743-7000) will fulfill your dreams. Here you can sleep in a spacious room decorated in salmon and teal and furnished with wickerwork rattan, dine in several very fine restaurants, bask beside the pool or on a pleasant manmade beach, play tennis and golf, or make arrangements with the concierge for charter fishing, diving or just about anything the Keys have to offer. The entire huge property is elegant but casual. Ultra-deluxe rates include a big gourmet breakfast buffet.

For moderate rates, you can have a basic motel room or a fully equipped efficiency at the **Valhalla Beach Resort Motel** (★) (MM 56.5, Marathon; 305-289-0616) and feel as if you are on a private island with a quiet Atlantic inlet and waving palms. The dozen units are strictly basic, but the tiny beach, little boat docks and considerable distance from traffic make this a quiet and special place.

Several motels and small hotels line the narrow but pretty Atlantic Beach at Key Colony Beach. The **Key Colony Beach Motel** (441 East Ocean Drive; 305-289-0411) offers small, carpeted, functional rooms for moderate prices, and you can dive into the large heated pool on those rare days when the ocean is too cold.

The **Ocean Beach Club** (351 Ocean Drive East; 305-289-0525) is a three-story affair with cool blue decor that suits its oceanside setting. Besides the deluxe-priced rooms, there are ultra-deluxe-priced apartments with fully furnished kitchens, a small pool and lots of beach chairs for sunbathing on the rare (for the Keys) strip of sand.

Sombrero Resort and Lighthouse Marina (19 Sombrero Boulevard, Marathon; 305-743-2250) offers bright, comfortable garden and waterfront units ranging from hotel rooms to suites with kitchens. Everything about the place is appropriately light and airily tropical, from the sparkling pool to the breezy restaurant and cheerful lounge. There are tennis courts, a proshop, sauna and 54-slip marina. Children are encouraged, making it a good family lodging. Deluxe to ultra-deluxe.

If you're looking for a bed and breakfast, and they are scarce in the Keys, try the **Hopp-Inn Guest House** (★) (5 Man-O-War Drive, Marathon; 305-743-4118), situated in an oceanside home. For a moderate-to-deluxe price you get one of four rooms with private bath and entrance, air conditioning, views of the ocean, good breezes and a full breakfast. Owners Joe and Joan Hopp also offer several apartments, without breakfasts but with full kitchens, at deluxe rates. Papayas grow right outside the door.

If you're in search of unique lodging, you might consider the double-decker houseboats at **Faro Blanco Marina Resort** (1996 Overseas Highway, Marathon; 305-743-9018). Securely moored, the boats are accessible from little private docks in a sheltered basin. These sedate blue-gray craft provide handsome quarters furnished formally enough for any ship's captain, and you can throw open the french doors to enjoy the comings and goings in the harbor. Cottages and condos also available. Prices are moderate to deluxe.

Reminiscent of old-time tourist cabins, **Conch Key Cottages** (★) (off Route 1 between MM 62 and 63; 305-289-1377) are located on their own tiny island accessible by a short causeway. This handful of rustic wooden cottages come in a variety of sizes; some have screened porches and all are within easy access of a pleasant little beach. Best of all, they are away from busy Route 1. Moderate to deluxe.

Knights Key Inn (★) (MM 47, Marathon; 305-743-9963) is a two-story unit of older vacation apartments, almost hidden alongside a neighboring campground, where you can dock your boat for free. If your moderately priced efficiency is on the west side, you have a great view of the Seven Mile Bridge. Rooms are old-fashioned with a slightly nautical decor, and the whole place is somewhat submerged in lush tropical flora. There is a small picnic area; a few retirees stay here all winter.

MARATHON AREA RESTAURANTS

Don Pedro (MM 53; 305-743-5247) demonstrates a creative use of a strip shopping center unit. Cuban cuisine is the feature of this sparkling blue-and-gray eatery located on an insignificant corner. All the entrées, such as *lechón asado* (roast pork), *boliche asado* (pot roast) and *picadillo* (a tasty hamburger dish), come with yellow rice, black beans, fried bananas and crispy Cuban bread. The very filling budget meals may be accompanied by tropical milkshakes or steamy, thick Cuban coffee and topped off with a dessert of flan, a traditional baked custard.

Brian's in Paradise (MM 52; 305-743-3183) has a menu with 12 large pages featuring humorous illustrations of Keys wildlife and something to eat for everyone. The emphasis is on seafood, the most popular item being the "Marathon meal" that provides a good way to sample local favorites—conch chowder, conch fritters, fried shrimp and Key lime pie. There are plenty of budget entrées as well as moderate selections, including the spit-roasted chicken entrée appealingly named "Bird of Paradise." The wide variety of sandwiches are served all day.

Search diligently for **Little Bavaria** (★) (MM 50, Gulfside Village Shopping Center, Marathon; 305-743-4833) and you'll be rewarded with a very authentic German meal of wienerschnitzel, pork *haxen* or bratwurst. Or try the sauerbrauten or curry sausage. The ordinary store space has been transformed into a charming European café with dainty lace curtains, a menu in German and English, a wide selection of imported German wine and beer and charming decor in white and Delft blue. Budget to moderate.

The art deco menu plus the comical cartoons of fictional chefs beaming at you from the walls hint that **Chef's** (Sombrero Resort, 19 Sombrero Boulevard, Marathon; 305-743-4108) is probably a fun place to eat. The small but well-balanced menu offers some elegant beef, seafood and chicken entrées; specialties include such delights as barbecued baby back ribs, blackened prime rib and fresh fish meunière. There is an open grill and a glassed-in dining area alongside the tennis courts. Moderate to deluxe.

The lighthouse that distinguishes Faro Blanco Resort is authentic, and so is the fine dining at the resort's restaurant, **Kelsey's** (MM 48.5, Marathon; 305-743-9018). Along with creative treatments of local seafood, this sedately casual place prepares roast Long Island duckling, veal shadows française with mushrooms and shrimp, and other continental gourmet dishes. The restaurant is lush with greenery, and its windows overlook the marina. Deluxe.

If you wind down 15th Street past where you think it ends and you'll come to **Castaway** (★) (turn toward ocean just below MM 48; 305-743-6247), a no-nonsense eatery on the working wharf where locals have been coming for several decades. There is a basic seafood menu with chicken and steak for the misguided, but the big come-on here is shrimp "steamed in beer—seconds on the house." They ply you with luscious hot buns dripping with honey even before you begin. Good variety of wines; moderate prices.

MARATHON AREA SHOPPING

You'll never have to go very far to find decorated T-shirts in the Keys; just about every shop has a selection. But if you go to **Handprints of the Keys** (★) (72 Coco Plum Drive, near MM 54; 305-743-4131) you can see how they are made. Prices are discounted here, and there's a good choice of these popular souvenirs, many designed by local artists.

Marine Jewelry (MM 54; 305-289-0628) manufactures gold and coral jewelry with nautical and sea-related themes, such as gold-capped shark teeth and gold Florida lobsters.

Being the largest populated area in the Middle Keys, Marathon has several shopping plazas and all the basic stores needed for daily living, as well as the usual souvenir dens. For originally designed, hand-painted Florida Keys skirts and handbags, stop at the **Brown Pelican Store** (K-Mart Shopping Plaza, MM 50; 305-743-3849).

If you are doing your own cooking, or you'd just like to peruse the catches-of-the-day, explore the collection of **seafood markets** along the wharves at the end of 11th or 15th Street, on the oceanside near MM 48. These are outlets for some of the area's serious commercial fishing.

MARATHON AREA NIGHTLIFE

The Ship's Pub (MM 61, Duck Key; 305-743-7000) overlooks the water beside the showy marina at Hawk's Cay. There's late-night dancing to all kinds of music.

For dancing Thursday through Saturday nights try the **Hurricane** (MM 49.5, 4650 Overseas Highway; 305-743-5755). There's usually a live band during the summer.

The Quay (MM 54, Marathon; 305-289-1810) is so popular that it has clones in Key Largo and Key West. You can enjoy the sunsets, full meals and tropical drinks at this wicker-furnished, brightly decorated Gulfside spot, where there's live entertainment Thursday through Sunday nights.

Good Times Lounge (19 Sombrero Boulevard, Marathon; 305-743-4108), in the middle of Sombrero Resort, has a variety of live performers who play deep into the wee hours of the night. Tropical drinks are the specialty at this cheerful poolside place.

You can dance or play darts as local and imported bands play soft rock and other music nightly at **Angler's Lounge** (MM 48.3, Marathon; 305-743-9018) at Faro Blanco Resort. This second-story nightspot has windows all around and a wonderful view of the harbor and bay.

Several arts organizations are active in the Marathon area, sponsoring or producing concerts and plays from time to time. For information on what may be going on during your stay, contact the **Marathon Community Theatre** (305-743-9368).

MARATHON AREA BEACHES AND PARKS

Sombrero Beach Park (★)—This free community park is mostly a generous windswept grassy area with a few palm trees and a long, narrow spit of sand along the ocean, offering one of the few public beaches around. Though not spectacular, it is a good place for some sun and relaxation and an ideal romping spot for children.

Facilities: Picnic areas, restrooms, playground. *Swimming:* Pleasant in usually clear, calm ocean water.

Getting there: The park is located on Sombrero Beach Road at MM 50 in Marathon.

Lower Keys Area

The Lower Keys, which begin at MM 40 just below the Seven Mile Bridge and extend to around MM 5, are *different*. They are different in geological makeup, in flora and fauna and even in ambience and pace from the rest of the Keys. Geologically, their fossil coral base is layered with a limestone called oolite (for its egg-shaped granules). Some of the islands of the Lower Keys are forested with sturdy pine trees, others with tall tropical hardwoods where orchids and bromeliads thrive. A number of endangered species, including the unique Key deer, struggle for survival on these low-lying islands.

Big Pine Key is the largest of the islands and second in area only to Key Largo in the entire Keys. Wildlife refuges and shopping centers share this island, the former protecting much of the unique plant and animal life, the latter offering necessary services for the people who choose to live in what seems a quieter, lonelier region than those on either side.

The Lower Keys boast the best beach south of the mainland and access to a fine protected section of coral reef offshore in the Atlantic. Though there are pockets of development, from collections of little frame houses to assorted elegant residences, frenetic modernization seems to have been held at bay. With some unassuming screened-in eateries, scattered modest lodgings and significant protected wild areas, this region offers more chances to experience the "old Keys" than any other.

Perhaps the most impressive sight in the Lower Keys is its initial access, the magnificent **Seven Mile Bridge**, spanning the sea between Marathon and Sunshine Key. The bridge that carries the Overseas Highway today is the "new" bridge, built in 1982 to replace the terrifyingly narrow but equally impressive structure that parallels it on the Gulf side. The old bridge, referred to as "the longest fishing pier in the world," crosses **Pigeon Key,** which you can't reach but can view from your lofty height above the sea. Once a railroad camp for Henry Flagler's crew, Pigeon Key is an important historic site; efforts are underway to preserve its natural state and historic old conch-style houses.

Unlike the upper and middle Keys, most of the Lower Keys seem to lie at right angles to the highway. Their geology, and hence their vegetation and wildlife, differ in many respects from that of their neighbors to the northeast. **Bahia Honda Key** (MM 37-38), for example, features some white sand beaches; many unusual species of plants and birds are found throughout the Lower Keys.

As you look across to the southern peninsula of Bahia Honda Key, you will see a magnificent section of the old **Flagler Bridge,** with the railroad trestle on one level and the automobile highway arching above it, a masterpiece of engineering for its day.

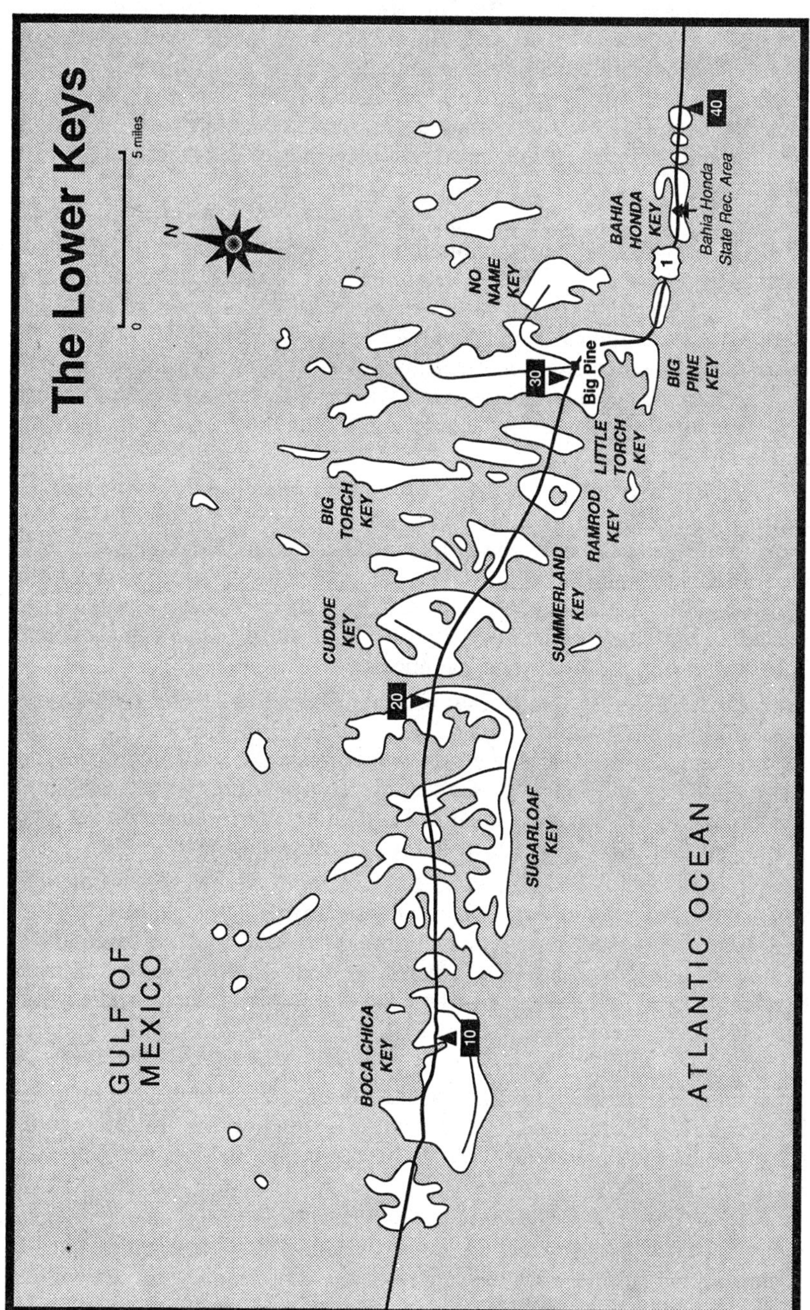
The Lower Keys
0
5 miles
N
GULF OF
MEXICO
ATLANTIC OCEAN
BOCA CHICA
KEY
10
SUGARLOAF
KEY
20
CUDJOE
KEY
SUMMERLAND
KEY
BIG
TORCH
KEY
RAMROD
KEY
LITTLE
TORCH
KEY
30
Big Pine
BIG
PINE
KEY
NO
NAME
KEY
1
BAHIA
HONDA
KEY
Bahia Honda
State Rec. Area
40

At MM 33 you arrive at Big Pine Key. Stop at the **Lower Keys Chamber of Commerce** (MM 31; 305-872-2411) for a lot of good information about this area. Big Pine Key is second only to Key Largo in size, but its character is quite different. Here are burgeoning subdivisions, good-sized shopping centers, freshwater sink holes formed in the oolic rock foundation of the island, and pine trees. The contest between development and the wild is apparent.

Living in uneasy relationship with the ever-growing population of Big Pine Key are the Key deer, a miniature subspecies of white-tailed deer that grow to be only about two feet in height. In the 1940s, the population almost disappeared, inspiring the establishment of the 7962-acre **National Key Deer Refuge** (headquarters at western end of Watson Boulevard; 305-872-2239). Occasionally you can spot the world's tiniest deer in the wilderness areas of the refuge, especially in early morning or late afternoon, but be warned that there are heavy fines for feeding or harming these endangered, fragile animals.

Not far from the town of Big Pine lies a good-sized freshwater rock quarry pond called **Blue Hole** (★) (2.25 miles north of Route 1 on Key Deer Boulevard), the only one of its kind in the entire Keys. It is inhabited by several alligators, who often lie near the shore, as well as turtles and various wading birds and fish. The nearby **Jack C. Watson Nature Trail** meanders through a typical Big Pine Key habitat of palms and slash pine and skirts a unique hardwood hammock.

Marine biologist Stan Becker will take you on a one-of-a-kind **Canoeing Nature Tour** (★) (off Route 1 at MM 28.5; 305-872-2620) of the Big Pine region. You may explore buttonwood forests rich with bromeliads, observe rare birds and Key deer, see the effects of wildfire (which is essential for regrowth), and become acquainted with much of the unique Lower Keys fauna and flora you might miss without a knowledgeable guide.

Only reachable by boat, **Looe Key National Marine Sanctuary** (★) (6.7 nautical miles southeast of Big Pine Key; headquarters at MM 37; 305-872-4039) is an exceedingly popular diving site. The spectacular coral formations of this five-square-mile area and the exceptionally clear waters make it a delight even for novice snorkelers. Several wrecked ships also lie within the sanctuary, including the 1744 British frigate *H.M.S. Looe*.

Captain Buddy's Family Fun Trips (MM 28.5; 305-872-3572; admission) will take you out among the islands and exploring the reef by power boat; reservations required. You can enjoy a sea kayaking adventure in the Great White Heron National Refuge by contacting **Reflections** (Big Pine Key; 305-872-2896).

By now you have probably noticed that some of the telephone poles along the Overseas Highway seem to be topped with great untidy piles of sticks and twigs. These are **osprey nests**. If you look closely, you will occasionally see a bird with its young. Ospreys are regular residents of the Keys; some seem uninhibited by the cars and 18-wheelers that constantly whiz beneath them.

Higher in the sky, on the Gulf side, floats a large, white, blimp-shaped radar balloon. This is **Fat Albert**, on the lookout for illegal drug traffickers and other inappropriate interlopers. It is moored to a missile tracking station on Cudjoe Key.

If you take a detour toward the Gulf on lower Sugarloaf Key, you'll get a glance at the **Perky Bat Tower** (★) (off Route 1 at MM 17). This Dade County pine curiosity was built in 1929 as the brainchild of Richter C. Perky, who hoped to get the menacing mosquito population under control by importing a population of insect-devouring bats to take up residence in this louvered bat condo. Some say the bats never arrived, others that they came and, not satisfied with their carefully designed accommodations, took off for preferable climes. At any rate, the novel structure still stands and is on the National Register of Historic Places.

Heading toward Key West, you will see increasingly less development and more mangroves. Here and there you'll spot folks fishing off the old bridges. The densest residential area surrounds the Naval Air Base on Boca Chica Key. When you reach Stock Island, you have arrived in the suburbs of Key West.

LOWER KEYS AREA HOTELS

Generic motels and small resorts appear here and there in the Lower Keys; rates are often lower than in nearby Key West. If you look hard, you'll also discover that some of the very best lodgings in this area are the hidden ones. If you'd like to rent a vacation home away from the highway, contact **Big Pine Vacation Rentals** (Route 1, Box 610-D, Big Pine Key; 305-872-9863). All the homes are on canals with boat dockage and fishing. Rates are moderate to deluxe; three-night minimum stay required.

There are three handsome duplex cabins on the Gulf side of **Bahia Honda State Recreation Area** (MM 37; 305-872-2353). Though the cabins are not really hidden, because you can see them from the highway, many visitors are unaware that the six gray frame units on stilts are available for rental. Unit rates are deluxe, but the fully equipped lodgings with spacious decks can accommodate up to eight people. Make reservations by phone or in person, up to a year ahead.

The motto of **The Barnacle Bed and Breakfast** (★) (Long Beach Drive, one and a half miles from MM 33; 305-872-3298), "barefoot oceanfront living with panache," says it all. The owners built their elegant home in the shape of a six-pointed star, creating a collection of interestingly designed, distinctive rooms around a central screen-roofed atrium where gourmet breakfasts are served. Guests stay in either of two rooms with private baths in the main house or in one of the two efficiencies in a many-angled annex. Deluxe.

Deer Run Bed and Breakfast (★) (Long Beach Drive, two miles from MM 33; 305-872-2800) offers three rooms, two moderate, one deluxe, with private baths in a very attractive Florida-style house with high ceilings, Bahama fans and good views of the ocean. A 52-foot verandah overlooks the sea and the natural grounds where raccoon and Key deer roam. The owner has cleverly decorated the outdoor area with driftwood and other jetsam deposited by the Atlantic currents onto the beach. Guests enjoy an outdoor hot tub and full American breakfasts.

If you'd like to stay near the area where the Key deer roam, contact **Canal Cottage** (Big Pine Key; 305-872-3881). This quaint, natural-wood stilt home is so far off the beaten path that you'll have to ask for directions when you call to reserve for a two-night minimum stay. Depend on Bahama fans and breezes to keep you cool here; everything is furnished, including breakfast food. Moderate.

The windswept, old-time one- and two-bedroom cottages at the **Old Wooden Bridge Fishing Camp** (★) (Bunta Risa at Bogie Channel, take Wilder Road at MM 30 and follow signs to No Name Key; 305-872-2241) are especially popular with anglers and divers who don't need a lot of amenities other than a comfortable, plain cabin, a full kitchen and access to the water. Rental boats are available, or stroll over to the Bogie Channel Bridge for some great fishing. Moderate.

"Tropical paradise" is a worn out phrase, but it really fits **Little Palm Island** (★) (offshore at MM 28.5, Little Torch Key; 305-872-2524). This five-acre island of waving palms and green lawns features 14 luxurious two-suite villas, each one facing the water. For the ultra-deluxe rate you enjoy generous thatched-roof quarters with abundant windows, Latin decor, a private sundeck, meals in the excellent restaurant, transportation from Little Torch Key and enough quiet to calm the most jangled nerves. If you want to go fishing, touring nature preserves, diving or sightseeing, Little Palm will make the arrangements; but if you want to stay around, you can sail, windsurf, browse in the library, get a massage or just luxuriate on the island once enjoyed by Harry Truman and other notables.

Sugar Loaf Lodge (MM 17, Sugarloaf Key; 305-745-3211) is one of the "full service" resorts with average but pleasant motel rooms and efficiencies, most of them facing the water. Full service here means not only a pool, restaurant and lounge, but a three-times-a-day dolphin show by long-time resident Sugar, a marina, mini-golf and fishing charters. It's also very convenient to Key West. Deluxe.

LOWER KEYS RESTAURANTS

The **Cedar Inn Restaurant and Lounge** (MM 31; 305-872-4031) is plain but a little less so than some of the other popular Lower Keys eateries. In fact, this one is just fancy enough to have oysters with caviar and sour cream for an appetizer. Fresh fish is served broiled, fried, stuffed or florentine. They also have stuffed lobster in season and a 'gator appetizer that most people try just so they can say they have. Moderate to deluxe.

Open for breakfast, lunch and dinner, the **Dip 'N Deli** (MM 31; 305-872-3030) is a nice place whose name tells all—there are fresh salads, 22 kinds of sandwiches, soups and lots of ice cream treats including old-fashioned sodas and milkshakes. Dinner features chicken and steak entrées. There's also lots of local chatter going on here, as well as the refreshing break from the ever-present seafood.

To get away from it all in style, plan to dine at the restaurant on **Little Palm Island** (★) (offshore from Little Torch Key, MM 28.5; 305-872-2524). You have to call ahead for a reservation; they will tell you when the boat will pick you up to take you to the lovely, luxurious island resort. If you're wise, you'll go in time to watch the sunset while sipping a cocktail beside the sandy beach or partaking of the fish of the day, yellowtail snapper filet, breast of chicken with fruit sauce, or any of the other continental entrées. Deluxe to ultra-deluxe.

Montes Restaurant & Fish Market (MM 23, Summerland Key; 305-745-3731) is a bare-bones place with plastic-covered round picnic tables and good old-fashioned fried seafood platters and baskets with french fries, cole slaw and sauce. Sit on the porch beside the canal and enjoy what you're supposed to eat in the Keys—conch chowder, conch salad, conch fritters, stone crabs and shrimp in beer. Moderate.

Mangrove Mama's (MM 20; 305-745-3030) is such an unlikely looking, side-of-the-road, banana-tree-surrounded eating establishment that you probably wouldn't stop unless someone recommended it—and plenty of Lower Keys folks do just that, with great enthusiasm. The floor is concrete, tablecloths are minimal, the chairs don't match and resident cats look longingly at your dinners. But the menu, though brief and to the point, is somewhat fancier than you'd expect, with such treats as baked stuffed shrimp and chicken and scallop Caribbean, sautéed with bacon and served in a creamy dijon sauce. The herb teas and homemade rolls are as pleasant a surprise as the handsome brick fireplace, used on very rare chilly nights. Moderate to deluxe.

LOWER KEYS SHOPPING

For all the basic necessities, the main place for shopping in the Lower Keys is the **Big Pine Key Shopping Plaza** (on Key Deer Boulevard just off Route 1 at MM 30).

Edie's Hallmark Shop (Big Pine Key Shopping Plaza; 305-872-3933) is far more than it's name implies. Here you'll find works by local artists and an excellent book section with top-notch vacation reading as well as a good supply of Florida and Keys books and guides.

LOWER KEYS NIGHTLIFE

The **Cedar Inn Restaurant and Lounge** (MM 31; 305-872-4031) has live entertainment some nights and occasional special events such as sock hops and the like.

For an evening with the locals, drop in at the **No Name Pub** (★) (north end of Watson Boulevard, Big Pine Key; 305-872-9115), a funky, run-down eating and drinking establishment with a carved-up wooden bar, over 70 kinds of beer, darts and pool. They may have a band, occasionally a pig roast and always the "best pizza in the known universe." This is a fun place that just about anybody can direct you to.

On Friday there's live rock-and-roll performed by local bands at **Looe Key Reef Resort** (MM 27.5, Ramrod Key; 305-872-2215).

Pirate's Lounge (Sugar Loaf Lodge, MM 17, Sugarloaf Key; 305-745-3211) is a typical resort-motel nightspot. This one has weekend entertainment and dancing, and boasts oversized piña coladas and strawberry daiquiris.

LOWER KEYS AREA BEACHES AND PARKS

Bahia Honda State Recreation Area—This southernmost state recreation area offers what many consider the best swimming beaches in the Keys—wider and leading into deeper water than most. Remnants of the undeveloped Keys remain in this beautiful park—silver palms, satinwood, dwarf morning glories and a number of rare birds such as the roseate spoonbill and white-crowned pigeon. You may camp in the wide open spaces (best choice during mosquito season) in view of a handsome segment of Henry Flagler's original old bridge, or in the shady hardwood hammock at Sandspur Beach.

Facilities: Picnic areas, restrooms, cabins, bathhouse, nature trail, concession stand, marina, dive shop, limited groceries; information, 305-872-2353. *Fishing:* Excellent, both in bay and ocean; guides available during tarpon season. *Swimming:* Excellent, both in the Atlantic Ocean and Gulf of Mexico.

Camping: There are 60 tent sites and 64 RV hookups; $24 per night ($10 more for hookups).

Getting there: Entrance on ocean side of Route 1 at MM 36.5.

Key West

Though not quite in the tropics, Key West is to all appearances a tropical island. Lying low on a shimmering sea, it boasts backyards lush with hibiscus, oleanders, frangipani and kapok and mango trees. Its generous harbors are filled with hybrid fleets of battered fishing craft, glass-bottom boats and handsome yachts. Date and coconut palms rustle like dry paper in the usually gentle and dependable breezes that come in off the sea. Heat pervades, but even in midsummer it's seldom unbearable. Key West is a small town sort of place where narrow streets are lined with picket fences and lovely old frame houses. At the same time, it's a traveler's haven with classy hotels and happy hours. The cul-de-sac of the Overseas Highway, it's unlike any other city in the United States.

Numerous well-known artists and writers, most notably Ernest Hemingway and Tennessee Williams, have found Key West a place of inspiration. The town boasts several Pulitzer Prize winners among its residents. Loafers have discovered Key West to be a comfortable spot for idling away the hospitably temperate days. Gays and others have found a tolerance for their lifestyles. Jazz performers, country-and-western singers and classical musicians have contributed to the sounds of the little city.

Each group has added color and contrast to the rich island tapestry. Today, Key West is a tourist town, one of the nation's chief travel destinations. Here most visitors have no trouble finding something to their liking. They can find tours, nightlife, souvenir shops, arts events, festivals and a nightly sunset celebration. Fishing, diving and boat trips to the Gulf Stream and tiny out-islands are added attractions.

It's easy to get around Key West; the entire island is only about four miles long and two miles wide. Stop in at the **Key West Welcome Center** (3840 North Roosevelt Boulevard; 305-296-4444) for a taste of the area. This is at about MM 4, but from here on you can stop counting Mile Markers and return to familiar street numbers.

By following Route 1 you will arrive in **Old Town**, the historic and main tourist area of Key West, just about where North Roosevelt Boulevard becomes Truman Avenue.This is a helter-skelter sort of place, with grand old Victorian houses, inviting alleys, junky souvenir shops, rocking and rolling bars, classy hotels, intimate guest houses, crowded marinas, street hawkers and incredible sunsets all tossed together into a colorful, noisy, artsy collage.

Away from Old Town, the remainder of the island includes settled residential areas, predictable shopping and a number of interesting sights that should pull you away from the tourist trappings. Here you are more likely to run into those descendants of old Key West and the lower Keys who proudly refer to themselves as "conchs." The original settlers were named after the giant shells that were so much a part of their sea-oriented lives.

Although Old Town is small enough for walking, and the whole island for biking, it helps to get oriented on one of several available tours. Besides, you'll pick up some very interesting history of this unique island city. The trackless **Conch Tour Train** (depots near the Welcome Center at 3850 North Roosevelt Boulevard and along Front Street; 305-294-5161) has been orienting visitors for over 30 years with 14-mile island tours, leaving at regular intervals daily. **Old Town Trolley Tour** (leaving from the Trolley Barn at 1910 North Roosevelt Boulevard, Mallory Square, the Welcome Center and most major hotels; 305-296-6688) meanders through the historic old streets, setting out about every 30 minutes.

If you prefer to get oriented on your own, stop at the **Chamber of Commerce** (402 Wall Street; 305-294-2587) and pick up a Pelican Path walking tour guide or Solaris Hill's *Walking and Biking Guide to Old Key West.*

You may have to wait in line to have your picture taken at the spot marking the **Southernmost Point** (ocean end of Whitehead Street). "Ninety miles to Cuba," reads the sign beneath the kitschy-looking striped buoy surrounded by folks with cameras.

The factory that was parent to the **Key West Cigar Factory** (3 Pirates Alley off Front Street; 305-294-3470) dates back to the mid-19th century. Though much smaller than the original establishments, this little shop is the place to watch cigars being hand rolled the way they've always been. Cigars are also rolled and sold at **Rodriguez Cigar Factory** (113 Kino Plaza; 305-296-0167).

History buffs will enjoy searching for the gun turret from the **Battleship USS Maine** (near drop boxes at the Post Office, Front and Greene streets). Not exactly hidden, but somewhat hard to find, this is a little monument to those who died in the tragic sinking that set off the Spanish-American War.

Take a look at the impressive **Old Stone Methodist Church** (Eaton Street at Simonton Street; 305-296-2392), whose two-foot-thick walls were made from solid limestone quarried right beside the sanctuary. Built between 1877 and 1892, the handsome church has a native mahogany ceiling and a teakwood chancel.

The most notable feature of Old Town is the architecture. Many of the beautiful old houses you see were built of wood by ships' carpenters in a blend of styles that came to be known as **conch-style houses**. Influenced by the varied backgrounds of their owners and the demands of the hurricane-prone climate, the result is an eclectic architectural heritage unique to this island city.

For an introductory sampling of these conch houses, start at the corner of Eaton and William streets, where two **Bahama Houses** stand side by side (703 Eaton Street and 408 William Street). These dwellings are the

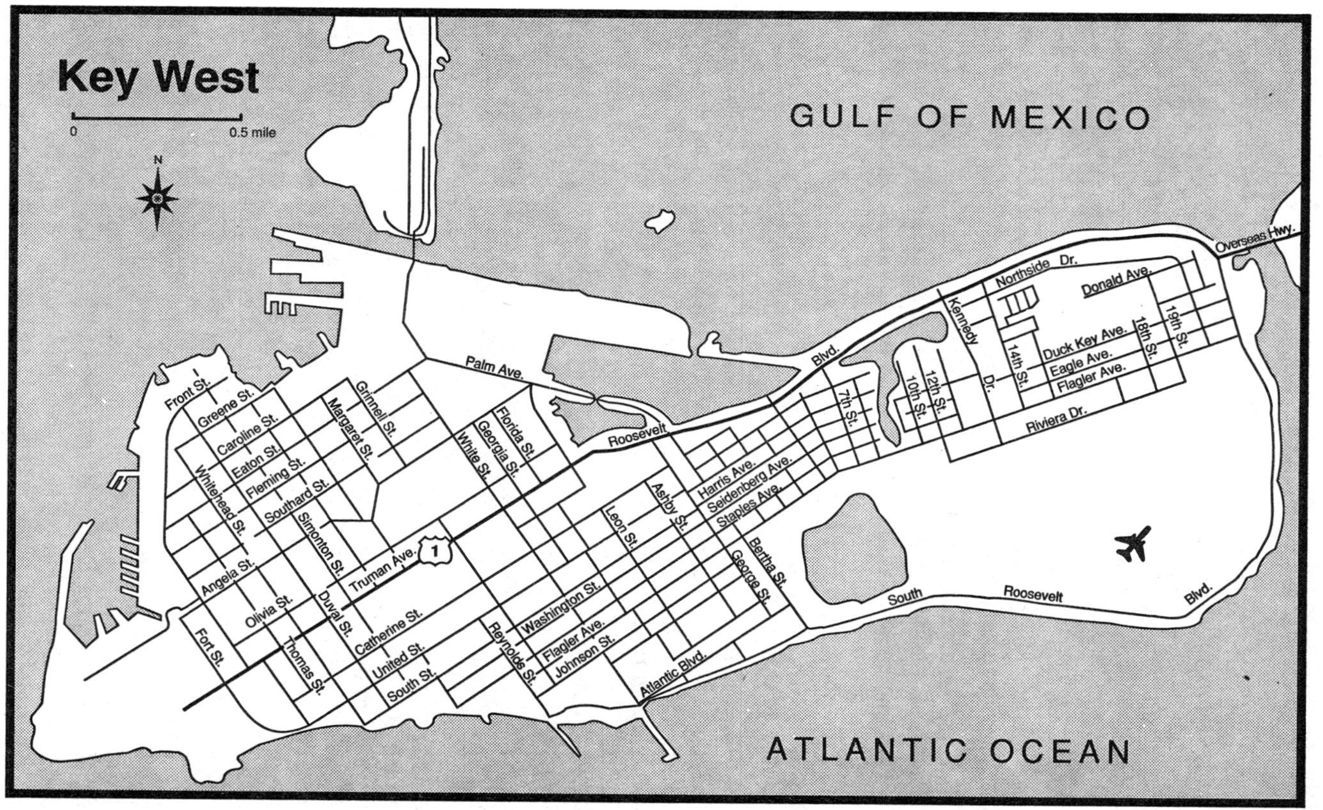
Key West
0
0.5 mile
N
GULF OF MEXICO
ATLANTIC OCEAN
Overseas Hwy.
Northside Dr.
Donald Ave.
19th St.
18th St.
Duck Key Ave.
Eagle Ave.
Flagler Ave.
14th St.
Kennedy Dr.
Riviera Dr.
12th St.
10th St.
7th St.
Blvd.
Roosevelt
Palm Ave.
Harris Ave.
Seidenberg Ave.
Staples Ave.
Bertha St.
George St.
Ashby St.
Leon St.
Atlantic Blvd.
Washington St.
Flagler Ave.
Johnson St.
Reynolds St.
South
Roosevelt
Blvd.
Florida St.
Georgia St.
White St.
1
Truman Ave.
Catherine St.
United St.
South St.
Grinnell St.
Margaret St.
Simonton St.
Duval St.
Thomas St.
Southard St.
Fleming St.
Eaton St.
Caroline St.
Greene St.
Front St.
Whitehead St.
Angela St.
Olivia St.
Fort St.

only ones known to have been shipped in their entirety to Key West from the Bahamas. Built in the mid-1800s by master shipbuilders, they feature unusual beaded siding, mahogany window sashes and broad verandahs.

Next door, the **Samuel Filer House** (724 Eaton Street), built around 1885, is a study in black and white contrasted with an etched cranberry glass transom and double-screen door. Only the front of the **Bartlum/Forgarty House** (718 Eaton Street) was floated over from the Bahamas on a schooner; the mid-19th century dwelling is constructed with wooden pegs.

The large **Richard Peacon House** (712 Eaton Street) was built in the late 1800s by the owner of Key West's largest grocery store. It has distinctive octagonally shaped verandahs and, some say, a ghost.

The **Audubon House** (Whitehead and Greene streets; 305-294-2116; admission) is a fine sample of early Key West architecture; its restoration inspired a city-wide interest in preserving other historic structures. Furnished with fine antiques of the 1830s—the period when John James Audubon visited the Keys—the three-story frame house is held together entirely by wooden pegs and is an excellent example of the shipbuilders' craft. It now serves as a museum housing an extensive collection of works by the famous painter/naturalist.

With delicate double balustrades, beveled glass and fan windows, ornate trim and 26 rooms, the neoclassical **Curry Mansion** (511 Caroline Street; 305-294-5349; admission) presents a three-story display of millionaire life at the turn of the century. Only the Bahama-style hinged shutters are common to other, less opulent homes of early Key West. Today the showcase house is open for tours daily, showing off the luxurious appointments and fine 19th-century furnishings.

Though many famous authors have spent time in Key West, none has left as strong a mark as Ernest Hemingway. He and his wife Pauline bought a fine old coral-stone house in which they lived from 1931 until the end of their marriage in 1940. Today, the **Hemingway House** (907 Whitehead Street; 305-294-1575; admission) is a tribute to "Papa's" life and work, for it was here that he created such masterpieces as *A Farewell to Arms* and *For Whom the Bell Tolls*. Tours are given daily, reflecting on Hemingway's works and his rigorous lifestyle. Through the marvelous house and luxuriant grounds roam sleek six-toed cats, said to be descendants of Hemingway's own; they lie irreverently on his works, snooze on his Spanish furniture and stalk the rooms that still reflect the writer's colorful personality.

At the **Key West Aquarium** (1 Whitehead Street; 305-296-2051; admission) you can touch a starfish or watch a shark being fed. Opened in 1934, the aquarium was the first visitors' attraction built in the Keys. Today the small but informative exhibit includes a turtle pool, shark tanks, an ever-growing experimental living coral reef and many other samples of Atlantic and Gulf underwater life.

If you've ever wondered how much a gold bar weighs or if rubies still sparkle after centuries on the bottom of the sea, visit **Mel Fisher's Maritime Heritage Society Museum** (200 Greene Street; 305-294-2633; admission). The place literally dazzles with gold chains, jewel-studded crosses and flagons, and great piles of gleaming coins, all treasures gathered by Fisher and his crew of divers from the sunken ships *Atocha* and *Margarita*. You really are allowed to lift the gold bar, though you can't take it with you.

Though nautical archaeologists may frown on treasure seeking today, "wreckers" were once an important part of Keys society, varying from honest salvagers of broken, stranded ships to clever and unscrupulous opportunists. At **The Wrecker's Museum** (322 Duval Street; 305-294-9502; admission) you can learn about this unusual 19th-century profession while also admiring Key West's Oldest House. Built around 1829, this nine-room pine structure houses period antiques, as well as ship models and sea artifacts. Of particular interest is a built-to-scale mid-Victorian conch-style dollhouse complete with a miniature mural of early Key West in its dining room.

Sporting an historically accurate facelift, the **Key West Lighthouse Museum** (938 Whitehead Street; 305-294-0012; admission) is a celebration of the seacoast. Climb the 88 steps to admire the beautiful Fresnel lens and enjoy unsurpassed views of the island and its surrounding seas. The museum houses a room restored to a turn-of-the-century style as well as photographs and other lighthouse relics.

The city of Key West grows many of its landscaping plants at the **Charles "Sonny" McCoy Indigenous Park** (Atlantic Boulevard at White Street; 305-292-8157), a showplace for trees and plants native to the region. You may wander inside the gates of the park during the daytime and learn to recognize the lignum vitae, silver palm and a number of tropical trees found only in the Keys.

The historic **West Martello Towers** (Atlantic Boulevard and White Street) are the enchanting home of Key West Garden Club's **Joe Allen Garden Center** (305-294-3210; donations). The remains of the once-upon-a-time fort, with its crumbling brick walls and arches and its massive banyan trees, create a pleasant, restful environment for permanent seed displays, numerous bromeliads and other tropical flora usually confined to greenhouses, and spectacular seasonal displays.

If you take the Conch Tour Train or stroll to the meeting of Margaret and Angela streets, you will see a remarkable **Bottle Wall** built by a Key West artist to keep people (and cars and fire trucks) from cutting through her yard. For a treat, drop by and meet **Carolyn Gorton Fuller** (★) (just strike the gong at the front door). If you buy her book, an artistic, adult coloring book that captures the spirit of Key West, she will show you her home and her eclectic and delightful works of art.

"I Told You I Was Sick," reads the straightforward message immortalized on a gravestone in the **Key West Cemetery** (Angela Street and Passover Lane; 305-292-8177). Due to the rocky geology of the island, many of the stone encased caskets rest above-ground, often carrying curious and, what seem now, humorous messages such as the one placed by a grieving widow: "At Least I Know Where He's Sleeping Tonight." History abounds in this enchanting and poignant spot too, as in the special memorial to those who died at the sinking of the U.S. Battleship *Maine* in Havana harbor in 1898. You may stroll the cemetery any time; tours are given on weekends.

From the top of the citadel of the **East Martello Museum** (3501 South Roosevelt Boulevard; 305-296-3913; admission) you can get a magnificent view of the island and the Atlantic, just as the builders of this 1862 Civil War brick fortress planned. Today the historic structure houses a large collection of Key West artifacts and serves as both a museum of Key West history and a gallery displaying the work of Keys artists. The fort's tower alone, with vaulted ceilings and spiral staircase, is worth a visit.

Few developments have caused so much controversy on this tiny island as the **Truman Annex** (main entrance at Thomas and Southard streets; 305-296-5601). Owned for decades by the Navy, the quiet, shady 103-acre parcel was the last big piece of undeveloped land on Key West when it was auctioned in 1986 to a wealthy Sikh from Maine. Now in the works are expensive condominiums, a complex of Victorian-style houses, marinas and luxury hotels, including a major hotel that will occupy a 27-acre island just off Mallory Square.

Today you can drive through the annex's wrought-iron gates, past the Bahama-style police with white pith helmets, and watch the new conch houses go up while the old ones tumble down. Here also is **The Little White House** (111 Front Street; 305-294-9988; admission), built in 1890, where President Harry Truman vacationed. The handsome white clapboard building has two facades and spacious porches enclosed with wooden louvers.

Recently rediscovered and unearthed from the sands, the **Fort Zachary Taylor State Historic Site** (★) (western point of island, off Southard Street; 305-292-6713; admission) is a treasure trove of Civil War weaponry and memorabilia. The excavations have revealed beautiful mid-19th-century arched brickwork, parade grounds and the largest collection of Civil War cannons in the United States. The park also contains one of the nicest little beaches, especially for sunset-viewing and boat-watching, in the area. A grove of trees provides some rare seaside shade.

Though Key West may seem all travelers and trolleys, there are several interesting natural spots where the flavor of the real Keys remains. One is the **Thomas Riggs Wildlife Refuge** (★) (South Roosevelt Boulevard, west of the airport; 305-294-2116). Behind a green chainlink fence stands an observation platform offering a view of the island's salt pond, where heron, ibis, gallinule and other resident and migratory birds gather. Phone the refuge number if the gate is locked.

The Garden Club of Key West owns a small but nicely laid-out and well-marked **Botanical Garden** (★) (Junior College Road and Aguro Circle) where you can get acquainted with some of the trees and other flora that grow in this distinctive region.

The glass-bottom sightseeing boat **Fireball** (north end of Duval Street; 305-296-6293; admission) and the glass-bottom boat of the **Coral Princess Fleet** (700 Front Street; 305-296-3287; admission) make regular runs to the coral reef in the Atlantic, as well as taking visitors on late afternoon sunset cruises.

Every visitor to Key West inevitably witnesses a sunset at **Mallory Square** (northwest end of Duval Street), a Key West institution that will make you feel like you're part of a Mayan ritual. You'll find bagpipers, jugglers, fire-eaters and people who think it's fun to stand on one foot for half an hour. As the great moment nears, a cheer rises from the crowd, reaching fever pitch as the sun hits the horizon.

KEY WEST HOTELS

As you might expect, in Key West you can find countless accommodations from bare-basics motels to outrageously expensive resorts. Especially interesting is the variety of guest houses, many of them remodeled Victorian homes from earlier Key West times. A few of the guest houses cater to gays only, and it's okay to inquire. If you want help finding a place to stay, contact the **Key West Reservation Service** (628 Fleming Street; 305-294-7713).

Quietly dominating the edge of Old Town, the soft pink, metal-roofed **Hyatt Key West** (601 Front Street; 305-296-9900) is a maze of well-lit stairs and balconies from which you can observe Key West's famous sunsets without the folderol of Mallory Square. The cool pastel decor suits the location beside a tiny private beach and marina. A pool, jacuzzi, exercise room, fine restaurants and indoor/outdoor lounge make this one of the choicest ultra-deluxe lodgings, and one of the most convenient for Key West sightseeing.

Pier House (1 Duval Street; 305-296-4600) has long been one of Key West's most popular hotels. It sprawls along the Gulf with rambling tin-roofed villas and acres of docks. Here you get all the goodies of an elaborate resort—superb restaurants, lively nightspots, a therapeutic spa—with that classic laid-back Keys mood. A small beach is soft and picturesque, the swimming pool expansive, and the grounds jungly. Old Town shops and sights are a short stroll away. Ultra-deluxe.

Don't let the "Holiday Inn" sign mislead you. **La Concha** (430 Duval Street; 305-296-2991) is unlike any chain hostelry you've experienced. This is a downtown Key West landmark seven-story hotel with a wonderful old-fashioned feel. Holiday Inn was smart not to clone it but to keep its dark woodwork and marble floors and furnish it with appropriate 1920s wicker and wood and hazy old seaside pictures. Walking down the hall and into one of the rooms is like stepping into grandmother's attic trunk. The pool and sundeck, rooftop lounge, restaurants and sidewalk saloon, however, are appropriate toasts to modernity. Ultra-deluxe.

Built in 1890 and featuring a handsome metal-roofed turret on one corner, **The Artist House** (534 Eaton Street; 305-296-3977) is one of many "conch" houses turned hostelry. For deluxe rates, guests may have one of six rooms with private bath, refrigerator and antique or period reproduction furnishings including four-poster or genuine brass beds. The jacuzzi resides in a lush garden among tropical plantings; breakfasts are continental. Rich period wallpapers and superb restoration make this an elegant lodging.

Open to women only, **Rainbow House** (525 United Street; 305-292-1450) offers ten, two-room suites. This Old Town inn serves breakfast poolside—lush landscaping adds to the charm of the pavilion and veranda. Sitting areas are furnished with wicker and the tropical-style bedrooms feature print bedspreads. Moderate to deluxe.

The **La Mer Hotel** (506 South Street; 305-296-5611) is one of many restored Victorian conch-style houses with ultra-deluxe-priced rooms. This one has contemporary furnishings and definite flair, with tropical plants, oceanview balconies and porches. A continental breakfast is served.

Adjacent to one of the few Atlantic beaches within walking distance of Old Town, **South Beach Motel** (508 South Street; 305-296-5611) offers 58 units ranging from moderate-priced singles to deluxe-priced ocean view efficiencies. This green pastel complex decorated with gingerbread and lattice work is shaded by palms and nicely landscaped with native plants. Popular attractions include an Olympic-size pool, large deck and a tanning pier. A dive shop on the property runs scuba and snorkel trips. Gay-friendly.

A 19th-century Victorian conch house, **Colours Key West** (410 Fleming Street; 305-294-6977) has 14-foot-high ceilings, hardwood floors and beautiful antiques. Bedrooms feature brass and wicker furniture, ceiling fans and, in some cases, balcony views of Old Town. A large clothing-optional pool is also popular at this 12-unit establishment favored by the gay crowd. Deluxe to ultra-deluxe.

After a major renovation of this 1880s-era classic revival building, the **Marquesa Hotel** (600 Fleming Street; 305-292-1919) has landed securely on the National Register of Historic Places. Each of the 15 rooms is luxurious and formal, with antique appointments, pastel walls, gleaming white woodwork and distinctive fabrics. Every corner is a masterpiece of workmanship. The property includes a fine restaurant and a sparkling pool. Ultra-deluxe.

Catering to a gay and lesbian crowd, the **Brass Key Guesthouse** (412 Frances Street; 305-296-4719) is a beautiful two-story, plantation-style house surrounded by verandas and tropical gardens. A beautiful pool and a spiral staircase leading up to the sundeck make this bed and breakfast particularly inviting. Fifteen rooms are furnished with English antiques, chenille bedspreads and ceiling fans. For extra privacy ask for one of the two cottage rooms. Deluxe.

Ethereal peach buildings trimmed in white gingerbread stand along a pretty beach at **The Reach** (1435 Simonton Street; 305-296-5000). This balmy address has lovely terraced suites with gleaming Mexican tile floors, Indian dhurrie rugs, ceiling fans and wet bars, and commanding views of the ocean, swimming pool and palm courtyard. The tin-roofed dockhouse is a choice spot to loaf.

The **Curry Mansion Inn** (511 Caroline Street; 305-294-5349) provides 21 rooms with private baths. Most are in the beautiful backyard annex that surrounds the pretty deck and pool, though several are in the fine old historic mansion itself. Furnishings are mostly top-of-the-line wicker, and every bed is covered with a handmade quilt. Rooms in the annex are all pastel and white, creating a cool, fresh feel even on the hottest summer day. Ultra-

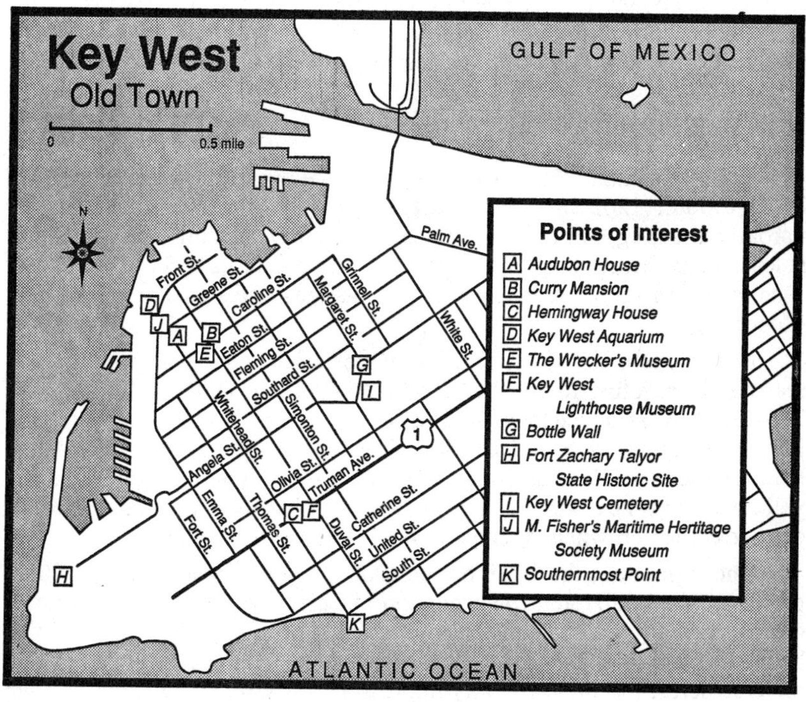

deluxe rates include complimentary happy hour, membership in a nearby beach club and a continental breakfast with various fresh-baked breads. Gay-friendly.

If you remember old-fashioned tourist courts, then you can indulge in a bit of nostalgia at **Key Lime Village** (727 Truman Avenue; 305-294-6222), a collection of 1920s and 1930s cottages surrounding an 1854 home. The accommodations are tiny but functional, including efficiency apartments and motel-type rooms with shared baths. There are no televisions or phones, but it's all very peaceful. Budget to moderate.

A member of the international Youth Hostel Association, the **Key West Hostel** (★) (718 South Street; 305-296-5719) has budget-priced dorm rooms for males, females and marrieds. All ages are welcome, but nonmembers must have a valid ID. There are full kitchen facilities and lockers and bicycles to rent.

Even if you don't choose to stay at the **Marriott Casa Marina** (Reynolds Street on the ocean; 305-296-3535), you should drop in and indulge in the Sunday brunch or at least explore the lobby of this 1921 historic landmark, created as the final resort along Henry Flagler's railroad. This handsome Spanish-style hotel radiates historic elegance. The pine floors gleam like glass. The french doors leading to a spacious loggia and the restaurant's restored mahogany coffered ceiling pay tribute to Flagler's dreams for the Keys. A beachfront restaurant, lighted tennis courts, pool and water sports center add modern luxury. Ultra-deluxe.

KEY WEST RESTAURANTS

The big sunken bar and the dark publike atmosphere make the **Full Moon Saloon** (1202 Simonton Street; 305-294-9090) a friendly and slightly uproarious eating and drinking place. You can get a full meal here until at least 4 a.m. Most of the fare is seafood, with emphasis on local specialties such as conch prepared in a variety of fashions and freshly smoked fish. Moderate.

Marvelous Gulf views, candlelit tables and soothing piano music are reasons for reveling in the **Pier House Restaurant** (1 Duval Street, 305-296-4600). As an added treat, the cuisine is consistently outstanding, relying heavily on innovative treatments of local seafood, fruits and vegetables. Musts here are the conch bisque, conch fritters with Key lime mustard sauce and yellowtail with key lime butter and papaya. A heady chocolate decadence dessert comes crowned with a fragrant red rosebud. Deluxe.

The sign above the **Crab Shack** (908 Caroline Street; 305-294-9658) promises "free crab tomorrow," but don't be discouraged if tomorrow never comes; the "all you can eat" spicy steamed shrimp is no hoax, if you dine between 5 and 9:30 p.m. Most of the meals here are moderately priced, and the crab selections are especially impressive for they include imports from

Maryland and Alaska as well as the local side-crawlers. You can eat inside or out in dining areas that are rustic and functional. There's a good assortment of combination dinners that include both seafood and meat.

The Buttery (1208 Simonton Street; 305-294-0717) keeps getting rave reviews from reviewers who enjoy raving, and who seem to also enjoy good food. White cloths, crystal, punched-tin lamps and a blue-and-white emphasis make this deluxe restaurant very attractive. Sit beneath the soaring skylight or under low ceilings to enjoy the elegant ways the Buttery prepares seafood, fowl and meats, especially veal, which the chef treats differently every night. Vegetarian pasta, yellowtail baked with bananas and walnuts, and a Caribbean seafood salad are some of the interesting menu items.

Pepe's (★) (806 Caroline Street; 305-294-7192) is like a wonderful old boathouse, outfitted in battered wood walls, tiller-top tables and rumpled fishing snapshots. Opened in 1909 by a Cuban fisherman, it moved from prominent Duval Street to a lonesome byroad. All for the better: except for locals, few know of the eatery's great burgers and gourmet coffees. There are also pork chops, steak and seafood, and creamed chip beef on toast for breakfast. A vine-covered patio offers outdoor dining. Moderate.

For a hearty moderate-priced meal, **El Loro Verde** (404 Southard Street; 305-296-7298), basically a small, cheerful, formica-boothed restaurant, offers traditional Mexican fare with a few Caribbean touches. There is a wide variety of domestic and imported beers to accompany the chips and hot and mild salsas; chalkboard entrées, such as fish Barbados with mutton peppers, vary from day to day.

Louie's Back Yard (700 Wadell Avenue; 305-294-1061) resides in a beautifully restored classical revival conch house with a tin roof, spacious verandas and airy 12-foot high rooms with polished floors and fine art. Best of all, though, is the view of the sea that you can enjoy from the deck or through the generous windows. Louie's deluxe-to-ultra-deluxe menu earns top rankings from food critics and includes such creative fare as roasted jerk chicken with a papaya-chili glaze.

For such succulent Cuban dishes as black beans and yellow rice, fried plantains, *picadillo* and those wonderful famous sandwiches of thick slices of meat and cheese on crusty Cuban bread, go to **La Lechonera** (3100 Flagler Street; 305-292-3700). Forget your diet; the theme here is pigs. Poster porkers line the walls, imparting such wisdom as, "a moment on the lips, forever on the hips" and "fat is beautiful." Budget to moderate.

The Rusty Anchor (★) (5th Avenue off 5th Street across from the dog track, Stock Island; 305-294-5369) is run by a local family who have turned a one-time leaky-floored shrimpers' bar into a favored eating spot for locals from Key West and elsewhere. Charter boat captains send their customers here because, as one said, "It's just the best," a good example of the word-of-mouth publicity that keeps folks coming. The location is unlikely, proving that the reputation of good seafood, well-prepared conch fritters and, surprisingly, barbecued baby-back ribs, are all it takes to make an open-air eatery a success. Moderate.

KEY WEST SHOPPING

Key West is the place to spend your money. The Old Town streets in the waterfront area are a mass of shops and boutiques offering everything from imported flamingos to artful fabrics. Visitors do most of their shopping in the dozens of glitzy and funky shops in Old Town; practical shopping is available in several centers in the newer areas.

Not quite all the sponge fishermen are gone from Key West, as explained on a continuous video at the **Sponge Market** (1 Whitehead Street; 305-294-2555). Elderly sponger C. B. McHugh demonstrates the harvesting and treating of sponges and tells their history on the film; the store has bins of these marvelous nonpolyfoam wonders.

Located in a historic old one-time waterfront grocery, the **Key West Art Center** (301 Front Street; 305-294-1241) is a cooperative for local artists. Works for sale include paintings and drawings of seascapes, sunsets and Key West street scenes, as well as sculpture and other art.

Brightly colored silkscreened fabrics and designer clothing are for sale at **Key West Hand Print Fabrics** (201 Simonton Street; 305-294-9535). You can watch the process of this local industry in the next-door printing factory.

Cavanaugh's (520 Front Street; 305-296-3343) has a wide variety of imported items for amazingly reasonable prices. This big store features furnishings and gifts from around the world, including Oaxacan pottery, Oriental accessories, Latin American treasures and African tribal artifacts. There is a selection of sporty clothing, but the main attractions here are the imports.

If you don't plan to go deep-sea treasure hunting yourself, you can arrange to buy an authentic piece of booty at **Mel Fisher's Treasure Exhibit and Sales** (200 Greene Street; 305-296-6533).

For exotic kites, colorful windsocks and just about any toy that flies, visit **Key West Kite Company** (409 Greene Street; 305-296-2535).

Fast Buck Freddie's (500 Duval Street; 305-294-2007) is a wonderful hodgepodge of a department store left over from the days before malls. Browse through racks of trendy tropical clothing, funny posters, fine candies, bathing suits, home furnishings and all sorts of gift items.

Haitian Art Co. (600 Frances Street; 305-296-8932) imports sculptures, carvings, papier-mâché and brilliantly colored paintings in handcrafted frames by Haitian artists.

The **Key West Island Bookstore** (513 Fleming Street; 305-294-2904) carries a large collection of literature about Key West and books by authors who have lived here. They also have new, used and rare volumes.

Lucky Street Gallery (919 Duval Street; 305-294-3973) is a marvelous cache of paintings, glassworks, pottery, jewelry, metal sculptures and pieces for the avant garde.

Those concerned with the environment will be interested in the **Greenpeace—An Environmental Store** (719 Duval Street; 305-296-4442), where all proceeds go to environmental campaigns such as saving whales, turtles and dolphins.

"Florida's Oldest Beach Bum" says the beat-up sign on **Lazy Jake's Hammocks (★)** (in the alley just east of the intersection of Elizabeth and Greene streets). The "bum" is Jake, a sunwashed fellow whose collage of old oars, boats, buoys, seashells, fishing nets (and hammocks, of course) continues across the alley.

Because it's away from the bustling commercial area, you might miss **Whitehead Street Pottery (★)** (1011 Whitehead Street; 305-294-5067), located in what was once a Cuban grocery. Every piece here is one-of-a-kind, including many beautiful and durable copper-red and raku art pieces glazed with metallic oxides.

KEY WEST NIGHTLIFE

If you wondered where the nighttime action was as you traveled down the Keys, you'll discover it's almost all here in Key West. Entertainment begins long before sunset and goes on far into the early morning hours. A number of nightclubs seem to spill right out through their open windows and doors and onto the street.

You should at least stick your head into **Sloppy Joe's** (201 Duval Street; 305-294-8585) because it has hooked onto the Papa Hemingway legend in as many ways as it can. Papa and Sloppy Joe were drinking buddies, apparently, and it's said that some of the tales that showed up in literature were founded on stories they shared in the backroom here. Just follow your ears and you'll find it most anytime of the day or night; there's live rock, rhythm-and-blues and other varied entertainment until 2 a.m.

Captain Tony's Saloon (428 Greene Street; 305-294-1838), "where everybody is a star," is said to be the location of the *real* Sloppy Joe's, and it just may be true. Anyway, the real star here is Captain Tony, a wiry white-haired codger who has polished his role as local character until it shines. Rowdy and fun, with all sorts of live performers, it's a Key West institution.

Two Friends Patio Restaurant (512 Front Street; 305-296-9212) features live Dixieland jazz, calypso and blues nightly in its big, popular open-air lounge, and the festivities sometimes spill out onto the street. There is a restaurant attached and a raw bar for late-night eating.

You'll find a bar, rock-and-roll and, of course, plenty of Jimmy Buffet music at the **Margaritaville Café** (500 Duval Street; 305-292-1435), where Jimmy, no longer "wastin' away," makes occasional impromptu appearances.

On the sunset deck of second-story **Havana Docks Bar** (Pier House, 1 Duval Street; 305-294-9541) you can get an eyeful of the Gulf and an earful of the Top-40 band entertaining the crowd. Dancing and revelry goes on late into the night. Cover on Wednesday and Friday.

There's weekend entertainment at the **Turtle Kraal Bar** (2 Land's End Village, end of Margaret Street; 305-294-2640), once a turtle cannery and now an old-style Key West eating and drinking spot. You can see turtles and other sea creatures here while you relax and have a drink.

The Top (430 Duval Street; 305-296-2991) has the best view of any night spot in Key West, from the top of the 1925 La Concha hotel. There's dancing and live music Sundays through Tuesdays, following, of course, the sunsets. Comedy acts are featured the rest of the week.

The arts are alive in Key West, too. A variety of popular and classical concerts, plays and dance programs are presented at the **Tennessee Williams Fine Arts Center** (5901 West Junior College Road; 305-296-9081).

The **Waterfront Playhouse** (Mallory Square; 305-294-5015) presents an assortment of plays, films, reviews and musical comedies throughout the winter and spring. **The Red Barn Theatre** (319 Duval Street; 305-296-9911) is a resident company presenting several productions during the winter season.

A number of artistic events take place as part of various long-running festivals during the high season, too. Contact **Florida Keys Fine Arts Center** (305-296-5000, ext. 362) and **Old Island Days** (305-294-9501) to see what's happening where during your stay.

GAY SCENE **One Saloon** (524 Duval Street; 305-296-8118) is a popular gay dance bar that attracts the leather and denim crowd. Dance to country music played by a deejay at this wood-paneled club decorated with old license plates. The saloon patio is also a popular retreat on balmy nights.

Mae's Westside Lounge (300 Southard Street; 305-294-8807), a women's bar located in a pastel pink Old Town building, features tropical plants, and famous women's sayings line the walls. There's dancing to recorded music and occasional bands, as well as a pool table, darts and basketball games. Relax outdoors on the patio.

From complimentary Sunday night barbecues on the patio to female impersonators in the Garden Bar, **The Copa** (623 Duval Street; 305-296-8521) is Old Town's biggest and busiest nightclub. Located in a converted theater, this establishment boasts nine rooms and accommodates up to 1200 guests. The heart of The Copa is a large dance room featuring disco played by a deejay. You can also watch comedy and music films in the Video Bar or play pool in the Pit Room. Although the crowd is predominantly gay in the summer months, The Copa is frequented by a mixed clientele during the winter season.

KEY WEST BEACHES AND PARKS

It's a surprise to many visitors that Key West has very few beaches, and those it does have are far from sensational. On the south side of the island, along the Atlantic Ocean, you can dip into the water or lie in the sun at one of several narrow public beaches that tend to get very crowded.

Smathers Beach—This city-owned beach is where locals lie in the sun in the daytime and take walks at night.

Facilities: Restrooms, watersport rentals, concession stands. *Swimming:* Nice water but rocky bottom.

Getting there: Off South Roosevelt Boulevard west of the airport.

Higgs Beach—This beach area is popular with families, as there are a number of recreational facilities nearby.

Facilities: Picnic areas, restrooms, bathhouse, playground, tennis courts, watersport rentals, concession stands. *Swimming:* Permitted.

Getting there: Located along Atlantic Boulevard between White Street and Reynolds Road.

The Sporting Life

SPORTFISHING

You can go sportfishing on a pricey, custom-designed charter or by joining one of the numerous party boats on a scheduled trip.

Tarpon, snook, redfish and trout are the four most popular fish that charter captains will help you locate in the western Everglades and Ten Thousand Islands region. Contact one of the following for a fishing trip: **Rod and Gun Club** (Everglades City; 813-695-2101), **Captain Dan** (Chokoloskee; 813-695-4573) or **Island Charters** (Chokoloskee; 813-695-2286).

For charter fishing in Biscayne Bay and the Atlantic Ocean in the vicinity of the Upper Keys, for such gamefish as amberjack, barracuda, bonefish, blackfin tuna and tarpon, contact **Club Nautico at Biscayne Marriott** (1633 North Bayshore Drive, Miami; 305-371-4252).

Charters and guides for fishing both the back country and ocean waters out of Key Largo can be had from **Back Country Adventures** (59 North Blackwater Lane near MM 105; 305-451-1247) or **The Sailor's Choice** (MM 100 at the Holiday Inn; 305-451-1802), among many, many others.

In Islamorada, there are also dozens of sportfishing outfits to choose from, including **Dux Spray Charters** (MM 83.5; 305-664-5214) and **Winter Hawk Charters** (MM 84, in the Holiday Isle Resort; 305-664-5567). **Holiday Isle Resorts & Marina** (MM 84; 305-664-2321) will make arrangements for both back-country and offshore fishing trips and charters.

In Marathon, charter booking services are offered by **The World Class Angler** (MM 48.3 at Faro Blanco Resort; 305-743-6139). **Marathon Lady Party Boats** (MM 53 at Vaca Cut, 305-743-5580) offers a variety of day and night fishing trips. For flats fishing join Captain Barry Meyer on the **Magic** (1000 15th Street; 305-743-3278).

In the Lower Keys, you can go tarpon fishing with **Outcast Charter** (MM 29.5, Sea Center, Big Pine Key; 305-872-4680). **Fantasy Charters** (MM 28, Big Pine Key; 305-872-3200) will take you offshore and reef fishing. Try backcountry fishing on the **Outcast** (MM 17, Sugarloaf Key; 305-745-3135).

From Key West you can go fishing for a few hours in the Atlantic or for several days on the Tortuga Banks; there are dozens of craft and fleets to choose from, such as **Yankee Fleet** (Land's End Marina, end of Margaret Street; 305-294-7009), **Sea Breeze Charters** (25 Arbutus Drive; 305-294-6027) and **MV Florida Fish Finders** (1 Front Street on Stock Island; 305-296-0111).

SKINDIVING

On any calm and beautiful day the sea to the east of Florida's Upper Keys is dotted with boats. They belong to the scuba divers and snorkelers who are captivated by the beauty of the continental United States' only living reef. Others search the remains of ships wrecked on that same lovely reef. Many communities in the Keys have dozens of scuba shops and dive centers designed to meet the needs of both novice snorkeler and sophisticated diver.

For scuba and snorkel trips via glass-bottom boat to the northern tip of the reef, contact the **Biscayne Aqua Center** (Convoy Point, end of Southwest 328th Street, east of Homestead; 305-247-2400) next door to the headquarters of the Biscayne National Park.

Route 1 in the Key Largo area seems like one continuous dive shop. To meet your diving needs, try **The Coral Reef Park Company, Inc.** (John Pennekamp Coral Reef State Park, MM 102.5, Key Largo; 305-451-1621), **American Diving Headquarters** (MM 105.5; 305-451-0037) or **Divers World** (MM 100.5; 305-451-3200). At Tavernier, try the **Florida Keys Dive Center** (MM 90.5; 305-852-4599).

Diving courses, gear and reef and wreck trips are available in Islamorada through **Lady Cyana Divers** (MM 85.9; 305-664-8717) and **Holiday Isle Resorts & Marina** (MM 84; 305-664-2321).

In Marathon, contact **The Diving Site** (MM 53.5; 305-289-1021) or **Tilden's Pro Dive Shop** (4650 Overseas Highway, Marathon; 305-743-5422) for reef trips, lessons and equipment.

Looe Key Reef Resort (MM 27.5, Ramrod Key; 305-872-2215) and **Cudjoe Gardens Marina and Dive Shop** (MM 21, Cudjoe Key; 305-745-2357) are full-service dive centers in the Lower Keys.

From Key West, you can scuba or snorkel by making arrangements with **Reef Raiders Dive Shop** (109 Duval Street; 305-294-3635) and **Key West Pro Dive Shop** (1605 North Roosevelt Boulevard; 305-296-3823).

BOATING

Boat rentals are available throughout the Keys. In Key Largo try **Jarmada Boat Rentals** (MM 107; 305-451-2628). In Islamorada, you can arrange boat rentals through **Holiday Isle Resorts & Marina** (MM 84; 305-664-2321) or go to **Robbie's Boat Rentals** (MM 77.5; 305-664-4351). **Boat Rentals at Poseidon Harbor** (MM 63, Conch Key; 305-289-1525) rents power boats and a glass-bottom skiff. In the Lower Keys, you can rent boats at **Dolphin Marina** (MM 28.5, Little Torch Key; 305-872-2685) and **Cudjoe Gardens Marina** (MM 21; 305-745-2357). Boat rentals are abundant in Key West, in places such as **Key West Boat Rentals** (617 Front Street; 305-294-2628) and **Club Nautico** (717-C Eisenhower Drive; 305-294-2225).

CANOEING

To explore the shoreline of Biscayne National Park by canoe, contact the **Biscayne Underwater Company** (Convoy Point, east of Homestead; 305-247-2400). For canoe rental, outfitting and guided trips in the eastern Everglades, try **North American Canoe Tours** (Route 29, Everglades City, across from the National Park Ranger Station; 813-695-4666) or **Glades Haven Recreational Resort** (800 Southeast Copeland Avenue, Everglades City; 813-695-2746). You can canoe the intriguing streams and ponds of the southern part of the Everglades through the **Flamingo Lodge Marina** (Flamingo; 813-695-3101). **Coral Reef Park Company, Inc.** (MM 102.5, John Pennekamp Coral Reef State Park, Key Largo; 305-451-1621) offers canoes for exploring the park area. In Marathon you can rent canoes at **Marie's Yacht Harbor Club** (MM 54, 100 Avenue I; 305-743-2442).

SAILING

In the Key Largo area you can rent sailboats from **Coral Reef Park Company, Inc.** (MM 102.5, John Pennekamp Coral Reef State Park; 305-451-1621). Sailing charters are available from **Witt's End Sailing Charters** (MM 100, Key Largo; 305-451-3354) and **Key Largo Shoal Water Cruises** (MM 99.5; 305-451-0083). In Islamorada you can book sailing cruises through **Holiday Isle Resorts and Marina** (MM 84; 305-664-2321). Go sailing out

(Text continued on page 368.)

Fort Jefferson

Like a scattering of tiny emerald beads, a cluster of coral reef islands dot the Gulf of Mexico 68 miles west of Key West. Ponce de León named them "Tortugas" for the turtles he found there; sailors called them "Dry" because they hold no fresh water. But the Dry Tortugas do hold a national monument, centered around a magnificent 19th-century fort.

To see **Fort Jefferson** (for information, contact the U.S. Coast Guard in Key West; 305-247-6211) from the air, surrounded by azure sea, walled moat and white sand, is like conjuring up a fairy tale, enriched with popular legends of pirate treasure. Walking through the open sally port and arched hallways, one steps into a vast area whose silence is broken only by seagull cries and the calls of migratory birds.

Fort Jefferson, from its perch on Garden Key, appears much as it did in its brief 19th-century heyday. German and Irish craftsmen, with the assistance of slaves, created the spectacular brick-and stonework from millions of bricks brought by sailing ships from Pensacola and Virginia, and granite and slate brought from New England. The eight-foot-thick walls stand 50 feet high and feature handsome arches and wide views of sea approaches. Fort Jefferson's half-mile hexagonal perimeter made it the largest link in the chain of coastal fortifications built from Maine to Texas in the first half of the 19th century. It encompasses almost all the land of its tiny key, creating the illusion that it floats on the glistening tropical sea.

Though at first glance the fort seems complete, it was never actually finished. Begun in 1846, work continued for 30 years, but Fort Jefferson's importance came to an end with the invention of the rifled cannon. When federal troops occupied the fort throughout the Civil War, they discovered its foundations were not built on solid coral reef as was originally thought, but on sand and coral boulders. The walls began to show cracks as foundations settled with the shifting of the sea floor.

Fort Jefferson's most inglorious claim to fame came in 1865. To this lonely and inescapable reef were sent the "Lincoln Conspirators," four men convicted of complicity in the assassination of President Abraham Lincoln. Most noted of these was Dr. Samuel Mudd, the physician who had innocently set the broken leg of John Wilkes Booth following the shooting of the president. Sentenced to life imprisonment at Fort Jefferson, Mudd was eventually pardoned following his gallant efforts at treating the almost 300 garrisoned men who were struck with yellow fever at the fort during the 1867 epidemic. Today visitors can explore Mudd's cell and envision the bleakness of his fate.

The Army formally abandoned Fort Jefferson in 1874, following more yellow fever and a serious hurricane; it never saw any military action. And many military men may have felt grateful, for duty at Fort Jefferson, where water was scarce, mosquitoes thick and hurricane winds ferocious, was not coveted. But fortunately for historians and travelers, President Franklin D. Roosevelt proclaimed Fort Jefferson a national monument in 1935, thus preserving its unique heritage and its spectacular architecture.

To visit Fort Jefferson, you must go by chartered seaplane with **Key West Seaplane Service** (5603 West Junior College Road, Key West; 305-294-6978) or by boat. The plane trip rewards visitors with breathtaking views of the shallow waters, shipwrecks and coral reefs off the tip of the state.

You can spread a picnic, pitch a tent in the shade of tropical trees or sunbathe on the tiny, pristine beach, but you must bring everything with you, for only restrooms are available on the island. An excellent self-guiding tour, introduced by an explanatory slide show, orients visitors to the wonderful wild fort that you may roam to your heart's content. Snorkelers need only wade out waist-deep from the little beach to behold the colorful array of marine creatures that dart among the patches of living coral in the crystal-clear Gulf water.

of Marathon with **Faro Blanco Marina Resort** (1996 Overseas Highway, Marathon; 305-743-9018) or aboard **Amantha** (MM 48.3, Faro Blanco Resort, Marathon; 305-743-9020). For catamaran cruises in Key West, contact **Sebago** (201 Caroline Street; 305-294-5687).

WINDSURFING

Windsurfers can find boats and lessons at **Caribbean Watersports** (Sheraton Key Largo Resort, MM 97, Key Largo; 305-852-4707) and **Coral Reef Park Company, Inc.** (MM 102.5, John Pennekamp Coral Reef State Park, Key Largo; 305-451-1621). Between Islamorada and Marathon, you can rent windsurfing equipment at **Pier 68 Boat Rentals** (MM 68.2, Layton; 305-664-9393).

You can rent windsurfing equipment and hobie cats from several companies who set up shop at Key West's public beaches along South Roosevelt and Atlantic boulevards.

HOUSEBOATING

To go houseboating in the southernmost Everglades and Florida Bay, contact **Flamingo Lodge** (Flamingo; 305-253-2241). Houseboat vacations in the Keys are available through the **Houseboat Vacations of the Florida Keys** (MM 85.9, Islamorada; 305-664-4009).

TENNIS

Many Keys resorts provide tennis for their guests. In Islamorada, the public is welcome to play at **The Net** (MM 81; 305-664-4122). In Key West you can play for no charge at **Bayview Park** (1310 Truman Avenue; 305-294-1346). There are also public courts at **Higgs County Beach** (Atlantic Boulevard between White Street and Reynolds Road).

GOLF

At Homestead, visitors are welcome at the **Redland Golf & Country Club** (24451 North Krome Avenue; 305-247-8503). At Key Colony Beach, near Marathon, the public may play at the nine-hole **Par 3 Golf** (turn off at MM 53.5 and go to 8th Street; 305-289-1533). On Stock Island, **The Key West Resort** (305-294-5232) has an 18-hole course with public tee-times.

BICYCLING

Bikeways parallel Route 1 intermittently down through the Keys.

BIKE RENTALS You can rent a wide range of bicycles at **Key Largo Bikes** (MM 99.5; 305-451-1910) and at the **KCB Bike Shop** (MM 53, Marathon; 305-289-1670). Bicycling is a good way to explore Key West;

bikes can be rented from **The Bicycle Center** (523 Truman Avenue; 305-294-4556).

Bicycles are for rent for exploring the **Shark Valley** day-use area of the Everglades National Park (Route 41, about 25 miles west of Florida's Turnpike; 305-221-8455).

HIKING

Residential development and the lack of sandy beaches limit hiking possibilities in the Keys. There are some intriguing trails into the Everglades, however, for both novice strollers and serious explorers.

EVERGLADES AREA TRAILS **Shark Valley Trail** (14 miles) in Everglades National Park leads hikers across a sawgrass waterway where they are sure to see alligators and a wide assortment of birds such as snail kites, wood storks and ibis. They may also observe deer, turtles, snakes and otter. Along the way is an observation tower that offers a good overview of the "river of grass."

Florida Trail South (27 miles) is a loop trail that begins at the Oasis Ranger Station on Route 41 west of Shark Valley. This wilderness trail, for experienced hikers only, plunges deep into the Big Cypress Swamp, which is actually a vast region of sandy pine islands, mixed hardwood hammocks, wet and dry prairies and mysterious marshes. Stunted bald cypress stand among the grasses; wildlife is abundant. Bring your own drinking water.

Elliott Key Nature Trail (7 miles) in Biscayne National Park varies in difficulty as it follows the "spite highway" (a road bulldozed by developers in the 1960s in an effort to keep the island from becoming a part of the national park), a boardwalk, an interpretive nature trail and some undeveloped areas. The trail, alternately paralleling bay and ocean, crosses some interesting hardwood hammock jungles. Access to Elliott Key is by private boat only.

Longer trails allow hikers to explore the coastal prairie and delve deeper into the mysteries of the Everglades. As they are sometimes under water, be sure to check at the ranger station or visitor center before starting out. Between April and October most trails are impassable. These trails include the following:

Pine Lands Trail (7 miles), beginning on the road to Long Pine Key, is a network of interconnecting trails running through an unusually diverse pineland forest. About 200 types of plants, including 30 found nowhere else on earth, grow here. Among the mammals spotted along the trail are white-tailed deer, opossums, raccoons and the seldom-seen, endangered Florida panther.

Snake Bight Trail (4 miles) commences about six miles northeast of Flamingo off the park road and heads due south to a boardwalk at Florida

Bay. Three miles along, it is joined by **Rowdy Bend Trail** (5 miles). The two make a good loop hike through a variety of terrains and flora.

Old Ingram Highway Trail (11 miles) begins at the Royal Palm Visitor Center and follows an old road through hammocks, sawgrass prairie, and pine forest. This flat hike is ideal for birdwatching. Look for deer along the way.

Bear Lake Trail (7 miles) begins three miles northeast of Flamingo at the end of Bear Lake Road. This raised trail was made with fill dirt from the digging of the Homestead Canal and heads due west, skirting a canoe trail and the north shore of Bear Lake.

The **Christian Point Trail** (3.5 miles), begins about 1.5 miles northeast of Flamingo, travels across coastal prairie and winds through mangrove thickets to the shore of Florida Bay.

Coastal Prairie Trail (14 miles) follows an old road bed leading to Cape Sable. This trail can be quite demanding, depending on ground conditions, as it progresses through open salt marsh and tends to flood. The trail begins at Flamingo and ends at Clubhouse Beach on the edge of Florida Bay.

KEY LARGO AREA TRAILS A hiking/biking path runs from Mile Marker 106 in upper Key Largo for about 20 miles. Not a wilderness trail, this is more of a walking route parallel to Route 1. It ties in with a short nature trail, passes the John Pennekamp Coral Reef State Park, follows an old road to a county park and also leads to some historic sites.

Transportation

BY CAR

From Miami, **Route 41**, the Tamiami Trail, heads due west through the middle of the Everglades, skirting the northern boundary of Everglades National Park. **Route 1** and the almost-parallel **Florida Turnpike** head toward Homestead and Florida City, where **Route 27** branches off into the heart of Everglades National Park. Route 1 and the slightly more northerly scenic **Card Sound Road** lead to Key Largo, where Route 1 becomes the **Overseas Highway,** continuing through the Keys all the way to Key West.

Note: Mile markers, often called mile posts, can be seen each mile along Route 1 in the Keys. They appear on the right shoulder of the road as small green signs with white numbers, beginning with Mile Marker (MM) 126 just south of Florida City and ending at MM 0 in Key West. When asking for directions in the Keys, your answer will likely refer to a Mile Marker number. We use them throughout the Keys, except for Key West, where street addresses are used.

BY AIR

Many visitors to the Keys and Everglades choose to fly to Miami (see Chapter Two for more information). However, there are two small airports in the Keys located in Marathon and Key West. The **Marathon Airport** is serviced by Air Sunshine, Airways International, American Eagle and USAir Express. Carriers at **Key West International Airport** include Airways International, American Eagle, Comair, Pan American Express and USAir Express.

The Airporter (305-247-8874) provides regularly scheduled shuttle service from Miami International Airport to Homestead, Key Largo, Cutler Ridge and Islamorada. **Upper Keys Transportation, Inc.** (305-852-9533) offers limousine service to Miami International Airport on a personally scheduled reservation basis.

BY BUS

Greyhound Bus Lines services Homestead (5 Northeast 3rd Road; 305-247-2040), Key Largo (MM 103.5; 305-451-2908), Marathon (6363 Overseas Highway; 305-743-3488), Big Pine Key (305-872-4022) and Key West (615½ Duval Street, rear; 305-296-9072).

CAR RENTALS

Avis Rent A Car (305-743-5428) is located at the Marathon Airport; **General Rent A Car** (305-743-6100) will arrange airport pickup.

Rental agencies located at the Key West airport include **Avis Rent A Car** (305-296-8744) and **Dollar Rent A Car** (305-296-9921). Pick up at the airport can be arranged through **Alamo Rent A Car** (305-294-6675), **Budget Rent A Car** (305-294-8868), **Hertz Rent A Car** (305-294-1039) and **Thrifty Rent A Car** (305-296-6514).

PUBLIC TRANSPORTATION

In Key West, the **City of Key West Port and Transit Authority** (627 Palm Avenue; 305-292-8165) operates buses that run the entire length and partial width of the island. Curiously, the route does not include the airport.

TAXIS

Taxicabs that serve the Key West airport include **A Better Cab Company** (305-294-4444) and **AAA Sun Cab Company** (305-296-7777). In Marathon, use the **Marathon Taxi** (305-743-0077).

WEST

COAST

CHAPTER SEVEN

West Coast

The West Coast is a Florida panther. Its beaches stretch tawny; its wilderness resists taming. And like the indigenous Florida cat, the Gulf Coast represents exotic intrigue and the continuing battle between the state's scenic wilds and civilization's growth gone wild.

Indian tribes settled near Crystal River, on this coast's northern tip, as early as 200 B.C. Relics discovered there have been traced to Mayan civilizations. More recently, tribes such as the Timucuans and the Calusas made their living in Gulf Coast Florida, eating fish and oysters and creating tools and burial mounds out of seashells.

The first "sightseers"—Spanish explorers such as Hernando de Soto, Ponce de León and Panfilo de Narváez—visited the West Coast in the early 1500s, long before Jamestown was settled. They found warring Indians, impenetrable swampland, vicious insects and suffocating heat that quickly discouraged European settlement.

In the following centuries, Florida's Gulf Coast became home to some intriguing, albeit unsavory, European adventurers. Back in 1772, one explorer called the Charlotte Harbor coastline area below Tampa, "a haunt of the picaroons of all nations." Like the rest of West Coast shoreline, Charlotte Harbor's honeycombed maze of islands, keys, shoals, inlets, bayous and estuaries made the waters a sailor's nightmare. And a pirate's dream.

Gasparilla is the awe-inspiring name one hears most in these parts when talk turns to pirates. Serious historians refute his existence, while treasure hunters never give up the faith. Whether or not he ever lived, his legend matches the adventurous spirit of West Coast Florida. You will see his name today from Cedar Key to Naples—on street signs, hotel fronts, trails and on a Charlotte Harbor island that bears his moniker.

War was a great settler of Florida's rugged frontier. During the Seminole Wars of the 1800s, Tampa and Fort Myers were selected as U.S. Army outposts because of their strategic locations. Soldiers returning from western Florida after the Seminole and Civil wars talked about the area as a balmy paradise. Pioneers became more plentiful.

By the late 1800s, the area began attracting wealthy entrepreneurs. In Tampa, Henry Plant was to Florida's West Coast what railroad tycoon Henry Flagler was to the East. Both were men of insight and power who recognized Florida for its recreational, health and wealth potential. Noting the rich vacationers Flagler was enticing to the East Coast with his railroads and hotels, Plant figured he could do the same in the west. After all, the Gulf Coast was blessed with the same semitropical climate and flora. Plus it had something the Atlantic side never would: seaside sunsets.

When Plant brought his railroad to Tampa in 1884, only a handful of staunch settlers lived there. He built a causeway over the bay and deep water piers for a seaport. In 1891, he erected his fabulous Tampa Bay Hotel. The opulent Moorish palace served as a bastion for wealthy vacationers until the Spanish-American War, when Colonel Theodore Roosevelt brought his Rough Riders to train on the hotel grounds. The landmark hotel today houses University of Tampa offices and a historical museum.

At the turn of the century, Plant built another resort palace, the Belleview Hotel, in Clearwater. Down the coast, the Gasparilla Inn was established on Gasparilla Island to house the Vanderbilts, DuPonts and other wealthy northerners during their winter stays. Teddy Roosevelt, Shirley Temple, Charles Lindbergh and others came down to the once-forbidden islands of Charlotte Harbor to fish and relax.

Meanwhile, industry had come to Tampa in the form of phosphate shipping and cigar making. In 1886, Vincente Martínez Ybor moved his tobacco factories from Key West to Tampa. An influx of immigrant workers followed to settle in Ybor City, a section of Tampa that is today a center of Cuban culture.

At the same time Plant was building Tampa into a city, inventor Thomas Edison was putting the name Fort Myers up in lights. At his winter estate, he grew the bamboo and goldenrod needed for his experiments.

While Plant and Edison brought notice to Tampa and Fort Myers, another name stands out in Sarasota: John Ringling. The circus man bestowed a legacy of culture to the fledgling town south of Tampa. A devotee of Italian arts, Ringling designed his palatial Sarasota home, Ca'd'Zan, in imitation of the Doge's Palace in Venice. In 1927 he brought his Ringling Brothers and Barnum & Bailey Circus to the area for wintering, thereby stoking the

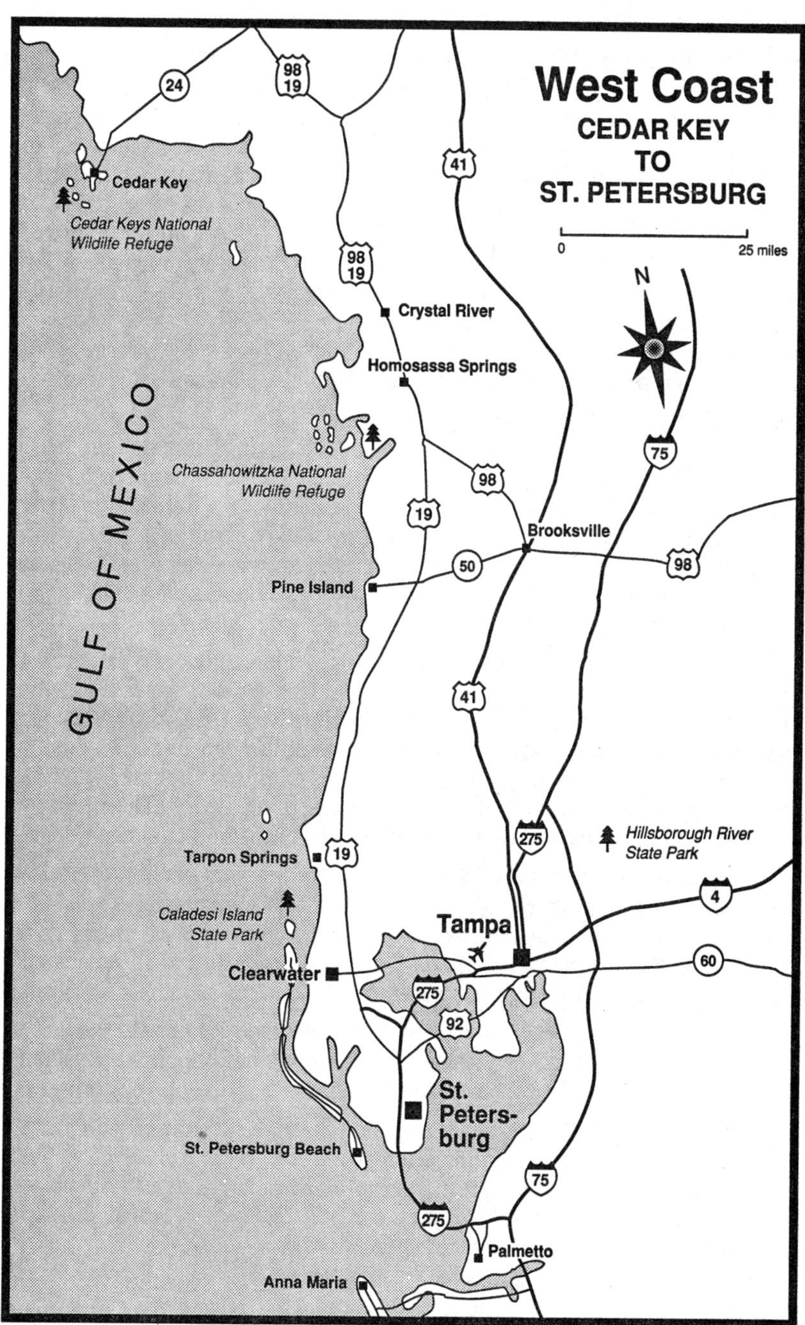
West Coast
CEDAR KEY
TO
ST. PETERSBURG
0
25 miles
N
GULF OF MEXICO
Cedar Key
Cedar Keys National Wildlife Refuge
Crystal River
Homosassa Springs
Chassahowitzka National Wildlife Refuge
Brooksville
Pine Island
Tarpon Springs
Hillsborough River State Park
Caladesi Island State Park
Tampa
Clearwater
St. Petersburg
St. Petersburg Beach
Palmetto
Anna Maria
24
98 19
41
75
98
19
50
275
4
60
92

city's economy. He built island causeways, hotels and an art museum, often using his circus elephants for construction.

In Naples, the 1920s brought an Ohio man named E. W. Crayton to develop this city that avid sportsmen had been keeping to themselves since 1887, when *Louisville Courier Journal* publisher Walter N. Haldeman discovered the area. On Marco Island, settler Bill Collier had turned his home into a fishing inn that in 1883 had advertised its rooms for "$1 a day. You furnish the meat." The '20s along Florida's West Coast not only roared, they boomed. By the next decade, tourism had developed into a bustling business that threatened to run amok, unchecked. Fortunately, the area's incredible natural endowment continued to bring lovers of the outdoors to the West Coast. Many of the islands, bays and villages were settled by vacationing fishermen, hunters and conservationists, who saw to it that wilderness areas were preserved.

A couple of decades later, bulldozers began again to threaten the fabric of tamed and untamed life on Florida's West Coast. Glitz brought the demise of much old architecture; developers' greed threatened wildlife. But during the 1980s, Floridians developed a renewed sensibility about their past, which gave pause to the bulldozers. A style of architecture recalling Florida's belle epoch was revived. Known as Old Florida style, it features white clapboard, tin roofs and airy verandas.

Today, the visitor to Florida's West Coast finds a pleasing balance between the wild and the wilds. In big-city Tampa, skyscrapers seem to shoot up overnight. The town's pace is set by whizzing jai alai orbs, zooming corporate successes and neon nightlife. Yet wildlife can be found even in this soaring metropolis, on the Serengeti Plains of Busch Gardens/The Dark Continent, where thousands of exotic animals roam freely. The old ways are preserved in parks, the renovated downtown area and at shrimp docks.

Much like the state's East Coast, cities on the segment of shoreline below Tampa are beginning to melt together, leaving little rural area in between. Yet each community has its distinctions. Sarasota, the cultured pearl in this string of gems, has been drawing educated, upscale young people with its arts and cultural attractions. Bradenton, its sister city, maintains a homier ambience.

Down the coast, beaches remain to be discovered; Charlotte Harbor cities hide quietly behind great resort villages that are popping up. Islands where pirates and powerbrokers once fled still shelter adventurous refugees.

Fort Myers and its environs comprise one of the fastest growing areas in the United States, but the reins are held tightly to control development. Naples sits in sophistication on the verge of Florida wilds at their best—Everglades National Park. Olde Marco Inn still receives guests at Bill Collier's place. It even provides meat these days.

St. Petersburg, once the butt of retirement-home jokes, now projects a younger, livelier image. Directly north of that city, Pinellas County has become one of the coast's most popular playgrounds, owing to such features as a futuristic pier and its swinging, sun-soaked beaches.

Along the way up the coast from St. Pete, you can find pockets of cultural diversity. In Dunedin, the squeal of bagpipes reaffirm a Scottish flavor; in Tarpon Springs, where icons weep and divers pick sponges, all the world is Greek.

Nature thickens and the glitz thins out en route to Crystal River, where the endangered one-ton manatee symbolizes the endurance of things wild. Attractions in this part of the apart-from-things world give window to old Florida soul: crystal clear springs, ancient Indian relics and funky mermaid shows.

Cedar Key, once a thriving port and now an artists' community, has reverted back to a time that reality-escapees find refreshing. Up in these far reaches of the West Coast, palm trees are joined by pines and oaks, beaches turn marshy and life seems simpler.

The satisfaction of Cedar Key's rediscovered way of life represents a new awareness in Florida development. Residents no longer feel that this area exists merely as a playground. A new sense of place has emerged on the West Coast of Florida that lauds the merits of being relaxed and homey. And wild as a Florida panther.

Tampa Area

DOWNTOWN To many, Tampa means Busch Gardens and Buccaneer football. But to those who take the time to explore, and to the accelerating numbers who are making this West Coast hub home, Tampa is seen as a sophisticated network of growth stemming from carefully nurtured agricultural and fishing roots. In downtown Tampa, there beats the heart of a thriving city. Dazzling corporate towers now rub elbows with spruced-up historic buildings and re-created street markets. The result is sophistication with a homey feel.

One of the biggest renovation projects undertaken was **Harbour Island**. Once weed-infested, today its cobblestone streets lead to a world-class hotel, luxury condominiums and the **Harbour Island Market** (813-223-9898), an indoor fantasy mall. The PeopleMover monorail carries passengers to and from the island and around the downtown area.

The neighborhood across the water from the island is also looking up. The **Franklin Street Mall** allows pedestrian outdoor shopping among restored boutiques that sit in contrast with Tampa's skyscraping and skyrocketing downtown commercial image. The **Tampa Theatre** (711 North Franklin Street; 813-223-8981) resides in the same neighborhood. Built in 1926, it has been revived to the original glamour that once earned it a reputation as "The Pride of the South."

A block away, sitting humbly amid Tampa's modern highrises, is the historic **Sacred Heart Catholic Church** (509 Florida Avenue; 813-229-1595). Completed in 1905, its Romanesque architecture features a remarkable rose window in front.

"Hands-on" displays at the **Museum of Science and Industry** (4801 East Fowler Avenue; 813-985-5531; admission) mean experiencing a hurricane and touching a shark's tooth. This, Tampa's largest museum, is an open-air facility that has fun with scientific phenomena.

The permanent collection at the **Tampa Museum of Art** (601 Doyle Carlton Drive; 813-223-8130) displays 19th-century Japanese prints, contemporary American paintings and pieces from ancient Greece, Egypt and Rome. The facility also hosts rotating humanities and art shows.

The long-standing landmark and historical anchor of Tampa is marked by the silver Moorish minarets of the **Tampa Bay Hotel**, now the University of Tampa administrative offices. The **Henry B. Plant Museum** (401 West Kennedy Boulevard; 813-254-1891; admission) within the university collects memorabilia from the days when its namesake settled Tampa with visions of luxury hotels in the early 1890s. Some of the wicker and imported furnishings from the opulent hotel are displayed in the museum. Also recalled in the museum's memory banks are the days when Teddy Roosevelt headquartered his Rough Riders at the hotel, to train for the Spanish-American War.

The 300-ton **José Gasparilla** (813-223-8130), the world's only full-rigged pirate ship, is docked on Bayshore Boulevard near downtown, for viewing.

Another pastime is watching the shrimp boats come in to unload their catches at the **shrimp docks** (22nd Street Causeway). If you don't catch any activity from the shrimpers, it's still a good place to watch waterfront activity and see gargantuan sea craft passing by.

For information on Tampa and its environs, stop in at the **Greater Tampa Chamber of Commerce** (801 East Kennedy Boulevard; 813-228-7777) or the **Tampa/Hillsborough Convention & Visitors Association** (111 Madison Street, Suite 1010; 813-223-1111), both downtown.

YBOR CITY AREA Visitors to Ybor City, the well-known cigar making center, can still see expert craftsmen roll cigars by hand and view factories as they operated in their heyday. Cobblestone streets, Spanish-tiled storefronts and wrought-iron detailing take you back to the days when Cuban, Jewish, German and Italian immigrants lived here.

The **Ybor City State Museum** (1818 East 9th Avenue; 813-247-6323; admission), once a Cuban bread bakery, depicts the history of the area near Preservation Park, a turn-of-the-century street of cobblestone and wrought iron. Three renovated structures demonstrate typical cigar workers' homes. In one, the **Ybor City Chamber of Commerce** (1800 East 9th Avenue; 813-248-3712) is housed. Stop here for a self-guided walking tour map of Ybor City.

At **Ybor Square** (8th Avenue and 13th Street; 813-247-4497) arts-and-crafts, antique marts, specialty shops and a nostalgia market are located where cigars were once manufactured. In the square at **Tampa Rico Cigars** (813-247-6738), visitors can still watch a craftsman roll cigars by hand.

While you're in the area, you might consider a sidetrip to the nearby **Bobby's Seminole Indian Village** (5221 North Orient Road; 813-620-3077; admission), which contains a community of chickee (thatched-roof) structures and a museum demonstrating the way of life of these long-time Florida residents. Sensational alligator wrestling and snake shows can be arranged for groups of 30 or more.

BUSCH GARDENS AREA **Busch Gardens/The Dark Continent** (3000 East Busch Boulevard; 813-987-5082; admission) remains the number-one attraction in the metropolitan area, number two in the state (after Disney World/EPCOT). The beer factory-cum-theme park takes visitors to 19th-century Africa via the 20th-century technology of a monorail system or skyride. The wilds are juxtaposed with the wild; jungle animals placidly roam the Serengeti Plains as thrill-seekers get dunked, spun and set on their heads by different amusement rides.

Tropical bird gardens, belly dancers, beer sampling and food and gift stands are all presented in exotic surroundings. Exhibits and rides carry Afri-

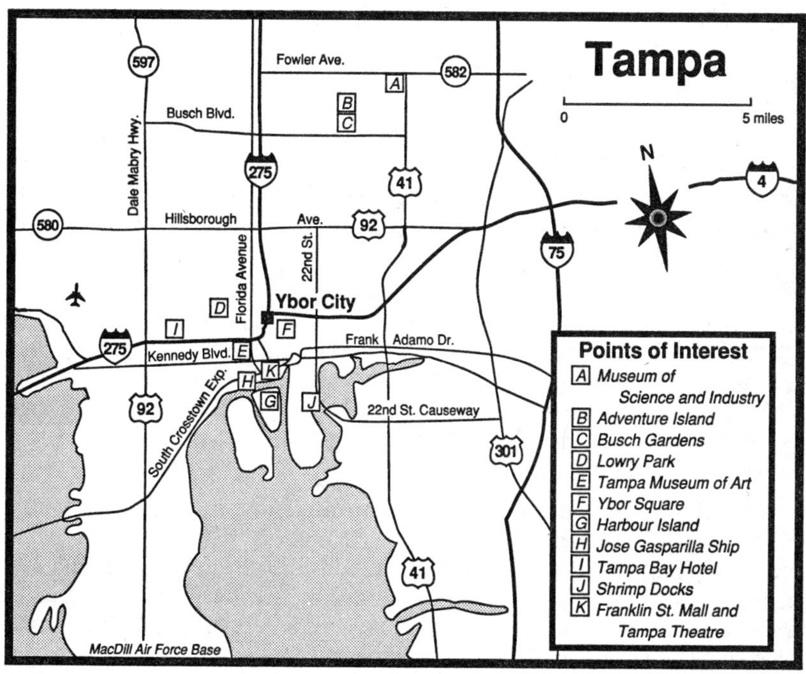

can handles: the "Python" and "Scorpion" are torturous roller coaster rides; an animal farm is found in Nairobi; visitors shoot the rapids on the Congo River; Stanleyville features a theater and log fume.

Nearby **Adventure Island** (4545 Bougainvillea Avenue; 813-987-5600; admission) is a ten-acre water theme park featuring an endless surf pool, water slides, innertubing chutes, beaches and picnic areas. The surf pool simulates the sea with manufactured churning. All is set in natural and man-made tropic surroundings.

Down the road, the **Mind's Eye Museum** (2207 East Busch Boulevard; 813-935-0736) is operated by the Brahma Kamari's Raja Yoga Center. Electronic video displays, halogen light shows and recorded commentary illustrate metaphysical tenets such as karma, reincarnation and God. Other displays define the soul and the history of religion through high-tech media. This psychic museum is a Western-world prototype of facilities throughout India.

At **Lowry Park** (7530 North Boulevard; 813-935-5503) storybook characters entertain the young and young at heart. This attraction is set up as a city park, replete with bubbling fountains, shade trees and picnic areas. From there, childlike fancy takes over. Foot bridges look like rainbows and ferris wheels spin. Safety Village is set up to look like a miniature town, complete with homes, a fire station and various shops. Here children learn the rules of the road in a universe their size. To top it off, there's even a zoo (admission).

TAMPA AREA HOTELS

Most of the accommodations in the city are chain hotels catering to the business traveler or overnight guest. Those looking for a fun-in-the-sun resort head across the bay to St. Petersburg and the necklace of islands that adorn it. If you plan on staying a while in the bay area, we recommend rooming there. For those seeking a few days of metropolitan stimulation and culture, we have found a few Tampa hotels that excel.

Overlooking intracoastal waterways, the **Radisson Bay Harbor Inn** (770 Courtney Campbell Causeway; 813-281-8900) is about the only place in Tampa you'll find a beach with your lodging. Private balconies in the 257 modern rooms overlook the bay or the city. Deluxe and ultra-deluxe tabs buy you lots of extras: restaurant, lounge, sailing and windsurfing, tennis courts and pool.

On the outside, the **Guest Quarters Suite Hotel at Tampa Bay** (3050 North Rocky Point Drive West, Tampa; 813-888-8800) looks like a Mayan temple dedicated to the god of bay waters. Inside the look is decidedly 20th century, with subtle shades, dark woods and modern conveniences. All 203 units are suites, renting in the deluxe and ultra-deluxe range. The facility provides swimming and hot tub facilities.

Holiday Inn Downtown–Ashley Plaza (111 West Fortune Street, Tampa; 813-223-1351) sits downtown on the riverfront near the Tampa Bay Performing Arts Center. Its 312 units include plushly carpeted rooms and suites decorated in modern mauves and teals. Moderate to deluxe.

On Harbour Island in the downtown hub, the **Harbour Island Hotel** (725 South Harbour Island Boulevard, Tampa; 813-229-5000) spells luxury in the form of 300 posh rooms with bay vistas, along with sophisticated clubs and restaurants. Dark woods panel the lobby areas, and moving sidewalks will carry you around the hotel. Ultra-deluxe.

With its gleaming mirrored silhouette towering near the bay, the **Hyatt Regency** (2 Tampa City Center; 813-225-1234) is easily Tampa's glitziest hotel. Formal and elegant, the lobby features a dramatic chandelier and waterfall that cascades down two floors. The 517 guestrooms are cushy and oversized, adorned with designer pastel draperies and plush carpets. Ultra-deluxe.

More homey and less glitzy is the family-operated **Tahitian Inn** (601 South Dale Mabry Highway, Tampa; 813-877-6721). You will find comfortable, clean rooms and a swimming pool at this moderate-priced motel.

Safari Resort Inn's (4139 East Busch Boulevard, Tampa; 813-988-9191) theme comes from its proximity to Busch Gardens. The lobby fits in with its luxurious rattan chairs and the bamboolike trim around the check-in area. The 99 rooms are decorated in jungle tones. There's also a pool, restaurant and lounge. Moderate.

Tampa also offers many budget-priced chain establishments such as **Days Inn Busch Gardens Hotel** (2520 North 50th Street; 813-247-3300) and **Red Roof Inn** (2307 East Busch Boulevard; 813-932-0073). The first features a pool and restaurant and the latter offers a jacuzzi.

TAMPA AREA RESTAURANTS

Local seafood—pompano, grouper, shrimp and stone crab—makes a culinary splash at most Tampa restaurants, washed with the new wave of American cuisine. Standing at the crossroads of Cuban, Spanish, Greek and Scottish subcultures, and influenced by its international port role, Tampa offers fare that tends to be continental while maintaining the homespun flavor of its surrounding agricultural communities.

Crawdaddy's Restaurant & Lounge (2500 Rocky Point Road, Tampa; 813-281-0407) is a theme eating spot done in poor white trash chic. Outside, you feel you've stumbled into the backyard of a Carolina mountain man. A tin smokehouse, long johns on the clothesline and a junked truck, together with the broken-down shacks that house the facility, are some of the props. Inside, things are considerably more comfortable and pleasant. Parlor lamps, curtained booths and carved highback chairs are designed to look aged and to provide an unique eating experience with picture-window views of the bay. The menu concentrates on seafood. Moderate.

Saltwater aquariums, exotic music and articles that have washed ashore give **The Castaway** (7720 Courtney Campbell Causeway, Tampa; 813-281-0770) its South Seas ambience. However, the food is mainly steak and seafood with some pasta and chicken dishes. Moderate.

Besides grilled steaks, **Chuck's Steak House** (11911 North Dale Mabry Highway, Tampa; 813-962-2226) serves snapper, swordfish, blackened shrimp and fresh Maine lobster. This beautiful, wood-adorned facility holds the added attraction of a glassed aviary. Diners with a window view here get to watch tropical birds flit among lush vegetation and waterfalls. Cushy booths and brass planters spread over several dining rooms. Moderate to deluxe.

Sushi and tatami fans can discover masterful Japanese cooking at **Kaoribana** (13180 North Dale Mabry Highway, Tampa; 813-968-3801). The restaurant holds true to Asian standards of beauty through simplicity with its blonde wood beams, lanterns and rice paper dividers. The floor seating offers the much-appreciated comfort of cushions you can lean back on. The moderate-priced menu also offers tempura, yakitori and teriyaki.

Jasmine Thai's (13248 North Dale Mabry Highway, Tampa; 813-968-1501) rendition of Thailand cuisine is dressed up with elegant touches. Offerings at this tiny restaurant include blackened chicken, garlic pork, squid with curry, Siam lobster and fancy duck. Moderate.

Although you may feel a little spooked when you first enter **Bern's Steak House** (1208 South Howard Avenue, Tampa; 813-251-2421), you have discovered Tampa's top shelf. The heavy, rococo decor gives it a slightly somber feeling, but be assured, things don't get any fresher than Bern's home-grown herbs and vegetables. Only the steaks and wine are aged, the latter comprising the largest selection offered anywhere in the area. Desserts are enjoyed upstairs in glass booths equipped with televisions and radios for after-dinner relaxation. Deluxe.

J. Fitzgerald's (4860 West Kennedy Boulevard, Tampa; 813-286-4400) serves dishes with names you'll need Julia Child along to translate: carpaccio with garlic vinaigrette, gravlax in dill-mustard sauce, vineyard snails with pernod under a brioche cap, grilled veal with morels in cream sauce. The surroundings mirror the upscale, deluxe menu with raspberry and mahogany touches. Deluxe.

Villanova By Lauro (4010 West Waters Avenue, Tampa; 813-884-4366) keeps customers satisfied with top quality Italian creations in the ultra-deluxe price range. From delightfully fresh salads (try the broccoli and hearts of palm with lemon dressing), to the al dente pasta dishes and incomparable veal specialties, to a selection of homemade desserts, every bite is memorable. Waiters in vests whisk past in a high-ceilinged, elegant atmosphere.

Dishes at **Selena's** (1623 Snow Avenue, Tampa; 813-251-2116) epitomize the Florida melting-pot effect. Creole and Sicilian are married together here to produce garlicked seafood with sides of sausage, red beans and rice. Furnishings are classic: refinished oak antiques and flowered wall-coverings. Moderate.

Volvos, BMWs and other trendy cars regularly crowd the streets around **Jimmy Mac's** (★) (113 South Armenia Avenue, Tampa; 813-879-0591). Set in a 1920s brick house of creaky wood floors and fireplaces, the ever-popular meeting place feels like a cozy family room. Known for its dressed-up burgers, it also features fried grouper sandwiches, steaks and great dessert coffees. Budget to moderate.

In the historic cigar factory district of Ybor City, restaurants principally feature Cuban food. The Cuban sandwich, Ybor City's gastronomic main-stay, creates a sense of friendly rivalry among restaurateurs, who all claim theirs is the best. Basically, this is little more than a sub sandwich. The difference is the Cuban bread, baked in yard-long loaves using a time-honored method that produces something totally unrelated to a sub bun. Other area specialties include Spanish soup, black beans and rice, paella, flan and Cuban coffee.

Tampa's **Silver Ring Café** (1831 East 7th Avenue; 813-248-2549) holds the reputation as maker of the best Cuban sandwich. These are produced in a showcase window for your entertainment. The decor of this long-established luncheonette is so old and out-of-date, it's "in." Seating is at a long formica counter, at tables or on stools facing little shelves along the wall. Antiques clutter the window, at this budget-priced eatery.

New Orleans ambience and food take Ybor City diners on a cultural departure at **El Pasaje Café Creole** (1330 9th Avenue, Tampa; 813-247-6283). Once a popular Spanish club, the restored building swings with jazzy background music, lively atmosphere, architectural drama and spicy Creole concoctions. The prices are budget to moderate for blackened fish, crawfish, jambalaya and crab cakes.

The **Columbia Restaurant** (2117 East 7th Avenue, Tampa; 813-248-4961) is both landmark and restaurant extraordinaire. The block-long building demonstrates a Spanish influence in its ornate tiling, archways, balconies and grand chandeliers. Although the waiters wear dinner jackets and musicians serenade tableside, the Columbia is casual and reasonable. Its menu is priced in the moderate range for traditional and inventive Spanish dishes: paella, steak *salteado*, and *boliche*, for example.

Latam Restaurant (★) (2511 West Columbus Drive, Tampa; 813-877-7338) is our favorite find in the city because of its incredibly inexpensive châteaubriand. But if you desire elegant atmosphere with your fine food, you will be disappointed. The eatery is housed in an unassuming facility with naugahyde decor. It also serves Cuban specialties. Budget.

TAMPA AREA SHOPPING

Harbour Island Market (601 South Harbour Island Boulevard, Tampa; 813-223-9898) features exclusive shops and luxury boutiques in an indoor marketplace. That's why it is such a pleasant surprise to find a place like **Everything's $1.00** (813-223-6847), which sells items of use and of little use, as promised, for a dollar.

Back Bay Outfitters (107 Franklin Street South; 813-221-0035) retails casual clothing and sportswear for men and women in downtown Tampa.

Old Hyde Park Village (1509 West Swann Avenue, Suite 100, Tampa; 813-251-3500) features upscale shopping in a restored historic setting. Many of the shops carry designer clothes, including **Polo/Ralph Lauren** (701 Village Circle South; 813-254-7656).

Westshore Plaza (Westshore and Kennedy boulevards, Tampa; 813-286-0790) is a popular Sun Coast shopping mall housing major area retailers plus an array of small boutiques and restaurants.

The **Swiss Chalet Gift Shop** (3601 East Busch Boulevard, Tampa; 813-985-3601) carries collectible figurines, T-shirts, citrus and other Floridiana.

For the best bargains in Tampa, head to **Fairground Outlet Mall** (6302 East Buffalo Avenue; 813-621-6047), where wholesale outlets sell shoes, jewelry and other items.

Antique hunters can hit the jackpot at **El Prado Antique Center** (MacDill and El Prado avenues, Tampa). Close to 20 shops cluster within a three-block stretch, selling treasures such as Tiffany silver and 19th-century art. **Village Antiques, Inc.** (4323 El Prado Boulevard, Tampa; 813-839-1761) is one such antiquarian, specializing in Americana.

Contemporary fine glass, silver and crystal are found nearby at **Smither's Gifts, Inc.** (3225 South MacDill Avenue, Tampa; 813-831-1280).

The merchandise in Ybor City ranges from antique glassware to loaves of crusty Cuban bread. At **Ybor Square** (8th Avenue and 13th Street, Ybor City; 813-247-4497) an old cigar factory, a stemmery and a warehouse have been converted into a historic shopping mall. One shop here, **Tampa Rico** (813-247-6738), hand rolls and sells cigars. Another, **Chevere** (813-247-1339) is a cache of cool and colorful cotton dresses, flowing skirts and other women's clothing from Central and South America. The always-crowded **Red Horse** (813-248-8859) carries out-of-date newspapers and magazines as well as postcards from around the world.

Buy your fresh Cuban bread at **La Segunda Central Bakery** (2512 15th Street; 813-248-1531) in Ybor City. Around back, you can watch the bakers at their task.

TAMPA AREA NIGHTLIFE

The **Yucatan Liquor Stand** (4811 West Cypress Street, Tampa; 813-289-8445) is a popular spot for live music, dancing and light shows. Cover.

J. J. Higgins (13254 North Dale Mabry Highway; 813-961-6810) offers an assortment of live entertainment nightly. Cover on weekends.

Country-and-western fans head 'em up for the **Dallas Bull** (8222 North Highway 301, Tampa; 813-985-6877). Cover.

The **Encore Bar** in the Ashley Plaza Hotel (111 West Fortune Street, Tampa; 813-223-1351) is the chic place to be seen after performances at the Tampa Bay Performing Arts Center.

Blueberry Hill (Harbour Island, Tampa; 813-221-1157) takes you back to the '50s with waitresses in cheerleading skirts and waiters in jock shorts. This bar/restaurant is decorated in neon and chrome, diner-style. Entertainment comes live or via a disc jockey.

Alternating between live rock and jazz, **Parkers' Lighthouse** (601 South Harbour Island Boulevard, Tampa; 813-229-3474) is a popular party spot that overlooks intracoastal waters.

Blues, reggae, and progressive music are featured at **Skipper's Smokehouse (★)** (910 Skipper Road, Tampa; 813-971-0666). Cover.

The Comedy Works (3447 West Kennedy Boulevard, Tampa; 813-875-9129) manufactures mirth with top-name entertainers.

The **Tampa Bay Performing Arts Center** (1010 North MacInnes Place, Tampa; 813-229-7827) houses three theaters in a 290,000-square-foot facility. Everything from Broadway musicals to local concerts are hosted at this first-rate complex.

For a gay country-and-western club, try **Moody's Café** (4010 South Dale Mabry Highway, Tampa; 813-831-6537). Inside there's a rough sawn frontier look and an attic's worth of old hats, pictures and other memorabilia decorating the walls. A disc jockey plays dance music.

If you're looking for offbeat local color, visit **Showtime USA (★)** (Route 41, Gibsonton; 813-677-5443), where you can mingle with circus stars and dance to live country music.

TAMPA AREA BEACHES AND PARKS

Hillsborough River State Park—This spot includes 3000 forested acres and a suspension bridge that spans the placid river. Within Hillsborough River State Park sits Fort Foster, a reconstructed Seminole War fort garrisoned by soldiers of the United States Second Artillery. Actually park service guides, they are dressed and equipped in exact replica outfits.

Facilities: Picnic areas, restrooms, canoe rentals; restaurants and groceries nearby; information, 813-986-1020. *Fishing:* Good. *Swimming:* Not safe in the river, but allowed in a pool.

Camping: There are 118 sites, 75 with hookups; $13-15 per night.

Getting there: On Route 301, six miles southwest of Zephyrhills.

Ben T. Davis Municipal Beach—A stretch of sand lying along the Courtney Campbell Causeway, the nine-mile drive bridging Tampa and Clearwater has pretty landscaping, and the sand is soft and white. This is the Tampa area's only saltwater beach, and the locals swarm here. True beach lovers go the distance to the other side of the Pinellas County peninsula across the causeway to the beaches of Holiday Isles.

Facilities: Picnic areas, restrooms; restaurants nearby, groceries a few miles away. *Fishing:* Good. *Swimming:* Good.

Getting there: The park lies right on the Courtney Campbell Causeway's east end where it approaches Rocky Point.

Simmons Regional Park (★)—A popular birdwatching and canoe area on 450 acres of bayfront and channel land. Visitors find a good model of mangrove life and a bird sanctuary. The sand beach is not wide but very natural. The fine but ungroomed sands are favored by locals who prefer seclusion to aesthetics.

Facilities: Picnic areas, playground, restrooms, showers; restaurants and groceries several miles away; information, 813-645-3836. *Fishing:* Saltwater; mangrove snapper and snook. *Swimming:* Good.

Camping: There are 100 sites, half with hookups; $10-12 per night.

Getting there: At 19th Street Northwest in Ruskin, off Route 41.

Bradenton–Sarasota Area

Home of America's most famous circus, Mediterranean-style villas and some of the best seafood on Florida's West Coast, the Bradenton-Sarasota Area is also the place to find bald eagles and bobcats, as well as best beaches and remote islands. A variety of historic attractions may even tempt you away from the waterfront.

To find one such attraction, you must drive out of town and into antebellum Florida. The **Gamble Mansion** (3708 Patten Avenue, Ellenton; 813-723-4536; admission), plastered with a mixture of sand, oyster shells and fresh water, remains a relic of southern Florida's sugar plantations. A tour through the late 1840's home will give you a look at the life of a wealthy planter. Period antiques sit in their proper setting within the spacious, columned mansion. Also on the premises in a visitor center, complete with exhibits on the mansion's history.

Snooty, a West Indian manatee weighing in at 850 pounds, is one of the main attractions at the **South Florida Museum** (201 10th Street West, Bradenton; 813-746-4131; admission). The complex includes artifacts of Florida history, science exhibits, a 16th-century Spanish chapel and a reproduction of Hernando de Soto's birthplace in Spain.

The **Manatee Chamber of Commerce** (222 10th Street West, Bradenton; 813-748-3411) is ready to provide more information on the sights of the area.

Peppered along Sarasota's waterfront lie islands ranging from glitzy to laid-back. To do an **island-hopping tour** of the Bradenton-Sarasota waterfront, follow Route 64 west from Bradenton through Palma Sola.

On your way to the islands, take a quiet sidetrip to **De Soto National Memorial** (75th Street; 813-792-0458; admission). You can drive to the point where the Manatee River meets the Gulf of Mexico, and where explorer de Soto purportedly met the New World. The view of old homes with landscaped spreads, not to mention the gumbo-limbo trees and cool Gulf breezes, is worth the drive. A visitor's center and interpretative trail tell the tale of the Europeans' arrival to this nation. In season, park employees dress in period costume to greet visitors with demonstrations and talks.

The first island you reach as you continue on Route 64 is **Anna Maria Island.** Anna Maria's personality is youthful and beach-oriented, and its twisty roads are dotted with beach shops and seafood restaurants.

South of Anna Maria lies **Longboat Key,** named for the long boat in which one of Hernando de Soto's scouts landed. The long island remains to this day a pleasant discovery. **Gulf of Mexico Drive** takes you on a tour of the island's exclusive shops and homes.

The next hop takes you onto **Lido Key**. To learn more about the sealife of Sarasota shores, visit **Mote Marine Science Aquarium** (1600 City Island Park, Lido Key; 813-388-2451; admission) at the island's northern end. Here you can see sharks, lobsters, seahorses and other species.

Headed south on John Ringling Boulevard, you will reach **St. Armand Key,** a round little island synonymous with shopping. Circus man and Sarasota developer John Ringling once envisioned this area as a fantasy circle of fine shops, restaurants and Italian statuary, and so it has developed. On the other side of "The Circle" stretch fluffy white beaches.

If you continue on Ringling Boulevard, you will cross the Intracoastal Waterway onto Sarasota's mainland. Here in **Sarasota,** the wild has been tamed and dressed up in tails. Considered the cultural center of southwest Florida, the city and its surrounding islands and towns show a vast appreciation for the arts, a sensibility inherited from John Ringling.

Downtown Sarasota looks as if it has discovered Florida's fountain of youth. Clubs, pubs, restaurants, galleries and quirky boutiques have been popping up in old, restored buildings. In the heart of the city, one of Sarasota's oldest attractions blends a love of nature and aesthetics. **Marie Selby Botanical Gardens** (811 South Palm Avenue, Sarasota; 813-366-5730; admission) spreads a banquet of exotic plant life that satisfies discriminating connoisseurs. The most brilliant display in the 15 gardens is the internationally acclaimed orchid center.

To scout out all that Sarasota has to offer, check with the **Sarasota Convention & Visitor's Bureau** (655 North Tamiami Trail; 813-957-1877).

Sarasota's greatest sightseeing attraction spreads bayfront at the northern end of town, on Route 41 near the airport. **The John & Mable Ringling Museum of Art** (5401 Bayshore Road; 813-355-5101; admission) and its 66-acre entourage of sights and gardens pay homage to a man who shaped the city's cultural destiny. The museum focuses on Baroque, Ringling's favorite type of art, but includes other styles as well. Original Rubenses, Velasquez and El Grecos demonstrate the circus man's love of travel and fine art. Classic Greek and Roman statuary graces the courtyard gardens.

The most impressive element on the Ringling grounds is **Ca'd'Zan,** Ringling's mansion, modeled after the Doge's Palace in Venice, with columned halls, ornately tiled towers and plazas, and breathtaking views from the living areas. Architectural elements and furnishings were shipped to the site from around the world. The 30-room mansion was completed in 1926 at a cost of $1.5 million.

Next door to the art museum sits **Asolo Theatre,** just as it once sat in a little town near Venice some centuries ago. When it came time to tear the building down, someone had the foresight to box up sections of the rococo-style, three-level theater. An antiquarian purchased the Asolo in its segmented fashion and later sold it to the Ringling Foundation, which had it shipped to Sarasota and pieced together.

A walk across the water-edged grounds at Ringling takes you to the **Circus Galleries,** a collection of displays and memorabilia that brings back the excitement and exotic feeling Ringling's shows once gave to the fledgling town of Sarasota. Displayed are ornate circus wagons, calliopes, costumes, photos, posters and exhibits featuring Tom Thumb, Emmett Kelly and other bygone circus celebrities.

After you leave the Ringling grounds, you might want to head south and hop over to **Siesta Key,** which can be reached by two bridges that cross the Intracoastal Waterway from Sarasota. **Ocean Boulevard** is where the action—and the beaches—are. Siesta's sands come from battered quartz rock, making them the whitest to be found, and some of the most popular.

As you leave Sarasota, there is one more island to hop on. To get to **Casey Key** (★), you must turn off Route 41 at Blackburn Point, although there are no signs to point the way. This is, no doubt, intentional, as the population of this ribbon of sand smacks of old money that wants to escape crowds. When you get to the island, turn left and wind along the residential road with its mansions and landscaped yards. The road takes you to **Nokomis Beach** and then to the south end bridge back to the mainland.

The city of **Venice,** farther south, is known for its clown school and shark's teeth. Named for Ringling's favorite city, the spot was once winter

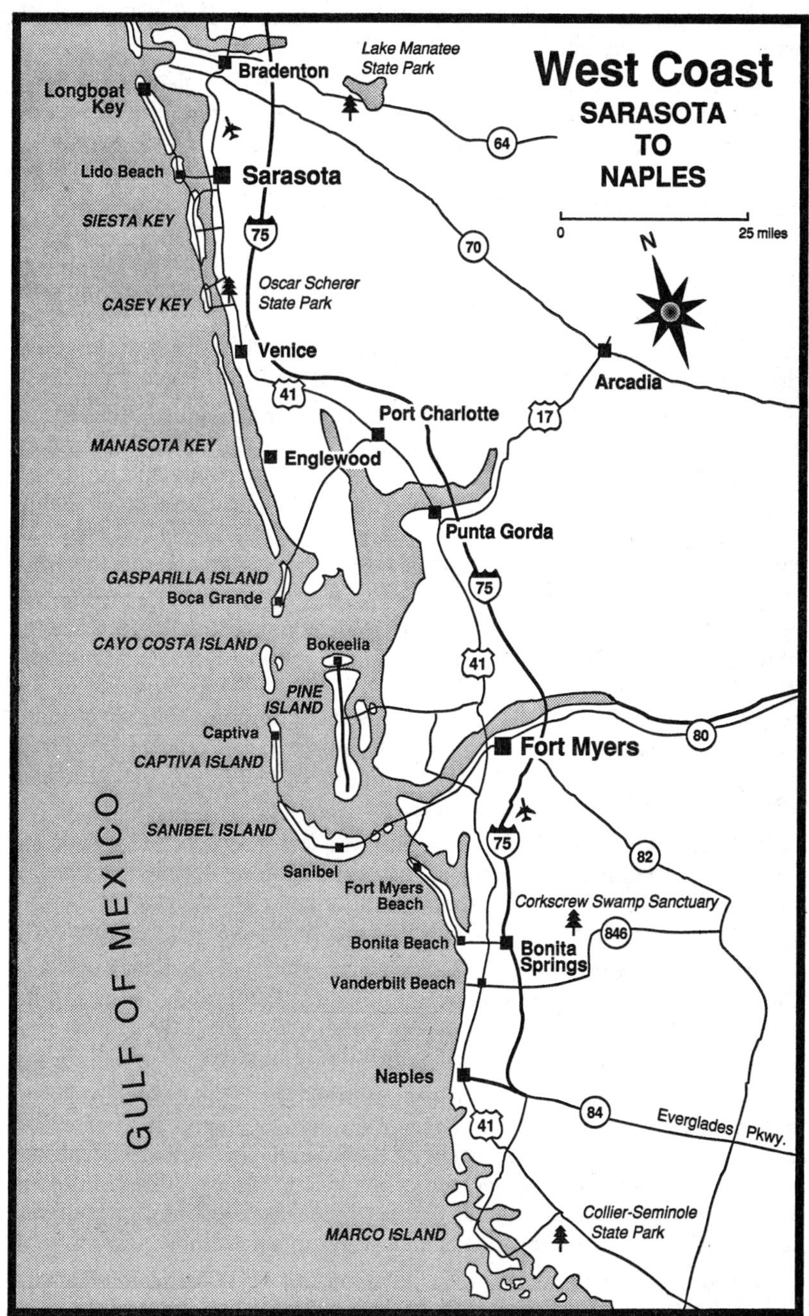
West Coast
SARASOTA
TO
NAPLES
0
25 miles
N
Bradenton
Lake Manatee
State Park
Longboat
Key
64
Lido Beach
Sarasota
SIESTA KEY
75
70
Oscar Scherer
State Park
CASEY KEY
Venice
Arcadia
41
Port Charlotte
17
MANASOTA KEY
Englewood
Punta Gorda
GASPARILLA ISLAND
Boca Grande
75
CAYO COSTA ISLAND
Bokeelia
41
PINE
ISLAND
80
Captiva
Fort Myers
CAPTIVA ISLAND
SANIBEL ISLAND
75
82
Sanibel
Fort Myers
Beach
Corkscrew Swamp Sanctuary
Bonita Beach
846
Bonita
Springs
Vanderbilt Beach
GULF OF MEXICO
Naples
84
Everglades
Pkwy.
41
Collier-Seminole
State Park
MARCO ISLAND

home to the circus. The Ringling Brothers Barnum & Bailey Circus still premieres in Venice each winter.

As for shark's teeth, **Venice Beach** is the gathering place for serious and amateur collectors who comb the beaches and waters to find the specimens that wash up here in abundance.

BRADENTON–SARASOTA AREA HOTELS

In a terra-cotta-and-white trimmed home on the river, **Five Oaks Inn's** (★) (1102 Riverside Drive, Palmetto; 813-723-1236) four comfy rooms are rented out bed and breakfast style. You'll feel as if you've come to visit your grandmother, with the full breakfast service, high ceilings, wainscoted living room and quiet surroundings that await you. Moderate to deluxe.

Touches of charm add specialness to a motor inn called **Bradenton Resort Inn** (2303 1st Street, Bradenton; 813-747-6465). The 200 moderately priced rooms are done in shades of gray and burgundy and furnished with white-washed oak pieces. Suites with kitchenettes are also available at a moderate to deluxe price. A keyhole-shaped swimming pool and fountain-graced reflecting pool garnish the grounds.

The most interesting accommodations in the immediate Bradenton vicinity lie offshore in Anna Maria Island's three communities of Anna Maria, Holmes Beach and Bradenton Beach, and on Longboat Key. At **Alamanda Villa** (102 39th Street, Holmes Beach; 813-778-4170), personality is defined with a Mediterranean flavor and large, modern rooms. The seven units look out on the beach and/or a wooden sunning deck. The hotel hides behind another building, so the rooms are not right on the main drag, though beach traffic can get pretty intense. Moderate.

Villa Del Sol (2502 Gulf Drive North, Bradenton Beach; 813-778-6671) offers miniature golf, a card room, a pool room, sunning deck with barbecue area, a swimming pool and 34 spacious guest rooms with its small beachfront. This moderately priced facility is a popular spot for families.

Sun 'n Sea Cottages (4651 Gulf of Mexico Drive, Longboat Key; 813-383-5588) look more like homes than cottages. Each of the units has its own neatly manicured yard, screened-in porch and carport. The beach area is small and seawalled to discourage erosion. Deluxe.

The highly acclaimed **Colony Beach Resort** (1620 Gulf of Mexico Drive, Longboat Key; 813-383-6464) caters to ultra-deluxe budgets and hedonistic fantasies. Townhouses and apartments (235 in all) are furnished with the most modern conveniences, including kitchenettes and marble bathrooms with whirlpool tubs. The grounds exude tropical lushness and recreational heaven with tennis, beach, fitness and swimming facilities.

Elegant upon first impression, **St. Armand Inn**'s (700 Benjamin Franklin Drive, Lido Beach; 813-388-2161) rooms are deluxe in price. You can rent a room, efficiency or suite here on the beach. The 116 units are decorated in subtle tones. The rooms' greatest features are their picture windows looking out on the beach. Extras include a lounge, coffee shop, pool and sundeck.

For residential bed and breakfast accommodations, **Our Hacienda (★)** (2803 Browning Street, Sarasota; 813-951-1920) offers two bedrooms in a Florida ranch-style home. The rooms are large, with brass-and-glass decor, and are budget-priced. A screened-in swimming pool and continental breakfast are added amenities. Two-night minimum.

The gay- and lesbian-friendly **Normandy Inn** (400 North Tamiami Trail, Sarasota; 813-366-8979) is a U-shaped, art deco-style motel in the heart of the city's theater district. A dozen moderate-to-deluxe-priced rooms are fully carpeted and some units come with mirrored ceilings and spas.

Azalea Apartments (330 Beach Road, Siesta Key; 813-349-7890) front the Gulf and Siesta's glorious beach. Despite its frenzied location, quiet is promised here. Shade trees protect patio sitters from privacy-busters. The six charming older apartments with linoleum floors rent at moderate to deluxe rates. During peak season, one-week minimum; off-season only four-night minimum.

A nice change of pace from the usual beachy accommodations on Siesta Key is a bed and breakfast inn called **Crescent House** (459 Beach Road; 813-346-0857). This historic home sits prettily across the street from the beach. Its architecture and decor is 1920s Florida: a pleasant blend of Victorian and wicker. The gingerbread building houses four guest rooms and a hot tub, with a sun deck. Continental breakfast is served daily on lacy tablecloths. Moderate.

Banyan House (519 South Harbor Drive, Venice; 813-484-1385) accommodates guests in a historic, residential setting at moderate prices. Nearby Sarasota's Mediterranean influence is evident in this neighborhood, with its red tile roofs and Spanish touches. Inside the home, the two guest rooms and seven efficiencies draw on an Italian motif, with some modern touches added. Continental breakfast, pool and a hot tub bring this '20s structure into the present day.

BRADENTON–SARASOTA AREA RESTAURANTS

A legend in its time, the **Crab Trap (★)** (U.S. 19, Palmetto; 813-722-6255) redefines native cuisine with a tendency toward the unusual: 'gator tail, soft-shell turtle, mullet, catfish, wild pig, Florida perch and, of course, crab. The surroundings are appropriately rugged and tropical; the prices are moderate.

Out-of-the-way but worth discovering, the **Sand Bar Restaurant & Lounge (★)** (100 Spring Avenue, Anna Maria; 813-778-0444) reigns as a local favorite. Casual dining on the deck beachside or in the picture-windowed dining room offers fried 'gator, Bali chicken, Cajun grouper, smoked salmon and caviar, soft-shelled crab and raspberry mousse cake. Moderate.

There's something fishy about the ambience and menu at **Moore's Stone Crab Restaurant** (800 Broadway Street, Longboat Key; 813-383-1748). Crab is the specialty, and Moore's freshness in that department cannot be beat, thanks to the owner's inventory of 3000 crab traps. Dine al fresco on the veranda or indoors with a water view. Florida lobster, scallops, clams, frogs' legs and shrimp keep the crab company on the moderate-priced menu.

Brick archways, wooden accents, wine racks and a long stretch of kudos decorate the walls at **Café L'Europe** (431 St. Armand's Circle, Lido Key; 813-388-4415). To complement the cozy dining room, continental cuisine is served at ultra-deluxe prices. Lunch offerings include banana pancake, veal with avocado, red snapper *belle meunière* and grilled sirloin. For dinner, choose from French specialties of the beef, pasta, poultry, veal, lamb and seafood variety.

Sashimi, tempura, tofu, teriyaki, Japanese bouillabaisse, egg rolls and octopus can be enjoyed at the sushi bar, or from a floor or chair seat at **Kyoto Japanese Restaurant** (1519 Main Street, Sarasota; 813-955-7899). Small, as are most of the eateries downtown, this slip of Asian culture packs a lot of authentic Japanese experience into its narrow set-up. Moderate.

Ristorante Bellini (1551 Main Street, Sarasota; 813-365-7380) is not just another Italian restaurant in a world of too many mediocre spaghetti houses. Some of the staff have a difficult time with the English language, which speaks well for its authenticity. Northern Italian cuisine is featured in a bright café atmosphere where unusual photographs and prints decorate the walls. The pasta, meat and seafood selections include *agnoloti* (dumplings stuffed with ricotta and spinach), *costoletta al ferri* (grilled veal) and snapper with wine and fresh tomatoes. Moderate.

For an incomparably fine dining experience, try **Carmichael's** (1213 North Palm Avenue, Sarasota; 813-951-1771). A historic landmark, the building was the '20s-era home of a Sarasota newspaper publisher. Restored to a lovely freshness, the restaurant itself is a must-see. Pastel stained-glass windows, a tiled fireplace and antique furniture lend esoteric touches to the tiny dining rooms. The fare is also unique. In this totally tame environment, wild game is featured in a deluxe range. Buffalo, wild duckling, king salmon, venison and other items appear on an ever-changing menu.

Sarasota comprises a large Amish population whose restaurants dot the city. Most are plain, cafeteria-style settings that serve the freshest of homegrown ingredients. One of the most popular is **Der Dutchman** (3710 Bahia Vista, Sarasota; 813-955-8007). All lunch and dinner specialties—roasted chicken, liver and onions, desserts and bakery goods—are homemade, even the noodles. Budget.

Good enough to make the top ten chart is the dizzying world of **Poki Joe's Greatest Hits (★)** (6614 Superior Avenue, Sarasota; 813-922-5915). The founder-owner-cook, once a musician, has decorated his walls with old 78 disks and Christmas lights. Hits of the 1930s and 1940s provide unique muzak. Sausage soup and spinach pie are some of the specialties; Poki Joe's also serves various forms of sandwiches, fish and steaks at moderate prices.

Old Florida meets new American at **Ophelia's On the Bay** (9105 Midnight Pass Road, Siesta Key; 813-349-2212). Cuisine is strictly new age. Lunch offerings include raw oysters, crabmeat salad, crêpe of the day and homemade chicken pie. The dinner menu provides eclectic temptations that range from classic cioppino to pompano in parchment. Patio seating is available overlooking the water. Moderate to deluxe.

Fresh and natural describes the food at **Wildflower** (5218 Ocean Boulevard, Siesta Key; 813-349-1758). The decor is just as healthy and bright looking. Have a breakfast of grilled tofu or a fresh fruit salad; a lunch of Mexican specialties or avocado Reuben; and a dinner of grouper, shrimp, sweet and sour tempe, steamed vegetables, or other healthful concoctions. Budget to moderate.

Pelican Alley (1009 Albee Road West, Nokomis Beach; 813-485-1893) serves unbelievably fresh seafood. The mood is comfortable and seaworthy. Locals and tourists alike head here for grouper, shrimp and novelty appetizers such as deep-fried artichoke hearts and pepperoncini. Moderate.

BRADENTON–SARASOTA AREA SHOPPING

Ellenton Antiques & Gallery (3711 Route 301 North, Ellenton; 813-729-1194) sells historic furniture and other antiques and art in an old red brick storefront.

Furry and dressed-up creatures reside at **Dolls & Bears** (9908 Gulf Drive, Anna Maria Island; 813-778-4456), a place for new and old-style collectibles from moderate to thousand-dollar price ranges.

Glassware, quilts, wicker, antique dolls and other collectibles await discovery at **Dotty's Depot** (1421 12th Avenue West, Bradenton; 813-749-1421), where about two dozen dealers are gathered under one roof.

When you say "shopping" in Sarasota, locals immediately free-associate **St. Armand's Circle** (813-388-1554). It reigns with the great shopping meccas of the world: 5th Avenue, Rodeo Drive, Worth Avenue, etc. The 100-plus shops and dining rooms cover every conceivable need. Price tags in many of the stores make shopping on "The Circle" strictly a spectator sport for many. Designer labels abound.

A few shops stand out for their unusual nature:

To satisfy the child in us all, visitors can stop in at **Big Kids Toys, Inc.** (24 South Boulevard of Presidents; 813-388-3555). Choose from a selection of games and toys that include a videotape titled *The Art and Science of Flirting* and a 1950 Seeburg jukebox.

Authentic boomerangs and aboriginal earrings are the sort of oddities you'll find at **Aussie Ltd.** (59 South Boulevard of Presidents; 813-388-1227), which also carries clothing, umbrellas and other things from down-under.

Galleries are Sarasota's shopping long suit. One selling unusual art at the Circle is **Sydney Hauser Gallery** (9 Fillmore Drive; 813-388-3021), featuring calligraphy.

Downtown Sarasota's restored storefronts have attracted the city's artists, who have opened many unusual boutiques and galleries in the area.

Sarasota Emporium (★) (1521 Main Street, Sarasota; 813-366-0954) takes a trip back to the head shop days of the '60s. Rock-and-roll posters, tie-dyed T-shirts, jewelry, greeting cards, erotica and paraphernalia are stocked.

Lovely gifts with a New Mexico Indian flavor are sold at **Santa Fe Trails Gallery** (1429 Main Street, Sarasota; 813-954-1972), including carvings, serapes, pottery, silver jewelry and paintings.

In Venice, **Basketville** (4011 South Tamiami Trail; 813-493-0007) is a huge facility that sells every sort of straw item ever woven. It also features woodenware, silk flowers and other gifts.

BRADENTON–SARASOTA AREA NIGHTLIFE

For entertainment local-style, stop in at **The Pub** (★) (760 Broadway, Longboat Key; 813-383-2391) to hoist a few with the fisherman crowd.

The **Club Bandstand** (300 Sarasota Quay, Sarasota; 813-954-7625) features decor and costuming from the '50s and music from a deejay spinning platters.

One of the most popular spots for nightlife in the Sarasota area is Siesta Key's **Beach Club** (5151 Ocean Boulevard; 813-349-6311). This bar has a college tavern atmosphere but is favored by a mixed group. Live entertainment. Cover.

Popular with the gay crowd, **Backstreet** (3709 North Tamiami Trial, Sarasota; 813-355-4388) is a dance club with a variety of live acts, including female impersonators. Located in a brick building near the airport, this establishment has video, disco and draft bars, as well as a billiard room. There is dancing to Top-40 music played by a deejay. Women are also welcome.

The performing arts flourish in Sarasota's rich cultural medium. The largest and most impressive center of the arts in this area is the **Van Wezel Performing Arts Hall** (777 North Tamiami Trail, Sarasota; 813-953-3366). The purple seashell-shaped hall hosts touring theater, music and dance companies.

Asolo Center for the Performing Arts (55 North Tamiami Trail, Sarasota) houses the professional troupe that once performed at the historic

Asolo Theatre on Ringling Museum grounds. The new facility is close by and is outfitted with two theaters plus film and television production studios.

Downtown's **Golden Apple Dinner Theatre** (25 North Pineapple Avenue, Sarasota; 813-366-5454) serves buffet dinner and theater in the musical/comedy vein.

Sarasota Opera House (61 North Pineapple Avenue; 813-953-7030) hosts major musical artists from New York.

BRADENTON-SARASOTA AREA BEACHES AND PARKS

Lake Manatee State Recreational Area—An inland 556-acre park featuring natural vegetation and a manmade reservoir, this spot shelters the endangered gopher tortoise, indigo snake and other indigenous animal life. There's a beach area on the lake.

Facilities: Picnic areas, boat rentals, hiking trails; information, 813-741-3028. *Fishing:* Good in the lake. *Swimming:* Good at designated area in the lake.

Camping: There are 60 sites, all with RV hookups; $10-12 per night.

Getting there: Located on Route 64 east of Bradenton.

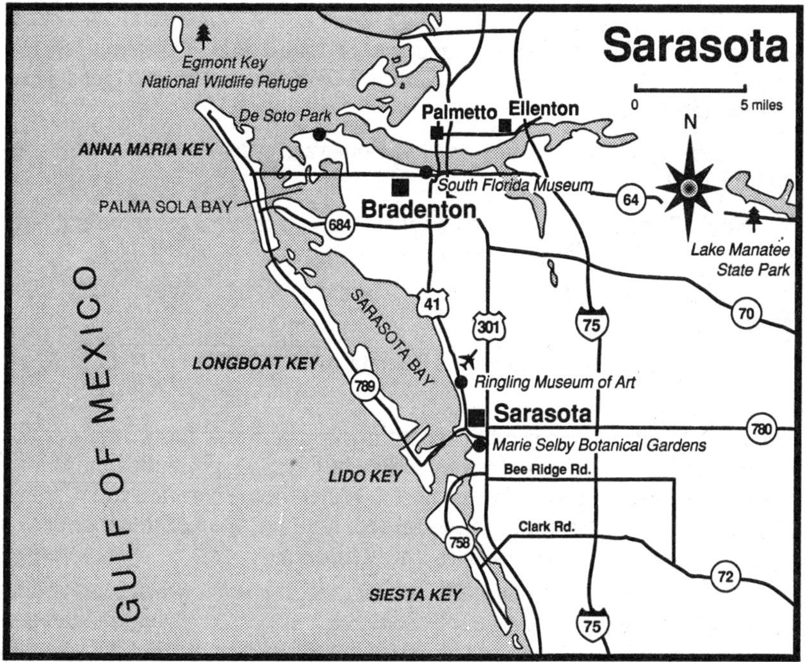

Egmont Key National Wildlife Refuge (★)—A remote island north of Anna Maria Island reachable only by boat. The threatened gopher tortoise abounds here, and the remains of a fort from the Spanish American War, built in 1900, can be seen. The two-mile by half-a-mile island draws serious shellers and beachgoers devoted to seclusion.

Facilities: None. *Fishing:* Good. *Swimming:* Good.

Getting there: The cheapest ride to the island, unless you have your own boat, is aboard the *Miss Cortez* (Cortez Road, Cortez; 813-794-1223), an excursion boat that operates every Sunday through Thursday.

The islands that front Bradenton and Sarasota show the Gulf a continuous run of sand. On these islands, all beach is public property. All accesses, however, are not. Each island has one or more marked public access points, often with parking facilities and other provisions. There are usually no perimeters to these beaches; they run into each other along the stretch of unbroken sand:

Coquina Beach—This is a long stretch of sand fringed in Australian pines at the south end of Anna Maria Island. The beach runs up the face of the island, connecting with Anna Maria and Manatee beaches.

Facilities: Picnic areas, restrooms, showers, lifeguard; restaurants and groceries nearby in Bradenton Beach. *Fishing:* Good off a dilapidated fishing pier on the Gulf side. Several fishing piers are located up the beach. Bradenton Beach City Pier at Cortez Road juts into the Intracoastal Waterway: sea trout, snapper and other local fish can be found here. *Swimming:* Great on Gulf side; avoid bay side. *Snorkeling:* Waters around the old pier contain sea life and fairly clear waters.

Getting there: Located on Gulf Boulevard at the southern tip of Anna Maria Island.

North Lido Beach—A natural, secluded area that invites birds and birdwatchers, this beachfront stretches a half mile.

Facilities: Picnic areas; restaurants and groceries nearby. *Swimming:* Great.

Getting there: Located on Benjamin Franklin Drive at Lido Key's northern end.

Lido Beach—This is really a continuation of North Lido Beach, which stretches the entire length of the island's Gulf face, onto South Lido Beach, which wraps around to the Intracoastal Waterway. There are more public facilities available here in this central location, but the beach continues on in much the same sugar fineness and whiteness.

Facilities: Picnic areas, playground, restrooms, showers, lockers, lifeguards, a 25-meter swimming pool, snack bar, volleyball; restaurants and groceries nearby. *Fishing:* Best at the southern end pass for sea trout, snook and snapper. *Swimming:* Good.

Getting there: Located on the 700 block of Benjamin Franklin Drive on Lido Key.

Siesta Key Public Beach—An island-long stretch of beach. The quartz sand on Siesta Key was judged first place by a national beach expert who studied the whiteness and fineness of beaches around the world. The water is clear and intoxicating as vodka here. For the bad news, it's often crowded. Condos crowd at the edge of the beach no matter where you go.

Facilities: Picnic areas, restrooms, showers, lifeguard, snack bar, tennis courts, playground; restaurants and groceries nearby in Siesta Village. *Fishing:* Good for local saltwater fish. *Swimming:* Excellent. *Snorkeling:* Great visibility, but not much to see. The best it gets is at Point of Rocks farther north on Crescent Beach.

Getting there: It's located along Midnight Pass Road at Beach Way Drive on Siesta Key.

Oscar Scherer State Recreation Area—Home to some of Florida's endangered and threatened species, such as the bald eagle, bobcat and scrub jay, this 462 acres of flatwoods is a naturalist's paradise. Fishermen enjoy this park for its versatility: both freshwater and saltwater life dwell in the confines of lake, creek and salt marshes.

Facilities: Picnic areas, restrooms, showers, canoe rentals; restaurants a few miles away; information, 813-483-5956. *Fishing:* Above the dam, freshwater fish such as bass and catfish; below the dam redfish and snapper are plentiful. *Swimming:* In the small freshwater lake.

Camping: There are 104 sites, all with RV hookups; $16 per night.

Getting there: Located off Route 41 south of Sarasota.

Casperson Beach—This Venice Gulf-front beach is known for its shark-teeth fossils and one of the longest fishing piers on the West Coast of Florida, measuring 750 feet. Lots of native vegetation—sea grapes, sea oats and palmettos—grow along this ribbon of beach with its grayish sand.

Facilities: Picnic area, playground, restrooms, showers, restaurants and snack bar on pier; groceries a few miles away. *Fishing:* Popular from the pier. *Swimming:* Good. *Snorkeling:* Divers frenzy for fossilized shark's teeth here.

Getting there: The beach is located at the southern end of Harbour Drive in Venice.

Charlotte County

Just because you've never heard of Charlotte County doesn't mean you should pass it by. People who really know Florida love this area's off-the-beaten-track locations like Gasparilla Island and Boca Grande Beach Park. Picturesque lighthouses, bird sanctuaries and fine art galleries reward travelers who take the time to explore this region. Laid back and low key, Charlotte County is nirvana for beachcombers.

You can enter Charlotte County from the north in the Port Charlotte area on Route 41. One of two **Charlotte County Chamber of Commerce** offices is found here (2702 Tamiami Trail, Port Charlotte; 813-627-2222).

To escape the beaten path and discover the true rural and seaside beauty of the area, jump onto Route 776 south of Venice and wind down the island road through **Manasota Key** (★) to Englewood Beach. You will enter Manasota at Manasota Beach, a popular coarse-sand beach to which the locals flock. The beach stretches the length of the island. At the other extreme lies **Englewood Beach**. In between, you'll experience a twisty ride among native vegetation hiding discreet private homes.

A truly hidden destination on this backroad tour is **Gasparilla Island** (★), reputed erstwhile headquarters of the West Coast's favorite pirate. Following Route 771, you will reach the toll bridge that takes you out to this island home of millionaires and tarpon enthusiasts. Past secluded mansions and private resorts, the road leads to the village of Boca Grande. Drive down **Banyan Street** with its canopy of gnarled and shady namesake trees.

Boca Grande Lighthouse Park lies at the island's tip where the remnants of a thriving phosphorus shipping business can still be seen in railroad bridge ruins. The 1890-era lighthouse overlooks the Gulf and the deep waters of Boca Grande Pass, where thousands of vessels congregate in the summer for tarpon fishing.

Back on Route 41, take Marion Avenue out of Punta Gorda, on a quick sidetrip to **Ponce de León Park**. The park is a wildlife area and popular fishing spot, with picnic facilities and a bird sanctuary. A monument with a cross marks the spot where many believe Ponce de León was fatally wounded in an Indian attack after trying to colonize the area in the early 1500s.

CHARLOTTE COUNTY HOTELS

Pelican Shore Cottages (★) (4076 North Beach Road, Englewood; 813-474-2429) reflect the natural, quiet island life around them on Manasota Key. The thick cypress wood siding has a salt-worn appearance that makes the eight cottage units seem as if they belong just where they are, sitting on the soft white beach of Manasota Key, tucked away among palms and pines between Englewood and Blind Pass beaches. Inside, dark wood and braided rugs lend a homey atmosphere. All units contain two bedrooms. Moderate. Weekly and monthly rates only.

Resort communities are the new wave in Florida vacationing. One such playground, **Palm Island Resort** (7092 Placida Road, Cape Haze; 813-697-4800), has settled its own, unbridged island. The experience starts on the mainland at Harbortown, where a swimming pool, marina and villas are situated. If this isn't far enough removed from civilization, a ferry boat takes those with Gilligan fantasies out to Palm Island to abide in luxurious efficiencies. The rooms provide airy, beautiful living that recalls Old Florida. A tram shuttles guests about the beaches, shops, restaurant, bar, pool and spa facilities. This type of vacation does not come cheap (deluxe to ultra-deluxe), but if you are looking for the ultimate in getaways, you'll find it in this 160-unit community.

If you go to **Gasparilla Inn** (5th Street and Palm Avenue, Boca Grande; 813-964-2201) during the winter—social season for the wealthy—chances are you'll be turned away. If you're around during off-season, do schedule at least a visit to this pale yellow palace that offers a yesteryear lifestyle. The rooms and cottages (140 units in all) remain as spartan as they were in the early 1900s. The civility of the era has been preserved at this unadvertised remnant of social graces near the beach. Ultra-deluxe.

CHARLOTTE COUNTY RESTAURANTS

Dine with a view at **Riverhouse Restaurant** (★) (5114 Melbourne Avenue, Charlotte Harbor; 813-629-0007). Neither well-advertised nor easy to find, this place is tucked behind a motel called Harbour Inn. The restaurant and lounge reflect a small town locale, in all its best connotations. But the menu is quite sophisticated: shrimp *à la aildo*, frogs' legs, baby back ribs, liver, etc. Deck dining with a superb outlook on the Peace River is available. Lunch offerings include burgers, salads and such. Moderate.

On Englewood Beach, **Barnacle Bill's** (★) (1975 Beach Road, Englewood; 813-474-9703) is famous for Dagwood-sized sandwiches that usually require a doggy bag. Picnic table casualness pairs up with budget prices.

The aptly named **Temptation Restaurant** (350 Park Avenue, Boca Grande; 813-964-2610) is a New Orleans-style place where white linen graces the tables and the murals depict the life of Boca Grande island and its people. Specialties include red snapper baked in a herb sauce, crab au gratin and linguine in shrimp sauce. Moderate.

Miller's Marina in Boca Grande, Lighthouse Hole (on Bayou Drive; 813-964-0511) is a favorite with both the locals and the boating crowd. The sea-cooled porch overlooks the activities of the marina below. The menu includes standard seafare, including all-you-can-eat shrimp nights once a week. Moderate.

A well-known eatery at Fishermen's Village, **Nightingale's** (1200 West Retta Esplanade, Punta Gorda; 813-637-1177) rises two stories, with dining on the first level and a raw bar upstairs. Salmon Monte Carlo, snapper amandine and soft-shell crabs are offered along with great sunsets. Moderate to deluxe.

Salty's Harborside Restaurant (3150 Matecumbe Key Road, Punta Gorda; 813-639-4151) at Burnt Store Marina features an elegantly nautical atmosphere. Seafood and landlubber specialties such as soft-shell crab, fried oyster sandwich, seafood croissant, salads, duckling, tournedos and lobster can be enjoyed with a dash of salt marinaside. Moderate.

CHARLOTTE COUNTY SHOPPING

Whimsical gifts, from pelican figurines to music boxes, are sold at **Silk 'N Sea** (3527-C Tamiami Trail, Port Charlotte; 813-625-5889).

Sea Grape Artists Gallery Co-op (117 West Marion Avenue, Punta Gorda; 813-575-1718) brokers the work of local artisans.

Fishermen's Village (1200 West Retta Esplanade, Punta Gorda; 813-639-8721) is the place to shop in Charlotte County. The shops carry an array of clothing, gifts and Florida souvenirs within the mall's restored dry dock shelter. You will find gifts with a difference at **The Fabric Gallery** (813-637-8949). Unique wallhangings, quilted exotic flora and fauna and other fine trinkets fill the shop. In the same mall, **The Scarlet Macaw** (813-639-8801) carries name-brand sportswear.

CHARLOTTE COUNTY NIGHTLIFE

Charlotte County is not known for its nightlife. Most entertainment is tailored to a senior crowd, except in the beach areas to which younger audiences gravitate. Cultural entertainment is just beginning to develop in this area.

In Boca Grande, **Laff-a-Lot Bar** (★) (Point Boca Grande; 813-964-2341) is a local hangout where island workers regularly meet to celebrate the end of the week.

The **Charlotte County Memorial Auditorium** (75 Taylor Street, Punta Gorda; 813-639-5833) hosts entertainers ranging from classic musicians to jazz bands.

CHARLOTTE COUNTY BEACHES AND PARKS

Charlotte County itself is hidden. Many travelers tend to pass it by, finding little of interest on its highway face. But the adventuresome who veer off the main thoroughfare find that the county's best side lies seaside. Its many beaches and islands offer remote havens of unfettered nature.

Manasota Key (★)—For those who can sacrifice convenience for seclusion, this long strip of beach fronting private homes is best mid-island at Blind Pass. The island, stretching between Venice and Englewood, is populated by private home owners but includes three public beaches. The one in the center is a largely neglected segment where the beach widens its shell-strewn sands. Pines and palms gather on the edges to separate it from the nearby road.

Facilities: Restrooms. *Fishing:* Good for snook, tarpon and redfish. *Swimming:* Good.

Getting there: Enter at either the south (Venice) or north (Englewood) end on Route 775.

Boca Grande Beach Park (★)—A white sandy beach with plenty of shade trees, this park lies at the southern tip of Gasparilla Island. Only the locals have discovered this patch of natural escapism.

Facilities: Picnic areas, restrooms; restaurants and groceries several miles away. *Fishing:* This island is famous for its tarpon fishing, especially in Boca Grande Pass at the southern end; also good local fishing from the North Pier and South Pier, both on Route 771. *Swimming:* Good.

Getting there: Located off Route 771 at the south end of Gasparilla Island.

Fort Myers Area

Island hopping provides one of the most enjoyable activities in this region. Within easy reach of Fort Myers are the resort islands of Estero, Sanibel and Captiva. While the first contains the sun-soaked community of Fort Myers Beach, Sanibel and Captiva offer world-class shell gathering and luxurious barrier-island beaches.

The adventure begins at **Pine Island**, the northernmost of the bridged islands. It is often called the "forgotten" island because its lack of beaches has left it behind in the condo race. By car, you enter the island from Cape Coral at **Matlacha**, where waterside fish houses demonstrate the island's way of life as it has remained for centuries. Before the bridge, stop at the **Pine Island Chamber of Commerce** (Pine Island Road; 813-283-0888).

To the north of Matlacha, **Bokeelia** (★) lies on an isle of its own, cut off from the rest of Pine Island by a creek. There's not much to see in this quiet spot except a few modern condos trying to make it in a town that hasn't yet woken to the times. Bokeelia serves as the mainland lifeline for some of the unbridged islands nearby. Cayo Costa, Cabbage Key and Useppa Island visitors use Bokeelia marinas as departure points.

These intracoastal islands still retain independence from the mainland and make for secluded and time-frozen destinations. **Useppa** is a private island that is home to a luxury members-only club. Passing it on the way to Cabbage Key, you'll notice the restored 1920s style that remembers the days when Teddy Roosevelt, Hedy Lamarr and Shirley Temple signed the guest book at its Collier Inn.

Cabbage Key (★) is a shred of island greenery dominated by a quaint inn and restaurant. A boater's pit stop, it offers nature and history lessons besides refreshments. Here, atop an ancient Indian shell mound, author Mary Roberts Rinehart built a home that now serves as the simplistic **Cabbage Key Inn** (Cabbage Key; 813-283-2278). A short nature trail takes you on a tour of this sand spit, after which refreshment within walls papered in autographed currency is a must.

Upper Captiva (★) sits just north of Captiva, having been separated by a hurricane of yore. This island of mostly private residences, waterside restaurants and a lovely beach makes for a refreshing escape. The departure point to this island is Captiva. For information on transportation to Upper Captiva, call 813-472-9223.

On the scenic causeway road to Sanibel Island, you'll spot the **Sanibel-Captiva Chamber of Commerce** (1159 Causeway Road; 813-472-1080).

A little known attraction on this island is hidden at the **Periwinkle Trailer Park** (★) (1119 Periwinkle Way, Sanibel; 813-472-1433). The long-time owner here is an avid exotic bird breeder and maintains a couple of aviaries. One sits outdoors for public viewing and is populated with flamingos, toucans, parrots and cockatiels. If you can persuade him, the breeder may show you his private rare collection.

Visit **J. N. "Ding" Darling National Wildlife Refuge** (1 Wildlife Drive, Sanibel; 813-472-1100; admission) for a look at uncaged bird life. This 5000-acre sanctuary is a nature-lover's mecca. You can drive, bicycle or canoe through the maze of estuarine wetlands to see roseate spoonbills, alligators, herons, armadillos, sea-grape trees, gumbo-limbos and buttonwood. Trails off the main road take you to quiet brackish pools populated with alligators snapping at egrets. An observation tower provides an overview of this wild world. A visitor's center offers education on the area's flora and fauna, and on the life of Ding Darling, the Pulitzer-Prize-winning cartoonist who took the area's waterfowl protection under his wing.

Captiva Island lies at the northern end of Sanibel across the Blind Pass Bridge. Though little is offered in the way of attractions, the drive through tunnels of untamed vegetation warrants a visit. Take a meditational pause at the **Chapel-by-the-Sea** (★) (11580 Chapin, Captiva), a romantic spot many choose for weddings.

Away from the islands, the attractions take a historic bent in the "City of Palms," Fort Myers. In downtown Fort Myers is found the **Metropolitan**

Chamber of Commerce (1365 Hendry Street; 813-334-1133). Nearby, housed in a former railroad depot, the **Fort Myers Historical Museum** (2300 Peck Street; 813-332-5955; admission) starts history buffs down the road to old Fort Myers and back to its days as a Calusa Indian settlement and Seminole War fort.

The **Thomas A. Edison Winter Estate and Botanical Gardens** (2350 McGregor Boulevard; 813-334-3614; admission) will not disappoint sightseers looking for a taste of history with their Florida sunshine. Located on a street flanked by the royal palms Edison planted to give the city its nickname, the Edison Estate spreads out along the Caloosahatchee River. The 1880-era house is actually two look-alike clapboard homes in which Edison and his wife lived and housed guests. More impressive is Edison's home-away-from-home laboratory, the museum of his inventions and the gardens he nurtured. In the museum, you'll see developmental stages of the phonograph, Edison's furniture creations and the Model-T Henry Ford custom-made for the inventor. The exotic botanical gardens feature a giant banyan tree and beds of goldenrod the inventor first planted for his experiments in discovering alternate methods of producing rubber.

FORT MYERS AREA HOTELS

The elegant **Sheraton Harbor Place** (2500 Edwards Drive, Fort Myers; 813-337-0300) overlooks the Fort Myers Yacht Basin near the downtown district. Done up in an impressive modern style, the 417 rooms offer plush comfort. The deluxe rates also get you an exercise room, three pools and whirlpool.

One of the few nonchain facilities in town, **Fountain Motel** (14621 McGregor Boulevard, Fort Myers; 813-481-0429) offers moderate rates, 19 reliably clean units, a swimming pool and its own brand of understated charm. Both overnight rooms and apartments are available. All are adequate in space and decorated in pastels with carpeting.

Close to Sanibel Island, the **Radisson Inn** (20091 Summerlin Road, Fort Myers; 813-466-1200) offers deluxe accommodations with a south-of-the-border theme. Plush and pleasant, each of the 153 units come equipped with a refrigerator and separate living and bedroom areas. Bar and grill, game room, bike rental, pool and whirlpool complete the services offered at this tidy property.

Sanibel's Song of the Sea (863 East Gulf Drive, Sanibel; 813-472-2220) captures the personal touches and ambience of a European hostelry: pink stucco walls with red tile roofs and statued gardens on a private beach. Guest accommodations are decorated with country French furnishings, tile floors and ceiling fans. Kitchen facilities, pool and jacuzzi, barbecue area and continental breakfast are included at ultra-deluxe rates.

(Text continued on page 406.)

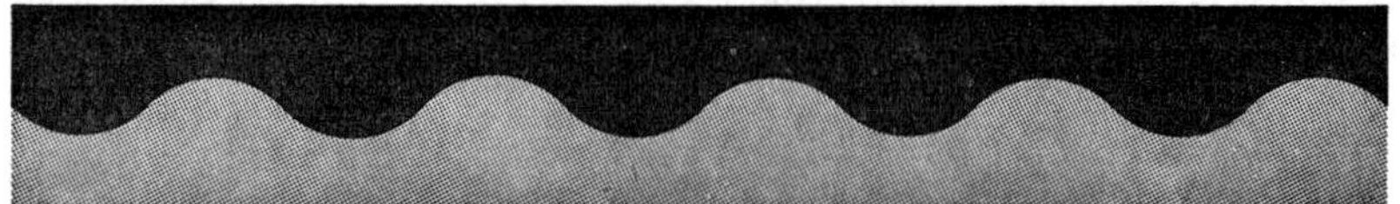

Collecting Seashells by the Seashore

It begins innocently, with a thumbnail-sized scallop blushing in the morning sun. You bend over to pick it up, to hold it in your hand and consider what a nice souvenir it would make of your visit to Florida's West Coast. You slip it into your beach bag and continue strolling down the beach.

Suddenly you are more aware of what lies at your feet than of anything else in this seashore world of wonders. The rest of your walk, alas, the rest of your beaching days is spent head down—eyeing cockles, conches, whelks and sand dollars. Your life has taken a new direction: you are shell-bent.

On **Sanibel Island**, the classic bent-from-the-waist shelling stance has been given a special name. Here in the Shelling Capital of the Western Hemisphere, the literally shell-bent are said to do the "Sanibel Stoop." The eastward hook on Sanibel's southern end allows it to snag shells the sea throws up from all directions. Its shelling fame has made it a prime destination for serious conchologists and amateurs for decades.

In early March, the island hosts an annual **Sanibel Shell Fair** that draws participants from around the world. Nearby, on the mainland, the **Fort Myers Festival of Shells** is celebrated every year. Along the West Coast, shell shows are also scheduled yearly during February and March in St. Petersburg, Treasure Island, Sarasota, Naples and Marco Island.

The best place to find shells on Sanibel Island is **Bowman's Beach.** Because of Sanibel's worldwide shelling reputation, however, the competition is fierce. Serious collectors are out before dawn in miner's hats and mesh slippers, equipped with flashlights, collecting bags and shovels, hoping to find a prize junonia or lion's paw left by the ebbing tide. These are the only vacationers in the world who cheer for bad weather. They pray for storms to bring caches of live shells onto the beach for easy pickings. Because of the popularity of shelling on Sanibel, the city has passed a law that limits the taking of live shells to two per species.

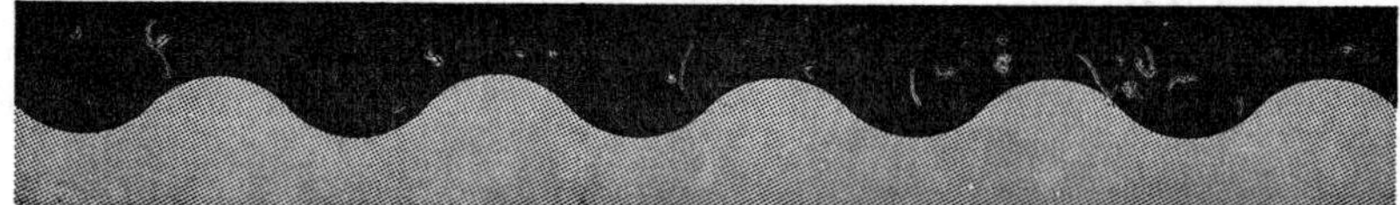

Although Sanibel boasts shelling ascendancy, the entire Gulf Coast attracts collectors. **Captiva Beach** also provides good shelling. Here you will actually find shin-deep piles of washed-up shells—all you have to do is sit in one spot and sift through to find your treasures.

In fact, this beach inspired Anne Morrow Lindbergh, author and wife of the famed aviator Charles Lindbergh, to write *Gift From the Sea* back in 1955. This book of essays compares different types of seashells with stages in a woman's life. You will find this slim volume, as well as a myriad of how-to-shell guides, for sale in most book and gift shops on Sanibel and Captiva.

To escape the hordes of the shell-bent on Sanibel, try some of the outlying islands for less-populated collecting. Shelling charters leave daily from Sanibel and Captiva marinas and resorts. A locally famous shell writer, **Captain Mike Fuery** (813-472-1015), works out of 'Tween Waters Marina on Captiva. He takes his shellers to **Johnson Shoals** off the coast of Cayo Costa, where they can find up to 60 different kinds of shells.

Cayo Costa and **Upper Captiva** islands, because of their seclusion, are popular shelling spots. The same goes for **Egmont Key**, north of Sarasota, and the **Cedar Keys National Wildlife Refuge** at the West Coast's northern extreme. The abundance of shells often comes in direct proportion to the absence of bridges and crowds.

For the less ambitious shell appreciator, there are easier ways to find shells than rising at dawn and mucking around in tidal pools. Hunt instead at the numerous shell shops scattered along the West Coast. The largest and most famous is North Fort Myers' **Shell Factory** (2787 North Tamiami Trail; 813-995-2141), which through the years has evolved from selling shells and coral to marketing jewelry, clothes, gourmet food and other gifts.

On Sanibel, both **Neptune's Treasures** (1101 Periwinkle Way; 813-472-3132) and **Showcase Shells** (1614 Periwinkle Way; 813-472-1971) are owned and operated by knowledgeable conchologists who share advice about their gifts from the sea.

Kona Kai Motel (1539 Periwinkle Way, Sanibel; 813-472-1001), a 13-room facility offers Hawaiian garden ambience in a location central to island shops and restaurants. Rooms or efficiencies are housed in Maui-inspired cottages with witch cap peaks. Rooms are moderate, efficiencies moderate to deluxe.

South Seas Plantation (Captiva; 813-472-5111) extends over one-third of Captiva Island. This is one of those provide-everything places where even the rich and famous find solitude. Rooms come in every shape and size, with price tags to match—generally in the deluxe and ultra-deluxe range, but package deals are available at lower rates. South Seas earns its reputation through attention to detail and by projecting to guests a fantasy island feeling.

The town of Fort Myers Beach lies on Estero Island, where hotels are plentiful as sand. Most accommodations lie along the main drag, Estero Boulevard. At the northern end of Estero you will find a less-discovered section of "The Beach," as locals call it. Occupying a good half block at the northern tip is the **Pink Shell Family Resort** (275 Estero Boulevard; 813-463-6181). Accommodation options include apartments, condominiums and cottages—170 units altogether. All are equipped with kitchen facilities. Units either front the Gulf of Mexico or Estero Bay on this narrow part of the island. Tennis courts, a pool on the beach, grass-roofed chickee huts, a fishing pier, game room and powdery beach are provided. The rooms are adequate, but the focus here is on outdoor activity. Rates are ultra-deluxe.

In the thick of things on Estero Island, **Beacon Court Motel** (1240 Estero Boulevard, Fort Myers Beach; 813-463-5264) is a small, family-type operation. Its 14 rooms are clean and comfortable at moderate rates. The one-level building is pretty in Gulf blue, and its wide balcony porch is generous, if not fancy or private.

Like a flower in a concrete jungle, **The Beach House** (4960 Estero Boulevard, Fort Myers Beach; 813-463-4004) blossoms among huge condominiums. The 14-room complex looks just as its name suggests: a blue-gray sprawling home with white shutters and trim. A breezy walk-through area is paved with bricks and draws you to its sea-walled private beach area. The rooms are small, and the place has an informal, unassuming appeal that induces immediate relaxation. Moderate to deluxe.

Leaving Estero Island, you cross an bridge to Lover's Key. **Days Inn at Lover's Key** (8701 Estero Boulevard; 813-765-4422) capitalizes on its romantically named location to suggest cozy getaways. The spot is secluded, but the chunk of concrete fails to elicit the proper emotions. The lobby and ground level public areas have a nice, open wall-less feel that one does not find enough of in Florida. But the rooms, even the penthouses, lack the proper ratio of decadence per dollar. The deluxe rates include a fully equipped kitchen in each of the 75 suites. The back bay view of the area's estuary waters provides an unique waterscape. Ask for a room with this view.

FORT MYERS AREA RESTAURANTS

Along Fort Myers and her islands, seafood is the favored fare, as well it should be. Since much of the area's transplanted population comes from the Midwest, meat and home cooking have found their place here as well. Continental and ethnic flavors also sweeten the melting pot.

The Veranda (2122 2nd Street; 813-332-2065), in downtown Fort Myers, maintains a southern regional style in a fine dining atmosphere. The restaurant is actually two antebellum homes connected by a courtyard garden. Entrées such as roast duckling and blackened fish are served with fresh honey molasses bread and pepper jelly. Deluxe.

If you seek the freshest down-home meal for your money, try **Farmer's Market Restaurant (★)** (2736 Edison Avenue, Fort Myers; 813-334-1687). The atmosphere is plain, but the food is like mom's, and the price for satiation dwells in the budget category.

Cape Coral—across the river from Fort Myers—boasts an Italian restaurant whose popularity brings knowing hordes despite a low profile. **Dario's Restaurant & Lounge** (1805 Del Prado Boulevard; 813-574-7798) satisfies any Italian craving. The comprehensive menu does veal, seafood, beef, poultry and pasta a dozen different ways each. Moderate prices in an unpretentious shopping mall atmosphere.

For barbecue at its roots level, go to **Hickory BBQ** (15400 McGregor Boulevard, South Fort Myers; 813-481-2626). Budget-priced meals of beef and pork sandwiches or ribs are served with the best sauce ever concocted. They smoke their meat on the premises of this spartan facility.

The names of Sanibel restaurants seem to change with the tides. One that has endured is **McT's Shrimphouse and Tavern** (1523 Periwinkle Way; 813-472-3161). Hidden from its busy location by natural vegetation, the triple-peaked building looks like an Old Florida home. The dining room allows outside views through latticed plexiglass walls. Ceilings soar and floors look as though they'd leave splinters in bare feet. The menu swims with mermaids, and dishes overflow with jumbo shrimp: shrimp marinara, shrimp Oscar, stuffed shrimp and all-you-can-eat steamers. The moderate menu also includes beef, chicken and fish dishes.

For relief from the tab-shock you experience at most Sanibel restaurants, check out **Island Pizza** (1619 Periwinkle Way, Sanibel; 813-472-1581) for budget-to-moderate pizza, sandwiches, baby back ribs and shrimp baskets, all served in a small but airy facility.

French restaurants often bring to mind condescending waiters and stuffy surroundings. *Au contraire* at **Jean-Paul's French Corner (★)** (708 Tarpon Bay Road, Sanibel; 813-472-1493). In a tiny room reminiscent of provincial inns, great food comes from humble surroundings. The staff is refreshingly casual; the food is a pure gift to the tongue—fine dishes such as filet mignon *au poivre* and sole stuffed with salmon mousse. Closed in the summer. Deluxe.

Timmy's Nook (Captiva Drive, Captiva; 813-472-9444) delivers the atmosphere of a neighborhood bar and eatery. Stone crab, fried grouper, cheeseburgers, beer and wine are enjoyed at wooden tables overlooking a marina. Moderate.

The idea behind the **Bubble Room** (15001 Sanibel-Captive Road, Captiva; 813-472-5558) is that "you use your five senses," explains a manager, referring to the three levels of whirring, blinking antique toys and trains, Christmas decorations and strands of bubble lights. Waiters buzz around in Boy Scout–type uniforms, pushing the restaurant's superb prime rib. A continental menu also features shrimp and mahimahi. Deluxe.

The place to settle a seafood hankering on Fort Myers Beach is indisputably **Snug Harbor Restaurant and Lounge** (645 San Carlos Boulevard; 813-463-4343). The experience begins with a stroll through brick-paved tropical gardens of hibiscus, screw pines and birds-of-paradise. Inside, the casual ambience is nautical in an uncontrived sense. The view out the window is of a shrimp boat rubbing gunwales with a luxury yacht. The seafood tastes as fresh as the flowers on the table look. Moderate to deluxe.

For a taste of authentic Greek food, try **Plaka Restaurant** (1001 Estero Boulevard, Fort Myers Beach; 813-463-4707). Served in the most casual of beachside atmospheres (the name means beach in Greek), this spot is a favorite. Gyro sandwiches, *moussaka*, spinach pie, baklava and all the Greek standards are offered at budget prices.

For a delicious sense of discovery, find **Café du Monde (★)** (1740 Estero Boulevard; 813-463-8088). The owners justifiably call this place "one of the best-kept secrets on Fort Myers Beach." A blend of Key West and California-of-the-'60s, Café du Monde stands out with its vegetarian quiche, avocado and turkey croissant sandwiches, and homemade broccoli and cauliflower soup. The atmosphere is as delicious as the food: a bricked courtyard that hides from busy Estero Boulevard behind a cement wall handpainted with roses. Umbrellas cover the oilcloth tables surrounded by potted plants and set with paper dishware. Budget.

The Mucky Duck (2500 Estero Boulevard; 813-463-5519) earned its reputation on nearby Captiva Island. This second in a series of British-inspired pubs continues its success at this historic beachfront location. Restored to a warm, country-style rendition of life in England, the menu blends Old World flavors with local specialties, offering fish 'n' chips, several preparations of shrimp and "whatever the fish." Moderate.

FORT MYERS AREA SHOPPING

Two exclusive Fort Myers shopping centers offer specialty merchandise in tropically landscaped settings. At **Royal Palm Square** (1400 Colonial Boulevard; 813-939-3900) check out **The Red Rooster Country Store** (813-939-7007) for country furniture, accessories and gifts.

At **Bell Tower Shops** (13499 Route 41 Southeast; 813-489-1221), the second open-air mall, you can find South American Inca jewelry, eel skin and other sophisticated gifts at **Lucia's Leather and Things** (813-489-4452). Distinctive bath articles from soap to knickknacks grace chic displays at **La Mom's Bath & Gifts** (813-489-2284).

Fort Myers' largest shopping center houses over 150 merchants. **Edison Mall** (Route 41 and Colonial Boulevard; 813-939-5464) hosts major retailers plus a multitude of specialty shops and food court eateries.

For discounted goods, shop at a local retail center, **Metro Mall** (Metro Parkway and Colonial Boulevard; 813-939-3132), or join bargain hunters flocking to **Fleamaster Fleamarkets** (4135 Anderson Avenue; 813-334-7001).

Touch of Sanibel Pottery (1544 Periwinkle Way, Sanibel; 813-472-4330) sells clayware thrown and fired on the premises. Their colors and designs are inspired by the island's flora and fauna.

For T-shirts with a difference, stop at **Wings Wildlife Boutique** (1700 Periwinkle Way; 813-472-2251). Unusual designs by local nature artists grace quality resort wear.

Schoolhouse Gallery (520 Tarpon Bay Road, Sanibel; 813-472-1193) stocks original paintings, sculpture and shelligrams; **Matsumoto Gallery** (751 Tarpon Bay Road, Sanibel; 813-472-6686), nearby, displays the work of island artists.

At **Discovery Bay** (7205 Estero Boulevard, Fort Myers Beach; 813-463-4715) you'll find a wide array of gifts including glassware, 14-karat jewelry and fashion jewelry.

For casual women's clothing, beachwear and accessories, try **Eastwind** (159 San Carlos Boulevard, Fort Myers Beach; 813-463-3232).

FORT MYERS AREA NIGHTLIFE

Rock bands play from a stage at the **Courtside Bar** (17260 Harbour Pointe Drive, Fort Myers; 813-466-2138) in Sonesta Sanibel Harbour Resort.

Wil's Landing Restaurant & Lounge (1200 Periwinkle Way, Sanibel; 813-472-4772) features karaoke three times a week. **The Crow's Nest** at 'Tween Waters Inn (Captiva Road, Captiva; 813-472-5161) swings nightly with rhythm-and-blues, soft rock and funk. Cover.

As far as theater, the Fort Myers area has just begun to develop. **Barbara B. Mann Performing Arts Hall** (8099 College Parkway, Fort Myers; 813-489-3033) hosts touring theater, music and dance troupes. The **Pirates Playhouse** (★) (2200 Periwinkle Way, Sanibel; 813-472-0006) presents intimate theatre-in-the-round productions by professional and community companies.

Fort Myers Beach is nightlife incarnate. Walk the beach or Estero Boulevard and stop in at the many clubs and bars for a people-packed and fun-filled evening out. One of the most notorious bars is **Top O' Mast Lounge** (1028 Estero Boulevard; 813-463-9424), where there's live music and dancing to popular tunes nightly.

The beachfront and rooftop action at **Lani Kai Island Resort** (1400 Estero Boulevard; 813-463-3111) draws lively crowds with rock-and-roll bands, Caribbean musicians and piano bar music.

Daytime and nighttime entertainment livens up **Pier One** (1000-A Estero Boulevard; 813-463-4242), where a deejay plays island and contemporary tunes in the high season.

FORT MYERS AREA BEACHES AND PARKS

Cayo Costa Island and Preserve (★)—This island of 640 acres can be reached only by boat. Because it is less populated than the lower islands, the shell pickings are great. Shell-studded white beaches run the length of the island on both the Gulf and bay side. All varieties of indigenous wildlife, including wild boars and bald eagles, thrive here.

Facilities: Picnic areas, outdoor restrooms, cold water showers; information, 813-964-0375. *Fishing:* Very good at the northern end where Boca Grande Pass separates the island from the famous tarpon mecca on Gasparilla Island. The pass that separates Upper Captiva from Captiva is named Redfish Pass for the fish found in abundance there.

Camping: Primitive camping is allowed; $13 per night. Twelve austere cabins also available.

Getting there: Many tours and charters out of Sanibel, Captiva and Pine Island will take you there.

Lighthouse Beach—Wrapping around the southwestern end of Sanibel Island, this beach benefits from Gulf and bay frontage. The sand is cushiony and shell-littered. The historic Sanibel Lighthouse sits here in old Florida glory. This is the most popular beaching spot for newcomers because it is easy to find.

Facilities: Restrooms; restaurants and groceries nearby. *Fishing:* Great fishing at the pier on the bayside for snook, shark, sheepshead and red snapper. *Swimming:* Good, but waters tend to be murky in this part of the Gulf.

Getting there: Located on the southeastern end of Sanibel Island where Periwinkle Way deadends.

Gulfside Park (★)—A secluded picnic area underneath Australian pines, this spot attracts folks looking for alligators in the canal that borders one side. The beach is narrow here but shell-strewn and relatively unpopulated. A stand of sea oats separates the beach from the picnic grounds.

Facilities: Picnic areas, restrooms; restaurants and groceries a few miles away on Periwinkle Way. *Swimming:* Good, gradual deepening.

Getting there: Located on Sanibel Island, at the end of Algiers Lane, off Casa Ybel Road.

Bowman's Beach—A long, secluded stretch of sand, probably Sanibel's finest. The shells are usually more plentiful on this northern end of the island, and the people less so. The Sanibel River cuts through, and two bridges cross its brackish waters. A short hike takes you past native jungle vegetation.

Facilities: Picnic areas, restrooms, showers, nature trails; restaurants and groceries a few miles away at Blind Pass; information, 813-481-7946. *Swimming:* Great.

Getting there: The beach is located on Bowman's Beach Road off Sanibel-Captiva Road.

Carl E. Johnson Park–Lover's Key (★)—A system of protected wetlands that covers three small islands—Lover's Key, Inner Key and Black Island. At Johnson Park, a tram takes you across wooden bridges and down sandy paths to view the area's unique mangrove ecosystem. The tram's destination is the beach and its picnic ground facilities on Lover's Key. Few have discovered this secluded beach spot shaded with pines and landscaped in native shrubbery. Hikers can also hoof it to the beach here, or north to Black Island.

Facilities: Picnic areas, restrooms, showers; restaurants and groceries several miles away in Fort Myers Beach or Bonita Beach; information, 813-481-7946. *Swimming:* Good.

Getting there: Located south of Fort Myers Beach on Estero Boulevard.

Koreshan State Historic Site—An historic and recreational park built on a religious theory. Founded by Cyrus Reed Teed, the Koreshan cult believed the earth was hollow and that the sun revolved in its center while life was contained around this nucleus. The Koreshans' legacy to this state was the introduction of exotic plants that continue to thrive here: avocados, mangos, royal palms and bromeliads.

Facilities: Picnic area, restrooms, canoe rental; information, 813-992-0311.

Camping: There are 60 sites, all with hookups; $14-16 per night.

Getting there: The park entrance is located right off Route 41, south of Fort Myers.

Naples Area

On the edge of the Everglades, the Naples area is one of the West Coast's more popular resort regions. Romantic beaches, grand cypress trees and wind-sculptured dunes are the region's calling card. Here you can choose between glamorous resorts and quiet inns. For a taste of contemporary Florida, check out the high-rise world of Marco island.

The fast-growing city of Bonita Springs sits south of Fort Myers along Route 41. Almost as old as Florida is the **Everglades Wonder Gardens** (Old Route 41, Bonita Springs; 813-992-2591; admission). This attraction offers a contained environment for viewing indigenous wetlands wildlife: the American eagle, toy deer, alligators, panthers and rattlesnakes. The non-live exhibits show their age with tinges of yellowing and fading, but therein lies much of the charm of this vintage tourist attraction.

Visit one of southwest Florida's finest wilderness refuges near Bonita Springs on Route 846 off Route 41. **Corkscrew Swamp Sanctuary (★)** (Sanctuary Road; 813-657-3771; admission) shelters breeding wood storks among its native plant and animal populations. Lakes of lettuce fern and 500-year-old cypress trees dripping with Spanish moss make you feel as though you have entered a different dimension of space and time.

The city of **Naples** sits prettily on a peninsula between the Gulf of Mexico and Naples Bay. The **Naples Pier,** a landmark that predates the city itself, juts out from golden sands at a perfect angle from which to view a sunset. Boutiques, fine restaurants and a perfect beach count as the city's greatest draws.

Not far from the pier, in old Naples, the **Palm Cottage (★)** (137 12th Avenue South; 813-261-8164) is one of the few remaining structures from the city's infancy days of the 1890s. It once served as winter home to *Louisville Courier Journal* editor Henry Watterson, and later as an annex to the town's first hotel. Today, the seashell mortar home serves as a museum and the home of the Collier County Historical Society. Docent-led tours are given daily.

The **Naples Chamber of Commerce** (3620 North Tamiami Trail; 813-262-6141) has more information on area sights.

Marco Island counterpoints soaring condominium towers with bald eagle nests. You can examine this island group's past and present on a ride aboard the **Marco Island Trolley** (813-394-1600; admission), an excursion back to the years of the ancient Calusa Indians, whose shell mounds have survived the onslaught of bulldozers and concrete. You'll also see a sample of the estuarine life of the Everglades' Ten Thousand Islands, of which Marco is the northernmost. For more information on the island, visit the **Marco Island Area Chamber of Commerce** (1102 North Collier Boulevard, Marco Island; 813-394-7549).

NAPLES AREA HOTELS

In Naples proper, the hostelries reflect the town's upscale, sophisticated image. North of the city, beach hotels show more personality and less expense. A sweet little five-unit place called **Inn on the Bay Motel (★)** (4701 West Bonita Beach Road, Bonita Springs; 813-992-2655) sits on the water. The building looks like a seaside shanty of white clapboard and blue trim. The comfortable, homey rooms are tabbed budget. The beach is within easy walking distance.

Down the road at Vanderbilt Beach, the **Vanderbilt Inn on the Gulf** (11000 Gulf Shore Drive North; 813-597-3151) has a location that best suits beach-goers. Metropolites, however, don't have far to go to reach Naples shops and restaurants. The simple two-story structure offers interior intrigue with a Florida-living motif in the rooms and a New Mexico-gone-tropic theme in the lobby. Deluxe to ultra-deluxe.

When the occasion calls for first-class accommodations with impeccable service, elegant rooms and tea served in the afternoon, **The Ritz Carlton** (280 Vanderbilt Beach Road, Naples; 813-598-3300) is the right choice. Hospitality that combines Old World graciousness with ultramodern convenience makes a stay here top notch. Tennis courts, golf course, fitness center, three miles of private beach and 463 rooms at ultra-deluxe rates are offered at this majestic Mediterranean palazzo set amid unspoiled coastlands and back bays.

Cove Inn Marina Resort (1191 8th Street South, Naples; 813-262-7161) rents 102 rooms with a lovely view of Naples Bay. The rooms huddle around a marina and boast some splashes of character, such as the cypress cross-section table in one of the efficiencies. Extras include a pool and chickee bar. Deluxe.

Victorian vacations await at **The Pavilion Club and Boat House Inn** (1170 Eddington Place, Marco Island; 813-642-7700). Paddle fans, french doors, rattan chairs, wooden shutters, sitting nooks and overstuffed pillows give the inn's 20 rooms their feel of old-time intimacy. Outdoors, the look reflects the hardships involved in settling this frontier; the inn's appearance is spartan dressed up with a few gingerbread touches. Deluxe.

NAPLES AREA RESTAURANTS

Fabulous blue vistas of sky and water and consistently fine seafood and steaks have kept **McCully's Rooftop Restaurant** (25999 Hickory Boulevard, Bonita Beach; 813-992-0033) popular through the years. The mood is relaxed elegance; the menu is moderately priced.

Riverwalk Fish & Ale House (1200 5th Avenue South, Naples; 813-263-2734) is found waterside in the Tin City shopping center. Casual, woody and open to the activity on the charter docks, it offers simply good seafood and a few chicken and steak entrées for dinner and sandwiches and salads for lunch. Moderate.

The Chart House (1193 8th Street South, Naples; 813-649-0033) serves fine food in a casual dining room with a stunning view of Naples Bay. Dinners feature prime rib, steak and seafood. Moderate to deluxe.

For a special night out, **The Chef's Garden** (1300 3rd Street South, Naples; 813-262-5500) cannot be beat. Creative cuisine using local produce and seafood has earned the restaurant top awards through the years. The setting is elegant, and the prices are ultra-deluxe on an ever-changing menu, with specialties such as grilled lamb chops in a rosemary sauce, grilled radicchio and romaine lettuce with pine nuts, and yellowfin tuna in a sesame vinaigrette.

For barbecue at budget prices try **Michelbob's** (371 Airport Road, Naples; 813-643-2877). Baby back ribs and barbecue chicken are favorites at this busy spot which offers bench seatings. New York steaks are another specialty.

The **Olde Marco Inn** (100 Palm Street, Marco Island; 813-394-3131) serves history with its fine German and French fare: *jaeggerschnitzel*, steak *au poivre vert*, grouper *à la meunière*, etc. The setting is a historical landmark where the island's founding father once lived. In a rambling home scenario, the inn sets tables in six dining rooms, each with its own personality: from the casual and sun-touched veranda, to the formal dining room with its cranberry glass chandelier, to the Audubon room decorated with wildlife prints dating back to 1850. Moderate to deluxe.

NAPLES AREA SHOPPING

Old Marine Marketplace (1200 5th Avenue South, Naples; 813-262-4200), a waterfront relic also known as "Tin City," has become a rustic mall housing high-class shops. For instance, **Things From the Sea** (813-261-3820) deals in quality nautical niceties.

The shops of **5th Avenue South** are strictly upscale. Check out **Gingerbread & Old Lace** (995 5th Avenue South, Naples; 813-649-5755) for fine consignment items such as art, handmade pieces and antiques.

The Southwest American Indian art sold at **Four Winds Gallery** (340 13th Avenue South, Naples; 813-263-7555) includes uniquely stylized and contemporary pottery, weavings and silver, gold and turquoise jewelry.

NAPLES AREA NIGHTLIFE

Located at the Registry Resort, **Garrett's** (475 Seagate Drive, Naples; 813-597-3232) is a popular weekend dancing spot with deejay music.

The **Naples Playhouse** (399 Goodlette Road; 813-263-7990) produces fine shows during its winter and summer seasons.

NAPLES AREA BEACHES AND PARKS

Barefoot Beach—A shelly spread of sand with little vegetation. Although the nearby condominium congestion seems to be creeping ever nearer, the beach stays relatively unpopulated and has an unsophisticated air about it. The sands somehow seem homier than its neighboring beaches.

Facilities: None; restaurants and groceries nearby.

Getting there: Located at Bonita Beach's southern end on Bonita Beach Road.

Delnor–Wiggins Pass State Park—A natural mile-long beachfront park where the Cocohatchee River lets out into the ocean. The narrow peninsula protects indigenous flora such as cactus, sea grapes, sabal palms, knickerbean and yucca. The lush white beach parallels low dunes and strands of sea oats. This area is protected to encourage turtle nesting. A trail at the southern end of the park takes you to an observation tower.

Facilities: Picnic area, restrooms, showers, boat launch, lifeguard; restaurants and groceries nearby; information, 813-597-6196. *Fishing:* Good at the north end along the pass for trout, snook and redfish; cast-netting for mullet in the bay. *Swimming:* Good.

Getting there: Located at 11100 Gulf Shore Drive North in Naples.

Lowdermilk Park—A shady city park with over 1000 feet of fine sandy beach where volleyball is a popular activity. This beach teems with teens on weekends. During the week, you'll find a different crowd, but a crowd nonetheless. Despite its masses, it's a wonderful place to spend a party day on the beach.

Facilities: Picnic areas, restrooms, showers, dressing rooms, snack bar; restaurants and groceries nearby. *Fishing:* The best spot is at the pier, south of the park. *Swimming:* Good.

Getting there: Located in Naples on Gulfshore Boulevard North at Banyan Boulevard.

Collier-Seminole State Park—On the edge of the Everglades, this 6470-acre preserve offers a taste of the area's salt marsh and hardwood forest wildlife to a limited number of visitors each day. Exhibits throughout the park include a replicated Seminole War blockhouse.

Facilities: Picnic areas, restrooms, nature trail, canoe and boat rentals, snack bar, some groceries; information, 813-394-3397.

Camping: There are 130 sites, 61 with RV hookups, and a backpacker camp; $13-15 per night.

Getting there: The entrance is located east of Naples on Route 41.

Tigertail Beach Park—This 31-acre Gulf-front beach sits on Marco Island apart from the conglomeration of condos. A system of wooden ramps takes you over the sea-coated dunes to a marvelous beach.

Facilities: Picnic areas, playground, restrooms, showers, windsurfing and sailboat rentals, snack bar; restaurants and groceries nearby.

Getting there: At the end of Hernando Drive on Marco Island.

St. Petersburg–Clearwater Area

Bordered by Tampa Bay to the east and the Gulf of Mexico on the west, this popular peninsula offers a wealth of opportunity. In addition to the urban attractions of St. Petersburg, there are beaches galore along the barrier islands that fringe the area.

DOWNTOWN ST. PETERSBURG The city of St. Petersburg lies on a peninsula across the bay from Tampa. Its pitted bay face smiles with calm waters and sunshine. Activity downtown centers around **The Pier** (800 2nd Avenue Northeast; 813-821-6164), an inverted pyramid-shaped structure that houses shops, restaurants and an observation deck. The view from here overlooks the seaside city in all its splendor and is especially scenic at night.

One office of the **St. Petersburg Chamber of Commerce** is located in the lobby of The Pier; another is nearby at 100 2nd Avenue North (813-821-4069).

One of the most impressive downtown features is the **Dali Museum** (1000 3rd Street South; 813-823-3767; admission), which boasts over 1000 prints and originals—including 93 oils—created by Spanish surrealist artist Salvador Dali. This collection of Dali's works, executed between 1914 and 1980, is contained within a spacious, modern garret.

The **Sunken Gardens** (1825 4th Street North; 813-896-3186; admission) is a pleasant surprise, with its jungle-like ambience. The grounds were created in a sinkhole from which the water was drained. The fertile pit was then landscaped with exotic plants and stocked with tropical birds. You'll see monkeys, crowned cranes, muntjac deer and hornbills wandering among bougainvillea, hibiscus and giant ferns.

From the Port of St. Petersburg (1st Street and 8th Avenue Southeast) you can board the one-day **cruise ship** *Sea Escape* (800-327-7400), to get a taste of the shows, buffets and relaxation that have made cruising one of the most popular forms of travel today.

SOUTHERN PINELLAS COUNTY Around the city's peninsular Gulf front, a thread of islands is woven to the mainland by five bridges. This thread, often known as the Holiday Isles, has developed into highrise heaven thanks to its gorgeous beaches and lucid waters. Pleasure seekers of all ages are attracted to this paradise playground where the most strenuous activity is building sandcastles.

The southernmost islands of this archipelago are the least populated. To make the island tour, take Pinellas Bayway across the peninsula that comprises Pinellas County, to Fort de Soto Park. North of the five islands that form the park, the town of Tierra Verde eases into the holiday carnival scene that its neighbor, **St. Petersburg Beach**, begins. Besides the wide beach and watersports action, other sights beckon the sightseer along this sandy rim.

From St. Petersburg Beach, the **island chain** along Gulf Boulevard includes Treasure Island, Madeira Beach, Indian Rocks Beach, Belleair Beach and Clearwater Beach. These Gulf-front islands are separated from the mainland by a narrow trickle of water that broadens at both ends.

Between Treasure Island and Madeira, a boardwalk with salty shops, restaurants and charter boats has cropped up at **Johns Pass Village and Boardwalk** (12925 East Gulf Boulevard, Madeira Beach; 813-393-7679). Patterned after a fishing community of yore, it pays tribute to the community's commercial fishing industry.

The **Suncoast Seabird Sanctuary** (18328 Gulf Boulevard, Indian Shores; 813-391-6211) works to restore sky-dwellers. You will find many species here, including the native cormorant, white heron, brown pelican and snowy egret.

NORTHERN PINELLAS COUNTY To get back to the mainland segment of Pinellas County, cross into Clearwater at the nicely landscaped Courtney Campbell Causeway. The inland Route 19 takes you along small peninsula towns. In one of them, **Heritage Park** (11909 125th Street North, Largo; 813-462-3474) comprises a collection of historic structures that reflect the area's pioneer days. One building, the McMullen-Coachman loghouse, dates back to the 1850s and is the oldest building in the county. Others include a sugar mill, railroad depot, school and church. At the museum period craftsmen wear authentic costumes, and exhibits demonstrate such folk crafts as rug hooking and loom weaving.

Nestled in the far reaches of Old Tampa Bay, **Philippe Park** (2355 Bayshore Drive; 813-726-2700) commemorates the three groups that settled in this area: ancient Indians, Spanish conquistadors and European settlers (who first introduced grapefruit to the New World at this spot). The large Timucuan Indian mound is listed in the National Register of Historic Places.

Dunedin is a Scottish-rooted city at the northern end of St. Petersburg's Pinellas County, where the peninsula attaches to mainland, reachable from Clearwater on Route 19A. Along the scenic bay drive, you'll begin to notice names like Aberdeen and Locklie on the street signs. The **Greater Dunedin Chamber of Commerce** (301 Main Street, Dunedin; 813-736-5066) hands out material on area attractions and accommodations.

If you seek the unusual in your sightseeing routines, consider **Noell's Ark Chimp Farm** (4612 South Pinellas Avenue, Tarpon Springs; admission). This home for retired zoo and circus primates features athletic apes and tame gorillas. You can't miss it: just watch for the big homemade sign that announces "Slow! Gorilla Ahead."

Tarpon Springs is Florida's Little Greece, an unexpected pocket of Aegean culture in a rural area of freshwater lakes and old southern neighborhoods. The community developed as a sponge divers' settlement in the 1890s. Along Dodecanese Boulevard one can still see the **sponge docks,** now used more by shrimpers than spongers. Shops and markets line the street, operated by Greek-American ladies and frequented by bearded sailors in Greek hats who converse in their ancestral tongue.

Spongearama (510 Dodecanese Boulevard, Tarpon Springs; 813-942-3771; admission), a museum that exhibits photos and memorabilia from the great sponging era, remembers the settlement days of Tarpon Springs. On display are animated scenes from the erstwhile world of sponge diving, including a walk-through sponge boat.

St. Nicholas Greek Orthodox Cathedral (36 North Pinellas Avenue, Tarpon Springs; 813-937-3540) is a relic of the Old World way of life. Its classic neo-Byzantine architecture features icon-studded walls, sculptured Grecian marble and a statue of the Blessed Mother that is said to weep.

In the **Universalist Church** (57 Read Street, Tarpon Springs; 813-937-4682), the works of landscape artist George Inness, Jr., are collected. While living in Tarpon Springs, this early 20th-century artist executed many of his most renowned works, inspired by the beauty and spirituality of his surroundings. When a hurricane blew out the church's stained-glass windows in 1918, they were eventually replaced with murals that Inness painted.

The **Tarpon Springs Chamber of Commerce** (210 South Pinellas Avenue, Suite 120, Tarpon Springs; 813-937-6109) distributes literature on things to see and do in the city.

ST. PETERSBURG–CLEARWATER AREA HOTELS

DOWNTOWN ST. PETERSBURG St. Petersburg's accommodations combine historical flavor with born-again energy.

Sitting with quiet majesty in an old residential downtown neighborhood, **The Heritage** (234 3rd Avenue North; 813-822-4814) wears its glamour like old money. The 70-room hotel was renovated in the 1980s to its '20s era birthright; rich mahogany bars and antique furnishings were liberated from years of paint. Subtle color tones in wallpaper, dhurrie rugs and polished oak floors lend a modern Florida look. Besides easy access to downtown attractions, The Heritage offers in-house benefits such as swimming pools, jacuzzis and a greenhouse atrium. Moderate to deluxe.

One of St. Petersburg's earliest homes, the **Bayboro House** (1719 Beach Drive Southeast; 813-823-4955) now stands as a bed and breakfast facility.

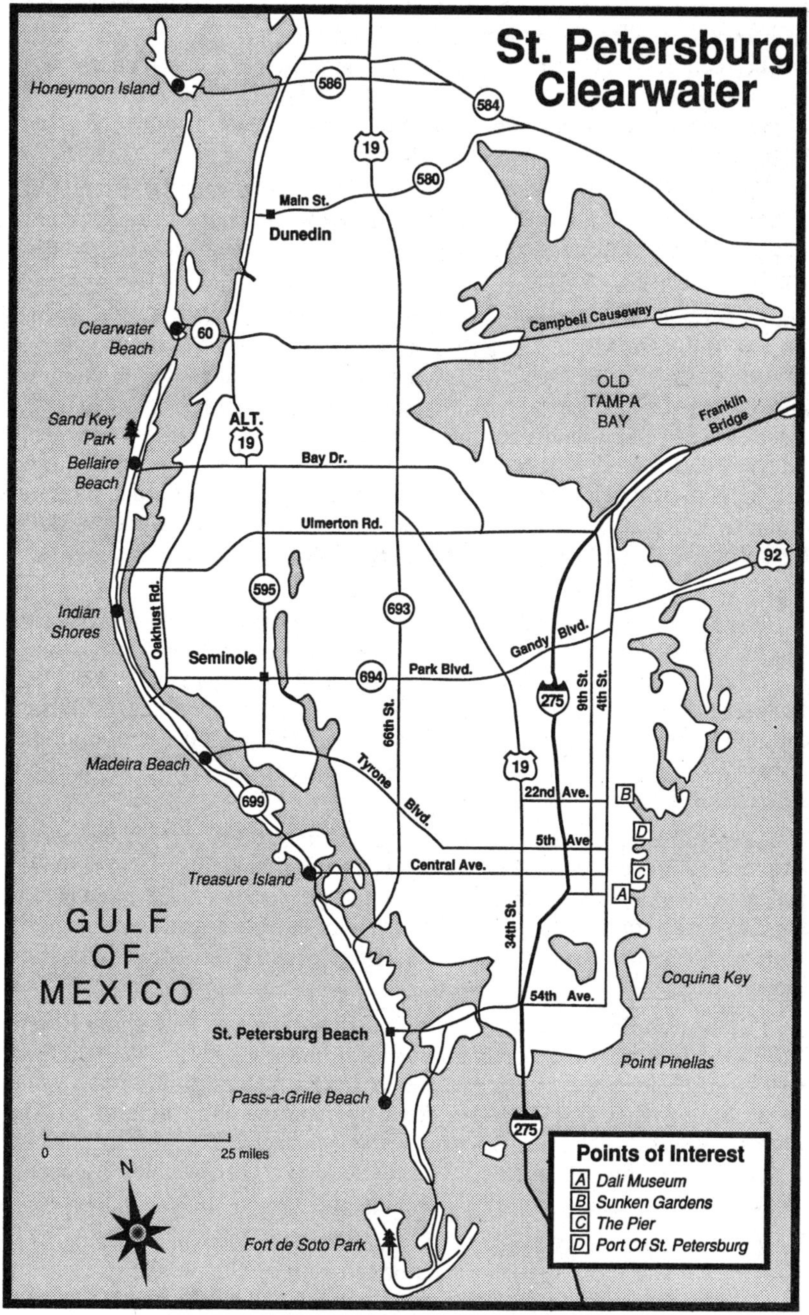

St. Petersburg Clearwater

Honeymoon Island
586
584
19
580
Main St.
Dunedin
Clearwater Beach
60
Campbell Causeway
OLD TAMPA BAY
Franklin Bridge
Sand Key Park
ALT. 19
Bellaire Beach
Bay Dr.
Ulmerton Rd.
92
595
693
Indian Shores
Oakhust Rd.
Seminole
Gandy Blvd.
694
Park Blvd.
275
9th St.
4th St.
66th St.
Madeira Beach
Tyrone Blvd.
19
22nd Ave.
699
5th Ave.
Central Ave.
Treasure Island
34th St.
GULF OF MEXICO
Coquina Key
54th Ave.
St. Petersburg Beach
Point Pinellas
Pass-a-Grille Beach
275
0
25 miles
N
Fort de Soto Park

Points of Interest
A *Dali Museum*
B *Sunken Gardens*
C *The Pier*
D *Port Of St. Petersburg*

The 19-room home, with its four guest rooms (all with private baths), was built by an early St. Petersburg settler in 1903. Its quirky old personality can be seen in its irregular architecture, asymmetrical windows and mixed bag of interior design styles. The front porch is white picketed, the steps edged in conch shells. A player piano, pump organ, marble tables and grandfather clocks furnish the inn. Moderate.

SOUTHERN PINELLAS COUNTY Accommodations of both skyscraper and mom-and-pop nature have mushroomed along the coastline in southern Pinellas County, fronting St. Petersburg Beach and nearby beach communities.

A historic masterpiece in cotton-candy pink, the **Don CeSar Beach Resort** (3400 Gulf Boulevard, St. Petersburg Beach; 813-360-1881) greets visitors to this beach town. It stands stately and fancifully to woo guests with complete resort services in the ultra-deluxe price range. Classic Florida resort style is embodied here. Built in the 1920s, when F. Scott and Zelda Fitzgerald supposedly visited, it was converted into an army hospital during World War II. An ongoing restoration now keeps the 277 rooms, plus restaurants, lounges, conference facilities and banquet halls, in prime condition. The Don's personality combines equal doses of Mediterranean, fairy castle and beach resort.

On Pass-a-Grille Beach low-key motels and beach houses line one side of Gulf Way, dusty sand beach the other. One colorful lodging option is the **Sunset View Guest House (★)** (1107 Gulf Way; 813-360-1333). For budget rates, you can sleep under a homemade quilt with sea breezes wafting through jalousy windows. Refrigerators come with each cozy room in this circa-1940 building that makes you feel right at home. Guests are allowed full use of kitchen facilities.

Ten miles southwest of St. Petersburg and 200 feet from the ocean, **Lighted Tree Guest House** (109 8th Avenue, Pass-a-Grille; 813-360-0373) has three budget-priced rooms done in Victorian, Florida and Egyptian motifs. Nestled in a jungle setting, this gay-friendly establishment features early American decor in the common areas. There's also a restaurant and bar on the premises.

Long Key Beach Resort (3828 Gulf Boulevard, St. Petersburg Beach; 813-360-1748) provides some architectural interest with its 44 beachfront rooms, efficiencies and apartments. Peaked roofs, a wooden observation sundeck and a rounded bay window front upgrade the court hotel look. The rooms are pleasant, the efficiencies not without character. Two pools, a poolside lounge and 180 feet of expansive beach comprise other amenities. Moderate.

A dramatic spiral staircase is the centerpiece of the elegant lobby at **Dolphin Beach Resort** (4900 Gulf Boulevard, St. Petersburg Beach; 813-360-7011). The moderate-to-deluxe-priced rooms, 173 in all, spread in a jagged low-rise building fronted by white beach and brightened by colorful sails and cabañas. The rooms are spacious and earth-toned with separate dressing areas.

Guests can tour the grounds via gondolas at the exotic **Tradewinds** (5500 Gulf Boulevard, St. Petersburg Beach; 813-367-6461). Housing 577 rooms, Tradewinds takes complete care of guests with four pools, a sauna, whirlpool, tennis and croquet courts, restaurants, wide beach and children's activities. Each room includes a wet bar, refrigerator and exclusive furnishings. Ultra-deluxe.

The rooms are furnished in a modern style at the **Breckenridge Resort Hotel** (5700 Gulf Boulevard, St. Petersburg Beach; 813-360-1833), with built-in white desk and bookshelves in the room I saw. Kitchenettes and balconies are provided in each of the 200 units. Lighted tennis courts, seaside eating and sipping, swimming pool and a fluffy beach complete the package. Deluxe.

A row motel called **Surfs Inn** (14010 Gulf Boulevard, Madeira Beach; 813-393-4609) shows a white face with a blue porte-cochère and colored shutters. The 25 rooms and efficiencies in this mom-and-pop facility are compact and front the pool and beach. Blue awnings and table umbrellas in the sunning area perk up this pleasant little place. Moderate.

Fresh little gingerbread cottages rent for budget-to-moderate rates at **Villa St. Tropez Motel (★)** (1713 North Gulf Boulevard, Indian Rocks Beach; 813-596-7133). The eight units sit across the street from the beach and include full kitchen facilities and a grassy sunning area with shuffleboard courts.

The **Holiday House Motel Apartments** (470 North Gulfview Boulevard, Clearwater Beach; 813-447-4533) lie low along blindingly white sands. Typically beach oriented, the 31 apartments won't win awards for interior decoration but are clean and roomy and provide full kitchen facilities. At moderate-to-deluxe rates you get a full apartment for what you would pay for a room at other hotels in the area.

Fine resort style at **Adam's Mark** (430 South Gulfview Boulevard, Clearwater Beach; 813-443-5714) is defined with accommodations and location that create a Caribbean atmosphere. The 206 modern rooms corner a wide stretch of beach and are custom designed with elegant tropical touches. Deluxe to ultra-deluxe.

NORTHERN PINELLAS COUNTY The city of Clearwater owes its existence to the **Belleview Mido Hotel** (25 Belleview Boulevard; 813-442-6171), built here at the turn of the century. The rambling mansion displays its heritage with clapboard and dormers, capped with peaks as green as the property's golf course. Green is also used on the interior, in the voluminous lobby and 350 guest rooms. Accents come in rich reds and mauves, with vintage touches such as Tiffany stained-glass ceiling panels, lobby fireplaces and brass fixtures. Elegance settles in here without pretentiousness; the surroundings inspire complete comfort. Ultra-deluxe.

A Swiss touch brushes the architecture of **Best Western–Jamaica Inn** (150 Marina Plaza, Dunedin; 813-733-4121). The 55 rooms sport peaked ceilings, marina views and blue and rose color schemes. The lobby and restaurant have red brick accents with chalet nuances. Moderate.

Those looking for a place to play in the Tarpon Springs area should consider a vacation at **Innisbrook Resort** (Route 19 South, Tarpon Springs; 813-942-2000). Serious golfers, tennis and racquetball whackers, and lake beachers congregate at this 1000-room facility. Rooms range from spacious to more spacious. The best of the ambience awaits outdoors in the woodsy, landscaped, lake-graced grounds. Deluxe to ultra-deluxe.

A crackling fireplace, wide wraparound porch and antique furnished parlor make **Spring Bayou Inn** (32 West Tarpon Avenue, Tarpon Springs; 813-938-9333) exactly the kind of place the words "bed and breakfast" evoke. The four guest rooms in this turn-of-the-century home either have shared or private bath, with continental breakfast served in the dining room. Moderate.

The Livery Stable (★) (100 North Ring Avenue, Tarpon Springs; 813-938-5547) is another bed and breakfast facility with 20 comfortable rooms and full breakfast. The white blockhouse building sits in an old residential area of town. Its rooms reflect age, but are clean and comfortable. Budget.

ST. PETERSBURG–CLEARWATER AREA RESTAURANTS

DOWNTOWN ST. PETERSBURG At the pier in downtown St. Pete, **Alessi Café At the Pier** (800 2nd Avenue Northeast; 813-894-4659) impresses with blond woods, a brass espresso machine and a showcase of sinful pastries. The moderate menu features Italian specialties and pizza.

SOUTHERN PINELLAS COUNTY Continental cuisine with a difference comes in moderate price ranges at **Good Times Continental Restaurant** (1130 Pinellas Bayway, Tierra Verde; 813-867-0774). The Old World influence takes a refreshing departure from France and Italy, to offer tastebud tantalization in the form of Hungarian chicken paprikash, beef stroganoff, filet mignon topped with glazed peaches and béarnaise, black forest cake and Czechoslovakian beer. All is served in a plain-looking facility with vinyl chairs and pool-hall paneling. (Closed in summer.)

On Pass-a-Grille Beach, **Hurricane Seafood Restaurant** (807 Gulf Way; 813-360-9558) seats you outdoors with a beach view, or inside its wood-accented, casual dining room. Seafood comes in every form imaginable at moderate prices.

Pelican Diner (7501 Gulf Boulevard, St. Petersburg Beach; 813-363-9873) serves budget homestyle meals in an authentic dining car atmosphere —authentic meaning this is a survivor of a bygone era, not a replica. Corroded chrome and vinyl counter stools, blue-and-white tiled walls and individual booth juke boxes are the setting; pork chops, liver and corned beef and cabbage are the fare.

Scandinavian specialties with names like *frikadeller* (meatballs), *medister polser* (seasoned sausage) and *hakkobof med log og speijlag* (beef topped with fried egg) taste as exotic as they sound at **Scandia** (19829 Gulf Boulevard, Indian Shores; 813-595-5525). Other meat and seafood dishes with more common names are also served in this Bavarian ski lodge setting. Prices are moderate.

Crabby Bill's (401 Gulf Boulevard, Indian Rocks Beach; 813-595-4825) is your basic beach seafood eatery where the food is terrific and the prices even better. The oyster stew is made to order, and the frogs' legs, catfish, shrimp, crab and fish have earned the place a reputation that means long waits. Budget.

Rolls of paper toweling hang on coat hangers above the tables at **P. J.'s Oyster Bar** (★) (500 1st Street North, Indian Rocks Beach; 813-596-5898). In an ultracasual atmosphere, oysters, clams, crab and shrimp are served in their unadulterated state (raw and/or steamed, hold the sauce). The menu also offers fried, broiled, baked or steamed seafood, sandwiches and blackened specialties. Budget to moderate.

For more than a decade, folks across Tampa Bay have made faithful sojourns to the **Lobster Pot** (17814 Gulf Boulevard, Reddington Shores; 813-391-8592), a place that can feed any lobster fetish. Danish, Maine, African and Florida lobsters, served unadorned or in creamy garlic or curry sauces, headline the menu. There are fish and prime steaks as well. Fresh flowers, candles and linens assure subtle formality amid fishing nets, mounted lobsters and other seaside decor. Deluxe.

A side dish of fun comes with your meal at **Julie's Seafood & Sunsets** (351 Gulfview Boulevard, Clearwater Beach; 813-441-2548). As the name suggests, this casual eatery sits across from the public beach, which calls for dusk rituals every night with happy hour specials. The moderate-priced menu offers wonderful seafood items and sandwiches. You may want to order the Ron Petrini sandwich: one bottle of Budweiser with two slices of white toast. Sit outside under an umbrella, in a room papered with business cards, next to a showcase of crab claws, or in an intimate boothed corner.

In Clearwater Beach, **Heilman's Beachcomber** (447 Mandalay Avenue; 813-442-4144) is known for its bargain southern-style dinners of fried chicken, gravy and mashed potatoes. Locals will also tell you that this is the best place in the bay area to get good stone crab. The ambience is simple, the menu diversified, the quality consistent. Moderate.

NORTHERN PINELLAS COUNTY For Italian in Clearwater, go to **Firenze Ristorante** (615 Cleveland Street; 813-442-6453). Light touches replace the heavy tomato sauce one sometimes associates with Italian. In a small main street storefront, moderate to deluxe dishes include linguine in clam sauce, steak, veal, chicken and seafood dishes.

Bill Irle Restaurant (1310 North Fort Harrison Street, Clearwater; 813-446-5683) serves German fare with fresh vegetable and seafood twists. The house salad is blessed with sprigs of watercress and a tasty sweet-sour dressing. Sauerbraten and schnitzel share the menu with *coquilles* of seafood Newburg and sole amandine. Plastic placemats top linen tablecloths, demonstrating the restaurant's mix of casualness and elegance. Budget to moderate.

Jesse's Dockside (345 Causeway Boulevard, Dunedin; 813-736-2611) is a class act near Honeymoon Island. Inside a gray clapboard-and-brick building the decor is very modern with pickled oak tables and rattan chairs set for marina views in one room, and a captain's stateroom motif in another. The moderately priced menu gives you a choice of preparation for your halibut, flounder, salmon, mahimahi, grouper or snapper: blackened, charbroiled, broiled, fried, island-style, stuffed, and so on.

A restaurant named **Molly Goodheads Raw Bar and Seafood** (400 Orange Avenue, Ozona; 813-786-6255) more or less invented the town of Ozona, between Dunedin and Tarpon Springs. The town's name gives you an idea of the whimsical nature of this two-floor one-time home. If it doesn't, then consider the stuffed deer wearing sunglasses, the bathtub full of beer and waitresses in T-shirts and shorts. The moderate menu offers seafood and burgers for lunch and dinner.

In Tarpon Springs, where many of the local dishes may sound Greek to you, **Louis Pappas' Riverside Restaurant** (10 West Dodecanese Boulevard; 813-937-5101) is renowned for serving ethnic dishes inspired by the city's Greek population. From the outside, the restaurant looks like a bank. Inside, the decor spews Greek feeling with family portraits, statues of gods and sponge-diving memorabilia. Besides authentic *pastitsio*, *moussaka*, lamb kebabs and other traditional Greek fare, Pappas does local favorites such as frogs' legs and blackened grouper. Moderate.

Less ostentatiously Greek than Pappas, **Costa's Restaurant** (521 Athens Street, Tarpon Springs; 813-938-6890) homecooks dolmades and octopus stew at budget prices. The small café goes light on atmosphere, with vinyl chairs and formica tables. But chances are you'll find more Greek locals than vacationers eating here.

ST. PETERSBURG–CLEARWATER AREA SHOPPING

The Pier (800 2nd Avenue Northeast; 813-821-6164), in downtown St. Petersburg, contains a variety of specialty shops that sell hats, curios and clothing, all in a high price range.

Glass Horizons (333 1st Street Northeast, St. Petersburg; 813-823-8233) is a good place to find artistic stained-glass creations in a complex called SPACE (St. Petersburg Arts & Crafts Emporium), a developing facility located downtown.

Lovers of books will find it difficult to leave **Haslam's Book Store, Inc.** (2025 Central Avenue, St. Petersburg; 813-822-8616), Florida's largest bookseller.

Out at Madeira Beach, **John's Pass Village and Boardwalk** (12th Avenue North and Gulf Boulevard; 813-397-8764) sets the mood of an old fishing village. Gift shops, resort wear outlets and numerous other stores congregate here. One shop, **The Bronze Lady, Inc.** (813-398-5994), is noteworthy for its clown motif. It specializes in clown paintings rendered by Red Skelton and also carries clown statuettes and other novelty items.

The **Wagon Wheel Flea Market** (7801 Park Boulevard North, Pinellas Park) overflows with goods at over 1000 booths.

Near the St. Petersburg-Clearwater airport, **Boatyard Village** (16100 Fairchild Drive, Clearwater; 813-535-4678) simulates nature's effect on seaside docks to create a trendy atmosphere for specialty shopping. Rusted tin, cracked windows and broken-down shacks house expensive boutiques. **Village Gem Shop** (813-539-6991) offers handmade jewelry crafted from rough and polished stones. Also here is the **Earthsea Studio** (813-536-6098), which creates sculptured and wheel-thrown stoneware pottery.

In the market for a new kilt? **Dunedin Scottish Imports** (1251 Pinehurst Road, Dunedin; 813-734-7606) claims to carry the largest stock of tartan in the world, along with china and its line of Gaelic delicacies.

Dodecanese Boulevard (Tarpon Springs) is a Hellenic marketplace in the tradition of old Tarpon Springs. Here you'll find natural sponges, as well as cotton and gauze fashions, olive oil, Greek olives and pastries with names like *kourambiethes*, *finikia* and *kataifi*.

Try **The Sponge Exchange** (Dodecanese Boulevard, Tarpon Springs), a theme courtyard mall, for fine, pricey gifts and clothing.

ST. PETERSBURG–CLEARWATER AREA NIGHTLIFE

At **Alessi Café At the Pier** (800 2nd Avenue Northeast, St. Petersburg; 813-894-4659), jazz and rhythm-and-blues bands jam outdoors overlooking the bay on weekend days and nights.

For that country twang in your evening, listen to the music over at **Carlis** (5641 49th Street North, St. Petersburg; 813-527-5214).

A St. Petersburg dinner theater features musicals and comedies: **The Country Dinner Playhouse** (7951 9th Street North; 813-577-5515).

Progressive jazz is featured at the **Hurricane Seafood Restaurant** (807 Gulf Way, Pass-a-Grille Beach; 813-360-9558) Wednesday through Sunday nights.

There's live entertainment nightly, mostly Top-40 stuff, at **Cadillac Jack's** (145 107th Avenue, Treasure Island; 813-360-2099).

Another hopping night spot is **The Beach Place** (2405 Gulf Boulevard, Indian Rocks Beach; 813-596-5633). Live entertainment; weekend cover.

Live rock-and-roll swings at **Seafarer Lounge** (12250 Ulmerton Road, Largo; 813-595-4892). Cover on weekends. Or hear live reggae rhythms at the colorful **Penrod's Palace** (★) (2675 Ulmerton Road, Clearwater; no phone). Cover.

Chuckles are the main course at **Ron Bennington's Comedy Scene** (401 Route 19 South, Clearwater; 813-791-4477) at the Rodeway Inn.

Visiting performing artists are sponsored at **Ruth Eckerd Hall** (1111 McMullen-Booth Road, Clearwater; 813-791-7400), home to the Florida Orchestra and the Florida Opera.

Showboat Dinner Theater (3405 Ulmerton Road, Clearwater; 813-573-3777), built in the shape of an actual showboat, stages musicals and comedies.

A popular gay dance bar near St. Petersburg, **Fourteen Seventy West** (325 Main Street, Dunedin; 813-736-5483) is a high-tech, high-energy establishment. Stainless steel, purple neon and laser shows set the tone for this club where there's dancing to Top-40 music played by a deejay. Special events include Saturday night drag shows.

In keeping with the Greek culture that is prominent in Tarpon Springs, **Zorba's** (508 Athens Street West; 813-934-8803) is the local favorite for belly dancing performances toasted with ouzo.

The Frog Prince Puppetry Center & Theatre (★) (The Arcade, 210 South Pinellas Avenue, Tarpon Springs; 813-784-6392) features professional puppet shows, workshops and exhibits.

ST. PETERSBURG–CLEARWATER AREA BEACHES AND PARKS

Twenty-eight miles of sugar sand sweetens Pinellas County's Gulf front. Its public beaches spread wider than anywhere else along the coast.

Fort de Soto Park (★)—A precious natural respite from the beach crowds lies on five road-connected islands at the southern tip of Tierra Verde. Hiking trails take you to cannons marking an uncompleted Spanish-American War fort and around quiet paths shaded by Australian pines and live oaks dripping with Spanish moss. Secluded areas are available at both East Beach and North Beach. The sand is coarse, shelly and booby-trapped with sand spurs. Natural vegetation along the beaches grows low to the ground: cactus, sea grape shrubs and sea oats. You get a true deserted feeling with none of the development on the northern islands to clutter the view.

Facilities: Picnic areas, restrooms, showers, snack bar; restaurants and groceries a few miles away in Tierra Verde; information, 813-866-2662. *Fishing:* Excellent from shore and the 1000-foot pier. *Swimming:* A three-mile area of the seven-mile-long beach is approved for swimming. At the north end, currents are dangerous.

Camping: There are 233 sites, all with RV hookups; $16 per night. Reservations must be made at the camp office in person or at the St. Petersburg County Building (150 5th Street North, Room 63, St. Petersburg).

Getting there: Located off Pinellas Bayway, south of Tierra Verde.

Pass-a-Grille Beach—A popular gathering place for young sunbathers, this strand of fluffy sand loops around the southern point of the island of St. Petersburg Beach. The long, wide beach is flanked by Gulf Way and its quaint homes and low-rises.

Facilities: Picnic areas, restrooms, showers, dressing rooms, snack bar; restaurants and groceries nearby. *Swimming:* Good.

Getting there: On Gulf Way on southern St. Petersburg Beach.

Sand Key Park—Like most of the parks in Pinellas County, this one is beautifully landscaped. The facility looks more like a resort than a city park, with lush greenery and beautiful sun-bleached blond sands. A rock barrier tumbles from the beach out into the Gulf at the southern end of the park.

Facilities: Picnic areas, restrooms, showers; restaurants and groceries a few miles away. *Fishing:* Good near the rocks and off pier; snapper, pompano and snook. *Swimming:* Good.

Getting there: Located at the northern end of Belleair Beach on Gulf Boulevard.

Caladesi Island State Park (★)—The English translation of this island's name tells the story: beautiful bayou. The park, set adrift from the hectic pace of Holiday Isles, must be reached by boat. Spread across 1400 acres, this natural island environment is frequented by families as well as being home to birds like great blue herons, snowy egrets and double-crested cormorants. The three-mile beach is wide and natural. The picnic grounds are shaded by sabal palms.

Facilities: Picnic areas, barbecue grills, playground, restrooms, showers, nature trails, lifeguard, snack bar; restaurants and groceries in Dunedin; information, 813-469-5917. *Fishing:* Good for snapper, snook and trout. *Swimming:* Good.

Getting there: Charters out of Dunedin or a ferry from Honeymoon Island (813-734-1501) take visitors to Caladesi.

Honeymoon Island—A small island connected to northern Dunedin by a causeway, this beach is practically immune from modern life. It's used mostly by locals. The sand isn't as fine as that of its neighbors, and large rocks make barefooting uncomfortable. The park's boast is its virgin slash pine stands populated by the endangered osprey, a native fishing bird.

Facilities: Picnic areas, nature trails, restrooms, showers, equipment rental; restaurants and groceries nearby; information, 813-469-5942. *Fish-*

ing: Good surf and pass fishing; snook, redfish, trout, whiting and tarpon. *Swimming:* Good.

Getting there: On Route 586, west of Route 19A in Dunedin.

Fred Howard Park and Beach (★)—This unique and hidden recreational area lies in the Greek community of Tarpon Springs. The park incorporates mainland picnic grounds and a wildlife sanctuary with an offshore beach. The two areas are connected by a mile-long causeway crossing waters blue as a Greek god's eyes. The two parts of the park portray completely separate worlds. The mainland area is sheltered in lovely old live oaks and carpeted in thick grass. The island is totally sand and sits open to the elements, with only cabbage palms and sea grapes by way of vegetation.

Facilities: Picnic areas, restrooms, showers, lifeguard; restaurants and groceries a few miles away in Tarpon Springs. *Fishing*: Good off causeway; trout, snapper, snook. *Swimming:* Great.

Getting there: Located on Howard Park Road near Tarpon Springs.

Crystal River–Cedar Key Area

Up past Port Richey, tourism attractions thin out. The slow pace along Route 19 often keeps travelers from discovering one of the nicest stretches of western coastline. Here Florida reverts to the personality of its youth, a kind of wild adolescence.

For a pleasant backroad sidetrip, take **Route 595 (★)** out of Hudson, north of Port Richey. This takes you through the town of **Aripeka,** where old, abandoned buildings sit by the side of the road.

En route to **Bayport**, you'll drive along rural roads through a canopy of trees. When you drive back to a crossroad at the Bayport Inn, swing up on Pine Island Drive to **Pine Island (★)**, a remote and exclusive spit of sand with a small park at its western end.

You'll return to the main road at **Weeki Wachee** (Route 19, Weeki Wachee; 904-596-2062; admission), a town whose main attraction and raison d'être (heaven help us) is an underwater mermaid theater. Here lovely, gold-clad young women perform complicated acrobatics in the crystalline waters of Weeki Wachee Springs.

North of Weeki Wachee, at **Yulee Sugar Mill Ruins State Historic Site** (Route 490, Homosassa; 904-795-3817), sits the remains of a sugar plantation in a tree-sheltered park. You can see the ruins of Florida's last standing sugar mill and its machinery.

At **Homosassa Springs State Wildlife Park** (Homosassa Springs; 904-628-2311; admission) you can enter an underwater fish bowl observatory and plunge over 50 feet deep in a natural spring to observe intermingling freshwater and saltwater life forms. Then a boat ride will take you through virgin Florida forest to see ospreys, turtles and other native Florida fauna.

More manatees are found in abundance farther north. These "sea cows," mistaken for mermaids by early sailors, have become synonymous with **Crystal River**, whose warm springs attract them. The endangered sea mammals come to winter here, and to entertain divers in the one place where humans are allowed to interact with the 2000-pound gentle giants. The mammoth vegetarians are known to encourage petting by rolling over on their backs.

The **Crystal River Chamber of Commerce** (28 Northwest Highway 19; 904-795-3149) distributes information on manatee preservation and area sights.

The **Crystal River State Archaeological Site** (3400 North Museum Point; 904-795-3817; admission) has been deemed an important ceremonial ground for ancient Indian cultures. Excavators have opened over 400 graves to find valuable prehistoric relics, including a sophisticated astronomical calendar system. Visitors can climb to the highest temple mound, which overlooks the river. A small museum displays pottery, arrowheads and other remnants of Indian societies dating back to 150 B.C.

Up on **Cedar Key** (★), Florida time moves in reverse. Once a thriving fishing and commercial center, it now boasts seclusion from the state's quickening pulse. The name "Cedar Keys" refers to a scattering of about 100 wildlife refuge islands, of which Cedar Key is the largest and only inhabited one.

The drive to this fishing village island accounts for its unspoiled nature. Once north of Crystal River, you feel as though you are driving to the ends of the earth. Towns are tiny and signs warn of bear crossings. At Otter Creek, take Route 24 to reach Cedar Key.

The **Cedar Key State Museum** (Museum Drive; 904-543-5350; admission) documents the days when trains operated on the island, before the hurricane of 1896 destroyed many of the cedar trees on which the local economy thrived. The museum also houses a seashell collection.

For more information, visit the **Cedar Key Chamber of Commerce** (in the Volunteer Fire Station, 2nd Street; 904-543-5600).

CRYSTAL RIVER–CEDAR KEY AREA HOTELS

Near Homosassa Springs Nature World and the Yulee Sugar Mill, **Riverside Inn** (Homosassa Springs; 904-628-2474) offers character as well as good location. The place is situated right on a river, from which it derives its personality. The marina atmosphere is complemented by stateroom furnishings in the 72 rooms. Golf courses, tennis courts, swimming pool, restaurants and lounges come with this resort and its moderate rates.

The antebellum South is re-created at **Plantation Inn & Golf Resort** (West Fort Island Trail, Crystal River; 904-795-4211), and southern hospitality reigns throughout the 142-room property. Golf is the sporting focus, but fishing and canoeing keep this secluded spot activity-filled. Columned white buildings house rather generic rooms with plush carpeting. Deluxe to ultra-deluxe.

Affordable accommodations are found at **Port Paradise Resort** (1610 Southeast Paradise Circle, Crystal River; 904-795-3111). Catering to the scubadiving trade that flocks to Crystal River, this resort offers moderately priced rooms, comfortable enough, all with efficiencies. The 100 rooms flank a marina where all the accoutrements for diving the springs are available.

The **Izaak Walton Lodge (★)** (Riverside Drive at 63rd Street, Yankeetown; 904-447-2311) began as a sportsman's lodge in 1923 and has been revived into a get-away-from-it-all bastion of hospitality. Dressed in a new tin roof and hunter green porch, the still-rustic facility sits on the river near a stretch of forested coastline. Budget and moderate rates are asked for the 12 units; a restaurant and lounge are located on the premises.

The Island Place (1st Street; 904-543-5307) testifies that Cedar Key has been discovered. Thirty luxury condo units decorated with exposed beams and designer touches simulate Old Florida with tin-roofed Victorian architecture. Prices for luxury are still lower here than in the rest of Florida, ranging in the moderate category.

Beach Front Motel (1st and G streets, Cedar Key; 904-543-5113) sits with unpretentious presence along a curve of rocky island shoreline. Its 23 rooms and efficiencies are comfortable and modern, most with waterfront views, priced in the budget category.

Island Hotel (2nd and B streets, Cedar Key; 904-543-5111) looks like an old frontier lodge, with its wooden two-story facade. Since this hotel is listed in the federal register of historic places, the mosquito netting over the bed, sepia photos and antique furniture in the rooms fit perfectly. There is air conditioning, but not a lot of other modern conveniences. Only six of the ten rooms have a private bath. A cedar-scented bar, gourmet seafood restaurant and lobby are outfitted with a pot-belly stove, church pews and other frontier-era furnishings. Moderate.

CRYSTAL RIVER–CEDAR KEY AREA RESTAURANTS

Bayport Inn (★) (4835 Cortez Boulevard, Brooksville; 904-596-1088) is an out-of-the-way roadhouse that serves good food in the moderate range. There's a warmth to the place, with its fireplace and booths, but what really attracts the locals is the downright good catfish, mullet, 'gator and frogs' legs.

K. C. Crump on the River (3900 Hall River Road, Homosassa Springs; 904-628-1500) resides in an 1870 home overlooking the Homosassa River.

Meat and seafood dinners done in creamy, fruity sauces are served to diners at rattan tables with commanding views. Moderate.

Except for locals, few attempt the lonely, sinuous nine-mile trek to **Peck's Old Port Cove** (★) (139 North Ozello Trail off Route 19, Ozello; 904-795-2806). There's not much here but crab traps and a little shack with a few rickety tables, along with the blue Gulf that falls off the horizon. Calvin Peck is famous for his fresh oysters, thick fried grouper and soft-shell crab sandwiches. The crabs are grown out back in Peck's blue crab farm—one of the few in the country. Budget to moderate.

For unpretentious seafood enjoyment in Crystal River, visit **Oysters** (606 Route 19 South; 904-795-2633). This restaurant is a favorite of the locals. The fresh seafood is prepared reliably, if not exotically. From mullet to seafood pasta, the many selections are budget-to-moderate-priced.

At **The Compleat Angler** (1 63rd Street, Yankeetown; 904-447-2319), don't be surprised to find a luxury yacht pulled up to the broken-down dock outside on the river. This country eatery has been discovered by jet setters in the know. In its restored fishing haven setting at Izaak Walton Lodge, the warm dining room features a rock fireplace and overlooks the Withlacoochee River. The moderate-priced menu specializes in fine meats, such as steak *au poivre* and châteaubriand, and fresh seafood, such as Cajun garlic scallops and oysters.

Cedar Key boasts a few food specialties of its own. Swamp cabbage (known in trendier terminology as hearts of palm) salads have always been associated with Cedar Key eateries. With its tenacity to fishing traditions, fresh seafood is the forte, especially crab, oysters, mullet and quahog clams. Sitting on the dock, **The Captain's Table** (Dock Street; 904-543-5441) looks as though it's been around awhile. Its name is spelled out in rope on the side of the building, and in broken letters atop the wooden structure. The menu makes a slight concession to non-seafood lovers, but the specialty is definitely Cedar Key-style seafood: mullet, oysters, crab fingers, stone crab and a combination platter for two that will appease even the hard-core shellfish fancier. Moderate to deluxe.

Seabreeze (Dock Street, Cedar Key; 904-543-5738) sits up on pilings over the water, surrounded by in floor-to-ceiling windows and spectacular views. The bill of fare is steak, chicken and seafood served every-which-way—including the traditional fried and broiled styles plus the fancier Florentine style. Laminated tables give this spot the requisite nautical appeal. Moderate.

The Heron (Highway 24 and 2nd Street; 904-543-5666) returns you to the old days on Cedar Key, when ladies wore long skirts—as the waitresses do here today—and food was flavored with homey touches. From the sculptured tin ceiling to the sturdy oak antique tables, time machine escape is served with specialties such as shrimp in anise-flavored tomato sauce and chicken in sour cream and bleu cheese. Moderate to deluxe.

Natural gourmet food describes the fare at **Island Hotel** (Main Street, Cedar Key; 904-543-5111). In deference to the survival of the state tree, no palm salads are served here. What you can expect to find in this diamond-in-the-rough facility is baked garlic, marinated tofu and Cedar Key soft-shell crabs. Moderate to deluxe.

CRYSTAL RIVER–CEDAR KEY AREA SHOPPING

For a cuddly souvenir of your Crystal River visit, try **The Manatee Toy Company** (631 Citrus Avenue; 904-795-6126).

Heritage Village (North Citrus Avenue east of Route 19, Crystal River) houses seven shops with a variety of antiques, collectibles, quilts and artsy clothing.

Cedar Key has become known for its artist residents. **Cedar Keyhole** (2nd Street; 904-543-5801) carries works of several local artists in the form of woodcarvings, pottery, folk art and macrame. Fine arts and American crafts are featured at the **Suwannee Triangle Gallery** (Dock Street; 904-543-5744).

CRYSTAL RIVER–CEDAR KEY AREA NIGHTLIFE

Up in the rural northern coastal regions, nightlife is limited to local taverns. A good place for imbibing and mingling in Homosassa Springs is the **Ship's Lounge** (904-628-2474) at Riverside Inn resort on the Homosassa River. Live bands play on weekends at **L & M** (2nd Street, Cedar Key; 904-543-5827), a laid-back local hangout overlooking a marina.

CRYSTAL RIVER–CEDAR KEY AREA BEACHES AND PARKS

The coastline gets marshier north of Pinellas County. The good news is the parks are more secluded.

Fort Island Beach (★)—You won't hear Crystal River locals talking about this out-of-the-way park, nor will you see signs advertising it. The beach is more natural than those developed farther south, but the sand is just as white and fine.

Facilities: Picnic areas, restrooms, outdoor showers, summer lifeguards, boat ramp; restaurants and groceries about ten miles away in Crystal River. *Swimming:* Good in roped-off area.

Getting there: Located at the western end of Route 44.

Chassahowitzka National Wildlife Refuge—A natural shelter for over 250 species of birds, as well as mink, otter, raccoon, bobcat, deer and alligator. Its 30,436 acres of estuarine habitat attract waterfowl by the millions. Other natural landscape here includes brackish marshland, swamps, island hardwood forests and oyster bars.

Facilities: Picnic areas, restrooms; information, 904-563-2088. *Fishing:* Excellent.

Getting there: The fragile environment is accessible only by boat. Headquarters are located at 1502 Southeast Kings Bay Drive in Crystal River.

Cedar Keys National Wildlife Refuge (★)—A closely guarded area that places its importance as a wildlife sanctuary above its role as a human resource. The refuge incorporates several offshore islands ranging in area from 6 to 165 acres, five miles from the town of Cedar Key. Over 50,000 nesting birds colonize here annually, including ibis, egrets, Louisiana herons and great blue herons. Birdwatchers also find white pelicans, roseate spoonbills and bald eagles migrating through the refuge. Because of its importance to wildlife, limited public use is allowed.

Facilities: None. *Swimming:* Good off the beach at Seahorse Key. (Closed to the public from March through June.)

Getting there: You must take a boat to reach the refuge. Many charters leave daily from the dock at Cedar Key.

The Sporting Life

SPORTFISHING

Deep-sea fishing is one of western Florida's most popular sports. Private charters and excursion boats are practically as plentiful as the grouper, shark, triple tail and flounder they seek. Here's a listing of a few:

In the Sarasota area, contact **Flying Fish Fleet** (Island Park, Sarasota; 813-366-3373). For deep-sea fishing from a head boat, try **Getaway Marina** (18400 San Carlos Boulevard, Fort Myers Beach; 813-466-3600). Party boat offshore fishing trips can be boarded at **Dalis Boat Charters** (1200 5th Avenue South; 813-262-4545) at Old Marine Market in Naples. **Florida Deep Sea Fishing** (4737 Gulf Boulevard, St. Petersburg Beach; 813-360-2082) offers offshore excursions. In the Crystal River area, contact **Robbie's Charters** (2060 South Melanie Drive, Homosassa; 904-628-3274).

SKINDIVING

You'll find plenty of scuba shops up and down the West Coast, but most of them take their clients to the East Coast or the Florida Keys. Gulf of Mexico waters are mostly cloudy and/or devoid of reef life. Terrific freshwater diving, however, is available at Crystal River, where spring-fed waters populated with manatees draw divers in droves.

A full-service diving shop in Tampa is **Scuba Unlimited** (4119 Gunn Highway; 813-960-7748). **Underwater Explorers** (12600 McGregor Boulevard, Fort Myers; 813-481-4733) is a qualified scuba instructor and dealer. **Advanced Aquatics** (3899 Ulmerton Road; 813-573-3483) serves the St. Petersburg and Clearwater areas. In Crystal River, **Port Paradise** (1610 Southeast Paradise Circle; 904-795-3111) features a full-service dive shop.

WINDSURFING AND SURFING

West Coast waters are generally too calm for anyone but the beginning surfer. Occasionally the waves on the beach that runs parallel with Captiva Road on Captiva Island swell into good rides. On the other hand, the entire coast makes for windsurfing fun, and many resorts rent equipment and offer lessons. Especially known for its fine winds and windsurfing competitions are the waters off the Sanibel Causeway on Sanibel Island. Many resorts rent sailboard equipment and offer instruction. These services are also found at shops up and down the coast.

In the Sarasota area, contact **Ocean Boulevard Sailboarding** (1233 Gulf Stream Avenue North, Sarasota; 813-364-9463).

Bradenton Beach Sailboat Rentals (1325 Gulf Drive North, Bradenton Beach; 813-778-4969) rents Hobies and G-Cats.

Windsurfing of Sanibel (1554 Periwinkle Way, Sanibel; 813-472-0123) provides full service to sailboarders. **Totally Windsurfing** (7859 Blind Pass Road, St. Petersburg Beach; 813-367-7059) teaches windsurfing and rents equipment.

BOATING

On Florida's West Coast, island hopping rates high on the activities list. Boating to unhitched islands for lunch is a favorite vacation activity. For those who prefer to do their own navigating, boats can be rented at many resorts and marinas.

Try **O'Leary's Sarasota Sailing School** (Island Park, Sarasota; 813-953-7505) for instruction and charters. **Don and Mike's Boat and Ski Rentals** (520 Blackburn Point Road, Osprey; 813-966-4000) rents jet skis, power boats and pontoon boats.

On Sanibel, power boats and pontoon boats can be rented at **The Boat House** (634 North Yachtsman Drive, Sanibel Marina; 813-472-2531).

In Naples, **G. R. Sailboats** (4892 Bonita Beach Road, Bonita Springs; 813-947-4889) rents Hobies and windsurfers. For powerboats, contact **Port-O-Call Marina** (505 Port-O-Call Way; 813-774-0479). In the St. Petersburg area, try **Jack's Boat Rental** (146 128th Avenue, Madeira Beach; 813-392-6912) or **International Boat Rentals** (17811 Gulf Boulevard, Redington Shores; 813-391-6308).

CANOEING

The area's state parks have some of the best waters for paddling along in unhurried enjoyment of natural surroundings. Most of the parks, including **Oscar Scherer State Park** (Route 41 south of Sarasota; 813-483-5956), **Koreshan Historic Site** (Route 41, Bonita Springs; 813-992-0311) and **Collier-Seminole State Park** (Route 41 east of Naples; 813-394-3397), also rent canoes. In addition, **Tarpon Bay Marina** (Tarpon Bay Road, Sanibel; 813-472-8900) rents canoes for touring J. N. "Ding" Darling National Wildlife Preserve.

BALLOONING

For a bird's-eye view of Florida's West Coast, take the sunrise hot-air balloon tour offered by **Trans-America Balloons** (North Port; 813-426-7326).

JOGGING

Running along the multitude of beautiful beachscapes in western Florida makes exercise almost painless. In Tampa, joggers enjoy the bay and stately home view along **Bayshore Boulevard**, a six-and-a-half-mile-long sidewalk route. This is also where the **Gasparilla Classic** is run each February in conjunction with the city's annual pirate festival.

GOLF

Public courses in Tampa include **Rocky Point Golf Course** (4151 Dana Shores Drive; 813-884-5141) and **Babe Zaharias Golf Course** (11412 Forest Hills Drive; 813-932-8932).

Sarasota is considered the birthplace of the American golf scene. Back in 1887, one of her first citizens, John Hamilton Gillespie, a Scotsman, cured his homesickness by building a two-hole link on what is now Main Street. Today, golf courses are uncountable here. Many are open to the public, such as **Bobby Jones Golf Club** (1000 Azinger Way; 813-955-8041) and **Sarasota Golf Club** (7280 North Leewynn Drive; 813-371-2431).

In Sanibel, **The Dunes Golf & Tennis Club** (949 Sand Castle Road; 813-472-3355) offers an 18-hole course with rentals and a pro shop. **River's Edge Yacht and Country Club** (14700 Portsmouth Boulevard, Fort Myers; 813-433-4211) is a lovely, fountained course.

Clearwater Golf Park (1875 Airport Drive, Clearwater; 813-447-5272) is a public course in Pinellas County. **Tarpon Springs Golf Club** (1310 Pinellas Avenue South, Tarpon Springs; 813-937-6906) is also a public course.

TENNIS

Several public tennis courts are located along the West Coast. In Tampa, **Riverfront Park** (900 North Boulevard; 813-253-6038) is a public facility with courts for tennis, racquetball and handball. Tennis courts are also found at **City of Tampa Courts** (59 Columbia Drive; 813-253-3782). In the Sarasota area, **Siesta Key Public Beach** (Midnight Pass Road, Siesta Key) and **Forest Lakes Tennis Club** (2401 Beneva Road, Sarasota; 813-922-0660) have public courts. **Sanibel Elementary School** (3840 Sanibel-Captiva Road; 813-472-0345) features four lighted courts. **St. Petersburg Tennis Club** (650 18th Avenue South; 813-894-4378) has 15 courts.

BICYCLING

A nature-view bike path runs through **Oscar Scherer State Recreation Area** south of Sarasota.

Twelve miles of bike path run the length of **Longboat Key** and onto **Lido Key. Boca Grande** on Gasparilla Island has a scenic bike path. **Sanibel Island**'s system of bike paths covers over 20 miles, providing access to all of the beaches, shops and restaurants. The path ends at the bridge to Captiva. You cannot ride over the causeway, however, so you must transport your vehicle.

You'll find paths in some areas of Fort Myers, notably on **Summerlin Road**, and in Naples as well, mostly around the beach areas.

Though established bike paths are not always provided in these areas, West Coast beach routes and city parks make for easy pedaling along flat terrain.

BIKE RENTALS Many large resorts rent bikes to guests as well as to the public, in addition to the following:

In the Bradenton-Sarasota area **Bicycle Center** (2610 Cortez Road, Bradenton; 813-756-5480) and the **Bike Shop** (5610 Gulf of Mexico Drive, Longboat Key; 813-383-5184) rent bikes.

On Sanibel Island, try **Island Moped** (1470 Periwinkle Way; 813-472-5248) or **Finnimore's Bike Shop** (2353 Periwinkle Way; 813-472-5577).

Trikes & Bikes (3451 Fowler Street; 813-936-1851) in Fort Myers and **Pop's Bicycles** (3685 Bonita Beach Road, Bonita Springs; 813-947-4442) in the Naples area have bike rentals.

In St. Petersburg Beach, you can rent bikes at **The Beach Cyclist** (7517 Blind Pass Road; 813-367-5001).

HIKING

Florida's West Coast offers the most scenic hiking along its hard-packed and often shell-strewn beaches. No established system of paths guides you along these sandy trails, fraught with wading birds, sand crabs and other beach life; most beaches are self-guiding. Off the beach, a few sanctuaries and state parks provide hiking opportunities that take you back to presettlement Florida.

Hillsborough River State Park Trails (8 miles) skirt river rapids, cross suspension bridges and penetrate forests of hardwood, oak, magnolia and sabal palm. Several species of wading birds and waterfowl can be spotted along these gentle hikes, as well as alligators, turtles and other freshwater fauna.

A system of easy trails has been established at the **Sanibel-Captiva Conservation Center** (4 miles total) on Sanibel Island. This area is a favorite for bird lovers; other types of indigenous fauna and flora also can be enjoyed from the trail and from the observation tower along it.

Cayo Costa State Park stretches for ten miles, allowing unparalleled opportunity for uninterrupted exploration of Gulf sands and bay mangroves. A short nature trail crosses from one side of the island to the other, where pine forests and cactus sandlands, white pelicans and an occasional wild boar can be seen.

Koreshan State Historic Site Nature Trail (1 mile) loops along the Estero River and through tropical gardens planted by religious settlers at the turn of the century. Avocado, mango, royal palm and sapote trees now grow wild here.

Collier-Seminole Trail (6.5 miles) winds through saltwater and freshwater marshland and mangrove forests. Rare finds here include a stand of native royal palms and the Florida black bear. This is the starting point of over 800 miles of the Florida Trail, which travels in starts and stops up to the northern Panhandle area of the state.

Boyd Hill Nature Trail (1101 Country Club Way South, St. Petersburg; 813-893-7326) features six trails through 245 acres of various Florida ecosystems.

Transportation

BY CAR

The Tamiami Trail, **Route 41**, marks the original path between Miami and Tampa, thus its name. For getting to know the area, this southern-bound route allows the best insight into the cross-section it dissects. It crosses most of the cities from Tampa to Naples mentioned in this chapter. **Route 75,** the major interstate from Georgia to Naples, is more often traveled by those looking at time schedules rather than regional personality. Tampa is connected to the Orlando–Disney World area via **Route 4. Route 19** stitches together the coastal cities from St. Petersburg north.

BY AIR

Three major airports service Florida's West Coast. Tampa is the coast's transportation hub; the Tampa International Airport is thereby the largest airport of the Gulf Coast. In Fort Myers, the Southwest Regional Airport also receives both international and domestic flights. The Sarasota-Bradenton Airport is a smaller facility.

Tampa International Airport is serviced by international carriers as well as domestic companies: Air Canada, American Airlines, Bahamasair, British Airways, Cayman Airways, Continental Airlines, Delta Air Lines, Mexicana Airlines, Northwest Airlines, Trans World Airlines, United Airlines and USAir.

Major transportation companies servicing the Tampa airport include **Central Florida Limousine** (813-276-3730) for Hillsborough County destinations and **The Limo** (813-572-1111) for Pinellas County.

Most of the major domestic carriers fly in and out of **Sarasota-Bradenton Airport**: American Airlines, Continental Airlines, Delta Air Lines, Northwest Airlines, Trans World Airlines and United Airlines.

Ground transportation from Sarasota-Bradenton Airport is provided by **Diplomat Taxi** (813-355-5155) and **Westcoast Airport Limousine** (813-355-9645).

Southwest Regional Airport carriers include: American Airlines, Continental Airlines, Delta Airlines, Northwest Airlines, TWA, United Airlines and USAir.

BY BUS

Greyhound Bus Lines depots along the West Coast are located in Tampa (610 Polk Street; 813-229-1501), Sarasota (575 North Washington Boulevard; 813-955-5735), Fort Myers (2275 Cleveland Avenue; 813-334-1011), Naples (2669 Davis Boulevard; 813-774-5660) and St. Petersburg (180 9th Street North; 813-895-4455).

BY TRAIN

Amtrak (800-872-7245) makes West Coast stops at Tampa (Nebraska Avenue and Twiggs Street), Bradenton (Manatee County Court House Bus Terminal, Manatee West at 12th Street West), Sarasota (City Hall Bus Terminal, Lemon Avenue between 1st and 2nd streets), St. Petersburg (3601 31st Street North), Clearwater Beach (Civic Center, 40 Causeway Road) and Clearwater (657 Court Street).

CAR RENTALS

Rental agencies located or with pick-ups at the Tampa airport include **Alamo Rent A Car** (813-289-4323), **Avis Rent A Car** (813-276-3500),

Budget Rent A Car (813-877-6051), **Dollar Rent A Car** (813-276-3640), **Hertz Rent A Car** (813-874-3232) and **National Inter Rent** (813-276-3783).

In the Sarasota-Bradenton area, the following agencies provide free airport pick-up: **A-Plus Car Rentals** (813-355-9621), **Alamo Rent A Car** (813-359-5540), **Avis Rent A Car** (813-355-5127), **Budget Rent A Car** (813-359-5353), **Dollar Rent A Car** (813-355-2996), **Hertz Rent A Car** 813-355-8848) and **National Inter Rent** (813-355-7711).

In Fort Myers, airport location and/or free pick-up service is provided by the following rental car agencies: **Alamo Rent A Car** (813-768-2424), **Avis Rent A Car** (813-768-2121), **Budget Rent A Car** (813-768-1500), **Dollar Rent A Car** (813-768-2223), **Value Rent A Car** (813-768-1200), **Hertz Rent A Car** (813-768-3100), **National Inter Rent** (813-768-1902) and **Sears Rent A Car** (813-768-2500). For used rental vehicles, call **Rent A Wreck** (813-337-1633).

PUBLIC TRANSPORTATION

To get around Tampa, **HART** (Hillsborough Area Regional Transit; 813-254-4278) runs dependably to most areas in the county. The monorail **PeopleMover** provides state-of-the-art transportation in the downtown Tampa business district and to and from Harbour Island.

In Sarasota, you will find comfort and reliability in **SCAT** (Sarasota County Area Transit; 813-951-5851) buses, which cover the in-town area and go to the beaches, Venice and Englewood. **LeeTran** (813-275-8726) buses provide limited service to Fort Myers Beach, eastern and northern Fort Myers, Edison Mall, Lehigh Acres and Cape Coral.

The **PSTA** (Pinellas Suncoast Transit Authority; 813-530-9911) operates buses with routes through downtown St. Petersburg and Clearwater. Service to other parts of the county is provided on a Dial-a-Bus schedule.

BATS (813-367-3086) city buses connect with PSTA routes to service St. Petersburg Beach.

TAXIS

Several cab companies serve the Tampa airport, including **Yellow Cab** (813-253-0121) and **United Cab of Tampa** (813-253-2424). **Diplomat Taxi** (813-355-5155) is the designated airport cab service at Sarasota-Bradenton. At the Fort Myers airport, try **Yellow Cab** (813-332-1511) for Fort Myers, Fort Myers Beach and Sanibel-Captiva destinations.

P A N H A N D L E

CHAPTER EIGHT

The Panhandle

It is curious that the section of Florida most accessible to the rest of the country should be its least known. "The Panhandle?" outsiders ask. "Is there really anything there?" Of course, there have long been visitors to Panhandle beaches, wise lovers of sand and sea who come in the summer months from Alabama, Georgia and Mississippi to work on their tans and romp in the crystal water or ride the occasionally challenging waves. They, and their ways of having vacation fun, explain why certain sections of the glistening shore have been dubbed the "Redneck Riviera."

Some retired folk have chosen to settle along this coast where the seasons change; many first fell in love with the place while stationed at Eglin Air Force Base (the nation's largest) or Pensacola's Naval Air Station. In recent years, Canadians have been heading this way in the winters, not minding the chilly sea breezes and thriving on the phenomenally low seasonal rates.

But the large majority of Florida's tourists skim across the Panhandle's eastern edge or zip through its inland middle on efficient allegro interstates, hastening to Daytona and Disney World and the pleasures of the tropics. In doing so, they miss one of the state's hidden treasures.

Over four centuries ago the Panhandle, already populated by Indian tribes hunting its hills and harvesting its waters, attracted some of America's first European visitors. Spanish explorer Hernando de Soto set out in 1539 to conquer Florida and search for treasure. He and his band of soldiers, horses, livestock and followers slogged through the swamps and woods along old Indian trails east of present-day Tallahassee and up into what would become Georgia. Tristan de Luna tried to set up a colony at Pensacola in 1559 and, if it hadn't been battered by hurricane and hardship, de Luna's village might have survived to beat out St. Augustine as the state's oldest permanent settlement. But de Luna was forced to give up, and much of the region remained inhabited by Indians, inspiring the Spanish to set up a chain of forts and missions from St. Augustine to Pensacola.

As later explorers made further attempts to tame the wild region, trades and treaties tossed the ownership of Florida back and forth between the hands of Spain, France and Great Britain for almost 200 years. When the British acquired the land in 1763, they divided it into two parts, East and West Florida, before returning it to Spanish hands twenty years later. The United States gained permanent ownership of the still-divided land with a final purchase from Spain in 1821.

Immediately, Andrew Jackson established a new territorial government, and the two Floridas merged. In 1824, Tallahassee was chosen as the new capital, not because of any intrinsic value but because it was about half way between Pensacola and St. Augustine, as confirmed by two delegates setting out toward each other from those cities. By 1840, steamboats were navigating the Apalachicola River and in 1845, Florida became a state. But the Civil War was still to come, and the Panhandle would feel its ravages for many years. Tallahassee escaped largely intact, however. Although federal troops occupied the city very briefly, this southern capital would remain the only one east of the Mississippi to avoid capture.

After the Civil War came reconstruction and its accompanying poverty. Though Tallahassee remained the capital and Panhandle ports flourished as the demand for wood and forest products grew, the state's real action lay to the south. As the East and West coasts of the peninsula boomed with development and tourism, the lands of the Panhandle came under the cultivation of sharecroppers and tenant farmers. The Panhandle story was more closely tied to the Deep South of Georgia and Alabama than to its own Florida family.

Today, much of the Panhandle still has a Deep South feel to it. Perhaps this is why tourists tend to pass it by for the distinctive glitter to the south. But though it still has remnants of plantations, small towns where natives speak in slow drawls and offer genteel hospitality, healthy pecan groves and more churches than you could ever count, the Panhandle has its own distinctions that make it truly Florida.

On the eastern boundary the swift and clean Suwannee River flows through deep woods of pine and oak and cypress. Near the western edge the Perdido and Blackwater rivers also run clean, dark-stained with tannin, dotted with tiny white sand beaches, meandering through rich forest lands. The broad Apalachicola River, once an important water highway, cuts the Panhandle nearly in two. These rivers and others, along with myriad creeks and streams, flow to the Gulf of Mexico, creating valuable estuaries and brackish marshes crucial to coastal wildlife.

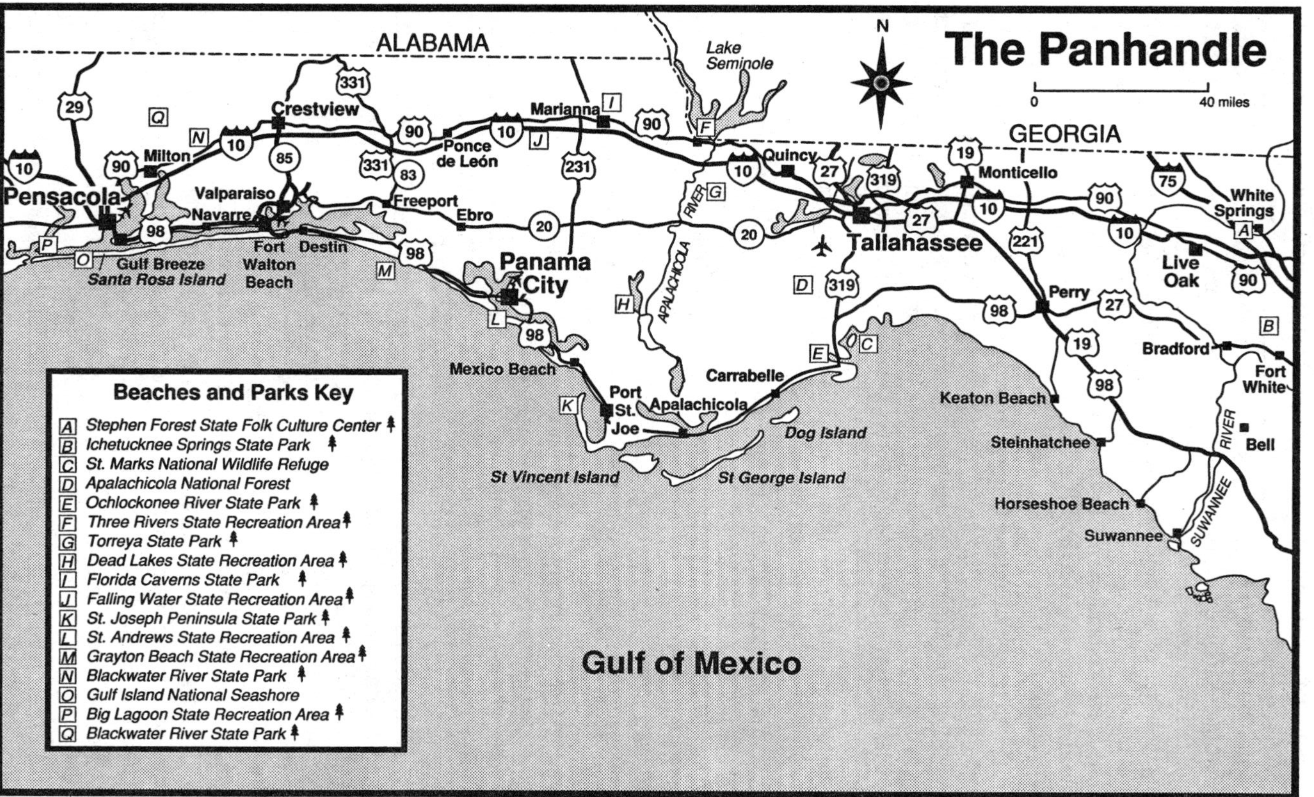
The Panhandle
N
0
40 miles
ALABAMA
GEORGIA
Lake Seminole
Pensacola
Milton
Crestview
Valparaiso
Navarre
Gulf Breeze
Santa Rosa Island
Fort Walton Beach
Destin
Freeport
Ebro
Ponce de León
Marianna
Panama City
Mexico Beach
Port St. Joe
Apalachicola
Carrabelle
St Vincent Island
St George Island
Dog Island
Quincy
Tallahassee
Monticello
Perry
Keaton Beach
Steinhatchee
Horseshoe Beach
Suwannee
Bradford
Fort White
Bell
Live Oak
White Springs
APALACHICOLA RIVER
SUWANNEE RIVER
Gulf of Mexico
Beaches and Parks Key
A Stephen Forest State Folk Culture Center
B Ichetucknee Springs State Park
C St. Marks National Wildlife Refuge
D Apalachicola National Forest
E Ochlockonee River State Park
F Three Rivers State Recreation Area
G Torreya State Park
H Dead Lakes State Recreation Area
I Florida Caverns State Park
J Falling Water State Recreation Area
K St. Joseph Peninsula State Park
L St. Andrews State Recreation Area
M Grayton Beach State Recreation Area
N Blackwater River State Park
O Gulf Island National Seashore
P Big Lagoon State Recreation Area
Q Blackwater River State Park

Several vastly differing sections of coastline mark the Panhandle's expansive contact with the Gulf. From the Suwannee's mouth to St. Marks lies the "big bend," a great marshy shore with almost no beaches, dotted with old-fashioned fishing villages and containing vast regions devoted to wildlife management. Westward toward Apalachicola and beyond, the protected shores of the bays abound in rich estuarine life; the waters produce a bounty of seafood and oysters that are world-famous. Here one must travel to the barrier islands or peninsulas for beachcombing and swimming; those who do so are rewarded with miles of dunes, abundant wildlife and fine Gulf waters.

From touristy Panama City westward lies the pièce de résistance of the Panhandle, a hundred miles of quartz sand and turquoise water said to be the whitest and clearest in the country. Visitors may choose their ways to enjoy this region, from the honky-tonk of overbuilt Panama City Beach to modest little villages to the towering condos and classy resorts of Destin and Fort Walton Beach to the pristine dunes of the Gulf National Seashore at historic Pensacola. With only minimal searching, you can even discover miles of beach that remain almost deserted.

An even more hidden part of Florida, however, lies inland, from the Gulf all the way to the Georgia line. Here meandering country roads wander through miles of rural countryside, sometimes rolling, sometimes flat and sprawling. At its heart is Tallahassee, a suddenly sophisticated capital city with two large state universities, respectable hills, oak-canopied roads and a lot of southern charm. At its back door lies the vast Apalachicola National Forest. In the hinterlands to the east and west are small towns, some poor, some prosperous, many reached only by lonely roads that travel in and out of forested areas, through scrub land and clear-cut woods, alongside murky swamps or past fine horse farms, hunting plantations and productive dairies. Peanuts grow well in the Panhandle, along with cotton and Spanish moss and hogs. Land still sells, in some places, for affordable prices.

Within this inland terrain, scattered like jewels dropped into unexpected pockets, clear fresh springs bubble up across the Panhandle. Some, like Wakulla and Ichetucknee, have been made easily accessible; others still wait to be discovered by adventurous visitors to the sparsely populated counties in which they lie. In recent years, scuba divers and snorkelers have been attracted by the challenge of the springs' crystal blue depths as well as their proximity to equally clear Gulf waters from Panama City westward.

Fishing has been a chief attraction of the Panhandle since the era of the Paleo-Indians; rivers, lakes, springs and marshes each offer up their unique prizes. Hunters thrive on the bounty of the deep forests and preserves.

So to those who ask, "Is there really anything in the Panhandle?" this chapter provides an answer. For the seeker of hidden destinations there is much. The greatest appeal of this land lies in the open spaces, the undeveloped fields and forests and beaches, the protected wetlands and unpolluted springs and rivers that can only be discovered by leaving the beaten path. In the Panhandle one can still walk in solitude, listen to mockingbirds and gulls instead of jam-boxes and, if one braves the backroads, drive for hours without seeing another car.

Eastern Area

Most tourists zip through the Panhandle's Eastern area on Route 10, or bypass it altogether as they head south. For the backroad-wanderer, however, hidden treasures of an undeveloped Florida wait to be discovered here. Just about any route you choose will take you through pine woods, past tree farms and pig farms, and along lonely roads whose miles seem to be inhabited by nothing but churches—some very old, others appearing to have been thrown up in haste overnight. Through it run rivers and streams, swift, dark, beautiful, and remarkably unpolluted.

Not to be missed, the **Stephen Foster State Folk Culture Center** (Route 41 and Route 136, White Springs; 904-397-2733; admission) celebrates the man who, though he never saw it, made the Suwannee River famous by setting it to music. "Old Folks at Home" ("Way down upon the Suwannee River . . ."), Florida's state song, and other familiar Foster melodies ring out from the park's carillon tower, entertaining the visitors who come to learn about the composer and area folklife through dioramas and exhibits. The riverside park is a beauty, full of trees and flowers and site of the remnants of a Victorian-style health resort where Teddy Roosevelt joined thousands of others to bathe in the smelly sulphur spring that flows into the Suwannee.

In traversing the Panhandle interior, you have a choice of routes. If you take Route 90 westward, the countryside becomes more rolling as it follows the old **Hernando de Soto Trail**. Historical markers explain that the Spanish explorer, along with 600 soldiers and assorted livestock and servants, trekked along mosquito-infested Indian paths here in 1539.

Today's travelers fare better, especially those who take the time to admire the Victorian and Greek revival houses in **Madison** and **Monticello,** where time seems to stand still. You can pick up a self-guided walking tour of Monticello at the **Chamber of Commerce** (420 West Washington Street; 904-997-5552). Drive around the square and gaze at the Jeffersonian-classic 1909-era courthouse, a dramatic domed structure built for only $40,000.

Routes heading south and southwest through this eastern area travel through vast areas of seeming nothingness—here tangled woods, there close regiments of planted pines, many clear-cut fields and acres of farmland. Much of the area is reserved for wildlife management. Along the eastern border flows the Suwannee River, its swift, clean water tannin-stained like tea and abundant in fish.

The greatest treasures are the springs, scattered like jewels tossed on a tattered quilt, occasional manifestations of the giant aquifer that lies beneath Florida. Some are unnamed, many unknown except to local folk. A few have been made easily accessible, incorporated into lovely parks such as **Ichetucknee Springs State Park** (Route 27 between Branford and Fort White; 904-497-2511) and **Hart Springs Park (★)** (Route C-344 southwest of Bell; 904-463-6486). For information on reaching **Charles Spring, Running Spring, Little River Spring, Peacock Spring** and other hidden beauties, you'll need a county map and advice, both of which are available at the **Suwannee County Chamber of Commerce** (601 East Howard Street, Live Oak; 904-362-3071).

Many roads lead to the coastal region known as Florida's "big bend." There are no great white sandy beaches here, which explains why much of the area is pristine and most of the little villages still keep to the business of fishing, maintaining a naturalness and a local charm. The marshy land and river estuaries attract numerous species of birds and the sunsets are spectacular. You can enjoy them from docks and porches in the Gulf-front towns of **Suwannee (★)**, **Horseshoe Beach (★)**, **Steinhatchee (★)** and **Keaton Beach (★)**.

From the coast, you can head back to the crossroads town of Perry. Here you can learn about Florida's remarkable lumber industry at the **Forest Capital State Museum** (204 Forest Park Drive; 904-584-3227; admission). There are dioramas showing how the cutting of giant cypress and pine was done in the old days and explanations of such futuristic wood products as rayon airplanes and cellulose clothing. Walk down a pine-needle path and enter the turn-of-the-century Cracker Homestead behind the museum. Washpots in the swept sand yard, grandma's mosquito netting, bare worn floors and a struggling garden carry you back to a time when life was simpler, and harder.

EASTERN AREA HOTELS

Numerous mom-and-pop enterprises provide lodging in the towns scattered throughout the eastern area. Many of them change hands often, and, like ladies in southern novels, may appear elegant on the outside while crumbling within. However, plenty of them are just fine, and most offer great bargains; just look over the room before committing yourself. The usual chains reside along the interstate routes.

In Live Oak, the **Econo Lodge** (Route 10 and Route 129; 904-362-7459) is an exceptionally fine budget motel with pool, jacuzzi and remote-control television. The pleasant rooms and abundance of towels put some higher-priced lodgings to shame.

The **Suwannee River Motel** (Route 41, White Springs; 904-397-2822) is a compact little outfit with 16 tiny, neat rooms for rates so low they seem from another era. When we were there, folks sat around chatting outside—about the friendliest little motel we've encountered.

"No frills" are the operative words at **Colonial House Inn** (Routes 75 and 136, White Springs; 904-963-2401), an interstate stopover with 28 nondescript but nicely renovated guestrooms. The design is typical motel, with one long stretch of single-floor rooms. Most importantly, rates are budget year-round.

For a roadside motel, consider the budget-priced **Friendship Inn** (Route 10 and Route 53, Madison; 904-973-2504). The wallpaper may not suit your taste, but the carpeted rooms are fresh and clean. There's an RV park on the same grounds, so you have access to laundry facilities and a nice pool under the pines.

For a budget rate you can get a good-sized, well-kept, carpeted room at the **Cadillac Motel** (Routes 19, 98 and 27-A, Fannings Springs; 904-463-2188), convenient to the nearby spring and the Suwannee River.

The old-fashioned fishing villages along the "big bend" of the coastline provide a variety of modest accommodations, most with kitchens, for people who come to fish or seek the serenity of this non-touristy, non-swimming beach area. Most provide fishing-guide services, and all offer peace and quiet.

Especially attractive is **Sexton's Riverside Motel** (★) (3rd Street and 1st Avenue, Steinhatchee; 904-498-5005), a set of small stuccoed cinder-block efficiencies. For a budget price you get two rooms, a furnished kitchen, a screened porch with a picnic table and a lovely view of the Steinhatchee River emptying into the Gulf.

Two miles from the Gulf, beside the Suwannee River, the **Suwannee Shores Motor Lodge** (★) (end of Route 349, Suwannee; 904-542-7560) offers 26 pleasantly ordinary units, some with kitchens, only a stone's throw from a marina and access to fine saltwater and freshwater fishing. Budget.

There isn't much beach at Keaton Beach, but there is a surprisingly nice motel constructed from modular housings, an addition to the successful restaurant next door. **The Old Pavilion Motel** (★) (end of Route 361; 904-578-2637) offers plenty of quiet, incredible sunsets, well-kept rooms with showers and a 500-foot pier over the Gulf. Budget.

EASTERN AREA RESTAURANTS

Menus are pretty predictable at the cafés and restaurants in the scattered towns of the eastern area—lots of good local seafood and fine examples of southern cooking. Even **The Brahman** (Route 90 West, west of Monticello; 904-997-3525) avoids the curries you'd expect from its owners, featuring, instead, liver and onions, golden fried quail, fried chicken and whole catfish. Budget.

"It's not Suwannee River country without catfish," proclaims the menu at the **Dixie Grill** (Howard Street and Dowling Avenue, Live Oak; 904-364-2810), and this is the place to try it. No filets here, just lots of big, crunchy, bony pieces served with homemade hushpuppies. You can order other seafood and steaks and dine in the plain café area or the fancy carpeted section. Budget to moderate.

The **Ship's Wheel Restaurant** (★) (end of Route 349, Suwannee; 904-542-2344) is typical of many budget-priced coastal restaurants that are worth the drive. The number of fishermen who eat here tells you something. Grouper, mullet and shrimp plates always come with hushpuppies, cole slaw and french fries, and there are chowders and oyster stew to fit the season.

A bit different from most "big bend" eateries, **The Old Pavilion** (★) (end of Route 361, Keaton Beach; 904-578-2637) offers gourmet items such as escargot over linguine, shellfish sautéed in garlic sauce, squid and lobster tails, along with the usual coastal fare. You dine over the Gulf, from whence come the items on the daily-specials chalkboard, and watch the shore birds fishing alongside the pier or flying home against a sunset backdrop. Moderate in price.

Roy's (★) (Route 51, Steinhatchee; 904-498-5000) delights diners who partake of the remarkable seafood platters, which include shrimp, scallops, deviled crab, oysters and crab claws at moderate prices. The salad bar features unlimited feta cheese and other Greek treats; steaming grits come with dinner if you wish. The place appears unassuming, but tinted windows offer wonderful sunset-viewing and shorebird-watching.

EASTERN AREA SHOPPING

Most of the eastern area towns are far enough away from shopping malls to be able to maintain healthy downtowns with assorted clothing shops, drug stores, hardware and even old-fashioned dime stores. If you long for some downhome, old-timey small-town browsing, you can find it. You may even find some antique bargains by getting off the beaten path; little shops spring up on town squares and in homes.

Handmade quilts, "gourd folks" and other craft items are featured at **L'Beth's** (Route 41, White Springs; 904-397-2650), a tiny cabin crammed full of antiques and collectibles.

Handwritten signs along the road announce "boiled peanuts," and, though an acquired taste, many folks get hooked on this north Florida delicacy. From the back of a truck or a tiny stand you can buy a steaming paper sack of these moist, soft-shelled, salty treats.

EASTERN AREA NIGHTLIFE

There are plenty of local drinking places along country roads and near little towns, but unless saloon-hopping is your style, you won't find much nightlife in this area.

One exception is **The Spirit of the Suwannee** (Route 129 just south of Routes 75 and 10, Live Oak; 904-364-1683), a huge park that puts on a variety of concerts and programs throughout the year. There are bluegrass festivals, story-telling events, clogging and square dancing, and other down-home entertainment.

For local color, latch onto one of the church suppers, fish fries or political rallies advertised from time to time on signs along the road. Most of these are money-raising events, so guests are quite welcome.

EASTERN AREA BEACHES AND PARKS

Suwannee River State Park—The Withlacoochee and Suwannee rivers meet in this quiet 1853-acre park, creating a rich variety of pine forest, hardwood hammock and sand hills. When the rivers are low, springs may be seen bubbling from their banks, crystal clear in the tannin-tinted waters. An old cemetery and Confederate earthworks recall the steamboat heyday when the area bustled.

Facilities: Picnic area, restrooms, nature trails; information, 904-362-2746. *Fishing:* Good for catfish, bass, panfish.

Camping: There are 31 sites, all with RV hookups; $10 per night.

Getting there: Just off Route 90, 13 miles west of Live Oak.

Hart Springs Park (★)—This 275-acre county park is built around one of the many surprising springs that seem to appear from nowhere in this part of the country. A small footbridge crosses the crystal clear run that flows to the Suwannee River, and cypress tress grow in the middle of the sand-bottomed swimming area.

Facilities: Picnic areas, restrooms, bathhouse, concession stand; information, 904-463-6486. *Swimming:* Wonderful, in clear, cold spring water.

Camping: There are 60 sites, some with hookups; $8-10 per night.

Getting there: Tricky, so go with map in hand. From Live Oak, head south on Route 129 to Bell; go west on Route 341 and continue on 341 when it heads south. At C-344 head west and go about eight miles to the spring (at four miles, C-344 jogs right, then left).

Ichetucknee Springs State Park—The heart of this lovely 2250-acre park is the crystal clear, icy cold Ichetucknee River and the series of springs that rise from the Florida aquifer to feed it. Canoeing and tubing are so popular here that folks often wait in line for entrance on summer weekends. The river winds through hardwood hammock and jungle-like swampland;

on quiet days folks floating on the river may spy otter, beaver, turtles or wading birds that make their homes here.

Facilities: Picnic areas, restrooms, dressing rooms, nature trail, canoe and tube ramps; information, 904-497-2511. *Swimming:* Excellent in springs and river. *Snorkeling:* Excellent.

Camping: Not allowed in the park but there are private campgrounds near each entrance of the park and camping in **O'Leno State Park** near Lake City.

Getting there: The south entrance is off Route 27 between Branford and Fort White; the north entrance is off Route 238.

Tallahassee Area

Unlike most Florida cities, Tallahassee is hilly, green and abounding in trees. More Deep South than tropical, its sights include the trappings of a fascinating state capital, the campuses of two state universities, the vestiges of plantation days, a bit of prehistory and a neighboring wilderness that comes right up to the city limits.

Because it's not on a major north-south route, Tallahassee isn't a tourist city. But despite its lack of tourist glitz, there's plenty to see and do here. Begin with a trip to the **Tallahassee Convention and Visitors Center** (200 West College Avenue; 904-681-9200), where you can arm yourself with brochures, maps and a self-guided walking and driving tour.

Most of the downtown sights are within walking distance of The Columns. Even so, you might want to use the **Old Town Trolley**. Designed primarily for local commuters, this colorful diesel-powered conveyance circles the downtown area, operating only on weekdays.

Near the Chamber of Commerce you'll discover the **First Presbyterian Church** (110 North Adams Street), a white-spired building that is Tallahassee's oldest house of worship. In 1838, the year it was built, townspeople sought refuge within its walls during Seminole Indian raids. Beautifully restored, even the galleries where slaves once sat still provide seating for worshippers.

Continue along Park Avenue for a few blocks and enjoy the fine antebellum homes that distinguish this lovely tree-lined promenade.

At the **Adams Street Commons** (200 South Adams Street) you'll find a serpentine, brick-paved block that has been redesigned and now features several fine hotels and restaurants, and some detailed landscaping.

Straight ahead stand two startlingly contrasting structures, the modern 22-story **Florida Capitol** (Apalachee Parkway and South Monroe Street; 904-488-6167), designed by Edward Durrell Stone, and the recently restored 1845 **Old Capitol** (904-487-1902), with its handsome dome and red-striped awnings. Tours of the new Capitol, including a scenic view from the top, are available daily. The Old Capitol is also open daily and houses exhibits of Florida political history.

One block from of the Old Capitol, on Apalachee Parkway, Florida's first major bank building, the **Old Union Bank** (904-487-3803) built around 1840, has been restored and is open Tuesday through Sunday for tours.

Two blocks west of the new Capitol, the **Museum of Florida History** (500 South Bronough Street; 904-488-1673) reflects a new interest in preserving the diverse and colorful story of the state. Here you'll see the interior of a citrus packing house, climb aboard a river boat, marvel over Spanish treasure and examine Indian relics.

Along nearby Martin Luther King Boulevard you can explore the **Old City Cemetery** (Martin Luther King Boulevard and Park Avenue), which has graves dating back to 1829, including those of pioneers and slaves and Confederate and Union soldiers. Adjacent to it, the **St. Johns Episcopal Cemetery** contains the graves of Prince Achille Murat, son of the King of Naples and nephew of Napoleon Bonaparte, and his wife, Madame Catherine Murat, great-grand-niece of George Washington. Several Florida governors are also buried here.

Within driving distance of downtown are **The Governor's Mansion** (North Adams and Brevard streets; 904-488-4661) and **The Grove** (North Adams Street and 1st Avenue). Modeled after Andrew Jackson's Tennessee mansion, "The Hermitage," the mansion is open for tours during the legislative session (late February to early April). The Grove, built in 1825 by an aide to Jackson, is the private residence of former Governor Leroy Collins.

The **Brokaw-McDougall House** (329 North Meridian Street; 904-488-3901), built in 1856, is a fine example of Classical revival architecture, distinguished by pleasing proportions and spaciousness. Six Corinthian columns support a second-story porch that overlooks grounds restored by landscapers to their 19th-century appearance.

The **LeMoyne Art Foundation** (125 North Gadsden Street; 904-222-8800) is also located in a restored antebellum home and features permanent collections of pottery, paintings, sculpture and photography by area artists. Occasional traveling exhibits also grace the rooms of this handsome house. The backyard garden is tended as a small showplace.

Florida State University and Florida A&M University both offer some interesting sightseeing. Once an all-black school, A&M houses its **Black Archives Research Center and Museum** (Carnegie Library; 904-599-3020) in one of Tallahassee's oldest buildings. Here you are greeted by an impressive display of photos of black Americans who have served in Congress; there is also a wide assortment of artifacts and exhibits on black culture and history. The **Foster Tanner Fine Arts Gallery** (904-599-3161), also on the A&M campus, presents the works of many black artists.

On the Florida State campus, the **University Gallery and Museum** (Fine Arts Building, Copeland and Call streets; 904-644-6836) features permanent collections of Japanese, Dutch and American painting, pre-Columbian artifacts and traveling exhibits.

If you'd like to see a museum-in-the-making, visit the **San Luis Archaeological and Historic Site** (2020 Mission Road; 904-487-3711). In the mid-17th century an Apalachee Indian town existed here, followed by a Spanish mission several decades later. Excavations are ongoing and explained to visitors by signs. Some of the uncovered artifacts are on display at the visitors center.

Tallahassee's most enchanting feature is its collection of **canopy roads,** lovely country byways that begin within the city limits and go for miles beneath towering live oaks draped with Spanish moss. Distinctive road markers designate these protected highways, which include Old St. Augustine Road, Miccosukee Road (Route 146), Centerville Road (Route 151), Meridian Road (Route 155) and Old Bainbridge Road.

If you'd like to get a glimpse of this entire area from the sky, you might check out **Captain Peper's Balloon Co.** (P.O. Box 3267, Tallahassee; 904-668-8200), which offers a variety of hot-air balloon flights.

For a fine trip down one of these Old South lanes, head northeast on Centerville Road. After eight miles of gentle turns, you will come to the 1859 **Pisgah Church**, a grand old meeting house with hand-hewn pews and clerestory windows. Continue beneath the oaks for another seven miles, and you will reach the old metal-sided **Bradley's Country Store** (Centerville Road, Moccasin Gap; 904-893-1647), little changed since the 1920s.

Many other interesting destinations lie outside the Tallahassee city limits. Just north of Route 10, the **Maclay Gardens** (3540 Thomasville Road; 904-487-4115; admission), built as a private winter retreat, present an astounding array of azaleas, redbuds, camellias, magnolias, amaryllises and other native flora in the spring months. The grounds, where something is always blooming, are open year round, the house from January through April.

The **Lake Jackson Indian Mounds** (north of Route 10 off Crowder Road and Route 27; 904-562-0042) look like a couple of ordinary hills in a park setting but are actually the remnants of an Indian village. It's a nice place to contemplate history and have a picnic. A nature trail leads to the remains of an old grist mill and irrigation lake.

Don't let the name of the **Tallahassee Junior Museum** (3945 Museum Drive; 904-575-8684; admission) mislead you; this wonderful combination zoo-park-farm-plantation provides information and entertainment for folks of all ages. It's hard to believe that only 52 wooded acres could communicate so much about north Florida in such a captivating and authentic manner. Be sure to take your children here, and if you don't have children, go anyway.

Located on the grounds of the Junior Museum is **Bellevue,** the former home of Catherine Dangerfield Willis, great-granddaughter of George Washington and widow of Achille Murat, Prince of Naples and nephew of Napoleon. The 1830-era home is a modest and excellent example of indigenous southern architecture.

At the southern end of Route 363, you will reach the **San Marcos de Apalachee State Historic Site** (904-925-6216; admission), at the confluence of the Wakulla and St. Marks rivers. A Spanish fort and mission stood here in the 17th century, and Confederate troops once occupied the area, too. You can see the old earthworks, pieces of walls and moats, and stroll a nature trail and boardwalk along the riverside. The visitor center displays artifacts from the fort's various eras.

In 1831 the **St. Marks Lighthouse,** located in the **St. Marks National Wildlife Refuge** (County Road 59; 904-925-6121), was built with stones from the old fort at San Marcos de Apalachee. One of the oldest lighthouses in the Southeast, its remarkable pineapple-shaped lens has served to guide ships from Civil War times to the modern age. Open in May only.

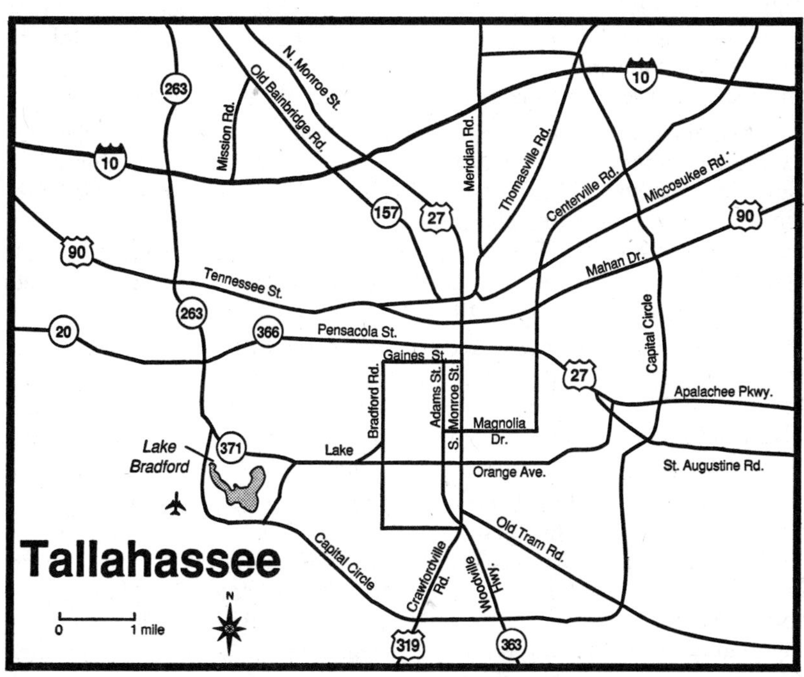

TALLAHASSEE AREA HOTELS

Ever since Tallahassee built its new state capitol building and spruced up its downtown, the ultimate place in elegant lodging has been **The Governors Inn** (209 South Adams Street; 904-681-6855), an amazing reconstruction of an old downtown business place, with high soaring ceilings and exposed heartpine trusses. Each of the 40 distinctive rooms is named for a Florida governor and furnished with appropriate antiques. Any head of state should be pleased to stay here, whether it be in a loft-bedroom overlooking a wood-burning fireplace or in a whirlpool-bath-equipped suite. Government and business folk keep the inn booked during the legislature's session, but if you can plan ahead and pay deluxe and ultra-deluxe prices, this is the place to stay. Amenities include continental breakfasts and complimentary cocktails in the pine-paneled Florida room.

In the downtown area, the **Tallahassee Sheraton** (101 South Adams Street; 904-224-5000) contributes its stature to the city's ever-reaching skyline. Many of the 245 rooms and 12 suites offer good views of downtown Tallahassee, the university campuses and the lush green countryside. The hotel offers all you'd expect, from large rooms to an assortment of eating and watering places. Decor is up-to-date and spacious. Deluxe.

If moderation suits your budget, but you'd still like to be near the center of town, consider the **Tallahassee Motor Hotel** (1630 North Monroe Street, Tallahassee; 904-224-6183). You'll know you're in an older motel, but the 92 rooms, endlessly strung out, are carpeted and clean. A nice pool and a lovely city park across the street set this place apart from other old motels, and the prices, even in the newer rooms, remain in the budget range.

Just about all the usual chain motels, from budget to top-of-the-line, can be found north of the city near Route 10 exits. **Cabot Lodge** (2735 North Monroe Street, Tallahassee; 904-386-8880) belongs to a small southern chain that offers more charm than most of its counterparts, and a continental breakfast, too. The 160 rooms reside in an assortment of yellow buildings with wide porches and green-and-yellow trim. There's an Old South feeling about the place, even though the rooms are modern. Moderate.

In the summer, you can save a lot of money by taking a room or suite at the privately owned dormitory, **Osceola Hall** (500 Chapel Drive, Tallahassee; 904-222-5010), on the edge of the Florida State University campus. This comfortably functional dorm is made up of two-room/one-bath suites. A food service, fitness facilities, sauna and pool are available. Budget.

Moorish architecture, hand-painted Toltec and Aztec designs and Spanish tile set the **Wakulla Springs Lodge and Conference Center** (Route 61, Wakulla Springs; 904-224-5950) apart from anything else north Florida has to offer. Built in 1937, this fine old hostelry overlooks Florida's deepest spring. Rooms look much as they did in the 1930s, with marble floors, area rugs and functional furniture. But you reach them by climbing broad marble steps, and you sleep in another era, in the quiet of a wonderful park full of wildlife. Moderate.

About 35 miles from town, **George's Lighthouse Point Resort** (Route 1, Box 3187, Panacea; 904-984-0171) has transformed itself from an ordinary motel into a riverside marina and lodge. Each suite is individually decorated, and many of them overlook the broad river. Boating and tennis are available at the resort. Two-night minimum. Deluxe to ultra-deluxe.

In 1985, a hurricane flooded the **Spring Creek Motel** (★) (25 miles south of Tallahassee at the end of Route 365 off Route 98, Spring Creek; 904-926-3751), so the clean, simple, concrete-block rooms now sport comfortable new furnishings, all handmade. There's little to do here but sit under the tall trees, eat at the excellent seafood restaurant next door and marvel at the freshwater springs that boil up in the middle of the nearby creek. It's a perfect place for quiet escape. Budget.

TALLAHASSEE AREA RESTAURANTS

Andrew's Second Act (228 South Adams Street, Tallahassee; 904-222-2759) has become one of the most popular eating spots in Tallahassee, especially during the legislative season. In this old setting with a new look, you might find a chalkboard special of duck teriyaki or sautéed grouper on a bed of linguine with lobster/sherry sauce and a host of other entrées from the popular Continental menu. Deluxe to ultra-deluxe.

Adams Street Café (228 South Adams Street, Tallahassee; 904-222-3444) opens in late morning for budget-priced burgers, sandwiches and other tasty lunch items. You'll see families, business folk and students here, delighting in the food and the prices.

If the display of luscious pastries doesn't stimulate your appetite, the menu at **Chez Pierre** (115 North Adams Street, Tallahassee; 904-222-0936) will. High-backed booths and flowered print tablecloths create a French café setting. You can enjoy chicken crêpes, onion soup, sautéed chicken breasts with mushrooms, and fish and scallops served in a lobster sauce. Moderate.

There are 120 items on the menu at **Bahn Thai** (1319 South Monroe Street, Tallahassee; 904-224-4765), all written in Thai and carefully explained in English. Despite its unassuming appearance and unlikely location among used car lots, diners wait in line for an hour or more to eat such traditional Asian fare as whole fish with hot sauce, sweet-and-sour shrimp and coconut milk soup. The menu, which includes Chinese dishes, is budget priced.

The Spartan (220 South Monroe Street; 904-224-9711) has been offering Greek food to Tallahasseans for years. Here you can choose souvlaki or spanakopita or try "Yorgo's Platter" for a wide sampling of Greek dishes. There is also non-Greek fare, such as beef Wellington and duck flambé with orange sauce. Seafood platters are popular at this intimate eatery, and include Florida lobster in season. Moderate.

Anthony's (1950-G Thomasville Road, Betton Place, Tallahassee; 904-224-1447), open for dinner only, offers traditional Italian dishes, as well as saltimbocca and fettucine Eduardo (a shrimp and crab combination in cheese sauce served over pasta). The high-backed wicker chairs and small tables make this an intimate place for romantic dining. Moderate.

Join the thousands of Tallahassee folk who have made a tradition of "fish dinners down at the bridge." "The bridge" is just below Panacea on the Ochlockonee Bay, and restaurants there are known for their excellent seafood. At **The Oaks Restaurant** (Route 98, south of Panacea; 904-984-5370), in spite of a seating capacity of over 200, you may still have to wait in line. This place serves up the usual platters with hushpuppies and grits; the shrimp boats, cold dinners and Florida lobster are added specialties. Moderate.

Diners at **Angelo's** (Route 98, south of Panacea; 904-984-5168) partake of sumptuous seafood "over the water," enjoying a spectacular view of the bay through huge windows or from the deck. The moderate to deluxe entrées include the usual seafood offerings, plus charbroiled seafood, creoles and stuffed fish. The grouper marguerite with a wine and cheese sauce reveals how this one-time fish camp has become sophisticated in recent years.

Not sophisticated, but worth the search, the **Spring Creek Restaurant** (★) (25 miles south of Tallahassee at the end of Route 365 off Route 98; 904-926-3751) concentrates on regional and seasonal "fruits of the sea" in a quiet setting under tall trees in the fishing village of Spring Creek. It's places like this that have finally put mullet on the list of respectable fish. Budget.

Some 18 miles northwest of Tallahassee is a place so hidden you'll find maps on the menus and business cards. Stashed down a dirt lane on 30 forested acres, **Nicholson Farmhouse** (★) (Route 12, 3.5 miles west of Havana; 904-539-5931) abides in a trio of marvelous old buildings. Start with a historical tour of the antique-filled farmhouse, built in 1828 by slave craftsmen and owned by the fourth generation of Nicholsons. Dine here, or in the home's original rustic smokehouse and its adjacent 1890s frame home. The place specializes in steaks that are "wet aged" at 34° for 21 days. The process works: this is some of the choicest beef in Florida. Moderate.

TALLAHASSEE AREA SHOPPING

Because Tallahassee serves as the major shopping center for north central Florida, just about anything you might wish to buy is available in the town's malls and shops. The fastest-growing area for specialty shops lies along Thomasville Road, serving the prestigious suburb of Killearn.

Betton Place (Bradford Road and Thomasville Highway) is the only shopping complex I've ever seen that made its home in a fine brick church building. The adaptation is clever and lovely, and the center features small specialty shops.

Market Square (Thomasville and Timberlane roads) also offers many specialty shops as well as an open-air market where local farmers bring their produce. Depending on the season, you may find anything from peaches to peanuts to fresh cane syrup.

Across from Market Square is a medley of specialty stores and restaurants called **The Pavilions** (1410 Market Street). One eye-catcher, **Narcissus** (904-668-4807), proffers snazzy women's swimsuits and elegant lingerie.

For anyone planning to explore the wilds of north Florida, a trip to the **Outdoors Shop** (2555 North Monroe Street; 904-386-4181) is the place to begin. Not only do they have everything you'll need for hunting, backpacking, camping or fishing, but they can tell you where to go and how to get there. They also carry a huge line of outdoor and sporty clothing.

If you're seeking souvenirs of substance, visit the gift shops at the **Museum of Florida History** (500 South Bronough Street; 904-488-1673) or the **Tallahassee Junior Museum** (3945 Museum Drive; 904-575-8684). Here you'll find items for children and adults ranging from T-shirts to history books to posters and calendars.

Antique shops abound in Tallahassee and in nearby Havana and Quincy. The serious connoisseur and the casual hobbyist can spend days browsing in small shops in private homes.

Bradley's Country Store (★) (Centerville Road, Moccasin Gap; 904-893-1647) is probably the only place of its kind to be listed on the National Register of Historic Places. Selling homemade sausage since 1910, the Bradley family also has stone-ground meal and grits, mayhaw jelly and other seasonal delights. A classy country store residing under ancient oak trees, Bradley's offers tasting samples of its famous sausage.

In the tiny town of Sopchoppy, artist **George Griffin's Suncat Ridge Pottery** (★) (Route 1, Box 30; 904-962-9311) features original pieces by a master potter.

TALLAHASSEE AREA NIGHTLIFE

Tallahassee nightlife is limited chiefly to quiet hotel and restaurant bars and noisy college gathering places. Big-name stars occasionally perform at the **Tallahassee-Leon County Civic Center** (505 West Pensacola Street; 904-222-0400). A few other night spots feature performances on an irregular basis. Check the Friday edition of the *Tallahassee Democrat*'s "Limelight" section for complete listings.

The Moon (1105 Lafayette Street, Tallahassee; 904-222-6666) is a big dance hall with four bars that features local acts and live music on some evenings and shows on others. Stars are booked on occasion. Cover.

Club Park Avenue (115 East Park Avenue, Tallahassee; 904-599-9143) features three bars, two dancefloors, a patio, video screens and deejay music. Drag shows entertain the gay crowd Saturday and Sunday nights. A mixed crowd frequents this brick walled, neon-lit club the rest of the week.

The **Tallahassee Symphony Orchestra** (904-224-0461) and **Florida State University's Symphony Orchestra** (904-644-6500) have full seasons of fine orchestral music. Students and faculty of FSU comprise the **University Opera** (904-644-6500); and baroque concerts are presented by the very popular **Bach Parley, Inc.** (904-877-6904). National and international artists appear on the **FSU Artist's Series** (904-644-5250) as well as the Tallahassee Community College's **TCC Artist Series** (904-488-9200).

The **Tallahassee Little Theatre** (904-224-8474) has been entertaining the community for almost forty years, and the **FSU Theatre** (904-644-5548) offers a full range of dramatic performances. Plays and concerts are also presented on the campus of **Florida A&M** (904-599-3000). In addition, the **Dance Repertory Theatre** (904-644-1023) at FSU gives annual shows.

TALLAHASSEE AREA BEACHES AND PARKS

Apalachicola National Forest—The largest of Florida's three national forests, this 557,000-acre preserve contains pine and hardwood forests, swamps, four rivers and a multitude of streams, springs and sinkholes. The variety is extraordinary, creating numerous recreational opportunities from wilderness canoeing to birdwatching to hunting and hiking.

Facilities: Several developed recreation areas with picnic areas and restrooms lie within the national forest. There are also semideveloped wilderness areas with picnic areas, fire pits, water and pit toilets. Hiking trails; information; 904-926-3561. *Fishing:* Excellent, in a number of rivers, lakes and streams. *Swimming:* Permitted at some recreation sites.

Camping: At **Silver Lake Recreation Area** there are 25 sites; $5 per night. Primitive camping is also allowed throughout the forest (no fee).

Getting there: A number of main highways and secondary roads—including Routes 375 and 65—offer access to the forest, which is located southwest of Tallahassee.

Lake Talquin State Recreation Area—This lovely, long lake, impounded in the gently rolling countryside, is most popular with local fishermen for the fine bass and other freshwater catches. Picnics and nature walks among tall oaks and pines and breezes off the water make it a welcome getaway place.

Facilities: Picnic areas, restrooms, nature trails; information, 904-922-6007. *Fishing:* Excellent in the large freshwater lake.

Camping: Not permitted, but available in three small county parks on the south side of the lake (off Route 20, follow signs); information, 904-487-3070. There are also some privately owned campgrounds in the area that offer tent sites and RV hookups. These include **Pat Thomas Park at Hopkins**

Landing (904-875-4544) with 30 sites, $5-10 per night; **Ingram's Marina** (904-627-2241) with 65 sites, $10 per night; and **Gainey's Talquin Lodge** (904-627-3822) with 60 sites, $15 per night.

Getting there: Located ten miles west of Tallahassee off Route 20.

Wakulla Springs, Edward Ball State Park—Spanish explorer Ponce de León is said to have wintered here, and one can easily see why he might choose this spot. The claim is that the beautiful spring is the world's deepest, and it was a favorite of swimmers and divers long before it became a state park. Boat trips along the Wakulla River allow visitors to see an unusual array of bird species. The wild beauty of the place explains why Hollywood has filmed a number of movies here.

Facilities: Picnic area, restrooms, bathhouse, lifeguards in swim areas, lodge, restaurant, glass-bottom boat and jungle-river cruises, nature trails; information, 904-222-7279. *Swimming:* Some of the best spring swimming in the state.

Getting there: Off Route 61, 13 miles south of Tallahassee.

St. Marks National Wildlife Refuge—One of the nation's oldest wildlife refuges, St. Marks encompasses thousands of acres of land and a large portion of Apalachee Bay. Visitors come chiefly for the wildlife, such as black bear, otter, alligator, white-tailed deer and raccoons, and for the thousands of migratory and native birds. The southern bald eagle is protected here, as are many other species.

Facilities: Picnic areas, restrooms, hiking trails, canoe access, observation tower, visitor center; information, 904-925-6121. *Fishing:* Excellent year-round in bay, lakes and rivers.

Camping: Not permitted on refuge, but available at the Florida Division of Forestry's **Newport Park** (Route 98 and 59, east of Newport; 904-925-6171). There are 30 sites; $8 per night. Bring your own water.

Getting there: Several routes enter the refuge; the main one is Route 59 off Route 98, south of Tallahassee.

Ochlockonee River State Park—This 392-acre park gives you a taste of the southern part of the Apalachicola forest without roughing it. The pine flatwoods are open here, providing good opportunities for spotting the endangered red-cockaded woodpecker and other birds. Deer, fox squirrel, bobcat and gray fox are attracted by the small grass ponds, bay heads and oak thickets; alligator warnings are posted.

Facilities: Picnic areas, restrooms, nature trails, scenic drive; information, 904-962-2771. *Fishing:* Both freshwater and saltwater. *Swimming:* Small protected beach on the Dead River, which is really quite lively as it empties into the Ochlockonee.

Camping: There are 30 sites, all with RV hookups; $10-12 per night.

Getting there: Off Route 319, four miles south of Sopchoppy.

Apalachicola Area

A Florida coast without beaches? Improbable as it sounds, that's what awaits along Route 98 in the Panhandle's Apalachicola Bay region. Protected by a distant barrier reef, this pretty stretch shows you what the Sunshine State looked like before the arrival of the unofficial state bird, the construction crane. The lack of beaches means minimal development, beautiful bayous, marshes, islands and quiet fishing villages.

For an interesting tour, take Route 65 at Eastpoint to **Fort Gadsden State Historical Site** (six miles south of Sumatra; 904-670-8988). The British built a fort here for recruiting blacks and Indians during the War of 1812. A short but bloody battle destroyed the fort a few years later, but Andrew Jackson established a supply base at the site in 1818 and Confederate forces occupied it during the Civil War. Little remains of the old fort, but the site includes a miniature replica, historical exhibits and a nice picnic area.

The Gorrie Bridge (Route 98) leads into Apalachicola, a struggling but charming old fishing and riverboat town with a glorious past. At the **Apalachicola Chamber of Commerce** (128 Market Street; 904-653-9419) you can pick up a self-guided walking tour brochure. Little remains of the town's cotton business (which dates back to the 1820s) except some historical markers and a crumbling warehouse, but the grand homes built by men who made their fortunes from cotton, lumber and sponges still stand in various states of glory.

You can tour **The Raney House**, where the Chamber of Commerce is located. The 1838 Greek revival mansion reflects the prosperity of its original owner, an Apalachicola cotton commission merchant. Built in the temple-pediment style, the house has four tall columns across the front. The wide halls, now displaying antiques and museum pieces, once served as breezy rooms during hot summer days.

Only two of Apalachicola's 43 original **cotton warehouses** (Water Street and Chestnut Avenue) remain. Compressed bales no longer stand in great piles, waiting for shipment around the world, but you can view the massive old buildings and imagine the dockside activity that followed a prosperous growing season. Next door stands the abandoned **sponge exchange**, a memorial to the days when the sponge trade at this port ranked third in the state.

Yellow fever was a serious problem during Apalachicola's early days. In an attempt to treat his patients by cooling them down, Dr. John Gorrie invented a machine for which all summer visitors to Florida must be grateful. At the **John Gorrie State Museum** (Gorrie Square; 904-653-9347; admission) you can see a replica of the first ice-making machine, the Gorrie invention that would one day lay the groundwork for modern air-conditioning. The small museum also features displays explaining the history and ecology of the bay.

Trinity Episcopal Church (Chestnut Avenue and Broad Street) was shipped in pieces from New York and assembled with wooden pegs in 1837 and 1838. The beautiful Greek revival building houses two historic organs, stained glass from several periods and a gallery designed for slaves who attended services here. Hand-stenciled designs grace the curved wooden ceiling. The church is on the National Register of Historic Places.

For a meditative visit, stroll under the moss-draped oaks in Apalachicola's **Chestnut Street Cemetery** (Route 98 and 7th Street), where you can find markers dating from 1832. Confederate and Union soldiers are buried here, as are a number of the area's leading citizens.

From the old waterfront area and **Battery Park** (Bay Avenue and 6th Street), you can watch the shrimp boats returning from a day's fishing, their nets spread out like dragonfly wings to dry. During oyster season the fishermen harvest the bay waters from their tiny boats, just as their fathers and grandfathers did before them, "tonging" with specially made long tongs for the shellfish that keep Apalachicola famous.

A large portion of the rivers, bays, bayous, marshes and islands of this region are included in the **Apalachicola National Estuarine Research Reserve** (headquarters at 261 7th Street; 904-653-8063). Though not really a traveler's destination, the headquarters will provide interested visitors with information on bird species, endangered animals, sea life and the importance of protecting the nation's ever-dwindling estuaries.

Westward from Apalachicola, Route 98 travels inland, returning to the coast at Port St. Joe, home of a monstrous and smelly paper mill. The town is attractive, though, and a short detour will take you to the **Constitution Convention State Museum** (200 Allen Memorial Way; 904-229-8029). Here talking mannequins reenact the finalizing of Florida's original constitution. Of interest, also, is a display of tools, china and personal items found at the site of short-lived Saint Joseph, an 1840-era boom town that was wiped out almost overnight by yellow fever and a hurricane.

APALACHICOLA AREA HOTELS

The little coastal towns along Route 98 to the east of Apalachicola have a number of mom-and-pop motels that cater to folks who enjoy the peace and quiet and the fine saltwater and river fishing. One of the nicest is **Sportsman's Lodge** (Route 98 and Route 65, Eastpoint; 904-670-8423), a big, sprawling place whose spacious rooms include kitchenettes. At your doorstep is a large marina where you can charter a boat for bay or deep-sea fishing. Budget.

The queen of Apalachicola's lodgings is the product of a million-dollar, historically faithful restoration of a circa-1907 wooden hotel. **The Gibson Inn** (Market and 4th streets; 904-653-2191), a handsome gray-and-white building, offers a choice of 31 rooms and suites, each individually decorated with period wallpaper, four-poster beds and antique armoires. The wrap-around double galleries invite rocking and relaxation. The lounge features a great old wooden bar, and the restaurant completes the gentle sense of stepping back in time that the entire Gibson brings off so well. Moderate.

You'll easily recognize the **Pink Camellia Inn** (145 Avenue E, Apalachicola; 904-653-2107) by its Pepto Bismol color and vast wraparound porches. Built in 1897, this cheery two-story house is simply adorable: four sunny guestrooms are stocked with antique beds, handmade quilts and artworks by the innkeepers who are also local artisans. Moderate rates include extra-large gourmet breakfasts and after-dinner homemade desserts.

You can dock your boat and clean your fish right at your door if you stay at the **Rainbow Inn and Marina** (123 Water Street, Apalachicola; 904-653-8139). The rooms are ordinary and only slightly musty, but the old waterfront location exudes a salt-air charm. Budget to moderate.

APALACHICOLA AREA RESTAURANTS

Florida's Panhandle coast is the place for seafood, and you won't find oysters better than those from the Apalachicola Bay. Most of the restaurants here serve everything the sea offers up; in fact, menus often seem cloned, featuring grouper, scallops, crab, mullet and whatever else is in season.

At **Julia Mae's Town Inn** (Route 98, Carrabelle; 904-697-3791) you'll get a big helping of oysters, along with french fries, hushpuppies and cole slaw. You may even meet the venerable Julia Mae, whose scallop burgers, Florida lobster, seasonal fish platters and stews and creoles have kept this slightly rundown café overlooking the marsh hopping for years. Moderate.

The Hut (Route 98, west of Apalachicola; 904-653-9410) is one more popular seafood-and-steak place that attracts folks who love Apalachicola oysters. Both local folk and visitors wait in line for the sumptuous seafood, beer and cocktails. Moderate.

At **The Grill** (100 Market Street, Apalachicola; 904-653-9510) you'll find local folks having a hearty breakfast (be sure to have some grits) or one of the downhome, moderate-priced, southern-cooked lunches or dinners. If you've forgotten what good hamburgers are like, you'll be pleased to find them here.

The restaurant at the restored **Gibson Inn** (Market and 4th streets, Apalachicola; 904-653-2191) brings elegance to this modest fishing town, with crystal, white tablecloths, brass lamps and probably the only official chef in the area, resulting in gourmet treatments of seafood, such as oysters *duxell* with brandied butter sauce or charbroiled dolphin with an avocado salsa. Lots of fresh vegetables and a varied menu make this a nice change for anyone tired of local fare; the ambience is old-fashioned and relaxed, the prices surprisingly moderate.

Three miles up the Apalachicola River from town, the **Anchor Room** (★) (200 Wadell Road; 904-653-9988) serves up wonderful local seafood to fishermen and river-boaters who do business at the marina next door, and to anyone else who has picked up rumors of this fish camp's dependable fare. Nothing fancy here, just a view of the river and plenty of hushpuppies. Budget to moderate.

APALACHICOLA AREA SHOPPING

The best shopping in the area is in Apalachicola, where local merchants still provide the personal attention so often missing in sprawling malls. Piggybacking on the Gibson Inn, the **Pied Piper Boutique** (54 Market Street; 904-653-8196) offers up-to-date women's styles.

Kristin Anderson sells her fine gold, silver and enamel "Kristinworks" jewelry at the **Long Dream Gallery** (32 Avenue D, Apalachicola; 904-653-2249). The shop also features pottery, textiles, glass and wood items created by top-notch craftspeople. The **Palmyra Gallery** (25 Avenue D, Apalachicola; 904-653-9090) specializes in trendy craft items from jazzy jewelry to cloisonné miniatures, as well as whimsical items such as dragons hatching from eggs and foam alligators.

APALACHICOLA AREA NIGHTLIFE

Except at occasional local lounges and roadside joints, nighttime is best for sleeping in this area. In Apalachicola local folks gather to drink at **The Hut** restaurant (Route 98, west of town; 904-653-9410). Or for a quiet cocktail you can sit at the antique bar or out on the porch of the **Gibson Inn** (Market and 4th streets, Apalachicola; 904-653-2191).

APALACHICOLA AREA BEACHES AND PARKS

Dead Lakes State Recreation Area—The thousands of dead trees still standing in the lake (formed when levees on the Apalachicola River blocked the Chipola River) give this 83-acre park its name. Two ponds, lake access, marshes and an abundance of longleaf pines make this an interesting spot for campers, anglers and nature lovers.

Facilities: Picnic area, restrooms, showers, nature trails; information, 904-639-2702. *Fishing:* Popular fishing site for bass, bream, perch and catfish.

Camping: There are 20 sites, ten with RV hookups; $8 per night.

Getting there: Located north of Wewahitchka along Route 71.

St. Joseph Peninsula State Park—Strung out on a long, pencil-shaped peninsula, this 2516-acre park provides gifts of the sea and shore usually reserved for barrier islands. With the Gulf on one side and St. Joseph Bay on the other, the seemingly endless stretches of white beach and high dunes

(Text continued on page 466.)

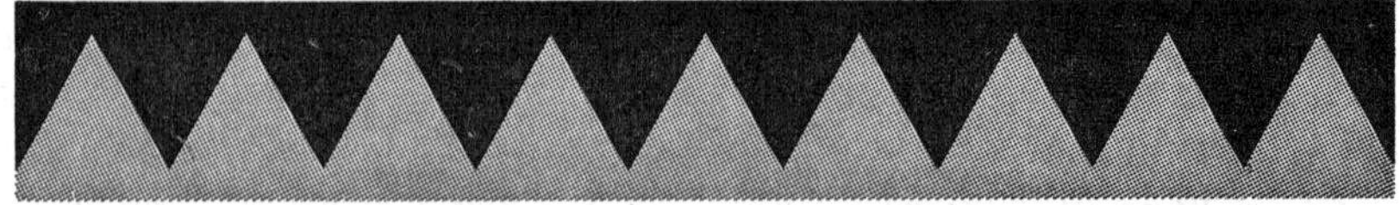

Apalachicola Area Barrier Islands

Look across the waters of St. George Sound and Apalachicola Bay and you will see a set of long islands hovering low on the brink of the horizon. Guarding some of the most productive fishing waters in the state and protecting the mainland from wind and storm, they provide nesting grounds for thousands of native and migratory birds. Their dunes and pinewoods harbor raccoons, ghost crabs, salt marsh snakes and diamondback terrapin. Their beaches glisten white and brilliant, attracting visitors in search of solitude and seashells.

Each of these barrier islands has a distinctive character. Easternmost, **Dog Island** lies about five miles across the sound from Carrabelle, boasting some of the highest and most unspoiled dunes in the state. Only a handful of residents live here year-round; only 100 houses and cottages stand among the dunes. Today most of Dog Island is a wildlife preserve, protecting at least 30 species of endangered animals, plants and birds. In the higher regions you can walk among ancient sand pines, rosemary and reindeer moss. The lower ridges are rich in slash pine, live oak, dune goldenrod, morning-glory and sea lavender. Black mangrove and marsh grasses thrive in the rich bayside estuaries.

Best of all, Dog Island provides lodging in its comfortable eight-unit **Pelican Inn** (★) (800-451-5294), one of Florida's most hidden hostelries. Rates are deluxe and you must bring all your food by boat or charter flight (which the inn will help you arrange), but the rewards are beachfront accommodations in fully equipped efficiency apartments with not even a streetlight to mar your enjoyment of the pristine environment. Daytrippers may come by their own boats or check dockside in Carrabelle for a varying schedule of ferry services provided by local skippers.

More accessible and more populated is **St. George Island,** a 25-mile-long narrow strip of land, much of which is being rapidly developed. It is reached by the St. George Island Bridge and Causeway, off Route 98 at Eastpoint. Nine glorious miles of undeveloped beaches and dunes,

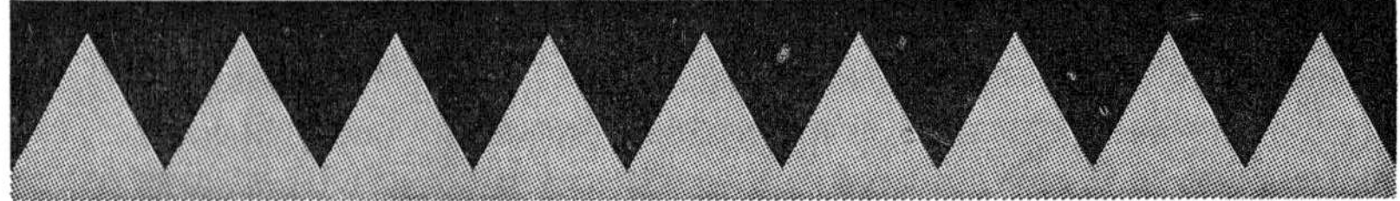

pine and oak forests, bayshore and sandy coves and saltmarshes have been set aside in the beautiful 1883-acre **Dr. Julian G. Bruce St. George Island State Park** (904-927-2111). A 2.5-mile hiking trail, beginning at the campground, leads through pine flatwoods and coastal scrub to Gap Point beside the rich bay waters. Amenities include observation decks, picnic areas and restrooms. Swimming off the glistening white beach is excellent. Surf and bay fishing can result in catches of redfish, ladyfish, Spanish mackerel, bluefish or pompano. Camping is allowed at 60 sites with RV hookups; $10 per night.

St. George's most interesting lodging is the **St. George Inn** (Franklin Boulevard and Pine Street; 904-927-2903), whose eight rooms feature cannonball beds, as well as French doors leading onto the broad wraparound veranda. Victorian in style and appearance, the moderately priced inn has both restaurant and lounge.

Little St. George (904-653-8063), an appendage to the main island but now separated by a manmade channel, lies to the west. Site of a 78-foot historic lighthouse, Little St. George is now a state reserve and can only be reached by boat.

Covering the entire 12,358 acres of a triangular shaped island, **St. Vincent National Wildlife Refuge** (★) (904-653-8808) is also accessible only by boat, for day use only. St. Vincent is unlike most barriers. Four miles wide at one point, it has 14 miles of beaches and 80 miles of crisscrossing sand roads and features several freshwater lakes and swamps. Almost 200 species of birds have been spotted; loggerhead turtles lay eggs on the beaches; bald eagles nest in the pines; alligators bask in the sun. Sambur deer and feral hogs recall the times when the island was a private hunting estate.

An outdoor kiosk at the town of Indian Pass (end of Route 30-B) provides information about St. Vincent Island. The refuge hosts an open house each October; otherwise you must get there on your own. If you do, your reward will be a rich experience of a varied natural Florida.

and the rich waters attract over 200 species of migratory and nesting birds. Scallops, octopi, crabs and flounder reside in the bay, small mammals in the marshes and dense woods. A 1650-acre wilderness preserve enhances the natural attractions offered by this beautiful park.

Facilities: Picnic areas, restrooms, nature trails, concession stand, marina, bathhouse; information, 904-227-1327. *Fishing:* Surf and bay fishing; crabbing and scalloping. *Swimming:* On miles and miles of beach.

Camping: There are 119 sites, all with hookups; $15-18 per night. Also available are moderately priced cabins that can sleep up to four people.

Getting there: Off Route 30, west of Route 90 near Port St. Joe.

Panama City Area

The white, sugary beaches, clear green, blue and turquoise Gulf water and the glitzy Coney Island-style attractions seem to keep the crowds of visitors to Panama City Beach occupied. However, there are a few other things to see and do should it rain, or if you've had too much sun. Stop in at the **Visitor Information Center** (415 Beckrich Road, Suite 205; 904-234-6575) for suggestions.

You'll have plenty to enjoy along Panama City Beach's Gulf-front road, which leads past neon motels, towering condominiums, beautiful beaches and a string of amusement park rides. Dragons and monsters and rattling roller coasters lure crowds to the **Miracle Strip Amusement Park** (12000 Front Beach Road; 904-234-9873; admission), while bumper boats, go-carts and video arcades draw them to **Fun City** (13626 Front Beach Road; 904-234-5507; admission).

For a quieter experience, visit the **Junior Museum of Bay County** (1731 Jenks Avenue, Panama City; 904-769-6128) and learn how Florida pioneers lived and worked. Stroll the nature trail or explore the log houses and the grist mill. A special room highlights hands-on activities relating to the current main exhibit.

You can feed dolphins, bait some crab traps and watch a shrimp net being reeled in aboard the **Glass Bottom Boat** (3605 Thomas Drive at the Treasure Island Marina, Panama City Beach; 904-234-8944). The company also offers shelling tours to prime spots on Shell Island.

You can discover a lot about the creatures of the sea at **Gulfworld** (15412 Front Beach Road; 904-234-5271; admission) as you watch stingrays and performing dolphins. There are also talking parrots, trained seals and a walk-through shark tank.

Also stop by the **Museum of Man and the Sea** (17314 Back Beach Road; 904-235-4101; admission), a small but impressive diving museum. You'll see 19th-century underwater equipment and sea-lab chambers used in modern oceanographic exploration, as well as treasures from Spanish shipwrecks and an informative display on underwater oil drilling.

Because the coast itself is the area's main attraction, treat yourself to an excursion to **Shell Island (★)**, a pristine state-owned island with seven miles of undeveloped beach and pine land. Sightseeing trips from Panama City Beach may be arranged through **Captain Anderson's Dinner Boat** (5550 North Lagoon Drive; 904-234-5940) and **Island Star Cruises** (6400 West Highway 98; 904-235-2809) as well as **Treasure Island Marina** (3605 Thomas Drive; 904-234-8944), which also offers glass-bottom boat tours.

For an entirely different outlook on the coast, **Coastal Helicopters** (12204 Front Beach Road, Panama City Beach; 904-769-6117) will take you up for a fine view of the white beaches and islands.

PANAMA CITY AREA HOTELS

With over 16,000 rooms to choose from in the Panama City area, from massive highrises to modest motels, decision-making can be tough.

Some of the best lodging buys are found near downtown Panama City, seven or more miles from the beach. For example, at the **Best Western Bayside Inn** (711 West Beach Drive; 904-763-4622) you'll find spacious rooms with blue-and-white appointments appropriate to the coast, some with efficiency kitchens and many with lovely views of the bay. Moderate.

Marriott's Bay Point Resort (100 Delwood Beach Road, Panama City; 904-234-3307) shows how $40 million can turn a country club into an exclusive resort. Most visitors stay in the luxurious 200-room pink hotel overlooking the Grand Lagoon; there are also villas to rent. Everything you need is on the grounds, including numerous restaurants, lounges, shops, pools, tennis courts and two golf courses. The only thing lacking is a beautiful beach, but the resort's own paddlewheeler will take you and your ice chest across St. Andrews Bay to pristine Shell Island for miles of white sand and crystal clear water. Ultra-deluxe.

For those who prefer being in the big middle of the Panama City Beach hubbub, the moderately priced **Bikini Beach Resort Motel** (11001 Front Beach Road; 904-234-3392) offers bedrooms and suites with all-electric, fully equipped kitchens. The decor is ordinary-motel, but the Gulfside rooms have nice balconies overlooking a fabulous beach.

For a luxurious escape from the glitz, the **Edgewater Beach Resort** (11212 Front Beach Road; 904-235-4044) provides guests with all the beauties of Panama City Beach in a classy, protected environment. With property extending from shore to shore, there are both tower and mid-rise condominiums featuring individually decorated apartments overlooking the turquoise Gulf waters and wide white beach. Intimate golf villas reside closer to the beach. Everything, from the excellent restaurants to golf and tennis and swimming pools, is reserved for the guests. Deluxe to ultra-deluxe.

If you like being where the action is, you'll appreciate the easy walk to shops, amusements, restaurants and fishing pier from the five-story **Osprey Motel** (15801 Front Beach Road, Panama City Beach; 904-234-0303). Though this popular beach area can get pretty crowded, you can escape to your private balcony and a spacious room, tastefully decorated and featuring a fully equipped kitchen. The moderate rates make it attractive to families.

Comfortably removed from Panama City Beach's main hullabaloo, the **Sugar Sands Motel** (20723 Front Beach Road; 904-234-8802) offers a variety of accommodations from single rooms to various-sized apartments. Best of all, the beautiful white beach is reasonably uncluttered, and the rates for the modest but well-kept rooms are moderate.

Just when you think Panama City Beach is nothing but motels and condos, you come onto the pretty blue-and-cream beach house that is **Cobb's Gulfview Inn** (21722 Front Beach Road, Sunnyside Beach; 904-234-6051). This bed and breakfast rarity is across the road from the dunes and the beach, but the grassy yard and the flowers, the lattice trim and the breakfast with homemade jams make this oasis a real treat. The five moderately priced rooms all have private baths.

PANAMA CITY AREA RESTAURANTS

It's said that people drive a hundred miles to eat amid the lush flora of **The Greenhouse** (443 Grace Avenue; 904-763-2245), an intimate Continental café in the Olde Towne Mini Mall in downtown Panama City. If you try the filet à la maison with sherried mushrooms and reduced cream sauce, you'll see why. Moderate.

The sign is fading but the aroma wafting out the door summons you through the leaded glass doors of **The Pasta Peddler** (448 Harrison Avenue; 904-763-0059), an unadorned downtown café in Panama City. In fact, the place smells so good that the lack of distinctive decor matters not. The homemade minestrone contains 15 vegetables; the broiled Italian sausage with green peppers and onions is a tasty addition to the moderately priced selection of traditional seafood, veal and chicken dishes.

The very popular **Harbour House** (3001-A West 10th Street; 904-785-9053) offers a pretty view of St. Andrews Bay, a few blocks from downtown Panama City. This family-style airy restaurant has a moderately priced seafood and beef menu, but folks come from all around for the budget lunch buffet, which offers 40 or more of the restaurant's specialties.

Marriott's Bay Point Resort (100 Delwood Beach Road, Panama City; 904-234-3307) is home to several excellent restaurants. For a dining experience rare since the passing of Florida's grand old hotels, get dressed up, stroll through the posh main lobby and spend a couple of deluxe gourmet hours in the hushed elegance of **Fiddler's Green,** whose high windows overlook the grounds and lagoon. At the ultra-deluxe **Terrace Court** you'll be served nouvelle cuisine by tuxedoed waiters; the rack of lamb is carved tableside. The moderately priced **Sunset Grill** offers traditional but excellent seafood entrées; you can watch the yachts slip in and out of the marina as you dine.

As you would expect, seafood tops the list of restaurant offerings in Panama City Beach. **Captain Anderson's** (5551 North Lagoon Drive; 904-234-2225) serves it up by the ton (the restaurant seats 600) quite successfully. Greek salads and homemade breads and desserts set this popular place apart from many of the seafood-platter establishments; so do the varied grilled fish and steak entrées. Moderate to deluxe.

The place for dependable, robust, large portions of pasta and veal is **The Italian Inn** (11040 Middle Beach Road, Panama City Beach; 904-234-0707). Mediterranean in style, the family-owned eatery is known for its veal scallopini and veal *valstanno,* stuffed with prosciutto and cheese. There's also fettucine, lasagna, spaghetti and stuffed shells laden with meat sauce. Moderate.

For a switch from fish, try the spicy red beans and rice at **J. Michaels** (5101 West 98, Panama City Beach; 904-785-9257), a nice old gray stucco place with tile floors, stained-glass windows, antique furnishings and a tin roof. Other Cajun specialties include sautéed oysters in a cup with an incredible secret sauce. You can also choose from many traditional southern dishes. Moderate.

Despite the deluxe prices and the medieval armor, the **Boar's Head Restaurant** (17290 Front Beach Road, Panama City Beach; 904-234-6628) is a casual, rustic, big-barn of a place for a leisurely, luxurious meal. The house specialty is prime rib, but they also chargrill and blacken fish and do lots of interesting things with shrimp and lobster. There's also an impressive wine list.

PANAMA CITY AREA SHOPPING

If teenagers can't find a seaside souvenir or a bathing suit in the Panama City area, they might as well give up. Dozens of stores that seem to be designed just for them are bulging with air-brushed T-shirts, sunglasses, crazy hats, beach toys and disappearing bikinis.

You'll find a variety of bargains from name-brand companies at the **Manufacturer's Outlet Center** (105 West 23rd Street, Panama City), where over a dozen stores feature clothing, shoes and stylish accessories.

The **Promenade Mall** (8317 Front Beach Road, Panama City Beach) is a festive specialty mall with pine siding and a red roof.

Anglophiles can have a great time among the china, tinned biscuits and English toys at the **British Pantry & Gift Shoppe** (437 Grace Avenue, Panama City; 904-763-9781).

Essentially a store for teachers, **The Learning Shoppe** (500 Harrison Avenue, Panama City; 904-769-8738) has a wonderful selection of educational toys and games for children of all ages.

PANAMA CITY AREA NIGHTLIFE

Much of the area's nightlife rocks during the summer months and hibernates in the winter. But you can find some things to do year-round.

The Rader family's Nashville-imitation **Ocean Opry** (8400 Front Beach Road, Panama City Beach; 904-234-5464) keeps drawing crowds to its big auditorium for country music and cornpone. They sing, they dance, they make you part of the family, and audiences love it.

Moonlight cruises are a good way to spend a balmy evening in these parts. You can go on a dinner-and-dancing or gospel-music cruise with **Captain Anderson** (5550 North Lagoon Drive, Panama City Beach; 904-234-5940).

U-Turn Sunburn Saloon (17283 West Route 98, Panama City Beach; 904-233-6625) is a hip place to be when the sun goes down—and much later of course. This beach bar has miles of wood floors, a swimming pool and live Top-40 or southern rock. Cover.

C Shell Lounge (Ramada Inn; 3001 West 10th Street, Panama City; 904-785-0561) entertains with anything from fashion shows to the remarkable steel band from a local high school. In summer there is a tiki bar on the deck overlooking the beautiful bay.

With decks over the beach and plenty of tropical drinks, **Pineapple Willies** (9900 Beach Boulevard, Panama City Beach; 904-235-0928) has a Caribbean feel. You'll hear a variety of live music and comedy routines reminiscent of a few years past. Cover.

With 20 bars, four levels (three inside) and perpetual day-and-night crowds, **Spinnaker** (8795 Thomas Drive, Panama City Beach; 904-234-7882) is one hot sand spot. Regular live bands include national artists like Three Dog Night and The Byrds. Cover. Closed during the winter.

PANAMA CITY AREA BEACHES AND PARKS

St. Andrews State Recreation Area—Its proximity to Panama City and its beautiful 1063 acres of beaches, dunes, pinewoods and marshes account for this being one of Florida's most popular recreation areas. It is bounded by the Gulf of Mexico, the Grand Lagoon and the ship channel so just about every water sport is available. The sand is like snow, the water clear as glass, the dunes rolling and covered with sea oats. A reconstructed "cracker" turpentine still can be found in the park.

Facilities: Picnic areas, restrooms, bathhouses, snack and grocery concessions, nature trails; information, 904-234-2522. *Fishing:* Two fishing piers and a jetty provide excellent year-round fishing for Spanish mackerel, redfish, flounder and more. *Swimming:* Excellent in clear Gulf waters and shallow pool behind the jetty.

Camping: There are 176 sites, all with RV hookups; $15 per night.

Getting there: Take Route 392 (Thomas Drive) off Route 98, east of Panama City, to the park entrance.

Shell Island (★)—This "adjunct" to St. Andrews State Recreation Area can be reached only by boat. There are no facilities, but there are seven miles of beach and wilderness, a pristine oasis where Panama City's condo skyline is almost out of sight and certainly out of mind. A number of charter boats will ferry you over from the mainland for a fee, which is well worth it, especially if you take along a cooler and an umbrella and spend the day.

Getting there: Information on boat charters available at St. Andrews State Park (904-233-5140) or local private boat tour companies.

Fort Walton Beach Area

Looking for a spot where alligators roam and traffic isn't crowding you all day? Then you've come to the right place. The Fort Walton Beach area is graced by beautiful salt marshes and miles of rolling dunes not yet leveled by overdevelopment. Wide expanses of turquoise water and sugary sand invite serendipitous strolls.

You'll find the alligators in rivers and streams that empty into Choctawhatchee Bay. This rich jungle wilderness, shaded by grand magnolia trees, also attracts birds and an abundance of other wildlife.

Long ago, steamers plied the bay's beautiful waters, carrying the cypress, pine and oak exploited from inland forests. Once the site of a giant lumber company, **Eden State Gardens** (north of Route 98 or Route 395, Point Washington; 904-231-4214; admission) still exhibits the remains of long ship-loading piers stretching into Choctawhatchee Bay. The main attraction, though, is a handsome two-story restored lumber baron's house, built in 1896 to look like an antebellum mansion and now filled with fine antiques. Broad landscaped lawns, shaded by moss-draped oaks, blaze with camellias and azaleas in the spring.

There is a small, homegrown **Historical Society Museum (★)** (115 Westview Avenue; 904-678-2615; admission) in the little town of Valparaiso, where you can learn how the Florida pioneers lived before the coming of the condos, and how the Indians lived in this historically rich region centuries before the pioneers came.

The chief attractions in Destin and Fort Walton Beach will always be the sand and the sea. For pointers on other sightseeing destinations, check with the **Destin Chamber of Commerce** (1021 Route 98 East; 904-837-6241) and the **Fort Walton Beach Chamber of Commerce** (34 Miracle Strip Parkway; 904-244-8191).

People who enjoy fishing the Gulf will like the small but interesting **Destin Fishing Museum** (east of Destin Bridge; 904-654-1011; admission), which presents video programs and includes a dry aquarium and an artifacts room displaying the history of the area's important fishing industry.

The preserved killer whale and huge mola mola (also headfish) make for interesting perusal at the **Museum of the Sea and Indian** (Beach Highway, also called Old Route 98, eight miles east of Destin; 904-837-6625; admission). The best part, though, is the great assortment of American Indian artifacts like Chief Osceola's dugout canoe and a corn grinder fashioned from a hardwood stump. You'll also find dozens of arrowheads, hoes and other tools and woven baskets.

For porpoise and bird shows and an underwater zoo, consider the **Gulfarium** (1010 Miracle Strip Parkway Southeast, Fort Walton Beach; 904-244-5169; admission). The Living Sea exhibit features sharks, moray eels, sea turtles and other exotic creatures in natural habitats.

The **Air Force Armament Museum** (100 Museum Drive, Eglin Air Force Base, Fort Walton Beach; 904-882-4062) presents seven decades of history through displays of aircraft, missiles and guns.

The **Indian Temple Mound Museum** (139 Miracle Strip Parkway, Fort Walton Beach; 904-243-6521; admission) explains the story of the Fort Walton area from the days of prehistoric peoples. Artifacts of the southeastern Indians and a series of exhibits appeal to all ages. The actual mound beside the small but excellent exhibit area is a National Historic Landmark.

Children and nostalgic adults will enjoy the restored one-room **Camp Walton School House Museum** (★) (107 1st Street, Fort Walton Beach; 904-244-3433; admission), which recall the days of spelling primers and hickory sticks. A pine-needle path leads to a restored old post office, with letters and magazines still waiting to be picked up from rustic wooden mailboxes.

FORT WALTON BEACH AREA HOTELS

There is much to choose from in the way of lodging in the Fort Walton Beach area, from simple beach cottages to elegant resort townhouses and condominiums. For detailed information on lodging in the quiet beach communities that lie along Route 30-A from Inlet Beach to Dune Allen and the more developed beaches from Four Mile Village to Frangista Beach, write the **South Walton Tourist Development Council** (P.O. Box 1248, Santa Rosa Beach, FL 32459; 800-822-6877).

For a grand experience of nostalgia wrapped in newness, rent a pastel pretend-Victorian cottage at **Seaside** (Route 30-A; 904-231-4224), a resort community built as an experiment in urban design and modeled on old-fashioned East Coast resorts. The town is so new it may not even be on your map, but you'll find it just west of Seagrove Beach. The frame houses are individually furnished and designed to a strict picket-fence-and-gingerbread code. Tennis courts, beach pavilions, pool, restaurants and shops are all part of the community. Deluxe to ultra-deluxe.

Destin claims to have more luxury condominiums than motel rooms, giving you plenty to choose from. Several large resorts offer golf, tennis and swimming pools as well as miles of beach, luxurious accommodations and the usual resort amenities. Chief among these is **Sandestin Beach Resort** (Highway 98 East, ten miles east of Destin; 904-267-8000). A mile-and-a-half farther west is **Seascape Resort** (Emerald Coast Parkway; 904-837-9181). Deluxe to ultra-deluxe.

Three golf courses, 21 tennis courts and a huge marina make **Bluewater Bay** (1950 Bluewater Boulevard, Niceville; 904-897-3613) the ideal resort for anyone who doesn't need the beach. Located across broad Choctawhatchee Bay from Destin, Bluewater offers beautifully appointed townhomes among the oak groves that set this place apart from so many sun-baked lodgings. Restaurant and shopping on the property. Prices range from deluxe to ultra-deluxe.

For deluxe-priced lodgings right on the beach, try the 38-unit **Sea Oats Motel** (Scenic Route 98, Destin; 904-837-6655). The carpets in these plain rooms have a few stains but are very clean, and all front the beach. Kitchenettes and picnic tables make this a good place for families on a budget.

Fort Walton Beach offers a number of the usual motels, but there is luxury to be found here, too. **The Breakers of Fort Walton Beach** (381 Santa Rosa Boulevard; 904-244-9127) has luxurious, fully furnished beachfront condominiums for ultra-deluxe prices. Along with a beautiful beach, the seven-story complex offers tennis courts, a grocery store, video store, exercise room with whirlpool and sauna and other amenities for convenience and contentment.

For a moderate room, try the **Leeside Inn** (1350 Highway 98 East, Okaloosa Island, Fort Walton Beach; 904-243-7359), across the busy highway from a nice beach park and next to a tiny piece of National Seashore land on the bay. The traffic is a drawback if you are trying to get to the beach, but you won't find a nicer room at this price, and the bayside rooms are amazingly quiet. Kitchenettes available.

FORT WALTON BEACH AREA RESTAURANTS

Word has it that **Nicks** (Route 1, Basin Bayou, Freeport; 904-835-2222) changes hands among family members every seven years, but the happy clientele of this rowdy and fun concrete block oyster house remains consistent. The drawing card is terrific fried, steamed and grilled seafood for moderate prices.

At the avant-garde community of Seaside, you can dine at **Bud & Alley's** (Route 30-A; 904-231-5900) on local seafood, pasta dishes, steaks and hearty soups. Their deluxe-priced dinners include such tempting fare as chicken breasts sautéed with leeks, prosciutto and lemon butter, marinated fish, grilled lamb chops and crawfish. The setting is upscale and airy—very Seaside.

If you want a bite without a big bill, the **Sip and Dip** (Route 30-A, Seaside; 904-231-4833) alongside the breezy boardwalk patio offers *muffuleta* and other creative sandwiches as well as old-fashioned soda fountain drinks.

Unless you are staying in Grayton Beach, you might miss the **Grayton Corner Café** (★) (Route 283 off Route 30-A; 904-231-1211), a casual old beach house facing the dunes. A sign warns that if the surf is good the chef may close early; otherwise he'll serve you grilled marinated seafood, oysters on the half shell, a great shrimp salad or creative sandwiches. Budget.

Bayou Bill's (Route 98 East, Santa Rosa Beach; 904-267-3849) makes up for its non-beach location by serving terrific seafood in a spirited nautical setting. Crowds wait cheerfully for the assortment of platters, blackened fish, steamed buckets and varied chalkboard entrées. Moderate.

The red beans and rice are so authentic at **Frank LeBleau's Cajun Kitchen** (Route 98 East, Santa Rosa Beach; 904-267-3724), you'll swear you're in Louisiana. Locals gather here under Frank's thousand gimmie-caps nailed to the ceiling to partake of gumbos, crawfish pie and barbecue, as well as big seafood platters. The Cajun breakfast omelettes are worth getting up for. Breakfast and lunch are budget-priced; dinner budget to moderate.

For fine dining in Destin, try the **Flamingo Café** (414 Route 98 East; 904-837-0961). The decor is an elegant black and white, from the checkered floors to the menus, which feature specially prepared seafood dishes such as grouper with mushrooms and artichoke hearts in a Madeira lemon sauce. Or try the veal steak with three sauces and citrus fruit, or the hot crayfish salad. Moderate to deluxe.

Enjoy the spectacular view of the Destin harbor and seafood prepared in a European manner with a touch of Louisiana, at the casually elegant **Marina Café** (320 Highway 98 East, Destin; 904-837-7960). The menu includes chicken, lamb and veal dishes along with local shellfish dishes. Moderate to deluxe.

Several decades ago, circus entertainer Harrison Thomas Babe took a bad fall during a show. He scooped up the insurance money, moved to Destin and opened **Harry T's Boathouse** (320 East Route 98; 904-654-6555). Harry died in 1974, but this zany place is a testament to his crazy escapades. There's a stuffed giraffe's head dead center as you walk in, plus great circus memorabilia parked all over the walls. Tucked inside a yacht club, the popular eatery features a waterfront patio and 120 moderately priced dishes, including chicken, fish, blackened steaks and pasta.

The Backporch (Route 98 East, Destin; 904-837-2022) is so popular with travelers that it sells its own T-shirts. The small menu features broiled, baked, steamed, chargrilled and fried seafood served in baskets and a nice smoked yellow-fin tuna salad. You can eat on butcher-block tables inside or at picnic tables on a deck right by the beach. Budget to moderate.

Scampi's (Route 98 East, Destin; 904-837-7686) is a three-ring-circus sort of place with a huge buffet, perfect for a family or a seafood-lover who can't make up his mind. The pretend pilings, nets and ropes may seem a bit hokey, but hungry diners flock to this big, noisy place. Moderate to deluxe.

All that fresh seafood you eat at **The Sound** (108 West Route 98, Fort Walton Beach; 904-243-2722) is plucked from the blue-green waters just out the eatery's backdoor. Sprinkled with plants and trees, this moderate-to-deluxe-priced spot overlooks the Santa Rosa Sound and serves up dishes like baked stuffed shrimp and sautéed grouper with dijon sauce and parmesan. There are also good steaks and prime rib.

Old photos and opera posters set the mood for the varied Italian cuisine at **Perri's** (300 Eglin Parkway, Fort Walton Beach; 904-862-4421). Veal fettucine dinners are a family specialty. The handsome brick building with green awnings features a cantina in the back. Moderate.

FORT WALTON BEACH AREA SHOPPING

There are shopping malls and strip centers in Fort Walton and Destin, as well as souvenir and shell shops in the more populated beach areas.

The most colorful shopping experience awaits visitors to **The Market at Sandestin** (5494 Route 98 East, Destin), a very trendy festival mall with lots of neon and color and many upscale shops, including **Classic Cargo** (904-837-8171). It's hard to pass by this store without stopping to gaze in the gleaming windows at the classic collections of fine designer china, crystal, silver and porcelain.

Sundog Books (Route 30-A, Seaside; 904-231-5481) offers some trashy beach reading, but its main stock consists of top-notch fiction and nonfiction and a good supply of wonderful children's books.

Modeled on a Mediterranean open-air market, colorful **Per-spi-cas-ity** (Route 30-A, Seaside; 904-231-5829) has a wonderful assortment of trendy casual clothes and gift and household items. Shop under canvas awnings to the accompaniment of classical music and sea breezes.

This That and The Other (★) (one mile east of Route C393 on Route 30-A, Santa Rosa Beach; 904-267-3190), hidden back among the trees, contains a treasure trove of early American antiques, china, quilts, salt-glaze pottery and weavings.

The Rainbow Connection (869 Route 98 East, Destin; 904-837-2055) features the varied colors and styles of "Kooler" sportswear, designed by a local manufacturer. With ten brilliant colors and over 50 styles, including some for children, the shop lives up to its name.

A seafarer's delight, **Armchair Sailor** (546 Route 98, Destin; 904-837-1577) stocks books on shipwrecks and pirates, sailing instruction and naval history. Navigational charts and instruments as well as nature guides are also featured at this nautical gold mine.

Florida Pottery (224 Eglin Parkway, Fort Walton Beach; 904-863-5181) smells of dried flowers and scented candles and features shelves and shelves of china, glass and other housewares, along with gift items and wicker furniture. Bargain hunters can have a heyday.

If beachwear and seaside souvenirs are something you can't resist, you'll love **Alvin's Island** (1204 Route 98 East, Okaloosa Island, 904-244-3913; and 1073 Route 98 East, Destin, 904-837-5178). Air-brushed T-shirts, shells that never saw a Florida beach, postcards for your friends and enemies back home—they're all at Alvin's.

FORT WALTON BEACH AREA NIGHTLIFE

The area swings, rocks or snoozes at night, depending on the season and the crowd. Some of the most popular year-round nightlife goes on at restaurants. **Bud & Alley's** at Seaside (Route 30-A; 904-231-5900) features live jazz and blues bands on summer weekends. There are outdoor movies and other entertainment at Seaside, too.

At **Harry T's Boathouse** (Destin Yacht Club, Route 98 East, Destin; 904-837-6716), overlooking the harbor, you can dance to a contemporary jazz-rock band or stroll along the docks. Lots of glass and many levels make this a delightful place. Cover.

Nightown (Palmetto Street and Azalea Drive, Destin; 904-837-6448), bright with laser lights, rocks with live bands and dancing. For a respite from the frenetic pace, you can escape to Nightown's second bar for a New Orleans-style mood and quieter music. Cover.

At **A. J.'s** (125 Destin Highway East, Destin; 904-837-1913) you can kick back under a giant tiki hut overlooking the bay. With live reggae or Caribbean vibes as a backdrop, who could ask for more?

Timbers Nitespot (1220 Siebert Street, Fort Walton Beach; 904-243-5400) is festooned with motion picture posters. Drop by early for a drink by candlelight, or late for dancing to live reggae and Motown music. Cover.

Yesterday's Lounge (Route 98 East, Destin; 904-837-1292) has a big dancefloor and a 1961 Cadillac on the roof, which lets you know that nostalgia is featured here, including occasional Elvis impersonations and a '50s- and '60s-era house band.

"Hog's breath is better than no breath" is the slogan of **Hog's Breath Saloon** (1239 Siebert Street, Fort Walton Beach; 904-243-4646), a wild and outrageously fun bar. Reggae and rock bands play regularly in this ramshackle building. Cover.

Mellow out at **Fudpuckers** (108 Santa Rosa Boulevard, Fort Walton Beach; 904-243-3833), a casual restaurant/bar with outdoor patios and live reggae, rock-and-roll or acoustic. Cover.

FORT WALTON BEACH AREA BEACHES AND PARKS

Drive the coastal roads through south Walton County toward Destin and Fort Walton, and you'll discover many miles of almost pristine coastline. Only an occasional highrise mars the vista. If you peel off Route 98 wherever you can, you will come to little pull-off roads where local folks park for a day at the beach. From Inlet Beach to Dune Allen there are bluff-like dunes overlooking the snow-white beaches and the turquoise Gulf.

Grayton Beach State Recreation Area—A sensational broad white beach and high dunes give this 356-acre park the reputation of being one of the loveliest on the state's coast. Boardwalks carry visitors across the ever-changing dunes and among the vital sand-holding sea oats. Besides the perfect beach and clear blue-green water, the park offers easy access to a brackish lake abundant in both freshwater and saltwater creatures, an extensive salt marsh, remnants of a pine forest and shady live-oak and palmetto hammocks.

Facilities: Picnic areas, restrooms, nature trails, vending machines; information, 904-231-4210. *Fishing:* In both the surf and lake. *Swimming:* Excellent, in blue-green clear Gulf waters.

Camping: There are 37 sites, all with RV hookups; $14 per night.

Getting there: Just east of Seaside on Route 30-A, at intersection of Route 283.

Henderson Beach State Recreation Area—Though there are no dunes here, this beautiful public beach has snow-white sand and crystal-clear water. It is also close enough to populated areas and the busy highway to guarantee wall-to-wall sunbathers during the summer months.

Facilities: Boardwalk, restrooms, showers, picnic areas; information, 904-837-7550. *Fishing:* Good for surf casting. *Swimming:* Excellent.

Getting there: At Destin, on West 98.

Rocky Bayou (Fred Gannon) State Recreation Area—This park reveals why not everyone in the Panhandle goes to the beach. Located on a gentle bayou off sprawling Choctawhatchee Bay, the restful park provides walks among the pines, oaks and magnolias, as well as access to excellent freshwater and saltwater fishing. The beautiful picnic area affords fine views of the broad bay.

Facilities: Picnic areas, restrooms, nature trails; information, 904-833-9144. *Fishing:* Excellent bay fishing and crabbing; freshwater fishing in Rocky Creek. *Swimming:* Nice, but not as sensational as the beaches across the bay.

Camping: There are 42 sites, some with RV hookups; $10 per night.

Getting there: Located five miles east of Niceville on Route 20.

Pensacola Area

Almost in Alabama, the Pensacola Area has just about everything you'd expect to find in Florida: alligators and historic districts, old lighthouses and Hispanic landmarks, memorable seafood restaurants and excellent fishing tackle shops. Come for the Dixieland scene and the Gulf islands. Stay to enjoy the Naval Aviation Museum and the national seashore. This area is one sleeper that will keep you wide awake.

The loveliest approach to the Pensacola area is via Route 399, along the sugar-white beaches of **Gulf Islands National Seashore** (see "Pensacola Area Beaches and Parks" section below). There are many places to cross the dunes on boardwalks or paths to enjoy the pristine beach.

West of the community of Pensacola Beach, with its water slides and amusement parks, the National Seashore extends for ten more miles. At the western tip of the island stands **Fort Pickens** (Fort Pickens Road; 904-934-2621), a beautiful 19th-century fortification built by slaves and incorporating over 20 million bricks. Geronimo was held prisoner here in the 1880s. The fort's museum features aquariums and nature exhibits.

About ten miles east of Gulf Breeze on Route 98 lies **The Zoo** (5701 Gulf Breeze Parkway; 904-932-2229; admission), the *only* accredited zoo in the Panhandle. You'll find over 500 animals, a petting zoo for children and a small botanical garden. Across the road, the folks at the **Wildlife Rescue & Sanctuary** (904-433-9453) will introduce you to pelicans, alligators, raccoons, owls and other wildlife.

Two miles east of Gulf Breeze, stop at the **Naval Live Oaks Visitor Center** (1801 Gulf Breeze Parkway; 904-934-2600) and stroll through a large stand of live-oak trees, the site where President John Quincy Adams inaugurated the first federal timber conservation program. There are exhibits on ship-building and information about the National Seashore.

As you cross over the handsome Pensacola Bay Bridge toward downtown Pensacola, you can admire the three-mile **fishing bridge** that runs alongside. It's said to be the world's longest fishing pier.

Stop at the **Pensacola Area Convention & Visitor Center** (1401 East Gregory Street; 904-434-1234) for helpful brochures, including a self-guided tour of the historic area and downtown Pensacola.

Nearby **Seville Historic District** (bounded by Bayfront Parkway, Tarragona, Romana and Cevallos streets) recalls the city's first century of European settlement. Within the district is the **Historic Pensacola Village** (bounded by Alcaniz, Government, Jefferson and Zaragoza streets)—an area brimming with charm, delightful architecture and mementos of days gone by. Stop first at the **Hispanic Museum** (Zaragoza and Tarragona streets; 904-444-8905; admission) and sign up for the village tour led by costumed docents. Along the way you'll spot such gems as a colonial well, a weavers' cottage, the French creole Barkley House, the Julee Cottage, a black history museum, the furnished Victorian Dorr House, the Colonial Archaeological Trail, the Museum of Industry and Commerce, and the Pensacola Historical Museum, located in Old Christ Church. **St. Michael's Cemetery** (Alcaniz and Garden streets) contains interesting graves dating from the early 19th century, including a replica of Napoleon's tomb.

Also here is the **T. T. Wentworth, Jr. Florida State Museum** (330 South Jefferson Street; 904-444-8586; admission), housed in the 1908 Pensacola City Hall. Inside these ruddy brick and clay walls are captivating exhibits—a funky Coca-Cola collection and over 100,000 of Wentworth's artifacts, including a bizarre petrified cat and shrunken head. Kids will love the third-floor children's museum with its giant aquarium, room of mirrors and the old ship.

Up Palafox Street, beginning at Belmont Street and continuing for over a dozen blocks, lies the **North Hill Preservation District**, a residential area filled with elegant homes reflecting the lumbering industry's turn-of-the-century heyday. Though none of the homes is open for public tours, the handiwork of gifted artisans and the wealth of the lumber barons make this an interesting area for driving or walking.

Downtown Pensacola is worth a turn, too, if only to admire the lovely wrought-iron work and balconies on the old store fronts in the **Palafox Historic Business District** along Palafox Street. If you'd like to see the catch of the day, turn off Main Street on B and C streets to the **fish markets**. The variety of seafood can be quite amazing.

In the old city jail building, you can view one of the changing exhibits at the **Pensacola Museum of Art** (407 South Jefferson Street; 904-432-6247).

To the southwest of downtown lies the vast **Naval Air Station** (take Route 98 to Navy Boulevard; 904-452-3604), home of the famous flying Blue Angels and the wonderful **Naval Aviation Museum.** From the first flying boat to cross the Atlantic to the Skylab command module and the newest fighter jets, this grand indoor/outdoor museum has exhibits that appeal to all ages. When it is in port, you can board the *USS Forrestall,* a World War II aircraft carrier that is still used for training.

A small piece of the Gulf National Seashore resides in the middle of the station and includes 40 acres of forest and historic **Fort Barrancas** (904-455-5167), across the bay from Fort Pickens. Drive past the **Old Pensacola Lighthouse,** which has been on duty since 1825, and Sherman Field, where the precision-flying Blue Angels take off.

PENSACOLA AREA HOTELS

If a condo is your preference, **Navarre Towers Condominium** (8271 Gulf Boulevard; 904-939-2011) has 56 nicely furnished highrise units for rent overlooking the beach at Navarre. When you get tired of swimming in the Gulf, there's a pool and tennis courts. Deluxe.

The refreshing gray-and-beige decor of **The Dunes** (333 Fort Pickens Road, Pensacola Beach; 904-932-3536) make even the hottest days seem cool at this handsome highrise. Overlooking the white sand and turquoise water, this understated art deco hotel has a café, outdoor and indoor pools and penthouse suites. They'll also entertain your children if you visit during the high season. Deluxe.

Bargains right on the sand are rare, but you can find one at the **Barbary Coast Motel** (24 Via de Luna, Pensacola Beach; 904-932-2233), where you can hear the surf from every room, all paneled in imitation weathered board. Functional and clean, the 24 units are moderately priced, and many have tiny kitchenettes.

Because it's on the sound instead of the Gulf, the plain but pleasant **Gulf Aire Motel** (21 Via de Luna, Pensacola Beach; 904-932-2319) falls into the budget to moderate range. It's close enough to the beach to be just fine for bargain hunters. Half of the rooms have kitchens.

Except for the spacious modern rooms, the **Pensacola Hilton** (200 East Gregory Street; 904-433-3336), incorporated into the 1912 L&N train depot, is a tribute to the past. Nostalgia reigns in the classic lobby, through the dining areas and into the ballrooms, where antiques and other period fixtures help to recall the early days of train travel. Views are grand from the higher story rooms above the old station. Deluxe.

Built into a block of warehouses near Pensacola's historic waterfront district, the **New World Inn** (600 South Palafox Street; 904-432-4111) features 16 rooms and suites, all named for historic personages of local significance, such as Andrew Jackson and Geronimo. Little history lessons and appropriate decor and furnishings make the inn interesting—each room reflects the nationality of its hero. Intimate architecture provides a secluded and elegant oasis on the edge of a struggling downtown. Moderate to deluxe.

Moderately priced rooms do exist downtown. The **Hospitality Inn** (901 North Main Street; 904-355-3744) provides comfortable rooms, renovated with wall-to-wall carpets and contemporary pastel draperies and bedspreads. The nondescript five-story building counts among its amenities a swimming pool. There are great shops within walking distance.

For something different from the many chain motels along Route 10, try **Leichty's Homestead Inn** (7830 Pine Forest Road at Route 10, Pensacola; 904-944-4816). The Leichty family shares its Amish-Mennonite heritage with the bed-and-breakfast guests by beginning the day with six-course breakfasts and ending it with traditional desserts. The gingerbread-style home is modern; the six rooms and suites, named for American patriots, recall a gracious past. Moderate.

Condos are going up on Perdido Key. For all the amenities from boat docks to tennis courts, try **Sea Spray** (16287 Perdido Key Drive, Pensacola; 904-492-2200), which features two- and three-bedroom highrise and condominium apartments for family groups only. Stays are usually for a minimum of four nights, but shorter times are available off-season. Prices are deluxe.

PENSACOLA AREA RESTAURANTS

"Eat, Drink & Flounder" advises the motto of Pensacola Beach's **Flounder's Chowder and Ale House** (800 Quietwater Beach Road; 904-932-2003). The menu is full of other such flounder puns, along with a selection of ordinary fare and a wide variety of hickory-grilled seafood. Okay, the place is corny, but it's fun, and the menu, designed by "Fred Flounder, Founder," has been a hit with beach folks for years. Moderate to deluxe.

Because it prides itself on very fresh, in-season seafood, **Jubilee** (400 Quietwater Beach Road; 904-934-3108) changes its menu every week. But it always features interesting combination dishes such as filet of chicken sautéed with crayfish or beef filets with artichoke hearts and crabmeat. A glorious overhead window and a lighted stairway give this casual spot an air of elegance. Moderate to deluxe.

An adjunct to a fish market in an area near downtown Pensacola known as "Seafood Village," **Patti's Seafood Deli** (★) (610 South C Street; 904-434-3193) attracts local folks to its bare-bones store by offering seafood in terrific sandwiches known as "Po-Boys," as well as gumbos, creole and platters. No hamburgers or chicken here, just fish right off the boats. You eat at spotless little tables and watch folks buying the latest catch to take home for dinner. Budget.

Several of Pensacola's more interesting restaurants have found their homes in restored buildings in the Seville historic district. Most lean toward international cuisine. For example, **Bodenheimer's** (304 South Alcaniz Street; 904-434-5588), with its old-style wallpaper and lace curtains, is a perfect setting for the German beer and bratwurst popular at lunch and the weekend dinners. There is always a demand for their shrimp Diane and shrimp Rothchild. Moderate.

Next door, a 60-year-old Scotto family portrait gazes down at you from the wall of the Capri Room at **Scotto's Ristorante Italiano** (300 South Alcaniz Street, Pensacola; 904-434-1932). Here you may select from a variety of homemade pastas, Italian stuffed snapper and other seafood dishes, as well as traditional chicken and veal offerings. The homemade cheesecake is irresistible. Moderate.

Restaurant reviewers and diners alike give **Jamie's** (424 East Zaragoza Street, Pensacola; 904-434-2911) continuous raves for the classic French cuisine and the selection of over 100 wines. The setting, in a cream-and-apricot Victorian cottage, is as much a drawing card as the splendid food. Deluxe.

Skopelos Seafood and Steak Restaurant (670 Scenic Highway, Pensacola; 904-432-6565) has proven for over three decades that a restaurant doesn't have to be next to the water to serve some of the best seafood possible. They also offer lamb, veal and steak, and add Greek touches to many of their entrées. Moderate to deluxe.

A part of New World Landing, an elegantly adapted warehouse near downtown Pensacola, **New World Restaurant** (600 South Palafox Street; 904-434-7736) has several handsome rooms that offer choices of decor. Whether you dine in the brick-walled Barcelona Room with its tall windows or in the Pensacola Room beneath a pressed-tin ceiling and huge historic photos, you can enjoy an array of Continental entrées like chicken *Escambia* (stuffed with ground veal and pine nuts then wrapped in dough and baked) and New York steak with mushroom and wine sauce. Try the death-by-chocolate dessert. Moderate.

You can eat aboard a non-ocean-going vessel at **The Yacht Restaurant** (Harbour Village Marina at Pitt Slip, Bayfront Parkway, Pensacola; 904-432-3707). The quick and hearty lunches appeal to business folk, and at night there is a wide assortment of seafood dishes and Cajun blackened entrées. Moderate.

Loosen your cuffs and practice your boardinghouse reach for a meal at the **Hopkins House** (900 North Spring Street, Pensacola; 904-438-3979), in the North Hill Historic District. You'll share a big table with whoever happens to be there, passing around heaping platters of fried chicken, roast beef, black-eyed peas and other southern dishes. This popular old house with a wide porch reminds you that family-style can be enjoyable. Prices are in the budget range.

McQuire's Irish Pub (600 East Gregory Street, Pensacola; 904-433-6789) is plastered with dollar bills signed by all the people who have delighted in McGuire's steaks, seafood and Irish music. It's hard to know whether the long lines are because of the food or the entertainment, but the atmosphere is exceedingly cheerful and the food excellent. Moderate.

PENSACOLA AREA SHOPPING

A number of small shops reside in restored cottages and mansions in the Seville Historic District (neighborhood of Zaragoza and Adams streets, Pensacola).

For top-quality paintings, watercolors, pottery and jewelry by local artists, go to the **Quayside Art Gallery** (15-17 East Zaragoza Street, Pensacola; 904-438-2363).

Handicrafts, antiques, collectibles, fancy coffees and imports are only a sampling of what you'll find Wednesday through Sunday at the **Quayside Thieves Market** (712 South Palafox Street, Pensacola; 904-433-9930) in a restored waterfront warehouse.

As you might expect in a historic city like Pensacola, there is an abundance of antique shops, over 30 at last count. The Visitors Bureau will provide you with an up-to-date list. One all-day prospect, the **9th Avenue Antique Mall** (380 North 9th Avenue; 904-438-3961) houses 38 shops under one roof.

Though Panhandle pecans drop from the trees only in the fall, you can buy them year-round in Pensacola at **J. W. Renfroe Pecan Company** (2400 West Fairfield Drive; 904-432-2083).

If browsing through dusty old volumes is your meat, go to **Farley's Old & Rare Books** (5855 Tippin Avenue, Pensacola; 904-477-8282). For bestsellers as well as gifts and tapes, try **Herron-King Bookstore and Art Gallery** (31 Hoffman Drive, Gulf Breeze; 904-932-6254).

The **Harbourtown Shopping Village** (913 Gulf Breeze Parkway, Gulf Breeze) is one of those designer-type shopping malls where it's as much fun to window shop as it is to spend money. You stroll outdoors in a village-like atmosphere past shops featuring clothing, gifts, jewelry and assorted other items.

If you're finicky about your fishing tackle, shop at **The Moorings** (655 Pensacola Beach Boulevard, Pensacola Beach; 904-932-0305), where the experts can custom-match you to a rod and reel. They'll outfit you accordingly, too, in classy seafaring or landlubber sportswear.

For quality souvenirs, books and materials on the history and ecology of the area, try the book and gift shops at the **Fort Pickens Museum** (Fort Pickens Road, Pensacola Beach; 904-934-2621), **Pensacola Historical Museum** (405 South Adams Street, Pensacola Beach; 904-433-1559) or the **Naval Aviation Museum** (Naval Air Station, Pensacola; 904-452-3604).

PENSACOLA AREA NIGHTLIFE

There *are* things to do at night in Pensacola, although the place is considered pretty quiet and sedate, especially for a Navy town. To see what's going on while you are in town, check the "Weekender" section of the Friday *Pensacola News Journal.*

For all-round fun, many locals and visitors head for **McQuire's Irish Pub** (600 East Gregory Street, Pensacola; 904-433-6789). Perhaps it's the crowd, perhaps the live Irish entertainment, perhaps the old-timey dark booths and the promise of "feasting, imbibery and debauchery" that make this pub so popular. Sure'n it's grand, and that's no blarney.

Flounder's Chowder and Ale House (800 Quietwater Beach Road, Pensacola Beach; 904-932-2003), where you can "eat, drink and flounder" overlooking the sound, has live entertainment several nights a week.

Jubilee (400 Quietwater Beach Road, Pensacola Beach; 904-934-3108) features a contemporary jazz band six nights a week. You can enjoy the relaxing sounds in the oyster bar or outside on the deck overlooking the water.

Since the late '60s **Seville Quarter** (130 East Government Street; 904-434-6211) has been one of Pensacola's most happening nighttime addresses. Located in the historic district, it boasts seven clubs with a wide variety of live tunes, from Dixieland jazz and county-western twang to high-pep disco. One price gets you into all the clubs.

The Office On Wright Street (406 East Wright Street, Pensacola; 904-432-7969) is a high-energy entertainment complex featuring a swimming pool, jazz piano bar, dance bar and cabana bar. The six-room club also offers a pool deck and rooftop terrace. Most of the music is deejay-generated, and female impersonators perform several nights a week. This gay club also attracts many straight guests.

Big name stars, circuses and concerts appear occasionally at the **Pensacola Civic Center** (201 East Gregory Street, Pensacola; 904-433-6311).

You can also find classical entertainment in Pensacola. The **Pensacola Symphony Orchestra** (904-435-2533) offers concerts. For information on the various community groups that present jazz, chamber music, ballet and opera throughout the year, contact the **Arts Council of Northwest Florida** (P.O. Box 731, Pensacola, FL 32594; 904-432-9906).

Theatrical performances are presented by the **Pensacola Little Theatre** (186 North Palafox Street, Pensacola; 904-432-2042), and the **University of West Florida Repertory Theatre** (11000 University Parkway, Pensacola; 904-474-2405). The handsomely restored **Saenger Theatre** (118 South Palafox Place, Pensacola; 904-444-7686) hosts a number of dance, music and literary events, some big-name.

PENSACOLA AREA BEACHES AND PARKS

Gulf Islands National Seashore—Fortunately for us and for posterity, Congress has set aside 150 miles of coastal land, including several barrier islands, from Santa Rosa Island to West Ship Island, Mississippi. In the Panhandle this includes six distinct areas—Perdido Key; the vast western Fort Pickens section of Santa Rosa Island; the Historic Forts section on the Pensacola Naval Air Station; the Santa Rosa day use area near Navarre Beach; the small Okaloosa area east of Fort Walton Beach; and the Naval Live Oaks area, site of the park headquarters, east of Gulf Breeze.

Facilities: Picnic areas, restrooms, lifeguards, self-guiding trails; bathhouses and outdoor showers in the beach sections; information, 904-934-2621. *Fishing:* Good surf and bay fishing and crabbing. *Swimming:* Excellent at Perdido Key, Fort Pickens area and Santa Rosa. Lifeguards on duty in some sections during the summer.

Camping: There are 200 sites, most with RV hookups; $10 per night.

Getting there: Located south of Pensacola; vast stretches of the park are accessible from Route 399.

Big Lagoon State Recreation Area—Because this 698-acre park contains beaches, salt marshes, dunes and pine woods, it is a good place to observe bird, animal and plant life. Boardwalks make many areas accessible, other spots convey a feeling of remoteness.

Facilities: Picnic areas, restrooms, bathhouses, nature trails, observation tower; information, 904-492-1595. *Fishing:* Excellent. Bluefish, redfish, flounder and sea trout in season. Crabbing and netting for mullet. *Swimming:* Several nice beaches on the lagoon, but the proximity to Intracoastal Waterway is a drawback.

Camping: There are 70 sites, many with RV hookups; $10 per night.

Getting there: Take Route 292-A southwest from Pensacola for about ten miles.

Inland Area

Florida's canoe capital, this tranquil area is the place to go to enjoy waterfalls, beautiful caverns, pine swamps and swinging bridges. The lack of bright city lights means you'll be able to see a lot more stars at night. A showcase for the state's past, you can explore the Panhandle's inland regions along major highways or country roads. Be prepared to make some detours to capitalize on what this area has to offer.

Along Route 90, **Quincy** is a pretty town whose shady streets and historic homes give the place a gracious antebellum charm. The downtown district has been revitalized and many of the old brick buildings sport fresh paint and clean awnings. This is a good place for antique-browsing. The **Quincy Chamber of Commerce** (221 North Madison Street; 904-627-9231) can help you enjoy the town.

You can pick up a "Historic Sidewalk Tour" of **Marianna** from the **Chamber of Commerce** (2928 North Jefferson Street; 904-482-8061). This is another Old South town with restored buildings and elegant historic homes.

Most visitors to Marianna come to see **Florida Caverns State Park** (Route 166, three miles north of town; 904-482-9598; admission; see the "Inland Area Parks" section below), where you can explore live limestone caves or arrange for some adventurous spelunking.

If you drive on up to admire the Victorian houses in Greenwood, you can rummage in the old cooler for a soda at **Pender's Store (★)** (Route 71, on the right just after the light; 904-594-3304) where local farmers have been buying feed and seed, work boots, dry goods and groceries from the Pender family since the last century. The heartpine floors and sturdy shelves date to 1869, when the place was built.

A number of springs bubble up in surprising places in the central inland region. An easy one to enjoy is at **Ponce de León Springs State Recreation Area** (Route 181-A south of Ponce de León; 904-836-4281; admission; see the "Inland Area Parks" section below). Two main boils below the concrete-walled pool produce 14 million gallons of crystal-clear water each day. Though the spring has never been proven to be a fountain of youth, the refreshing swimming and the tall cypress trees impart a sense of tranquility and well-being.

Sinkholes, or sinks, are also common in Florida. Their evolution begins when the weak acids in rainwater seep through cracks in limestone beneath the ground, forming a cavern. If the surface collapses, the cavern, filled with water, is revealed and the result is a sink. The one at **Falling Waters State Recreation Area** (Route 77-A, three miles south of Chipley; 904-638-6130; admission; see the "Inland Area Parks" section below) is unique, for its underground cavern is also fed by stream waters falling down a 100-foot smooth-walled chimney, resulting in the state's only natural waterfall.

By leaving Route 10 at Greensboro and winding down Route 12, you can visit **Torreya State Park (★)** (Route 271; 904-643-2674; admission; see the "Inland Area Parks" section below) and stroll the pretty walkway to the 1849-era **Gregory House.** This remnant of Florida's steamboat days was transported across the Apalachicola River from its original plantation setting. The classic Greek revival house is filled with 19th-century antiques, including a bedroom suite belonging to the original owner's daughter. Be sure to explore some of the park as well. The rare torreya tree is making a comeback here, and the high bluffs offer fine views of the river.

In the late 19th century, Chautauqua religious leaders selected DeFuniak Springs as their winter headquarters. A portion of the **Chautauqua Auditorium** (Circle Drive) with its handsome colonnaded dome is still in use. Stop in here for information on the town and the current Chautauqua renaissance (it houses the **Walton County Chamber of Commerce**; 904-892-3191). As you round the lake on Circle Drive, you will see a number of turn-of-the-century homes, the 1896-era **St. Agatha's Episcopal Church** and the tiny **Walton-DeFuniak Library** (904-892-3624), elegant reminders of Florida Chautauqua's 40-year heyday.

The **Bob Sikes Library** (Route 90, east of Crestview; 904-682-4432), a handsome brick building with curving staircase and marble floors, houses local Indian artifacts as well as tributes to the former Congressman, who sponsored the Gulf Islands National Seashore.

West of Crestview, Route 4 leads into the **Blackwater River State Forest,** so named for the beautiful tannin-stained river that meanders through dense woods. A number of sideroads make for varied exploration of this wild natural region.

Milton, called the "canoe capital of Florida" because of its easy access to the rivers and creeks in the Blackwater Forest, is a restored turn-of-the-century town with an interesting history rooted in lumber and shipping. Pick up information at the **Milton Chamber of Commerce** (501 Stewart Street Southwest; 904-623-2339) and take a stroll along the Blackwater River.

INLAND AREA HOTELS

Generic motels in budget and moderate price ranges can be found wherever Route 10 is crossed by a major highway. Many of the inland towns also have a variety of mom-and-pop lodgings, and most of them are budget. If you want luxury, you'll have to stay in Tallahassee or head for the coast.

Seminole Lodge (Legion Road, two and a half miles north of Sneads; 904-593-6886) is more like a motel than its name suggests, but its location on the shore of Lake Seminole makes its ten rooms popular with fishermen and anyone who enjoys wonderful views of the water. The rooms are old-timey, spacious and well-kept; even the ones with kitchenettes are budget-priced. There are boats to rent, a picnic area and a big park nearby.

Although **Tomahawk Landing** (★) (Off Route 87, 12 miles north of Milton; 904-623-6197) is primarily a camping spot for canoeists, the wide variety of cabin accommodations makes this a delightful place to stay and experience the Blackwater Forest area. You can put your whole family in a screened shelter or escape to the lantern-lit honeymoon cabin on the banks of the Coldwater River for a budget rate; or, for a moderate charge, live it up in one of the air-conditioned deluxe cabins in the pine woods, with a fully equipped kitchen and a fireplace to keep things cozy in the winter.

On the banks of the Apalachicola River, the **Morgan Motel** (Route 90, Chatahoochee; 904-663-4336) is an unpretentious establishment with clean, carpeted rooms at budget prices. Just one mile from the Three Rivers Recreation Area, this motel is popular with the angling crowd.

INLAND AREA RESTAURANTS

During the day you know that the cars and pick-ups parked at Parramore Landing belong to folks out fishing. In the late afternoon you can join the ones who come ashore for fried catfish, shrimp or scallops at **Parramore Restaurant** (★) (off Route 271, 12 miles north of Sneads; 904-592-2091). Even landlubbers eat at this rundown but popular fish-camp café restaurant. If you've never had cheese grits, try them here. Budget to moderate.

Tony's Restaurant (4133 Lafayette Street, Marianna; 904-482-2232) is one of those hometown eateries where gossip gets traded and plates get piled with budget-priced fixin's such as ham steak and crisp-fried catfish with hush puppies. Roomy booths and checkered tabletops provide a sunny ambience, and fresh-cooked field peas, string beans, candied yams and buttered carrots ensure a wonderful aroma.

It's said that lots of politicking goes on at **McLain's Family Restaurant** (Routes 10 and 85, Crestview; 904-682-5286), which means that local folks like this high-ceilinged roadside stopping place. Budget to moderate specials of fried chicken and broiled seafood make this a nice alternative to the neighboring franchises along the interstate route.

Looking for Cajun food like jambalaya or gumbo? Craving fried catfish, broiled halibut or grouper? Or perhaps you'd just like to try a country buffet featuring fried chicken and a dozen salads, side dishes and desserts. If so, why not stop in at **Grandma's Restaurant** (5887 Route 90, Milton; 904-626-8788). Set in an old wood barn, this paneled, antique-furnished dining room is a good budget-priced choice.

INLAND AREA SHOPPING

Graceville is synonymous with shopping. Bargain hunters come from all points in search of good deals on name brands at the **VF Factory Outlet** (Highway 77 South and West Prim Avenue; 904-263-3207) and the **Grace-**

ville Factory Stores (904-263-4500) next door. You can spend a day hunting for shoes, toys, jewelry, clothing, leather goods, cosmetics and more.

With 3000 square feet of antiques and collectibles, **Second Hand Rose** (7080 Route 90 East, Milton; 904-623-0627) is a great place to explore Florida's past. This shop is particularly strong on furniture, jewelry and crystal.

Stop by **Etc.** (17 North Madison Street, Quincy; 904-875-1864) for women's suits, dresses, belts, jewelry and other career essentials.

In the late fall you may see signs for pecans. If you miss them, you can get plenty, shelled or unshelled, from **Lundy's Pecans** (★) (Route 89 north of Milton; 904-623-0652) in November and December. Lundy's also has blueberries in July. And don't forget to try the boiled peanuts sold along the road. After the first shock of biting down on one of these soft, warm, chewy legumes, you may become a believer. We did.

INLAND AREA NIGHTLIFE

Inland towns roll up their sidewalks early, so folks in search of serious nightlife either make do with local bars and pool tables or head for the coastal cities. The best entertainment probably happens in the forests and preserves, where no lights interfere with stargazing and campers can listen to the rustling of nighttime critters hunting for their dinners. Mockingbirds sometimes sing all night long.

INLAND AREA PARKS

To travelers who hug the coastline or zip through the Panhandle on Route 10, inland area parks will remain hidden. These parks are worth the short detours, however, as they offer a variety of natural phenomena found nowhere else in the state.

Three Rivers State Recreation Area—The three rivers are the Chattahoochee and Flint, which merge above Lake Seminole, and the Apalachicola, which flows out of it. The lake is the result of the flooding of a river swamp; many dead trees rise above the water, guaranteeing fine fishing. The park is somewhat hilly, with grassy shoreline-slopes in some areas, and deep and diverse woods abundant in deer, gray fox and raccoons elsewhere.

Facilities: Picnic areas, restrooms, fishing dock, nature trails; information, 904-482-9006. *Fishing:* Excellent for bass, catfish, bluegill, perch and bream. *Swimming:* Permitted.

Camping: There are 65 sites, many with RV hookups; $8 per night.

Getting there: Take Route 271 north off Route 90, west of Sneads.

Florida Caverns State Park—This park is beautiful both above and below ground with its disappearing river, magnolia forest and dry cavern.

Tours among the spectacular cavern's stalactites and stalagmites are available daily.

Facilities: Picnic area, restrooms, nature trails, visitor center; information, 904-482-9598. *Fishing:* In the Chipola River. *Swimming:* Refreshing spring swimming in Blue Hole.

Camping: There are 32 sites, all with RV hookups; $12 per night.

Getting there: Off Route 166, three miles north of Marianna.

Ponce de León Springs State Recreation Area—This 443-acre park reveals one of the small, pretty Florida springs that has been developed for swimming, snorkeling and diving. Like so many of these jewels, the spring creates an oasis in the dry, sandy inland region. Several trails lead you through surrounding pine woods.

Facilities: Picnic area, restrooms, nature trail; information, 904-836-4281. *Swimming:* Refreshing spring swimming.

Getting there: Off Route 90, just east of Ponce de León.

Falling Waters State Recreation Area (★)—This small 155-acre park boasts the state's only natural waterfall, which actually starts at ground level and falls 100 feet into a mossy sinkhole to disappear into the ground. The tiny, lush region around this curiosity and the other ordinary sinks in the park provide a pleasant respite from the surrounding dry and sandy terrain.

Facilities: Picnic area, restrooms, nature trail; information, 904-638-6130. *Swimming:* In a small manmade lake.

Camping: There are 24 sites, all with RV hookups; $10 per night.

Getting there: Three miles south of Chipley off Route 77.

Torreya State Park (★)—This unusual park is named for the rare torreya tree that has made a comeback after near-extinction. In an almost magical setting, a trail winds up and down ravines and forested bluffs, rising as much as 150 feet, shaped by the Apalachicola River winding along the northwestern boundary. Because of the rapidly changing elevations, a wide variety of distinctive plant communities resides here. Many trees and plants commonly found in the Appalachian regions of north Georgia thrive, along with the rare Florida yew and the U.S. Champion bigleaf magnolia. A restored antebellum plantation house recalls the days when the river was an important waterway for steamers.

Facilities: Picnic areas, restrooms, hiking trails; information, 904-643-2674.

Camping: There are 29 sites, many with RV hookups; $10 per night.

Getting there: Off Route 10 between Quincy and Marianna. Take the Bristol exit (Route 12) off Route 10 and head southwest to Route 271; go north to the entrance.

Blackwater River State Park—This heavily wooded park on the southern edge of the 183,155-acre **Blackwater River State Forest** stands as a sort of mystical microcosm of its larger neighbor, with deep, dark areas of pine swamp hardwoods, white cedar and a wide variety of other flora. While the river is not really black, it is as dark as strong tea, stained by the tannin from cypress trees and decaying leaves; the water, however, is unpolluted and clear, dotted with broad white sandbars. Oxbow lakes, swamps, dry hills, ponds and swamps attract abundant wildlife to the park; wildflowers and birds lure nature-lovers year-round.

Facilities: Picnic areas, restrooms, nature trails; information, 904-623-2363. *Fishing:* Catfish, bream and other freshwater fish. *Swimming:* Excellent river swimming off a sandbar beach.

Camping: There are 30 sites, all with RV hookups; $10 per night.

Getting there: Off Route 90, 15 miles northeast of Milton, west of Floridale.

The Sporting Life

SPORTFISHING

Both freshwater and saltwater fishing opportunities are abundant in the Panhandle. Charters, boat rentals and guide services can be found just about anywhere water runs deep enough for a skiff. Fleets of fancy deep-sea craft carry parties out into Gulf waters for marlin, sailfish, black-fin tuna, barracuda, king mackerel, shark, and dolphin (the fish, not Flipper, the mammal!). Inland lakes and rivers teem with large-mouth bass, bream, panfish and catfish, while coastal areas produce speckled trout, redfish, Spanish mackerel and more.

The following companies offer deep-sea and/or bay charters: **The Nixie** (87 5th Street, Apalachicola; 904-653-9081), **Sportsman Lodge** (Magnolia Bluff, Route 98, Eastpoint; 904-670-8423) and **Marquardt's Marina, Inc.** (Route 98, Mexico Beach; 904-648-8900).

On Panama City Beach, try **Captain Bob Zales' Zodiac Charter Fleet** (3605 Thomas Drive; 904-235-2628) or **Davy Jones Charters** (Anderson-Davis Pier; 904-234-5979). In Destin, go to sea aboard **Emmanuel** (Route 98; 904-837-6313), or **Paper Tiger and Silver Lining** (Sweet Jody Docks; 904-837-5536). In Pensacola, you can charter the **Party Boat Chulamar** (1101 Gulf Breeze Parkway; 904-434-6977), or contact **Abundant Charters** (2112 Pullman Circle, Pensacola; 904-453-5885).

If you want a licensed guide to introduce you to some areas unknown to most tourists, try the following: **Pace's Fish Camp** (River Road, Steinhatchee; 904-498-3008), **Shell Island Fish Camp** (Shell Island Road, St. Marks; 904-925-6226), **or Elrod's Fish Camp** (12 miles east of Destin, near Santa Rosa Beach; 904-267-2318).

Freshwater boat rentals and/or guide service can be found in any inland town within casting distance of a river or a stream. You'll see their signs along the road. Availability depends on the season and the guides are often natives who have been fishing their favorite spots all their lives. On the Steinhatchee River, **Ideal Fish Camp** (Route 51, Steinhatchee; 904-498-3877) rents open fishing craft and **Westwind Fish Camp** (Route 51, Steinhatchee; 904-498-5254) has flat-bottom boats.

SAILING

Yacht charters are offered by **"Sheila M"** (St. Andrew Marina, Panama City; 904-234-5480). In Fort Walton, **Adventure Watersports** (1320 Route 98 East; 904-244-5222) rents catamarans, pontoons, runabouts and wave runners. For sailing out of Pensacola, contact **Break Away** (Harbor Village; 904-438-1711).

WINDSURFING

Sailboarding is hotly pursued along Florida's northern Gulf beaches. For rentals, check with **Bay Windsurfing** (2226 Thomas Drive, Panama City Beach; 904-234-0963), **Rogue Wave Windsurfing** (171 Brooks Street Southeast, Fort Walton Beach; 904-243-1962) or **Surf and Sail** (15 Via de Luna, Pensacola Beach; 904-932-7873).

SKINDIVING

The choice of experiences for divers in the Panhandle is broad indeed, from exploring wrecked ships in the Gulf to cave-diving in deep hidden springs. The less daring can rent snorkeling equipment and lazily watch fish in a blue spring. Many outfitters provide equipment and exploration trips in salt and freshwater, as well as scalloping, shelling, spear fishing and/or instruction.

To explore more than two dozen hidden springs in the eastern area, contact **Spring Systems Dive Center** (Peacock Road, Luraville; 904-776-2310) or **Branford Dive Center** (Route 27 and the Suwannee River, Branford; 904-935-1141). In Tallahassee, organized dive trips can be arranged through **Coral Reef Scuba** (1362 Lake Bradford Road; 904-576-6268 and 2020 North Point Boulevard; 904-385-1323).

For Gulf and bay exploration, as well as some spring diving, try **Apalachicola Divers Supply** (119 Water Street, Apalachicola; 904-653-9521), **Captain Black's Dive Center** (301 Monument Avenue, Port St. Joe; 904-229-6330), **Hydrospace Dive Shop** (3605 Thomas Drive, Panama City; 904 234-9463) or **Panama City Dive Center** (4823 Thomas Drive, Panama City Beach; 904-235-3390). In the Fort Walton area, try **Aquanaut Scuba Center** (Route 98, Destin; 904-837-0359), **Fantasea** (Route 98 East, Destin; 904 837-6943), the **Scuba Shop** (348 Miracle Strip Parkway, Fort Walton Beach

904-243-1600) or **Captain J. Dive Shop** (301 Highway 98, Destin; 904-654-5300).

Dive Mart (5501 Duval Street, Pensacola; 904-494-9800) and **Scuba Shack** (719 Palafox Street, Pensacola; 904-433-4319) explore Florida's westernmost waters.

Spring exploration in the central area is offered by **Aqua-Lin, Inc.** (Cypress Springs Road, Vernon; 904-535-2960), **Morrison Springs Diving Facility** (south on Route 81, Ponce de León; 904-836-4223) and **Vortex Spring Inc.** (Route 81 north of Ponce de León; 904-836-4979).

CANOEING AND TUBING

Milton calls itself the canoe capital of Florida, and you'll know why when you see hundreds of canoes on the Blackwater River or Coldwater Creek on a holiday weekend. There's canoeing on other Panhandle rivers and spring runs, too, from the Suwannee to the Perdido, and much of it can be handled by novices. There's no better way to explore the waters of hidden Florida.

Rental companies usually provide shuttle services and often rent tubes and rafts. To canoe the Suwannee River and the eastern area runs, try the **Spirit of the Suwannee Canoe Outpost** (off Route 129 north of Live Oak; 904-364-1683), **River Run Campground, Inc.** (Route 27 east of Branford; 904-935-1086) or **River Road, Inc.** (on the Suwannee at White Springs; 904-397-2945).

In the Tallahassee area, try **The Canoe Shop** (1115-B Orange Avenue; 904-576-5335) or **TNT Hideaway Inc.** (Route 98 at the Wakulla River, St. Marks; 904-925-6412).

To explore the western Panhandle rivers, try **Andrew Jackson Canoe Trails** (P.O. Box 666, Baghdad; 904-623-4884), **Adventures Unlimited** (12 miles north of Milton on Route 87; 904-623-6197), **Blackwater River Canoe Rental** (Route 90 east of Milton; 904-623-0235) or **Bob's Canoes** (Highway 191 northwest of Milton; 904-623-5457). **Adventures Unlimited, Perdido** (Route 84 at the Perdido River; 904-968-5529) offers canoeing on Florida's western boundary.

In the central inland area, try **Chipola River Canoe Trail** (Route 28, Marianna; 904-482-4948), **Cypress Springs Canoe Trails, Inc.** (Cypress Springs Road, Vernon; 904-535-2960), and **Sasquatch Canoe Rentals** (Route 90 east of Crestview; 904-682-3949).

HOUSEBOATING

To explore the Suwannee River, begin at its mouth on one of **Miller's Suwannee Houseboats** (off Route 349, Suwannee; 904-542-7349) for one-day to one-week trips.

GOLF

The Panhandle climate and a wide variety of courses attract golfers year-round. In Tallahassee, the public can play at the **Helaman Park Municipal Golf Course** (2737 Blair Stone Road; 904-878-5830) and the **Seminole Golf Course** (2550 Pottsdamer Road; 904-644-2582). There is a public course at **St. Joseph's Bay Country Club** (off Route 98, Port St. Joe; 904-227-1751). In the Panama City area try **Signal Hill Golf Course** (9615 Thomas Drive, Panama City Beach; 904-234-5051).

The elegant resort **Seascape** (100 Seascape Drive, Destin; 904-837-9181), in the Fort Walton area, opens its championship course to the public. You can also play at **Bluewater Bay** (Niceville; 904-897-3613).

In the Pensacola area you can tee off at **Green Meadow Par 3** (2500 West Michigan Avenue, Pensacola; 904-944-5483) or the **Tiger Point Golf & Country Club** (1255 Country Club Road, Gulf Breeze; 904-932-1333). Golfers traveling the inland areas may play at **Florida Caverns Golf Course** (2601 Caverns Road, Marianna; 904-482-4257), **The Dogwoods Country Club** (Highway 177-A Northwest, Bonifay; 904-547-9381) and **Tanglewood Golf & Country Club** (Tanglewood Drive, Milton; 904-623-6176).

TENNIS

Many of the resorts and local country clubs provide courts for their guests and allow the public to play for a fee. Included in this list are **Holiday Golf & Tennis Club** (100 Fairway Boulevard, Panama City Beach; 904-234-1800) and **The Dogwoods Country Club** (Highway 177-A Northwest, Bonifay; 904-547-9381). **Sandestin** (Emerald Coast Parkway, ten miles east of Destin; 904-267-8000) opens its courts to the public. You can also play at the **Shalimar Pointe Tennis Club** (2 Country Club Road, Shalimar; 904-651-8872) and at the **Pensacola Racquet Club** (3450 Wimbledon Drive; 904-434-2434).

BICYCLING

Narrow roads and hot weather discourage many folks from biking in the Panhandle. On Pensacola Beach, the **Michael J. Kennan Memorial Bike Path** provides four miles of safe and scenic biking that will eventually be linked to a path traversing the Gulf Islands National Seashore.

Three guides to biking in the Panhandle have been designed by the **Florida Department of Transportation** and may be obtained from the department at 606 Suwannee Street, M. S. 12, Tallahassee 32301. These include suggested routes from downtown Pensacola to the Gulf Islands National Seashore, a loop tour from Tallahassee to Monticello and back, and a tour from Tallahassee to St. Marks.

BIKE RENTALS Rent your bicycles at **Beach Things** (13226 Front Beach Road, Panama City Beach; 904-234-0520), **Bob's Schwinn** (415-G

Mary Esther Boulevard, Fort Walton Beach; 904-243-5856) or **Paradise Bicycle Rental** (715 Pensacola Beach Boulevard, Pensacola; 904-934-0014).

HIKING

Though most visitors to the Panhandle do their primary walking on the beaches, there are other hiking opportunities available. Almost every state park and recreation area contains at least one nature trail. The Florida Trail Association is in the process of creating unbroken hiking trails from Pensacola to Lake Okeechobee; several existing Panhandle trails are already part of the system. Because altitudes seldom go above 300 feet, most hiking is easy, especially in seasons when temperatures cool down and the mosquitoes disappear.

TALLAHASSEE AREA TRAILS **Stoney Bayou Trail** (6 miles) and **Deep Creek Trail** (12.7 miles) allow exploration of the vast St. Marks National Wildlife Refuge. These loop trails begin near the visitor's center off Route 59 south of Newport. Deep Creek Trail leads deep into coast swampland where you are likely to encounter wide varieties of birds and wildlife.

Ridge Trail (3 miles) and **Otter Lake Loop** (9 miles) lie in a secluded western portion of the St. Marks National Wildlife Refuge where ospreys nest. Both these loop trails begin and end at the Otter Lake Recreation area east of Panacea off Route 98.

St. Marks Trail (16 miles) begins off Route 98, and travels through beautiful and remote areas of the St. Marks National Wildlife Refuge to Route 319, five miles east of Sopchoppy.

Apalachicola Trail (22 miles) begins where the St. Marks Trail ends, near Sopchoppy. It crosses four rivers and explores both wilderness and scenic areas that display much of north Florida's natural phenomena.

The **Trail of the Lakes** (9 miles) is a loop trail which links up with the Florida National Scenic Trail in the western part of the Apalachicola National Forest. It begins at the Carmel Lake Recreation Area 15 miles south of Bristol. Good place for a family hike to get a sampling of the forest's flora and fauna.

APALACHICOLA AREA TRAILS **St. Joseph Peninsula Trail** (18-mile loop) begins at the ranger station in the T. H. Stone Memorial State Park and travels through the St. Joseph Peninsula Wilderness Preserve. You can make an interesting loop by going one way along the beach and returning through the interior. This will provide opportunities for shelling as well as observing marsh and piney woods wildlife. It's a long walk, but not difficult.

PANAMA CITY AREA TRAILS **Pine Log Trail** (3 miles) is an easy loop trail popular with birdwatchers. It begins at the Pine Log State Forest Headquarters, off Route 79, south of Ebro.

INLAND AREA TRAILS **Torreya State Park Hiking Trail** (7 miles) is a loop trail that traverses ravines, bluffs and streams and goes through hardwood forests unique to Florida. The short **Apalachicola River Bluffs Trail,** incorporated into this loop trail, passes Confederate gun pits and offers good views of the river.

Jackson Red Ground Hiking Trail (21 miles) runs through the center of Blackwater River State Forest. The trail traverses forest and swamp and crosses the Blackwater River.

Sweetwater Hiking Trail (4.5 miles) begins at the Krul Recreation Area near the intersection of Routes 191 and 4 and crosses Sweetwater Creek on a swinging bridge.

Transportation

BY CAR

Traveling with dispatch across the Panhandle is accomplished by driving the interstate highway **Route 10,** which is intersected by north-south **Routes 75** and **19** and many roads winding down from Georgia and Alabama and up from the coastal cities and towns. The slower but more scenic **Route 98** follows the curves of the coastline, while old **Route 90** parallels Route 10 through the inland towns.

BY AIR

You can fly into airports at Tallahassee, Panama City, Fort Walton or Pensacola. Airlines serving the **Tallahassee Regional Airport** include Delta Airlines and USAir.

Panama City-Bay County Municipal Airport is served by American Eagle, Delta Atlantic Southeast, Northwest Airlink and USAir Express. Ground transportation is provided by **Deluxe Coach Service** (904-763-0211).

Fort Walton Beach (Eglin Field) is served by Delta Atlantic Southeast and Northwest Airlines.

Airlines serving the **Pensacola Airport** include Continental Airlines, Delta Airlines, Eastern Airlines, Northwest Airlines and USAir. There is no shuttle transportation service from Pensacola Airport into town.

For a wider choice of schedules, you might consider flying into Jacksonville (see Chapter Four) and driving west.

BY BUS

Greyhound/Trailways Bus Lines serve the major cities and many of the small towns across the Panhandle. In Tallahassee, the station is at 112

West Tennessee Street (904-222-6614); in Panama City at 917 Harrison Avenue (904-785-7861); in Fort Walton Beach at 105 Chestnut Avenue Southeast (904-243-1940); and in Pensacola at 505 West Burgess Road (904-476-4800).

CAR RENTALS

You'll find car rentals at each of the Panhandle airports. In Tallahassee, try **Avis Rent A Car** (904-576-4133), **Budget Rent A Car** (904-575-9192), **National Inter Rent** (904-576-4107), **Hertz Rent A Car** (904-576-1154) or **Alamo Rent a Car** (904-576-6009).

Rentals are available at the Panama City Airport from **Avis Rent A Car** (904-769-1411), **Budget Rent A Car** (904-651-9600), **Hertz Rent A Car** (904-763-2262), **National Inter Rent** (904-769-2383) and **Snappy Car Rental** (904-785-8808).

At Fort Walton Beach Airport you can pick up a car from **Budget Rent A Car** (904-651-9600), **Hertz Rent A Car** (904-651-0612) or from **National Inter Rent** (904-651-1113). For a better rate but more inconvenience try an **Economy Rent A Car** (904-678-6223) "rent a heap cheap."

Car rental franchises at the Pensacola Airport include **Avis Rent A Car** (904-433-5614), **Budget Rent A Car** (904-478-8445), **Hertz Rent A Car** (904-763-2262) and **National Inter Rent** (904-432-8338). You can save with **Ugly Duckling Rent A Car** (904-939-3973).

PUBLIC TRANSPORTATION

Public transportation is limited in the Panhandle and is used mostly by folks going to and from work. In Tallahassee, contact **Taltran** (904-574-5200) for bus schedules. The **Escambia County Transit System** (904-436-9383) provides local bus service in the Pensacola area.

TAXIS

Several cab companies serve the Tallahassee airport, including **Yellow Cab** (904-222-3070). At the Panama City airport, you can use **Yellow Cab** (904-763-4691). The airport in Fort Walton Beach is served by **A-1 Taxi** (904-678-2424) and **Checker Cab** (904-244-4491). At the Pensacola airport, taxi service is available from **Green Cab Co.** (904-449-3018), **West Hill Taxi Co.** (904-438-5621), **Warrington Taxi** (904-455-8506) and **Yellow Cab** (904-433-3333).

Index

Hotel, restaurant and trail names have not been included here unless cited as a sightseeing or historical attraction.

Also Available From Ulysses Press

HIDDEN BOSTON AND CAPE COD
This compact guide ventures to historic Boston and the windswept Massachusetts coastline. 228 pages. $7.95

HIDDEN COAST OF CALIFORNIA
Explores the fabled California coast from Mexico to Oregon, describing over 1000 miles of spectacular beaches. 468 pages. $13.95

HIDDEN FLORIDA KEYS AND EVERGLADES
Covers an area unlike any other in the world—the tropical Florida Keys and mysterious Everglades. 156 pages. $7.95

HIDDEN HAWAII
A classic in its field, this top-selling guide captures the spirit of the islands. Winner of the Lowell Thomas Award. 420 pages. $14.95

HIDDEN MEXICO
Covers the entire 6000-mile Mexican coastline in the most comprehensive fashion ever. 444 pages. $13.95

HIDDEN NEW ENGLAND
A perfect companion for exploring from Massachusetts colonial villages to the fog-shrouded coast of Maine. 564 pages. $14.95

HIDDEN PACIFIC NORTHWEST
Covers Oregon, Washington and British Columbia. Seattle sightseeing, Oregon beaches, Cascades campgrounds and more! 528 pages. $14.95

HIDDEN SAN FRANCISCO AND NORTHERN CALIFORNIA
A major resource for travelers exploring the San Francisco Bay area and beyond. 444 pages. $14.95

HIDDEN SOUTHERN CALIFORNIA
The most complete guidebook to Los Angeles and Southern California in print. 516 pages. $14.95

HIDDEN SOUTHWEST

Explores Arizona, New Mexico, southern Utah and Colorado. Native American sites, campgrounds and desert adventures galore! 504 pages. $14.95

CALIFORNIA
The Ultimate Guidebook

Definitive. From the Pacific to the desert to the Sierra Nevada, it captures the best of the Golden State. 504 pages. $13.95

DISNEY WORLD AND BEYOND
The Ultimate Family Guidebook

Unique and comprehensive, this guide to Orlando's theme parks and outlying areas is a must for family travelers. 300 pages. $9.95

DISNEY WORLD AND BEYOND
Family Fun Cards

This "guidebook you can shuffle" covers Orlando's theme parks with a deck of 90 cards, each describing a different ride or attraction. $7.95

DISNEYLAND AND BEYOND
The Ultimate Family Guidebook

The only guidebook to cover all Southern California theme parks. Includes three chapters of daytrip possibilities for families. 240 pages. $9.95

FLORIDA'S GOLD COAST
The Ultimate Guidebook

Captures the tenor and tempo of Florida's most popular stretch of shoreline—Palm Beach, Fort Lauderdale and Miami. 192 pages. $8.95

FOR A FREE CATALOG OR TO ORDER DIRECT For each book send an additional $2 postage and handling (California residents include 8% sales tax) to Ulysses Press, 3286 Adeline Street, Suite 1, Berkeley, CA 94703. Or call **1-800-377-2542** or 510-601-8301 and charge your order.

About the Authors

Stacy Ritz, author of the Miami chapter, has also written Ulysses Press' bestselling *Disney World and Beyond: The Ultimate Family Guidebook.* She is the co-author of *Hidden New England* and *Florida's Gold Coast: The Ultimate Guidebook.* A regular contributor to the *Miami Herald* and the *Fort Lauderdale Sun Sentinel*, she has also written for the *Washington Post*, *Orlando Sentinel* and *Miami Herald.*

Candace Leslie was raised in Florida and holds a degree from Florida State University. A member of the Society of American Travel Writers, she has written for *Reader's Digest*, *Diversion* and other publications throughout the United States. She wrote the introductory section of *Hidden Florida* as well as the Keys/Everglades and Panhandle chapters. Candace Leslie is also author of *Hidden Florida Keys and Everglades* and other books.

Marty Olmstead, who wrote the East Coast and Gold Coast chapters, is a member of the Society of American Travel Writers. A resident of Sonoma, California, she writes about the Wine Country and other travel topics for a variety of national and regional publications. Olmstead is a feature editor for the *Marin Independent Journal.*

Chelle Koster Walton, author of the Central Florida and West Coast chapters, is a freelance writer based on Sanibel Island in Florida. A member of the Society of American Travel Writers, she writes regularly for the *Miami Herald* and *Fort Lauderdale Sun Sentinel*, and is a contributing editor for *Caribbean Travel and Life.* She also authored *Caribbean Ways: A Cultural Guide.*

About the Illustrator

Timothy Carroll has illustrated several other Ulysses Press guides, including *Hidden New England* and *Hidden Southern California.* His artwork appears frequently in *Newsweek*, *Esquire*, *Spy*, the *Boston Globe*, *San Francisco Focus*, *Premiere* magazine and the *Washington Post.* His current hobbies are travel and credit cards.